CW01064432

Praise fo:
Red Road to Fr:
A History of the South African Co... ...., 1921–2021

'Lodge provides a richly detailed history of the party's vicissitudes and victories; individuals – their ideas, attitudes and activities – are sensitively located within their context; the text provides a fascinating sociology of the South African left over time. Lodge is adept at making explicit what the key questions and issues are for different periods; and he answers these with analyses and conclusions that are judicious, clearly stated and meticulously argued. Without doubt, this book will become a central text for students of communism in South Africa, of the party's links with Russia and the socialist bloc, and of the Communist Party's changing relations with African nationalism – before, during and after three decades of exile.'

– Professor Colin Bundy, Green Templeton College, University of Oxford

Red Road is a fascinating and dispassionate history of 'the party' and its role in the South African liberation struggle. Lodge tackles the big questions without flinching, while also capturing the nuances of a complex context. He presents a detailed and integrated narrative of a century of struggle, which does not shy away from the many controversies involved.

– Professor Janet Cherry, Nelson Mandela University

'A master of the historical yarn, Tom Lodge tells the amazing story of the enigmatic, resilient and chameleonic South African Communist Party. Detailed, meticulously researched and a page turner, the book effortlessly navigates the twists and turns of the red road travelled by idealists and realists who found themselves members of a party that sought to build a society run by workers. Why was the party leadership unable or unwilling, over a century of political activity, to fly the red flag consistently high and instead chose to tie the fate of the vanguard of the working class to that of a nationalist movement, the African National Congress? What are the chances of the party realising its supreme goal of a socialist society given the current situation? These are the questions that Lodge deftly and incisively addresses through a close and critical study of all the scholarly sources and his own independent research. This book is arguably the definitive history of the SACP to date. A must-read for all militants, historians and those interested in understanding the continued influence of the party in South African politics.'

– Dr Trevor Ngwane, University of Johannesburg

'Whether traversing well-trodden routes, paths less travelled or uncharted territory, this tour de force, drawing on the author's renowned knowledge, skills and critical acumen, illuminates how and why South African communists achieved remarkable influence and outreach on the precarious road to freedom.'

– Ronnie Kasrils, author, former minister, former member of the Central Committee of the SACP, former member of the National Executive Committee of the ANC

'*Red Road to Freedom* is the first comprehensive account of the century-long history of the Communist Party by one of the most authoritative scholars of South African political history. From the early socialist groups and international influences that contributed to the party's formation, to its embrace of national liberation and progressive Africanisation, its reorganisation underground, the armed struggle and exile years, and finally its still unfolding relationship with successive ANC-led governments post-apartheid, [...] [it] reflects on the critical role played by communists in South Africa's freedom struggle [...] and their lasting influence on black politics.'

– Arianna Lissoni, History Workshop, University of the Witwatersrand

'Tom Lodge takes us on a century-long tour of the history of the South African Communist Party, through the fractal coastline of this party's ideological evolution, to the hinterland of its organisational dynamics and relations with other actors. He's qualified to be our tour guide because he knows this history so well. [...] This book was worth waiting for – it's so refreshing and a welcome addition to what is unfortunately a thin literature on the history of SACP. Like his previous books, this one is set to be compulsory reading for anybody interested in the anatomy and fate of post-apartheid South Africa.'

– Professor Eddy Maloka, Visiting Professor at the Wits School of Governance & CEO of the African Peer Review Mechanism

'A scholarly *tour de force*. Lodge brings to light forgotten episodes, fresh insights and challenges to some standard appraisals, always with an empathetic understanding of the tens of thousands of men and women who were part of this century of struggle.'

– Jeremy Cronin, author, SACP political bureau member and former deputy minister

RED
ROAD
TO
FREEDOM

A
HISTORY
OF THE
SOUTH AFRICAN
COMMUNIST PARTY

1921 - 2021

TOM LODGE

Ⓙ JAMES CURREY

First published in Africa and India by Jacana Media (Pty) Ltd in 2021
10 Orange Street, Sunnyside, Auckland Park 2092, South Africa
www.jacana.co.za

First published in Rest of World by James Currey in 2022; paperback edition 2024
an imprint of Boydell & Brewer Ltd,
PO Box 9, Woodbridge, Suffolk IP12 3DF (GB)
and Boydell & Brewer Inc.,
668 Mt Hope Avenue, Rochester, NY 14620–2731 (US)
www.boydellandbrewer.com
www.jamescurrey.com

The financial assistance of the National Institute for the Humanities and Social Sciences
(NIHSS) towards this publication is hereby acknowledged. Opinions expressed and those
arrived at are those of the author and are not necessarily to be attributed to the NIHSS.

British Library Cataloguing in Publication Data
A catalogue record for this book is available from the British Library

ISBN 978-1-84701-321-7 (James Currey hardback)
ISBN 978-1-84701-360-6 (James Currey paperback)
ISBN 978-1-4314-3134-2 (Jacana paperback)

The publisher has no responsibility for the continued existence or accuracy of URLs for
external or third-party internet websites referred to in this book, and does not guarantee
that any content on such websites is, or will remain, accurate or appropriate

Cover photo: Armour against mine workers, Johannesburg, Wednesday, 15 March 1922.
In this picture, 'Whippet' tank A387 is on its way down Main Street to Fordsburg Square
to support the army's assault on the strikers' headquarters. It broke down later and had to
be towed away. It was the army's only tank, purchased from Britain after the First World
War. The army's main firepower deployed that day were the artillery guns stationed
outside the miners' mansions in Parktown and Westcliff.

Cover design by publicide

Set in Ehrhardt MT Std 10.5/14pt

This publication is printed on acid-free paper

Contents

Preface

CPSA leadership meeting in Cape Town, 1930. Bottom row, left to right: Bill Andrews, WH Harrison, Sidney Bunting. Johnny Gomas is holding the Lenin portrait. Second row includes Gana Makabeni, standing above Harrison. Rebecca Bunting is in the third row, fourth from the right. In the top row, Douglas Wolton is fourth from right.

I began work on a history of South African communists in 1984. I had recently completed a book that was mainly about popular resistance to apartheid during the 1950s. In the course of researching this topic, it became clear to me that in the key places in which organised opposition by black South Africans had been most effective, communists had played a major role in establishing the networks and local leaderships that had mobilised effective campaigning. The great set pieces of anti-apartheid 'struggle' of the 1950s, beginning with the Defiance Campaign, were the product of social movements that combined the forces of workplace organisation with neighbourhood politics animated by 'bread and butter' preoccupations through the 1940s. This combination was especially effective in Port Elizabeth and East London as well as across the townships of the East Witwatersrand, each a locality in which trade union and community leadership were fused in the same people. Take these people and their followers away, and the history of the 1950s would have been different.

I collected the evidence for how these leaderships emerged and how these networks evolved from reading decades-long sequences of local daily newspapers, then, much more than now, a rich resource for social historians. In the pages that were directed at black readers, those that reported on events in townships or 'locations', in the occasional reports of public agitation over local grievances, communists were conspicuous personalities. They would continue to supply community leadership during the 1950s, publicly visible as ANC organisers. In the early 1980s, in the existing scholarship that addressed the history of black South African political movements, communists were, however, almost unmentioned. From the evidence I had assembled to tell the story of *Black South African Politics since 1945*,[1] I concluded there was another book that should be written, about the Communist Party and its contribution to South Africa's history.

At that time there were four really authoritative texts for any serious reader about the South African Communist Party's history. Eddie Roux's *Time Longer than Rope* supplied a gracefully written history of black South African struggles for freedom up to the mid-1940s, the time it was written.[2]

The party's development is a central concern in Roux's narrative, and his treatment of its course through the 1920s and 1930s was informed by his own experience as a party activist in Johannesburg as well as his personal friendships with many of the principal characters. Roux left the party at the end of the 1930s, disaffected by the factionalism and expulsions that followed a succession of strategic changes ordered by Comintern officials. Jack and Ray Simons's luminous and voluminous *Class and Colour in South Africa* was also shaped by the authors' personal engagements in the story they were telling, for both of them helped lead the party in Cape Town through the late 1930s and 1940s.[3] As with Roux's book, their focus was much wider than just the Communist Party, though to a much greater extent than Roux they wrote with a conviction that, to use Bill Freund's phrase, 'the national question and the labour question were closely intertwined'.[4] From this perspective, the party's historic achievement was its movement away from its initial preoccupation with building a class vanguard around white labour to forming an alliance with African nationalism, and in the process transforming it into a radical and militant political movement. The Simonses' book is at its richest when it is grounded upon their own recollections of Western Cape labour movements, in which Ray Simons was so central a figure. The story I learned from local newspapers in East London and Port Elizabeth parallels their own analysis, though they derive their evidence from other vicinities. But their story ends, in 1950, with the party's dissolution.

Jack and Ray Simons were less critical of the Comintern than Eddie Roux; in particular they viewed Moscow's injunction in 1928 that the party should work towards a 'Native republic' as a positive step. In contrast, Eddie Roux's view was that the command was superfluous and damaging, as the party was already enlisting black South African support through building trade unions. Trotskyist views of the party's development have tended to take this argument as their starting point; their contention is that in attempting to secure alliances among African nationalists, the party would again and again fail to exploit opportunities to strengthen a workers movement.[5] The most detailed treatment of Comintern's relationship with its South African affiliate hadn't been published when I began my research, but Sheridan Johns's thesis on the topic was already well known, based as it was on a huge body of Comintern documentation in the public domain.[6] His argument was that the party became wholly subject to external directives from 1928 through the early 1930s, directives that were shaped by Soviet strategic priorities and were often completely impractical and that led to the party's near destruction. Subsequent scholarship by Johns and the Russian historians Apollon Davidson and Irina

Filatova, drawing upon more recently accessible Comintern archival material, elaborated but largely confirmed Johns's (and, indeed, Roux's) arguments about the Native republic thesis as an imported doctrine.[7] In contrast to this view, the Simonses actually attributed the authorship of the slogan and its underlying rationale to a South African communist, James La Guma.

Shortly following the publication of *Class and Colour*, a succinct official history, *Fifty Fighting Years*, appeared.[8] Michael Harmel, its author, was the party's main theorist through the 1950s, and the main personality in shaping its programme in 1961, *The Road to South African Freedom*. This employed the concept of internal colonialism in developing a theoretical justification for the party's engagement with the Congress movement. Harmel had a particularly clear conception of the road to socialism as passing through distinct stages. As a historian his own view of the party's earlier development was influenced by its current trajectory and his understanding of the party's support in 1928 for a 'Native republic' was broadly favourable. Unlike the Simonses, who suggested that the party's efforts to ally with African nationalism at the end of the 1920s arose from a sensible reading of local conditions rather than being prompted by orders from outside, Harmel viewed Comintern's role positively, in setting the party on a 'correct' course, determined by the local application of Leninist anti-imperialist doctrine, something that wouldn't have happened if the South African communists had been left to their own devices. Harmel was quite critical of the Simonses' book, however, lamenting their concentration upon 'personalities rather than social forces' and what he took to be their failure to appreciate the theoretical grounds for the party's support for national liberation. Harmel's text itself is very much about what he calls 'the clash of ideas' and their dialectical effects, and his type of 'historicism' eschews anything anecdotal.[9] *Fifty Fighting Years* becomes especially thin on detail after the party's prohibition, though, to be fair, in 1971 it would have been very dangerous to make public the party's hidden history as a clandestine formation.

Generally, these early writings about the party were dismissive about the struggles of white workers. For example, from their perspective the Rand Revolt was a 'reactionary' tumult, dominated by Afrikaner nationalists. In Harmel's book the ending of the strike is represented as 'the decisive defeat' of white labour 'as a force independent of the bourgeoisie'. This view is also reflected in a later study by another party member, Rob Davies, until recently a South African cabinet minister, whose doctoral study of white labour depicted their actions in 1922 as a defensive 'economic class struggle' conducted by a 'supervisory new petty bourgeoisie'.[10] But fresh insights began to accumulate as a consequence of archivally based historical reconstructions of South African working-class movements starting in the 1970s – a reflection of the duration of archival restrictions as well as a fresh academic interest at South African universities in labour studies prompted by the emergence of a new black trade union movement. This union movement's own journal as well as the campus-based History Workshop movement drew in a range of disciplines. South African labour researchers paid close attention to shifts in the labour process as well as the social world of the workers they encountered. The formation of workers' solidarities and the gestation of their collective action were understood as complex products, not easily reducible to the lexicon of 'materialist analysis', and not simply attributable to the efforts of formal organisations such as trade unions. It was a scholarship that often put its protagonists at odds with Althusserian-inspired 'structuralists' whose focus on capital and its 'fractions' accorded little space to the exploration of the detail of popular movements or the influence of ideas. FA Johnston wrote a pioneering archive-based study of the Industrial Workers of the World, a black syndicalist group.[11] He also undertook the first scholarly study of the 1922 strike, a study that emphasised the structural insecurity of a vulnerable and unskilled white workforce.[12]

Increasingly, historical work addressing South Africa's early labour movements has explored the interstices and even the reciprocal influences between white and black workers' struggles, as well as the degree to which both in the first decades of the twentieth century were shaped by internationally influential certainties about the proximity of capitalism's defeat: here Jonathan Hyslop's work on white labour leaders and Lucien van der Walt's study of syndicalism have been transformative.[13] Allison Drew's biography of Sidney Bunting also merits mention here as the best biographical study of the formation of one of South African communism's founding fathers.[14] A detailed history of the South African Bundists still awaits an author.

My own work on the party stalled in the mid-1980s. I wrote up my initial research on the party's activities during the Second World War, then a relatively under-researched area, but on returning to Johannesburg from the sabbatical I spent in Britain where I undertook my initial interviewing, I became diverted by a present-day insurrectionary movement. In any case it had become clear to me that the secret history of the party's recent development would be closely guarded, and for good reasons. Since the party's unbanning in 1990 and the return to South Africa of most members of its exile community, however, conditions have changed, and the practical reasons for the party to conceal its history since 1950 have lost their force. Nearly fifty members of the underground party have now published memoirs, and several of these veterans have donated their archives to university libraries: a considerable proportion of the party's internal records have become freshly accessible in the last couple of decades. A large selection of the Comintern archives in Moscow is now available online. In other former communist countries, formerly closed records can now illuminate the various kinds of solidarity and support that were offered to South African communists. The availability of new archival resources and readier first-hand informants has prompted a revival of writing about the party. David Everatt's study of the construction of a non-racial political movement in the 1950s filled in some of the gaps in our knowledge of the party's reconstruction after its banning.[15] Mia Roth's history draws on South African official archives as well as Comintern records to present a different interpretation the party's pre-1950 journey; unlike earlier writers, she concludes that it remained a movement emotionally tied to white labour with its African adherents patronised and disregarded.[16]

Probably the most influential of the more recent studies of the party's development is Stephen Ellis's investigation of the party's relationship in exile with the ANC, *External Mission*.[17] Drawing on a range of archival resources including East German records, Ellis argued that the party prospered in exile and that it completed a process of controlling and directing the ANC that had begun in the 1950s; and that, moreover, this was largely detrimental. In particular, Ellis attributed to the party's influence the evolution of an authoritarian political culture in the larger movement. Eddy Maloka's history of the exiled party – which is about to appear in a third edition – presents a very different view of the party. Drawing upon what appear to be the party's own archival records, he suggests that the party's situation in exile was often precarious and that its influence within the ANC was quite limited, not least because of its tiny size.[18]

Even from this brief overview, it should be clear that in writing this book I have been building on formidable foundations constructed by other researchers. So, what am I adding to what we already have?

In general, I have tried to identify the different social groups in which the party found its support and from whom it recruited its leadership. Secondly, a recurring question I address through the narrative is when did the party make a difference; when was its presence important in shaping broader political developments?

Turning to the chronology, I pay more attention to the party's pre-history than is the case with earlier organisationally focused treatments. One conclusion that I have drawn from this is that the party was shaped by a range of socialist traditions and that their influence persisted. I place greater emphasis than earlier writers on the party's first contacts with black South Africans and I suggest than these were decisive. On the great debate about the 'Native republic' I find the view of the party as a Moscow proxy unpersuasive, though it was also true that when Comintern got its way, the effects were indeed damaging. The party's engagement in popular front politics after 1935 has been largely uncharted: this book supplies fresh detail. In the 1940s I propose that the party became a key actor in the formation of black working-class politics, but that this process was also divisive and difficult and by no means inevitable. Hitherto unused archival materials as well as the insights from an increasingly candid genre of autobiographies make possible a much fuller picture of the secret party of 1952 to 1965. Despite its concealment and tiny numbers, its intellectual impact on black South African mainstream politics was considerable. On the exile period, one of my key preoccupations was to map out the activities of the party's recruits and more informal following inside South Africa. I also explore the scope and nature of its broader influence and, in doing so, I have reached different conclusions from both Stephen Ellis and Eddy Maloka. Finally, I have tried to bring the story up to date, attempting to assess the degree to which communists both inside and outside government have shaped and influenced policy in successive ANC-led administrations.

In researching and writing this book I have benefited from various kinds of help and camaraderie.

Over a long time a number of people answered my questions patiently and openly, and I can now record my thanks for their generosity and their time. They include Miriam Basner, Rusty and Hilda Bernstein, Brian Bunting, Jeremy Cronin, Bettie du Toit, Barbara Harmel, Willie Kalk, Indres Naidoo, Essop and Meg Pahad, Ray Alexander and Jack Simons, Bernard Sachs, Albie Sachs, Albertina Sisulu, Walter Sisulu, Ben Turok and Douglas Wolton. I hope I have not misinterpreted what they have told me. I am also indebted to fellow researchers who shared their own interview transcripts with me: Iain Edwards, Bob Edgar and Milan Oralek. A number of other researchers have placed their interview transcripts in accessible archive collections: I list these in detail in my bibliography, but I'd like to make a special mention here of Sylvia Neame's transcribed interviews, conducted through the 1970s and 1980s. Together with the documents she has preserved, these embody a treasure trove for any research on South Africa's liberatory politics, assembled by one of its magisterial historians.

Another key group of people guided me through the archival repositories I visited, often identifying relevant materials and unearthing key documents. In particular, without the support of Gabriele Mohale, Elizabeth Marima and their former colleague Michele Pickover at the University of the Witwatersrand, constructing the research base for this book would have been impossible. I am also very grateful to the librarians who maintain the newspaper holdings at the Johannesburg Public Library: the library's press collection is magnificent, unparalleled and under-appreciated. Here Mr Mashaba was my kindly guide. I am similarly obligated to Karen Ijumba at the Rivonia Museum's Liliesleaf Archive, to staff at the Mayibuye Centre at the University of the Western Cape, the University of Cape Town's Jagger Library, the Luthuli Centre at the University of KwaZulu-Natal's Westville campus, the Rivonia Museum, the Borthwick Centre at the University of York, the British Library at St Pancras, the South African National Archives, and the Czech National Archives in Prague. I must also thank Warren Siebrits and Lucia van Zyl in Johannesburg, who allowed me and helped me to photograph the judge's copy of the evidence books from Bram Fischer's trial, which Mr Siebrits purchased in May 2017.

Often ideas and arguments in this book were developed through correspondence, conversations, and other kinds of promptings from friends, colleagues and scholars who work in the same field. Particularly useful and encouraging in this respect were my exchanges with Francis Antonie, Peter Biller, Belinda Bozzoli, Colin Bundy, Luli Callinicos, Allison Drew, Jonty Driver, Iain Edwards, Irina Filatova, Baruch and Yael Hirson, Peter Hudson, Sheridan Johns, Ronnie Kasrils, Paul Landau, Stephen Louw, Anthony McElligott, Hugh Macmillan, Shauna Mottiar, Bill Nasson, Sifiso Ndlovu, Sylvia Neame, Milan Oralek, Neil Robinson, Noam Pines, Jeremy Seekings, Alf Stadler, Karel Sieber, Raymond Suttner, Mark Stein, Charles van Onselen, Harry Wilson, Nic Wolpe and the organisers and participants of seminars and lectures held at the universities of Limerick and York as well as the Centre for Civil Society in Durban. Lucien van der Walt generously shared with me his files of *The International*, saving me from what would have been an expensive visit to the South African Library in Cape Town. Two sabbaticals, one granted by the University of the Witwatersrand in 1984 and one by the University of Limerick in 2017, supplied some of the time I needed to undertake the research and writing. I must also acknowledge for their gracious hospitality and lively engagement my host institutions where I spent these research leaves: the Centre for Southern African Studies at the University of York and the Centre d'Etudes d'Afrique Noir at Sciences-Po, Bordeaux.

Publishers willing to make commitments to long research-based monographs are becoming unusual. I have been really fortunate in the support I have enjoyed from members of the team at Jacana. Their backing has been the most important consideration in making this book happen, from their commissioning of the title ten years ago through their long wait for its completion to their sympathetic engagement in the final crafting of the text as well as the care and thought they have directed at the book's design. Working with Maggie Davey, Bridget Impey and Russell Martin has been so rewarding.

Finally, working on a big book is enriching in all kinds of ways but many of the costs of the process are absorbed by the author's family and household. My last thank-yous are for Carla, Kim, Guy and Amie for their interest and their encouragement and their tolerance during my absences and disengagements from other things that matter.

ONE

Just like Russia: Revolutionary Socialists in the Cape and the Transvaal, 1890–1921

I. W. W.'S IN SOUTH AFRICA.

Organization Established Among the Natives at Durban.

JOHANNESBURG, Union of South Africa, July 18.—At the preliminary hearing of S. P. Bunting, former Provincial Councillor; S. Hanscomb, and a man named Tinker, who were arrested on July 7 for complicity with the threatened uprising of the natives in South Africa, held here today, it was testified that Bunting presided at 'various meetings at which the natives were urged to organize against the capitalists.

It was also stated that a branch of the Industrial Workers of the World had been established among the natives at Durban.

The New York Times

Published: July 19, 1918

Report in the New York Times *on SOP Bunting's trial after the 1918 sanitation workers' strike. At the time the IWW or 'Wobblies' were a major news story in the United States, hence the interest here in their South African manifestation.*

'**O**ur conditions are more Russian than British', an editorial asserted in a socialist weekly newspaper published in Johannesburg in 1919.[1] It was a claim that South African revolutionaries liked making, especially when they were in sympathetic company. 'The situation in South Africa is almost identical to that in Russia,' South African visitors informed Comintern leaders when they met them in Moscow in 1921.[2] Accordingly, South African socialists were swift to employ an imported demonology to describe their own local adversaries. The ex-servicemen who broke up the meetings the International Socialists tried to hold outside Johannesburg's City Hall were 'Decembrists'.[3] The Citizen's Protection League, an organisation pledged to maintain public services in the event of lightning strikes, was Johannesburg's version of the 'White Guards', warned *The International*.[4]

These sorts of contentions and the terminology accompanying them were not simply used for rhetorical effect; they reflected sincere convictions. After all, Jewish Russian emigrants from the Russian Pale were well represented in the group of men and women that formed a communist party in Johannesburg that year; presumably they knew what they were talking about. In any case, you didn't have to be Russian to spot certain obvious similarities between pre-revolutionary Russia and imperial South Africa. In Russia a socialist revolution had just happened, despite the country being only 'on the verge of developing industrially. In Russia, the workers ... are mainly a peasant class ... not class conscious.'[5] So too in South Africa, where '"the proletariat" in practice includes not only the industrial workers but the small peasants and landless agriculturists', just 'like that of Russia'.[6] South African natives were abused abominably, the anarchist shopkeeper Henry Glasse reported from Port Elizabeth, in a letter he wrote in 1905 to Prince Kropotkin; they were compelled to carry passes with them at all times, 'à la Russia'.[7] In fact, nineteenth-century Russian visitors to South Africa suggested that comparisons between the respective situations of Russian peasants and black South Africans worked in Russia's favour.[8] Even so, South African communist leaders such as Sidney Bunting made a point of describing South African peasants as 'serfs'. Bunting's usage was not so careless; before deciding to travel to South Africa, while serving articles in London, he wrote a 300-page 'treatise' on Russian imperial expansion.[9] It wasn't just communists who noticed parallels in social relationships between the two countries. Charles Pienaar, visiting Russia in 1925 as the London-based South African trade commissioner, noted approvingly the similarities in peasant land tenure he observed in 1925, during the era of the New Economic Policy, and the policies that prevailed in 'our 'occupation' farms in the Northern Transvaal'.[10] There were also the more obvious coincidences of geography and distance. Bill Andrews, a South African engineer who joined Comintern's executive in 1923, took a train from Moscow to the Crimea. He observed how 'around Alexandrosk the colouring and general appearance of the country resembles the South African veld in mid-winter – minus the kopjes. The train runs through one vast brown plain.'[11]

Yet Johannesburg, the chief setting for this volume's narrative, was hardly St Petersburg. It did not resemble an imperial metropolis. It had no marble palaces or grand public spaces. In their place stood corporate buildings like the nine-storey Corner House, Johannesburg's first skyscraper, headquarters of Rand Mines, and the new luxury shops that catered for the city's managerial class: Stuttaford's Romanesque revival department store and Cuthberts' shoe shop with its pagoda-style corner tower. And in this global mining centre, the engine room of what Lenin himself had recently proclaimed to be capital's ultimately destructive imperial phase, the 'hidden abode' of production would be especially well concealed. After all, as one visitor to Johannesburg noted, 'there isn't much to see above ground at a gold mine', only the 'pithead gear, a few sheds, [and] a maze of railway sidings'. The city itself had its man-made landscape as its most conspicuous backdrop, 'the yellow mine dumps, table topped, … in line upon the skyline like the truncated hills of some titanic mole'.[12] Other than these artificial hillocks, the city had few attractions for sightseers. Indeed, in 1910, when the British socialist Tom Mann toured Johannesburg, the first stop in the itinerary his hosts organised was a visit to the cemetery in Braamfontein. This was not to pay homage at the tombs of any previous heroes, but rather to inspect the graves 'kept in readiness', thirty or so freshly excavated pits awaiting the bodies of the white mine workers who would die that week from accidents in their shifts or from phthisis in their beds. There were a number of larger trenches as well, in which dead African workers were 'dropped in', five at a time.[13] At that time the average working life for a white miner was seven years, for their black workmates somewhat less. Five years later, in 1914, Tom Mann made a second excursion to Johannesburg and on this occasion there were indeed heroes' graves, trade unionists shot dead by armed cavalry in the middle of the city, during a strike in 1911.[14] As in Russia, strike movements and workers' protests in South Africa would be suppressed with armed force, most notably in 1922. Norman Herd, the first chronicler of the great white miners' rebellion of that year, remembers how as a small child he was sitting on the verandah of his parents' hillside cottage in Durban, watching a train 'panting up the slope'. It was 'packed with Khaki-clad men ... shouting and cheering without restraint', the Durban Light Infantry, on its way 'to crush a strike in Johannesburg'. And Herd, too, couldn't resist a Russian comparison, commenting how the smoke that 'drifted from the muzzles of the guns across a wrecked and cratered landscape was as meaningful in its vagueness as Turgenev's smoke'.[15]

IN SOUTH AFRICA, organised socialist activity can be traced back to as early as 1890. In that year in Port Elizabeth a local storekeeper named Henry Glasse formed a Socialist Club. Glasse had been living in Port Elizabeth since 1881 after his arrival from England. In 1886 he had translated into English a pamphlet by Prince Peter Kropotkin, *The Place of Anarchism in Socialistic Evolution*, and his own writings published by the Freedom Press in London confirm his commitment to anarchist beliefs.[16] In a letter written to Kropotkin from Port Elizabeth in 1905 he mentioned his experiences in working alongside South African 'natives', among whom, he suggested, 'you could still find the principle of communism – primitive communism – such brotherly love ... such help for one another ... unknown among "civilised" people'. They were sorely 'ill treated', he noted, 'not allowed to be on the streets after 9 p.m., in the land that was once their own'.[17] Writing in 1912 in the *Voice of Labour*, a syndicalist weekly published in Johannesburg, Glasse proposed that for white South African workers to 'pretend' they could fight their battles separately from 'coloured wage slaves' was 'simply idiocy'.[18] Glasse established his Socialist Club in Port Elizabeth in 1891 but no records survive that can tell us about its activities.[19]

Other early groups inclined to acknowledge that white, black and coloured workers might share common class interests included a cluster of Jewish trade unions that began to be established in Cape Town in 1898. Here the presence of coloured artisans helped prompt predispositions to build organisations that crossed communal lines.[20] Working against such promptings, though, was the importation of a British model of 'craft unionism' which, in seeking to confine entry into skilled trades to people who had served lengthy formal apprenticeships, often excluded local craftsmen, becoming effectively mono-racial.[21] Meanwhile, in Johannesburg, an International Independent Labour Party was formed in 1899 though it collapsed with the outbreak of the South African War.[22] James T Bain, a Scottish engineer, who was influenced by William Morris and was an acquaintance of Prince Kropotkin, was one of its leaders. Bain saw himself as a revolutionary socialist but his radicalism was tempered by racial defensiveness: the party's appeal to 'Workers and the General Public' included both condemnation of 'Bastard Jingoistic Imperialism' and a demand for the maintenance of 'the Transvaal as a white man's country'.[23] A cluster of various craft-based unions enlisted different groups within the workforce on the gold mines before the war. A more all-embracing Witwatersrand Mines Employees and Mechanics Union, a 'shadowy and small organisation', drew its inspiration both from the American 'Knights of Labour' and British socialist 'New Unionism', urging workers to form one big union, an assembly of different crafts and skill levels. Its formation was prompted by fears that the Chamber of Mines planned to sponsor a massive immigration of skilled workers to reduce local wages. James Bain was one of its key personalities. The union had friendly relations with the Kruger administration and opposed the Uitlanders. A succession of well-publicised scandals contributed to its collapse in 1895.[24] Meanwhile, a Knights of Labour had existed in Kimberley: it was anti-capitalist but also opposed to the diamond mines employing cheap coloured labour.[25] More prosaically, a Trades and Labour Council established itself in Johannesburg in 1895.

At the South African War's end, in 1902, with the revival of gold-mining, fresh immigrants from Australia and the United States as well as demobilised ex-soldiers from Britain and the Dominions would bring fresh ideas. Between 1901 and 1903, 114,000 immigrants arrived in South African from Europe.[26] On the Witwatersrand by 1904, the white population was 123,000, more than double its pre-war level.[27] The white population in this region included more than 20,000 white mine workers, many of them recently arrived from Cornwall, California and Australia: the mining industry was the single largest employer. Nearly 4,000 whites worked on the railways around Johannesburg in 1913 and another 25,000 white workers were employed in small factories and workshops.[28] The black or African workforce on the Witwatersrand was concentrated on the mines: there were nearly 200,000 African mine workers in 1910 after a decade in which the Chamber of Mines had struggled to recruit Africans. This was partly because during the South African War African peasants had occupied deserted white farms and seized stock and were reluctant to enter into mining contracts. The Chamber accentuated its difficulties in recruiting Africans by reducing wages for African workers from pre-war levels.[29] For three years between 1904 and 1907, 60,000 indentured Chinese workers were brought in to alleviate labour shortages on the mines. White South African and British trade unionist opposition to the employment of Chinese workers persuaded the newly elected government in the Transvaal and an ascendant Liberal administration in Britain to agree to repatriate the workers in 1907. South African labour leaders believed that Chinese workers represented a much greater threat to local white skill monopolies than Africans, and they claimed that from the time of their introduction Chinese workers were replacing whites.[30] African workers on the mines were migrants, recruited on annual contracts, housed in enclosed compounds, and paid a small fraction of white worker wages. White wages had to cover comparatively higher levels of subsistence, which were partly the effect of the costs of supporting urban households using imported goods.[31] Outside the mines, more urbanised African workers were confined mainly to domestic service – there were 37,000 African 'houseboys' in Johannesburg – and menial labouring jobs. The African share of the off-mine industrial workforce in Johannesburg was minor, amounting to only 6,000 employees in 1912.[32]

Before the First World War, then, the non-mining working class on the Witwatersrand was mainly white and still substantially first-generation immigrant, though, increasingly, locally born Afrikaners were joining the less skilled sections of the industrial workforce. In the two other main South African cities, Cape Town and Durban, the picture was different. In the Cape Colony the 1904 census registered nearly 50,000 coloured workers in industrial occupations, mainly unskilled but including considerable groups of artisans especially in the tailoring and garment industries, who would have been living mainly in Cape Town or Port Elizabeth.[33] Of 830 trade unionists counted in Cape Town in 1907, 173 were coloured.[34] In Durban, ex-indentured Indian workers constituted entire workforces in certain factories before 1910 and were in the process of joining the ranks of skilled workers despite their exclusion from apprenticeships.[35]

On the Witwatersrand, a Trades and Labour Council, revived in 1902, assembled a group of mainly skills-based craft unions as well as the Transvaal Miners' Association (known from 1913 as the Mine Workers' Union). The Miners' Association from 1907 was essentially an industrial union, and its leader Tom Matthews, together with Bill Andrews of the Amalgamated Engineers, favoured a more confrontational approach to worker organisation than the generally more conciliatory craft union principals who opposed any political activism by trade unionists beyond immediate job-related concerns.[36]

Like many of his fellow workers, Tom Matthews was a Cornishman, who during his American experience had become a socialist and a convert to the American model of industrial unionism. He was also exceptional in his South African work setting for his relatively benign attitude towards African workers; he told the 1907 Mining Commission that as an idealist and a socialist, he believed 'in treating the Native as a White man'.[37] It was Bill Andrews who would become the dominant figure on the left end of the political spectrum embodied in the council's leadership. By this stage of his life, Andrews had a formidable presence; a patrician-looking labour aristocrat, he was described as 'stately' and 'careful of his dignity'.[38] He was born into an artisanal family in Suffolk and brought up as a Methodist, schooled in chapel and through an ambitious course of bedtime reading of the English classics chosen by his dressmaker mother. Andrews would join a generation of labour leaders that included men who read for pleasure, autodidact intellectuals who maintained bookcases among their few possessions.[39] He served his apprenticeship as a trainee fitter from the age of 13 and arrived in South Africa in 1893 on a 'miner's ticket' to find work on the mine at Geldenhuys Estates. Here he helped to form a branch of the Amalgamated Engineers.[40] Military service during the South African War interrupted his ascent within the trade union movement. Before the First World War, though favouring wider kinds of class mobilisation than the defensive craft-based concerns of many Council leaders, Andrews's militancy was confined by racial exclusivism. He was ready in 1907 to restrict Africans from operating boilers, for instance, on grounds of safety; and in 1908 he called for whites to be given preference when unskilled labour was needed, because whites were citizens and voters, and hence more likely to uphold and defend 'standards' that would guarantee 'the general welfare of the community'.[41] With the restoration of representative government in the Transvaal, voting and electoral politics were becoming key preoccupations for this early generation of trade union leaders. The Trades and Labour Council sponsored its own candidates in Johannesburg's municipal elections in 1903 and 1904.[42]

Australian experience supplied especially important models, imported into South African by men with backgrounds of militant Australian trade unionism.[43] Australian gold miners had combined tough class insurgency with racial sectionalism, beginning with their opposition to the importation of cheap Chinese labour into Australia in the 1850s – a political struggle that would be replicated more successfully in South Africa between 1904 and 1907. More generally, many if not most immigrants from the imperial Dominion could be expected to share the racial prejudices that helped justify British imperial expansion. 'White labourism' was a transnational ideology, not specific to South Africa.[44] What was striking about the Australian experience was the combination of social democracy with racial exclusivity. That a Labour Party administration had enacted significant reforms (while opposing Asian immigration) ensured that the Australian experience would supply a key framework of reference for leaders of the South African labour movement. In 1905 a Political Labour League, inspired by a parent body in New South Wales, was established by Peter Whiteside, an ex-Australian engine driver and president of the newly re-established Trades and Labour Council between 1902 and 1904; he was a 'fervent racist' and an early opponent of the Chamber of Mines' plans to import Chinese labour.[45]

Meanwhile, a Labour Representation Committee in 1905 brought together delegates from trade unions and the Trades and Labour Council, a local branch of the (British) Independent Labour Party (ILP) and other more exotic groups based among recent European immigrants, some of whom were influenced by Marxist ideas. These included the syndicalist-inclined Italian Socialist Group; the Vorwärts Club, constituted by German Social Democrats; the Friends of Russian Freedom; and the Jewish Bund.[46] The Bundists began arriving in South Africa in 1900, bringing with them from the Russian Pale their own strategic vision of a socialism brought about by an insurrectionary labour movement constituted by industry-wide unions.[47] Bundists formed the Friends of Russian Freedom in 1905 in reaction to that year's reports of the pogroms that followed the revolutionary upheaval in Russia. The Friends were a Jewish 'self-defence' movement; initially, though, their most frequent adversaries were not anti-Semites but rather bands of Zionist youth paramilitarily predisposed like them.[48] The Bund opposed the Zionists' aim of a separate territorial Jewish state; it sought cultural rights and civic equality for Jews within the countries in which they lived. The experience of Russian anti-Semitism inclined the Bund to oppose racial discrimination in general.[49]

The Bundists would make a lasting contribution to the evolution of South Africa's revolutionary socialists, arguably reinforcing predispositions to extend organisation beyond white workers. First-generation Jewish immigrants, many of them with experience or knowledge of the Bund, would for a while outnumber workers of British origin in the Communist Party's predecessors. In 1905, Bundists were at the radical end of the spectrum of South African labour politics. The more staid ILP favoured the 'socialisation of the means of production', but its solidarities did not extent to embracing the doctrines of universal brotherhood upheld by its parent body in Britain. The British ILP was a parliamentarian party; loosely accommodating ideologically, it included Marxists in its following but its leadership was generally reformist. Bill Andrews, who was one of the people who established the group, was beginning to read Marx at that time, though he was probably exceptional in this. During its short existence, the South African branch of the ILP championed exclusively white suffrage and opposed the local presence of Chinese labour,[50] in this way joining the mainstream of the South African labour movement.[51]

The Labour Representation Committee would supply the organisational foundations for the South African Labour Party, which was formed finally in 1909. Like the British body from which it borrowed its name, the committee was a broad group ideologically speaking, including Marxist and anarchist revolutionaries and more reformist socialists within its fold, but most of its membership would agree that skilled jobs should be restricted to whites and the existing numerical ratios of black and white workers should be retained.[52] When it was formed, the Labour Party accepted coloured members in the Cape, where coloured people were enfranchised subject to various qualifications[53] and also sometimes belonged to cross-racial craft unions. Coloured membership of the Labour Party was conditional on the acceptance and 'upholding' of 'white standards', that is, white wage levels.[54] At its formation, it should be noted, the Labour Party called for Indian repatriation.[55]

On the Rand, craft union leaders could be ambivalent on the issue of racial job reservation. Their chief preoccupation was to maintain the status and leverage enjoyed by highly skilled workers who had served lengthy apprenticeships against any efforts by employers to 'dilute' or fragment the labour process so that skilled jobs could be broken down and undertaken by less skilled replacements, white or black. By comparison, the Transvaal Mine Workers' Association was quite explicitly committed to racial job reservation – a reflection of the extent to which by the 1900s white mine workers were no longer undertaking productive tasks underground, but were increasingly supervising African operatives such as drillers – 'hammer boys' – instead. Indeed, in 1907 a government report concluded 'that the mines are independent to a great extent of the skilled miner'.[56] In these circumstances white miners were much more vulnerable to replacement by low-paid African migrant workers than were genuine craftsmen who had qualified through lengthy apprenticeships. More generally, before the First World War most white trade unionists and most labour political leaders were predisposed to defend racial privilege.[57]

MORE RADICAL AND EMANCIPATORY inclinations were evident in this early phase of white working class politics. In Johannesburg a short-lived Socialist Labour Party constituted itself in 1902 and began distributing writings of Karl Kautsky and Daniel De Leon, though unlike both Kautsky and the American syndicalist, it totally rejected electioneering. De Leon would be an abiding influence on the South African left. A former teacher and one-time Columbia University lecturer, Daniel De Leon joined the leadership of the American Socialist Labour Party in 1891. His thinking was shaped both by Marx and by Social Darwinist ideas about pre-historical collective communalism. Social evolution, De Leon would argue, had reached the stage at which political institutions were no longer needed; industrial society could function creatively without any coercive order. The vehicles for revolutionary change would be all-industry unions. The Industrial Workers of the World, which De Leon helped to establish in 1905, was a practical expression of this vision. Workers' control would establish itself through the general strike.[58] De Leon did not, however, rule out the option of such 'political' activism as contesting elections, and indeed the Socialist Labour Party had originally constituted itself as an electorally focused body. After 1912 the American syndicalists would be split by strategic disagreements between DeLeon's Detroit-based group and the more purist and more anarchist-influenced Chicago-centred Syndicalist League, which rejected electoral politics as harmful.

The leader of the Socialist Labour Party in Johannesburg was Jock Campbell, apparently 'the first socialist to make propaganda among African workers'; he spoke of the 'unity among all wage slaves'.[59] In Cape Town, a Social Democratic Federation (SDF) was constituted in 1904, again mainly by demobbed soldiers. Wilfrid Harrison, an ex-guardsman turned pacifist who worked as a carpenter, was one of its key personalities, combining imaginative vision with, to use the phraseology of one of his contemporaries, 'grit and pluck'. Harrison described himself as a 'philosophical anarchist', and though the early Federation[60] had connections with the Marxist British group of the same name, its anarchist predispositions may have been strengthened by membership drawn increasingly from artisan Jewish immigrants, normally residents in what were still multiracial slum neighbourhoods, for not all politically animated Jewish arrivals were Bundists or Zionists and, in any case, several of the South African Bundists appear to have been influenced by anarcho-syndicalist ideas before their arrival in South Africa.[61] Harrison himself was in contact with Kropotkin's associates in London by 1910.[62] The SDF published a monthly newspaper, the *Cape Socialist*; it opened a soup kitchen in the mainly coloured area of District Six; and it agitated on behalf of the unemployed. Other activities undertaken by its hundred or so members included a choir, picnics and debates: the Federation was not a militantly activist agency. It did oppose white labour exclusivity, contesting the colour bar in trade unions, and enlisted coloured members and addressed its followers at meetings that drew mainly black crowds in a range of languages including isiXhosa. The SDF was largely Cape Town-focused, though a more short-lived De Leonite Social Democratic Party led mainly by Jewish immigrants organised the first May Day demonstration in Johannesburg in 1904.[63]

In 1908, the SDF condemned the draft Act of Union as an 'insult to the coloured races', the only white-led South African political organisation to do so.[64] More conspicuously perhaps, in that year it hosted a visit to Cape Town by Keir Hardie, the British ILP MP, after the leaders of the local Trades and Labour Council had withheld their hospitality.[65] The SDF leaders' willingness to associate their group with Hardie was another quite explicit commitment to the ideal of racial equality. Hardie had visited Pretoria, Johannesburg and Durban, attracting fiercely hostile public receptions in those centres because of his support for equal rights for Indians and the sympathy he expressed for the Natal Africans' grievances that led to the 1906 Bambatha rebellion. Hardie had also proposed that unions should welcome African workers, explaining that if they were to succeed in obtaining the same pay rates as whites, white vulnerability to competition from cheap labour would cease.[66] Despite its anarchical predispositions, the Federation contested elections in districts with coloured voters, at least once successfully, with Morris Alexander winning a municipal seat with the help of coloured as well as Jewish voters in District Six in 1905.[67] In District Six the Federation enjoyed electoral support partly as a consequence of the backing of John Tobin, a local coloured businessman and founder of the African People's Organisation (APO). Tobin was normally a supporter of the white Afrikaner Bond, but he encouraged coloured voters to elect more left-wing or racially liberal candidates in those districts that the Bond did not contest.[68] The Federation also set up a general workers' union with its offices in District Six to facilitate coloured recruitment though Jewish Bundists were its most evident supporters.[69]

Jewish Bundists would have helped to persuade the SDF to hold a meeting in Cape Town to express solidarity with Russian revolutionaries; in 1907 it also collected funds and, together with the Friends of Russian Freedom, organised a programme for Sergius Riger during his visit. Riger was a member of the Bund's Russian central committee.[70] Olive Schreiner sent a message from London to be read out at this meeting in solidarity with the Russian rebellion. Subsequently, Schreiner, who had been friendly with Karl Marx's daughter

Eleanor, wrote to the SDF her 'Letter on the Jews'. In this communication she condemned the Russian pogroms and identified Karl Marx, 'the great German socialist', as an emblematic Jewish figure in European political reform, ensuring herself a lasting place in the South African communists' canonical pantheon.[71] While visiting Johannesburg later in his tour, Riger tried to persuade his hosts in the Friends of Russian Freedom to set up a formal South African branch of the Bund but he encountered resistance; they felt 'there was no place for this in South Africa'.[72] Meanwhile, in an unusual foray into militant activism, in 1906 the SDF organised interracial demonstrations among unemployed workers, including a march on parliament. Several of the meetings degenerated into riotous looting sessions, much to Harrison's mortification. Raiding a bakery, 'throwing armloads of bread into the scrambling clutching hands of cheering workers' during one of these unruly tumults supplied the first experiences of activism for the teenage Jimmy La Guma, later a key figure in the early history of the Communist Party.[73] Harrison himself preferred educational and cultural work to direct action; he believed that 'socialist education' was the most effective way of countering racial prejudice – white workers needed to be persuaded.[74]

Between 1908 and 1912, a weekly newspaper, the *Voice of Labour*, would supply the main platform in Johannesburg for an alternative left politics to the defensive concerns of white labourism.[75] Another ex-South African War serviceman, Archie Crawford, edited *Voice of Labour*. Crawford had been, until his dismissal for organising protest against retrenchments in 1906, a fitter in the railway workshops in Pretoria and, briefly, a Johannesburg city councillor after his election in 1907. He had belonged to the Independent Labour Party and was a member of the Labour Representation Committee. *Voice of Labour*, at least when it came to defining its editorial principles, rejected any organised activity based on racial distinctions,[76] though the content of its columns often reflected the casual, everyday racial condescension that probably characterised most of its readers: interracial class solidarity did not require 'kissing a black brother or inviting him to tea'.[77] Crawford and his associates as members of the Labour Representation Committee were present at the foundation of the Labour Party. In October 1909, when the party held its first conference, ideological and programmatic differences led to the withdrawal of many of the real socialists, including Crawford and the *Voice of Labour* group, the Johannesburg Socialist Society, the Cape Town-based Social Democratic Federation and a Social Democratic Party with a branch in Durban and a few followers in Pietermaritzburg. The Durban Social Democrats corresponded with Henry Hyndman's Social Democratic Federation, the first British

Marxist party, whose members believed that mass suffrage would make viable a parliamentary route to socialism. A new Socialist Society in Pretoria also stayed outside the Labour Party. It was started during Wilfrid Harrison's stay in the city when he was working as a carpenter on the new Union Buildings. The Pretoria Socialists confined their activities to a weekly discussion club, notwithstanding the local presence within their midst of one exiled Russian anarchist, Davidoff, who was apparently an advocate of assassinations and other violent sorts of 'propaganda by the deed'.[78]

Archie Crawford had proposed that the Labour Party should reject racial distinctions but, as we have seen, the party incorporated racist restrictions into its programme from its inception. Indeed, its first president, the printer HW Sampson, tried unsuccessfully to persuade the party at its foundation to support the geographical partition and total segregation of Africans from whites.[79] Even so, despite the departure of the more radical groups whose leaders had belonged to the Labour Representation Committee, the Labour Party retained a left wing which included at least a few Marxist socialists. The relative overall political weakness of labour was evident in the 1910 Union elections when the Labour Party won only three out of 13 seats it contested (from a total of 121 constituencies). James Bain stood as one of its candidates, contesting the Pretoria North seat against his mine-owner employer, Sir Thomas Cullinan, calling for expropriation of the mine and denouncing the authorities' 'studiously contemptuous' treatment of white workers. He won 538 votes, nearly a third of the poll.[80] Overall, the Labour Party drew 12.74 per cent of the vote in the Transvaal and a slightly smaller share in Natal. Subsequent by-elections raised its parliamentary representation to six; Bill Andrews was the victor in one of the by-elections, in 1911, in Germiston, arguably becoming South Africa's only socialist parliamentarian.[81] Andrews's biographer, Jack Cope, who was commissioned to write his book in the 1940s by the Communist Party, maintained that as early as 1907 Andrews 'was beginning to doubt the white labour policy' and quoted from his maiden speech in parliament in 1912 on railway workers, in which he observed that 'the black man will not submit to being herded into a compound and treated like a slave'.[82] Unusually among his associates in the ILP, Andrews did not oppose the arrival of Chinese labour and, as we shall see later in his career, would maintain friendly contacts with the local Chinese community.[83] Even so, Andrews's socialism could still be shaped by racial considerations: in another parliamentary intervention, one year later, Andrews called upon the authorities 'to substitute white youths for Africans on maintenance of telegraph lines in his constituency'.[84] Disagreements persist about the extent to which Andrews personally held racialist beliefs, but there can be no doubt about his willingness then and indeed later to garner political support by appealing to racial sensitivities.[85]

WITHIN THE MORE CONFINED arena of labour politics, the Labour Party's more radical non-parliamentary rivals could sometimes appear effective and popular, despite counting their organised following in tens or hundreds compared with the Labour Party's 16,000 paid-up membership.[86] A syndicalist-led local branch of the Industrial Workers of the World (IWW) was established in January 1911, building on a general workers' union that had been formed the year before by the Transvaal Trades and Labour Council and inspired by a visit to South Africa in 1910 by Tom Mann sponsored by the council. Tom Mann had been the general secretary of the ILP in Britain in the 1890s. Between 1903 and 1910 he worked in Australia, helping to lead the syndicalist Victoria Socialist Party. During his visit to South Africa, Mann had called upon his hosts in at least one speech to invite Africans to join the industrial unions he was proposing: 'Whatever number there are, get them all, and if there are another 170,000 available, white or black, get them too.'[87] The IWW's leaders were associated with the *Voice of Labour* and included Jock Campbell, Archie Crawford and, most centrally, Andrew Dunbar, a Scottish blacksmith, sacked from the railways in 1909 after leading a strike. He then became a tramway worker in Johannesburg. Echoing Mann's views, the IWW claimed to embrace all workers, regardless of colour or skill, and explicitly declared its hostility to craft-based unionism, breaking links with the Trades and Labour Council. It was also openly syndicalist, loyal to the Chicago wing of the American movement, and hence determinedly anti-parliamentarian.

In two illegal tram strikes in Johannesburg in January and May 1911, precipitated by management's efforts to impose an unpopular inspector, the IWW succeeded in building a following across almost the entire tramway workforce. Because of efforts by the authorities to forcibly suppress picketing, conflict between the police and strikers together with their supporters, including their wives, developed an insurrectionary quality when strikers erected barricades and assaulted police and would-be scabs with pick-handles. Archie Crawford's lover, Mary Fitzgerald, was dubbed by the press 'Pick-handle Mary' for her combative contribution to these encounters. The IWW subsequently sponsored a 'pick-handle brigade' to break up Labour Party meetings. The IWW's influence spread to Pretoria railway workers, already organised in a general workers' union, led by a one-time adherent of the Dutch social democrats, Hessel Poutsma. This was a union that claimed to welcome all workers irrespective of race, and indeed in later years it recruited coloured and even a few African members in the Cape.[88] The IWW would lose its force and its following in the aftermath of the sackings that succeeded the second tram strike, but momentarily a more radical and professedly socially more inclusive unionism had seemed to be making a real impact on a significant segment of the industrial workforce.

More widely as well, outside the sectarian community of self-consciously organised syndicalism, white workers appeared set on a politically confrontational trajectory. As an official report noted at the end of 1913, 'It is no exaggeration to say that to many of these men ... loyalty to their union has taken the place of loyalty to their government or to their employers.'[89] That year on 27 May, the mine workers' union had declared a strike in protest against the actions of the aptly named EH Bulman, the new manager at New Kleinfontein near Benoni, who had been deployed intentionally to extinguish union militancy. He had dismissed several workers, replacing them with non-union members, and cancelled the Saturday half-day holiday. The local strike committee included men who described themselves as socialists and even syndicalists; one of these was George Mason, also the chairman of a local Labour Party branch, an ex-carpenter from Durham. The miners were soon joined by engine drivers and the stoppage spread across the Witwatersrand, turning into a generalised demand for union recognition.

For James Bain, recently appointed organiser of the Transvaal Federation of Trade Unions, who helped to ensure the generalised backing the Kleinfontein miners received, the dispute supplied 'the opportunity to launch the full-scale attack on the mineowners for which he had waited so long'.[90] He was elected as secretary to the strike committee and would escalate the strikers' demands to include an eight-hour day which would include the time spent in the lifts descending to the shafts, thereby effectively and intentionally ensuring the transformation of the local protest into a wider revolt.[91] Several veterans of bitter Australian labour disputes also joined the committee, including J Forrester Brown, the Mine Workers' Association's East Rand organiser. Archie Crawford and Mary Fitzgerald began to play a conspicuous role, addressing meetings, and Crawford would edit the strike newspaper, which helps to explain its inclusion of syndicalist poetry as well as writing by Kropotkin. In Benoni, the strike committee took over the Grand Theatre as its headquarters, replacing the Union Jack with the Red Flag. In between its rallies, strikers were treated by sympathetic local cinema owners to free showings of *Quo Vadis* and *Les Miserables*.[92] The *Strike Herald* published lists

24

that named scab workers and reported violent assaults on them approvingly. On 2 July the strike attracted power workers in Vereeniging and on 4 July a general strike was announced at a meeting in Fordsburg's Market Square. By this stage 18,000 workers were on strike. Soldiers and armed police broke up the Market Square gathering, and in reaction crowds looted gun shops and set fire to the offices of *The Star*, using dynamite charges, as well as the railway station. An African watchman died in the station fire. The next day, British army cavalry lined up outside the Rand Club fired into a crowd, killing as many as 25 immediately and hurting hundreds more, of whom 12 died later in hospital. On the day after, negotiations between the strike leaders and General Smuts, the Defence Minister, enabled the workers to claim a victory; the authorities promised that grievances would be investigated, compensation would be paid to the families of dead and wounded strikers, and no one would be victimised. In the days following the agreement 9,000 African mine workers went on strike but were forced back to work by soldiers and armed police.[93]

In the second half of 1913, a series of minor wildcat stoppages accompanied the expansion of the railway workers' union, which by the end of the year had registered 9,000 members. The railway workers' union collaborated with the Federation of Labour (the renamed Trades and Labour Council) in producing a Workers' Charter calling for union recognition and the repeal of anti-strike legislation. On 8 January 1914 the union initiated a strike to prevent retrenchments, which was supported the following week by a general strike call from the Federation. Leaders made their political intentions quite clear. As one of their spokesmen declared: 'This is war to the knife. It is definitely a war of the classes. There is no distinction as to race, creed or colour ... I can promise you the end of the fight will be victory for the workers and the end of the government.'[94]

This time, though, the government was better prepared. During the preceding year, the final stages had been completed in setting up a Union Defence Force. The authorities no longer had to depend on a colonial garrison, and could mobilise regular soldiers in overwhelming numbers, five times as many as in 1913, as well as calling up commandos and declaring martial law. Four thousand soldiers laid siege to the Johannesburg Trades Hall. The police arrested strike leaders and on 28 January deported nine of them, including Hessel Poutsma and several of the men who had been conspicuous in the mine workers' stoppage in the previous year. Retrospectively, the government enacted a deportation law; its action on the 28th was in fact illegal but it effectively broke the strike. The arrival of the deported strike leaders in London was greeted by crowds totalling half a million in a massive demonstration of support, the biggest of its kind up to that time.[95] Meanwhile, in South Africa, 700 railway workers lost their jobs after retrenchments.

As the report cited above suggests, officials and government leaders viewed these events as serious challenges to the state's authority, interpreting them as the outcome of revolutionary conspiracies. The most authoritative research on the 1913 strike movement is dismissive of this view.[96] A few syndicalists certainly played a role in the strike's leadership, but their contribution was hardly decisive, Elaine Katz argues. Certainly, James Bain was influential, for without his contribution it was less likely that what began as a local dispute would have broadened into such a major conflagration. But Bain did not share Crawford's and Fitzgerald's 'revolutionary absolutism', his biographer thinks.[97] Bain was no syndicalist, as he revealed in his brief encounter with Jan Smuts during the strike, when he tried vainly to interest Smuts in a scheme to place miners in an agricultural settlement.[98] And most strikers were not really revolutionaries, not in a conscious sense. In so far as strikers viewed themselves as participants in an insurrectionary movement, this was largely a consequence of the South African rulers' predisposition to treat labour protest as illegal rebellion and hence to use armed force from the outset to repress it. That Jan Smuts, the Minister of Defence, represented the government in negotiations with the workers was itself significant. Though an Anglophile, Smuts had little sympathy for industrial workers.

For syndicalists and other radical socialists, the strikes did appear to confirm that white workers had the potential to supply the cutting edge to a liberatory movement against capitalism, not least because of the strikers' own usage of socialist iconography. As one newspaper report observed of Benoni on 8 July 1913: 'the Red Flag has been supreme ... it waves from hundreds of houses and stores'.[99] Socialists on the left as well as officials in government were very ready to read into white workers' unrest symptoms of revolutionary consciousness, even if most of these workers were more probably hoping 'for recognition within the existing order'.[100]

Whatever their underlying motivations, the 1911–14 strikes were politically significant for any history of the South African left because of their political effects. The first and most obvious of these was the enlargement of the Labour Party's support. It contested the Transvaal Provincial Council's elections in which the party won 26 seats. Labour's organised followers in 1913 were augmented by a significant expansion of Jewish membership; Jews joined in considerable numbers that year, prompted by fears of enforced deportation that were triggered by the government's new legislation enacted after the strike, and their fresh presence in the Labour Party is likely to have strengthened its left wing.[101] Key members of the Socialist Labour Party also joined the Labour Party in 1912. The Socialist Labour Party was a syndicalist group formed at roughly the same time as the IWW in 1910 but differing from it in its acceptance of electioneering as an accompaniment to industrial action, following Daniel De Leon's Detroit-based group. Eddie Roux, whose father, Philip, was one of its leaders, describes the Socialist Labour Party as a faction that existed within the Labour Party from its inception; by 1914 Philip Roux was secretary of the Labour Party's Bezuidenhout Valley branch.[102] In 1912, the Labour Party affiliated to the Second International, and the acceptance of its anti-war resolution adopted that year at the Stuttgart conference created new space within mainstream Labour for more radically predisposed socialists.[103]

A second effect of the strike movement was its impact in shifting to the left key individuals within the labour movement, most notably Bill Andrews, who helped to mobilise the general strike in 1914. In a subsequent parliamentary debate Andrews defended the rights of black workers 'to organise and combine', later telling his Labour Party colleagues that black people should be included in any national community that had abolished the class system. George Mason moved leftwards even further in advocating interracial trade unionism, as did Forrester Brown, another of the mine workers' officials; both men were probably prompted by the African strikes that had followed the white mine worker stoppage. Mason in 1916 actually claimed that he had asked African workers during initial stages of the strike in Benoni to lay down their tools and demand more pay; 'they responded almost to a man', he insisted 'and the mine was stopped'.[104] This may have been true, for Smuts justified the 1914 deportations by suggesting that certain deportees had 'tampered with the natives' in 1913, implying that they had encouraged African workers to join their action.[105] There may have been other white calls for black solidarity action. After the suppression of the African strikes, the Native National Congress (later the African National Congress) angrily objected that black strikers were paying the penalty for 'doing what their white overseers told them to do'.[106]

Sidney Bunting, one of the successful Labour candidates in the 1913 Provincial Council elections, was also impressed by the black strikes. As he noted in his manifesto, Africans were 'bound to organise soon', though at present they remained 'allies, or rather tools of capitalism against the white worker'.[107] Bunting, an attorney, had actually been present at the Rand Club shootings; he was a member of the Club at the time although he resigned shortly afterwards. In September 1912, the Labour Party's newspaper, *The Worker*, argued that the 'right to combine' applied to all men, irrespective of colour, and in November the paper suggested the treatment meted out to Indians protesting against taxes and restrictions showed a 'sinister resemblance' to the government's actions on the Witwatersrand in July.[108]

IT WAS INTERNATIONAL WARFARE, not local racially based concerns, that supplied the grounds for the decisive split in the labour movement between revolutionary socialists and white labour. The Labour Party's membership of the Second International committed it to a principled opposition to war. In September 1914, in reaction to the outbreak of the First World War on 28 July, a War on War League assembled at a meeting in Johannesburg and began publishing a weekly four-page *Gazette* until its enforced closure by the censor eleven issues and two months later. Its supporters included a majority of the Labour Party's executive, 11 out of 15,[109] a telling indicator of the way in which the 1914 strike had radicalised a section of the party's leadership, though noticeably many of the trade union officials held back. In occupational terms, the League's leadership was mainly in the hands of a group of well-educated professional men, including Colin Wade, a dentist; the pharmacist Philip Roux; and Sidney Bunting, who interrupted his attorney's practice to edit the *Gazette*. The *Gazette* serialised Kropotkin's *War and Capitalism*, but its framework of intellectual reference was accommodating: Walt Whitman and Mark Twain were just as likely to be cited in its columns as Karl Liebknecht and Rosa Luxemburg, the leaders of the Gruppe International or the Spartacus League, the left wing of the Independent Social Democrats in Germany. And a sizeable proportion of the League's personalities were genuinely principled pacifists, opposed to all wars, not just imperialist ones, men like the Reverend RJ Hall, the chairman of the local Workers Educational Association.[110] The anti-war group also signed up 7 out of the party's 23 elected Provincial Council representatives and the party's new organising secretary, Ivon Jones, recently sacked from his post as a bookkeeper at the power station in Vereeniging because of his evident sympathy with the 1913 strikers. Support for the League within the labour movement tended to coincide with more racially conciliatory attitudes, though there were exceptions. Andrew Dunbar forecast in the *Gazette* an unhappy homecoming for soldiers returning from the war: 'When you come back you'll find a nigger doing your job for half a dollar a day.'[111] In fact Dunbar would shortly become an assertive advocate of cross-racial class solidarity and may have supported such views in 1914 but, even so, he could still use the everyday racist common sense that prevailed in the white labour movement when it suited him.

On their return to South Africa in January 1915, the men who were deported in 2014 would mostly join the pro-war camp. Labour Party branches remained solidly pro-war, especially after the German sinking of the liner *Lusitania*, an action that prompted anti-German riots and lootings in Germiston. This was Bill Andrews's parliamentary constituency, and he refrained from actually joining the League though he opposed the war in parliament and at League meetings as well as contributing to the League's funds. He told his biographer later that his reluctance to associate himself with the League publicly was because 'he envisaged [a] war of liberation on behalf of workers', but that might have been an *ex post facto* rationalisation.[112] The League also drew in people from outside the Labour Party, including genuine pacifists as well as individuals from the Cape Town Social Democratic Federation, despite the fact that the Federation itself only adopted an anti-war policy in 1916.

The League was not uniformly Marxist though it included Marxists in its followers. In the case of one of its key principals, Ivon Jones, his intellectual development at that time can be tracked through his correspondence. At this stage, Jones was mixing his reading of tracts from the radical but non-Marxist British left with Leo Tolstoy, then the key authority in his principled pacifism. He still retained his Unitarian faith, a bond that helped to cement his friendship with the mine workers' leader, Tom Matthews.[113] A personal history of strong religious conviction was a common feature of this first generation of South African socialist radicals – in Bill Andrews's case, after losing his faith 'to fill up [the] space of religion came socialism and the trade union movement'.[114] Ivon Jones shared with Andrews a Methodist childhood. He was the son of a shopkeeper in Aberystwyth. His upbringing was shaped by his family's engagement in the Welsh cultural revival. Leaving school at the age of 14, he worked as a shop assistant but, influenced by his friend and patron, the scoutmaster, Unitarian and local historian Eyre Evans, Jones embarked on a programme of serious reading. By 1903, at the age of 20, he was a regular contributor to the Welsh-language columns of the *Welsh Gazette*, while managing the family grocery. Diagnosed with tuberculosis, he travelled to New Zealand, supposedly a healthier climate, en route encountering Russian revolutionaries among his fellow passengers. Six years of wool sorting and apple picking did little to improve his health, and in 1910 he took up an invitation from his brother to help run his shop in Kroonstad. Later he managed a coal agency in Boksburg. He learned bookkeeping at evening classes and then found a post at the Victoria Falls and Transvaal Power Company's office in Germiston. Here he joined the Labour Party, becoming the local branch secretary and forming a friendship with Bill Andrews, another serious reader and autodidact. Jones's upbringing, faith and frailty helped foster his puritanical self-control, but he was also warm and affectionate with his friends, and from the beginning of his South African sojourn he would write about Africans sympathetically, encountering them first as customers in Kroonstad at his shop in Boksburg. 'If honesty, trust and fidelity count for anything, the Basuto is in the main a credit to his maker,' he reported in one of his weekly letters to Evans.[115] In Germiston, his initial political activism was shaped by his moral outrage at the treatment of white workers; one of his letters home includes a horrified commentary on the effects of phthisis so evident among his new comrades in the Labour Party.

The party itself, at its annual conference in December 1914, anxious to avert any divisions, decided that opposing or supporting the war should be a matter for individual conscience; after all, it was quite clear that South Africans were not going to be conscripted. Over the next year, a pro-war group gathered momentum within the party, gaining support as the party broadened its membership, recruiting small farmers, traders and professionals. In March 1915, the League published a pamphlet, *Keep the Red Flag Flying*, warning of the efforts of the pro-war group to win over rank and file. The pamphlet itself was explicitly socialist and quoted from the *Communist Manifesto* while the Labour Party's newspaper, *The International*, in its first issues cited Marx's 'Eighteenth Brumaire' and the German socialist Karl Liebknecht, reflecting perhaps the League's support from many of the Jewish ex-European socialists who had joined the Labour Party in recent years.[116] The Labour Party held its conference on 22 August and pro-war leaders were led by newly styled Major Frederic Creswell, one of the Labour MPs elected in 1910, fresh from his military service in the South West African expedition, 'every button of his uniform glowing with military ardour'.[117] At a meeting packed with militarist delegates from recently resurrected branches, the one-time pit-head manager Creswell forced the resignation of the anti-war executive by demanding a pledge of loyalty to war aims, a demand supported from the floor.

A short-lived International League of the South African Labour Party embodied a forlorn effort to remain within the party as a critical minority but one month later, on 1 October, the League re-established itself as a separate body, the International Socialist League (ISL), claiming the loyalty of most of the Johannesburg branches of the Labour Party. At its first conference on 9 January 1916, 32 delegates representing 400 members elected a nine-member management committee. At this meeting the ISL claimed branches in Benoni, Germiston, Johannesburg Central and East, Krugersdorp and Durban.

In attendance as well was a group of 'fraternal delegates' from the Pretoria Socialist Society. The Pretoria Socialist Society was fully absorbed into the League that year, though a full ISL branch in Pretoria was not constituted until 1918. In Cape Town, the Social Democratic Federation remained an independent group, and Harrison, who had joined the War on War League, remained a leading figure within it, continuing to contest elections in its name. The Durban Social Democratic Party remained outside as well, because its leadership wanted a firmer rejection of white labour exclusivity from the ISL.[118] The ISL started its own branch in Durban, holding regular Sunday meetings in the public gardens. It was chaired by a Norwegian businessman, Sophus Pettersen, the owner of a whaling station. Given the presence at the League's helm of former senior Labour Party officials, as well as a member of parliament, Bill Andrews, and important trade union leaders including (briefly) James Bain, as well as Forrester Brown, the Mine Workers' Association secretary, J Clark and J Crisp, respectively secretary and chair of the boilermakers and engineers, and CB Tyler, the builders' main organiser, the ISL's emergence appeared, at leadership level at least, as a significant defection from the Labour mainstream.

Opposition to the war and internationalist class solidarity were the animating concerns in the ISL's formation. But the issue of local class solidarities was addressed quite explicitly at the outset of the League's development. At the Labour Party conference in 1914 during a debate about coloured membership, Bill Andrews observed that 'the working class of this country are native people', and sooner or later the party would have to recruit them.[119] In its new newspaper, *The International*, Ivon Jones suggested that racial exclusion was a critical issue dividing it from the Labour Party: 'Internationalism which does not concede the fullest rights which the native working class is capable of claiming will be a sham. One of the justifications for our withdrawal from the Labour Party is that it gives us ... freedom to deal ... with the great and fascinating problem of the native ... Not until we free the native can we hope to free the white.'[120]

In its early public meetings, to judge from a report in *The International* on a gathering addressed by Andrew Dunbar, the former IWW activist and now a member of the ISL elected leadership body, a 'little knot of native and coloured men' was often in attendance.[121] In March, George Mason spoke at an ISL meeting about 'trade unionists and the native question', advising those present not to waste time 'arguing against the prejudice of white workers' but rather to help black workers 'train and organise themselves'.[122] Two of the Africans present were named in the report, 'Letanka' and 'Mvataza', both journalists and hence already known to the meeting's organisers. In June 1916 the ISL hosted its first African speaker at a meeting in the Trades Hall, inviting Robert Grendon, editor of the Native National Congress newspaper, *Abantu Batho*, to discuss 'the link between Black and White'. Middle-class African nationalists like Grendon were not usually considered as potential allies by ISL leaders, and the latter often characterised the 'parsons and lawyers' at the Congress's helm as reactionaries.[123]

Yet just how generally welcome was the presence of even working-class Africans at ISL meetings is questionable. At its first conference in January 1916, an occasion for agreeing upon and spelling out policies, Sidney Bunting's introduction of a petition of rights for natives prompted 'extremely keen' discussion. Dunbar took Bunting's side; in his view, there was no 'native problem', only a worker problem. Not everybody agreed, and Colin Wade referred to 'biological evidence on the intellectual development of the native as compared to the white'. Bunting's resolution was adopted, though, and the League at its inception would support the abolition of 'all forms of native indenture, compound and pass systems' as well as the 'lifting of the native worker to the political and industrial status of the white'.[124] The implication in this phrase that Africans should obtain political rights, the vote in other words, was in fact the most contentious issue, and its acceptance was for Bunting a significant victory.[125] The resolution was subject to Colin Wade's implicitly segregationist qualification that the numbers of native workers should not increase and that natives should be helped 'to free themselves from the wage system'.[126] *The International* itself published an article in March 1916, excoriating capitalism's erosion of the 'natural social apartness of white and black'. Another *International* editorial suggested that cross-racial 'industrial cooperation' would lead to 'healthy social segregation'.[127] Following this logic, Andrews suggested that 'intermixture of race' – cross-racial marriage – was 'not likely to be more general when industrial, political and educational equality are attained'. Indeed, they were less likely to happen because 'A community living on a higher social plane than we do can be safely trusted to discontinuance any practice contrary to the wellbeing of the Commonwealth'.[128]

These were not settled views, however. Bunting remained outspokenly critical of Wade's amendment, suggesting that if Karl Marx had lived in Johannesburg, he would have formed his association of working men 'not on the well paid craft unionists who themselves batten on native labour ... but rather on such class conscious elements as he could find among the black workers'.[129] Though he was initially drawn into Labour politics in 1913 through witnessing the massacre outside the Rand Club, Bunting's background probably helped to distance him emotionally from the preoccupations of white trade unionists.

Sidney Bunting came from a distinguished Methodist lineage; his father was a prominent Gladstonian liberal. He arrived in South Africa in time to fight on the imperial side in the closing stages of the South African War and then opened an attorney's practice, joining the Rand Club and drawing an income from his family's estates in Natal. His first political engagement was involvement in the White Expansion Society, a body led by Sir Patrick Duncan. The brutality of the 1913 strike's armed suppression was for him a decisive point, though he had already begun to form friendships with Labour Party politicians, for example Philip Roux and Ivon Jones. A close observer of the 1913 strike, Bunting was impressed by what he perceived as supportive actions at the time taken by black mine workers. He aligned with the ISL after the Labour Party split on the war issue. A so-called mixed marriage with Jewish and Lithuanian-born Rebecca Notlewitz may also have helped to shape his evolving 'negrophilism', as he would call it. By early 1917, Bunting was ready to acknowledge that when black workers joined unions, they would embody 'not merely auxiliaries in the white man's fights, but on the contrary as constituting in this country the bulk of the working class, in whose cause the more fortunate few should rather consider themselves as in their turn the auxiliaries'.[130]

Meanwhile, Colin Wade himself succeeded in winning a municipal electoral seat in Germiston as an ISL candidate in November 1915, though his campaign emphasised local issues and made no reference to the disagreements that provoked the split with Labour; indeed, he both accepted and proposed to extend the existing pattern of residential segregation.[131] In the national elections, one month earlier, Andrews lost his parliamentary seat, obtaining only 82 votes. At this stage, the League was still represented in the Transvaal Provincial Council by Sidney Bunting and five other ISL members.[132] The League published a manifesto for the November municipal elections in Johannesburg; its proposal for 'strict supervision of White and Native housing' as well as the 'development of Klip Spruit as Native Township' suggested acceptance of existing segregationist policies.[133] One of the ISL's candidates in Johannesburg, J Clark, the boilermakers' trade union secretary, won a municipal seat with 721 votes. He was also a provincial councillor and was expelled from the League in 1917.[134]

On the issue of racial equality or, as the League's founders expressed it, 'the native problem', at the time of its foundation the ISL's leadership incorporated a spectrum of views. There were people attending its first conference who believed that racial differences were biologically entrenched. In the middle of the spectrum there were the more widely shared views that Africans were culturally primitive and needed 'upliftment' through mobilisation in a white-led class struggle.[135] Finally there was an emerging minority, including Bunting, who were beginning to acknowledge that black workers might embody the main force in bringing about any rupture with capitalism. The League was similarly eclectic in its imagining of the actions through which socialism might be reached. The notion that a post-revolutionary South Africa would restore to Africans a rural arcadia of self-governing agricultural communities that would 'retain all they produce and even produce more than they retain' remained compelling for many Leaguers. The language quoted here was that of Bunting, who was ready to concede as late as 1919 that in a South African socialist system 'native wage labour' would 'certainly not' constitute an 'outstanding characteristic'.[136] Forrester Brown, the secretary of the mine workers' union, had a more straightforward proposal; his union, he maintained, really had no choice. Sooner or later they would be forced to organise 'natives', on the basis of equal pay for equal jobs. Wartime experience had already shown how easy it was for mine owners to replace white workers with cheaper Africans. In any case 'it was their duty to bring him [the African worker] to the level humanity intended him to be'. [137] In its early public appeals, though, ISL propaganda about cross-racial class solidarity was often phrased in a way that pandered to existing prejudices. For example, a May Day leaflet in 1917 warned readers that the world's workers were 'combining irrespective of language and colour'. Even in South Africa, 'the nigger boys will soon be combining and showing the cuff and collar men points in solidarity'.[138]

Otherwise, the language of the pamphlet was within the accepted conventions of revolutionary socialist rhetoric, including standard syndicalist phraseology. Self-professed syndicalists such as Philip Roux or Andrew Dunbar were an important grouping within the ISL leadership. If we keep this in mind, Baruch Hirson's comment that 'the new League was as reformist as the parent body' seems overstated.[139] Syndicalists belonged to the revolutionary socialist family but they disagreed with communists about the state, which they believed would always be controlled by a dominant group. Hence, they argued, revolutionaries should not seek to capture state power but rather destroy it, replacing it with self-managed associational activity for which present-day trade unions were embryonic agencies. Unions, or rather one big 'industrial' union constituted mainly by the unskilled or semi-skilled workforce, would be the main vehicle for revolutionary action through a general strike. Among themselves syndicalists disagreed as to whether electioneering and parliamentary agitation could be a useful accompaniment to such action or, rather, distracting or corrupting.[140]

How widely these arguments were understood among the 400 or so people who belonged to the ISL is unclear, but traces of their influence are discernible in early statements by several ISL leaders. Bunting, for example, writing in September 1915, proposed a new approach that would 'cut government right out, and looks to organised workers themselves to call the tune'.[141] The language of one of the 1916 conference resolutions, calling for 'the organisation of workers on industrial or class lines ... as the most effective means of providing the necessary force for the emancipation of the workers', can be read as evidence of a syndicalist vision.[142] A critical assessment in *The International* of the Easter Rising in Dublin suggested that armed revolt could only lead to 'death on the barricades'; workers should rather depend upon their only weapon, their labour, and in deploying industrial unionism they would embody 'a new socialist commonwealth', replacing the old order with 'social regeneration'.[143] However, the ISL's founding conference turned down a proposal by the delegation from Benoni that the League should adopt the constitution of the (syndicalist) Socialist Labour Party of America. This, together with rejection of language about a post-war workers' uprising to abolish the capitalist system, as well as the ISL's continuing commitment to electoral activity, might indicate that 'more conservative interpreters of Marx' prevailed at the conference.[144] Even so, Ivon Jones in 1916 did write to the American Socialist Labour Party, requesting their literature, and noting the 'marvellous influence' that De Leon's works and the American party's philosophy had 'exercised' in South Africa; indeed, De Leon was Marx's 'true successor', he believed.[145] At this stage, Jones and Bunting were only beginning to read Marxist literature systematically, and in South Africa American-style syndicalism supplied the most readily available Marxist–influenced writing in English. Many of Lenin's most important writings were yet to be translated into English. After learning Russian, Ivon Jones would write a summary of *What Is to Be Done* in the British party's *Communist Review* in 1924.[146]

But the presence of Russian and Yiddish-speaking Bundist socialists within the ISL makes it likely that within the organisation there were Marxists who drew their sources of inspiration not from American syndicalism but from the competing strands of European socialist and revolutionary politics influential at the time. In 1907, Jock Campbell was circulating leaflets by Kautsky.[147] Bill Andrews's biographer Jack Cope suggests that in the 1900s he and other left-wing white labour leaders admired German social democracy. Indeed,

Andrews recollected in the 1940s that he and most of his associates 'looked with envy on the German Social Democratic Party', taking them 'to be the last word in revolutionary politics'.[148] He believed then 'that parliamentary action would place the workers in power', though whether Andrews retained such optimism after the outbreak of the war seems unlikely. He remained at odds with syndicalists within the ISL, however, in his advocacy 'of fighting elections to provide them with a platform'.[149] The ISL's application to join the anti-war European socialists who convened the Zimmerwald Conference in September 2015, an application that was accepted, would have placed the organisation within a Marxist political grouping in which the dominant voices were often Russian, including the Bolsheviks and the Mensheviks, though from September 1915 through 1916 the most frequently and admiringly cited external authority was Karl Liebknecht – *The International* even went so far as describing WH Andrews as 'the Liebknecht of South Africa'.[150] However, to judge from the books and pamphlets offered for sale or excerpted in the early issues of *The International*, 'the conversion to Marxism was slow'.[151] Authors appearing in this way in the newspaper included Leo Tolstoy, Peter Kropotkin, and Fenner Brockway as well as British left-wing humanitarians such as ED Morel and HN Brailsford. Sponsorship of a 'left cadet' movement for schoolboys suggests that pacifism remained a key commitment for certain League members.[152] For young people, the ISL also maintained a socialist Sunday School; Sidney Bunting, after helping with one of its sessions in February 1918, noted that 'as usual' it had been an unrewarding experience.[153] By 1917, the doctrinal canon represented in summaries, excerpts, briefer quotations and approving citations in *The International* had narrowed. Over the year the most discussed or cited authority was Marx, who made eight appearances, closely followed by Daniel De Leon with seven. Lenin was quoted four times and both Karl Kautsky and Karl Liebknecht twice. Most of the other authorities who supplied space-fillers were either British or American Marxists. The newspaper contained no quotations from Rosa Luxemburg; she was the only other major Marxist theoretician besides Lenin to write thoughtfully about South Africa, in her case using its recent history as an example of capital's destruction of peasant economies.[154] Sidney Bunting may have read her by this stage.[155]

Electoral campaigning was an early preoccupation for the ISL, though its membership probably understood its purpose in different ways and, of course, certain syndicalists within the League were opposed to any electoral participation even if only for propaganda purposes. League leadership generally favoured electoral participation; after all, it provided opportunities for publicity as well as a measure of legal protection; 'it [was] "the shield" that protects the organisation'.[156] Initially, with the ISL contesting national, provincial and municipal elections, electioneering required a major mobilisation of supportive activity and material resources. The results were hardly encouraging. Colin Wade stood in the Troyeville by-election against Frederic Creswell in January 1917, collecting 32 votes against Creswell's 800, the ISL's lowest poll to date. This time, Wade campaigned on an anti-capitalist and anti-war manifesto, which also reminded voters that 'native workers are here to stay'.[157] More obliquely, Andrews in that year's Provincial Council elections defended himself against 'the catchvote alarum that I want to give the vote to kaffirs', by conceding that his opponents were correct and that he did indeed stand for political equality, though he held back from explicitly calling for black enfranchisement.[158] In any case, as he explained later, political power – voting – was 'quite a secondary matter' compared with collaborative class action.[159] Neither he nor Sidney Bunting succeeded in winning seats. Aside from elections the League had three main strategic focuses for its early activities. Firstly, it invested considerable effort into opposing the war and associated 'jingoism'. Secondly, as might be expected from the presence of so many heavy-weight white labour officials in its leadership, it aimed to reform and radicalise the white trade union movement. Thirdly, a group of ISL leaders were concerned, from the outset, to draw Africans and other racially subordinate communities into working-class politics. As Ivon Jones had observed after the Troyeville election, 'the great mass of the proletariat … happens in South Africa to be black'.[160]

Anti-war activities included the weekly socialist Sunday School, 'the Commune of the Young', three of them in fact, specially intended to counter the influences of patriotic militarism promoted by 'khaki-worshipping' in classroom lessons and through such youth organisations as the Boy Scouts.[161] More assertively, the League undertook several leafleting campaigns to oppose military recruitment and other war-related activities. These propaganda campaigns would have represented laborious commitments for a small organisation. For example, in two weeks a 'Leaflet Distribution Corps' organised by the Johannesburg branch delivered house-to-house or handed out nearly 19,000 leaflets across all the main white working-class residential areas.[162] The leaflets contained proposals for making education a people's concern, as well as denouncing the 'empire idolatory' that was replacing more normal kinds of instruction in wartime schooling. In that year the League contested school board elections in Johannesburg: of four ISL candidates, Sidney Bunting did best, obtaining 930 out of 8,000 votes.[163]

Charles Tyler's efforts to establish a building workers' union which would accommodate all the relevant trades in the construction industry and which would be open to African workers belong to the second group of activities; it was mainly directed at white workers though a few Africans did join the new union. Tyler was a leading De Leonite and he had belonged to the Socialist Labour Party.[164] Meanwhile, ISL members who held senior positions in the Mine Workers' Association worked to strengthen local branches and broaden membership among less skilled workers. The League itself was heavily critical of negotiations between the Association and the Chamber in which, for the remaining duration of the war, the mine workers' union's officials (including the ISL's Forrester Brown) agreed on a no-strike policy in return for raised minimum wages, a fixed ratio of white and black workers, and a check-off system, the last commitment effectively a form of employer recognition.[165] The limits of ISL influence within white labour were especially evident in the failure of the new South African Trades Union Congress, formed at the end of 1917, to embrace the principles of industrial unionism, an objective that had been a major preoccupation for ISL-affiliated trade union officials through the preceding year.[166] ISL advocacy of industrial unionism in this context was clearly inspired by a syndicalist vision. An industrial conference organised by the ISL in September 1917 and attended by 45 delegates (including three Africans) referred to an ideal situation in which 'the one Industrial Union will become the Parliament of Labour and would form an integral part of the International Industrial Republic'.[167]

MEANWHILE, THE LEAGUE pursued its third objective of widening the communal parameters of working-class politics by including within its programme of weekly public meetings at the Trades Hall topics calculated to appeal to Africans. This was a modest beginning: reports in *The International* suggest that attendance at such gatherings included a dozen or so Africans at most, probably drawn mainly from the aspirant middle-class circles who were engaged in the Native Congress. Africans began attending ISL public meetings in the Trades Hall in March 1916.[168] In March 1917 'a large sprinkling' of Africans were present at a public event organised by the ISL to protest against the Native Affairs Administration Bill. Important local Congress members were there, including Saul Msane, the main speaker. As *The International*'s report commented, 'It was gratifying to see how easily the whole audience caught up the spirit of forgetting for the time being that there was such a thing as colour.' The report also mentioned a contribution from another African speaker, RC Kupan. He held up a document containing 'the Constitution and Rules of a native union', recently started in Johannesburg but since suppressed.[169] Prompted perhaps by this intervention, a more ambitious effort to mobilise Africans started with a less public event on 19 July 1917. This was the first assembly of an ISL-sponsored group that would name itself the Industrial Workers of Africa (IWA). Present were 30 men, 20 of them Africans, gathered in Neppe's Building on Fox Street, in a furniture shop owned by an ISL supporter, just opposite the Marshall Square police station.

At least two of the Africans present were police informers, and through their reports preserved in police files we can track the details of the IWA's progress. At this first meeting, the Africans in attendance were asked where they worked, just to check that there were no policemen present. One of the white men present explained why the meeting had been called. 'Natives' were the working class of South Africa, and they should have the same rights as white men. They needed political rights so that they could be free from the pass laws and they needed other rights as well. The organisers of the meeting, they said, could not 'themselves' at this stage 'do anything for a native'. The Africans present would have to make their own meetings, and once they had taken such an initiative, then members of the socialist movement could offer help and advice. Strike action would be a key ingredient in any successful action to obtain rights, especially strike action on the mines. Indeed, African mine workers should belong to a union. Before dispersing, all those present agreed they would reassemble in the same place, every week, at the same time.[170]

Reassemble they did, every week, their discussions copiously recorded in the notebooks kept by the police spies. In the first few sessions, Andrew Dunbar seems to have led the discussions, though through the sequence of meetings for which there are records of the white ISL members, Sidney Bunting was the most regular presence. At the next meeting, Dunbar opened the session by drawing a diagram on a blackboard to represent capitalist injustice; he used it to demonstrate how it was that 'working men, black and white men ... do all the work ... produce everything'. All the workers, black and white, should 'fight against the capitalists and take them down from their place'. First, African workers should refuse en masse to register their passes: 'Native Affairs cannot arrest the whole lot of them'.[171] More in this vein characterised discussions at further encounters during August, again with Dunbar (it seems) supplying much of the impetus, though by 16 August one of the Africans present made the recommendation that a first step in 'making the natives organise' would be a leaflet in African languages. This was a good idea, Dunbar responded;

indeed he had been sending socialist leaflets to an Indian, 'Gandi', who was busy in Durban, mobilising Indian workers. This meeting also included an exchange between Bunting and another of the Africans about the Native National Congress: Bunting asked what sorts of people attended its meetings and was told its followers were mainly 'exempted natives, shareholders and a couple of lawyers'. Too middle class, Bunting observed, not the sort of people that might struggle against class injustice.[172]

In fact, younger Congress members were often named among those present, and when the meetings set up a formal organisation, on 27 September, initially calling itself the Society of the Industrial Workers of the World, Congressmen and one of the police spies joined the elected committee. The name change to the less unwieldy Industrial Workers of Africa was decided on 11 October at a particularly well-attended session in Neppe's shop, at which there were 50 Africans present.[173] One explanation of the original decision about the name is supplied by Eddie Roux in his biography of Bunting. 'When asked what they wanted', those in attendance had said 'Sifuna zonke' (We want everything).[174] Discussion at subsequent gatherings during October and November focused on the approval and production of a leaflet co-written by Saul Msane and Hosea Phooko in collaboration with two of the ISL people, Ivon Jones and Barron Wright. The text was short but to the point:

> Native workers! Why do you keep in slavery? ... Why are you kicked about and spat upon by your white employers? ... Listen ... It's because you are workers of the World. It's because your employers want to be rich through you. It's because they buy and pay the Government and the Police to make you worthless so they will be able to make you work for them ... You do all the work; without you they cannot live. You are their life. Take note of that. You are oppressed and milked and you are their cows they live on. There is only one way of freedom, Native Workers! Unite! ... Bind yourself in a chain of being workers. Wake up ... It is now dawn. Ho! You have long been sleeping and the white men robbing your strength for nothing ... Come let us fight against these many passes that cause the trouble and also fight against the low wages.[175]

The organisation also began to be formalised with the production of membership lists and the eliciting of voluntary financial contributions. To judge from the records kept by the police, membership peaked in late 2017 at 67 people. Bunting was able to tell the meeting on 15 November that the ISL had paid for the printing of 10,000 copies of the leaflet, though IWA members themselves collected money towards its costs as well. Plans and schemes for the distribution of the leaflets would supply the main business considered by the group through the next few months. A fundraiser social was held on 9 March 'with black and white men singing on the stage, the piano and the violin played by a white man and a white girl'.[176] The white violinist may well have been Bunting himself, a talented violinist, for, as his letters to his wife Rebecca indicate, he undertook much of the preparatory work for the 'kaffir concert', as he called it.[177]

The money raised at the concert was used to support the travel required to circulate the leaflet. In March 1918, police identified a 'strange well-dressed' IWA organiser addressing a group in a room in one of the compounds at Consolidated Reef Mine, and reading from the leaflet.[178] The police report named the visitor as Reuben Kapan, one of the first members of the IWA, and probably the same man as the RC Kupan who had spoken about an earlier attempt at building an African union at an ISL meeting in March. Kapan was a travelling salesman; he made his living hawking patent medicines outside mine compounds, and for some months now he had been distributing leaflets while selling his stock. A report on January 1918 in the *Rand Daily Mail* confirmed that the leaflet was in wide circulation across the mining compounds.[179] At a meeting on 15 March, one of the people in attendance claimed that the leaflet had helped to cause a stores boycott, in protest against inflationary price rises at the concessionary shops operating just outside mining compounds. If this was the case, it was probably not intentional. The League, while providing sympathetic commentary on the boycott in its newspaper after it happened, also suggested that the effort directed into its organisation was misplaced: workers were 'robbed' at the point of production, not as consumers. However, its editorial conceded, 'the solidarity displayed is the significant thing, for the boycott was "marvellously unanimous"'.[180]

The boycott started on 10 February, spread through the eastern Witwatersrand and by the 14th was being enforced with pickets before these were broken by mounted police. Whether the circulation of the leaflet really helped to precipitate the compound store protest is of course uncertain but, significantly, at about this time the police began warning Neppe about allowing his space to be used for the IWA's meetings. Neppe apparently had the 'proper funks', Bunting confided to his wife on 19 February, but even so the IWA continued to meet in his hall.[181] The League itself had decided to move its own offices out of the Trades Hall after the governing white trade union officials, in reaction to the ISL's meetings, decided in September 1917 to ban black people from their headquarters. It would also establish its own office in Neppe's Building at 54 Fox Street. For its annual conference the League's leadership prepared a special statement on 'International Socialism and the Native' for discussion by branch delegates. It called for the ending of passes, contract labour and compounds, and for 'the lifting of the Native workers to the political and industrial status of the whites'. White workers' racial prejudices were 'suicidal' and really constituted 'the only native problem'.[182]

THE LEAGUE'S APPARENTLY enthusiastic sponsorship of a black workers' organisation at the cost of friction with white union leadership reflected wider changes in its political orientation and social make-up. During 1917 events in Russia provided a fresh source of external inspiration. Ivon Jones would supply a running commentary on the Russian developments, writing in March about 'a bourgeois revolution' in St Petersburg, 'but arriving when the night of capitalism is far spent'.[183] *The International*'s coverage of the Russian Revolution soon began to highlight the role of Lenin as well as Trotsky, and its writers were quick to identify themselves and the League with the Bolshevik cause. As an article entitled 'Lenin on Top' proposed in August, 'From all accounts the situation is developing in favour of the principles advocated by Lenin. Every week proves him to be right.'[184] Bill Andrews was in England at the time, having left South Africa to attend a peace conference in Stockholm sponsored by surviving anti-war socialist groups, and he established contact with Maxim Litvinov, the Bolsheviks' emissary in London. By a happy coincidence, Litvinov was attending a Labour Party conference at which Andrews was present and they stayed in the same hotel; their first encounter was accidental, it seems.[185] Encouraged by this contact, Jones wrote to Andrews, suggesting that he should advise Soviet leaders 'that no consul be appointed for the Russian Revolution in South Africa, without first consulting the International Socialist League'.[186] If Andrews offered such advice, it evidently had no impact. When the South Africans made their first discreet effort to open direct consular relations with the Soviet Union in 1925, South African communists were kept ignorant.[187]

Admiration for the Bolsheviks and even such personal connections as Andrews's meetings with Litvinov did not immediately result in a strategic shift in the League's outlook. After all, very little of Lenin's strategic thinking was available to English-speaking League members; it is most unlikely that from 1917 the ISL's outlook became 'deeply coloured ... by the teachings of Lenin', a claim made by Andrews's biographer.[188] Andrews himself at that time was still broadly influenced by syndicalist currents; from his tour in Britain that year he drew his most important lessons from a visit he made to the Clyde, hosted by the Scottish Labour Party, where he encountered the 'direct representation' of workers' politics in the 'industrial unionism' for the Shop Stewards' Movement.[189] The first extensive reference to any of Lenin's arguments in *The International* was on 30 November 1917, a direct quotation from an article Lenin wrote in a Swiss newspaper outlining Bolshevik disagreements with the anarchists on the necessity for the state to continue to exist after the revolution.[190] Before then a total of three quotations from Lenin had appeared in *The International* columns, all in 1917, one of them a condemnation of Karl Kautsky's and German social democracy's support for the war, used as a space-filler.[191] Although throughout 1918 *The International* supplied a running commentary on Russian events, it provided no real insights into the ideas that made Lenin distinctive as a Marxist revolutionary strategist. A short biography that appeared in the newspaper in February 1918, translated from Norwegian by Sophus Pettersen, simply noted that Lenin was 'famous for his knowledge of the agrarian problems in Russia'.[192] It was only in 1919 that *The International* began advertising English translations of his writings. *State and Revolution* was available to *The International*'s readers in 1920.

As Lucien van der Walt's careful reading of Ivon Jones's journalism about the Russian events has shown, the Leaguers' understanding of what was happening was shaped by the syndicalist precepts that had up to then been such an important influence among them, a misunderstanding that was shared by left-wing English-speaking commentators in other places as well.[193] 'Not only Marx, but De Leon, his successor, is also vindicated by Russian Labour,' Ivon Jones observed just after the Bolsheviks seized power.[194] So, the October Revolution was not a seizure of state power, for 'the socialists do not want to be responsible for the Political state'.[195] Soviets were a Russian form of industrial union.[196] Lenin and other Bolshevik personalities were not aspirant rulers, but simply delegates of the council of workers, which itself was engaged in the destruction of the state and the replacement of 'the government of men with the administration of things'. At the time, such perceptions were not unreasonable. In 1917, Lenin himself was arguing that 'soviets were a higher form of democracy than an ordinary parliament' and the vehicle through which a proletarian dictatorship would be realised.[197] Even as late as 1919 Lenin was telling Arthur Ransome 'how far and how early De Leon had pursued the same train of thought as the Russians'.[198]

This view of what was happening in Russia may not have been accepted by every syndicalist within the ISL. The League's unqualified praise for the Bolsheviks estranged a section of the former adherents of the Socialist Labour

Party.[199] It is also likely that within the ISL there were growing numbers of members who were better informed about Bolshevik strategy and aspirations. There was an upsurge of ISL recruitment within Johannesburg's poorer Jewish neighbourhoods, especially in Ferreirastown, where recent immigrants from the Russian Pale of settlement were concentrated, most of them manual workers or shop assistants.[200] Bernard Sachs's memoir of growing up in these districts recalls the 'extravagant rejoicing' in Ferreirastown that greeted news of the Tsar's abdication, when 'Jews danced in the street and embraced'.[201] A Yiddish-speaking branch of the ISL would constitute itself in September 1917. Membership would peak at between 500 and 1,000, rather more than its parent body's following. A pamphlet it published in Yiddish in 1919 on the Russian Revolution had a print run of 7,000.[202] The branch opened a library of socialist literature in an old hotel in Jeppe Street and conducted study classes. The members undertook a major fundraising drive to buy a printing press for *The International* as well as collecting money for 'white and coloured locked-out workers'. The branch self-consciously modelled its structure on the Jewish section of the Bolsheviks, the *Yevsektsiya*, a body established in Russia after the revolution which promoted the use of Yiddish and supported various other expressions of Jewish cultural autonomy while opposing Zionism.[203] Within its leadership there were veterans of the Bundist Friends of Russian Freedom as well as anarchists, and the Yiddish-speaking branch would become sharply divided between syndicalist purists who wanted the ISL to withdraw from electioneering and any participation in parliamentary bodies, on the one hand, and defenders of 'political action', on the other, both ready with appropriate textual authority from Lenin.[204] The growing presence of this group within the ISL probably helped to diversify the range of socialist thinking within the League, but it was also important for a while at least for another reason, because it weakened the influence of the white labour aristocracy within the ISL's following. White trade unionists apparently objected to being called 'comrade' by the Yiddish speakers.[205] Tensions with white unionists may have been a consequence of the branch's insistence on building connections with black workers as well as reflecting anti-Semitic prejudices, directed especially at 'Peruvniks', the derogatory term used by anglicised Jews to refer to recent immigrants from the Pale.[206] The police records identify certain Yiddish ISL branch members, notably Israelstam and Kessler, as frequent participants in IWA meetings.[207] In June 1917 an editorial in *The International* maintained, perhaps rather too optimistically, that 'sympathy for the Russian revolution' had as its local corollary 'the solidarity of labour irrespective of race or colour'.[208] It is likely that members of the Yiddish-speaking branch would offer strong support for such contentions and for the ISL's efforts to mobilise black workers in the IWA.

The IWA itself was chiefly active in the same geographical vicinity as the ISL's new Jewish branch, the poorer multiracial districts of central Johannesburg, from Ferreirastown to Bezuidenhout Valley. It may have succeeded in attracting a few mining compound residents to its meetings, as its ISL sponsors had hoped, but many of the people actively involved in the Association were more urbanised people, probably mainly employed in small workshops and services. This reflected wartime growth in the African urban workforce; while the number of Africans in the mining industry remained level, between 1915 and 1919 Africans and coloured people employed in manufacturing rose nationally by 50 per cent, from 60,000 to 90,000.[209] The individuals named as IWA leaders were not always workers, though; indeed, one contemporary perception of them was that the Association 'was composed chiefly of young intellectuals'.[210] The three most frequently cited organisers, William Thibedi, Hamilton Kraai and Alfred (Fred) Cetiwe, were relatively well educated, almost certainly mission school graduates. Thibedi, a teacher, was the son of a clergyman, an upbringing which he evidently rebelled against, to judge from the strong vein of anti-clericalism that featured in his reported speeches.[211] 'Comrades,' he would cry, 'we must kick out the missionary and the clergyman. I know because my father is a ——— clergyman.' 'I know what I am talking about. What is the missionary doing for us? He educates us and then leaves us alone to starve. He points to the sky and tell us, "By and by, after you're dead, you'll have enough to eat and fine clothes to wear!" That's not good enough for us! We want food to eat and clothes to wear today. Am I right?'[212]

Hamilton Kraai worked as a foreman in a wholesale store. Cetiwe was a picture framer's assistant. Given the social backgrounds of these people, it is not surprising that despite the intentions of the ISL organisers to set up a body distinct from the 'middle-class' Congress and more determined to wage class struggle, IWA and 'second-echelon' Congress leadership overlapped. Hamilton Kraai was a Congress member at that stage. So, too, probably was Herbert Msane, often mentioned in the police reports, who was the son of Saul Msane, a senior Native Congress leader. Meanwhile, Horatio Bud-M'belle was the nephew of Isaiah Bud-M'belle, another top Congress official. On 28 December 1917, twenty IWA members and six members of the Transvaal Native Congress as well as six members of the coloured African People's Organisation, whose local organiser, Talbot Williams, was also an IWA participant, decided to form a joint committee 'to devise ways in which our labour organisation can succeed in the labour market'.[213]

THE CONNECTIONS BETWEEN the IWA's leadership and local Congress notables are a reflection of the same considerations affecting educated urban Africans that helped to radicalise a segment of the provincial wing of the Congress movement, the Transvaal Native Congress, after the First World War. During and just after the war, industrialisation and the consequent increase in the African population on the Witwatersrand had attracted a substantial group of relatively well-educated people, a community of at least a thousand or so, many of them clerical workers or teachers drawn to Johannesburg by hopes and ambitions for a better life. In 1917 and 1918 such expectations were especially unlikely to find fulfilment. As one official report noted in 1921, 'a large majority [of members of the Native Congress] is comprised of natives who have acquired a certain amount of education only to find the professional, clerical and skilled avenues of employment closed to them'.[214] Disappointed expectations about finding higher-status employment would have been compounded by sharp price rises after 1917, a desperate housing shortage, harshly administered pass laws, and police liquor raids. Women in even 'respectable' households undertook home brewing to augment the family budget; at least one Native Congress member of that time interviewed in 1979 could remember using the income from beer sales to pay for school fees.[215]

The local application of pass laws was extended to African women around Johannesburg just before the war, and during the war the numbers of African women present locally expanded swiftly. Passes may have been a particular focus of disaffection because of their especially severe policing on the Rand in this period.[216] Then there was the housing shortage. In 1918 there were 10,000 Africans without accommodation in Johannesburg's compounds, municipally administered African locations and African freehold areas. These people crowded into the multiracial slum districts, and they would have included a disproportionate share of this 'aspirant petty bourgeoisie' population.[217] This was a group aiming to achieve an urbane 'civilised' lifestyle but they were finding their prospects for securing middle-class comforts and status blocked. In this setting they were particularly predisposed to identify with and take up more widely shared grievances and, more importantly, to react to then by joining or even leading militant action.

On 8 June 1918, African municipal labourers living in the Vrededorp compound, sanitation workers or so-called bucket boys, refused to go to work. In the previous month, municipal workers from several compounds had asked for an increase, taking their cues from recent successful strikes by white municipal engineers and, more unusually, from black employees in the nearby railway workshops. The authorities' refusal of any wage increase for the sanitation workers was delivered to the compound on 1 June; maybe, they were told, they would get a small increment when they renewed their contracts the following year. These were the lowest-paid workers on the Rand but also very vulnerable; it took them a week to decide to take action. The police were the first to react to the strike, arresting 50 of the workers, and the municipality immediately afterwards recruited replacements, but these too went on strike. The protest spread to other compounds despite another 150 arrests and subsequent convictions with hard labour sentences under Masters and Servants legislation. These events prompted a meeting of the Transvaal Native Congress (TNC) on the evening of the 19th. We know what happened at this and subsequent TNC assemblies because, once again, police informers were present taking notes, in fact the same men who had joined the IWA. Here it seems that the initial inclination of the senior Congress leaders to petition the Governor General and otherwise restrict their support for the strikers to organising legal assistance was overridden by more militant speakers who included IWA members. The meeting decided that other compounds across the Reef should be persuaded to join the strike. Talbot Williams of the APO took fright and defected at this point, visiting the office of the magistrate who had imprisoned the strikers, making a 'signed confession' and undertaking to try to halt the protest.[218] He died later that year, one of the thousands of local victims of the global influenza epidemic.[219]

On 19 June the TNC held a more public meeting attended by about a thousand people, including a dozen or so whites – ISL members, it seems. After angry addresses by even the more moderate leaders, a resolution was moved from the floor to call for a general increase for black workers of a shilling a day. The IWA's Herbert Msane proposed the formation of a secret committee to direct the protest drawn from IWA and TNC principals: workers would strike on 1 July, for a shilling a day and against the pass laws. In general, the police informers suggested, a group of IWA members including Hamilton Kraai and Alfred Cetiwe were the main voices advocating militant methods. As Levi Mvabaza, one of the TNC leaders who had been attending ISL meetings during 1917, noted: 'The capitalists and the workers are at war everywhere in every country… The white workers do not write to the Governor General when they want more pay. They strike and get what they should.'[220]

Over the next two weeks, disagreements within the TNC between militants and the 'Black-coated respectables' appear to have weakened the commitment to strike on 1 July, particularly after the authorities released the arrested sanitation workers.[221] The ISL itself counselled against strike action in *The International*, arguing on 21 June that more preparation was needed for an action which would certainly draw military-style repression.[222] In offering such advice, the ISL leaders were acting as 'responsible revolutionaries', according to Bill Andrews's biographer.[223] On 1 July, though, certain workers did indeed go on strike, followed on 6–7 July by several thousand mine workers at two compounds until they were forced underground by police wielding bayonets. The striking mine workers may have been influenced by visits to their compounds by IWA members earlier in the year, and mine workers seem to have been present at public meetings addressed by IWA men. John Higginson, citing police records, has suggested that the miners were responding directly to William Thibedi's challenge: 'Friend, are you a worker?'[224] In that same month, the Prime Minister's hosting of a TNC delegation and the appointment of a commission of inquiry helped to deflect any further protest for the time being. The Moffat Commission reported in September, recommending wage increases for certain groups, the abolition of night passes for women, and a number of other concessions. Meanwhile, following their arrest on 6 July, ISL and TNC leaders as well as IWA men were put on trial in September, after being detained without bail, charged with incitement to violence, the first time blacks and whites had been charged together as a consequence of shared political activities.[225] The ISL leaders charged included Sidney Bunting, who, the prosecutor claimed, had instructed an IWA man, Luke Massina, to visit compounds and persuade the 'Natives to organise and strike'.

The trial ended when Luke Massina, who had been arrested with the others but then turned state evidence, admitted perjury, telling the court that the sworn statements that he had supposedly signed and that the prosecution had submitted as his 'evidence-in-chief' were false and that he had never signed them.[226] Massina was in fact a 'double agent', originally employed by the Native Affairs Department to attend IWA meetings, but almost immediately he had told his new IWA comrades about his assignation.[227] According to this trial testimony, he actually joined the League. Even so, it is most unlikely that Bunting was in any way an instigator of the 'bucket boy' strike. As he told the court, serious revolutionary socialists were not really interested in 'instigating petty organised rabble strikes for a mere rise of pay', a comment that underlines the social and cultural distance that still separated even the more 'interracial' white ISL leaders from their protégés in the IWA.[228] At the trial, the defence for the accused men argued, probably truthfully, at least with respect to the white ISL defendants, that their first knowledge of the bucket strike was from reading press reports.[229] However, at the same time, Bunting's defence, together with his co-accused, probably downplayed the extent of the League's and the Association's implication in the events. Though the sanitation workers were acting on their own initiative, the records of the earlier IWA meetings do indicate that Bunting and others were hoping their efforts would culminate in a general strike movement, and it is possible that parts of Massina's original testimony were truthful, though in *The International* at the time, Leaguers advised that a general strike would be 'an undertaking for which no sufficient organisation as yet' existed.[230] The League had been working closely with both Thibedi and Talbot Williams before the strike. Thibedi is likely to have been the more energetic of the two. As one of his later comrades explained, not quite admiringly, he was a busy personality who 'scurried all over the place all the time like a mouse'.[231] Significantly, William Thibedi was included among the speakers at the open-air meeting the League held in Johannesburg on May Day, a meeting that was directed especially at black and coloured workers. The gathering drew about 200 people, mostly it seems coloured workers.[232]

This was not the end of the TNC's excursion into the politics of mass action, and the IWA continued its efforts to prompt the nationalist body to move along confrontational courses. In line with the Moffat Commission in the months that followed, the Chamber of Mines held back from proposing a general increase of wages. In March 1919, after various fruitless encounters with employers on the wage issue, the TNC at a mass meeting on 30 March resolved in favour of further protest, this time directed at the pass laws. In the words of the police witness: 'It was therefore agreed that passes be thrown away, as passes are the foundation on which the refusal of the Europeans is based.'[233] The pass campaign opened on 31 March with a large crowd assembling outside the main pass office in Johannesburg, addressed by a group in which IWA leaders were conspicuous: the by-now 'familiar figures' of Horatio Bud-M'belle, Alfred Cetiwe and Hamilton Kraai. They told officials that because wage increases had been refused, they would not carry passes. Hundreds of people subsequently handed in their passes at a meeting in Von Brandis Square and anti-pass pickets then fanned out to collect thousands more passes outside factories and businesses. Large meetings and similar pickets, especially outside municipal compounds, were broken up or dispersed by mounted police in the following days. Anti-pass protesters were also beaten up by striking white municipal workers who at that time had formed a 'Board of Control' at the City Hall. Despite hundreds of arrests, the protests spread to envelop most of the East Rand by mid-April. Specially mobilised Mounted Riflemen escorted arrested protesters to the magistrate's court in Johannesburg after several efforts by excited onlookers to rescue them.[234] In court, the accused were often defended by Sidney Bunting. He was on one occasion physically attacked by a group that included white municipal strikers, who frogmarched him 'face-downwards' down the street.[235] Though willing to defend passive resisters without charge, Bunting may have had reservations about any support for a pass campaign; recent preceding editorials in *The International* had made it quite clear that the League should not concern itself with the 'civil disabilities of Indian storekeepers, African lawyers and coloured middlemen'.[236] Even so, in the months running up to the anti-pass movement, League leaders had remained on friendly terms with the Native Congress, and Bill Andrews had actually addressed a Congress meeting in December 1918. Yet shortly after this friendly gesture, Bunting reassured *The International*'s readers that nothing had changed in the League's view of Congress: 'it forms an admirable buffer enabling the ruling class to stave off the real emancipation of the natives.'[237]

During this tumult, Congress moderates became increasingly nervous. A Congress delegation had in fact been summoned to Pretoria by the Director of Native Labour, Colonel Pritchard. He had told them that the government was considering granting much larger numbers of pass exemptions and that he would explore with the relevant officials in Johannesburg the possibility of the provision of more housing and a relaxation of restrictions on home brewing. Moreover, those who had given up their passes would have a week's grace to collect duplicates without any penalty or payment. The TNC's Mabaso reported these prospective ameliorations at a meeting on the 6th, and was apparently subjected to a critical cross-examination by the IWA's William Thibedi. Thibedi had no right to speak to him in such a way, Mabaso protested; he was just a youngster who would get everybody into trouble. Mabaso then declared the meeting closed after somebody else accused him of being bribed and a group attempted to rush the platform.[238] In the days that followed, despite the IWA's urgings to the contrary, the TNC leadership seems to have decided to accept the settlement offered by Pritchard and it withdrew its sponsorship from the protest, which ended desultorily in the second half of April 1919. As we shall see, the IWA remained active and an effective catalyst agency both on the Witwatersrand and elsewhere, with William Thibedi, by now a full member of the ISL, playing a major role in its leadership, for example by chairing an IWA meeting on 27 June.[239] On 27 July Thibedi addressed a meeting convened for 'all labourers'. He told those present he had left the Native Congress, for its leaders didn't use money properly: 'they use it for themselves, and we, the working men, get nothing'.[240] The workers must separate from Congress and form their own organisation, he said. But most people at the meeting disagreed, and the assembly broke up inconclusively. More encouragingly for Thibedi and his comrades, that month *The International* reported an influx of fresh membership for the IWA.

THOUGH THESE PIONEERING efforts to construct an organised African working class-oriented group have assumed a retrospective importance, not least because of the role the IWA played in helping to prompt and shape wider movements of protest, they were not a major preoccupation for most of the ISL's membership at the time. We are so well informed about them because of the presence of the police informers, who left an archival paper trail. But the reports of ISL presences at IWA and TNC meetings suggest the engagement of a dozen or so people, a small minority in an organisation with a membership of around 400. Bill Andrews's position on black South Africans was probably typical: to be sure, as he explained in a contribution to *The International* shortly before his departure for Europe, black people were part of the working class and should be organised, in parallel unions if this was more practical, but they themselves should do this. They were 'not to be considered passive creatures waiting for their White brothers to emancipate them'.[241] Sidney Bunting and Ivon Jones generally received support for their views and actions at the League's decision-making bodies, and it was probably not the case that deep fissures existed within the organisation over attitudes to black workers. Indeed, in January 1919 at the ISL annual conference delegates adopted a proposal that the League should add to its declaration of principles the phrase 'special attention being paid to native workers'. Opponents of the resolution were worried that this might make recruiting among Afrikaners more difficult, for them a task that should be the main priority given the near-total absence of Afrikaans-speaking membership of the League. Despite this concern, support for the proposal was in the end unanimous among the 39 delegates. Two members of the IWA contributed to the debate, both making speeches, appealing for white worker solidarity and referring to Congress as a 'capitalist gang'. The municipal workers' strike 'nearly succeeded', they said, despite having no organisation. What was needed was more 'socialist education'.[242] As we shall see, it would remain the case that active engagement in building a black socialist movement would continue to be limited to a small group of enthusiasts.

At the same meeting Bill Andrews was elected as the League's full-time secretary-organiser, though he had in fact been playing this role for some months before, shortly after his return from Britain. He would also become the ISL's press manager.[243] Andrews had stayed in Britain until mid-1918, and

51

during his time there he visited Clydeside to learn about the shop stewards' movement, the Clyde Workers' Committee, a group influenced by syndicalism. Andrews's radicalism would have been reinforced by his exclusion from the inter-allied labour conferences by the British Labour Party. On several of his public appearances in Britain he called for equal treatment of black workers.[244] Andrews had arrived back from England equipped with fresh moral authority as a consequence of his conversations with Litvinov, which he wrote up in a pamphlet, *The Workers' Revolution in Russia.* 'If I were in Russia I would be a Red Guard,' he told an audience assembled for his homecoming.[245] Andrews was the League's third full-time organiser. The post had been held by Ivon Jones until he became too ill with his tuberculosis. Jones was then replaced by Tinker, a typographer who was one of Bunting's co-accused in the 'bucket strike' trial. Tinker resigned in November 1918 because of his syndicalist-inspired objections to the League's electoral activity. On Andrews's appointment, the post was salaried at £15 a month, and simply raising funds for such expenses required considerable effort.[246] In one of his letters to his wife, Bunting mentioned canvassing for donations, visiting 15 addresses with a net catch of £1.[247] Friendly Jewish traders were a key source of funds, to judge from advertisements in *The International* – benefactors included party members such as 'Comrade H Glazer, Expert Ladies and Gents Tailor' and hairdresser EA Vella, whose appeal to readers to 'Help a RED make a living' appeared in the paper's columns during the second half of 1920.

Notwithstanding any declarations of intent about paying special attention to black workers, Andrews's activities would focus on white workers. From late 1918, he was busy urging the formation of shop stewards' committees up and down the Reef among the trade unionists assembled in the mining workforce. In February, Andrews was 'deputed' by the ISL's executive or management committee to offer his assistance to white tramway strikers in Pretoria. He proposed they should turn the tables on their obdurate employer and assume responsibility for running their own tram service, taking in the fares and holding them in trust: 'Lock out the Council' should be their slogan.

Andrews was not simply reacting to opportunities on his own. In late November a group of ISL members began meeting to consider the 'coming wave from Europe'. For those who participated in these deliberations, the Russian Revolution and the appearance of workers' soviets in Berlin, Munich, Budapest and Vienna were signals that 'the time had come to secure the role of the working class in SA'. Workers' councils should be brought together in each significant South African city 'for the ultimate purpose of exercising [workers'] control'.[248] 'The Soviet is the only practical politics in South Africa', for 'every general strike on the Rand brings us to the brink of revolution'.[249] In December the League announced a 'Preparedness Campaign' that would take as its inspiration 'the Great Push in Europe', a reference to events in Germany and Austro-Hungary.[250] In Johannesburg, a 'Preparedness Committee' began meeting weekly. In Pretoria, the strikers in the end did nothing, but on 1 April 1919 Andrews made the same suggestion to engineers and power and tram workers in Johannesburg who had stopped work in protest against retrenchments. The strikers should seize control through their own council, he advised. This time the workers were more receptive. A 'Provisional Board of Control' or 'Soviet' – the latter term was actually used by the strikers – occupied the City Council chambers and restored power supplies and public transport for ten days, charging fares and paying workers, before handing back direction of the services after the council capitulated on its proposed retrenchments. The Board chose as its chairman James Bain, then the leader of the striking power workers. The Johannesburg Soviet was an exclusively white initiative, though Andrews as well as Charles Tyler and Andrew Dunbar in their addresses to the strikers had each suggested that the Soviet should represent and embrace all workers, irrespective of race, a view that Bain seemed to echo in one of his speeches at the City Hall.[251] It was advice the strikers disregarded; they offered no support to the simultaneous African anti-pass protest and even promised the councillors whom they were about to eject from the City Hall that they would help in dealing with the 'native unrest' and act quickly against any 'outrages' directed at white women or children.[252] To be fair to Andrews, in February he had succeeded in persuading the South African Industrial Federation – the new incarnation of the Trades and Labour Council – to protest against the harsh treatment meted out to African strikers in Bloemfontein.[253]

Even before the Board of Control handed back to the councillors their usurped authority, Sidney Bunting published a fierce condemnation of its actions. This was no 'Soviet' – proper workers' councils did not announce their intention to hand back power once grievances were addressed, he pointed out in an editorial on 4 April. But in any case the Board was hardly representative of most workers: 'Where were the masses ... the underdogs', the delegates of the 'sanitation boys', for example? If the Board's attitude to black workers was only 'benevolent neutrality', that would be one thing, but the fact was that Board spokesmen had been outspoken in their willingness to help suppress any native 'outrages'. This was a 'lynching affray', led by labour's aristocracy, not a workers movement. 'The Johannesburg lunchtime crowd, many of them no doubt, fresh from cheering Bolshevism in the Town

Hall, not only jeered at the outrages but helped to catch and belabour any male or female Native luckless enough to be abroad at the time ... 'Native Menace' indeed! ... Who are the menacers but the whites armed to the teeth, who are the menaced everytime, if not the timid, unarmed defenceless blacks, who voluntarily collect all sticks whenever they hold a meeting.'[254]

Andrews did not defend the Board's actions at that time, though twenty years later he wrote warmly about the episode, eschewing any reference to a 'soviet'. Rather, retrospectively, his emphasis was on the comparative efficiency of the Board's operations and the general approval it elicited from 'the humbler citizens of Johannesburg'.[255] Eight months later, he made the same kinds of points about an even shorter-lived Durban 'Soviet', which had secured the reinstatement of a town clerk who belonged to the Municipal Employees' Association.[256] Here the Board of Control's 'possession' of the City Council's offices lasted just eight hours before it handed back control. Even so, Harry Haynes, one of the leaders of the 1913 mine workers' strike who was the main instigator of this undertaking, claimed afterwards that 'proletarian discipline ... under the dictatorship' was wonderful; it ensured that everything 'worked like clockwork', he insisted – even the police cooperated.[257]

Back in Johannesburg, Ivon Jones seems to have assumed the role of peacemaker, arguing that Bunting's characterisation of the white workers as a labour aristocracy was wrong. As events had just demonstrated, they certainly had the capacity to establish a proletarian dictatorship, and when that day would come they would discover very quickly that 'unless within twenty four hours after the revolution the whole proletariat experienced the joyousness of freedom ... the revolution founders'. But to hold back from efforts to enlist their engagement would be mistaken, for the 'white proletariat ... is the engine of revolution in South Africa'.[258] Even so, they should have tried to elicit black workers' participation in their council, for 'such experiments can only be successful by forcing the whole proletariat to capture control'.[259] It is likely that Jones's position reflected the predominant sentiment within the League at that time. References to the 'Soviet principle of worker's control' was a central theme in the election manifesto the League issued before the 1920 elections.[260] As one contributor to the party paper pointed out, the aim of a proletarian dictatorship was now 'becoming practical politics'.[261] An official report presented by League representatives in Moscow in 1921 referred to the Johannesburg 'Soviet' as a useful experiment and omitted any reference to its offer to help suppress any black protest. The Board was conceived with the intention of 'giving the rank and file a taste of their own power'. Its leaders, however, 'wisely reckoned that as a permanent institution under capitalism the Soviet was impossible'.[262]

The assertiveness of white trade unionism at this time certainly reinforced the League's disinclination to write off white workers as a potential revolutionary force. In 1920 the number of strikes peaked, 66 stoppages with an average duration of nine days involving 105,658 workers, and trade union membership would reach 132,754. The number of strikes would in fact fall in 1921 – there were 22 in all – though the numbers participating, 107,507, remained considerable.[263] Despite the encouraging signals the League leadership discerned in white labour militancy, in their vision of how a revolutionary change might happen they warned that white workers would not emancipate themselves until they had 'conquered all race prejudice'. In a document the League prepared for its 1919 annual conference, it developed its argument further. Soviets would be indispensable, because even if white workers were sufficiently present in parliament to enable that body to assume some of the roles of a dictatorship of the proletariat, local councils of workmen would be needed to ensure that the 'great bulk of the proletariat' who were disenfranchised could assume control. The most pressing task for the ISL, the document concluded, was 'to awaken and inspire our native fellow workers to grapple with their responsibility' and to encourage white workers 'to educate, organise and cooperate with their native workers at their place of work'.[264]

In 1919 this did not seem an utterly hopeless prospect. In that year there was at least one success in inducing joint action by white and black workers, but it would happen in Cape Town, not Johannesburg. It would involve Hamilton Kraai and Alfred Cetiwe, who together had moved from Johannesburg to the Cape after the collapse of the anti-pass campaign. Shortly after their arrival in April or May 1919 they had begun recruitment for a local branch of the Industrial Workers of Africa in the main African location, Ndabeni, drawing support there not from the ISL, which had no branch in Cape Town, but rather from a syndicalist group, the Industrial Socialist League.[265] The Industrial Socialist League had broken away from the Social Democratic Federation, which its founders perceived as ineffectual and 'academic', insufficiently 'in the vicinity of the proletariat'.[266] They also objected to the Federation's electoral orientation: the Federation regularly contested municipal elections putting up its own candidates to contest District Six, the stronghold of the African People's Organisation's Dr Abdullah Abdurahman, who, in Harrison's words, was 'really no representative of his people'.[267] The Industrial League was 'ultra-syndicalist' in that it adhered to the purist position of rejecting any electoral participation, even for propaganda purposes.[268] Wilfrid Andrews in his autobiography would disparage the Industrial Socialists' efforts to build a syndicalist movement among coloured sweet workers, efforts chiefly characterised, he dismissively maintained, by 'tea parties and rather desolate propaganda meetings'. Though they opened an office in District Six, 'the common people were not much concerned', Harrison suggested.[269] That may have been so, but the League also rented a hall that could accommodate up to 400 people, and at its opening on 12 January 1919 speakers from the League and local trade unions addressed a full house, including 12 sailors, adherents of the Industrial Workers of the World, the 'Wobblies'.[270] They also enjoyed some initial success among railway workers, holding meetings in Parow, a suburb next to Cape Town's railway workshops.[271] The Industrial Socialist League opened a branch in Johannesburg, which Andrew Dunbar joined in early 1919, thereby earning his expulsion from the ISL. At the beginning of 1920 the Yiddish-speaking branch of the International Socialists followed Dunbar's course, defecting from the parent body in protest against its continuing adherence to electoral participation and joining the Johannesburg Industrial Socialist League.[272] It had failed to persuade the International Socialists to delete its 'political action' commitment after a 28-to-2 vote by delegates at the party conference. This decision followed several months of debate. As Ivon Jones observed in an editorial, the issue had become 'the touchstone which divides anarchism from revolutionary socialism'.[273] Whether all the Yiddish-speaking branch members left the ISL at this time is unclear. Probably not, for there would be plenty of evidence of the residual influence of Bund socialism, and individual former Bundists continued to shape the ISL and its successor. In October 1920, the Industrial Socialist League renamed itself the Communist Party of South Africa, the first but not the last entity to use that title.

Harrison's disparaging comments notwithstanding, the Industrial Socialist League was in fact busy and assertive in Cape Town, holding as many as five open-air meetings a week as well as publishing a monthly newspaper, *The Bolshevik*. Henry Glasse was an occasional contributor, his writing rare evidence of the now decades-old continuity of a South African radical socialist tradition. They may not have enlisted much engaged support in District Six, though police informers reported that their meetings there in their new Socialist Hall were well attended, but they did succeed in establishing a degree of influence within the Cape Federation of Trade Unions and they were particularly active around the dockyard.[274] In the Federation, the key personalities were AZ Berman, who was elected treasurer of the Federation in 1919, and F Lopez, secretary of the tramway workers' union. Both artisans, they were fairly typical of the Federation's following – youngish workmen.

They managed to obtain support for resolutions at the Federation's congress in favour of industrial unionism, for joining Profintern, the Red International of trade unions, and for the abolition of capitalism, though the Federation, generally a conservative craft union body, would act later on none of these. The Industrial Socialist League favoured joint class action across racial divisions, and it helped the Industrial Workers of Africa to get started locally.

The League had supported another African union as well, the Industrial and Commercial Workers' Union (ICU), led by a Nyasa immigrant, Clements Kadalie, which had started a branch in the docks in January 1919. The IWA's membership would overlap with the Cape Native Congress in Ndabeni and it began to compete with the ICU, claiming dock workers as its first recruits. It held its first meeting in the docks in July, arranged with the Industrial League's support. In December, the Cape Federation of Trade Unions (CFTU) called a strike in protest against food exports, blaming them for local inflation. For two weeks, from 17 December, 3,000 dockers stopped work; these were members of the CFTU's white and coloured affiliates as well as the ICU and IWA, both of which agreed to add a wage demand for African workers to the proposed export ban. The ICU claimed a local following of around a thousand dockers but local press reports suggest the IWA was a serious rival; on the second day of the strike, Hamilton Kraai addressed a meeting attended by 800 people in Ndabeni.[275] Disappointingly, the strike had a ragged ending when coloured and white workers returned to their jobs after the cessation of exports was conceded. The IWA managed to extract a vague undertaking from the mayor to investigate wage levels and it announced the strike to be at an end, provoking charges of betrayal from Kadalie. It was a discouraging finale to what had been the first serious 'interracial' class action. But it may have left a legacy, for, as one commentator pointed out two decades later, 'to this day, the Cape Town dockers, with their stevedore unions, remain among the best organised and paid groups of African workers in the country'.[276] But there were no further reports of any undertakings by the Industrial Workers' Association's Cape Town branch. In 1922 Hamilton Kraai was working for Clements Kadalie as a translator, helping him to sign up an ICU following in East London.[277]

FOR THE FINAL PHASE in the active history of the Industrial Workers' Association, we must return to Johannesburg. Here, leadership of the Association and the International Socialists now overlapped in the personality of William Thibedi, who wrote and circulated a recruitment leaflet for the IWA in July 1919, describing it as 'your native council'.[278] At that point, the IWA was apparently still recruiting 'fresh members' in Johannesburg.[279] However, there is no evidence to indicate that the Association undertook any further agitational work, for in the second half of 1919 it seems to have functioned as a discussion club rather than a proto-union. In Johannesburg on May Day, police broke up an assembly of 4,000 African workers, though whether they were responding to a call from the IWA is unclear.[280] The following year, when African mineworkers went on strike on 17 February 1920 demanding wage increases, at most the Association may have influenced events indirectly. It may have been the case that IWA members continued to visit compounds in the months before the strike.[281] We do know that in the preceding days certain of the strike leaders had habitually attended Native Congress meetings in Vrededorp at which IWA members may have been among the speakers.[282] There is at least one contemporary description of a white orator addressing blanketed mine workers 'from the kraals' before the strike, asking his audience: 'Why do you allow the white man to sit around in those buildings? They are yours.'[283]

The strike was a major event, the largest South African mine workers' strike until 1946,[284] bringing out at one stage or another a total of 71,000 men. The workers' grievances stemmed from the same inflationary considerations that precipitated the store boycott in 1918; and, indeed, several local mine-store boycotts immediately preceded the strike. The workers' determination was accentuated by an unusually severe drought in the reserves during the winter of 1919. There were other motives as well: during the war white labour shortages had encouraged black workers informally to undertake more skilful tasks and they expected recognition for this at the war's end.[285] Strike leaders were often the most skilled black workers, 'boss boys' and often literate.[286] Though strikers used trade union methods – picketing, for example – all the evidence indicates that their mobilisation depended on pre-existing and older networks of ethnic and kin solidarity.[287]

Deployment of mounted riflemen and arrests of identified ringleaders brought the strike to an end, and shortly in its wake the Chamber announced wage increases, which had in fact been planned but not publicised before the strike began. During the strike the League issued a leaflet addressed to white mine workers, calling upon them not to scab. 'White workers, do you hear the new army of labour coming?' it began.[288] The leaflet was reprinted in the daily newspapers but failed to persuade any sections of its intended readership, though it probably helped to dissuade voters from supporting the League's five candidates in the March 1920 general elections – their highest tally was achieved by Bill Andrews, who received 78 votes. The leaflet was condemned by the leaders of what was now called the South African Mine Workers' Union, and two ISL members who tried to distribute the leaflet at particular shafts were arrested and later forced to resign their jobs by their fellow workers. One of these was Joe Andrews, vice chairman of the Mine Workers' Union at Crown Mines, by all accounts a popular figure.[289] It seems likely that Joe Andrews's expulsion was supported mainly by relatively recently recruited shaft workers, 'Dutch Afrikanders', for he had the backing of older, more experienced workers at the mine. Significantly engineering union officials tried vainly to persuade their members not to scab at the nearby power station, which was also affected by a strike by the black workers.[290] Ivon Jones claimed in a report he wrote in 1920 for the recently formed Comintern, that before the strike 'leaflets were distributed in the mine shafts by Communist sympathisers among the miners' – he was probably referring to Andrews and his comrades.[291] Actions of this kind indicated considerable courage and conviction but it was significant that the ISL was addressing its leaflet to white workers; there was clearly no channel through which it could communicate directly with the strikers.[292] Dispiritingly, the Mine Workers' Union executive at the time of its attack on the ISL leaflet included Forrester Brown, then still a League member. During the municipal workers' strike in 1918, former and present League members, including Forrester Brown, seem to have acceded to the South African Industrial Federation's offer in July to recruit 'labour battalions' to help the government in the event of any further African unrest. By the time of the African mine workers' strike, Forrester Brown's ISL membership was only 'nominal', it seems.[293]

CONFINED MAINLY TO A supportive role during this major upheaval on the Witwatersrand, the International Socialists were better placed elsewhere to provide leadership in a pioneering labour movement. In Kimberley, Sam Barlin, an ex-Bundist trade unionist from Johannesburg, helped to set up a Clothing Workers' Industrial Union. One of its recruits was a teenage tailor, Johnny Gomas, later in the 1930s a key figure in the Communist Party's history. In December 1919 the union won a strike after employers had reneged on a wage increase it had negotiated for its several hundred members.[294] Gomas and the union secretary, Fred Pienaar, were among the 27 coloured men who joined the local branch of the ISL.[295] Barlin also established a Horse Drivers' Union among coloured workers in Kimberley; their strike was weakened by scabbing by white railway workers, though African workers brought in to replace the coloured strikers 'returned whence they came' after meeting trade unionists.[296] The local ISL branch that was set up in mid-1919 was led by coloured trade unionists.[297] It would publish a leaflet directed at coloured voters during the 1920 elections.[298] In East London, ISL members in 1920 were engaged in supporting 'the trade union movement among the natives there', probably a reference to the recently formed local ICU branch.[299] In the previous year, *The International* had printed an appeal for support for striking Indian waiters in East London.[300] More tellingly, perhaps, the League was also busy among Indian workers in Durban. In early 1917, members of the local ISL branch in Durban encouraged the formation of an Indian Workers' Industrial Union. Originally founded by Gordon Lee, then the Durban chairman of the ISL, and formerly an adherent of the Industrial Workers of the World, the union swiftly elected its own Indian leadership and recruited across a range of trades in which Indian workers were concentrated in the city, including the docks, clothing factories, laundries, hotels and tobacco processors.[301] The union's secretary, Bernard Sigamoney, already well known as a cricketer, and a former high-school headmaster, was present at the ISL's annual conference in January 1918 where he denounced a new regulation that segregated Indian passengers on trains. The union ran educational classes and embarked on a scheme to translate articles from *The International* into Tamil, Telegu and Hindi, for at that time very few Indian workers spoke English. The union supplied leadership to a waiters' strike in June 1919, and in October 1920 was also involved in an action by 120 tobacco workers employed by a Natal Indian Congress leader, RB Chetty. In the tobacco factory, the union together with the ISL attempted to radicalise the workforce. Bill Andrews, then on a visit to Natal, made a speech calling for the formation of Soviets, though the workers and local leaders were inclined to keep their sights on the wage issue and, indeed, succeeded in negotiating an increase – for them a victory, if not a significant gain for the syndicalist leadership of the union. The workers' victory was partly a reflection of their success in mobilising community support; they formed neighbourhood committees that raised funds and discouraged scabbing. Meanwhile, the ISL had called on white workers not to scab, an appeal ignored by the local federation though supported by the Building Workers' Industrial Union.[302] Shortly after the strike, Sophus Pettersen stood for the ISL as a candidate in the Provincial Council elections; he failed to win a seat but drew a respectable share of the Indian vote. The Durban branch of the League itself had recruited 'several Coloured and Indian comrades' by March 1918.[303]

Ivon Jones, convalescing from his illness in Durban, had been helping to reinforce the ISL's local presence, joining Bill Andrews on speakers' platforms. While Bernard Sigamoney and Gordon Lee were assembling their Indian trade union, he and a former Social Democratic party member, Laurie Greene, had drafted a leaflet in isiZulu, Sesotho and English, *The Bolsheviks Are Coming*. They printed 10,000 copies, according to the subsequent trial record. Much of its content was taken up with condemnation of Allied intervention in Russia. 'The hope of the workers is coming from Bolshevism', for the 'free commonwealth of labour' lay in Russia. Here in South Africa, all workers should ready themselves for 'the world-wide republic of labour'. They should get ready by combining 'in the workshops ... as workers, no matter what colour'. Jones and Greene were charged under the Riotous Assemblies Act. Jones was compelled to leave his sanatorium and Laurie Greene's wife was dismissed from her job managing a café, the Greenes' main source of income. At the trial in May, witnesses included Josiah Gumede, secretary of the Natal Native Congress, who informed the court that under any Bolshevik dispensation 'we natives should be made slaves'. Under cross-examination, Ivon Jones claimed he had never visited an African township or a reserve; he 'was not addressing African peasants, but sought only to organise the working class, black and white'. He denied any incitement to violence; on the contrary, his leaflet reflected a programme that led away from violence: 'We claim that the native workers, left to themselves, blindly groping in conditions that are increasingly trying, are liable to follow the mistakes of all inexperienced workers by relying on crowds for their strength instead of upon their labour ... To avoid in the industrial field the territorial strife of the pioneer and tribal days, that is our aim.'[304]

In publishing the leaflet, Jones told the court, they were 'trying to make the native fit for control', for they did not 'consider they are fit at the present time to rule the country; that is why we have to carry on propaganda'.[305] White and black workers 'combining in the workshop does not mean intermarriage', he added.[306] Despite these explanations, the two men were convicted and sentenced, though at the end of August their convictions were overturned on appeal to the Supreme Court. As the Judge President noted, 'in the circumstances existing at the time', he could find nothing in the pamphlet 'which created, in his mind, either alarm or excitement'. It was the sort of thing 'they were all very familiar with', and in any case propaganda of that kind was hardly prohibited.[307]

JONES RETURNED TO JOHANNESBURG shortly afterwards and began running a literacy class for African workers, the first evidence we have of any extended conversational encounters between him and Africans.[308] A rather different source suggests that at the time of his leaflet, Ivon Jones's attitude to African workers was influenced by instrumental considerations rather than any kind of emotional empathy. In April 1919, a police informer posing as a prospective member met Jones during an arranged appointment at the Balcony Tea Room in Johannesburg. He told Jones that he was a man who had 'been living among natives for some time' and who as a result of this experience could never bring himself to 'acknowledge absolute equality with them'. Jones was apparently able to reassure him. The Leaguers, he admitted, were 'only using the native in a selfish way to further their own ends'. By inciting Africans to strike, they knew that if Africans achieved higher wages, white wages would rise as well, for no white man would work 'for a lower wage than natives'. Wages were the key: 'the destruction of the passes is merely a side issue which appeals to the native mind'. If true, the report does rather confirm the absence of any really intensive engagement by the ISL's leadership in the 1919 African anti-pass protests in Johannesburg, and the degree to which by this stage the IWA was acting independently from its founding sponsors.[309]

Also present at this meeting were two Russians, Leo Lapitsky and Israel Sosnovick, whom the League had been entertaining during their stay in Johannesburg. During their visit they were hosted by one of their compatriots, Michael Wolberg, who had left Russia after various conspiratorial exploits and, on arriving in South Africa, discovered he possessed an unexpected talent for business. By the time he reached Johannesburg in 1917 he was a wealthy entrepreneur. He joined the ISL all the same, but kept his membership discreet, continuing to move in elite circles, successfully prevailing on the mayoress to accept an appointment as patron of the Russian literary circle he established. South African archival records refer to his arrest in 1918, though for what reasons is unclear. He was freed after Maxim Litvinov made representations on his behalf through the British.[310] In 1919, shortly before the time of the Johannesburg Soviet, he was able to use these connections to arrange a public meeting inside the City Hall – normally forbidden territory for the ISL – to be addressed by the two Russian exiles, both of whom had worked for the Soviet administration in the Ukraine briefly before the German invasion of 1918.[311] What he had billed as a talk by now-remorseful revolutionaries that would be directed at exposing Bolshevik atrocities was attended by 6,000 people. To the mounting consternation of the dignitaries assembled on the platform, Sosnovick read out, and Wolberg translated word by word, a pre-agreed script which was celebratory rather than condemnatory in tone, concluding with a rendering of 'The Internationale' 'on the huge city hall organ'. There were subsequent calls for their arrest, but any such move was forestalled through pressure from the 'Board of Control', that is, the 'Soviet'. Lapitsky and Sosnovick subsequently visited Cape Town before their deportation. Wolberg accompanied them back to Russia, a lengthy and difficult journey, which he described in detail in a report he submitted to the offices of the recently formed Communist International one year later in April 1920.[312] He also brought with him to Moscow bound copies of *The International* and supplied the Comintern officials with a profile of the League. He assured them it was a serious revolutionary agency, capable of drawing thousands to its meetings, and emphasised its key difference from the Labour Party as a group that did 'not recognise any kind of difference based ... on skin colour', that 'conducts militant propaganda among dark skinned comrades' and that 'managed to form a rather strong organisation among them as a branch of our party'.[313] Wolberg's report evidently attracted attention from the highest level of the Russian party's leadership; in the volumes of Lenin's published *Miscellany*, there is a note requesting a copy of the report.[314]

The League already viewed itself as an adherent of the Bolshevik line, Wolberg reported, and when the police visited its offices at 45 Fox Street, they would tear off from the walls posters of Lenin and Trotsky. In fact, shortly after Wolberg joined the League, it had indeed in January 1918, at its annual conference, declared itself in support of the Bolsheviks; this was when Andrews was instructed to contact Maxim Litvinov on the party's behalf. In September that year at the World War's end, the League turned down a conciliatory invitation from the Labour Party to rejoin its fold, explaining that its revolutionary socialism and its engagement with black workers constituted irrevocable differences.[315] As we have seen, the accompanying decision to contest elections separately from the Labour Party prompted the defections of the more doctrinaire anti-parliamentarian syndicalists to form a rival communist group in Johannesburg. By this stage the differences between Leninist Bolshevism and syndicalist understandings of revolutionary processes were beginning to become clearer. They were, after all, quite plainly evident in some of the literature that was by now being offered for sale in *The International*. For example, readers could purchase Lenin's pamphlet on *The Soviets at Work*, translated a year after its original publication in *Pravda*, in which he defended the retention of well-paid bourgeois technicians and the necessity for repressive state measures, including forced labour. Lenin's strictures on 'the problem of increasing discipline' and his views on the necessity for 'compulsory labour for all' were the subject of an admiring article reprinted from Melbourne's *Labour Call*.[316] In case readers had missed the point, the same issue of the ISL's newspaper carried a harsh critique of anarchism, written by the ex-Glaswegian IWW activist, JM Gibson. Anarchists were a group who represented 'a menace to the socialist objective'; indeed, they were 'at one with the bourgeoisie'.[317] A few months earlier in September 1918, *The International* dismissed any objections to Lenin's dissolution of the Russian Constituent Assembly (in which Bolsheviks were in a minority) as 'parochial'. *The International* reproduced Lenin's justification: as an expression of democracy, the Soviet was much more effective than institutions of 'representative government' because its 'thought and will' reflected the feelings of local organs, 'always functioning and therefore always reflecting the thoughts, desires and will of the small communities they represent'.[318]

In June 1920, the Communist International at its conference spelled out its 21 conditions for affiliation, including insistence that it would recognise and support only one communist party in any one country. Also by now quite evident was Comintern's endorsement of Leninist vanguardism and the Bolsheviks' seizure of state power as well as its hostility to syndicalism and its support for using electoral platforms in pre-revolutionary struggles, though the ISL's *International* continued to project a vison of an industrial republic created and embodied by big unions. During 1920, both the ISL and the Industrial Socialist League in Cape Town applied for affiliation. Bill Andrews told his biographer that the League's application was accepted 'without difficulty' that year.[319] Correspondence in the Comintern files suggests, though, that the League was still waiting to hear about its acceptance in March 1921. This may have been an effect of the difficulties in communication between Moscow and Johannesburg. In July 1921 the League sent delegates to the Comintern's third congress who participated in its proceedings; this rather does imply that it had by then achieved formal recognition.

THE LEAGUE'S PRESENCE at Comintern's congress was the final act in South African communism's pre-history. Four features of this genealogy of South African revolutionary socialism traced out in this chapter are conspicuous, and each of them merits more emphasis than they have received in the standard historical treatments.

First was its debt to anarchist syndicalism, initially inspired by the ideas of Peter Kropotkin and then reinforced by the thinking of American syndicalists brought into South Africa through successive waves of migration of workers from other parts of the English-speaking world. Syndicalism would remain influential within the South African left; its notions of a socialist commonwealth brought about through industrial action left a strategic imprint that would shape South African politics for decades, long after the specific injunctions of Daniel De Leon had been forgotten. Migrants from Australia and elsewhere also brought with them an ideology of 'white labourism', not a specifically South African programme. However, this racial sectionalism was by no means an uncontested way of perceiving the new setting in which white workers found themselves as they established their communities along the gold-bearing reef of the Witwatersrand.

For a second important dimension of the working-class politics that preceded the Communist Party's formation was its fluidity on the issues of race and cross-communal solidarity. Bill Andrews is an exemplary case in his inconsistency and ambivalence on racial issues, intuitively and emotionally finding his sense of community within the confines of white industrial neighbourhoods and yet intellectually ready to recognise that the real working class included black South Africans. In both Johannesburg and Cape Town, De Leonite syndicalism prompted socialist organisers to start building wider class-based fraternities, and this chapter has traced in detail the construction of syndicalist groups that enrolled black workers in both cities, arguably in each case helping to shape much larger movements of worker insurgency among mine workers in the one and dock workers in the other.

A key role in extending the social reach of radical working-class organisations was played by Jewish immigrants, particularly those with previously acquired familiarity with revolutionary ideas and networks in the Russian Pale. Among newly arrived first-generation immigrants, the Jewish Labour Bund would remain influential in promoting their engagement with left-wing groups in South Africa. Further arrivals of Jewish immigrants would bring important reinforcements to the Communist Party in the 1920s and 1930s. They maintained a reflexive set of political practices that, arguably, shaped South Africa's wider oppositional politics profoundly. They would make a lasting contribution to the evolution of South Africa's revolutionary socialism, initially reinforcing its predispositions to extend organisation beyond white workers. These people sometimes arrived in South Africa ready to replicate the organisational formations in which they had been engaged in Lithuania, formations in which Bundists had played the pioneering role. In Johannesburg, Bundist ideas about an insurrectionary labour movement in a South African setting fused with syndicalist predispositions that were shared more widely within the white labour movement in the 1910s and

1920s. One long-term effect of Bundist strategic reliance on organised labour was South African communists' neglect of, indeed disinclination to mobilise, peasant support, an aversion which can be traced back through its history to the Bundist dislike of Russian rural populism – a reaction to the Narodnik movement's anti-Semitism. Bundists were conspicuous in the Lithuanian Communist Party and, in an increasingly repressive political climate for Jews, admiration for the Russian Bolsheviks increased. As we shall see, left-wing Jewish emigrants to South Africa often had personal experiences that predisposed them to view Russian communism sympathetically.

The fourth dimension of this story about South Africa's embryonic socialism is the degree to which it was shaped by black people. To be sure, South African revolutionaries depended initially upon imported visions and an immigrant lexicon. None of its pioneering personalities drew their inspiration from any ideas about pre-colonial arcadias or from the African resistance to imperial conquest. As this chapter suggests, men like William Thibedi and Hamilton Kraai began adapting and domesticating these exotic visions and applying this foreign lexicon to their own circumstances and needs, and, in doing so, they assertively established their role as active agents in indigenising a South African socialist lineage.

TWO

CPSA: Early History, 1921–1926

Mineworkers gather outside the magistrate's court in Johannesburg, February 1922. Note banner with the call for 'White workers of the World to unite for a White South Africa'. The same slogan appears in several photographs taken around this time in different vicinities.

It would take three meetings over the course of 1921, in January, March and August, to assemble the different Marxist revolutionary groups that existed in South Africa into a broader Communist Party that itself would achieve Comintern recognition. Towards the end of 1920, reacting to the Comintern's conditions for affiliation, the International Socialist League (ISL) invited a range of organisations to attend its annual conference in January 1921 to discuss the formation of a Communist Party. This invitation succeeded in eliciting the presence at this meeting of spokesmen from several groups including the Johannesburg branch of the Industrial Workers of Africa (IWA); the Indian Workers' Industrial Union; the Marxist Club, a group that emerged out of disagreements within the Durban Social Democratic Party (SDP); and the Poalei Zion, local representative of the socialist flank of the Zionist movement; as well as various white trade unionists and individuals from the Labour Party. Andrew Dunbar also attended on behalf of his Communist Party but then walked out after the meeting refused to repudiate electoral activity.

Those who remained agreed on a statement that maintained that as South Africa was not in a revolutionary situation, the role of the party would be to openly propagate communist principles and to try to shape or direct the local labour movement. Under the circumstances, an illegal movement was not a practical option, 'too easily betrayed and corrupted by police spies'.[1] The statement repeated the League's earlier rejection of any connection with the Labour Party and welcomed the Comintern's endorsement of electoral participation. Socialist unity would exclude anarchists, the new party would be disciplined and centralised on the Comintern model, and it would not sanction any autonomous branches. League delegates disagreed sharply over a proposal from Sidney Bunting that they should support Afrikaner nationalism to an extent, given its anti-imperialist potential; a majority decided against such a course.[2]

Bunting also presented a second proposition, that the League should support a set of African struggles, not just workers' demands but also opposition to landowners, the Natives Land Act, pass laws and campaigns for the franchise. However, this did not imply endorsement of African nationalism. In accepting this plan, delegates would also decide by 40 votes to 29 that at no time could a Communist Party 'identify with any nationalist or other bourgeois party' and hence could not 'support its programme'. To be sure, Comintern's expectation, spelled out in its conditions, was that in colonial settings communist parties should help 'national and colonial liberation movements', a corollary of Lenin's view expressed at the recent Comintern congress that anti-colonial movements might play 'a much more revolutionary part than we expect'.[3] However, in the League's view at this time, this condition would be fulfilled by a South African Communist Party supporting or even leading broad struggles for African rights, including peasant-based movements, but not by alliances with 'nationalist native organisations'.[4] On the contrary, *The International* editorialised, the League did 'not believe in "restoring the land ... to its rightful owners"'.[5] A five-person Unity Committee was chosen that included Bill Andrews and Sidney Bunting to decide on aims and rules for the proposed new party. It drafted a manifesto which set out as the party's most 'immediate task' the establishment of 'the widest and closest possible contact with workers of all races and to propagate the Communist gospel among them, in the first instance, among the industrial masses, who must provide the storm troopers of the revolution, and secondly among the rural toilers'.[6] The first point in the committee's draft constitution set the tone for the rest of its content: the new party would accept the Comintern's 21 points; and organisational structure would be strongly centralised with decision-making power between congresses vested in a central executive.

Shortly after this first meeting, Andrew Dunbar's Communist Party split and most of its adherents, though not Dunbar, together with part of the Cape Town Social Democratic Federation (SDF) constituted themselves as the United Communist Party, as a grouping that was in broad agreement in accepting Comintern's conditions as well as acknowledging the inevitability of any post-revolutionary state. This new group was represented by Wilfrid Harrison at the meeting summoned by the ISL's Unity Conference on Easter Sunday, 27 March; by this stage Harrison had moved sufficiently from his original anarchist moorings to be able to support the 21 points with 'unqualified acceptance'.[7] The syndicalist rump of the Communist Party also sent people to the Easter meeting at which they encountered representatives of Poalei Zion, the Marxist Club, the Durban SDP, the SDF and, of course, the ISL. Compromise with the ISL was made easier by the League's decision to boycott the February 1921 general elections in South Africa – League candidates who contested the poll in Natal did so as independents.

The IWA and the Durban Indian unionists were not represented separately at this meeting, though Bill Andrews in a letter written on 27 April to Sam Barlin, then in Moscow, observed that things were 'looking better' as far as the 'Communist movement' was concerned, because 'the natives [had] formed what they call a "Little Group" in Natalspruit [outside Johannesburg] and wish to become a branch of the new Communist Party'. William Thibedi headed this group, Andrews reported. In the following year, Andrews suggested, it might be possible to send an African worker to Russia, though for the time being, 'there is no native worker … in whom we have absolute confidence'.[8] This was a little surprising, for aside from the IWA group that the League had sponsored, it had also been running its own weekly night school for Africans since April 1918.[9]

Andrews was writing to provide Barlin as well as Ivon Jones and J den Bakker with the necessary credentials to attend the upcoming Comintern conference as League delegates. Jones had been living in Russia for almost a year after leaving South Africa in November 1920 to recuperate from an especially severe spell of tuberculosis. In Nice he met Karl Radek, Comintern's secretary, who suggested he should travel to Moscow to attend the next Comintern conference. By this time, Michael Wolberg had reported on the League and Jones would make the journey to Moscow as its representative. While in Nice he wrote a report, 'Communism in South Africa', which he would present to the Comintern's executive on the League's behalf. The League, Jones explained, 'imbued with the ideas of De Leon', was the largest of the various socialist groups in South Africa, active especially around Johannesburg, 'the industrial university of the African native'. Jones's report emphasised the League's engagement in the 1918–20 African workers' struggles and its role in setting up the IWA. It also drew attention to the way that the Native Congress had 'timidly' disengaged 'from the mass movements of its own people'. In South Africa, he insisted, 'the national and class interests of natives cannot be distinguished one from the other'. The African workers' struggles that the League had been supporting themselves embodied a 'revolutionary nationalist movement in the fullest sense of Lenin's term'.[10]

One year later, writing to Trotsky on 2 June 1921, Jones set out his argument even more emphatically: 'In South Africa, economic and political crisis will be the result of the awakening of the black proletariat … native workers are a perfect material for a socialist revolution. But they are illiterate … But the Comintern should not have any doubts. Native workers are beginning to understand and master the idea of a Workers Organisation.'[11] Jones would join the Comintern's executive as a 'consultative member', after being elected in July 1921 at its third congress. Here he urged that its executive should pay serious attention to the 'negro', a proposal that was accepted but not acted upon subsequently,[12] though Comintern's chairman, Grigory Zinoviev, in an earlier session with the South Africans had suggested it might be a good idea 'to organise a commission to study the question about the Blacks'.[13] Zinoviev's comment may have been influenced by the debate at Comintern's second congress on alliances with anti-colonial national liberation movements, in which Lenin and the Indian delegate Manabendra Roy had disagreed over whether communists could ally with bourgeois democratic nationalists.[14] The League's delegation at the third congress had set out its stall in a rather more reserved and apologetic phraseology than the language used by Jones when he wrote to Trotsky. In South Africa, the 'negro race' had 'a very primitive character' and this characteristic explained 'the consequently exclusively white character of the Communist Movement'. Even so, 'the logic of class struggle' compelled communists 'to place the question of solidarity with the native workers in the forefront of its propaganda with white workers'. Direct approaches to African workers were difficult, however, for 'there [were] hardly any native linguists among the white communists'. These considerations implied that 'the small white working class should be regarded more as a purchase hold for the direct action of the Comintern'. In the longer term, 'South African natives offer good material for the Communist movement'.[15] As the language being used suggested, even among Leaguers for whom cross-racial solidarity was common sense, cultural condescension towards Africans was reflexive. An anonymous article in *The International*, written probably by Jones, implied that even under socialism, a working class would remain white-led: 'Under proletarian control the natural goodwill born of interdependence that undoubtedly exists between the white mechanic and his black helper, the white miner and his hammer boy, white railwayman and native cleaner, at the place of work, would be reflected on the political plane.'[16]

Two weeks after Comintern's third congress, 14 delegates, all of them white, from the League and the United Communists helped to found the Communist Party of South Africa (CPSA) proper at a third conference held in Cape Town between 30 July and 1 August 1921. Poalei Zion and the Marxist Club sent friendly and supportive messages and were counted as participants in the proceedings despite their physical absence.[17] The Durban Social Democrats held back. They could not accept most of Comintern's conditions, objecting especially to point 13 concerning periodic 'clearances' of petty bourgeois elements that might penetrate parties functioning in legal settings.[18] In their understanding of the 21 points an illegal organisation

71

was in any case an absolute requirement, and that was unacceptable.[19] They survived as an electorally oriented body into the mid-1920s, holding a council seat in Durban's municipality, which they first obtained unopposed in 1919. Delegates adopted the Unity Committee's manifesto and constitution unaltered despite objections from certain Cape Town delegates to the party's centralised structure. Aside from the decisions about organisational structure, the proceedings included 'a long discussion' on 'how best to organise and do propaganda amongst the native and coloured workers'.[20] The conference was interrupted on the evening of the 31st by a public meeting in the City Hall which attracted an audience of 2,000 to listen to speeches by Bill Andrews, Sidney Bunting, Wilfrid Harrison and Frank Glass. Most of the audience were not white, Bunting noted in his letter home that evening, adding that Bill Andrews in his speech was 'sound but not up to form – perhaps the coloured audience put him off'.[21] Delegates elected a nine-person executive with Charles Tyler as chairman, Andrews as secretary – a paid post with a monthly salary of £35 – and Bunting as treasurer.[22] In his new capacity as party secretary, shortly after the conference, Andrews wrote to Comintern's headquarters. A new Communist Party of South Africa had been formed based upon acceptance of the 21 points; it was now applying for affiliation.

Despite the absence of Africans at the August meeting, the arguments and declarations that accompanied the new party's formation suggested that their enlistment into its following, if not leadership, would be a priority. But at its first meeting after the founding conference, the Johannesburg branch of the CPSA 'hesitated' on the question of accepting Africans who had applied for membership. Argument about the issue preoccupied participants for another three sessions.[23] William Thibedi did in fact join the CPSA at the time of its formation but he was the only African to do so, it seems, for he was not accompanied by any of his fellow members from the Industrial Workers of Africa.[24] Nor were there indications of recruits from the Indian and coloured unions that ISL activists helped to start in Durban and Kimberley except for Bernard Sigamoney, who shortly afterwards would leave South Africa to undergo pastoral training in Britain as an Anglican priest. Presumably the other members of the putative Natalspruit branch mentioned by Andrews earlier that year were found wanting in one way or another and were excluded.

IN THE FIRST COUPLE OF years of its history, the CPSA would concentrate its energies mainly on building support among white workers. Given the very different predispositions that the ISL was signalling to Comintern through 1920 and 1921, this orientation needs explaining. The weakening and final disappearance of the IWA during this period was possibly one consideration. From mid-1920, with the local effects of global recession prompting militant reactions from a still-formidable white labour movement, even Sidney Bunting acknowledged that black workers needed to have visible organisational strength before whites could acknowledge them as 'worthy fellow labourers in the common cause'.[25] The departure from the ISL at the beginning of 1920 of most of the members of its Yiddish-speaking branch probably strengthened the influence of the English craft unionist grouping within the League and its successor. This is rather confirmed by the profile of the new party that Ivon Jones provided for Comintern. In his letter he supplied commentaries about 24 prominent party personalities. These biographical notes offer helpful insights into the social nature of the party's leadership and following. All of Jones's sketches are of men; yet Rebecca Bunting was elected as a member of the executive, seemingly at that time the only woman active in the party. The 24 men on Jones's list included Thibedi and Sigamoney but otherwise all the rest were white. The dentist Wade, the attorney Bunting and the bookkeeper Jones were, broadly speaking, from professional or white-collar backgrounds. The rest were mainly skilled artisans, including four fitters, two tailors, an engine driver and three tramwaymen, as well as builders, cabinet makers and two mine workers. They were mainly aged in their thirties and early forties. The names suggest that they were chiefly of English immigrant origins or descent.[26] Six of the nine executive members were from the ISL and the Witwatersrand as were most of the 300 or so of the CPSA's members.[27] Though Jones included in his profiles Charles Tyler, Sam Barlin and Abe Goldman, each with experience of trying to recruit African or coloured workers into unions, most of the people he described would have been active in the League's efforts to shape and influence the white labour movement. In effect, the rupture with the syndicalists in 1920, which had prompted the departure of many of the Yiddish speakers, had resulted in the CPSA's main predecessor becoming a body constituted mainly by 'English' artisans.

Externally derived policy considerations may also have helped to persuade the CPSA to concentrate on winning over white workers. The third congress of the Comintern, from 23 June to 12 July 1921, adopted resolutions that acknowledged 'the ebbing of the revolutionary wave in Europe', a situation which justified cooperation with labour movements and parties through the formation of 'united workers' fronts'. This was a shift from an earlier, more aggressive repudiation of any alliances with social democratic groups, a position in fact implied by the 21 conditions adopted at the previous congress in 1920; at that time the Red Army's successes in Poland had created hopes that communist parties might seize power in other European countries.[28] In Britain, on the other hand, calmer counsels prevailed after the third congress and the party was expected to try to affiliate to the Labour Party. Though its successive efforts were rejected, the Communist Party there was rather successful in 'capturing' local branches of the Labour Party despite its members being formally prohibited from joining in 1922.[29] With respect to South Africa, as we have seen, Comintern officials between the two congresses, between mid-1920 and mid-1921, appeared to encourage the League to engage more with black South Africans; Zinoviev's comment can be interpreted in that light. But by the time the CPSA was founded, the Comintern line had shifted and the South African party would have been expected to follow the course set by Lenin at the third congress and attempt to build a 'common front of all [workers'] parties', advice that Jones relayed back to Johannesburg in his report on the Third International.[30] Though the South African communists would wait until 1923 to decide in favour of applying for Labour Party affiliation, they would in late 1921 move their office back to the Trades Hall, where Andrews was in any case already based, an unwelcoming environment for any black visitors. As Eddie Roux explained in his biography of Sidney Bunting, most members of the new party's leadership felt 'their main work was among the [white] trade unions and the Trades Hall was a strategic centre'.[31]

As Bunting would confide to his wife in 1923, 'our old policy of liberation to the native workers has been dropped', though in this letter his comment suggests that this was a leadership decision, not a reflection of membership sentiment.[32] He may have been right at least with respect to membership outside Johannesburg; after all, in Cape Town in late 1921 Wilfrid Harrison put himself up as a municipal candidate, representing the party against Dr Abdurahman in ward seven. Abdurahman retained his seat comfortably, but the attempt by communists in Cape Town to secure coloured electoral support suggests the party's rather different social orientation here from that in Johannesburg. In Cape Town the party's weekly public meetings in Adderley Street were generally 'faithfully supported' by 'native and coloured elements', an attendance that was evidently valued by the local leadership.[33]

In any case, even without any strategic promptings from Comintern, and even if the party had retained all the Yiddish-speaking supporters who had joined the League, it is very likely that in late 1921 and early 1922 South African communists would have aligned themselves with the mainstream white labour movement, given the early signals of impending confrontation between white mine workers and their employers. In 1922, out of a workforce of 200,000, about 20,000 gold miners were white. By 1922 they were generally less skilled than they had been nearly ten years earlier, at the time of the 1913 strike. During the war, the division of labour had resulted in the increasing fragmentation of skilled work and more delegation of tasks to Africans (who in 1922 formed two-thirds of the semi-skilled workforce) – changes that were reflected, as we have seen, in the assertiveness of black workers in 1920. In 1922 white miners no longer performed any productive tasks, it seems, though as holders of blasting certificates they retained a racial monopoly on the handling of explosives.[34] As Sidney Bunting had pointed out five years beforehand, in 1917, many of the white overseers 'could not, even under the best conditions, drill a 36 inch hole correctly in eight hours'.[35] The 1913 strike had replaced employment contracts for whites with set wages together with incentives calculated on the basis of 'efficiency per boy per fathom a day', an arrangement that accentuated the exploitative nature of the relationship each white worker had with the drillers and other black workers whose operations he directed as a 'ganger'.[36] White workers were increasingly likely to be recently urbanised Afrikaners – maybe about half the white workforce in 1922. So the newer workers often came from farm backgrounds in which black people were subjected to extreme kinds of command. White workers in 1922 were more likely to live in suburban family dwellings, another consideration affecting their attitudes to black workers, from whom they were completely separated socially.[37] They still thought of themselves as skilled workers, and, arguably, their supervisory role required skills, knowledge and experience that the Chamber of Mines still needed in the process of gold extraction.[38]

Following a strike in 1917 in which white miners objected to the introduction of coloured waste packers, negotiations between management and the mine workers' union led to the Status Quo Agreement of September 1918 in which the Chamber of Mines promised there would be no further displacement of white workers through increases in the supervision ratio. During 1918 and 1919 white workers (in contrast to black gold miners) gained better wages, shorter hours and cost-of-living supplements, and in so doing, of course, they became increasingly expensive for employers. Through 1920 these increased costs could be offset as the internationally fixed gold price was abandoned but in 1921 the global price of gold fell. On 8 December, the Chamber decreed that the numerical ratio between white and black workers underground would change and 2,000 semi-skilled whites would lose their jobs. The remaining more skilled white workers, the gangers, would have their pay cut. The Chamber's announcement also suggested that further reorganisation of underground work would follow. After a bad-tempered halt to discussions with the mine workers' union, the Chamber warned that the Status Quo Agreement would end on 31 January.

Within the union a militant leadership was emerging in the Council of Action, constituted by men who had led unofficial or wildcat strikes at City Deep and Langlaagte between November 1920 and January 1921. Two of the strike leaders, Ernest Shaw and Percy Fisher, had been fined and suspended from their branch office positions in the mine workers' union. In response they formed the Council of Action. With the assistance of Bill Andrews, council members subsequently helped to form a Johannesburg section of the Red International. Andrews understood the council to be a militant rank-and-file movement of the kind he had been trying to promote since his return from the Clyde. Shaw was a CPSA member with previous involvement in the League and the Social Democratic Federation; as with Fisher, not a party member, he had a syndicalist background. Lerumo's official history of the Communist Party, written fifty years later, refers to Percy Fisher and Harry Spendiff as communists, but all the reliable contemporary evidence indicates they were not.[39] The party had only a few adherents in office-holding positions in the mine workers' union despite a communist, J Forrester Brown, holding the general secretaryship. The mine workers' strike movement was politically diverse and independent.

Most communists, certainly in Johannesburg, perceived white mine workers as a key group: advanced workers, capable (despite their racial prejudices) of standing at the forefront of any South African revolution as a vanguard formation against capital.[40] And when the miners lost their initial battles and capitalism succeeded in reducing white workers to the 'African's standard', then they would surely recognise their true class interests and abandon 'false ideologies'. Interracial solidarity would then expand accordingly – of this, most communists in Johannesburg, at least, were certain.[41] In key respects the mine workers' union embodied the kind of industrial unionism that Bill Andrews among the CPSA leadership had been especially striving to promote within white labour over the previous decade. Indeed, there is evidence that the Council of Action itself was a product of the League's earlier encouragement of a shop stewards' movement,[42] and there were striking similarities between its manifesto and the 'Preamble' adopted by the Industrial Workers of the World. These resonances included the council's envisaging of 'direct industrial action … used to institute a Republic of Industrial Workers'.[43]

In the days before the strike, the Communist Party's leadership agreed that they would join the white workers in their struggle against the Chamber 'under all circumstances'. In the long term, they suggested rather hopefully, 'circumstances would compel Africans and white workers to recognise identity of interests'.[44] Sooner or later, white workers would realise that 'there is not and never was a white South Africa ... Natives at starvation wages, that is the thing to attack: that is what ruins the white standard ... There is ... no future for white workers under capitalism.'[45] All the same, communists were emphatic that white miners were quite 'justified in fighting to keep up the numbers and pay of holders of blasting certificates'. They were, though, somewhat surprised by the union leadership's readiness for confrontation with the Chamber. Indeed, on the day the strike started, communists were attending a picnic they had arranged at Florida Lake. Though they were later accused by the government of being key instigators of an insurrectionary strike movement, during the early stages communists believed that the strike would end in defeat, and in the columns of *The International* they insisted that 'conditions on the Rand were not ready for the step to a Soviet Republic'.[46] The official strike leadership was supplied by the top echelon of the Mine Workers' Union, which was politically close to the Labour Party. There was a Central Strike Committee which directed local strike leaderships. The Communist Party would seek to influence the strike mainly through the council, a body whose individual members would become increasingly influential in the later stages of the strike, though the council itself rarely met as a caucus. Early during the strike, Council of Action members began organising their own meetings in strike centres.

The strike began on 10 January: 24,000 workers responded to the union's call, just about the entire white workforce on the mines across the Witwatersrand together with other groups of workers in the collieries. In the case of the collieries, as a contributor to *The International* noted at the time, the absence of the white workers made very little difference; three weeks later coal output was at normal levels.[47] After two weeks, commando units – that is, strike-supporting militia – began appearing at every strike centre, even in the smaller villages. This was after the first breakdown in negotiations between the official strike leadership, the 'Augmented Executive', and the Chamber. During these talks the council, basing itself in Andrews's office at the Trades Hall, directed a steady stream of excoriation at the executive, critical of its willingness to enter talks so early. The first month of the strike was relatively peaceful and orderly as negotiations proceeded, and they very nearly reached an agreement. After the talks finally ended in deadlock, the government called for a return to work and for the owners to reopen the mines, the latter a signal to the Chamber to send in scab labour, a move halted within a day by forceful picketing. The pickets were supported by the workers' commandos, including mounted armed horsemen, some of them initially formed with local police encouragement as a precautionary measure in case of any African rebellion.[48]

Armed white men and Africans were involved in skirmishes in Fordsburg on 13 February, and on the following day Bill Andrews and five council members were arrested and held for a week on incitement charges. A commando parade assembled on the Union Grounds in Johannesburg on 15 February, at a demonstration involving around 10,000 people, including groups of women bearing banners with at least one displaying the slogan 'Workers of the World, unite and fight, for a White South Africa'.[49] On the day the council leaders and Andrews were released, the government banned the commandos from attending strike pickets. In enforcing this proclamation, police attacked a commando in Putfontein on 27 February, arresting several men. Subsequently the commando assembled outside Boksburg prison where the police's captives were being detained, and police fired upon them, killing three while they were singing 'The Red Flag'. In the following week the Augmented Executive attempted to arrange a meeting with the Chamber and then, after the Chamber's rebuff, called for a ballot on the strike's continuation. In reaction to this, the militants in the council meeting on the evening of 4 March decided to assume overall control, summoning the commando leadership to the Trades Hall and calling for a general strike for 7 March. During the following week, commando leadership began to displace union officials in local leaderships as the strike transformed itself into an insurrection. Commandos attacked Africans on 7 March.

After a declaration of martial law on 10 March, the South African military used artillery and aircraft to destroy the strike headquarters in Fordsburg, siting the guns in the gardens of wealthy Parktown, the neighbourhood containing the mine owners' mansions. Weaponry on a similar scale was directed at the other main concentrations of armed strikers in Benoni, Boksburg and southern Johannesburg. As Ivon Jones observed afterwards, this was the first use of aircraft, 'the supreme capitalist weapon', in the suppression of an industrial conflict.[50] Two of the key council leaders, Percy Fisher and Harry Spendiff, died during the Fordsburg assault, probably by their own hands. Nearly 5,000 strikers were arrested and 953 were subsequently charged. Four men of the 18 sentenced to death would be hanged, though most sentences were abrogated in May 1924, shortly before the general election. In the violence accompanying the strike, 250 people were killed, including 44 Africans, with the remaining recorded fatalities more or less evenly divided between 78 strikers who were killed, 76 soldiers and policemen who died, and 62 white residents who were caught in the cross-fire in different localities.

EVEN FROM THIS BAREST outline of events it should be clear that despite the emblematic presence of revolutionary socialism in the strike movement, as in earlier battles between white mine workers and their employers, this was a class insurgency in which the Communist Party's contribution was incidental rather than decisive. Jack Cope, when writing Bill Andrews's biography, believed that 'Communist leadership was in the ascendancy' during the strike and that Andrews supplied a 'guiding hand' to the council.[51] This is probably an exaggeration, and in any case the extent to which even the council supplied coordinated leadership in the strike's latter stages was limited. Only eight communists were among the 67 miners who were convicted after the strike, six of these on relatively minor charges, for bearing weapons and the like, for which they received brief prison terms or, in two cases, fines; the other two were sentenced to two years.[52] One communist was killed during the strike, 'Comrade D Nortje, killed by natives in the fighting'.[53] Later, communists suggested that Nortje's death was a consequence of Chamber-sponsored *agent provocateur* activities.[54] Both during the strike and afterwards, for many Communist Party leaders the strike's meaning was clear: it was a major offensive against capital with all the associated heroic class militancy that should characterise such epic conflicts.[55] For his part, Ivon Jones, writing in Moscow at the time, remained undecided as to whether this was a 'last revolt of a non-revolutionary white working class driven to arms by the very insecurity of their economic position against the native masses' or, rather, an event which might have more emancipatory implications.[56]

Communists in Cape Town were more critical. Speakers at their open-air meetings who supported the strike encountered a barrage of heckling from Industrial and Commercial Workers' Union (ICU) and African People's Organisation (APO) supporters assembled in mainly coloured crowds. The ICU's leader, Clements Kadalie, declared at a meeting on 12 March that any success for the strikers would mean 'the retarding of our people'. In this confrontation the ICU pledged its loyalty to the government, for 'white workers had declared war on black workers'. This was quite evident in the 'brutal slaughter of innocent black men and women who had shown no hostile attitude to the white miners'.[57] Influenced by such reactions, Frank Glass, secretary of the Cape Town branch, wrote in *The International* that white workers' racism rendered them ineligible for any leadership role in a unified working class.[58] But in Moscow, Lenin himself followed the rebellion's development day by day, calling for reports on the strikers' progress. Lenin had, of course, drawn upon South African evidence in developing his theoretical work on imperialism and, even after its publication, kept up his reading on South Africa – in 1920, for example, he ordered Davidson Don Tengo Jabavu's *The Black Problem*.[59] Lenin suggested to Zinoviev that the Communist International should send somebody to South Africa to gather first-hand evidence about this suppression of such an important workers' uprising in what was, after all, such a key outpost for imperial capital. Ivon Jones volunteered for this mission, but in the end funds were unavailable. Jones had helped to draft a fiery appeal on behalf of the mine workers for Comintern's executive to endorse, but this was 'suppressed' apparently, a 'lost opportunity', Jones believed.[60] Two months after the strike Lenin himself was too ill to have any influence in setting Comintern priorities, for at the end of May he would be incapacitated by a stroke.

So, why could communists who were committed at least in theory to non-racial class solidarity ally themselves so unconditionally with a movement defending racially coded job reservation? Long after the event, Andrews's biographer could write that 'although the call for a white SA which became the chief slogan in the dispute appears reactionary on the surface it was nevertheless founded upon sound working class instinct'. It was not anti-native, he insisted.[61] Part of the answer is in the communists' own understanding of how white workers would eventually recognise such solidarities – through a dialectical process, they suggested. As Andrews observed before the strike, 'It will only be when by bitter experience white men find out the hopelessness of their colour bar that it will be possible to talk to them.'[62] In any case, as even Sidney Bunting was ready to acknowledge, what the workers were defending in their efforts to maintain 'the colour bar' was really 'civilised standards', in other words full livelihoods that any worker should be able to maintain, rather than the 'serfdom' meted out to black workers.[63] Strikers actually drew parallels between their struggle and the fight against slavery in the United States.[64] So party spokesmen were ready to endorse even the strikers' slogans, albeit with qualifications. 'Communism alone can make South Africa a white man's country', in so far as 'that Communism alone can secure to every worker – whatever his colour – the full product of his labour'.[65]

Which features of the strike movement helped to sustain the party's support, aside from the consideration that some of its members were involved directly? First and foremost, probably, was its militarised character, which, even before the fighting started, brought to the strike an insurrectionary dimension, literally embodying the strikers as class warriors. Communists were swift to characterise the commandos as 'Red Guards of the Rand', in doing so self-consciously drawing parallels between this South African rebellion and the militarised formations that had undergirded successful socialist revolution in Russia and so nearly effective workers' uprisings in parts of Germany.[66] As Jeremy Krikler has pointed out in his luminous reconstruction of the strike, it was a reasonable enough comparison.[67] First World War experience as well as the skills learned in combat shaped the outlook of militarised radical political groups across Europe's revolutionary tumults. In South Africa, Krikler's research suggests that World War veterans supplied much of the leadership of commandos, a view that undercuts earlier assumptions in the revolt's historiography about their formation reflecting Afrikaners' 'backward looking republicanism'.[68] Eddie Roux's account, based partly on his own observations, suggests that 'it was in the commandos that most of the anti-native feeling found expression'. He maintained that the commandos were 'Afrikaner nationalists to a man'.[69] Krikler's research suggests, however, that Afrikaner republican nationalism was only one strand in the revolt and was not prevalent. The commandos, up to 15,000 of them, were ethnically mixed (with respect to the white population) in their composition; indeed, there was even a Sinn Fein unit. They sometimes included strikers' wives and there were women's only commandos. One, led by a Communist Party member, Eva Green, attempted to occupy the Johannesburg telephone exchange.[70] A women's commando in Newlands on 6 March proposed blowing up the local railway station. In general, the extent to which women acted out of conformity with their customary domestic roles was an arresting feature of the insurrection – for communists, another signal of its liberatory portent.[71]

To sustain his argument, Krikler considers the ways that the commandos mimicked British army drill, procedure and organisation. But they did elect their officers, a feature that might indicate syndicalist sources of inspiration.[72] The commandos' formation, in the early stages of the strike, was a clear indication that strike leaders, at least at the intermediate levels of the movement, were prepared for the authorities to use military force against them; nearly from its inception, then, the strikers were ready to challenge the state's authority. Influenced as it was by its own residual syndicalist traditions, it was very easy for the party to view the strike as an expression of revolutionary industrial unionism.[73] As Jones would observe, it was, after all, 'the first great armed revolt of the workers on any scale in the British Empire'.[74] Evidently trying to make amends for his earlier condemnation and reflecting upon the strike's 'place in working class history', Frank Glass wrote in 1924, paraphrasing Lenin in 1905: 'It was a great revolution and by no means a chaos, because there was, albeit unsuccessful, an armed revolt of the Rand workers, because for a space, workers' commandos, workers' military units, the prototypes of the future Red Army in South Africa, flitted before the eyes of the World Proletariat ... The commandos will be reborn and will win.'[75]

Then there were the strikers' beliefs and ideas. This was a self-professedly anti-capitalist rebellion. It expressed its identity and ambitions through socialist slogans and symbolism: the strikers' insignia was a red rosette; at the first funeral of the men killed by the police, the coffins were enfolded in red flags; and the commandos' horses were dressed in red trappings.[76] Even the less radical members of the strike's leadership – the senior trade union officials – used language that was unequivocal in its moral condemnation of capitalists as a class. In Benoni, on the evening of 11 January, a crowded assembly called for the mines' nationalisation, calls echoed at later gatherings such as at Johannesburg's Union Grounds when those present adopted a resolution favouring an 'equitable distribution of the profits which are a direct result of our labours'.[77] Certainly the strikers were racist – to use Krikler's phrase, 'class ideology sat uncomplicatedly with racism'[78] – but this was a common feature of working-class rebellions in the English-speaking world in which, all the same, socialist language expressed profound beliefs. As Krikler puts it, the strikers were fighting for a world in which 'white labour would have a special claim'.[79]

Support for the strike was animated also by empathy and camaraderie. For the men and women in the party in Johannesburg, the strikers were fathers, brothers, friends and neighbours. In Willie Kalk's case, for instance, his brother was in the Jeppe commando. And as he recalled more than fifty years later, 'although it was a white workers' strike that was anti-black largely, it was fighting against a bigger enemy, the Chamber of Mines'. As he put it, rather hopefully, here was the 'dialectic at work'.[80] More detached and middle-class observers such as Bunting may have been ready to argue that the miners had lost the skills that had once made them indispensable, but during the strike such detachment was difficult for communists in Johannesburg. Living as they did in the same communities, calls for solidarity from the strikers' hustings could move them only one way. As Bernard Sachs recalled, writing after three decades about a meeting he attended as a Young Communist:

> From this rostrum the men from the mines, many of them in advanced stages of phthisis, would pour out all their pent-up hatred of those they held responsible for their misfortunes. There is something strange about the oratory of men who are in the advanced stages of phthisis. Their lungs are eaten away by the dust they absorb daily thousands of feet deep down in the earth. But their voices have quite an unexpected metallic ring, and for a

moment you are taken aback. The intermittent coughing which interrupts the flow of words is most dramatic in its effect. I often felt that to create the right atmosphere there was little else needed of these phthisis men to do but to mount the rostrum and just cough.[81]

With respect to the 1922 strikers' racial outlook, Johannesburg-based communists were insistent that this was a transient consciousness: epiphenomenal, as it were. After all, they already had witnessed instances of interracial class solidarity working the other way, that is, black workers supporting white-led strikes: the dock workers' strike in Cape Town was a case in point.[82] They could draw reassurance from the efforts of certain strike leaders, Percy Fisher in particular, to restrain his comrades from attacking black bystanders, and indeed from Fisher's quixotic attempts to persuade strikers to encourage their African fellow workers to demand triple wages.[83] Within the ISL itself there were veteran mine worker organisers who were outspoken critics of racial prejudice: Harry Haynes was an especially eloquent example.[84] Writing early in the strike, Ivon Jones reported to the Comintern that there had not been 'a single instance … cabled in the reports, of attacks by white workers on the negro working masses', a restraint that he attributed to the party's influence. In fairness to Jones, one of the telling features of the strike was the way its leadership did not represent black workers as enemies, eschewing, for example, any depiction of them as scabs. Strikers made no effort to picket mines or in any way discourage African workers from going underground, and they declared their opposition to the Chamber's repatriation of African workers to their homes for the strike's duration.[85]

Jones's assessment would, however, be overtaken by events. On 7 and 8 March there were coordinated and savagely brutal attacks on Africans by commandos. One of these attacks was on the Primrose workers' compound, in which eight men were shot dead – a reaction to the earlier deployment by mine managers of their African workforce as armed guards on the mine's railway siding to forestall a sabotage attack. Africans used as army auxiliaries in other settings – as stretcher bearers, for example – also died during the insurrection. In the other cases, the targets of white armed assaults, both on the East Rand and in Johannesburg, seem to have been chosen randomly: crowds of people outside workplaces or shops. One explanation offered by Jeremy Krikler is that these racial attacks constituted 'a last desperate attempt by a besieged working class to assert its community with a "white South Africa" that despised them, and that was shortly to attack them militarily'.[86] Harsher verdicts on the strikers' actions insist that racial aggression was intrinsic to the strike's development from its inception, and that the commando movement in particular was inspired by a backward-looking evocation of a pastoral rural setting in which 'white men ruled by force'.[87]

This was not the perception of most communists present at the time, even those who were among the group who felt that the party's main focus should be with black workers. Ivon Jones, not of course a witness to events, could still, writing after the strike, represent the racial attacks as 'tragic conflicts of minor character [that] occurred between Black and white workers', not expressions of any of the main dynamics of the conflict.[88] Other communists, contributors to the British weekly *Dreadnought*, maintained that attacks on Africans were mainly the work of hooligans and provocateurs.[89] Even Sidney Bunting would argue after the strike that police and mine managers had armed 'native workers' and deployed them as guards with the deliberate intention of provoking strikers to attack Africans.[90] Writing twenty years later, Jack Cope maintained his view that violence was police-instigated, suggesting that the 'simultaneous' outbreak of violence in different centres as well as its sudden ending had all the hallmarks of a 'trick'.[91] But Krikler's examination of one of the major attacks, the commando raid on Primrose Compound, makes it quite clear that this was an operation planned by local strike leadership.

The authorities raided the party's office on 10 March, damaging its printing press and confiscating records that were subsequently cited in a commission of inquiry which eventually made it clear that the party's role was at best supportive rather than central to the strike's direction.[92] The police arrested and detained Bunting and Andrews. Over the rest of the year the communists would lose about a hundred of their members.[93] However, the formation of a Strike Prisoners' Release Committee supplied a focus of activism for the newly formed Young Communist League, its 20 or so adherents, schoolboys mainly, undertaking a chalk-and-sticker campaign and holding street corner meetings in Jeppe, Fordsburg and Benoni as well as trying to dissuade their classmates from attending army cadet meetings.[94] Towards the end of the year the party itself was beginning to draw in fresh recruits, setting up new branches in Springs and Jeppe and succeeding in winning a series of trade union secretaryships.

Subsequently, communists would campaign for clemency for the men accused of capital charges, including Carel Stassen, who would be hanged for murdering two Africans in Sophiatown on 8 March.[95] At the beginning of 1923, Comintern would condemn the impending executions with a resolution signed by Karl Radek, which forecast that white workers would not give up their fight and that, moreover, they would 'learn how to draw the native workers into the struggle against South African capitalism'.[96] Such optimistic perceptions were informed probably by the analyses supplied by key South African communists. Sidney Bunting wrote his own considered assessment of the rebellion and its meaning. In fact he wrote two texts on the topic, one of which was published by the party and subsequently translated into Russian, in which he suggested that the revolt 'was not a proletarian revolution' but rather 'a prelude'. But the miners' 'rage was right i' the main', he suggested, quoting Robert Browning. Any repeal of the 'colour bar regulations' on the lines suggested by the Chamber would 'not benefit the native worker', in fact 'rather the reverse', presumably because the Chamber would seek to reduce all workers to a common state of even greater immiseration. In his second text, which remained unpublished, he wrote more reflectively on the meaning of the slogan 'White South Africa'.

> This phrase can no doubt be interpreted in two ways, as the bourgeois claim to European possession of the land and the enslavement of its native inhabitants, and as the white working class demand to survive, at a standard of living fit for a European. Thanks to the men's instinctive grasp of the position and to communist propaganda, the latter, the proletarian sense, eventually prevailed. As the struggle increased its intensity it became clarified, and at the height of the conflict it was only the ignorant and unorganised of the miners that still felt it to be an anti-native affair. The dominant inspiration was the class struggle against tyranny and the solidarity of the working class.

Even so, Bunting concluded, the strike's real vulnerability was the absence of 'any solidarity between whites and blacks'. But, he reasoned, even if 'whites had called out the blacks', the latter 'would not have responded', a consequence not so much of racial prejudices, but a gulf created by lower standards of living. Common action would arise only when such differences began to be addressed by 'bridging the differences between the conflicting sections'.[97] The implication in his argument was that such white workers remained a potentially revolutionary force and that material circumstances might yet prompt such common action. At this juncture Bunting really did believe that eventually white workers' racial hostility would recede, even among recently proletarianised Afrikaners; indeed, he maintained in his published pamphlet, white worker hostility to black workers was already on the wane. In promoting cross-racial worker solidarity, communists should take care to propose a 'levelling up' of wages: 'equal pay for equal work'.

That present-day capitalism could not afford universal wages on the level paid to white workers was so much the better; communists should not be concerned to seek measures 'to make capitalism tolerable to one or another section of workers'.[98] Meanwhile Ivon Jones, reporting again to his fellow Comintern executive members predicted, accurately enough, that 'a political revulsion' among white workers might result in a Labour–Republican bloc. In such a development, he suggested, Bill Andrews could assume a leading role, and such a united front, supported by communists, would be a strong 'anti-imperialist force'.[99] In a setting in which mine owners appeared to have won a complete victory and were able to enforce wage cuts, several thousand redundancies among white semi-skilled workers and their proposed increase in ganger quotas, it was understandable that communists convinced themselves that white mine workers would continue to be capable of class insurgency. Bunting himself claimed that new union officials were all 'good militants' and 'industrial disputes' were simmering: 'the Capitalists are presuming too much on their armed victory'.

BUNTING WROTE SOME OF these reflections during travels in Europe between June and December 1922. He attended the Comintern's congress in November as a party delegate and also spent time in Germany and in Britain. Lenin had recovered sufficiently to address the congress, and he had apparently read Bunting's paper on colonial labour after its publication in *Novy Vostok* (New East); he asked to meet Bunting but then became too ill for any appointment.[100] Originally Jones, Bunting and Andrews were nominated to represent the party at the conference, but then they were told that only one delegate would be allowed and Bunting apparently was Zinoviev's preferred choice.[101] In any case Jones was too ill to attend and Harrison was having passport difficulties. The conference was in November, but Sidney and Rebecca arrived two months early. Sidney spent the time writing a paper on the 'colonial labour front', arguing how it might be possible to develop joint class action between white and black workers on the basis of calls for equal pay for equal work. Bunting's argument was not confined to South Africa. At that stage the party was under the loose supervision of the Anglo-American Colonial Group, a Comintern office that attempted to guide and coordinate the North American, British, Irish, Indian, Australian, Egyptian and South African parties.[102] In line with their conception of united fronts, Comintern strategists at this time were beginning to focus on national liberation movements as the key vehicle that could move colonial societies towards socialism. This was a corollary of the second Comintern congress's 'theses' on 'the negro question', which proposed that the exploitation of black people was an effect of imperialism. Bunting's view was that nationalist bodies were at best 'stepping stones' and that in South Africa, at least, 'subject races' needed to be 'organised as workers'. Bunting was critical of the theses on the negro question, which he felt were 'chiefly applicable to conditions in the United States'. In particular he was worried by the recommendation that communist parties should invest effort in compelling white unions to accept black members; advice that he felt was impractical in the South African setting, in which most white unions were craft-based and hence exclusionary on the basis of skill. As he wrote to Zinoviev after the conference, the best way to 'break the white workers' prejudice' would not be to agitate for Africans ('typical raw natives') to be admitted into the Amalgamated Engineers, for example, but rather 'to confront the whites with the spectacle of strong organisations of black workers'.[103] Meanwhile, during Bunting's absence, the British socialist Tom Mann made a third visit to South Africa, this time hosted by the League. His tour included an appearance at the ICU conference. Mann was critical of white worker racialism, though he added his voice to those calling for mercy for Carel Stassen and his comrades.[104]

At this stage it was still possible – and, indeed, even expected – that national sections of the Comintern could respond critically to injunctions from Moscow-based officials. In any case, Bunting was in general supportive of the Comintern's united front policy. Indeed, the associated recommendation that working class mobilisation could initially be around their reformist 'immediate needs' offered for Bunting an authoritative justification for his own backing of the white miners' strike.[105] Moreover, he and Ivon Jones, now a respected Comintern official, were at that stage arguing on roughly the same lines, though by the time of his visit to Moscow, Jones was staying at a sanatorium in the Crimea. A sequence of letters by Jones to Comintern officials, prompted by Comintern plans for a Negro Race Congress, urged that the 'Negro race question' was best addressed by 'draw[ing] negroes into the class movement'.[106] He also emphasised that organisers should take care to select delegates 'in touch with the labour masses'. As he explained, through their South African experience, communists had learned that 'as soon as a Negro attains any measure of education he becomes spoilt as a proletarian and loses touch with the negro working masses because he is immediately snatched up to be a lawyer's or agent's tout'.[107] The key task for communists in Africa generally was to secure control of any newly formed native unions and forestall the prospects of their being 'pocketed by bourgeois agents'. This would 'have far more effect in the fight against Imperialism than any Congress'.[108] Bunting was more critical than Jones of the proposed conference. As he reported later to his party, its organisers in the Negro Commission were chiefly 'weak' and its justificatory 'thesis' was the 'result of some inexplicably keen manoeuvring in a purely American direction'. In particular, as we have seen, he was alarmed by the language suggesting that communists should try 'to compel the trade unions to admit negro workers'.[109] The term 'negro' was used at Comintern to refer both to African Americans and black Africans. It was apparently a South African delegate – it could only have been Bunting – that had persuaded the congress to include a discussion of the 'negro question' in its agenda. Bunting was ready, though, to concede to African Americans or, at least, 'the more advanced negroes of America' the task of forging 'a real link' between the European proletariat and colonial Africa.[110]

Most of the leadership in the South African party would have been hostile to any such counsel in the year that followed the suppression of the Rand Rebellion. In April 1923, the party would decide to support the electoral pact between the Labour Party and General Hertzog's National Party. The support was qualified. As an editorial in *The International* explained, a coalition government constituted by Labour and Afrikaner nationalists would not make much material difference to their rank-and-file supporters, who would 'sooner or later' reject bourgeois leaders and opt for a real workers' party. Hence an electoral victory for the Pact 'would be a spur to working class consciousness'. Given these sorts of considerations, any active effort to build or encourage black trade unions was hardly likely to be a priority.[111] In any case, many of the key party leaders viewed white workers as a vanguard group and recent events only solidified such beliefs. A sequence of letters Sidney Bunting wrote to Rebecca, then staying in Cape Town, are especially useful in supplying a contemporary record of the kinds of sentiments that prevailed among most party leaders.

Writing to Rebecca on 19 April, Sidney confided that within the party leadership he was feeling very isolated and the office atmosphere was most inhospitable.[112] The other party leaders had no time for his report on the Comintern conference, and efforts he had made to secure Bill Andrews an invitation to join the Comintern executive alongside Ivon Jones had fallen flat: Andrews was ungracious, telling Bunting, 'I don't want to go to Moscow, as I don't want to meet a lot of niggers there.'[113] This was a few days before the South African party's own conference. There were various efforts to include issues related to black workers on the agenda but discussion of such moves 'was boycotted here', at the head office, where the prevalent sentiment was:

'we have got a hold on the [white] trade unionists now and must nurse them.' Most of the new members that had been recruited recently, Bunting believed, were 'racially prejudiced', but such feelings were as strong in Andrews as among the new white working class comrades, he thought. Indeed, most of the executive, in fact, were anti-colour, 'ignoring of all', except for 'white propaganda about white matters'.[114]

In fact, the party's second congress, on 28 and 29 April 1923, did adopt a few resolutions about black workers although, as Bunting had predicted, delegates generally paid more attention to white political preoccupations. They agreed to apply for affiliation to the Labour Party – their application was rejected two months later – and, regardless of whether their application was accepted or not, the communists resolved they would work for an electoral victory for the Pact, though their expectation was that Labour would not accept any cabinet positions in a Nationalist-led government.[115] The day after, Sidney wrote to Rebecca noting that the new executive was 'rather markedly anti-native ... though they adopted for submission to the Comintern the native demands I had proposed'. Andrews evidently was reassured 'that the party shall not be a Black party'. Bunting's commentary suggests that the distinction between perceiving that white workers were a vanguard group whose support was essential and outright antipathy to Africans was often in practice blurred. Andrews himself said little apparently during the proceedings, preferring his allies to speak for him. Frank Glass in this role 'was more reactionary than I have ever heard him' and he was supported by several of the new trade unionists. Glass had been serving as the party's full-time organiser on the Witwatersrand from January 1923. Not all the new members were racialists, though. One new recruit was in fact the mayor of Springs, Jack Allen, 'one of the nicest new members', also a Labour Party man, and 'he did not at all support the anti-nigger talk'.[116] The following day Andrews told Bunting that he was 'the last of the negrophiles'. They had got rid of the others in the conference elections, and now there was only Bunting left. The 'old policy of liberation to negro workers had been dropped', Sidney concluded mournfully in his nightly report-back to Rebecca. In the party office William Thibedi 'gets sworn at when he puts his head in'.[117]

We only have Bunting's reports on such exchanges, though we know from Andrews's own correspondence that relations between the two men had been frosty since 1918, if not before.[118] In fact it seems as if the party's white labour orientation at that time was less determined than Bunting perceived or Andrews claimed. Frank Glass, dismissively characterised by Bunting as 'Andrews' pupil', was at best an uncertain ally, capable of sudden shifts of course. His own writings do not suggest that he was a racialist; quite the contrary.[119] The Young Communists within a year of their formation in May 1922 were directing their efforts at bringing '"native youth" into the organisation'.[120] This was after an initial attempt to reach out to Afrikaners. They actually succeeded in setting up an all-Afrikaans-speaking group in Germiston, but it became inactive after six weeks.[121] By November 1923 the Johannesburg branch of the Young Communists decided that recruiting Africans should become their 'main task', a decision that followed quite a sharp debate led by Eddie Roux and Willie Kalk arguing in favour and opposed by Solly Sachs, an engineering student at Wits University and already an authoritative figure because of his grasp of Comintern doctrine.[122] From their formation, Young Communists had debated the 'Colour question', if we take Roux's memoirs as our main source, though other accounts through much of 1922 suggest that the League's activism was chiefly focused around solidarity with the imprisoned miners.[123] They were also busy opposing the influence of the Boy Scout movement as well as fostering a 'Young Workers' Sporting Association' with separate sections for boxing, tennis and hiking, activities inspired by a model propagated by the Young Communist International.[124] Whether the League should concentrate on black workers was in fact sufficiently divisive for Eddie Roux and Willie Kalk to seek a ruling from the Young Communist International, which they obtained in their favour in November 1923. So whatever misgivings may have remained among their members, the Young Communists were now committed to working among black South Africans.

During 1923, neither young communists nor their elders would make any significant attempts to actively enrol or mobilise black South Africans. To be sure, they did issue a leaflet condemning the Bulhoek Massacre after police fired on a millenarian African movement in the Eastern Cape. But most of party's energies were invested in efforts to build a united front that could embrace white labour organisations. Communists in Benoni supported Labour in municipal elections, though a communist candidate, Jessie Chapman, stood in one ward in which Labour offered no opposition to the Smuts-supporting South African Party councillor, possibly a reflection of a reciprocal *de facto* local alliance.[125] Jessie Chapman's 'electoral address' focused mainly on the wage reductions and dismissals that had affected white mine workers as well as calling for unemployment relief at a 'recognised white standard'.[126] Without a local branch of their own organisation, communists constituted a militant grouping within the Labour Party in Boksburg. In Cape Town, in the absence of Labour candidates, communists also contested municipal council elections, in one case performing quite creditably; here their electioneering attempted to reach beyond the concerns of white South Africans.[127] The establishment of communist-led unemployment committees in Johannesburg and Benoni also chiefly targeted white working-class communities, though the corresponding formation in Cape Town embraced coloured workers as well.[128] Bunting's letters indicate that working with the white unemployed was a major focus of whatever party activism was happening at the time.[129] The unemployment movement owed its public visibility to Harry Haynes, one of the leaders of the 1913 miners' strike in Kleinfontein and a principal personality in the 1920 Durban Soviet. Haynes and two other men chained themselves to the balustrade of the public gallery in parliament so they could harangue General Smuts without being removed easily, a tactic they borrowed from the British women's suffragette movement. Smuts was apparently 'livid with rage', because of the inevitable delay in expelling Haynes and his noisy comrades from the chamber.[130] A newspaper for the unemployed, *The Torch*, appeared, though only once. In Benoni an 'Unemployed Commando' formed itself to picket the various public works projects provided by the authorities for white unemployed workers at three shillings a day – 'scab work', the movement's leaders insisted. A third visit from Tom Mann, a four-month tour between October 1922 and February 1923, added a powerful voice to the advocacy of a cross-labour alliance. Mann also addressed the ICU's third annual conference, suggesting to ICU members that they could expect global support from workers 'on the basis of genuine brotherhood'.[131]

In line with the Comintern's united front prescriptions that Bunting had brought back from Moscow, during 1923 communists adopted a more sympathetic position to African National Congress (ANC) as well as acknowledging the ICU's potential as a force in mobilising black workers. As Bunting now dutifully conceded, 'national liberation is, in the case of the subject races, the necessary introduction to proletarian revolution'.[132] Probably with the same logic in mind, an *International* editorial suggested that communists should support the (Afrikaner) National Party 'even to the extent of joining that party'. After all, a Nationalist regime was much less likely than any Smuts-led government to join Western allies in any fresh war against Russia.[133] A Russian famine relief effort elicited a surprisingly generous response – not just from whites, to judge from the lists of donations printed in *The International*. The party could send 837 bags of maize and £1,300 to Russia. Thus evident public sympathy for Soviet Russia and fresh civilities from local Labour Party leaders may have helped to sustain optimism about the possibility of local cross-racial class solidarity. When they looked for it, communists thought they could find evidence of changing attitudes in the wider movement. After all, even the Labour Party had welcomed coloured delegates at its most recent conference 'and good class conscious ones too'; the meeting was in fact presided over by a Communist Party member, the mayor of Springs, Jack Allen.[134] And for a brief period later that year, the Mine Workers' Union through its Propaganda Committee began a public discussion of whether it should open up a section for recruiting black workers as trade unionists. This would be an 'epoch-making' turn-around, *The International* noted hopefully, and one that appeared to be supported by 'prominent officials' as well as a well-attended 'aggregate meeting' in Johannesburg.[135] In the end the union's executive rejected the proposal; it evidently failed to engender any significant rank-and-file support. But that the union had considered such a move so publicly was a significant advance, Bunting suggested.[136] Or, as Bill Andrews suggested, 'the fact that the question [had] moved from purely academic to the practical plane is an indication that opinion and circumstances are changing'.[137] Andrews would retain his optimism throughout the rest of the decade. To be sure, he allowed, despite progress in removing barriers that blocked the entry of 'non-Europeans' into the registered union movement, 'certain affiliated unions' were still unwilling to countenance such a prospect. He was philosophical about this: 'It may be said that these facts reveal inconsistencies and contradictions which is of course true. Life itself is not simple. It is composed of a whole series of compromises, contradictions and apparent inconsistencies. The relationship between man and man, to say nothing of woman, is complex and full of unresolved problems.'[138]

IN MID-MAY 1923 Sidney Bunting had taken over *The International*'s editorship and the party's secretaryship when it was finally decided that Bill Andrews would travel to Moscow to take up his position on the Comintern executive; the invitation had become a summons. He sailed on 15 May. Andrews's departure certainly strengthened Bunting's hand, but, as he told Rebecca, within a couple of weeks other party leaders were complaining that he was 'giving too much attention to native grievances'.[139] Among his critics was Frank Glass, who had been 'rather cross' when Bunting had taken over from Andrews; he wanted the job himself, apparently.[140] In fact, Bunting was conscientious in sticking to the party line on white-oriented united front activity, despite increasingly evident dissatisfaction among communists in Cape Town who objected to the pro-white labour orientation.[141] Rebuffed in their application for Labour Party affiliation, communists remained active in Labour Party branches and, indeed, in August that year party speakers joined Labour personalities at public meetings to support the sole candidate opposing the South African Party's incumbent in the Turffontein by-election in Johannesburg. As Bunting explained, it was quite unnecessary to know anything about the candidate, Major Hunt, who was probably in most ways 'unacceptable on [his] own merits'; it was sufficient that if elected he would vote against the government.[142] Later, in early 1924 Bunting would write supportively about the Labour Party's efforts to attract trade union affiliates; after all, if unions were to 'adhere' to the Labour Party, they might yet 'help to make it more proletarian'.[143]

Meanwhile, in Moscow, Andrews was accorded significant status, presiding at a meeting of the British Commission at which the organisation's heavyweights, Bukharin, Béa Kun and Zinoviev, were present, and more routinely working with Lozovsky, head of the Red International of Labour Unions, Profintern.[144] During his six-month stay in Moscow he seems to have kept his own views about South African strategic priorities to himself. Indeed, to judge from his reporting about his Russian experience, he appears to have spent a lot of time on various sightseeing excursions. However, he did have several meetings with Zinoviev, maintaining 'close contact' with Comintern's leader throughout his visit, he claimed.[145] The only detail he supplied about any of the Comintern executive meetings he attended was an occasion when the South African party was reproved for its insularity, that is, for not paying sufficient attention to other left-wing movements elsewhere in Africa.[146] Shortly after his arrival, Comintern would begin preparations for a major 'negro' conference timed to coincide in 1924 with its own fifth congress. The South African party was expected to be the main agency through which the Comintern 'would reach the negroes of Southern Africa'.[147] 'We do not doubt that you are beginning the work among the natives with energy', Comintern informed the South African leadership in November with a note of asperity that would characterise many of its future communications with Johannesburg.[148] Bunting's response was uncharacteristically defensive. Finding suitable 'negro' delegates among the local community of educated Africans was very difficult.[149]

That might still have been the case in 1923. But the party's social reach was becoming more extensive. By early 1924, the Young Communists were helping the ICU to establish its new office in Johannesburg. They also persuaded two key local ICU personalities to join their ranks, Thomas Mbeki and Stanley Silwana. Mbeki, it would seem, was either already or about to become a police informer.[150] But while Young Communists began cultivating an alliance with African trade unionists, the party still remained committed to seeking an accommodation with white labour. Communists did not put up its own candidates in the general election, explaining that they would support the Pact alliance between Labour and Afrikaner nationalists.[151] This was not the time to split opposition to Smuts, the party's manifesto explained, though communists should not expect radical reforms from the Pact in power. Jack Allen, the mayor of Springs, did stand as a candidate for the Labour Party, resigning from the Communist Party just before the campaigning began.[152] The party published a manifesto, a rather quixotic document given that it was sponsoring no candidates of its own. It told its supporters that Labour Party candidates 'should be strictly held to certain planks'. These included demands that had a particular salience for Africans, such as the 'abolition of pass and passport laws and mineworkers' records of service rights' and the extension of certain rights and entitlements 'to all classes of workers'. This inclusion of rather generalised language, which in fact referred to the needs of African workers, was a concession to the Young Communists' growing influence.[153] Communist support for the Pact was not reciprocated; indeed, both the Pact partners were publicly hostile to the party, though apparently Labour politicians were actively 'canvassing Communist votes in private'.[154] The Nationalists in particular were careful to dissociate themselves from the party. Local Nationalists closed down a party meeting in Vrededorp, threatening to attack the platform if the speakers took up their places, and subsequently writing to *The Star* newspaper to defend their action: there was no room for the Communist Party in South Africa, they explained.[155]

Whether the party's main strategic orientation should remain directed at winning over white workers was the key issue at the party's conference in November 1924. By this stage, the Pact administration had been in power for five months. Two Labour Party members would accept positions in General Hertzog's cabinet. Colonel Creswell took up the portfolio for defence and labour, a 'logical result of his political career', while his colleague Tom Boydell became the Minister for Posts and Telegraphs and Public Works.[156] In accepting these positions in a 'bourgeois cabinet', communists maintained, the Labour Party had entirely abandoned its working-class character.[157] Their position was arguable. Certainly, Creswell would introduce quite significant reforms during his ministry, beginning with the shortening of the working week, restrictions on employing children, and changes to the law on miner's phthisis: increased rates of compensation for white workers afflicted by the disease, and specialised medical treatment and more limited provisions for sick black workers, a one-off payment and a free rail pass home.[158] Probably more objectionable from the perspective of the Communist Party were the measures enacted in 1925 and 1926 to protect both skilled and unskilled white workers from the threat of being replaced by cheaper black workers, the Wage Act of 1925 and the Mines and Works Amendment Act of 1926, which supplied legal force for the 'colour bar' on the mines. In fact, the numbers of white mine workers as a proportion of the workforce would remain level, through the Pact administration, absolutely and proportionately less than its total before the First World War. White miner wages stagnated during the Pact administration, declining in real terms. At most the legislation checked the reduction of the white workforce that had begun after the 1922 strike. The Wage Act accorded to the Minister of Labour the power to set the same minimum wages for black and white workers, by means of which he could threaten to raise black wages to white levels, effectively – and intentionally – removing any incentives for employers to substitute black workers for whites.[159] Also, during the early months of the Pact government, officials spelled out a new policy making the South African Railways a preserve of protected and privileged employment for unskilled whites. In September 1924, communists contested local elections, putting up candidates in Johannesburg, Benoni and Cape Town, and declaring themselves to be representatives of 'the working class only' – but of all workers, 'whatever their race or colour'.[160] For communists, Labour in government was an unedifying spectacle; indeed, Labour's Afrikaner nationalist colleagues could sometimes appear more conciliatory. In his autobiography Eddie Roux recalls the party sending a deputation to meet Tielman Roos, then Minister of Justice, to complain about police instigation of hooliganism at party meetings by reform school inmates. Roos was unexpectedly welcoming and even sympathetic, speaking warmly about Sidney Bunting's anti-war stance.[161]

At the conference in November 1924 Frank Glass led the argument in favour of another effort to obtain Labour Party affiliation. At this juncture Glass and others believed that as the left wing of a labour movement in power, communists would have leverage to extract reforms.[162] This was odd. Glass may have been impressed by a very militant white building workers' strike in his home base of Cape Town, and his views were also shaped by his continuing activity in the unemployment movement. Even so, he had just contested municipal ward nine in Johannesburg, standing against Labour. Andrews was less assertive in arguing in this vein but certainly agreed; he seconded Glass's motion. But opposition to Labour Party affiliation was generalised; one of the speakers criticising such a move was Solomon Buirski from Cape Town. Within the Cape Town group there was apparently a spreading perception that 'the non-Europeans were the real proletariat' and united frontism –

at least with respect to the Pact – had generally been unpopular within the local party.[163] The leadership elections at the conference brought three Young Communists into the management committee, including Eddie Roux, who was appointed as Bunting's deputy in his new role as party chairman. Their presence reflected a change in the party's active following. The Young Communist League (YCL) itself was expanding, recruiting sufficient numbers during 1923 so that by the beginning of the following year it had fully fledged branches in Germiston, Benoni and Cape Town, in addition to its original base in Johannesburg.[164] The party was now smaller, younger, better educated, and less likely to include experienced trade unionists from the skilled working class. As the Young Communists noted, their constituency was unlikely to include many white apprentices: 'the bulk of South Africa's youth, both black and white, stands outside industry'.[165] In fact, at this point the League was building its following chiefly among white apprentices: the new Germiston branch, mainly Afrikaans speaking, was entirely made up of 'young industrial workers'.[166] Andrews retained the Communist Party secretaryship, and Frank Glass continued to look after the party finances, but the new programme adopted in November 1924 suggested that in future fresh efforts would be directed at African workers. Communists were now formally committed to building industrial organisation among all workers, 'irrespective of colour'. Yes, they would still seek a united front, but this would be a front of all workers, 'to bring the European and the helot workers together in a united army',[167] rather than an alliance with sectional white politicians. The conference opposed any further attempt to seek Labour Party affiliation; the Young Communists led the opposition to Frank Glass's proposition that they should make another attempt. The programme included a list of demands. These for the first time explicitly spelled out communist commitment to the extension of the Cape qualified non-racial franchise throughout South Africa. The programme also called for free compulsory education, votes for all white women, and the more familiar maxim of equal pay for equal work.

This was hardly a charter for radical social upheaval. To be fair, most communists probably favoured more universal kinds of enfranchisement. As a commentary in *The International* had noted, most Africans were already 'exceptionally well qualified' to make sensible decisions on polling day.[168] Recruitment of Africans remained selective and limited, though the 1924 conference would later be perceived by party historians as a decisive moment in the party's Africanisation.[169] Certainly, tactical and strategic priorities were now different. In February 1925 Bill Andrews resigned from his editorship of *The International* as well as the secretaryship; as he explained, 'a difference over tactics has led to his resignation from office'. While he agreed that all workers should be unionised 'regardless of colour', he disliked the new emphasis on organising Africans.[170] He may also have been uncomfortable with the party's uncompromising antipathy to the Pact administration; later that year he would accept appointment to the government's new Economic and Wage Commission.[171] This was a consequence of his secretaryship of the South African Association of Employees Organisations, formed in 1924 and renamed the Trades Union Congress (SATUC) in 1925. He had been elected into this position largely as a consequence of support from the engineers and the building workers. In effect he became the top official in the most significant white labour body. As Minister of Labour, Frederic Creswell perceived that he needed to acknowledge Andrews's authority and hence he included him among the commission's six members. On the commission Andrews would help draft a minority report calling for reforms in the treatment of black labour, calls that would be disregarded.[172] Andrews would remain a senior trade unionist throughout the next two decades. In 1925 he was one of a small group of loyal communists now on the party's margins who were still influential in the white labour movement.

Frank Glass, who gave up his post as the party's treasurer, was less diplomatic than Andrews in explaining why. Africans, he suggested, 'could not possibly appreciate the noble ideals of communism'.[173] As we have seen, Andrews remained a party member, but Frank Glass left the party, one in a wider exodus at that time that included several influential figures in white labour, including Harry Haynes. Glass charged that the party had become anti-white; in the following months he organised the Tailors' Union's affiliation with the Labour Party, as well as working for SATUC as its treasurer.

AT THE BEGINNING OF 1925 the party started sponsoring a night school in Ferreirastown.[174] The main organiser of this undertaking was William Thibedi, the IWA veteran, by then also an ICU shop steward.[175] Earlier he had asked the party to sanction his establishment of a Christian Communist School – 'to bore within religious circles'.[176] Meanwhile, the Young Communists organised their own Euro-African debating society, hoping presumably to attract rather better-educated Africans than the workers who would be taught basic literacy in Thibedi's classes. Contributions from African readers began appearing in the columns of *The International*.[177] But at this stage, the party held back from direct organisation of Africans into unions or from any real effort to set up branches in areas in which they could expect to recruit among Africans.

Instead, communists engaged more actively with African organisations, and especially with the ICU, encouraged by the ICU's proclaimed intention of mounting a 'crusade' for 'One Big Union' to embrace all African labour.[178] In fact, just as the efforts to support a Pact victory and achieve some kind of working alliance with the Labour Party had been the party's main objectives from mid-1922 to the general election in 1924, its developing engagement with the ICU would become its chief preoccupation during the next two years, until the end of 1926. Here, communists continued to defer to Comintern's united front policy and in this they were at least partly inspired by external models. For example, party strategists drew parallels between their increasing involvement with the ICU and the Chinese party's willingness to defer to and refrain from competing with the nationalist leadership supplied by the Kuomintang.[179] Indeed, Bill Andrews actually appeared as a speaker at a local Kuomintang conference in Johannesburg.[180] The Kuomintang had an established presence in South Africa from 1920, with an office in Fox Street, one block away from the communist headquarters.[181] Its officials were 'on very good terms' with the Communist Party, La Guma noted in a memorandum for Comintern, and the Kuomintang could be relied on to send 'strong Fraternal' greetings to every party congress.[182] Bill Andrews's contacts with Chinese community leaders dated from before the First World War.

Andrews also spoke at the ICU's formal opening of its new meeting hall in Johannesburg in September 1925, reassuring his hosts that as a 'representative of a very considerable section of the white working class', many white workers welcomed the ICU efforts to draw 'native workers' into organised labour.[183] During 1925 and 1926 Sidney Bunting, Eddie Roux and Solly Sachs appeared quite often as speakers at ICU-sponsored gatherings. Roux in particular developed a friendship with Kadalie, though even the more reserved Bunting would concede to Roux that the ICU leader was 'not yet a bad lot'.[184] But connections with the ICU went well beyond such habitual protocols, for during 1924 and 1925 cross-membership began to draw the party closer to the ICU as it recruited key office-holders. Thomas Mbeki and Stanley Silwana joined the Young Communists in 1924, and during that year Mbeki emerged as a pivotal actor in establishing an ICU presence in the smaller centres of the Transvaal, drawing in farm workers as well as more urban people. Meanwhile, Silwana worked as a clerk in the union's office in Cape Town. Eddie Khaile, the ICU's financial secretary, also joined the Communist Party. Here, during 1925, local communists Solomon Buirski and Joe Pick recruited two senior ICU office-holders, James La Guma, the organisation's national secretary, and its Cape provincial secretary, John Gomas.[185] La Guma's first political experience was as an unruly teenager participant in rioting triggered by a protest organised by the Social Democratic Federation. Gomas had joined the ISL's Kimberley branch in 1919, and may have maintained his affiliation on returning to Cape Town, for Harrison notes in his autobiography that 'one La Guma, a Cape Native, was already casually associated with us'.[186] In 1926 five party members belonged to the ICU's National Council.[187]

Though they occupied conspicuous positions in the ICU, communists did not function as a caucus; several joined a more cautious faction when it came to tactical decision-making; and others helped constitute a more aggressive 'Ginger Group of Young Bloods'.[188] Even so, their influence was considerable. In April 1926 the ICU moved its headquarters from Cape Town to Johannesburg and this helped to make the organisation more accessible for the Communist Party. Arguably, the party's growing influence was evident in Clements Kadalie's growing propensity to employ anti-capitalist rhetoric. Though increasingly on friendly terms with individual communists, Kadalie remained sceptical about communist ideas.[189] But communists within the ICU may have shaped the movement strategically. Helen Bradford has argued that the ICU's movement into the smaller towns and the countryside reflected a new conviction among African communists that 'land and peasant questions were of the utmost importance'. The language is from the party's 1925 conference at which Eddie Khaile told his new comrades that 'The natives especially in the country districts are ripe for organisation'.[190] The party set up an Agrarian Department in May 1926; three of its six members were ICU officials: Gomas, La Guma and Khaile. A programme of immediate demands included land for peasants, nationalisation of estates and repeal of the Masters and Servants Act. By mid-1926 African communists were sufficiently numerous to constitute a No. 2 Group within the Johannesburg branch, meeting in Ferreirastown, organising a lecture series, and both writing and soliciting African-language contributions to the party newspaper – content aimed at the new rural following that the party hoped to attract. Much of their educational activity was directed at the ICU, to which most members of the group belonged, though they also looked forward to changes in their own organisation. As one of their speakers, Joseph Phalane, explained: 'I am a Communist not because there are white people in the Communist party but because that is the Party that will make us free. We want a black Communist Party.'[191]

Promptings from the party were especially evident at the ICU's annual conference in mid-1925 when it adopted a new constitution that included language from the Industrial Workers of the World in its preamble. James

La Guma probably helped to draft the document.[192] It was also the case that General Hertzog's introduction in parliament of draft segregationist legislation in 1925 helped to induce a leftward shift in the ICU's leadership. After meetings with General Hertzog, the ICU had enthusiastically supported the Pact during its electoral campaigning. Yet the union's leaders would refrain from matching their angry rhetoric with any intentional change in tactics, refraining from sponsoring strikes, continuing to petition government, and still occasionally using the racially irredentist language of Garveyism, language that the party condemned when it was used by the ANC. The Communist Party was indulgent, though, ready 'to make a fuss of the ICU' as a guest at its fourth congress held in Cape Town between 26 and 28 December 1925. Here old and new African and coloured communists were conspicuously present, including William Thibedi as well as John Gomas, Eddie Khaile and Stanley Silwana, accompanied by fresh local recruits, who were mentioned in the conference report only by their surnames: Gaba, Madase-Shumba and Gamsu. Thibedi would join the central executive at this conference. Despite the presence of African communists, the discussions at the meeting included an argument over whether the party should defend the right of Africans to walk on pavements; certain delegates felt this was an issue on which silence would be more tactful.[193] In an more encouraging vein, in April 1926 Clements Kadalie spoke at a party public meeting, making warm comments about the Soviet Union and calling on African workers to take part in May Day demonstrations.

The mutual cordiality between the two organisation's leaderships would not last very long. There were several reasons for its breakdown. The first of these was a fresh source of external agency. The increasing influence communists appeared to enjoy within the ICU alarmed liberal and non-communist socialist circles in Johannesburg. Mabel Palmer, a Fabian and former suffragette, invited Winifred Holtby, the British novelist and Independent Labour Party luminary, to undertake a four-month public speaking tour of South Africa, between February and June 1926. Mrs Palmer was well connected: she counted Bernard Shaw, Sidney Webb and HN Brailsford among her friends. Palmer knew Kadalie slightly and introduced Holtby to the ICU leadership at a meeting in Durban. Impressed by this encounter, Holtby promised to explore whether she could find sources of support in Britain. In Johannesburg, Holtby stayed with Ethelreda Lewis, herself the author of a best-selling novel and screenplay, *Trader Horn*. Lewis was a Smuts supporter, but she was also a critic of restrictions on 'native rights in their own native land'. Politically, she was also activated by passionate antipathy to communism, and she was determined to persuade the ICU leader that there could be 'better, safer, more stable friends for himself than white Communists'.[194] During Winifred Holtby's visit, Ethelreda Lewis and her guest agreed that Holtby would on her return to Britain try to secure support for the ICU from non-communist socialists. True to her word, back in London Winifred Holtby met Arthur Creech Jones, secretary of the Transport and General Workers' Union. Creech Jones then began corresponding with Kadalie, advising him to join the International Confederation of Free Trade Unions. For Kadalie, the prospect of external backing and recognition from such an authoritative body arose at a time when local expectations of comparable kinds of acknowledgement were being disappointed. It was becoming clear that despite his own affable relations with Bill Andrews, his application for affiliation with the South African Trades Union Congress might be turned down, a disappointment that was finally confirmed in mid-1927 though it already seemed quite likely.[195]

Meanwhile, the ICU was finding it increasingly difficult to pay the bills for printing its own newspaper on the party's press; indeed, by November 1926 the press's manager, not a communist, was refusing to print any further issues of the *Workers' Herald* and had on one occasion thrown the ICU's copy out of the window into the street. A speech Andrews made in Pretoria praising Hertzog for his consideration of white workers' problems was a further source of Kadalie's disillusionment with the communists. A more immediate worry for Kadalie was the criticisms directed at the ICU's leadership by its own communist officials. In March 1926 James La Guma compiled a report on the way in which, in its financial arrangements, the ICU was violating its own rules; he also called for reorganisation of the union into industrial sections. £600 had been lost in the preceding year because of 'inefficiency, dishonesty and unconstitutionalism on the part of the branch and other officials', La Guma charged. He was especially censorious about some of the provincial secretaries, particularly in the Orange Free State and the Eastern Cape, for their misuse of funds. He also criticised Kadalie himself, in his case not for corruption but for autocratic behaviour: 'It seemed that a dictatorship is in embryo.' Provincial secretaries should be transferred each year between differences provinces, he recommended, and Kadalie should cease his editorship of the *Workers' Herald*.[196] Meanwhile, the Communist Party's newspaper, now named the *South African Worker*, carried reports by Laurie Greene in Pietermaritzburg, who had become an ICU member, on rank-and-file complaints about the leadership's inactivity and its preference for legalistic methods. The branch had been at odds with the provincial office over its refusal to forward subscriptions to Durban. As Greene pointed out, most members were too poor to pay their subscriptions and were in any case disinclined to pay for lawsuits when they should be using 'industrial power'.[197]

In Johannesburg, African communists active in the ICU were calling for the union to set up sections for specific industries and, indeed, William Thaanyane, an ex-railway worker and a member of the Ferreirastown Group, on his own initiative set up a communist-led organisation for African railway workers.[198] Such urgings as well as calls from Johnny Gomas for the establishment of a shop stewards' movement were implicitly threatening to the kind of leadership exercised by most top ICU officials. More explicitly, the *Worker* began publishing critical comments about top-echelon venality within the union. In retribution, Thibedi lost his position as an ICU shop steward for sending reports to the communist paper.[199] Police reports indicate an increasing fractious relationship between the communist-led ICU branch in Johannesburg and the ICU headquarters; at the end of October, Kadalie himself instructed the Johannesburg branch to end its preparations to commemorate the Russian Revolution.[200] In September, communists believed they had succeeded in persuading Kadalie to accept an invitation to attend a Comintern-sponsored Conference of Oppressed Nationalities, to be held in Brussels, under the auspices of the League Against Imperialism, an opening event in a new campaign against imperialism. For the Comintern, anti-colonial politics had acquired a fresh strategic importance. The communists would supply the necessary funding, presumably with help from the Comintern. Creech Jones counselled Kadalie to turn down the invitation, advice which in the end he accepted, though initially he prevaricated. He may also have received vague hints about rewards for any turn against the communists.[201] Meanwhile, both La Guma and Eddie Khaile were urging the ICU to call for a general strike to protest against the recent enactment of colour bar legislation, a proposal Kadalie felt would be reckless.[202] By November, Kadalie was openly attacking the Communist Party, calling it a 'Second Master'.

On 16 December, at an ICU National Council meeting, Kadalie announced he would not be travelling to Brussels. He accused the party of interfering in his organisation. A final source of irritation was that La Guma had accepted the party's nomination to attend the Brussels meeting without seeking permission from Kadalie.[203] La Guma's report had ensured he would have few allies at this meeting, but in any case he was more widely unpopular within the organisation, being perceived as an officious bureaucrat.[204] After an angry exchange with La Guma, the Orange Free State's organisational secretary, A Maduna, proposed that no office-holder within the ICU could be a member of the Communist Party. La Guma had highlighted Maduna's venality in his report. The council approved the motion and on the next day four communists who were senior ICU office-holders were expelled: James La Guma, Thomas Mbeki, Johnny Gomas and Eddie Khaile. In a press interview Kadalie explained that the communists were guilty of meddling.[205] Mbeki rescinded his party membership and continued to work as an ICU organiser, as did Stanley Silwana.

Kadalie nevertheless remained on friendly terms with Bill Andrews. Andrews spoke at an ICU rally on 5 April 1927.[206] At this stage the ICU was still committed to seeking affiliation with the Trades Union Congress (SATUC), and in this venture ICU leaders perceived Andrews as an ally within the SATUC leadership. Kadalie also asked Frank Glass, who had left the party in early 1925, to help with the task of auditing the ICU accounts, a necessary preliminary for any kind of local or international affiliation; more generally he hoped Glass would help out with the financial and administrative tasks that hitherto La Guma and Khaile had undertaken. Glass would work as the ICU's temporary financial secretary for the next 18 months, through 1927 and the first half of 1928. Glass was no longer a party member, but he still probably thought of himself as a communist and it is likely that he helped to ensure that the ICU would still occasionally use anti-capitalist phraseology in its programmatic statements.[207] It may have been these rhetorical flickerings that prompted Creech Jones to write to Kadalie in September 1927, warning against 'being sidetracked by the Communists', and repeating earlier advice that the ICU should not 'embarrass itself by affiliation to the League Against Imperialism'.[208] Ethelreda Lewis was especially exasperated by Glass's recruitment. She'd been away from Johannesburg when Kadalie extended his invitation to Glass, and, as she informed Winifred Holtby on her return to Johannesburg, she discovered 'that a certain dangerous person called Glass (an ex tailor who is a communist) has been making hay while the cats [were] away, and worming himself into positions of indispensability'. Glass 'had always been clever enough to keep close to Kadalie', Lewis complained.[209] Frank Glass had in fact known Kadalie for much longer than Lewis, supporting the ICU's early efforts to organise its following in Cape Town in 1920.[210]

Kadalie remained on good terms with individual communist personalities. Sylvia Neame has suggested that the real reason for the break with the party was not any profound antipathy to the communists in general but rather Kadalie's deteriorating personal relationship with James La Guma.[211] Andrews would remain in Kadalie's good books even after SATUC turned down the ICU's application for affiliation. Andrews himself had worked hard to attempt to persuade his fellow unionists to consent to an ICU affiliation, suggesting in January 1928 that the ICU should reduce its claims about its 100,000 paid-up membership so that white trade unionists would not fear they would be overwhelmed by the ICU's numbers. In any case, he argued, such an adjustment would make affiliation more affordable for the ICU. 'More propaganda was needed', however, 'before affiliation could take place', he conceded.[212] In that same year, 1928, Andrews led an ICU deputation of aggrieved African postal workers, negotiating on their behalf in a meeting with the Minister for Posts and Telegraphs, a concession that prompted the subsequent expulsion of the minister, the Labour Party's Walter Madeley, from the cabinet.[213] At the ICU's April 1927 conference, Sophus Pettersen appeared as a fraternal delegate, as an organiser of the Seamen's Union. Pettersen had in fact helped the ICU establish a presence in Durban's docks. Kadalie favoured Pettersen's attendance at the conference – after all, his presence there was a mark of recognition from white labour – but he was excluded by a narrow vote from the conference all the same because he was a communist.[214] For at this meeting the ICU decided that there should be no cross-membership between the two organisations. That it took a whole morning to debate this decision is noteworthy for the number of communists who belonged to the ICU was small, around 100 or so, 50 of them on the Witwatersrand.[215] Two months before, in February, the entire ICU branch in Vereeniging was disowned after it had objected to the expulsions, possibly a consequence of personal loyalties because the branch had originally been established by William Thibedi, then trying to organise coal miners in the vicinity.[216] A portion of its membership reconstituted themselves as a communist formation. Almost by accident, for the party's leadership had not anticipated this rupture, the communists were being drawn and prompted into a new kind of politics. They could no longer extend their influence through an alliance with the ICU. Instead they would have to build their own following. Intuitively they looked to the workplaces where black people were assembled as labourers, but over the next few years they would find most of their African support not really in factories or compounds but in townships, in the places in which black South Africans lived.

The next chapter will take up the story of this transformative experience. Here, we need to interrupt the narrative, to consider just what sort of organisation the party had become by the end of 1926. What was its size and what kinds of people constituted its active membership? How was it led and governed? How did it fund itself? To what degree did it enjoy influence among other groups? What were the strategic conceptions that animated its leaders at the end of 1926? And what was the nature of its relationship with the wider international communist family?

BY THE END OF 1926, the Communist Party of South Africa had an organised following of not more than 400, roughly the same size of membership it had started with in 1921.[217] It was rather smaller than the organised community of revolutionary socialists that had existed just after the First World War. As we have seen, the Yiddish-speaking branch of the ISL by itself claimed a paid-up following of between 500 and 1,000 in 1917. Most of the CPSA's membership was concentrated on the Witwatersrand. At this time, party leaders spoke about a long-term aim of 'becoming a mass party ... the largest working class party in the country', and from the end of 1925 they hoped to achieve that goal through enrolling black members.[218] However, for the time being the party still preferred to work more selectively, influencing movements such as the ICU, not through efforts at mass recruitment of its rank and file but rather through support and assistance as well as selective enrolment of key office-holders. The party also retained through its individual members a degree of influence among white trade unions; its members held office in several key organisations. Nevertheless, there is not much evidence that the Communist Party's trade union office-holders either tried very hard or really succeeded in trying to influence white trade unions or trade union coordinating bodies to follow party prescriptions – not after 1922. Bill Andrews may have been rather unusual in this respect. Between 1921 and 1924 the party committed itself to attempts to construct a united front with the Labour Party, attempts that were rejected dismissively. The party's performance in parliamentary and municipal elections made it quite clear that its political following among white workers was inconsequential, notwithstanding the presence in its leadership of widely respected trade union leaders. Between 1921 and 1926, the party newspaper's print run was usually between 2,500 and 3,000, mostly disposed of through sales outside workplaces, a major obligation for party members.[219] In 1921 the paper had 1,500 subscribers but this proportion fell in the next few years.[220] *The International* was not written in a style to elicit mass readership, though this was an era when working-class leaders were autodidacts and often read ambitiously. A circulation of 3,000 and perhaps a wider readership suggest that the party's ideas may have been reaching a substantial section of the white labour elite.

Who belonged to the party? Its membership was certainly younger than in 1920, a consequence of the establishment of a Young Communist League whose founders had joined the party leadership. Given the League's concentration in Johannesburg on high-school-related campaigning as well as the conspicuous role played by university students such as Eddie Roux and Solly Sachs in its leadership, it is likely that the party's white membership was becoming increasingly drawn from educated and professional people, mainly men. In Cape Town the trend may have been different. In 1923, the Young Communists were holding public meetings in Salt River, reportedly drawing audiences of 300, mostly apprentices.[221] Meanwhile, the trade unions in which party members were most likely to officiate were based in the emerging manufacturing sector, particularly clothing, often employing quite recent Jewish immigrants from the Russian Pale. The Anglo–Australian white labour aristocracy in the workforce on the mines and in the associated engineering trades were less central to communist leadership than they had been at the time of the party's inception. The elected branch delegates who attended the fourth congress at the end of 1925 included the Johannesburg group, led by Bunting, an attorney. His companion delegates included a young leather worker (Willie Kalk), a botany student (Eddie Roux), a journalist (Bernard Sachs), a trade unionist (Jimmy Shields) and an ex-teacher (William Thibedi). Cape Town's delegates were coloured (Johnny Gomas), African (Eddie Khaile), Indian (P de Norman) and white Jewish (J Pick). Benoni was represented by Jessie Chapman, together with former mine worker Jimmy Shields from Johannesburg, who embodied the party's remaining connections with the white labour establishment. As is evident from this list, black South Africans formed part of the party's membership and were beginning to join its leadership. The earliest identifiable African communists tended to come from relatively genteel backgrounds and were well educated. William Thibedi would have been a case in point. But by the end of 1926, the party was beginning to draw in larger numbers from former ICU branches in smaller towns in the Transvaal. These new entrants would have included labourers, service workers and farmhands, often people without schooling. In Johannesburg by 1926 the party was running a night school for illiterate people and, in doing so, supplied an easily accessible portal for the first time since the IWA for entry into the communist movement of Johannesburg-based African workers.

Although by this stage the South African communists perceived themselves as Leninists, the party's organisation was loose and open, quite different from Lenin's conception of a vanguard party. It was not secret, it did not rely on a cellular structure, and its base level of organisation was not workplace-rooted. Its aspirations for developing into a mass movement, though unrealised, suggest a different conception of how it should organise. It was hardly disciplined in the Leninist sense, remaining tolerant of a diversity of thinking within leadership; disagreements over policy were open and surfaced in the party press, as in the case of Wilfrid Harrison's objections to the united front. There was an effort at 'Bolshevisation' in 1926. Solly Sachs returned that year from his sojourn at the Lenin School filled with fresh enthusiasms. In fact, at that stage 'Bolshevisation' would be quite limited in its application to local conditions, reduced to the regularisation of agendas for the monthly aggregate meetings, and the establishment of a clear dividing line between members and sympathisers, well short of the reforms Sachs himself had proposed to Comintern officials.[222] Sachs perceived that the relationship between Comintern and its South African affiliate was too casual. He also suggested it would be 'highly expedient' to send some Africans to train in Moscow. The 'nearest and most essential task', Sachs urged, would be the organisation of strong 'native unions'. But the party could not afford to pay organisers, as it spent 'all its resources' on the newspaper.[223] It is likely that at this juncture Comintern officials did not pay much attention to this advice: in the records there are letters about Sachs's work in Moscow at Krestintern, the Peasant International, to which he had been assigned. Sachs, 'despite being quite a trustworthy comrade … is not sufficiently active in the party'.[224]

How did the party finance its activities? International affiliation did not bring in substantial additional resources. This is obvious enough from the Comintern's records. In 1921, ISL delegates to Moscow received some help in paying for their fares in returning to South Africa, though it seems they funded their journey to Moscow themselves.[225] But, generally, the South African requests for help were disregarded. At the time of the 1922 strike, Ivon Jones was complaining to the Comintern secretary that South African appeals for aid had barely received consideration, except for a five-minute discussion at a budget committee meeting eight months previously.[226] At that time, Jones reported, the party was only able to pay for *The International* because it ran its printing press at a profit; this was the major source of party income apart from membership dues. Two months later, Jones noted that the South African party, 'the most active of the British colonial parties', continued to be omitted in any 'allocation of material and moral support'.[227] When Andrews travelled to Moscow in 1923 to join the Comintern executive, the South African party paid for his travel expenses, with some difficulty, because it had to undertake various kinds of fundraising.[228] At its fourth congress at the end of 1925, delegates agreed that members of the management committee would be paid, but in fact the older practice of party officials working part-time and unpaid continued.[229] In January 1926, as Solly Sachs admitted in his report to the Comintern, even *The International*'s editor worked on the paper in his spare time, not for payment.[230] *The International*'s sales did not pay for the expenses of its production nor were these offset significantly by the advertising that began to appear on the back pages in 1923 and 1924 from such friendly sources as 'Comrade H Glazer, Expert Ladies and Gents Tailor'. As we have seen, the donations to the party during this period were local, often from the shopkeepers that traded in the vicinities that constituted the communists' heartlands: Ferreirastown, Rosettenville and Fordsburg. In late 1926, Bunting was writing to the Comintern to ask yet again for assistance. In 1925, the party had bought a new printing press which replaced the press damaged by police during a raid on the party's office in 1922. A series of appeals and social events had raised money to pay for the press, but there remained a debt of £750. Supposedly, the debt was meant to be paid off through profits from other work, and the party had hired a manager to run the press as a commercial operation. The manager was now refusing to print the ICU's newspaper, the *Workers' Herald*, because of unpaid bills over several months; the party needed to find £400 to placate him.[231]

In her history of the Communist Party, Mia Roth has suggested that towards the end of 1926 and through 1927 the party's financial fortunes improved, and she notes that it made no requests to the Comintern for funding during 1927. Other signals, she thinks, that the party suddenly became comparatively wealthy were a series of journeys that party officials made to Europe as well as its ability to move out of the Trades Hall and rent its own office space. Her explanation of what she understands to be its comparative prosperity during this time is that through the agency of Frank Glass, the party was able to siphon funds out of ICU accounts. This ICU funding allegedly ended up in a Standard Bank account in Cape Town controlled by a close associate of Sidney Bunting's. She notes that in writing to Eddie Roux in December 1926, Bunting referred to a 'regular scramble for free trips'. Glass, she suggests, did not really resign from the party in 1925 and this was only a subterfuge that enabled him to remain close to the ICU.[232]

Kadalie, it is quite true, did indeed complain that the communists stole ICU money. His contentions, though, probably had their origins in a dispute with James La Guma over the control of funds in a bank account maintained by the Cape Town headquarters of the ICU, which he accused La Guma and other officials of transferring into another account used by Cape Town's ICU branch.[233] In an argument with Roux, Kadalie did not repeat this accusation. Writing on 10 October 1928, he angrily denied Roux's suggestion that the ICU's financial administration had a history of malpractice:

> You say also the finances of the ICU were bad long before and that you did not like to expose us then. If that is correct, any sensible person will agree with me that your party is rotten to the core since it connived a crime.

> Of the finances of the ICU, your Party only got its information from La Guma, Khaile and Gomas. None of them can say anything ill against me … You are deceitful, because your Party got a lot of moneys from the ICU through your printing press.[234]

Ethelreda Lewis, as we have seen, disliked Frank Glass intensely and she was convinced that he had remained a communist. She suggested to Winifred Holtby in a letter written in April 1928 that Glass had stolen hundreds of pounds from the ICU while pretending to manage the union's accounts.[235]

It is true that the party during 1927 would raise the funding for at least one journey to Europe, the fare for the ANC president Joshua Gumede's travel to Brussels.[236] But the other expeditions were either, as in Bill Andrews's case, financed through the trade union organisations that he represented at the various meetings he attended or paid for by host organisations. James La Guma may well have had his fare to Brussels paid by the League Against Imperialism; his later travels were certainly arranged by Comintern. Bunting's comment about 'free trips' rather implies trips for which the party did not have to raise funds. We know from comparative experiences of other communist parties that Comintern financing of its non-Russian affiliates peaked in 1927, the year when the British party received £40,000. For the Russians, the British imperial parties had acquired a fresh significance strategically and the South African one may have benefited from this.[237] We also have a comprehensive picture of the ICU's accounts from the balance sheets prepared by Frank Glass. From May to October 1927, head office income from ICU branches totalled £6,203; expenditure, mainly on salaries and printing, was slightly higher; altogether the ICU had in its accounts credit balances totalling nearly £1,500.[238] Indeed, after nearly a year of Glass's management, the ICU's National Council noted 'with pleasure the improvement made in the financial position'.[239] At about the same time the party was compelled to halt publication of its newspaper temporarily because it could not afford it. If the party through Glass was stealing from the ICU, it seems unlikely that it would have been unable to pay its printing bills, which would have totalled a small fraction of what the ICU was normally spending. The ICU's own in-house historian, incidentally, insisted that when communist officials ran the ICU's finances before 1926, they did so honestly, and that the major abuses were not in head office but elsewhere after the expulsion of communist office-holders.[240]

So, THE PARTY HAD no money. Did it have influence?

If elections are a measure of a group's political impact, then during this period the Communist Party as well as its main predecessor, the International Socialist League, had little support among enfranchised white workers. Occasionally, successful candidates in municipal wards were exceptions in a general picture in which communist candidates rarely achieved more than a hundred votes. But in a setting in which white workers shared a sense of fierce class identity and emphatic camaraderie, sustaining them through very violent confrontations with employers and the state, communists and revolutionary socialists could sometimes inspire workers' behaviour and the way they understood and represented their struggles. This was certainly the case with the workers' council movement – the 'Soviets' of 1919. And though most mine workers in the 1922 strike were probably fighting for recognition and incorporation into the existing social order rather than for a new Commonwealth, there was a section of the mine workers' leadership that was more radical, an insurrectionary core that included communists. Even so, the main importance of the white mine workers' rebellion for the communists was its impact on the party and the way it shaped its strategic thinking rather than as an event over which they exercised decisive agency. During the uprising most communists were spectators and, more occasionally, active supporters, but only a few were key actors. And their support for the Labour Party–Nationalist Pact electoral campaign in 1924 had no impact at all on Labour–Nationalist campaigning; the party had no leverage; and even key communist trade unionists were excluded from Labour platforms.

Indeed, even at this stage, communist revolutionaries could make stronger claims about shaping the course of black South African collective action, if not always intentionally. The Industrial Workers of Africa (IWA), though hardly controlled or directed by the ISL, was nevertheless the League's creation and ISL members played a leading role within it and subsequently joined the Communist Party. The IWA's propaganda was in wide circulation before the 1918 compound store boycott as well as the sanitary workers' strike, and IWA members may have been visiting compounds before the African mine workers' strike in 1920, though by then the group had lost momentum and at best they might have been just one source of external prompting among many. Meanwhile, the limits of ISL influence among white mine workers at that time were all too evident in the almost complete disregard of their appeals to white workers not to play the part of scabs during the African strike. Later on, from 1924, Communist Party members would hold key positions in the ICU's leadership, sometimes as a consequence of the party recruiting them after they had reached the ICU's upper echelons. Though IWA members had helped to mobilise the dock workers' strike in 1920, the event which accompanied the ICU's formation, subsequently communists who helped manage the ICU would fail in their efforts to reform the organisation or persuade their fellow principals to embrace more strike action. Arguably, this was because they misunderstood the character of the movement they had joined, as Sylvia Neame has suggested, seeking to foster a particular 'class basis' for the movement that it could not have, given the inchoate nature of its main constituencies.[241] Individual communists such as Thomas Mbeki made a significant contribution in extending the ICU's reach to smaller towns and farms in the Transvaal and the Free State, but this was not a consequence of the party's directives; before 1928 the party paid very little attention to the people it called 'rural toilers'.

The Communist Party's leaders were certainly much more committed to supporting the class mobilisation of black South Africans than is suggested in some of the early historical analyses of the party's predecessors and its own initial development. Sheridan Johns, for example, writing in 1965, concluded that 'the disagreements between the labor and socialist groups of white workers in the Transvaal were offset by their near unanimity on the question of non white labour'.[242] The evidence in this chapter indicates a diversity of views on this question particularly among white labour elites, both before and immediately after the party's establishment. And even those personalities who remained convinced that winning over white working-class leadership should be the party's first aim, acknowledged that most Africans were workers and without their involvement any struggle would quickly founder. Bill Andrews emerges in this story as a much more ambiguous figure than the simple white racist paternalist who is caricatured in several treatments. As he himself once pointed out, people are complicated and inconsistent; and Andrews himself, as well as his comrade and friend Ivon Jones, exemplifies the way in which the precepts they drew from the universalising claims of revolutionary socialism were often at odds with the sectional and racist common sense that patterned their immediate daily lives. Even Sidney Bunting at this point in his life had little real empathy with the African workers he so desperately wanted to draw into his organisation.

All the same, occasional or even everyday racist reflexes did not detract from the sincerity or the commitment with which men such as Bunting, Jones or Andrews acted upon externally derived beliefs in bringing about cross-racial class solidarity. The sources of such beliefs were also complicated. One possibility is that the '"Africanisation" of the party was foretold in part by its strong syndicalist bent evident at its founding'.[243] But a less doctrinal basis for non-racial class solidarity might have been the earlier experience of being at the receiving end of racial discrimination among the Bundist immigrants who joined socialist movements on their arrival in South Africa and who were conspicuous both in the ISL and the early CPSA. And there were also other kinds of common sense derived from ordinary life in South Africa that cut across the habits and attitudes engendered by segregation. For example, a significant number of founder communists were or had experience of working as shopkeepers, running small trading ventures in which Africans were customers rather than subordinates and in which interchanges with them might be characterised by civility and even warmth, as Ivon Jones's letters from his Free State store indicate.[244] But for many white communists at that time, class solidarity with Africans was prompted more by their cerebral adherence to revolutionary theory than any particularly moral aversion to racism. After all, as Bunting once explained, they were not in the business of alleviating 'the civil disabilities of Indian storekeepers, African lawyers and coloured middlemen'.

So what were the communists intentionally trying to achieve in this early phase of their existence?

Within the party and even within its leadership there were different strategic conceptions. Though programmatic statements suggest that at the time of the party's formation communists were generally agreed that electoral participation allowed for opportunities for propaganda and supplied protection against repression, they looked forward to fundamental revolutionary changes that would result from class action in and around workplaces. But individual communists still at times seemed to believe in the possibility of achieving meaningful reforms through institutionalised political participation, as in the case of Bill Andrews's willingness to join an official commission in 1925. After all, this was the generation that, with respect to its English-speaking members, were often politically socialised through reformist white labour parliamentarianism in Australia. This kind of argument supplied a rationale for supporting the Labour Party pact with the Nationalists: that communists could reinforce a Labour left wing, which could then extract meaningful concessions. More usually, communists maintained that workers had first to become frustrated with parliamentary representation before they would turn to the party.

More generally, De Leonite syndicalism – 'cutting government right out' – was the default strategic perspective of the party's founders, who looked forward to a time when workers' councils instituted during a general strike would replace the state for ever. As Lucien van der Walt has argued and as the primary sources consulted for this chapter confirm, anarchist and syndicalist ideas were common currency among the people who formed the party in 1921, and for several years afterwards syndicalist ideas would continue to animate the organisation. Between 1917 and 1922, communists didn't see the advent of an industrial uprising merely as a long-term objective; working to achieve the advent of proletarian dictatorship was 'practical politics', they insisted.[245] Such optimism was a consequence of the conceptual assignment to ostensibly militant white workers in mining and heavy industry of a vanguard role, as Ivon Jones expressed it in 1919, that of 'the engine of revolution in South Africa'. Most communists agreed that the working class was mainly black and that ultimately white workers would have to draw upon black support, and most – not all – were convinced that sooner or later white workers themselves would acknowledge this logic and act upon it. They disagreed among themselves about the details of how black workers might best be organised and whether this should be a priority or a more secondary activity. Bunting was exceptional in his early scepticism about white workers leading a unified class struggle and in his willingness to speak openly about black workers participating as the key constituency in a revolutionary movement, not simply as 'auxiliaries', though this was not a position he maintained consistently.

To an extent the party's strategic and tactical decisions were influenced by its affiliation with the Communist International. Its efforts in 1923 to ally with the Labour Party were partly a response to Comintern's generalised injunctions favouring the formation of united fronts, a reflection of more conciliatory shifts in Soviet international relations that accompanied Lenin's New Economic Policy. The party was less willing to ally itself with African nationalist organisations and, as we have seen, its leaders were often heavily critical of the ANC, though Bunting was to soften his position after visiting Moscow in 1922. For the communists, the ICU was a more amenable partner in any kind of front. But while willing to concede to the ICU the task of organising black workers industrially – before their expulsion, communists viewed the ICU primarily as an industrial organisation, not as a broader political movement – communists believed that they themselves should be organising African workers politically as members of the working class, disclaiming any interest in mobilising peasants, for example. Their narrowness of focus may have been partly a consequence of the Bundist heritage that had animated much of the party's rank and file. At this stage, also, South African communists were hostile to nationalism more generally. As Roux would later acknowledge, they had not read Lenin extensively. In particular, Johannesburg-based communist leaders had not paid any real attention to Lenin's contention in mid-1921 that 'in the impending decisive battles in the world revolution', anti-colonial movements would 'initially' direct themselves to the goal of 'national liberation', but would then 'turn against capitalism'. Colonial toilers – peasants – 'will play a very important revolutionary part', Lenin had insisted.[246]

Though South African communists would sometimes concede that African nationalism might be a 'disguised class struggle', they were normally more dismissive of African nationalism, preferring to deride its 'rudderless opportunism' which most often supplied 'an admirable buffer' between the government and oppressed black South Africans.[247] At this point the nature of Comintern itself, then more ideologically open than it would become later, made it quite easy for the party to engage with external directives selectively and adaptively. In the early 1920s, South Africa was not considered important enough for Comintern to dispatch any visitors to it, despite Jones's urgings after the 1922 strike. As Solly Sachs would observe in January 1926 during his visit to Moscow, the relationship between the South African party and the Comintern was weak, and in his view insufficiently organised.[248] Even so, as was evident for the commentaries and reports in the party's newspaper, the South African communists paid plenty of attention to developments in Comintern policy, and both Jones in Moscow and Bunting while visiting made efforts to redirect the International's 'theses' on the 'negro question'. When Andrews visited in Moscow the following year, he refrained from arguing with his hosts, but then he was probably more comfortable than Bunting with Comintern's strategic prescriptions, at least with respect to how the party should work with black South Africans; that is, through alliances rather than competing with black-led organisations through recruitment. Even after the 1926 rift, Andrews remained on good terms with ICU leaders. During this period, as later, Comintern's influence over its South African affiliates was moral rather than exercised through any kind of leverage. As Bryan Palmer observes in his study of American communism, in the early 1920s foreign communists 'looked to the Russian revolutionaries for guidance' and usually accepted advice willingly: 'crude dictation and unassailable directives were not generally the mode of interchange' between the Comintern's headquarters and its national affiliates, at least not yet.[249] And, of course, for the South Africans, the sense of being members of an epochal global movement was all the more important given their marginal political status domestically. As we have seen, there were no material benefits from this association: as contributors to *The International* noted ruefully, no 'Moscow Gold' had arrived in Johannesburg. But, as the following chapter shows, Comintern would soon become much more assertive in engaging with its South African section.

THREE

Native Republic, 1927–1932

*Sidney and Rebecca Bunting campaigning for African votes in the Transkei in 1929. Gana
Makabeni (in suit and tie, on right) accompanied the Buntings as their interpreter.*

In March 1927, James La Guma travelled to Moscow. He was the first black South African communist to meet Comintern's leaders. Their encounter with him would reshape the party's character profoundly and its effects would be enduring.

The original purpose of La Guma's journey was to represent the Communist Party of South Africa (CPSA) at the First International Congress Against Imperialism and Colonialism in Brussels, an international meeting organised by the Workers' International, a Comintern-linked trade union assembly, held on 10–14 February 1927. The Congress's purpose was to set up a League Against Imperialism, a body intended to help Comintern build connections with anti-colonial nationalist movements. While in Brussels he was invited by officials from Comintern's British Secretariat to visit Moscow.[1] Apparently La Guma impressed the officials he encountered in Brussels. As one of the Indian participants remarked after the meeting, here was a 'negro delegate who did not believe in the professions of his white colleagues'.[2] Self-educated, mercurial, ambitious and imaginative, La Guma had considerable gifts for leadership, though, according to one of his friends, he could also be an 'irritable fellow, ratty', that is, short-tempered.[3] He could deliver speeches in three languages, English, Afrikaans and German, and composed songs as well.[4]

Shortly after his arrival, La Guma presented a brief report on 10 March, supplying the Anglo-American Secretariat with an overview of South African political organisations, including a profile of its South African affiliate. Subsequently at a meeting with the British Secretariat of the Comintern a resolution was prepared on South Africa, urging the party to advocate full South African independence and to try to build a left wing with Afrikaner nationalism.[5] On 16 March, La Guma offered a more argumentative perspective to the Comintern Praesidium. South African party leaders, he told the Comintern officials, had for some time been trying to agree on a programme that could build the widest worker support. 'The difficulty was that we have all these conflicting elements to reconcile', for, he explained, any platform that might attract black workers would risk alienating whites. He finished by asking 'whether there will be any advice coming from the assembly this evening'.[6]

There would indeed be advice, from no less than Nikolai Bukharin, at that time Comintern's general secretary, who had been, within the Soviet Union's leadership, Stalin's key ally in his feud with Trotsky. Bukharin made a point of attending the meeting on the 16th and proposed that it should reject the resolution prepared on the 11th; it was too general, he noted, and failed to offer a helpful 'line' for the South African party to follow. What was needed, he said, was a clear message that would spell out the party's position on 'the national question, in other words the race question, [and] the relationship between black and white workers'. 'That is the most important question', he insisted. The party, he added, should make demands, 'such as a demand for a Negro republic independent of the British empire, or in addition for autonomy of the national white minorities, etc.' Overall, he concluded, the Comintern should 'say very clearly that in the struggle between the Negroes and the whites that it is on the side of the Negroes'. Any resolution that failed to register these points would be opportunistic and 'politically incorrect'. A better resolution should be prepared, he advised, preferably by 'a small committee of three comrades'.[7] The Praesidium agreed. Shortly after this meeting, La Guma would leave Moscow to return to South Africa, and so would not be a member of the group designated to write the resolution. He was back home in South Africa by April.

That La Guma had left Moscow before the resolution was drafted deserves emphasis because several authorities suggest that together with Bukharin he was one of the main architects of what would be for the party a major strategic shift.[8] La Guma's biography, written by his son, suggests that he had quite an extensive conversation with Bukharin *before* the Praesidium meeting and that Bukharin's recommendation that the South African party should work for a 'Negro republic' echoed the earlier exchanges he had had with La Guma.[9] La Guma's recollection of this meeting is sharply focused: Bukharin, who received him at the Communist Party headquarters, was hospitably 'genial'. They met in a room stacked with old newspapers and dusty books. Bukharin had his trousers held up with an old necktie, and was wearing 'scuffed slippers'.[10] Bukharin spoke English easily enough so they would have needed no interpreters, though in any case La Guma was fluent in German, another of Bukharin's languages. Simons and Simons also argue that La Guma was a key figure in the slogan's conception, suggesting that his attendance at the Brussels conference was a turning point in persuading him that South African communists should be conducting an anti-imperialist struggle.[11]

117

Their view was partly informed by Douglas Wolton, one of the main actors in the story that will unfold in this chapter. In Wolton's view, it was La Guma who had taken the initiative. 'I would say that La Guma raised the whole issue in the sharpest possible manner in Moscow. He discussed the question at considerable length with Bukharin and Max Petrovsky [head of the Anglo-American Secretariat],' he wrote to Jack Simons.[12] Similarly, in 1975 Wolton told Brian Bunting that the impetus for the slogan came from South Africa and that it was not imposed by Comintern.[13] Petrovsky himself told the South Africans in 1928 that the resolution 'was prepared with the help of Comrade La Guma'.[14] Sidney Bunting, then the CPSA's general secretary, also believed that James La Guma prompted the resolution, that 'the slogan would never have been born' if La Guma had not travelled to Moscow, and, moreover, that La Guma himself 'was a bit of a racialist'.[15] La Guma had certainly co-drafted and signed a resolution on behalf of the South African delegates in Brussels which called for the right to self-determination. The resolution included in its phraseology the demand of Africa for the Africans, not language customarily used by the party, though it contained nothing about a Negro or Native republic.[16]

Sheridan Johns's research, based upon Comintern records, indicates that the slogan's genesis was more protracted and complicated and that it was an outcome of general Comintern policy with respect to the 'Negro Question'.[17] At its fourth congress in 1922, Comintern adopted a set of 'Theses on the Negro Question'. These maintained that people of African descent worldwide were politically animated chiefly by the exploitations of imperialism. US Negroes were especially likely to have revolutionary predispositions, living as they did in an advanced capitalist country as an 'oppressed nation',[18] and hence they should be the main agencies for communism within the Negro world. Accordingly, Comintern established its Anglo-American Secretariat, which would broadly concern itself with anti-colonial and anti-imperial initiatives in the British Empire and Dominions as well as in Ireland, Argentina and the United States, and which replaced the British Secretariat. In 1927, the Secretariat established a Negro subcommittee which drafted a resolution on US Negro self-determination, calling for a 'Negro Soviet Republic' in the areas of the 'Black Belt' in the South where African Americans constituted a 'compact mass of farmers on a contiguous territory', a proposal that echoed Stalin's own definition of a nation.[19] By 1925, Stalin himself was taking a particular interest in the African American students who were beginning to arrive to study at the University for Toilers of the East. With this background in mind, it was obvious for Johns that the

Stalinist conception that shaped Comintern policy developed for African Americans 'was taken up by the Comintern and extended to South Africa'.[20] More recent research based on the Comintern's archive attributes the first application of the phraseology of a Negro republic to Max Petrovsky, a key figure in developing the original concept of a Negro republic with respect to the United States. Petrovsky, whose real name was David Lipetz and whose other Comintern aliases were Goldfarb and Bennett, was an ex-Bundist, and this experience may have fostered a special preoccupation with ethnic or racial self-determination issues.[21]

Other Soviet foreign policy concerns may also help to explain Bukharin's interest in the affairs of the South African party. During the mid-1920s Bukharin believed that it was on capitalism's 'colonial periphery' that it was most vulnerable, and in colonial settings communists should encourage peasants, whatever proletarians were available, and the native bourgeoisie to constitute 'a single nationalist revolutionary current'.[22] More particularly, given a recent sharp deterioration in relations with Britain which prompted fears of military conflict, a revolutionary struggle in South Africa might distract Britain from sponsoring any aggression against the Soviet Union. Soviet perceptions of Britain as a threat were partly a consequence of propensities to view the Baltic countries, Poland and Romania, each perceived as hostile to the USSR, as British allies.[23] The South African resolution itself would be drafted by the Negro Commission, a subcommittee within the Secretariat, as Johns established, citing as his source the subcommittee's African American vice chairman, Harry Haywood. Haywood did inform Johns during his research that members of the subcommittee had spoken to La Guma during his visit.[24] But whatever his role may or may not have been in the initial conception of the resolution, James La Guma would be an enthusiastic advocate for its adoption and embrace and, as we shall see, certainly helped to elaborate its content later on.

The new resolution was approved by Comintern's Political Secretariat on 22 July 1927 and sent to South Africa on 9 August. The resolution noted that the South African party was weak, but 'the present intensified campaign of the government against the natives' represented a fresh opportunity to build a following among African 'peasants and workers'. It was among these groups that the party should be principally active. For this purpose it needed the kind of programme that could attract mass African support, though it should also maintain and not lessen 'its work amongst the white population'. The party should fight against all racially discriminatory laws and regulations, but it should do more than this. Its immediate slogan should be 'an independent

119

black South African Republic as a stage towards a Workers and Peasants Republic with full autonomy for all minorities'. The party itself should become a predominantly African organisation and it should 'do everything possible to help the native comrades into the leadership'.[25] In essence, and in this formulation, the slogan suggested that in South Africa the main task for communists was to support a struggle of an anti-colonial character. That the party should base itself among peasants and workers – the ordering was not accidental – implied that a land-hungry African peasantry would be the largest group mobilising in such a struggle – the 'motive force', so to speak.[26] The black republic would be a transitional political order, a staging point in further progress to socialism. It would probably not, however, embody a 'bourgeois democratic republic', not in the sense of a liberal democracy, given the effective absence of an African bourgeoisie, in Comintern's view, though peasants would own their land – as was the case in the Soviet Union during the implementation of the New Economic Policy, a policy of which Bukharin was by 1927 the key champion. But in its initial conception the Native republic would require an alliance with African nationalists. In La Guma's words at that time: 'to be revolutionary a national movement in conditions of an imperialist yoke need not necessarily be composed of proletarian elements, or have a revolutionary or republican programme, or a democratic base'.[27]

IN CERTAIN RESPECTS, given the features of the broad political setting, it made sense for the South African communists to become a more African- or black-oriented organisation. Since 1924, as we have seen, an Afrikaner Nationalist and Labour Party 'Pact' government had institutionalised concessions to white workers, which had the effect of bureaucratising leading sections of the white trade union movement as a consequence of the provisions of the Industrial Conciliation Act, encouraging the development of a hierarchy of hundreds of officials.[28] The Act also excluded any prospect of registration for African unions. Prime Minister Hertzog's circular of October 1925 expected official departments to substitute 'civilised' for 'uncivilised' labour; as a result, the number of Africans employed on the railways nearly halved between 1924 and 1933.[29] Wage legislation in 1925 instituted a minimum wage, which eroded the comparative advantage for employers of employing Africans; meanwhile, municipalities were allocated extra funding to find jobs for unskilled whites paid at the new minimum rate. The government's rural policies brought a million-plus African labour tenants with their families under the demanding provisions of the Masters and Servants Act. Crop failures in 1925 and 1926 accentuated their hardships while in towns there were wage cuts for Africans. In 1926 taxation was extended so that every adult African male was expected to pay £1 a year and households in the countryside ten shillings for every hut occupant. These were the measures to which rural Africans reacted with a tide of rebellious protest and which swelled the rural following of the Industrial and Commercial Workers' Union (ICU). In November 1925 Hertzog announced a new legislative programme, a series of proposed laws that would remove the Cape African franchise, curtail still further African access to freehold land-ownership, and make 'exemptions' from the pass laws more restrictive for middle-class Africans. The bills were dropped in 1929 because at that time Hertzog could not obtain the necessary two-thirds parliamentary support for them, but the threat they posed up to then had a politically radicalising effect on relatively educated Africans who might have hoped to join the small elite of property owners and professionals. As the ICU leader, Clements Kadalie, himself noted, in 1925 and 1926 ex-teachers began joining his organisation in significant numbers, attracted not least by the better salaries it paid branch office-holders, positions in which they predominated.[30]

In 1927, for the CPSA to direct itself at building a mass base among Africans in the cities, let alone in the countryside, would represent a challenge, but not an undertaking for which it was completely unprepared. In January 1927, the Communist Party had just 400 members, 350 of whom were white, according to its own records.[31] La Guma supplied a slightly different picture when he spoke to the Comintern Praesidium on 16 March. He thought there were about 100 'negroes' in the party (he seems to have included coloured and Indian members within this group). Membership, he said, was concentrated in Johannesburg and Cape Town. In Johannesburg, the Young Communist League (YCL) had resolved in November 1923 that its 'main task' would forthwith be 'the organisation of African youth'.[32] Most of the African members, La Guma suggested, were recruited from and had been active in the ICU before their expulsion in December 1926, a development that followed La Guma's efforts to check top-level corruption in the union.[33] La Guma himself and four other communists had held key positions within the ICU's leadership. There were several ICU communists in Port Elizabeth before the expulsions.[34] That the party had any black membership was a consequence of sustained effort by a group led by Sidney Bunting, a group which until 1924 had been a minority within the CPSA in believing that 'non-Europeans' were the 'real proletariat'.[35] The party's Youth League was especially persistent in trying to recruit Africans, and indeed it was two of its converts, ex-schoolteacher Stanley Silwana and labourer Thomas Mbeki, who had helped to set up the ICU in Johannesburg.

Among South African communists, Sidney Bunting was an early advocate of African rights and was active in trying to enrol black South Africans into the International Socialist League (ISL), well before the CPSA's formation. It was due to his insistence that the ISL published a leaflet supporting African mine workers during their strike in 1920. Shy and formal, Bunting was not a man who made friends easily. Hyman Basner, in the party leadership in the 1930s, grew up next door to the Buntings' modest home in Doornfontein. In his autobiography he supplies a brief portrait: a 'rasping voice' and 'eyes kept firmly looking at the ground', kindly enough, but a personality without charm, Basner remembered. The kindliness extended to his legal practice; Basner noted Bunting's 'sentimental reluctance to charge proper fees',[36] a restraint that helped to explain why he and his wife Rebecca lived in Doornfontein, even at that time a shabby locality.[37] Even so, his sincerity must have resonated with African workers in the party's following, whom Bunting himself described as often 'ignorant and half civilised ... unable to speak any but their native languages'.[38] In these classes, Bunting may have appeared 'paternal', a word used about his manner with black South Africans by his critics;[39] but with one or two African communists, Bunting developed enduring and reciprocal friendships, especially with the trade unionist Gana Makabeni, who was a frequent visitor to the Bunting household. When Bunting walked across the mine dumps to visit Makabeni in his house, his sons accompanied him to play with the children of Makabeni's neighbours – at that time exceptional behaviour for a white South African family. During the doctrinal rifts that followed the Comintern's intervention, most of the key African unionists would remain unwaveringly loyal to Bunting. In matters of doctrine, though, Bunting would always be uncomfortable. Eddie Roux, friendly with Bunting before he joined the party because Bunting knew his father, suggests that Bunting was well out of his depth in the Comintern's 'Whirlwind of Theory' – here he was a 'blundering novice' and his almost 'complete lack of doctrinal knowledge let him down'.[40]

Eddie Roux himself was no theoretician, at least not of the sort that would earn him approval among the party's orthodox thinkers. All the same, he would play an important role in the party's history in this period. After helping to form the Young Communist League with his friends Willie Kalk and Bernard (Bennie) Sachs, he had convened a study group to work its way through the first volume of *Capital*. He found he could not accept Marx's theory of value; for him, its assumptions seemed to be at variance with obvious economic facts.[41] His intellectual independence was very much a product of his background, for Eddie had been brought up in a household in which ideas mattered. His father, Philip, a founder of the ISL while working as a chemist, discovered rationalism as a young man and had given up his Calvinist faith, discarding his Afrikaner identity as the son of a Free State farming household at the same time. Philip first became a 'patriotic Britisher by association', fighting on the imperial side in the South African War, before encountering socialism in 1911.[42] Roux grew up in an affectionate but argumentative family and eventually quarrelled with his father over his political activism, for by 1922 Philip had become an 'armchair socialist'. In any case Philip Roux belonged to the party faction that opposed Bunting's efforts to recruit Africans. When Eddie refused to give up his role in the Young Communists, he was locked out of the family home in Bez Valley. By that stage, aged 20, he was a student at Wits. He found lodgings in nearby Jeppe, sharing a room with an anarchist, and supported himself through working as a part-time demonstrator at Wits University. It was Willie Kalk who first drew him into friendships with Africans. Eddie started attending ICU meetings and fundraiser dances with two of the union's organisers, Thomas Mbeki and Stanley Silwana. He met Kadalie and was enchanted by him.[43] At their first encounter Kadalie took the copy of Swinburne's *Songs before Sunrise* and 'in his gentle high-pitched voice' read some of the verses from 'Messidor':

> Let all that hunger and weep
> Come hither, and who would have bread
> Put in the sickles and reap

Despite his busy political life, Roux graduated from Wits with first-class honours and was by 1926 already working as a junior lecturer in the Botany Department. By 1927 he was at Cambridge, the recipient of a three-year Exhibition Scholarship.

From 1925 Johannesburg activists held a twice-weekly party night school in a church in Ferreirastown, using passages from Bukharin's *ABC of Communism* for literacy lessons. Roux's recollections are that at this stage the party's African following was mainly drawn from semi-literate but relatively urbanised workers in light industry. The first African unions that the party established in Johannesburg after the break with the ICU in the opening months of 1927 were among workers in laundries, furniture workshops, clothing factories and a mattress company,[44] though the African communists had been willing to organise workers neglected by the ICU before the break; this was the case with the setting up of an African railways workers' group in late 1926.[45] The party's activities, it was true, were focused on urban workers, not the countryside, but its previous connections with the ICU would have given its African members access to networks that indeed extended into the kinds of communities engaged in the sorts of agrarian uprisings envisaged in the Comintern resolution. Indeed, it was African party members, particularly Thomas Mbeki, who during 1926 began building ICU branches constituted by African labour tenants on farms in the Eastern Transvaal. Their efforts were prompted by tenant protests against the application of the 1926 Masters and Servants Act, which extended to 180 days the period during which they had to work on the landowners' fields.[46] But despite these initiatives, it was still the case that the most extensive claims the party could make in leading or, at least, influencing organised labour were with respect to white trade unions; it retained a hold on important positions in the white labour coordinating bodies in Johannesburg and Cape Town. And there remained within the party, even among its younger members, people who, in Roux's words, 'feared and disliked Natives',[47] or, more commonly, people who felt for practical purposes, as in the case of Solly Sachs, that Africans and whites should be organised separately.[48] Though only 25, Sachs was already a formidable figure, organising shop assistants since his teens, while studying at Wits and joining the Central Committee as its youngest member. Sachs was freshly returned from a visit to Moscow where he had absorbed the most recent Comintern prescriptions for 'Bolshevisation'; he wanted the party to be reorganised on a cellular basis.[49] Later in 1927, Bill Andrews, the party's most prominent white trade unionist, would write a recommendation to the executives of the South African Trades Union Congress (SATUC) and the Cape Federation of Trade Unions (CFTU), advising them to reject an ICU application for affiliation, and arguing essentially that such a development would open up rifts within the white labour movement. This was still at a time when, at least in theory, communists were seeking readmission into the ICU.

Not surprisingly, then, when the Comintern resolution arrived in Johannesburg in August 1927, it was rejected by the party's Central Executive Committee. One of those who voted against it was Johnny Gomas, a coloured labour organiser who worked in Cape Town. For him, a communist 'schooled in the tradition of the International Socialist League, believing in the class struggle as analysed by Marx', supporting a separate black state seemed a repudiation of basic theoretical precepts.[50] Bunting subsequently wrote to James La Guma explaining the committee's decision; the slogan 'would antagonise the European section of the working class' and the authors of the slogan evidently had 'insufficient knowledge of the situation in South

Africa, especially the widespread apathy of the native masses'.[51] A more definite consideration of the proposal was postponed until the party's congress in January 1928. The argument about native apathy may have come from Bunting himself, for one year later in his address to the Comintern executive he maintained that the 'native agrarian masses as such have not yet shown serious signs of revolt' and hence to identify them as a moving force of revolutionary struggle would be misconceived.[52] Bunting believed that Bukharin underestimated the degree to which black South Africans were already proletarianised; supporting a mainly rurally based nationalist movement would be a distraction, he felt. Bunting was either dismissive about or unaware of the labour tenants' rebellion on South African farms, in which several of the party's African members had been involved as ICU organisers. This was despite the fact that he personally worked quite closely with African members, teaching regularly at the Ferreirastown night school, where, despite his formality, Oxford accent and general 'awkwardness and angularity', his charges 'worshipped him'.[53] But when it came to leadership, African members were still on the margins. Thomas Mbeki, the main African communist in the ICU, had in any case resigned from the CPSA so as to retain his ICU position; he may also by this time have been working as a police informer, though that defection may have come later.[54] Eddie Roux, who might well have been better informed than Bunting about the scope of ICU activities in the countryside – he was one of the few white communists who enjoy relaxed friendships with African comrades such as Thomas Mbeki as well as being close to Bunting – was, of course, studying in Britain during 1927 and 1928.

On 1 December, James La Guma on his second visit to Moscow – he was in Europe to attend a follow-up meeting in Brussels of the League Against Imperialism, accompanying the ANC president, JT Gumede, on this journey and on his subsequent tour of the Soviet Union – reported the lack of any progress on the resolution to the Anglo-American Secretariat. The Central Executive Committee, which with one exception (Johnny Gomas) was entirely 'European', he noted, was 'not in as close touch with the masses as they should be' and were not 'gauging the situation correctly'.[55] In reaction, the Secretariat dispatched a telegram to Johannesburg: the party should 'accept the resolution … as the line for their every-day practical work'.[56] This reproof failed to arrive, apparently, possibly as a consequence of Comintern's decision to transmit it via London.[57] At the party's congress most delegates were opposed to the resolution, although, tactfully, the 'thesis' was referred back to the new Central Executive for further consideration. Early in 1928, the party published a pamphlet on its aims entitled *What Is This Communist*

Party, which maintained its traditional emphasis on 'class conscious agitation' together with collaboration with any nationalist movements such as the ANC only 'in so far' as they supported the aim of 'conquest of political power by the workers'.[58] After further urging from Comintern officials, the Central Executive Committee held a special meeting on 15 March, to which La Guma was invited.

By 15 March, the party leadership had received a more explicit version of the Native republic argument from Comintern's headquarters, drafted apparently during La Guma's second visit to Moscow with his help.[59] In particular, the South Africans were told, the 'national question in SA is based upon the agrarian question [and the] ... black peasantry [is the] basic moving force in alliance with and under the leadership of the working class'. Moreover, the communists should pay particular attention to 'embryonic organisations among the natives'. They should especially cultivate a relationship with the African National Congress (ANC), seeking to reorient it into 'a fighting nationalist revolutionary organisation'.[60] This need not imply embracing a proto-bourgeois movement, for, as Comintern had noted in its draft 'Thesis on the Revolutionary Movement in the Colonies and Semi Colonies' – a much more general document prepared for its Congress which had also been sent to the Central Executive Committee – alliance with the USSR might enable revolutionary groups in colonial territories to avoid 'the stage of the domination of the capitalist system'.[61]

Most of the South African leadership remained unconvinced. The meeting on the 15th began with La Guma reporting on his most recent visit to Moscow. He arrived wearing the fur hat and heavy overcoat he had purchased in Moscow, treasured souvenirs he brought home together with the colour poster of Lenin which, for the rest of his life, would hang alongside the picture of his father on the parlour wall of his home in District Six.[62] He told executive members that he had been 'instructed' that ten places had been offered for South African students at the University for the Toilers of the East. Meanwhile, the Secretariat was expecting a 'very careful investigation of its resolution'.[63] At the Praesidium meeting that he attended, Bukharin had observed that white South African workers, 'soaked as they were with imperialist ideology', could not constitute the main revolutionary force.[64] In the discussion that followed, slogan supporters were confined to La Guma and Douglas and Molly Wolton. Douglas Wolton had first known La Guma in Cape Town as an ICU organiser after he had joined the party there in 1924 while working at the *Cape Argus*. As the district secretary he encouraged African recruitment in Cape Town. He had visited Johannesburg during the 1922 Rand Revolt, attending strike meetings, and 'realised it was a ridiculous situation when there were so many native miners for the strikers to turn against them'.[65] An ex-telegraph operator at the post office and a relatively recent immigrant from England, he had been appointed as the party's newspaper editor in December 1927, directing its content at black readers for the first time.

For Douglas Wolton, the slogan 'Workers of the World Unite' was under South African conditions too abstract; worker unity would only come after a proletarian revolution.[66] And, as Molly, Douglas's Lithuanian-born wife, whom he married in 1925, noted, 'Even a Native Bourgeois Government and the limited freedom secured would be an advance on present conditions'.[67] This was not the view of the Africans who had joined the Executive Committee after their election at the congress. The slogan was racialist and might simply place power in the hands of self-serving chiefs, they maintained. Meanwhile, white trade unionists were reluctant to discount white labour entirely. Solly Sachs believed prospects for a successful African nationalist movement were remote, for 'all subjected people were becoming proletarianized and there were no middle class or petty bourgeois elements among natives'.[68] The discussion extended over a further two meetings. Those present managed to reach agreement on which African students they should send to Moscow, five rather than ten at first, because that was as many as they could afford to divert from organisational work. There were also difficulties with the prospective students' passport applications. The party's first African recruit, William Thibedi, was refused a passport on each of his three separate applications between 1927 and 1929.[69] At the end of the third meeting, Bunting took up the point Sachs had made earlier: there was no native bourgeoisie in South Africa and 'the stage of nationalism need not necessarily be gone through'.[70]

The Executive Committee remained divided, and finally settled on a compromise. Majority and minority reports would be submitted to the Comintern and the party would send two delegates to the International's sixth World Congress scheduled for August. Bunting would be the first delegate, but he would be accompanied by Rebecca, also elected as a delegate, and Eddie Roux, then still completing his doctorate at Cambridge. The minority report would be written by the Cape Town branch where, according to James La Guma, apparently most black or coloured members supported the slogan,[71] including Johnny Gomas, though in other ways he remained loyal to Bunting. But he had been an ally of La Guma's in his efforts to address the venality of the ICU leadership; like La Guma he'd been a full-time organiser of the ICU in Cape Town as well as member of the party and its predecessor since 1919. He'd begun work as a tailor, and his record included a conviction for theft from his employer in 1920, a lapse from respectability which troubled some of his more law-abiding white comrades.

NOTWITHSTANDING THEIR OPPOSITION to the slogan, during the first half of 1928, in their 'everyday practical work' the South African communists' activities appeared to follow to a considerable extent the courses envisaged by Comintern's leadership. For a brief period even, an alliance with African nationalism seemed a practical option, following the election to the ANC's presidency of JT Gumede, who had returned from his attendance at the Brussels meeting predisposed to make common cause with the communists in an anti-imperialist movement. Gumede was elected as ANC president in mid-1927 and in this capacity was invited to the Soviet Union. This was an excursion arranged and paid for by the South African party,[72] and James La Guma had accompanied him on his tour. Gumede was hosted by the civil war hero Marshal Budenny at a special banquet held in his honour, and subsequently met Stalin.[73] He returned deeply impressed with achievements that he claimed represented 'the key to freedom'. On 27 February 1928, Gumede attended a meeting of the party's executive and he allowed communists to share the platform at various public meetings he addressed. He chaired an ineffectual Free Speech Defence Committee set up to oppose prospective sedition legislation. This committee also included Douglas Wolton as its secretary. In April, however, a joint meeting between the ANC and the ICU repudiated the ANC's 'association' with the Communist Party; opposition to Gumede's move leftwards had been mounting, particularly from the ANC's House of Chiefs, and though Gumede himself remained on friendly terms with party leaders, even being tempted to join their organisation,[74] he would be displaced in ANC leadership elections in 1930. After April 1928, Gumede had considered leaving the ANC and setting up a branch of the League Against Imperialism, but communists advised him against this.[75] Bunting had discouraged La Guma from setting up a branch one year earlier. Aside from not wishing to sponsor any direct rival to the ANC, Bunting was worried that a communist-sponsored local version of the League would attract hostility from the Trades Union Congress.[76]

On 25 March, a coordinating committee for a new Federation of Native Trade Unions (FNTU) was set up, chaired by Ben Weinbren, with William Thibedi as its full-time paid organiser and James La Guma as its secretary. In Moscow in July, Eddie Roux wrote a memo for Comintern officials providing details of the Federation's membership. He claimed the five affiliates between them had a membership of 1,163.[77] At the same time the party began to actively recruit an African membership, setting up branches in Sophiatown, Evaton, Potchefstroom and Vereeniging that would be wholly constituted by Africans, as well as smaller clusters of members grouped into a South Eastern Transvaal branch. In Vereeniging, the party took over a disaffected ICU branch that had been led by communists whom the union had expelled;[78] a popular night school helped to swell its local organised following. In 1929 and 1930 Vereeniging communists were active in local protests against a new lodger's tax and new local regulations that required African women living in the townships to carry passes.[79] A local member of the party, Rapatana Tjelele, also helped to establish an embryonic steelworkers' union.[80] In Potchefstroom the party grew after Bunting had succeeded in obtaining an acquittal for Thibedi, who had been arrested earlier on an incitement charge. As in the case of Vereeniging, the party's popularity and membership would grow to over 1,000 during 1928 as a consequence of communists' engagement in local opposition to the municipality's introduction of lodgers' fees in the African township. Party headquarters directed Edwin Mofutsanyana and Shadrach Kotu in June 1928 to work as organisers to set up a night school. They did their best to instil a systematic structure, but in the end 'We had a big loose party and we called them communists'.[81] The lodgers' fees were a measure that women especially viewed as an assault on their families, as children over the age of 18 living at home would now be taxed and in effect have to seek permission to live in the location. The party supplied more legal support in trials of people who refused to buy the permits and local communists, many of them women, organised meetings and a procession of 300 to the court building when non-permit holders were charged. In this vicinity, it was the party's prestige and its apparent embodiment of an alternative source of authority and power to a repressive local administration that were the sources of its local appeal. As Josie Mpama, one of the local party leaders, recollected much later: 'When one man asked … why he should join, the answer was given that he would be able to carry a briefcase, like the organisers do.'[82] Josie Mpama herself looked after Edwin Mofutsanyana in Potchefstroom; he lodged with her and later they would live as man and wife.

Elsewhere many of the party's new followers, in the south-east Transvaal for example, were farm workers, attracted to the party for much the same reasons that such people were at that time flocking to the ICU. Meetings among these groups were often held 'in a religious atmosphere', the party's Central Committee noted in mid-1927,[83] a mood to which the party's own African organisers responded with their own usage of religious terminology and biblical parallels: 'we speak of the love that you Christians speak of and we believe we should protect that love', Edwin Mofutsanyana reassured his listeners at one party rally.[84] These efforts enabled the party to record substantial increases in its membership. By mid-1928 it claimed an organised following of 1,750, 1,600 of whom were not white, and by the end of year the total had risen to 3,000.[85] Such claims need to be interpreted in their context: the party was concerned to demonstrate to Comintern that it was taking the injunction to build an African following seriously. A visiting Comintern official found in 1931 that membership claims of a similar order were often based on 'one-time contacts' and were hence likely to be seriously inflated.[86] This may have been the case earlier; ballooning local memberships, such as those registered by party organisers in Potchefstroom were more likely to reflect transient local excitement rather than durable commitment. As the party itself noted retrospectively in 1932, these local followings were usually based on 'loose and indefinite' relationships; the 1,000 people signed up at Potchefstroom were all recruited at a single meeting, and many of these too were farm workers rather than location residents.[87]

Mia Roth's archival research in South African Department of Labour files suggests that the trade unions the party established in 1927 and 1928 may also have been rather chimerical. In December 1928 one of the department's inspectors undertook a check on information about the unions he had received from Ben Weinbren, the FNTU's chairman. The inspector reported he could find no information about where these groups were active and he was sceptical about their membership statistics.[88] When he visited the FNTU's office (in the building also used by the party as its headquarters), he could find no books to show evidence of paid-up members.[89] In fairness, the absence of paid-up members does not mean that African unions did not have followings. The ICU also struggled to collect subscriptions from its members, as William Ballinger discovered when he tried to put its organisation on a more systematic footing.[90] Despite their poor record-keeping, more senior officials were not so dismissive about these efforts by communists to build African trade unions. CW Cousins, the Secretary of Labour, writing to his minister in January 1929, suggested that the Federation's attempts to form new unions appeared 'to be attaining a fair measure of success'.[91] This view was shared by Chief Inspector Ivan Walker, in writing in May 1929 to the Undersecretary in the ministry, and noting that the 'native employees' in the affected sectors were 'all fairly well organised' and enjoyed 'some sort of working agreement' with the relevant 'European' unions. Within these workforces, Walker continued, a 'small band' of communists were 'wielding an influence out of all proportion to their numbers'.[92] William Thibedi supplied a detailed breakdown of the numbers concerned in a letter he wrote to Moscow at the beginning of 1929. The largest FNTU affiliate, he reported, the laundry workers, had a membership of 800, followed by 600 furniture workers and 400 clothing workers.[93] These were hardly strategically powerful groups of workers, as Grossman has pointed out;[94] African workers in heavy industry often lived in compounds, less accessible to organisers. But as we have just seen, officials perceived communist trade unionism as a significant development. Indeed, they saw it as a threat that should be deflected through reform. As Ivan Walker suggested to the Secretary of Labour in August 1929, recognition of the rights of Africans to organise would have 'got far' in 'minimizing trouble and counter[ing] the efforts of the Communists'.[95] In general at this time, the senior officials in the Department of Labour favoured bringing unionised African workers within the scope of the Industrial Conciliation Act, not least because if wage determinations applied to black workers, this reduced the likelihood of them displacing whites.[96]

It was also the case that the party's new emphasis on building African unions coincided with a growth in Transvaal manufacturing, especially in undertakings linked to rising consumption, such as baking, laundry, clothing and furniture, and these industries increasingly recruited Africans. The new Wage Board determinations applied to all workers irrespective of race and until 1929, when restrictions were introduced requiring applications to be signed by all supporters, African unions could apply quite easily for a wage investigation to the Board. For white registered unions in this industry, it was in their interests to encourage African unions so as to prevent white workers being displaced by cheaper black replacements. Accordingly, communist white officials in these bodies sometimes played a leading role in setting up or supporting parallel organisations for black workers.[97] This was especially the case in those sectors of industry in which registered white unions could not use skill scarcity as a source of leverage with employers. They had two choices, either to support the organisation of black workers to prevent their own members being undercut or to try to block the entry into their industries of workers prepared to accept lower wages. As in the case of white tailoring workers, their inclination to adopt the first course of action and encourage the activity of a black parallel body, the African Clothing Workers' Union, was partly a consequence of their own members, recently arrived Jewish immigrants, themselves experiencing discriminatory attitudes from supervisors and employers.[98] The African clothing workers actually stayed away from work in solidarity when the white tailoring workers went on strike, but their action was not reciprocated one year later when they downed tools in protest against employer action against their own union leaders. Subsequently the Clothing Workers formed a parallel liaison with Solly Sachs's Garment Workers. This clothing workers' protest strike does show how vulnerable African workforces were even in the industrial sectors in which they had made most advance. As Sidney Bunting noted, most union members performed the least skilled work, being employed as sweepers or messengers and suchlike, not working on machines. Significantly, in Germiston the Clothing Workers' Union leader whom the factory owner dismissed in the incident that precipitated the strike was a presser, one of the few semi-skilled machinist positions assigned to Africans. The Clothing Workers' Germiston following numbered about 200, but at not one workplace were more than ten of its members employed.[99] In such settings employers could replace dismissed workers very easily.

SIDNEY AND REBECCA Bunting travelled to Moscow in July to attend the Comintern's sixth congress and to challenge the arguments running through the Native republic resolution. In London, they were joined by Eddie Roux and they all then travelled together, breaking their train journey in Berlin 'where the Reds had fought on the barricades on May day weeks before'. They took a walk through the Tiergarten Zoo, eating cherries. Once in Moscow, 'cold-shouldered by some of the Negro delegates' who had been told they were 'typical white South African chauvinists',[100] they had time for more sightseeing before the congress proceedings began. They watched Eisenstein's *Battleship Potemkin* and they visited the Palace of Culture and Rest, and tried not to pay any attention to the 'importuning beggars' on every street corner.[101] They attempted to arrange a special appointment with members of the Anglo-American Secretariat but 'we couldn't find anyone in authority who was prepared to speak to us'.[102]

Bunting's first presentation at the congress on 23 July engaged directly with Bukharin's notion that black South Africans were chiefly peasants. They were not, he said; rather they were mainly migrant workers in an industrialising economy, a viewpoint that echoed Rosa Luxemburg, though he may not have been aware of this. Comintern's references to colonial 'masses' were racially condescending: the colonial working class were full proletarians. His speech provoked Bukharin as well as Petrovsky to attack him as a social democrat, which was at that stage becoming a damning label in Comintern's lexicon. There were even more harmful perceptions. The African American Harry Haywood understood Bunting to be saying that in South Africa the 'road to socialism would be travelled under white leadership'.[103] Bunting stood his ground; such misrepresentations should be 'repudiated and disavowed', he told the delegates and, indeed, 'the wrong impression given by Comrade Bukharin's speech should also be definitely removed'.[104] Rebecca Bunting and Eddie Roux were equally combative. Rebecca two days later reprimanded the assembly for its under-representation of women. This was symptomatic of a more general predisposition in the communist movement to assign to working-class women auxiliary support roles rather than making them communists who could be brought into 'the heart of party work'.[105] Meanwhile, Roux offered more criticisms of the Native republic argument for 'presupposing the presence of a native bourgeoisie and the absence of a large class of white proletarians capable of becoming the allies of the natives in their struggle'. But Roux appears to have had second thoughts, informing the Negro subcommittee (by then the Negro Commission) on 11 August that disagreements now existed within the South African delegation; he now believed they had not paid sufficient attention to the proposed programme.[106] As he explained, later, 'I must have been trying to convince myself that the slogan was theoretically correct.'[107] At this meeting, Petrovsky, head of the Anglo-American Secretariat, criticised the South Africans for their apparent belief that the party could 'simply organise the masses of proletarianized Negroes directly into the Party itself'.[108] In September, in a letter he wrote to the party leadership after his return to Britain, Roux conceded that 'we knew very little about agrarian conditions' and that any slogan that might succeed in efforts to 'rally the main mass' would have to be 'nationalistic'.[109] As he noted in a separate letter to Douglas Wolton, 'it was time for the CPSA to put its theoretical house in order … Our reaction to the slogan showed we were not up to date in Leninist theory.'[110] Subsequently he confided to Wolton that he had become 'quite reconciled' to the slogan, which now seemed to him 'perfectly logical' and really meant only 'what we have been saying all the time in a slightly different way'.[111]

On 11 August, the Negro Commission had delegated a group to draw up a resolution addressing the South African arguments.[112] Bunting and Roux were asked to join this group. Bunting refused to soften his position. He saved his most developed argument for an address to the congress on 20 August. In South Africa, as in most African colonies, he argued, 'there is as a rule no native bourgeoisie'. For this reason, he continued, 'class struggle is practically coincident and simultaneous with the national struggle'. Accordingly, there was 'no very great point or virtue in emphasising the national aspect of the struggle as more fundamental'. Africans were rapidly becoming proletarians, and, as yet, the 'native agrarian masses as such have not yet shown serious signs of revolt'. The resolution urged communists to 'boost up' the ANC, though this was 'a moribund body'. Meanwhile, the party was enjoying successes in 'rapidly organising militant trade unions'. Workers and 'some peasants' were 'pouring into the party'. The slogan could only distract the party from this course while unnecessarily alienating white labour. At present, he concluded, they were against the creation of any 'special nationalistic slogan at all'.[113]

In line with this argument, five days later, the South Africans proposed an amendment to the slogan. They should mobilise for 'an independent workers and peasants republic', in which 'all toilers' would enjoy equal rights. A movement for a specifically Native republic 'risks race war', they explained, and in any case 'no native nation exists today, there are only various rival tribes'.[114] Their audience was unreceptive and in certain cases derisive. Referring to a comment by Rebecca Bunting on whether 'natives' had stronger claims to the land over 'aboriginal hottentots', Manuilsky of the Soviet Communist Party retorted that if white comrades were unwilling to fight for native rights, then 'Who knows? They too may well be driven into the sea', a comment that according to Harry Haywood, chair of the Negro subcommittee, 'brought the house down'.[115] At this point, then, the South Africans realised their efforts were futile, for it was now clear, in Roux's words, that the Comintern leadership would 'allow of no modification in the slogan'.[116]

Finally, congress at the beginning of September voted in favour of a resolution on 'the South African Question', jointly drafted by the group mandated by the Negro Commission on 11 August (though certainly without Sidney Bunting's active participation). The text supplied a more elaborate restatement of Comintern's original directive, 'final instructions for the South African Party', as it were.[117] This opened with a description of the South African economy's 'generally colonial character'. To be sure, there was no 'negro' bourgeoisie, not as a class – just a few traders and thin stratum of intellectuals. Even so, the leaders of the main 'negro' trade union, the ICU, having expelled the communists, were 'now endeavouring to guide the negro trade union movement into reformism'. All this background represented an 'exceptionally complicated but favourable position for the CPSA'. It should reorganise itself 'on shop and street nuclei basis' and orient its activities mainly towards 'native toilers'. It should acknowledge that the 'national question', based upon the agrarian question, 'lies at the foundation of the revolution in South Africa'. The Native republic slogan was correct, notwithstanding the party's 'stubborn opposition' to its adoption. As well as continuing its work in organising African workers into trade unions, and while not neglecting white workers, the party should 'pay particular attention to the embryonic national organisations, such as the ANC', participating in them and seeking to transform them into 'fighting' bodies. Moreover, the party 'should immediately work out an agrarian programme', elaborating 'concrete partial demands' and setting up peasants' organisations and trade unions for farm workers.[118]

On his way home, acknowledging that the 'slogan' was now 'law', Bunting used most of the time on his two-week sea journey back to Cape Town diligently writing his own rationalisation and defence of the Comintern line. The result of his efforts was a pamphlet, *Imperialism and South Africa*, in which he now conceded that black workers experienced 'an extra subjection', that of racial as well as class oppression; that whites of all classes 'had their heel on the neck of the blacks as a whole'. National liberation was therefore a distinct task, he admitted, though given the absence of a native bourgeoisie, it and class struggle 'tend to telescope or coincide'. Be that as it may, communists called for a 'South African Workers' and Peasants' Republic', which in effect meant 'a government very predominantly native in character' with rights for everybody and 'consequently all necessary protection for racial or national minorities'.[119] Bunting explained the meaning of the Native republic slogan in much the same way in a letter to *The Star*. Delegates at the congress, he suggested, 'intended ... to emphasise this Native character of South Africa of any reorganisation of South Africa on non-Imperialist lines and to discountenance any covert "White chauvinism" ... that might still lurk concealed'. But the Native republic would exclude no one, he insisted, and 'It is disproportionate to boggle overmuch over a phrase to the detriment of the overriding struggle for real independence'.[120] It was very much in this vein that the party's seventh congress approved the Native republic slogan in December 1928, in an elaborate formulation which foregrounded the final objective of a Soviet republic and surrounded the Native republic phraseology with a thicket of qualificatory language. The party now stood for 'self-determination of the African peoples', that is, their complete liberation from imperialist as well as bourgeois and feudal or semi-feudal rule and oppression, whether 'British' or 'South African'. The party would work for

wresting of power for a Workers' and Peasants' Soviet Republic wholly independent of the British or any other Empire, and comprising all the toiling masses, whether natives or otherwise ... under the leadership of the working class, with the slogan of 'An independent South African Native Republic as a stage towards the Workers and Peasants' Republic, guaranteeing protection and complete equality to all national minorities' (such as Europeans); leading to the reconstruction of the country and the rehabilitation of its people on a non-Imperialist Socialist basis.[121]

Self-determination would in effect mean the end of bourgeois rule; as Bunting informed Roux, 'this language about "stages" represented sociological rather than chronological sequences'. In truth, the notion of a 'stage' was simply 'verbiage', he believed.[122]

The congress had opened with a tea party and picnic in the Buntings' garden and was an event in which Sidney appeared still very much at the party's helm. In its detailing of the party's tasks, the programme supplied no indication of any really new activities though it was accepted that the party should follow Comintern's prescription for the reorganisation of the party on a 'shop or street nuclei basis' with the formation of 'factory groups'.[123] Even so, the vote in favour of the programme represented at best a precarious compromise between the 28 delegates, of whom only 10 were white.[124] Several white labourites actually voted against it. One of them, Wilfrid Harrison, maintained that the Native republic was generally opposed by Cape Town communists, but because 'a few negrophilists' in Johannesburg accepted it, 'we had to fall in'.[125] He and his comrades had written to the British party to complain about the slogan but heard back from a resigned Harry Pollitt, the British Communist Party's general secretary: 'Comintern has endorsed it and I can do nothing.'[126] Harrison had travelled to the meeting with Johnny Gomas as the other delegate, chosen, he thought, 'because Johannesburg wanted a native to represent Cape Town'. He sardonically recollected Bunting 'playing the Bohemian by inviting all the Bantu and their women for tea'.[127] For people like Harrison who believed that African culture and achievements 'haven't got much further than an assegai or reed hut', any talk of African leadership of the party was sentimental.[128] In fact, three Africans were elected onto the Central Executive Committee alongside six whites, the same proportion as in the previous year,[129] when the main African trade union organisers, Makabeni, Khaile and Thibedi, had joined the party leadership.[130] Some of the original African members of the party remained unhappy with the slogan as well. Before the congress both Douglas Wolton and James La Guma had maintained their correspondence with the Anglo-American Secretariat, remaining heavily critical of the Bunting line; Wolton claimed that Bunting was responsible for various unspecified 'hostile acts ... to stem the development of non-Europeans within the Party'.[131]

When two white South Africans who had arrived in Moscow for training,

Willie Kalk and Victor Danchin, met members of the Secretariat, they were told that Bunting clearly did not take the slogan seriously. Their riposte, that the majority of the party was against the slogan, and that black workers were quite ready to fight alongside whites, would only have served to confirm the Secretariat's suspicions.[132] Kalk and Danchin had been chosen by the South African party for Moscow studies to help make up the shortfall caused by their inability to find the full quota of ten African students – 'three years holiday at the workers expense', James La Guma observed in a letter he wrote to the Secretariat.[133] In mid-December 1928, the Secretariat cabled Johannesburg, with the immediate purpose of objecting to the South African party's recent efforts to improve relations with the ICU – it had in fact been asked to do this the previous year by Comintern. The party's relationship with the ICU in this period was ambivalent. Despite the expulsion of Communist Party members at the end of 1926, Kadalie maintained contact with individual communists. During La Guma's first visit to Moscow, in 1927, the Comintern, with Bukharin's approval had passed a resolution instructing the South African party to try to repair relations with the union, working inside it to persuade members to press for the annulment of the expulsions.[134] A later command was that the party should attempt to build opposition to Kadalie's leadership within the organisation, an injunction the communists seem to have ignored.[135]

The more important message of the cable was a recommendation for the postponement of the congress until the arrival in Johannesburg of Comintern's emissary, for there was evidently need for more clarity on the slogan.[136] The cable arrived too late for any change in plans, but it was certainly the case that even among the slogan's supporters there was disagreement about its meaning. Indeed, Molly Wolton enlivened the congress proceedings with the suggestion that the Native republic should follow the USSR model and be a federation of republics, for in South Africa 'we have various tribes with different languages, different traditions and customs'. Only one Native republic 'would not meet the situation'.[137] Her proposal elicited no support; for the time being, with Bunting invoking Comintern's doctrinal authority,[138] despite any remaining misgivings they may have retained, delegates ostensibly accepted the prospect of 'native rule', which would quickly 'merge into that of the Workers and Peasants Republic'.[139]

DESPITE ATTEMPTS TO INTERPRET 'native rule' in a way that might just be acceptable to the more old guard white trade unionists whom the party still kept within its fold, tactically from 1929 the party did alter course. This was most obvious in the communists' forays into the countryside. As we have seen, African organisers had already been busy recruiting farm workers during 1927 and 1928, but now building rural support was no longer merely a secondary concern. This was signalled when Sidney Bunting declared his candidature for the Transkeian African vote in the June 1929 parliamentary elections. At its congress, the party had in fact decided to contest two seats in which non-white votes were decisive: the Cape Flats, where Douglas Wolton would try to attract African and coloured support, and Thembuland in the Transkei, where out of an electorate of 3,487, 1,711 Africans were qualified to vote, mainly by owning land freehold.[140] The Buntings bought a second-hand baker's van in February and at the beginning of March began their electioneering, accompanied by Gana Makabeni, who would interpret Sidney's speeches into isiXhosa, using his licence as a translator fairly freely it seems. Makabeni was Transkeian-born and so could enter the territory freely.[141] This would not be a campaign carefully calibrated to meet the particular concerns of the small group of relatively educated and well-off Africans who were enfranchised: 'lawyers' clerks, teachers, recruiting clerks, etc', as Bunting dismissively characterised them.[142] Non-voters too, the Buntings enjoined, should turn up at the polling stations to underline the election's unfairness.

Bunting used his speeches to explain the local operations of a capitalist system that had turned territories like the Transkei into 'the principal labour recruiting and breeding annexer for the Chamber of Mines'.[143] In the text of the surviving copy of one of his speeches there is a cursory reference to 'the slogan of a South African native republic'. Above all else, he explained, this would mean votes for everybody, and redistribution and 'full restitution' of the land to the 'land workers and the peasants'.[144] As Wolton commented to the Buntings shortly after the campaign, 'you preached it [the slogan], but don't believe in it'.[145] In an address outside the Umtata Show Grounds, Bunting took as his text Jesus' injunction in the Temple, that 'It is written, my house shall be a house of prayer, but ye have made it a den of thieves'. So too in South Africa, in a setting in which seven-eighths of the land was owned by the white minority, 'Plunder is the order of the day'. Meanwhile, Rebecca Bunting reminded her listeners at the same meeting that Mr Payne, Bunting's main opponent, had said, 'it would be a sad day for South Africa when native women stop working the land'. However, she noted, 'Mr Payne does not suggest that his party if it gets into power will be giving land to women to work on.'[146] The Buntings and Gana Makabeni were arrested twice, and on both occasions were charged with trying to foment racial hostility. After they were convicted and fined the first time, several hearings would interrupt their subsequent campaigning before the second case collapsed. For historians, the transcripts of various witness statements supply a rich if not always reliable record of the campaign. It seems a bit unlikely that Gana Makabeni would have used his interpreter's discretion to suggest that 'Europeans would take the trousers off the Natives and take his balls as well'.[147] It is quite probable, though, that Bunting did refer disdainfully to those 'Natives' who thought they 'are quite content as they are', as 'mere flunkeys, blacking the masters boots and aping his talks'. 'Their minds have been dulled', he observed, 'enslaved in the mission schools'.[148] This was hardly the sort of language calculated to appeal to the mission school graduates likely to predominate on the voters' roll, but for Bunting these were not his target: as he explained to Roux, 'most of the voters are "good boys"'.[149] Even so, the Buntings took care to meet those chiefs who would receive them, for, as Rebecca remembered thirty years later, 'the attitude of the chiefs was quite good at that time'.[150]

As might be expected, Bunting's progress through Thembuland provoked alarmed commentary in the Bhunga, the advisory assembly in Umtata. As Councillor Mda warned, Bunting was 'preaching to my people what is called Communism. They are told in Xosa that they shall be equal. Has that ever existed? Right away from the time when God created man and woman he made them not equal.'[151] That Bunting was able to poll 2,890 votes, 12 per cent of the total so he could retain his deposit, was quite impressive, and rather better than Douglas Wolton's tally of 930 on the Cape Flats.[152] Photographs of the open-air meetings in Thembuland suggest well-attended events, with most of the (exclusively male) audiences wearing shabby clothes and sitting on the ground – hardly the kind of people who might have attended mission school or acquired freehold land, the necessary qualifications for voting, and certainly not lawyers' clerks or teachers. 'Our speeches became the talk of the whole district,' Bunting claimed,[153] and he may well have been right. Even seven decades later, Bunting's biographer Allison Drew could find local informants with accurate memories of what Bunting had said. Bunting's share of the vote was probably affected by the heavy police presence at every meeting he held as well as the restrictions that accompanied the two trials. Without such threatening attention from the authorities, his poll might well have been larger, as he himself argued after the campaign.

Following the Thembuland campaign, the party continued its efforts to mobilise a rural following through its launch on 25 August of a League of African Rights. As Eddie Roux explained to the Comintern executive later, the intention of the League was that it should serve 'as an auxiliary organisation to spread the influence of the Communist Party among the Native peasantry and toilers in the small towns and country districts'. Direct enrolment in the party for 'these politically immature elements' was impractical, he suggested, but even so these people showed 'considerable enthusiasm for the national cause and are anxious to join an organisation'.[154] The communists persuaded JT Gumede to take the presidency of the League and certain other more adventurous ANC officials to join the League's leadership. Gumede accepted this role 'in his individual capacity', for the ANC conservatives were increasingly hostile to 'the menace of Communistic propaganda', to quote one of them speaking at the Non-European Christian Ministers' Association.[155] The League was inspired apparently, Roux recalled later, by advice Roux and the Buntings had received in Moscow; they were told that trained communist revolutionaries should reach a popular constituency through a 'mass organisation' – advice in line with Petrovsky's view that the party should not attempt to recruit directly into its ranks 'the masses of proletarianized Negroes'. Bunting had experimentally set up an initial branch of the League in Manzana, near Engcobo, during his Transkeian campaigning. The idea was that the organisation should be 'designedly innocuous', its 'prime objectives' being the extension of the Cape franchise to the other provinces and free education. At its formal launch, the League announced its intention to collect a million signatures for a petition which would also call for an end to the pass laws. It adopted as its slogan 'Mayibuye iAfrika' (May Africa come back).[156]

According to Roux, the League's co-secretary, the new organisation 'was a big success' from its inception, and it was able to capitalise especially on rural disaffection in Natal, drawing in previous supporters of the ICU, 'which was breaking up'. Here, particularly, 'there were thousands who were still politically-minded and looking for just such an organisation'.[157] The petition forms seemed to be attracting a ready response, he claimed. The petition was 'couched in the form of a demand', Roux explained to the Comintern,[158] and indeed the language used in the League's publicity was assertive rather than supplicatory.[159] However, its calls for an extension of the restricted Cape franchise did fall rather short of the universal suffrage that might be expected in a fully democratic 'Native republic'.[160]

Whether the League always succeeded in finding the receptive following Roux claimed for it is questionable. Gana Makabeni had been appointed its rural organiser, and his letters to Bunting from Mpondoland indicate that, though initial meetings he held were well attended, it was difficult to form branches or get people to commit 'to be active or to sign first' the petition. Interestingly, he also discovered that what the people he encountered really wanted was 'to join Bunting's party as they call it'.[161] The most 'attentive' people at meetings, Makabeni found, were 'illiterates', and on the whole 'intellectuals' were much less willing to support the petition.[162] Mia Roth cites police reports from Pietermaritzburg to the effect that only 80 people had signed the petition by the end of October; the local branch of the League put up a poster that denounced as cowards people who had refused to sign.[163] Police reports for two meetings convened for Sidney Bunting's visit to Kimberley supply details of modest crowds, 100 or so at first and then doubling by the end. At both meetings, when members of the audience asked questions, they began by expressing concerns about Bunting's motivation; who was sending him and paying his expenses, and so forth. However, when one 'resident' declared that 'Mr Bunting was a snake in the grass and that he was leading the natives astray', there was an 'uproar', which would have led to 'bloodshed' had not the police been present. Quite a number remained behind to sign the petition.[164]

The Comintern's emissary, Paul Merker, or, to use his real name, Boris Idelson, was present from between April and July to witness the League's progress. On 25 September he wrote a generally critical report on the South African party for the Comintern executive. The report made no explicit reference to the League. With respect to the party's activities in rural districts, Merker was dismissive; the work 'has practically not begun', he observed. He did concede that Bunting's electoral campaigning had elicited 'great enthusiasm'. However, though in certain vicinities thousands had joined the party, the leadership had failed to 'organise them on the basis of political and economic demands'. Instead, Merker complained, in what might have been an oblique reference to the League, the party had 'confined itself to general agitation'.[165] He was also critical of the party's general organisational state. Its executive meet too infrequently and there was insufficient division of labour within its bureaucracy. White membership was shrinking, and with respect to the 'Negro comrades ... we still have a process of becoming'. Often they were capable enough but 'the situation is not such as would favour their development'. In addition, the party was in dire straits financially; indeed, Merker had 'never come across a party as poor as that in South Africa'. But the most serious shortcoming was 'the failure to understand our position on the national question'. Education was needed, not just with respect to black comrades. Tellingly, the library holdings in the party's head office contained 'nothing of Lenin'.[166]

In addition to Merker's censures, by mid-October Comintern's executive had learned about the League. Aitken Ferguson of the British party had already written to Moscow about the League, an undertaking that he characterised as 'anti-Bolshevik' and reflective of 'the essentially liberal nature' of the South African communists' outlook.[167] The Comintern executive dispatched a telegram to Johannesburg, scolding the party for its use of 'auxiliary organisations' and instructing the South Africans that the 'struggle ... must be waged not through petitions, but in a revolutionary manner'. Instead the party should organise mass demonstrations under a set of militant slogans. A later communication from the Comintern executive included a more explicit condemnation of the League. This was an example of the party abandoning its independent role. The League 'bears the character of a political party with a reformist programme', a programme that would 'eclipse' the party's own aims. Indeed, the League's programme 'shows the extent to which the Party was lagging behind the Native movement'. The evidence for native 'revolutionary determination' was abundant: this was no time for a 'mild reformist programme, well within the framework of South African legality', the Comintern executive maintained.[168] This commentary followed an initial response by Roux to the Comintern telegram in which he explained that in their context the League's demands were not reformist and that signing a petition was an act 'demanding a certain amount of courage'. Indeed, the League's organisers experienced 'great difficulty' in persuading people that they would not be prosecuted if they signed. And in any case, in forming the League, the party believed it was following the Comintern line, as well as advice and suggestions from Comrade Merker. Meanwhile, the party was worried by the possibility it might be made illegal; the formation of the League as a front organisation seemed a sensible precaution.[169] At roughly the same time, the party began to develop a relationship with Lekhotla la Bafo, the Basotho Council of Commoners, an anti-colonial movement based at Mapoteng, Lesotho, the birthplace of its founder, Josiel Lefela, who had been annoying British officials with a series of 'impudent letters' since Lekhotla's formation in 1919.[170] From 1928 Lefela became a regular contributor to the Sesotho columns of the *South African Worker*.[171] William Thibedi was the first contact between the party and Lefela, who had worked in South Africa as a mine worker. Lefela met Kadalie in 1926 and visited the party offices shortly afterwards.[172] The association between the party and Lekhotla remained informal through most of the 1930s, maintained mainly by Lefela's friend, Edwin Mofutsanyana, and was ignored by Comintern.[173]

Was the Comintern justified in believing that in the prevailing circumstances in the second half of 1929 the League of African Rights was much too cautious a venture, a 'right opportunist mistake', and that the party should have put itself at the head of 'an agrarian revolution' and a militant struggle for national liberation, as it was arguing in December?[174] And was it more generally correct that the South African communists were failing to respond adequately to local conditions? Comintern's letter referred to strikes ('which rapidly assume a political character') in Durban as well as riots, boycotts and refusals to pay tax, all symptoms of an insurrectionary climate which its leaders maintained the South African communists should exploit more systematically. These were references to actual events. For example, a major confrontation between Africans, the police and white civilians on 17 June 1929 in Durban followed an unruly demonstration outside the municipal beer hall during the course of a boycott. Major police raids in November also in Durban sought to intimidate tax defaulters with a major show of force. A Communist Party branch was first established in Durban when party members working within the ICU were trying to build support among dock workers. The branch was reportedly defunct by 1926 and stopped existing in 1927.[175]

The party then revived its presence in Durban in 1928, recruiting among ICU yase Natal members or ex-members, and concentrating its activities in Mobeni township where the municipality had raised rents. And not just in Durban. One of its new ex-ICU recruits was one of the union's organisers of labour tenants around Pietermaritzburg, the former schoolteacher Gilbert Coka, who had attended Bunting's night school classes in Johannesburg and who was, according to the party's main organiser in Pietermaritzburg, the storekeeper and former ICU member Laurie Greene, a 'born orator'.[176] But the party's local support was more conspicuous in Durban. Here for a period it benefited from an uneasy alliance with the ICU yase Natal leadership. According to William Ballinger, the communists were initially so successful in their 'agitation' that George Champion, the ICU yase Natal's leader, 'threw in his lot with the CP', claiming that in making such an alliance he would prevent 'their propaganda from going too far'. The ICU yase Natal was in the ascendant during the beer hall boycott, but the careful balance that Champion tried to maintain in his relationship with his new allies was captured in the public marches his followers staged – red-uniformed ICU militiamen, a brass band, and flags at the front of the procession, the Union Jack and the Soviet banner.[177]

This conflict between the authorities and African residents in Durban reflected an increasingly repressive political climate nationally at the end of the 1920s. The onset of the global depression in 1929 would halt the growth in manufacturing that had drawn black workers into factories during the

1920s, and in general industrial output and employment would fall until 1933. In 1929 the National Party won an electoral majority; it maintained its pact with Labour, but within the coalition it was more powerful and could dictate terms on policies affecting Africans, though white workers too would be severely affected by unemployment. There were to be new taxes on urban residents, including African women for the first time, and the extension of pass requirements through the 1930 amendments to the Urban Areas Act. In 1932, the Native Service Contract Act tightened controls on rural Africans and restricted their movement to towns. The imposition of lodgers' fees in Potchefstroom in 1928 and in Vereeniging in 1930 was an early portent of what was going to become a more general effort to expand African taxation receipts. As we have seen, these localised developments helped the Communist Party acquire substantial, if loosely organised, followings in these centres.

That there was a potential mass following for a more revolutionary movement – Comintern's view at the end of 1929 – was an assumption that would be tested shortly. But the actions it was prescribing by the end of 1929 were different from the original directives that accompanied the resolution as they were phrased the previous year. In 1928, the CPSA had been instructed to work with nationalist organisations – specifically the ANC – and seek to transform them into fighting revolutionary bodies. Arguably, this was what the CPSA had been attempting to achieve through setting up the League, which did after all include ANC personalities in its leadership, and in any case in the Western Cape it had indeed been engaged in building a militant following for the local ANC.

Now the communists were being told to dispense with any 'auxiliary' formations and put themselves at the helm of a militant struggle for national liberation. This shift was not really prompted by any change in local conditions or any fresh opportunities; indeed, any commentary on these is completely absent from Merker's report. Rather, it was a consequence of a new strategic line that began to shape Comintern policy from the beginning of 1929.[178] Essentially the new line was a move leftwards, precipitated partly by the attack by the Kuomintang on its former Communist Party ally in China in April 1927 as well as a deepening rift between the party and social democratic groups ('social fascists') across Europe. There was also the more general belief that capitalism was entering a 'third phase' of acute contradictions, a central issue in the emerging rift between Bukharin and Stalin.[179] Bukharin's Comintern policies were under fierce attack from Comintern's sixth congress; in effect, for communists any kinds of organisational alliances were now expressions of 'right deviationism', especially those with social democrats, 'the moderate wing of fascism'.[180] For these reasons, alliances with leaders of nationalist or any reformist groups were now anachronistic, acceptable only in the form of 'united fronts from below', as the British party informed the South Africans on 10 December[181] – that is, efforts to enlist the support of the mass following of nationalist groups while refraining from any cooperation with their leaders.[182] As the South African communists would learn later, Comintern's view at this point was that 'united front tactics' that 'consisted of appeals to the reformist leaders to take part in the common struggle' would cause the party 'to lose its individuality'.[183] But given the doctrinal fluidity in Moscow, local efforts to interpret the Native republic slogan's practical implications were unlikely to engender Comintern approval. Indeed, as one reading of the Comintern archival record by Russian historians suggests, South African leadership would almost certainly have been found at fault whatever course of action they might have chosen. This was a period in which 'the centre' in Moscow was 'tightening its grip' over affiliated communist parties, and one goal of the general line 'was getting rid of the old generation of communists in foreign communist parties', especially those who, like Sidney Bunting, believed they could exercise their own strategic judgement, picking and choosing those Comintern prescriptions that appeared relevant and rejecting others.[184]

Bunting, who would continue to lead the party as its chairman and treasurer during 1929, remained determined to exercise his own discretion. He disregarded the Comintern's order to dissociate the party from the League and continued to sanction joint activity with the League through the rest of 1929 and into the early months of 1930.[185] In this he had the support of Albert Nzula, one of the African communists who had joined the executive after Bunting's return from Moscow. Nzula wrote with some asperity to members of Comintern's executive on 11 December 1929, complaining about their 'vilification of us'. 'We know the forces we are up against,' Nzula added, 'and we do not only do our best but better than, if we may say so, you can teach us when it comes to local details.'[186] As Nzula also reminded Comintern, on 10 November a joint meeting in Johannesburg burned an effigy of Oswald Pirow, the Minister of Justice, who had just succeeded in enacting an amendment to the Riotous Assemblies Act. The burning had 'shocked even Pirow's opponents', Nzula reported. The amendment enabled the minister to banish any individual who he believed might be fostering hostility between 'Natives and Europeans'; communists believed, correctly, the new law would be used against them.

On 16 December 1929, Dingaan's Day, the Communist Party together with League and ANC leaders and sections of the ICU sponsored anti-pass demonstrations and meetings in a number of towns. Between 4,000 and 10,000 people joined a procession in Johannesburg, the biggest public protest in the city for some time.[187] One person died after a white bystander fired a gun into a crowd assembled in Potchefstroom to listen to speeches by Edwin Mofutsanyana and JB Marks. Encouraged by the scale of this mobilisation, the party called for a general strike and pass burning on 1 May, for which it printed tens of thousands of leaflets, but they evoked only patchy participation. The League itself was weakened when Gumede lost the ANC presidency in April and his conservative successor disavowed any continuing joint activities with communists. In any case, in an increasingly precarious economic climate with rising unemployment, African workers were unwilling to join any political strikes. The nascent African trade union movement that communists had been building since 1926 was in no state to initiate such activity, even if workers had been receptive. One of its key organisers, William Thibedi, had been removed from the FNTU leadership at the end of 1929 and suspended from the party after allegations of venality, allegations which Bunting believed were probably unfair, and probably motivated by his opposition to the Native republic slogan.[188] He was reinstated later in 1930 in response to calls from rank-and-file membership.[189] His replacement was to be Albert Nzula. Nzula already held a leadership post, and had been elected as the party's assistant general secretary at the end of 1929.

One of the new 'intellectuals' who had been joining the party recently, Albert Nzula was recruited by Douglas Wolton in Evaton in 1927 while he was then teaching at the Wilberforce Institute. Nzula had no real experience in organising unions, though he worked briefly at the ICU office as a clerk. Wolton viewed Nzula as the party's 'most promising recruit',[190] later writing of his 'brilliant knowledge of socialism and in particular the national question'.[191] Roux was more reserved, describing him as 'brilliant and unreliable'.[192] He was certainly self-confident, insisting that he should be allowed to address what were mainly white-attended public meetings held by the party outside the Johannesburg City Hall.[193] Assigned the role of becoming a trade unionist and lacking any real qualifications in this capacity, he was amenable to Wolton's preference for emphasising unionism's political functions rather than workaday issues of wages and conditions.[194]

The Federation could claim no successful strikes during 1929 and there were no reports of its expansion outside Johannesburg – probably a reflection of economic circumstances. Indeed, Merker had noted in his report in September 1929 that within the 'Federation of Non-European Workers there was complete disorganisation', although, in the face of all evidence to the contrary, he insisted 'the outlook is very good'.[195] Roux also commented in his letter to Comintern in October upon the Federation's weakening because of internal divisions and its inability to build organisation in 'the big industries'.[196] He was evidently unimpressed by an appeal in the party newspaper *Umsebenzi* on 29 August to African mine workers to form one great mine workers' union.[197] The South African mine workers' historian VL Allen has interpreted this exhortation as an indication that some progress had already been made, though the initial work had been done by Thibedi, at that stage at odds with the Federation's leadership.[198] But even if its embrace was beginning to include African mine workers, communist-led African organised labour was hardly in a state of development in which it could address the new directives it received in April 1929 from the Red International, Comintern's labour affiliate. South African unionists should 'strive to transform the economic struggles into political struggles and strike out for self determination', for the unions 'must be a leading part of the struggle to create a negro republic in SA', they were told.[199]

OUTSIDE JOHANNESBURG, PROSPECTS for such transformations may have seemed a bit brighter during 1930. Eddie Roux, having returned from Cambridge, based himself in Cape Town, where for a short time until his dismissal for political activities he worked for the government's agricultural department. He persuaded Bunting to allow him to edit a weekly isiXhosa version of *Umsebenzi*. Bunting paid for the press from his own savings. He had been funding the CPSA from his personal bank account for some time,[200] though the party was now receiving fresh funding from Comintern – £12,000 that year, according to Albert Nzula.[201] According to Roux, the press was a useful investment; the new paper had a circulation of 5,000 and reached many readers in the smaller rural centres, not just in the Western Cape. In a letter to the party's leadership in November 1930, Roux supplied a list of the paper's agents in 'new areas', selling several dozens of copies in fresh centres for the party, including Oudtshoorn and Port St Johns. These places, he suggested, should be the locations for 'the building up of branches'. Despite the difficulty of translating Marxian doctrinal phraseology into isiXhosa, Roux had done his best, he explained, 'to keep the policy of the paper as near to that of Comintern as possible'.[202] He and his more knowledgeable local helpers settled on the isiXhosa word *ungxowankulu* for 'capitalist' (literally 'the man with a big bag'), rejecting as anti-Semitic the more normal rendering of *majuda*, a term that reflected Xhosa encounters with local Jewish storekeepers.[203] A visiting official from the Red International, who met only Roux and Gomas and one other trade unionist during his stay in Cape Town, insisted that Roux should find space for his own ponderous take on the new party line; the article, 'stiff with jargon', Roux thought, was completely unintelligible and probably for this reason did no harm.[204] These efforts attracted friendly interest from Russian linguistic academicians though Comintern officials were apparently less enamoured: in particular Roux's preference for the League's 'Mayibuye iAfrika' slogan over any references to the Native republic invited their disapproval.[205]

In the smaller towns in the Western Cape, party activists during 1930 found ready adherents to their calls for strikes and meetings, animated by the Native republic slogan but also prompted by very particular local conditions that supplied a receptive setting. In the Western Cape, communists had been adhering to the course prescribed by the Comintern in 1928 rather closely, if not intentionally. Johnny Gomas, Elliot Tonjeni and Bransby Ndobe, coloured and African communists expelled from the ICU, had joined the provincial ANC and set up a string of rural branches in the Boland. Arguably, in the Western and Eastern Cape, the ANC was more susceptible to radical direction than elsewhere, largely because here the African elite focused its political attention on the franchise rather than relying on the ANC 'for its organised political life'.[206] Communist entry into rural activism in this region coincided with a local agricultural setback when employers attempted to cut wages in response to lower world prices. Communist-led ANC branches included a group in Worcester with 800 members, mainly coloured farm workers.[207] Here was quite a good example of party activists attempting to organise agricultural labourers systematically around their specific concerns, a task that Merker's report suggested the party had neglected.[208] Around Worcester during 1929 a drought had helped cause a decline in already bad living conditions; wages were down as farmers began to import African contract labour into the area; and these circumstances induced increasing numbers of coloured farm workers to try to find jobs within Worcester itself, on the railways and with the municipality. As a consequence, during 1929 and 1930 there were rising numbers of unemployed living in the town's location, itself increasingly overcrowded because the council refused to sanction any house building.[209] Liquor raids by the police to check the illicit brewing that for many families was an increasingly important source of income were another source of local grievance. As noted above, Elliot Tonjeni and Bransby Ndobe, both communists, had already set up ANC branches among farm workers during 1928, helped by Johnny Gomas. Tonjeni led a mass demonstration through

Worcester on May Day. Five days later a second demonstration ended in riots and shootings, resulting in five deaths. Subsequently the provincial ANC disowned the movement and expelled the communists. Tonjeni and Ndobe then established their own 'Independent ANC', adopting as their programme the three demands popularised by the League of African Rights: land, free education and the vote.[210] After a series of strikes, the two were banished at the end of 1932, Tonjeni to the Eastern Cape under the Riotous Assemblies Act and Ndobe to Basutoland. After their departure and a prohibition on Sunday meetings the movement subsided. In exiling Tonjeni, the authorities succeeding only in displacing his political activism, not ending it, at least not for a while. Moses Kotane, writing as late as April 1934, found around Cradock and Tarkastad two groups of Tonjeni's followers affiliated to the Independent ANC – the sort of people, he thought, who should be in the party.[211]

During 1930, communists also succeeded in building a new following in Durban, where they had set up their first township branch two years previously. In Natal generally, recent taxation rate increases for Africans were especially high and in Durban, as noted above, armed police were used to conduct tax raids in November. In that month 8,000 people were searched for proof of payment receipts in the labour compounds near the docks. Rather unexpectedly, the Communist Party had won a City Council seat in February 1929 in a municipal by-election, with the election of Sophus Pettersen, one of the CPSA's founders and a key funder of the party; he was also someone who could organise travel to meetings in Europe for party delegates willing to work as stokers or seamen.[212] In fact, Pettersen's standing as an independent workers' candidate was unopposed on election day because his opponent in Durban Point's ward four was disqualified on a technicality. Within the ward, Pettersen owned several businesses, and in his campaign he had won white trade unionist nominations as well as promises of support from Indian ratepayers, who formed a significant proportion of the voters in the ward. He lost the seat shortly afterwards when the council decided that as one of their key contractors, he was ineligible.[213] Among his other properties, Pettersen owned an office building in which for a while he provided the party with free premises.[214] Pettersen had easy access to the docks and was a familiar figure in the compounds, where he addressed workers' meetings.

Roux suggested that it was in Durban in 1930 that *Umsebenzi* sales were most buoyant, and it is likely that this was a reflection of local sentiment after the taxation raids.[215] During that year, the Communist Party was able to offer inspirational leadership to an African working-class constituency that had become disillusioned with the ICU yase Natal. An alliance between the union

and the Zulu royal house had proved to be unpopular and had failed to shield
unemployed men from eviction from the city for having no visible means of
subsistence – a new power under the 1930 amendment to the Urban Areas
Act which the local municipality started using. The recent engagement of
local ICU leadership in the newly established Advisory Boards also helped to
detach them from the concerns of the 'labouring poor'.[216] A freshly invigorated
local Communist Party was able to enlist in its ranks a significant number of
lower-level ICU officials, and thousands of the union's rank and file would
join the party's informal following: this was much larger than the hundred
or so Durbanites who had formally joined the party. A decision by the party
to end the year with a militant protest against the pass laws involving mass
pass burnings on Dingaan's Day, 16 December, failed to garner much support
in the party's more established bases – only 150 passes were burned at the
Johannesburg meeting although Potchefstroom registered a more impressive
300.[217] In any case, local responses to the pass-burning call did not always
signify a locally established party presence. A first-hand account of pass
burnings in Pretoria suggests that they were instigated by four groups, the
ANC, the ICU, the 'Radicals' and the 'Garveyites'.[218] In Durban's Cartwright
Flats, the customary venue for ICU gatherings, the communist-led turnout
for the event was exceptional. In the words of a police report, 'a huge crowd,
many of them ICU adherents', running into thousands of protesters, handed
in their passes to party organisers together with tax receipts, collected in
bags, ready for burning in a bonfire.[219] As Sifiso Ndlovu has pointed out, the
speeches delivered at the meeting, as recorded by the police, effectively rooted
the idea of the black republic in local Zulu nationalist iconography as well as
in all-too-recent memories of land dispossession:

> I am native. I am standing in the country of my birth. This country of ours
> has been stolen. These people have stolen our country and are ruling it.
>
> Dingaan was a Communist, and he will be there on the Day of Dingaan
> … This is the day when we will not forget those who will put them [whites]
> in hell.
>
> … either you – the black man of this country – are going to have a
> Black Republic of Africa, or that you are going to be exterminated.[220]

The police broke up the meeting before the burnings could begin, and during
the confrontation three people were killed. Johannes Nkosi, the party's
main organiser in Durban, a former cook and farmhand, died subsequently
in hospital with a fractured skull, most probably from wounds inflicted by

policemen after they pulled him off the lorry from which he was addressing the crowd.[221] In the aftermath of the Durban protest, 200 of 'the most active communists' were deported. For example, in February 1931 the leader of Durban Clairwood branch, Abraham Nduweni, was banished to Standerton for two years under the Riotous Assemblies Act. His branch had been formed in November 1930 when Nduweni led his ICU branch into the Communist Party.[222] A secret underground local party leadership did function for a while, though its leadership included at least one police agent.[223]

In both Durban and the Western Cape, there was thus plenty of evidence of communist willingness to engage in assertive actions, well outside 'the framework of South African legality'. Even so, the Comintern's assessment of the party's performance remained disparaging. For example, on 25 April 1930, the Comintern's Praesidium informed the CPSA leaders that they were still 'committing serious mistakes of a Right opportunist character' and had yet to carry out activity linked to the 1928 resolution, especially with respect to 'the return of the land'.[224] A later directive instructed them more precisely on this issue. On white farms the party should form trade unions from white sharecroppers and labour tenants, and in the Transkei it should accord a leading role to landless peasants, forming special organisations for them – arguably just what Gana Makabeni had been attempting to achieve in Mpondoland.[225] A letter in September 1930 complained that an earlier set of instructions dispatched in May (and in fact not received in Johannesburg) spelling out 'Immediate Tasks' had not 'been seriously considered'. Meanwhile, the party's 'contact with the masses' was 'limited to chance meetings'. There was a refusal 'to select and train negro cadres', a comment on the party's reluctance to dispatch the full quota of ten African students.[226] An earlier draft of this letter was even more severe. Recruiting was haphazard and mainly took the form of 'taking down names at meetings in masses'. 'It is a communist Party only in name', because of the 'lack of Bolshevik leadership'.[227]

Not all the criticism of the party's leadership was directed from Moscow. The party's African membership had been changing since 1927 and a larger group of relatively well-educated men were joining the party, several of them ex-teachers, a social group about whom Bunting had expressed general reservations in the past. Their entry into the party postdated the earlier disagreements between Bunting and white working-class leaders about the importance of building African membership, and so they were much less inclined than the early African communists to acknowledge Bunting's moral authority. Albert Nzula, JB Marks and Edwin Mofutsanyana can be viewed as part of this group, though Mofutsanyana, who had qualified as a teacher, had actually worked as a mine clerk, joining the party after a friend and a colleague – Jacob Majoro – was charged following a skirmish at a railway station. He was also inspired to become a communist after watching William Thibedi interpret a speech by Jimmy Shields to a crowd in Vereeniging. JB Marks's father was a coloured railway worker in Ventersdorp, a 'staunch member of the ANC'; his mother was a Mosotho.[228] He had been recruited into the party while teaching in Potchefstroom after meeting Molly Wolton on a visit. He already belonged to the ICU but had not been very active.[229] Despite Bunting's record of early efforts to build a following among black workers, new African members were irritated by what they took to be condescension in his manner and were willing to interpret his resistance to change as paternalistic, even racist.[230] As one of the newer recruits, Moses Kotane, observed, 'my little intellect always brings me to the conclusion that Bunting was in the Party for creating a title for himself'.[231] Not in fact an 'intellectual', at least in the sense of the way the party used the term to describe people's social background, Kotane had been recruited in 1929 by Nzula. Self-taught, not formally educated, he was already by the time his white comrades got to know him an 'insatiable reader' and would demonstrate an aptitude for doctrinal engagement ,'our cleverest African theoretician'.[232] His initial encounter with Bunting was unfriendly, apparently, and it seems to have left a lasting impression. As he wrote later in an autobiographical statement completed during his Comintern-sponsored training in Moscow: 'the Bunting group ... did not want any Negro in the leadership, they were either considered spies or place seekers'.[233]

Meanwhile, Sidney Bunting's relationship with Albert Nzula, never warm, deteriorated, partly as a consequence of his disapproval of Nzula's drinking. Nzula was probably an alcoholic but Bunting's reaction was accentuated by his own puritanical standards when it came to personal behaviour, and these shaped his relationships with several of his African comrades.[234] Later, Bunting's antipathy to Nzula would be used against him as evidence of his supposed favouring of the 'removal of native functionaries from the leadership'.[235]

Complaints about Bunting helped to feed Comintern's antipathy, especially after the Woltons arrived in Moscow in July as members of a British delegation to the Red International's conference; they had left South Africa one year before, shortly after Douglas Wolton's electoral campaign on the Cape Flats. A report from Solly Sachs would have supplied further grounds for Comintern chastisement. Sachs was writing on 8 October 1930 after a four-month absence from South Africa while attending labour meetings in Hamburg and Moscow. He returned to Johannesburg, he wrote, to find the party 'in a worse state'. No serious work was being undertaken by its leadership because 'all the time is taken up by faction fights'. At executive meetings, 'Nzula, the most able and loyal member of the party was drunk', but he had been 'driven to drink by party leadership'. His own defence of 'the correctness of the [Comintern] line … was received with sneers'. Nor could he persuade the party 'to elicit … interest in the plight of the Railwaymen'.[236] In that month rumours about the extent of hostility to Bunting within the party leadership reached Cape Town. On behalf of the Cape Town branch, Johnny Gomas wrote to Johannesburg to express his comrades' support for Bunting.[237]

The extent of Bunting's backing within the wider reaches of the party was insufficient to bolster his position at the congress held in December 1930. Shortly before its convening, Douglas Wolton had returned from Moscow, equipped with fresh authority as the bearer of a set of Comintern orders which he may have helped to draft.[238] He had been working in various parts of Comintern's bureaucracy for the previous six months. These orders were in the form of a letter on 'How to Build a Revolutionary Mass Party', subsequently reprinted in *Umsebenzi*.[239] At the conference, Wolton very much presented himself as Comintern's delegate.[240] After a review of the various 'right opportunist errors' that the party had persisted in making, the Comintern edict called for the reorganisation on its 1924 model, that is, 'Bolshevisation', with the placement of active members in workplace groups; and as for the 'revolutionary trade unions incorporating political demands', they should be the party's first organisational priority.[241] The leadership would be chosen *en bloc*, and Wolton himself selected a slate that excluded the Buntings. Aside from himself, three other whites would join the new Central Committee; they included Solly Sachs, Eddie Roux and Lazar Bach, a recent recruit to the party, very much a Wolton protégé, and a recent immigrant from Latvia. Bach's communist experience predated his arrival in South Africa in 1929[242] and, according to Roux, he had an 'amazing knowledge of Comintern doctrine and a Talmudic delight in its intellectual subtleties'.[243] Commitment to African party leadership was signalled with the addition to the committee of 23 Africans. For several of the new leaders, the conference offered an opportunity for doctrinal recantation. Albert Nzula, for example, admitted that he 'was one of those who was in favour of the League of African Rights, but that was due to a total misunderstanding of the party line … while we were still yapping about a petition, the masses of Worcester prepared actually to carry out a militant revolutionary struggle'. Eddie Roux was also fairly contrite, recalling that he and the Buntings had in Moscow been demonstrably 'almost completely ignorant of the fundamental principles of Communist propaganda', though he remained critical of their hosts for the uncomradely way they were treated. The formation of the League was a mistake, he conceded, and 'Comrade Bunting is not a Leninist, definitely not'. Subsequently, he himself had 'made a lot of serious mistakes' in his editing of the newspaper. On a more upbeat note, Douglas Wolton reminded the delegates that with struggle between imperialists becoming fiercer, and an 'unparalleled wave of depression' then prevailing, they could look forward to 'a rise and deepening revolutionary struggle of the masses'. Organisational form must now be given to the 'considerable advance in political understanding of the new Party line' they had achieved. They should avoid, however, the 'Left wing tendency to make a heroic gesture without any organisational preparation', as had happened recently in Durban, he suggested.[244] Sidney and Rebecca Bunting attended the conference, and Sidney was in no mood for contrition: 'Faith in the native masses does not mean that every black, any more than every white, is a genius or paragon.' He would not regret being relieved from executive responsibilities, for 'he could not work with Comrade Wolton and some of the party wreckers'. Rebecca also spoke out. They had followed the Comintern line loyally, departing from it only when the challenges were too great. 'How can we speak of nuclei in the factories ... The Executive [had] tried its best to get into the [mining] compounds.'[245]

Work on 'Bolshevisation' of the party's structure began straight away with a re-registration of the party's Johannesburg membership with the intention of weeding out non-activists and the placement of the remaining adherents into groups, mainly based in clothing and furniture factories – the groups were going to be, in fact, very small. There was another group for people who could not be assigned to work groups who lived in African locations, and there were provisional (and probably only aspirational) concentrations to accommodate gold miners.[246] All these clusters were meant to report every week to the district committee and maintain 'iron discipline' in collecting dues and selling the party paper – for which editorial work and printing were shifted back to Johannesburg, where Wolton could ensure propriety in its content. Eddie Roux continued to edit the paper, helped in this role by Molly Wolton, and Moses Kotane was offered full-time employment as its compositor. As a consequence of this closer supervision, 'Imprecor' language[247] and features derived from Moscow began to replace the articles that had built an African readership previously under Roux, and circulation halved that year.[248] As Kotane once put it, the Woltons 'spoke a language none of us understood'.[249]

An activist programme of demonstrations followed Comintern's schedule of 'international days' around particular themes of the groups, beginning with demonstrations on 9 March, the 'International Day of Struggle against Unemployment'.[250] Johnny Gomas's and Eddie Roux's contribution to this particular event was to throw leaflets from the public gallery into the chamber at the House of Assembly. Roux then travelled to Durban where he started a night school and sold copies of *Umsebenzi* at ICU meetings at Cartwright Flats.[251] He was jailed briefly after disobeying a magisterial order to leave Durban. Outside the established centres, the party's efforts to mobilise rural people were modelled on very recent Soviet Union experience. For instance, Gana Makabeni was told, with respect to his work in the Transkei, that the party's programme should distinguish 'between rich, middle and poor native farmers', distinctions that the party's African organisers found very hard to recognise on the ground.[252]

Among the growing population of unemployed urban workers, the party could claim some success in extending its influence. Roux recollects that from the beginning of 1931 the 'serious' work of the party lay with the unemployed, white and black.[253] The party set up unemployed workers' committees, one in Durban with 22 members, two in Johannesburg with 250 participants, and six in Cape Town, with 1,341 members altogether, though these groups were hardly stable entities; membership turnover was high, as organisers admitted.[254] Working with the unemployed was a Comintern injunction, and this was one area in which the party might reasonably expect to make some headway in drawing in a new white working-class following. For white unemployment was rising sharply, a consequence of the impact of global depression on the South African economy, peaking at 40,000, or 20 per cent of the white workforce in 1933, and only returning to 1930 levels in 1936.[255] On May Day, the party assembled a large crowd outside the Rand Club, mainly unemployed people and, to judge from the use of an interpreter evident in a press photograph, mostly African, shouting the slogan 'We want bread'. After efforts to force an entry, ten men were charged with public violence.[256] Most of the organisational work in this sphere was undertaken by Issy Diamond and Molly Wolton. Both of them would enliven any of the party's platforms and engendered a ready response from white workers. Issy Diamond owned and ran a barber's shop, 'a mecca for ex convicts' and revolutionaries of all stripes, a kind of 'indoor Hyde Park'.[257] According to Roux, 'right wing deviations peppered his speeches' but such lapses hardly worried his audiences. His particular way of dealing with the inevitable question – 'Would you allow your sister to marry a kaffir?' – was to reply, 'Ah, but you don't know my sister.'[258]

Molly was quick with hecklers as well, 'brilliant in repartee' and popular with audiences because she was also pretty, 'all pent up energy like a coiled spring, all fire and fury when it came to public speaking which she loved'.[259] They tried very hard to ensure that such demonstrations were multiracial, by bringing together into single processions separately assembled groups of white and black demonstrators. Usually by the end of the event most of the white participants had left.[260] Work among the white unemployed was actually implied in the Comintern's new directives that Wolton had brought back from Moscow; these had called for a 'united front' between 'native toilers' and the 'poorer section of the white workers'. In 1931, the Politburo circulated a set of notes that supplied further doctrinal justification for activity in this vein. These suggested among other things that Afrikaners had 'an instinctive antagonism to finance capital' and the party should seek to lead them into a 'genuine struggle for independence upon a real democratic basis'.[261] If we are to believe claims by Makabeni, however, work among the unemployed during 1932 increasingly focused on white workers, not Africans, and black speakers at such events registered only a token presence.[262]

IN FACT, THE PARTY'S efforts to win support among unemployed Afrikaners at best achieved temporary expressions of racial fraternity, as in December 1932 when a multiracial Christmas Eve procession walked through the streets soliciting gifts of food for the workless from local businesses. However, a more enduring white constituency for the party was consolidating itself through the formation of the Jewish Workers' Club. Established in 1929, the Club's membership was drawn mainly from recently arrived immigrants from the Baltic states, Lithuanians especially and also Latvians. For these new arrivals, the Club's premises in Upper Ross Street, Doornfontein, often supplied a welcoming social centre as well as practical support, including English classes. As Ray Adler recalled, 'we were looking for a home, we couldn't speak the language, and we wanted to be active'. Ray Adler had been active in the illegal Communist Party in Lithuania before arriving in Johannesburg in 1928 aged 20 to work as a dressmaker.[263] In the early 1930s the Club had an active membership of around 300. It was anti-Zionist and Marxist in orientation and often drew its participants from people 'nurtured' in the traditions of Russian communism,[264] or at least with backgrounds that predisposed them to be sympathetic to the Soviet Union. There was Matya Ozinsky, for example, who spent her childhood in the Ukraine after leaving Lithuania, living in an area where 'we had a lot of pogroms, not from the Red Army [but from] the White Army'.[265] Or Dora Alexander in whose village 'there was no school until the Bolsheviks came; the first school was created when the Bolsheviks came'.[266] Or Eli Weinberg, whose Russian civil war experience included his adoption as a mascot by Red Cossack cavalry. He joined the party in Latvia as a teenager and remained loyal to it despite refusing to obey a command to shoot an informer. He was arrested by the Latvian authorities and tortured before his departure for South Africa in 1929.[267] The Club's members collected money for Gezerd, the fund that helped to finance settlement in Birobidzhan, the Jewish autonomous region in the USSR.[268] Its members' previous experience in the clandestine revolutionary politics of the Baltic states also shaped their behaviour in the South African party to which the Club deferred. As we shall see, the Club's adherents would supply useful support for Wolton's Bolshevisation undertakings, and they were often also more familiar with Comintern doctrines than their South African-born comrades. It was members of the Club who supplied much of the readier participation in two new front organisations which the party set up in 1931, the Friends of the Soviet Union and Ikaka la Basebenzi (Workers' Defence), providing both organisations with the strong-arm muscle required on two occasions to forcibly exclude Bunting's supporters.[269] Ikaka was established as the local branch of International Red Aid, which was supposed to provide protection and legal support for victimised workers; by 1933, Hyman Basner suggests, its operations were centred in his lawyer's office, paid for mainly from his firm's income.[270] The Friends of the Soviet Union enjoyed some success in building bridges for the party, especially in the more friendly quarters of non-communist white labour after the organisation began in 1933 organising annual delegations of South African trade unionists to visit the Soviet Union.[271] It would only really flourish during the Second World War.

Comintern officials and local party leaders would later adopt a disparaging view of the influence of the Jewish Workers' Club within the party, suggesting that its members were foreigners who failed to engage themselves in local issues, and who introduced doctrinal 'trouble from outside'.[272] This was an exaggerated caricature at best. There is plenty of evidence to suggest that a striking number of these recent immigrants brought with them from their homeland social adaptability and sensitivity to injustice that prompted them to find common cause with black South Africans. For example, on the sea journey to Cape Town, Dora Alexander prepared herself by reading *Uncle Tom's Cabin* in a Yiddish translation, the only book she could find that seemed to her to be vaguely relevant to her new homeland. African dockers loading coal in Walvis Bay, who were supervised by a 'white overseer with a long whip', appeared to her as a re-enactment of Harriet Beecher Stowe's story: 'I stood on the boat and I said, you're going to South Africa and you're going to help rid the world of that'.[273] Arriving in Cape Town or Johannesburg, these young men and women often found work in occupations such as tailoring, millinery or shop-working, livelihoods in which Africans were beginning to make inroads, and they lived in neighbourhoods, such as Doornfontein or Fordsburg, that were still at that stage multiracial. Issy Heymann, a key figure in the Club's history, reached Johannesburg in 1931, having left Lithuania because 'there was no prospect for a Jewish boy'. He found work in a mining concession store in Springs, learning Shangaan and Zulu so that he could speak to his customers. Ben Weinbren persuaded him to join his shop workers' union. He encountered Eddie Roux at the Club, who asked him to sell the party newspaper outside the compounds and in the townships, for, as he explained, 'I could speak the lingo, you see, and there I was a very popular chap'. He sold the paper for two years before joining the party in 1936.[274]

At the ninth congress, Rebecca Bunting observed that the party had already struggled to form workplace groups and that its efforts so far had been unrewarding. Under its new leadership, efforts to extend the party's influence to mining compounds did continue into 1931, and indeed in August, when Nzula wrote an 'organizational report' for the Comintern, he asserted that the party had succeeded in building three gold-mine groups, one at City Deep with 30 members, one with seven members at Crown Mines and another of two at Robinson Deep. The City Deep group was in fact the nucleus of mine worker organisation that Bunting stated he had formed in January 1931.[275] There were also 40 members of the Brakpan party district who were miners but who had yet to be organised in workplace groups. However, Nzula warned, the mining groups were new and their progress would depend 'upon the proper combination of legal and illegal work in them'.[276] With his original claims to have recruited mine workers, Bunting may have been exaggerating; as Mia Roth has suggested, he had strong reasons at the beginning of 1931 to try to improve his standing in the party.[277] Nevertheless, both the Buntings had routinely sold the paper inside mining compounds during the 1920s; as Rebecca explained much later, at that time the authorities were more relaxed, though by 1931 'they wouldn't allow us in'.[278] More than two years later, in August 1933, Moses Kotane would report to Comintern that the party had recently succeeded in recruiting 'some *livingbeings* in the mines … *very very few*, but livingbeings'; Kotane's phraseology suggests that previous party claims about engaging African mine workers were overstated.[279]

In fact, most of the available evidence indicates that during 1931 the party's efforts to build or even sustain organisation among black workers, either directly or through unions, were unsuccessful, at least around Johannesburg. Part of the difficulty was Douglas Wolton's insistence that the renamed African Federation of Trade Unions (AFTU) under Albert Nzula's secretaryship should eschew any class collaborationist activity, such as efforts to make representations through the Wage Board.[280] In January 1931, William Thibedi was finally dismissed from the trade union office and the Federation increasingly functioned as a front for the party, essentially as a political movement. Party directives discouraged collaboration between its affiliates and their white 'parallel' registered unions, and Nzula himself did nothing to try to win support within the Trades and Labour Council, accusing it of sabotage and betrayal when he was invited to address its conference. During 1931, the AFTU affiliates dwindled. In the following year, one of the strongest of the African unions, the clothing workers' union led by Gana Makabeni, was ordered by the AFTU to break its links with the registered Garment Workers' Union (GWU), led by Solly Sachs, supposedly because the GWU withheld strike pay from black workers locked out for supporting a strike by the white garment workers. The party expelled Makabeni in March 1932 after he refused to break links with the GWU.[281] Later that year the GWU would attract hostility from the party leadership for its use of Industrial Conciliation Act procedures, a central plank in its strategic approach. James La Guma was expelled from the party after a strike led by a new branch of the GWU in Cape Town ended in disaster. His expulsion was due to working with the Trades and Labour Council to try to involve the labour inspectorate in a settlement – an action which his party critics described as 'formulating opportunistic deviations and fractional tendencies'.[282] It was La Guma's second rift with the party. In 1929, he had withheld his support from Douglas Wolton's efforts to win the election on the Cape Flats, and instead worked for the rival National Party candidate as his election agent. He later published a self-critical apology for his 'political opportunism' on this occasion, but he did not explain why he had done this.[283] The strike itself was a reaction to a wage cut, though for its organisers it was also 'a demonstration of militant Red Trade Union activity'.[284] It was undertaken at a time of widespread retrenchments in the industry and it drew support initially from only a quarter of the factory's workforce, though Johnny Gomas claimed that participation grew to nearly half.[285] The party viewed it as sufficiently important to send Lazar Bach down to Cape Town to advise the local union leadership. Bach's advice, it seems, was confined to telling the Cape Town organisers that they shouldn't take money from the GWU that Solly Sachs had offered because Sachs was about to be expelled.[286] Bach's advice was rejected, though the GWU money only extended to one week's strike pay. La Guma's expulsion came after he had called on the party to investigate Bach's role during the strike.[287]

Solly Sachs was expelled from the party in September 1931 at the same time as Sidney Bunting, Fanny Klenerman, Bill Andrews, Ben Weinbren and CB Tyler. Sachs's offence was to have held back the Garment Workers from participating in the party's May Day proceedings outside the Rand Club, taking his comrades on a picnic instead. Undismayed by his expulsion, Sachs continued to lead the GWU, a body largely constituted by Afrikaner women with an African parallel body, and Sachs himself would continue to be characterised by government politicians as a communist.[288] Indeed, Sachs himself continued privately to think of himself as a communist, as he once told Harry Pollitt. Bunting's supposed deviationism included his efforts to persuade the leadership to reinstate William Thibedi as well as various 'opportunistic acts' such as defending in court unemployed demonstrators arrested during a May Day demonstration.[289] He had also appeared in public with ICU and ANC leaders. His expulsion was preceded by various abusive encounters, including one meeting, a 'veritable Witches Sabbath', as one of those in attendance recalled: 'everybody shouting Bunting down and calling him "Lord" Bunting as he tried to make himself heard. An elderly woman, whom Bunting had befriended over years, turned her posterior towards him, with her dress held high.'[290] Douglas Wolton may have been responsible for the mockery of Bunting's supposedly aristocratic origins. Bunting's father had been knighted and had actually turned down a peerage. Wolton started calling Rebecca 'Lady Bunting' at public meetings well before Bunting's expulsion.[291] Weinbren and Charles Tyler, the leader of the builders' union, were supposedly guilty of reformism and class collaboration, while Andrews, the party's most influential figure in white organised labour, had spoken at a Labour Party event on May Day, effectively therefore supporting 'social fascism'.[292] For the rest of the 1930s Andrews continued to hold senior positions in the Trades and Labour Council, being elected as its secretary in 1933 and serving on its executive for the next two decades. Bunting continued to try to persuade the Comintern executive to intervene and rescind his expulsion, and in doing this he could still muster support from African branch secretaries who had remained members. Minutes survive of a meeting of 'Communist delegates' that assembled in November 1932 and resolved to write to Moscow. In attendance were branch secretaries from Vereeniging and Brakpan.[293]

A few months before Bunting's expulsion, in June 1931, the leader of the Bloemfontein branch, 'the most active Communist in the Free State',[294] Sam

Malkinson, was also expelled. That there was a branch at all in Bloemfontein was mainly a consequence of Malkinson's work. Malkinson was a Jewish Lithuanian immigrant. He had first arrived in Bloemfontein in 1914, accompanying his mother from Kaunas, after being invited by a wealthy uncle who had made his fortune selling supplies to British soldiers during the South African War. His uncle promised his mother 'he'd make a man' of Sam and he put his 17-year-old nephew to work on his potato farm as a supervisor. Paid two shillings a day and mistreated in other ways, Sam ran away after witnessing his uncle sjambokking an African worker. After various efforts in Johannesburg to find work as a bookkeeper, a trade he learned at school, Sam joined the army, determined to travel to Europe and make his way home to Russia. He spent nearly three years fighting in Flanders and was wounded. He failed to reach Russia; the authorities insisted he should return to South Africa where he had enlisted. While recovering from his wounds, he had followed the news about the Bolshevik Revolution with mounting excitement and he started attending left-wing political meetings after he arrived in Cape Town. He joined the party in 1921 and returned to Bloemfontein in 1923 to work as an accountant; he'd gained a qualification while in England. There, in his words, he began 'preaching on a soap box in the location' and assembled a party branch, entirely African, with the help of Bunting and former ICU members, including his chief collaborator, Isaiah 'Ntele.[295] In 1926 a local branch of the ICU attracted a mass following during a campaign for a minimum wage for local workers. The branch fell apart later in the decade, racked by internal feuding and demoralised when one of its leaders turned state evidence in a trial that followed confrontations with the police.[296] So Sam Malkinson could build on earlier networks, and on working days he could even draw a crowd of 400.[297] For the first time he found confidence as a speaker and acceptance among people he admired: 'I loved the Basotho – intelligent people, logical, gentle.'[298] He was banned from attending gatherings under the Riotous Assemblies Act in November 1930 after being arrested for sedition, but he continued to help lead the branch, working through 'Ntele.

Sam Malkinson used to visit Sidney Bunting at his home; he'd travel to Johannesburg every so often because he 'kept the books' for the party and each year prepared its financial report. Sam admired Bunting, 'made a hero of him' and maintained with him a lively correspondence, typed on a red ribbon. He was too far from Johannesburg to participate in the 'theoretical wars' but he fell out with Douglas Wolton all the same. For Sam Malkinson, Wolton seemed 'a typical Englishman', 'one who sulks if he doesn't like something'. He once asked Malkinson why he hadn't organised the Bloemfontein communists into factory groups, and 'he sulked' when Malkinson told him 'there were no workers in Bloemfontein' – not factory workers, that is; 'there was only the railway'. Malkinson's exclusion happened in stages. He'd annoyed Wolton by challenging his directives on how the Bloemfontein branch should be reorganised. Then he was dropped from the party leadership, now named the Politburo – news that Eddie Roux had to take to Bloemfontein to explain to his local comrades, which he did somewhat half-heartedly. While Malkinson's ostensible failing was his lack of theoretical clarity, the real reason may have been his criticisms at Politburo meetings of Albert Nzula's drunken behaviour and anti-Semitic language.[299] The Bloemfontein comrades, mainly Africans, were unconvinced by the reasons Roux offered and demanded Malkinson's reinstatement. They also submitted their own complaint about Nzula, who they said had been writing letters about party matters to an ex-party member in Bloemfontein who they thought was now a police informer.[300] This insubordination was sufficient for Malkinson to be expelled for fractionalism and, in Roux's words, 'the Bloemfontein branch was destroyed'.[301]

ALL THE SAME, IN JULY 1931 Comintern's leadership pronounced its satisfaction with the party's 'successful struggle for the line', noting how in the recent May Day demonstration the party had 'passed on from parliamentary and petition forms of action' to more revolutionary methods. 'All the necessary conditions exist for the successful development of the revolutionary struggle in South Africa under the leadership of the CP.'[302] Comintern also offered praise for the party's apparent successes in their work with white workers. However, South African communists still needed to make a decisive break with white trade unionists and chauvinists such as Andrews, Comintern's memorandum cautioned, for this was written two months before his expulsion. They also needed to make the organisation of African mine workers, dock workers and farm labourers their priority in trade union work.[303] As noted above, Nzula, recently arrived in Moscow one month later, wrote about the party's progress, claiming it had established a range of workplace groups around Johannesburg. The party's membership now totalled 5,000, with Africans outnumbering whites by 25 to 1, he calculated, including three groups in the Transkei, in Umtata, Engcobo and Libode, though here the organisation was 'still suffering from the Bunting influence and has made little headway because of this among the peasantry'. Overall, peasants made up only four per cent of the party, and most of its followers were 'industrial', though this category included shop workers, gardeners and domestic servants.[304]

Albert Nzula would never return from Moscow. Selected for studies in Moscow because of his intellectual aptitudes, he was at first a promising pupil at the University for the Toilers of the East and even collaborated with his tutors in helping to write a book on *Forced Labour in Colonial Africa.* Interestingly, in his references to South Africa in this book, he includes quite a critical treatment of the African Federation of Trade Unions' 'left sectarian line which blocked understanding of workers who are influenced by reformism'.[305] He attributed the AFTU's decline to the effects of ignoring the everyday needs of workers.[306] He also provided Zulu lessons to the translator, IL Snegirev, who subsequently dedicated his anthology of Zulu folk tales to him.[307] But his drinking continued despite drying-out spells in a sanatorium and, alarmingly, when drunk, it seems he expressed anti-Stalinist views. He died in Moscow in January 1934 after an evening of heavy drinking and falling into a ditch and catching pneumonia.[308] There were rumours that his death was contrived, but Edwin Mofutsanyana, whose time in Moscow overlapped with Nzula's last year, was certain that Nzula died of drinking, for it had reached unprecedented levels. He did confirm that Nzula could be critical of Stalin. Comintern officials discouraged his return to South Africa until he had overcome his alcoholism and calmed down ideologically, and proposed that he should spend some time in the United States. The alternative understanding of Nzula's death, that he was murdered, is supported by reported testimony from at least one of Nzula's acquaintances. Jomo Kenyatta, in Moscow at the same time as Nzula, told CLR James that he had seen Nzula being escorted from a meeting by two security officials and that Nzula had never reappeared.[309]

Meanwhile, back in South Africa, campaigning against the 'right danger' constituted by disaffected groups now became a focus of party activism, and Jewish Workers' Club members were deployed to disrupt meetings held by Bunting and his supporters.[310] Bunting himself held back from any organised opposition to the party leadership, refraining from joining Thibedi's Communist League and contesting his expulsion in letters to the Comintern; interestingly, Comintern replied to him, denying that he had been expelled. The idea that there was a coherent 'Buntingite' opposition reflected doctrinaire assumptions about the 'right dangers' confronting the international communist movement, though Bunting would also be accused of consorting with Trotskyists. In April 1932, Wolton informed Comintern of the activities of 'expelled right wing communists who attempted to capture' the Friends of the Soviet Union; this was after Bunting and some of his supporters had attended one of its meetings; they were summarily expelled from that body as well.[311] A stroke caused Bunting to abandon his legal practice, and for a while he would earn a living as a viola player in a cinema orchestra before becoming a caretaker in a Johannesburg apartment building. Gana Makabeni remained a faithful defender of Bunting, and on one occasion was beaten up for his loyalty by JB Marks.[312] He was not alone in this. A meeting of Bunting's African sympathisers, held in November 1932, included the chair and secretary of the Brakpan branch, the secretary of the Vereeniging branch, and representatives of AFTU affiliates.[313] Those present were mainly disaffected members rather than people who had been expelled, though several of them had lost their positions as a consequence of their branches being 'frozen' in Wolton's reorganisation. Bunting himself would die in 1936, not of a broken heart as one might have expected,[314] but rather from a cerebral haemorrhage. Eddie Roux attended the funeral for the party, an act of solidarity which displeased the party's Moscow-based monitors.[315] Gana Makabeni was among the speakers; he was there, he said, for the African workers.[316]

Back in October 1931, Comintern's Political Secretariat wrote approvingly to the party about its expulsions of 'the right opportunist chauvinist Bunting clique' and also sent a new set of resolutions that changed the wording of the call for a Native republic. Now the South African party should work for the 'rights of the Zulu, Basotho, etc. nations to form [their] own Independent Republics'. These would then unite in a federation under a workers' and peasants' government.[317] This phraseology implying an ethnic federation was accepted by South African Politburo members at the end of the year.[318] The other change was the disappearance of any language about stages.[319] In effect, national revolution would simultaneously be a proletarian movement – a significant leftward shift since the 1928 protocol. Willie Kalk, freshly returned from his training in the Soviet Union, was quick to interpret the new spirit: at the party's Central Committee meeting of December 1931, he 'demanded' the exposure of 'the ICU and the ANC as counter-revolutionary'.[320]

Nzula's claims about the party's membership were checked in mid-1932 by a visiting Comintern official, Eugene Dennis (later, the general secretary of the American Communist Party). The figure of 5,000 actually applied to the number of membership cards the party had issued over its entire history to date, he found. In addition, Dennis discovered party membership had fallen during 1929, a consequence of inactivity in the previously very large branches in Vereeniging and Potchefstroom and it fell further through the next two years, with the attrition especially sharp in Durban in 1930 because of deportations. Seventy-five new 'native' workers were recruited in Johannesburg in 1931, Dennis established, but only a few attended any further meetings. By the end of 1931 there were only 60 members, he thought, though thereafter there was a 'slight increase to over 200'.[321] More detail about his investigations surfaced in a letter written by a Comintern official in 1934: 'We were told that the Party had 2000 members and 9 trade unions, groups on the mines, but investigations and inquiries proved otherwise. They went about rural areas collecting names and claiming that these were party members.'[322] Dennis's impression that membership had dwindled was partly corroborated by Johnny Gomas's testimony at a Central Committee meeting in December 1931: in Cape Town at that time, he said, the party's active following was down to 20, mainly white.[323] Falling membership did not appear to discourage party leaders. Indeed, it was possible to interpret the decline as evidence that they were on the right track, particularly if you shared Douglas Wolton's 'blind optimism', one of his personality traits noticed by Eugene Dennis.[324] As Wolton explained to the Comintern leadership in a letter dated 7 April, 'the former loose character of the Party organisation has begun to be transformed'.[325]

Dennis's later reports were more reassuring. Dennis was not a Moscow-based functionary. He had arrived in South Africa in early 1932, at the age of 28 a veteran of harshly suppressed efforts to organise fruit pickers in California, during which he had been jailed six times.[326] His supervision of the South African party was protracted and he would only leave the country in November 1934.[327] A friendly manner helped him with the more independent-minded local comrades, and even Eddie Roux found him a 'very likeable fellow'.[328] In South Africa his instructions were to help the party set up a youth league and prepare for illegality by building an underground apparatus.[329] In fact, as we have seen, a youth wing had existed since 1923. He was also to encourage the formation of a mass unemployment movement and urge the building of party groups on farms and mines. In October, in writing about his stay in South Africa, he proposed that there had been improvements since his arrival. He took the credit for reconstituting the membership, for when he arrived the party was all-white, he maintained, a claim that he made repeatedly in his later life, and that he may have believed.[330] The party that year had signed up 500 new people altogether and retained 400 of them, he reported. It was doing good work on coal mines in Natal, and on the trade union front there were new affiliates among harbour workers and on the Durban-based whaling fleet. The party was also making inroads into peasant communities in southern Natal. He registered certain failings: the fact that only half the new membership had been placed in 'functioning nuclei' and that the party still really had to form strong connections with the white unemployed. All in all, however, Dennis told his employers, he was witnessing the real beginning of a Bolshevik party.[331]

For once, local party leaders were more candid. Their view, expressed in a Central Committee resolution in July, was that 'the Party was lagging behind the revolutionary agitation of the masses'. Its groups or cells remained mainly residential. The AFTU affiliates had 'completely collapsed', membership was 'stationary', and the Young Communist League was 'non existent'.[332] Unless there had been a dramatic change between July and October – and this seems unlikely – Dennis's report was misleading and probably self-serving. If anything, by the time he was writing the party was even further from the goal of bringing workers in key industries into its fold. For after his expulsion, William Thibedi formed a Communist League, one of several groups in contact with the exiled Trotsky to be formed by people whom the party expelled at this time. Thibedi's League managed to win support among the nascent industrial groups that he had helped set up for the party at Crown Mines and City Deep. The Central Committee's admission about the AFTU's disintegration was at odds with a report in April 1932 in *Umsebenzi* about an AFTU meeting attended by representatives of farm workers and peasants as well as factory delegates. In fact, as Department of Labour officials confirmed, the supposed conference was a meeting of the Jewish Workers' Club and there were no African workers in attendance; the report was a complete fabrication, it seems.[333]

An assessment of the South African communists by Harry Pollitt, published at the end of 1932, reckoned that the membership of AFTU affiliates was down to 200, though he gave the party credit for 'some success among the miners'.[334] Pollitt was also critical of the effect of expulsions and the way that 'the red trade unions in practice set themselves against the white workers as a whole'.[335] In Cape Town, the party had ignored the existence of an established union with mass support among black dock workers (a reference to the group originally set up by the ICU?) and formed its own, a good example of its propensity to ignore the necessity to work within and win over reformist groups by forming fractions.[336] In the unions, the rejection of any methods of struggle except for communist-led strikes was only isolating the Red leadership from the masses, Pollitt concluded.[337] Pollitt's article was not derived from first-hand knowledge; he was using information he obtained from Eugene Dennis, it seems.[338] Meanwhile, in December 1932, victims of the Politburo's purge dispatched a memo to Moscow to state their case. It was signed by Gana Makabeni. They charged that the party had 'become mainly a white man's affair, almost completely in the hands of the Jewish Workers

Club (mostly petty bourgeois)'. The AFTU was 'merely a slogan'.[339] There were no Africans at that year's May Day meeting in Johannesburg. To be sure, *Umsebenzi* reported on various 'huge successes', but these 'are not known to people in the supposed areas'.[340]

AT THIS JUNCTURE, ARGUABLY at one of the lowest points in the party's fortunes, let us interrupt the narrative to address key questions that have preoccupied earlier writers about this history. From 1927, for much of the next decade, the Communist International would help shape the Communist Party of South Africa's overall sense of purpose as well as the way it organised itself and the tactics it adopted. In analytical treatments of the Communist Party in this period, critical assessment has focused on two main issues. The first is to do with agency. Did the party lose its local decision-making capacity in this period? Were the changes in strategic purpose defined in the various Comintern directives that arrived between 1927 and 1936 coerced or imposed, or were they in accord with predispositions and beliefs held by sections of the party? Secondly, were the strategic directives arising from Comintern's 'new line' helpful in meeting the needs arising from local conditions?

Was the Comintern's strategic line imposed? For writers who have relied chiefly on Comintern sources, Comintern policy reflected the needs of Soviet foreign policy. Consequently, in Sheridan Johns's phraseology, the struggle for an independent Native republic was a 'made in Moscow' product.[341] In 1928, the South Africans were 'forced' to adopt the Native republic slogan.[342] The slogan was determined by Comintern thinking about African Americans.[343] After its sixth congress, Comintern assumed direct control of the South African party and for the next decade the party would be subject to its will.[344] Various 'lines' were formulaically conceived and 'foisted' upon South Africa with no detailed understanding of local conditions affecting their conception.[345] What was transferred to South Africa in 1928 was an ultra-left policy that had its origins in Soviet internal politics.[346]

A second set of writers stress James La Guma's contribution to the original conception of Comintern's resolution during his two visits to Moscow. They also emphasise the extent to which a receptive group existed within the party, particularly among recent well-educated African recruits. South African misunderstandings of Comintern directives and local mistakes in their implementation were also to blame for the party's failures during the decade.[347] More positively, in South Africa as in other settings, comparative research has suggested that local communists were able to interpret Comintern prescriptions 'to make sense in the diverse conditions they encountered'.[348]

Whether Comintern officials would have drafted something rather like the Native republic programme without La Guma's participation does seem quite likely, given the parallels they perceived between the situation of black South Africans and African Americans. La Guma was no theorist, as is quite evident from his own writing at the time. Viewing his role as decisive – as Sidney Bunting did at the time – is probably wrong. But the extent to which South Africans were forced into compliance is debatable. As the Simonses argue, Comintern had moral authority but no real leverage, though their contention that it was the South African party's 'strong tradition of internal democracy' that would have blocked any external effort at coercion is questionable.[349] Under Bunting's leadership the party implemented the resolution selectively and defied Comintern instructions, with respect to the League of African Rights. Initially, at least, until 1930 it was possible for party leaders to interpret the Negro/Native republic thesis in a 'flexible and pragmatic' vein, just as in the United States.[350] Comparisons between South African communist experience and the only other substantial African communist organisation, the party in Algeria, suggest that the South Africans were relatively successful in resisting the Comintern new line: Bolshevisation was introduced considerably later than in Algeria.[351] At later stages the South African party ignored or became divided over more sectarian revisions of the Comintern line, and acted against Comintern guidelines on an everyday basis, for example in attempting to collaborate with other groups. From the mid-1930s, distance, poor communications and the extent to which Comintern relied on British intermediaries also detracted from its effective authority. The limits to Comintern's ability to control its South African affiliate were rather similar to its only partial authority with respect to the British party, where Comintern's main reliance was on persuasion and inducement rather than harder, more coercive kinds of control. In general, parties that operated as legal entities in their domestic settings were less susceptible to dictation from Moscow.[352] Even so, because of the influence of African Americans within Comintern in the late 1920s, the Moscow-based leadership was considerably more willing to intervene authoritatively in the case of the South African party than was the case in its relationship with other communists in the British Dominions. Notably, the Australian and Canadian parties were pretty much left to their own devices in developing policies concerning their own indigenous populations.[353]

Was it a sensible command in 1928 that the party should look to an African peasantry as the 'motive revolutionary force' and that it should ally itself with

African nationalists, whether 'from above' or 'from below'. Left-wing critics of the Comintern line argue that Bukharin's scheme at best drew supportive evidence from South Africa selectively, that the South African communists were already making significant progress in organising Africans on the basis of their working-class identity, and that in effect the Native republic introduced the notion of a staged progress towards socialism, which drew the party into alliances with bourgeois-oriented African nationalism. As Drew has noted, 'by introducing the language of stages, the thesis had limitations as a mobilising device for socialism'.[354] The Simonses and Lerumo, writers who themselves were key figures in developing later justifications for subsequent alliances between communists and African nationalists, offer favourable assessments of the underlying logic of the Comintern's programme. For instance, the Simonses maintained that the programme was a theoretically sophisticated response to four key changes: the state's incorporation of the white labour aristocracy, African proletarianisation, the Africanisation of the party's following, and wider African militancy.[355] Martin Legassick, writing in the late 1960s, noted that in colonial settings calls for self-determination were not necessarily bourgeois, for, given the weakness of local bourgeois groups, the 'consummation of nationhood falls to others'.[356] Following Amílcar Cabral, he suggested that in such settings, intellectuals in developing a national culture will draw upon peasant folk beliefs and even proletarian preoccupations. In 1927–8, the 'climate was ripe' for the party to build an African following around calls for national liberation, he argued.

At the time of Comintern's first draft resolution on the Native republic, the South African party was still confining its explicit aims concerning African political rights to an extension of the Cape franchise to the other three provinces. The Comintern's authority seems to have been needed to secure the party's embrace of Africans as prospective full citizens – though, as we shall see, this commitment would weaken after the turn to popular frontism in 1936. Comintern's characterisation of South Africa as a typical colonial setting in which most Africans were peasants was misguided, but it did encourage the South African communists to pay more attention to people living on farms and in the smaller towns, where they began recruiting vigorously. Left to itself, the South African party might not have developed in this way: Sidney Bunting was convinced that there was no potential for rural revolt. On the other hand, Bunting made a real effort to build a rural following for the party when told to do so, and the League of African Rights found its most ready following in the area in which he had mounted his electoral campaign. Comintern's call for its disbandment was indeed destructive and demoralising. The League enjoyed some success in reviving and extending older rural ICU networks, and had it continued, it might have supplied support for Gumede and those of his allies within the ANC who were conspicuous in its leadership.[357] The more radical 'Bolshevised' version of the programme implemented from 1930 under Douglas Wolton's authority ignored the fragility of the organisational gains the party had made in the 1927–9 period. These gains were partly the effect of the party's efforts to meet external prescriptions, and they were certainly largely undone by the move to base organisation on workplace units and to reject as reformist any use of officially sanctioned procedures, a corollary of viewing trade unions primarily as revolutionary political instruments. Before Bolshevisation, the official archival evidence shows that the party's trade unions were weak, but as senior government officials noted, in the circumstances communists had enjoyed 'a fair measure of success' in their early efforts to build African unions. Whatever the scale of their success in this domain, most of their achievement would soon be undone by the application of Comintern's directives.

FOUR

Factions and Fronts, 1932–1939

Makapele Amapasi !

Eddie Roux drew and printed this linocut, one of a series he produced while editing the party newspaper, part of a more general strategy to make the paper more appealing to African readers.

As we saw towards the end of the last chapter, Gana Makabeni suggested that reports in *Umsebenzi* referred to fictional events. It is a comment that raises an important methodological issue for researchers. Any effort to track the history of the party through the period of the 1930s has to address the difficulties posed by the source material. Most of the existing narratives of the party's development in this period rely heavily on Eddie Roux's books, written after he left the party, and Roux (like the party's own historians) tended to reproduce reports from *Umsebenzi* uncritically. Yet, if we are to take Makabeni's observation seriously, it is likely that certain *Umsebenzi* stories were inventions. Roux was also of course writing from his own memory, and was retrospectively very critical of the direction the party took after 1928, and had no reason to exaggerate or misrepresent the party's activities, except with respect to his own contribution perhaps. As is evident from Eugene Dennis's communications, the reports by the observers dispatched by Comintern were not always truthful either. It does seem sensible, therefore, to attempt to find other sources to document the party's activities, not just its own press and the memories of its own membership. As we have seen from Mia Roth's research on communist trade unions, when the party's claimed activities are cross-referenced with official government archival sources, the results suggest that party-derived information can be misleading. Following this logic, Roth is sceptical about the reported events that Roux and more orthodox party sources attribute to one of the key activist episodes of this time, its decision in 1932 to put up JB Marks as a 'demonstrative' candidate in a by-election in Germiston. On this venture, she could find no relevant coverage in the Johannesburg press.[1]

Marks may have been chosen because he was, in the view of Eugene Dennis, 'an effective mass agitator'; and within the party's African following in Johannesburg, both with workers and the 'intellectuals' (Marks himself had been a schoolteacher), he enjoyed 'considerable influence'. This may have been because, unlike several of Douglas Wolton's allies on the Politburo, he could show 'strong conciliatory tendencies'; evidently this feature of his personality was not an asset in Dennis's view, though it may explain why he was widely liked.[2] He had an untidy personal life and was always short of money: 'It's agony! The way money comes and goes,' he used to say, adding: 'And you're horrified when you wake up to find who's lying next to you.' As one of his friends, Hyman Basner noted he had as well the saving 'grace of humour'.[3] The party's decision to contest the election symbolically was equally canny. It was the first poll in which white women had the vote. It also represented a key test for the increasingly unpopular government: the election would receive plenty of public attention. The seat had been held by a member of the Labour Party but, given the party's loss of support resulting from its participation as a junior coalition partner in the Pact government and also because of the recent arrival in Germiston of tens of thousands of landless Afrikaner migrants, National Party organisers were determined to establish an urban beachhead by taking the seat. In fact, both the main white parties, the ruling National Party and the main opposition, the South African Party, would provide vigorous support from their top-echelon leadership for their local candidates. Unlike its earlier forays into electoral politics among black or coloured voters in the Cape, here the communists were intervening in a major arena for mainstream white politics.

The by-election campaigning took place over October–November 1932. The party organised public meetings for whites in the market square and at the railway workshops – where they had more success, Roux claims, as the workers were chiefly English-speaking, and 'were prepared to give the Communists a hearing'.[4] Railway workers may have been especially receptive because they had been severely affected by local retrenchments since the advent of the depression.[5] But for the party, non-voters were their main target, for in Germiston's African location they were hoping to exploit local dissatisfaction over lodgers' fees, following the same course they had taken in Vereeniging and Potchefstroom. Barred from the location, communist organisers held meetings outside the location fence: Roux recollects 'huge crowds' in attendance. *Umsebenzi* carried reports of Marks's speeches, in which he told his audience that the white candidates represented imperialist slavery. As well as the lodgers' permits, Marks referred to other local grievances including the poll tax and beer raids.[6] For good measure, *Umsebenzi* also carried a report that detailed the eight basic demands around which it was seeking to mobilise residents in Germiston location; these included opposition to imperialist war preparations against the Soviet Union and the Chinese people.[7] Eddie Roux describes one of these meetings, on 16 October, at which he was present, accompanied by Molly Wolton and by 'stalwarts from the Jewish Workers Club and girls in their bright cotton frocks'.[8] They began their speeches, which focused on the lodgers' fees, with the help of an interpreter. Then the police arrived with their own 'unofficial supporters', who began heckling. What had been an orderly gathering degenerated into a 'rough and tumble',[9] and Roux and his comrades on the platform were arrested. Subsequently, the Attorney General dropped the charges, of resisting arrest and incitement. At a later meeting white hecklers shouted out death threats, a development that prompted one of the more excitable party leaders in Johannesburg to order the men from the Jewish Workers' Club to arm themselves with revolvers, an injunction they sensibly seem to have ignored.[10]

Roux was then assigned the task of attending the official nomination meeting to announce the party's candidate. After a surprised magistrate informed him that Marks was ineligible, Roux was escorted out of the building, only to be delivered to a group of National Party 'toughs' who beat him up. For his pains, he was banished from the Witwatersrand for a year, together with other party leaders and Solly Sachs, who had attracted official displeasure in Germiston earlier for his role in a strike by the garment workers. Roux went into hiding. The bans were withdrawn subsequently after the party applied to the Supreme Court to test their validity.[11] The party continued its meetings outside Germiston location and during polling day 'collected votes for its own demonstration candidate', using forms it had distributed earlier.[12] Three thousand forms were collected in Marks's favour, it was claimed. After the election party activists tried to sustain the lodgers' permit protests. A communist-organised meeting on 18 January was broken up by police and municipal labourers assembled for the purpose by the location superintendent. On 25 January another meeting, inside the location and this time not party-organised, was broken up by armed policemen who fired their weapons.[13] An elderly woman subsequently died of gunshot wounds.[14] That brought to an end any protests against the permits. Encouraged by what it perceived to be the success of this initiative in the general election of 1933, the party announced six more demonstrative candidates, though *Umsebenzi* contains no details of any campaigning on their behalf.[15]

Did any of this happen? Is there any evidence that offers independent corroboration of Eddie Roux's memoirs of these events? There are other first-hand recollections. Ray Adler, when interviewed by Colin Purkey and Leslie Witz in Johannesburg in 1990, remembered attending the meeting on 16 October. She was one of the girls in bright frocks from the Jewish Workers' Club that Roux mentioned: 'a handful of us came to support him'. She described the police creating a 'disturbance'. She remembered JB Marks's campaign as essentially light-hearted: 'it was a joke,' she said, though that could have been an effect of Marks's manner, for he was funny and unassuming – in fact rather a surprising personality for the party to promote at that time.[16] The first really full narrative of Roux's experiences on nomination day is contained in Bernard Sachs's memoir, published in 1949. Roux's two books published before Sachs's account provide much less detail on this episode. Sachs's version, written ostensibly at least from an eyewitness perspective, contains details that are in none of Roux's accounts, neither the two earlier versions nor the later narrative included in his autobiography.[17] In 1981, Eli Weinberg wrote about his own recollections of the Germiston campaigning, again supplying fresh anecdotal material.[18]

In fact, the Johannesburg press offered plenty of reportage that confirms every detail of the incidents described in each of Roux's three narratives and, indeed, provides a quantity of additional information.[19] The first press report was about an evidently tumultuous public meeting in Germiston's market square in which police had to protect the speakers, Molly Wolton and JB Marks, 'the native "Red" candidate', from an attempt to rush the platform by a hostile group of unemployed white men. There were half-a-dozen fist fights in which 'several women, obviously Communist sympathizers, made good use of their feet on those who were attacking their friends'.[20] Roux's attempt to nominate Marks as a candidate for the by-election 'helped to relieve the formal proceedings' of their customary dullness, according to the *Mail*'s local correspondent. The magistrate was in fact notably civil. He told Roux that it was no use arguing, he had to abide by the law, but he would 'make a note' of Roux's application. The report includes a photograph of Roux being 'frog-marched' down the street outside the court after being 'pummelled'; the photograph shows the police and the mayor attempting to restrain Roux's escorts.[21] As might be expected, Roux's and Solly Sachs's banishment elicited fresh press attention, especially because Oswald Pirow, the Minister of Justice, supplied his own justification. The effort to nominate a black candidate was not simply a 'merely amusing' incident, Pirow insisted; it was 'something that went far deeper', an insult to the people of Germiston and evidence that the communists 'had lost all sense of proportion'.[22] Eddie Roux meanwhile kept the story going by defying his ban and appearing at various meetings as well as eluding a police search for him over the next two weeks, efforts that predictably earned him the sobriquet of the 'scarlet pimpernel'.[23] 'An extraordinary amount of time has been spent trying to find Mr Roux,' a police spokesman complained – an exasperated comment that suggested the local police command did not share Pirow's view of the threat to civic order that Roux supposedly embodied.[24] He was finally arrested on arriving at one of the party's Sunday afternoon meetings that communists had been holding outside Germiston location 'for some months past'.[25] The party's proxy election in the township attracted commentary as a 'curious feature' in the *Mail*'s coverage of polling day. Arthur G Barlow's report refers to a 'march-past' outside the main polling station by 'native women', dressed in their Sunday best, 'on their way to protest at the town office at some new regulation in the location'. It was an indication, Barlow thought, of 'the effectiveness of Communist propaganda'. Barlow also referred to the 'straw' election the party conducted, and their announcement to have collected 3,000 votes for their 'native "candidate"'.[26]

Aside from vindicating the integrity of Roux's recollections, the press reportage indicates that the party's engagement in Germiston's election resonated quite widely across different local communities. The location meetings were popular and, as the *Mail*'s reports tell us, had been held over several months, beginning well before the announcement of the by-election. It was evident that the party tapped into local grievances, manifest in the hostility to the police; several of them were injured when members of the crowd attacked mounted constables who attempted to halt a party open-air meeting on 13 November.[27] The procession of black women marching past the voting station on polling day offered telling confirmation of the party's success in linking its claims for universal enfranchisement to such local grievances as the lodgers' permits, poll taxes and liquor raids. The reference to the women involved in the skirmishing between the party and unemployed men at the earlier meeting reported in the *Mail* is to *white* and *local* women, and their presence on that day at a party-sponsored occasion merits commentary.

There was in progress at the time of the election a fiercely contested strike by white female garment workers at a local factory at which on several occasions armed and mounted police broke up picket lines, using their batons against women who themselves were 'assaulting' scab workers.[28] The strikers were reacting to a recent effort by garment factory owners to bring Transvaal wages on a par with the much lower scales that prevailed in the Cape, in line with a recent Wage Board determination. They also decided to sack a number of African pressers, the only African machine operatives employed in the industry and the group of African workers that often supplied leadership to the nascent African Clothing Workers' Union, a body that until recently had been communist-aligned; as we have seen, the party expelled its leader, Gana Makabeni, just before the strike. The picket line attracted reinforcement from people whom the police identified as male members of the Jewish Workers' Club, who doubled up as muscular reinforcements for Ikaka la Basebenzi (Workers' Defence – the local branch of International Red Aid, a party front organisation).[29] The local branch organiser of the Garment Workers' Union (GWU) may have been a communist according to the police; and it does seem quite likely, given the presence of the Workers' Club's Ikaka activists, that the party had sanctioned support for the strike, notwithstanding their recent expulsion of the GWU's secretary, Solly Sachs. The party maintained a loyal 'fraction' within the GWU in Germiston, which, while opposing Sachs's leadership of the union, favoured militant strike action and, indeed, criticised Sachs for his neglect of the plight of locked-out African clothing workers. So, for the duration of the strike, hostilities with Sachs were suspended, and during August and September party leaders from Johannesburg, including Eddie Roux and Issy Diamond, attended union-organised meetings and picket lines in Germiston.[30] Sachs himself continued to share public platforms with communists and, indeed, continued to perceive himself as a communist. He was quoted comparing the police's treatment of the strikers with the behaviour of pre-revolutionary Russian Cossacks 'employed to ride down working girls'. One day, he promised, there would be a Soviet in Germiston.[31] This is the context that helps to explain the presence of local white women at the meetings addressed by John Marks. Their railway-worker husbands were evidently not in attendance, but railwaymen at a Labour Party meeting in Germiston supported a protest against the ban on Roux as well as that on Sachs.[32] The bans themselves followed a meeting between Oswald Pirow and the local employers in which he agreed to banish Sachs in return for employers reducing their wage cut. Associating Sachs with the communists by extending the ban to cover them as well was a clumsy effort to render it more publicly acceptable.[33] In Germiston, then, in 1932, the party achieved a measure of success in orchestrating responses across segmental social divisions, managing more by accident than by design to interweave African community-based protest with engagement in working-class action outside the factories.

The other references by Eddie Roux to on-the-ground party efforts to extend its organisation among Africans and to establish a local campaigning presence included activity led by Lazar Bach in Natal during 1932, and continuing attempts in Johannesburg to support and mobilise unemployed workers, white and black, as well as opposition to police 'pick-up' arrests around Johannesburg at the end of 1933. In Durban, by mid-1932, 'the movement, there, what was left of it, was now entirely underground'.[34] Roux suggests that Lazar Bach, because of his experience in Lithuania, had particular gifts when it came to clandestine work. Though he concedes that Bach's reports about his achievements were overstated, he does seem to believe that the communists managed to establish an organised base in Pinetown, 15 miles from

Durban's centre. Here the initial organisers were able to undertake agitation and leafleting in country districts, calling for a tax strike. The branch was in Pinetown because it was the locality to which the authorities had deported one of the leading figures in the 1930 pass protests, James Mbete, unusually a Xhosa speaker, not a local man.[35] The leaflets were printed by Mike Diamond, Issy's brother, a local party member who was arrested along with two of the Pinetown organisers, Mbete and E Dhlamini. Another African party organiser in Pinetown, James Ncwangu, was convicted in August 1932 for urging people not to pay taxes. Finally, in Durban, Bach claimed to have set up a Seamen and Harbour Workers' Union, which attracted support from African and white sailors, principally Scandinavians, on whaling boats. Douglas Wolton in his memoirs also mentions this body as being formed at this time, though he locates it in Cape Town, and the white members in his account are Italian fishermen.[36] All these activities were referred to in Eugene Dennis's report to the Comintern's headquarters, cited in the last chapter. Roux suggests that Durban's communist activism subsided after Bach's departure at the end of 1932, though a further report by Dennis indicates that Bach was still working in Durban in mid-1933,[37] and Roux himself would revisit and spend time in Durban in 1934. Bettie du Toit's memoir includes recollections of a visit she and Roux made to Durban in 1935 to organise a solidarity strike at the Consolidated Textile Mill in support of a strike by textile workers in Industria, Johannesburg. They appealed to Indian and African workers to form a new union in defiance of the existing registered body that had withheld support.[38]

Meanwhile, in Johannesburg, communist-sponsored activism included a soup kitchen in Ferreirastown, which ended on 15 April 1933 after police arrested a group of unemployed Africans collecting money from door to door to support the kitchen; the men tried to resist arrest and 'a general fight began'.[39] A communist party organiser, Stephen Tefu, was convicted for public violence on this occasion. Two weeks later, on May Day, Gideon Botha, the white mine workers' organiser who had replaced Issy Diamond as the party's preferred leader for the movement of the white unemployed, led a demonstration 2,000-strong.[40] The crowd, *Umsebenzi* reported, one-third white and two-thirds African, originally assembled separately but then united to march on the Carlton Hotel where the marchers believed a group of cabinet ministers were visiting. Later outside the City Hall, Botha and Tefu both spoke as well as Josie Mpama, who, according to the *Rand Daily Mail*'s report, addressed her audience 'fluently and got a good hearing'.[41] However, in a sequel to this event at a meeting that evening, the communist presence was opposed by a section of the white crowd and then the police baton-charged, singling out any Africans present. From then onwards, according to Roux, 'joint activity of black and white unemployed was practically impossible'.[42] Subsequent party campaigning that year in Johannesburg was confined to protest against a new practice in which police with 'motor vans' visited locations over weekends and conducted arbitrary arrests, bringing 'batches' of Africans before magistrates the next day on minor charges. In December 1933, posters appeared around Johannesburg with the wording 'To Hell with the Pick-Up'. Mass meetings were held on 16 December and Roux was again arrested and charged with incitement. What progress the party made in the formation of location defence committees as advocated in *Umsebenzi* is unclear. In January the party called for a united conference on native disabilities, inviting a range of liberal groups and personalities, including the ICU's William Ballinger and the Rev. Ray Phillips – possibly a sign that by itself the party had not succeeded in generating much organised activity on the issue.

THAT COMMUNIST LEADERSHIP in Johannesburg was willing in January 1934 to make joint cause with liberals and American missionaries may have been an early indication of a strategic shift towards popular frontism. In several European countries during 1934, local communist parties on their own initiative began to seek alliances with groups that they only recently had been characterising as social fascists – well in advance of Comintern's switch in favour of 'United Fronts from Above' in mid-1935. In Johannesburg, more pragmatic tactics may simply have been the effect of Douglas and Molly Wolton's departure and the appointment of Moses Kotane as party secretary. The Woltons left Johannesburg at the close of 1932 after Douglas emerged from a four-month prison sentence; he had been found guilty of criminal libel in one of his *Umsebenzi* columns. On his release he was banished from Johannesburg. The Woltons travelled to Cape Town: Douglas had been assigned the task of organising a training school in the 'southern districts' for 'workers and peasants'.[43] He was active in other ways in Cape Town, helping to support an AFTU-aligned 'minority group' or fraction in the registered Cape Tramway and Bus Workers' Union, and he was arrested with other local organisers while leafleting on the Grand Parade.[44] In May he was sentenced to another prison term, this time for three months. During his confinement Molly became very ill with a heart complaint and a nervous breakdown. She also became convinced that the authorities might deport her to Lithuania, a not unreasonable fear. There were other difficulties: Molly had arrived back from Moscow in 1931 with their baby, and in Cape Town 'the Comrades could no longer continue to maintain her'. On release, Douglas was offered a job by his brother on a Yorkshire newspaper, and he and Molly together with their infant child left South Africa on 5 September without obtaining approval from the Politburo. Subsequently Wolton was charged by the British party with violation of discipline following complaints from South Africa; he replied indignantly, referring to his 'record of carrying the Comintern banner alone in 1927 when the entire leadership was fighting against it'.[45] Wolton's absence from Johannesburg had the immediate effect of an upturn in *Umsebenzi*'s fortunes. Eddie Roux was able to exercise independent editorial control from the end of 1933 and encourage 'a style more informative, less vituperative and less violently dogmatic'. He also tried to include features that might attract readers among the African intelligentsia. In 1933 the party made a special effort in trying to build support among African teachers, starting a cyclostyled magazine for them, *Indlela Yenkululeko* (The Road to Freedom), circulating it among Fort Hare students whom Eddie Roux visited in mid-1933, camping on a hill-top beside the campus and delivering a sequence of lectures.[46] Roux also curtailed any mockery of religion in the newspaper, as this had proved to be unpopular with African readers.[47]

Even by the standards exercised by Comintern visitors, Wolton had 'strong sectarian tendencies', though Eugene Dennis, writing in June 1933, thought that he was overcoming them. Despite Wolton's departure, doctrinaire adherents of the supposed Comintern line (as it was locally interpreted) remained influential in the party's leadership. After the 1931 expulsions, there were no open doctrinal disagreements within the party for a couple of years, but in 1934 the inner tensions resurfaced. Moses Kotane was a key agent in this. Kotane had undergone training at the Lenin School for a year from late 1931 and during 1932, and on his return to South Africa he was appointed party secretary in Johannesburg. It was a role that he took on warily. As he explained to his Comintern sponsors shortly before his return to South Africa, he felt that his one year's training was insufficient preparation: 'I am supposed to supervise the Communist Movement in South Africa. How can I? For today I may be right but tomorrow I'll find myself unconsciously on the Right-wing and next in the Centre, in short, from one extreme to the other. I have heard Communists speaking about political estimation, and changing tactics with changed conditions, to me all these remain a riddle to be solved.'[48] His professed modesty notwithstanding, Kotane was by then writing with a degree of self-confidence that would have marked him out among any group of South African communists. Five months later in a letter to Moscow, he criticised South African party leaders for trying to exercise too tight a control over the party's front organisations and its aligned trade unions, making them too dependent and 'irresponsible'.[49] In August 1933, Kotane noted in another report to Comintern *Umsebenzi*'s recent revival in fortunes, evident in 'increased correspondence and *actual buying* of the paper by the masses', though he also warned about the 'tactlessness' of certain comrades that could ruin all the good work done recently.[50] At the end of 1933, Kotane travelled across South Africa visiting the different party centres and on 23 February 1934, writing from Cradock, he supplied the Politburo with the insights he had gathered from his tour. What he had learned, he wrote, was that, ideologically, the party had 'become too Europeanised', too theoretical, and 'beyond the realm of realities'. Too many of the party's members were 'ideologically … not South Africans'. They were not interested in the country they were living in: 'their hobbies are "the German situation and the Comintern", "Stalin and Trotsky" and "the errors of various Com. Parties"'. There was too much pretentious usage of 'International Press Correspondence phrases and terminology'. The party needed to become more Africanised – more familiar with 'the language of the Native masses'. The majority of Africans were 'more national conscious than class conscious'. Even so, Kotane had found, when speaking to them carefully, 'so far' he had 'always succeed[ed] in bringing them around to my point of view e.g. on the question of the poor whites'. The party needed to adapt its approach in communal settings in which 'national oppression, discrimination and exploitation confuses the class war'.[51]

KOTANE'S LETTER COINCIDED with another set of criticisms sent to the Politburo, this time jointly signed by 12 members of the Johannesburg party district. Most of the signatories were white, though the group also included Josie Mpama, who had moved from Potchefstroom following her marraige with Edwin Mofutsanyana. They made their attack more personal than Kotane's, suggesting that 'a clique' constituted by the Woltons and Lazar Bach had pursued 'a wrong policy of a leftist nature' and reduced the party to an isolated sect. They were especially critical of Lazar Bach and included in their missive a list of various 'adventurist indiscretions' (including unspecified efforts to wage guerrilla warfare in Natal) and an attempt to remove Kotane from his post by 'methods of intrigue and wire pulling'.[52]

By May, the feuding between Kotane's and Bach's respective supporters was open and sufficiently serious for the Johannesburg District Committee to hold a three-day meeting with the aim of reconciling the fractions. On this occasion, to judge from the list of those who attended, Kotane's supporters were the largest group in attendance and Bach's attempt to call for a vote of no confidence in Kotane was rejected. In a lengthy speech, Kotane condemned outright what he called 'the ridiculous extremes' to which Bolshevism had been taken in South Africa, procedures (he said) that had 'smashed' everything the party had built. On his return from Moscow, he told the meeting, Kotane had investigated the various claims that party leaders had made about membership and '95 per cent of these statements were untrue'. Any sensible arguments to organise first before mounting actions were denounced as reformist and social democratic, he complained. 'These people thought that a revolution could be brought about just by issuing leaflets' but even the party's publicity arrangements barely existed. In the office he had found huge piles of unsold copies of *Umsebenzi*, for there was no longer any network of agents to sell them. He then referred approvingly to Roux's recent efforts to revive the newspaper, which were opposed by Bach, he suggested. Kotane went on to reiterate his arguments about the need to nativise the party's ideology. In the past, there had never been a real black leadership, he noted. 'The native leadership of 1931–32 (so-called) consisted of nothing but boys. They had no opinions of their own.' Things were better now, he thought, but essentially Bach's opposition was 'a fight against Native leadership'. The party needed to restore its branch structure and 'to start a united front revolutionary movement'.[53]

At that stage, external authority still favoured Bach. In June 1934, Comintern's Political Commission approved a fresh 'Resolution on South Africa'. It noted the party's success in building its influence among the broad masses of toilers and the years 'of severe struggle against the survivals of Buntingism'. The resolution emphasised the continuing requirement for the party to organise itself on the basis of factory cells, to build its own fractions within reformist organisations, and to prepare for illegal work – essentially, a repetition of Comintern's 'new line'. It should remain wary of any proposals for united fronts with national reformists, including ICU leaders. The factory should remain the main centre of any struggle against fascism.[54] For good measure, the Moscow officials also prepared a set of draft statutes for the party which emphasised that recruitment should be selective and accompanied by a careful vetting process. Policy discussions should 'not lead to the illegal apparatus of the party organisation and the Party workers losing their conspiratorial concealment'. Meanwhile, 'the slightest element of factional struggle' should be countered with 'merciless struggle'.[55] Comintern could not have supplied a more explicit repudiation of Kotane's arguments. His position became additionally weakened by JB Marks's and

Edwin Mofutsanyana's return to Johannesburg fresh from their courses at the University for the Toilers of the East. Both would become key allies of Lazar Bach, who for a while appeared to be ascendant. Mofutsanyana, for example, would condemn the anti-pick-up campaign and efforts to solicit support for it from 'reformist' personalities, as 'the logical continuation of Buntingism'.[56] Much of the expressed disagreement between Bach and Kotane hinged around different interpretations of the meaning of the Native republic, with Bach castigating Kotane for retaining the notion that the republic would be a stage that preceded a workers' and peasants' government.[57] Kotane's call for a front which would be an alliance rather than an array of communist-directed 'fractions' in other organisations was also evidence of his weak appreciation of what the party's leading role should be. For *Umsebenzi* readers the dispute was most visible in a set of exchanges about whether or not a black bourgeoisie really existed: Kotane's view was that it did not, and that even the black petty bourgeoisie was not a truly exploitative group, and hence alliances with the ANC's leadership might be a viable course. The party at that stage had set itself against any such alliances; indeed, the Politburo resolved on 27 October 1934 that the ANC 'was an organisation of the comprador feudal bourgeoisie', with 'a history of treachery to the masses'.[58] This was view echoed by JB Marks: the ANC was the institution of the native bourgeoisie, a group of parasites.[59] Denial of the existence of the native bourgeoisie led to a denial of a struggle against national reformism, *Umsebenzi* readers were instructed by Comintern's Zusmanovich.[60] Kotane was branded a petit-bourgeois national reformist and a series of expulsions targeted his supporters. Kotane and Roux also both lost their positions on the Politburo in September.[61] Roux was also removed from the editorship of *Umsebenzi*.

Bach's doctrinal authority and his predominance on the Politburo through mid-1934 to mid-1935 did not decisively shape party activities. These became increasingly oriented towards the kinds of alliances that matched Moses Kotane's understanding of what the party should be doing, to judge from *Umsebenzi* reportage during this period. *Umsebenzi* continued to be edited by Eddie Roux – for Kotane, a key ally. At the beginning of March 1934, for example, 3,000 people attended a Sunday evening open-air meeting on the steps of Johannesburg's City Hall, a venue that the party would make its own for the rest of the decade. It was a CPSA-sponsored meeting and Roux spoke on behalf of the party. Other speakers included Johanna Cornelius, who was then president of the Garment Workers' Union, a body with which the party had had strained relationships since Solly Sachs's expulsion. Eddie Roux was among the speakers. More surprising was the presence on the platform of Bill

Andrews. The meeting was the first of a series of assemblies directed at building a 'United Front Against Fascism and War'. Jewish Workers' Club members were well represented in the audience, though the main intention was to attract Afrikaans-speaking workers, to whom a leaflet was addressed, warning against the Greyshirts, a local fascist militia.[62] To judge from interviews, anti-Greyshirts activism would soon become a central preoccupation within the Workers' Club. The reports may have exaggerated the numbers gathered at what were to become weekly meetings. But for the party they represented a significant change. Bill Andrews's presence that Sunday suggests that Comintern's cautions against alliances with 'national reformists' were being ignored by party supporters. Later that month, Andrews was present at an 'Anti Pick-Up' conference in Sophiatown assembled by the party; he was there to express support for opposition to the police's arbitrary arrests from the Trades and Labour Council. Gana Makabeni was also present, representing the African Clothing Workers' Union; he cautioned that more organisation was required before they could turn the United Anti-Pick-Up Committee into a national revolutionary movement. Edwin Mofutsanyana for the CPSA pointed out that there were too few people in attendance. In the same issue of *Umsebenzi* (24 March) a report referred to a legal victory won by African furniture workers who had refused to work overtime in October; their appeal against conviction under the Masters and Servants Act was conducted by George Findlay, a Pretoria-based lawyer who would help lead the party in Pretoria during the next decade. Findlay conducted a prosperous legal practice; his office in Cape Town had employed Robert Kadalie, Clements's brother, as a clerk and he had defended the ICU leader against the efforts to deport him in 1927 besides taking briefs in other ICU-related cases.[63] Clearly, by this stage the party's trade unionists were once again prepared to work through existing legal procedures.

That African workers could win such a victory reflected the more promising circumstances for African trade unionists created by the industrial growth that had been in progress since 1933, the year the South African government allowed the South African pound to find its value independently of the global price of gold, effectively creating the conditions for an industrial boom. The value of industrial output more than doubled between 1933 and 1939.[64] Industrial expansion brought with it a rise in African urban employment, also more than doubling in private industry between 1932 and 1939, for instance.[65] There was renewed and increased support within elite liberal circles and within the Department of Labour for African trade union recognition.[66] The negotiations that accompanied the decision to leave the gold standard resulted in a 'Fusion' government between Smuts's South African Party and Hertzog's Nationalists. This development precipitated the formation of a more uncompromisingly republican breakaway 'Purified' National Party under the leadership of Dr DF Malan. Malan's Nationalists would start systematically to build an organised following among white Afrikaans-speaking workers, sponsoring their own ethnically exclusive nationalist unions for this purpose. The price for Hertzog's participation in the coalition was the revival of his segregationist bills that had been shelved in 1929. In essence, then, Fusion policies supplied the conditions that favoured African labour organisation and at the same time reintroduced proposed legislation that was perceived as a fresh threat by African leadership groups across the political spectrum. An improved climate for African labour organisation was reflected in the revival of former affiliates of the AFTU, some of them under the leadership of Max Gordon, a member of the (Trotskyist) Workers' Party, and others under the leadership of Gana Makabeni, who remained outside the Communist Party. Gordon's revival of the Laundry Workers' Union began with a successful approach to the Wage Board to obtain arrears for members who had been underpaid since a wage determination in 1932. By 1937, out of a workforce of 1,400 in Johannesburg, 1,100 belonged to the union. Gordon led a cluster of seven unions by the end of the 1930s, called the Joint Committee. It would have a combined membership of 19,920 by the end of the 1930s while Makabeni's group, the Coordinating Committee, had an affiliate strength of 4,000. Both groups benefited from changes in Wage Board rules in 1937 that made it easier for representatives of African organisations to apply for wage determinations. In Gordon's report in 1937 he noted that most claims against employers that year, more than 300, were settled after negotiations with Department of Labour officials.[67] Gordon was actually employed and funded by the South African Institute of Race Relations in his capacity as a trade union leader from January 1938.

On 27 April 1935, *Umsebenzi* published a letter from AK Mokgatle, describing the forcible removal by municipal authorities of tenants from Sophiatown. What was needed was a united front between residents, landlords and stand-holders, who were often ordinary African workers who had managed to buy some land and erect property. Meanwhile, Eddie Roux offered his own views on the existence of the African bourgeoisie. 'It is true', he conceded, 'that some Congress leaders are petty bourgeois' and 'trying climb upon the back of their fellow Africans'. But to view them as an organised capitalist class was ridiculous; moreover, among the African petty bourgeoisie there were 'fellow travellers' who would 'travel a very long way with the workers and the peasants'.[68] The argument would continue over the next six months, accompanied at the same time by various expulsions of Moses Kotane's supporters for 'reformist activities' and 'fractionalism'.[69] Meanwhile, 'Anti-Fascist' activity did seem to enjoy some success in drawing white trade unionists into party-sponsored activity. Communists in Johannesburg were engaged both in leading and in organising solidarity activities (including demonstrations outside the factory and the jail) in a strike for recognition in June–July 1935 by the new Textile Workers' Industrial Union (TWIU), an organisation composed mainly of Afrikaner women.[70] TWIU leaders were on the platform speaking in Afrikaans at an Anti-Fascist meeting in Pretoria alongside Gideon Botha.[71] One of the new union's organisers, Bettie du Toit, joined the party at this time and in 1936 was sent to Moscow to study at the University for the Toilers of the East in 1936–7.[72] Nor was anti-fascism at this stage a concern limited to the party's white membership. Calls for solidarity with Ethiopia during the Italian invasion may have tapped into African nationalist sentiment. A recently reinvigorated party branch in Durban attempted to persuade dock workers to refuse to load Italian ships and circulated a leaflet in isiZulu: 'Ezase Ethiopia'.[73] Sixty dockers refused to handle locally derived meat exports destined for the Italian army; they were dismissed and replaced. The party also tried to instigate a consumer boycott of those local butchers involved in supplying the exported meat. According to Eddie Roux, *Umsebenzi*'s circulation during the Hands Off Ethiopia campaign reached 7,000.[74] This was a venture in which the party was demonstrating a certain independence. The Communist Party's call for international sanctions against Italy was at odds with Soviet policy. For the Soviet Union, isolating Nazi Germany was the priority, and hence Dmitry Manuilsky, one of Comintern's secretaries, discouraged any attempts to boycott Italian trade among Comintern affiliates.[75]

Between 25 July and 20 August 1936, Comintern held its seventh congress, which formally endorsed a strategic switch in favour of the international communist movement joining forces with social-democratic and even bourgeois political parties in a 'broader united front' against fascism. Communists should abandon the 'false conception' that all bourgeois parties were fascists; indeed, in the circumstances they had an interest 'in retaining every scrap of bourgeois democracy'. Comintern's formal policy shift at its congress had been preceded by various signals since Hitler's accession in 1933. In Britain, for example, the party had been instructed to form a united front with the Independent Labour Party at the end of 1933, despite the continuing official Comintern opposition to such alliances. As one commentator has noted, the shift away from the post-1928 new line of 'class against class' hostility was 'fitful' and Comintern directives during 1933–5 were inconsistent.[76] Even so, Robert Naumann, an official in Comintern's Anglo-American Secretariat, was expressing concern as early as February 1936 about the South African party's hostility to 'oppressed people's nations'. Nor was the party being helped by the 'incorrect line' fed to it by the likes of Comrades Zusmanovich and Potekhin, Naumann added. This simply inflamed the factional struggle.[77] Moreover, there were 'practically no Boer or English workers in the party', Naumann complained in a subsequent memo; rather, the 'European section of the Party primarily consists of Jews (the great majority) Letts, Lithuanians, etc., who emigrated from the Baltic countries and are but little concerned with the country'.[78]

On 14 September, Roux and Kotane cabled Comintern's headquarters to request Moscow's intervention. The South African party, they charged, was split 'from top to bottom' as a consequence of the 'mass expulsions' of Kotane's supporters. Subsequent telegrams from Marks and another member defended the ejection of the five 'undesirables'.[79] On 23 September representatives of the two rival groups were instructed to travel to Moscow. Lazar Bach had gone to Moscow in response to an earlier summons in time to attend the Comintern congress, despite advice against going from Louis Joffe. He would be reinforced in October by two of his supporters, the Richter brothers, Maurice and Paul, both members of the Johannesburg District Committee. Moses Kotane's journey took longer and he only reached Moscow on 6 November, travelling for three months. Roux declined the Comintern summons as he was facing a court case, this time for calling King George V a parasite during Jubilee celebrations.[80] JB Marks was also expected to arrive in Moscow but he decided to end his journey in Paris after also being warned by French communists. Bach collaborated with Zusmanovich in writing a speech for Josie Mpama, then studying at Toilers of the East and appointed as the party's delegate at the conference. The speech replicated Bach's established views about the Native republic and in Moscow it was received badly, being interpreted as sectarian dissent from the new Comintern policy.[81]

While waiting for Kotane's arrival, the Comintern authorities sent Bach and the Richters on study courses and appointed André Marty, then heading the Anglo-American Secretariat, to lead an investigative commission into the South African party.[82] The commission would function intermittently for nearly two years, but for the South African visitors its most decisive sessions were held between 13 and 19 March 1936, the first occasion when representatives of the two groups would debate their arguments in front of Marty and his colleagues. Before these sessions the commission had drafted a resolution which it expected the South African party to adopt at its next congress. This statement opened by noting 'the big role' that the Native republic slogan had played in the struggle against right opportunism. 'But new conditions today' had made the slogan 'inexpedient', and at odds 'with the employment of united front tactics'. Moreover, the South African party's leadership had been wrong to 'mechanically identify' the tasks of national liberation with workers' and peasants' revolution. They had also erred in adopting a hostile attitude to national reformists, including the 'anti-British republican movement of the Boers'.[83] Marty's views about the potential of such a movement reflected his understanding of the 1922 Rand Revolt, a revolt that, though it had failed 'to find the slogans to get the native workers into the strike', 'was never against the Natives'.[84] Essentially, then, before the discussions were held, the commission had already decided the key outcomes. On 13 March, Marty opened the meeting with a series of criticisms of the South Africans, focusing on their failure to send delegates to Comintern's recent congress, and on the mistakes arising from their 'scholastic discussion' of the Native republic. Not all the blame was directed at the South Africans. Russian experts at the University for the Toilers of the East, Potekhin and Zusmanovich, who had collaborated with Albert Nzula, had helped to promote a sectarian line within the trade union movement, Marty continued. The party had developed hostile relationships with both African and Afrikaner nationalism, underestimating the possibility that both might be allies in working-class struggle. In an obvious reference to Latvian-born Lazar Bach's role in the leadership, Marty advised that in future the party should select leaders 'who have been indisputably connected with the country'. Indeed, of the 150 people who currently belonged to the party, 'and I am not sure about that', about half were 'foreign'.

Only after these preliminaries were the South Africans allowed to speak about their differences. Clearly sensing the direction of the proceedings, Lazar Bach struck a conciliatory and self-critical note, suggesting that now that they understood the implications of the seventh congress decisions, both sides in the dispute could work together. Maurice Richter was more recriminatory and defensive: 'I think I would be dishonest now if I said that I have regained all faith in the opposition.' Kotane was much more truculent; at the start of the proceedings, after Marty's opening address, he asked why the comrades in Moscow did not find the 'patience to listen to what we are quarrelling about'. Because, Marty told him, 'we have very old experience about fratricidal struggles, and you are here in the house of a doctor'.[85] Kotane was willing to express a measure of contrition – 'we have realised the danger and harm we have done the party', but his views about his adversaries remained unforgiving: 'I reached a stage where I hated some people personally. Why? Because they distorted what I said. I hated them personally and politically. You get this in a struggle, when you fight with people who twist and turn things and you develop that way.'[86] He also made it quite clear who his friends were, speaking with sympathy about Eddie Roux's intellectual independence, and using as an example the issue of 'biology', on which Roux 'had his own views' – a reference to Roux's inability to accept the theories of the Soviet agrobiologist Trofim Lysenko.[87] Kotane was evidently quite willing to respect Roux's authority in this area of his professional expertise. With respect to the party's current African leadership, Kotane was dismissive. They were not really leaders, he said; they were simply 'people who do what they are told'.[88] Even with respect to his own role, 'I was not a real secretary, I was just a name … I was editor of a paper, but you know I never saw the paper until it was published.'[89] He himself would prefer to be out of the leadership; instead, 'let me do some work'.[90] Kotane's opinions about the quality of African leadership were ruefully endorsed by Bach, who admitted to the commission that 'we do not train Native cadres, but automatically put them into leadership'.[91] Roth suggests that Kotane's testimony effectively discredited Bach and the Richter brothers at the commission.[92] Kotane's comment about Africans in the party's top echelon is corroborated by Roux's retrospective view about the African Politburo members of that time, 'who despite coaching, remained bewildered and subservient'.[93]

For members of the commission, some of the most revealing testimony came from Josie Mpama, then visiting Moscow as a student. She aligned herself with neither group; indeed, as she explained, in the doctrinal dispute, for rank-and-file members like herself, 'I did not know who is right and who is wrong'.[94] When he became secretary of the party, Kotane became effectively isolated from its African followers: 'Comrades come to Moscow to be educated and yet when they get home, they drag him and put him among the whites … nobody could see him…'[95] What had in fact happened was that on his return from Moscow in 1932, Kotane was advised by other party leaders to avoid public appearances so as to escape police attention, a sensible enough precaution. He had stayed secluded for a while, living in a house in Sophiatown. Meanwhile, despite the supposed organisational changes introduced by Wolton, 'Our party is still based on a territorial basis, we have no factory nuclei' and 'We do not get workers where they work'. She was critical of the Bach group's view of the African nationalist leadership, for 'We must not run away from the fact that though they are reformist they have influence over the masses'.[96] On the other hand, she said, it was quite wrong of Eddie Roux to allow the inclusion in *Umsebenzi* of articles 'that should not appear' about the native bourgeoisie.[97] With respect to the party's own leadership, she agreed with Kotane: 'I do not know all the European comrades, but I know the Natives and, as a matter of fact, I do not see four or five people who could take over the leadership.'[98]

After five days of these recriminatory exchanges, Marty brought the session to a close: 'We can and must finish now', he ruled. The discussion and factionalism must stop; whoever tried to continue it 'must immediately be exposed'. From henceforth, South African communists must concentrate on building a racially united trade union movement and on defending the rights of all native peoples. *Umsebenzi*'s editorial board should be reconstituted and some of the key figures ejected from the movement – Bill Andrews, for instance, should be welcomed back, he advised.[99] Meanwhile, a more detailed list of actions was contained in a set of proposals that had been prepared; these needed to be accepted without equivocation. The Secretariat's programme, to which Marty was referring, was extensive. In addition to the measures Marty mentioned, it also stressed the work that the party should undertake to win 'Afrikanders, especially the poor and middle farmers' away from fascist influences. This could be achieved, the programme suggested, by the party calling for confiscation of the land of the big land magnates. The party should seek to 'build a very broad people's front' while also supporting the Labour Party, though it should not hold back from criticising the Labour Party for its shortcomings, albeit 'in a very friendly form'. The party should retain its antipathy to 'Trotskyite fascists'.[100] And, Marty warned the South Africans in his parting words, 'I advise you ... to drop the Independent Native Republic question and turn to another question.'[101] From now on the party should promote three main demands: bread and work for all workers, land for Africans and poor whites, and rights and liberties for all. And the backbone of the effort to take these demands forward was to be 'trade union unity'.[102]

The commission's report was less than a complete vindication of Kotane's position, though Kotane's biographer later maintained that 'Kotane's view' was 'seen to be in consonance with the united front line'.[103] For example, the injunction to build a racially united trade union movement was at odds with Kotane's own view that labour was best organised 'by developing a parallel movement'. At that stage, Kotane counselled, 'there is no question about unity'.[104] In fact, Marty had been sharply critical of both sides' behaviour and the commission would assign to the British party the task of guiding the South Africans in the correct interpretation of the new line. The British party should invite a couple of the South African party's leadership to London, and together with members of the British Politburo and George Hardy, the British Communist Party's representative on the commission, they should 'discuss fully the essential questions ... and communicate the results of this discussion' to Comintern's executive.[105] This arrangement would become routinised between 1936 and 1939, with the British party supervising and sometimes actively directing the South Africans through a subcommittee set up in its Colonial Department.[106] Marty's colleague in Comintern's Anglo-American Secretariat, Robert Naumann, supplied the liaison between London and Moscow and would himself provide a series of critical commentaries.[107] George Hardy would become the new Comintern emissary to South Africa. He had already been visiting South Africa for this purpose, arriving at the beginning of 1936.

Unlike Lazar Bach and the Richter brothers, Kotane would be allowed to return home, in August. Two months after Kotane's departure from Moscow, Bach and the Richters appeared before Comintern's International Control Commission, accused of Trotskyism, mainly because while in Moscow they had shared a room and corresponded with someone who had later been identified as a Trotskyist. Bach was also accused of concealing from the party that his father had been convicted by Soviet courts for speculation. Bach had already aroused suspicions after officials discovered he had written the supposedly sectarian speech that Josie Mpama delivered at the seventh congress. The commission's view that Bach's and the Richters' 'fractional disruptive work' in the South African party was connected to their role as Trotskyist 'double agents' would soon become a new orthodoxy.[108] After they were found guilty, the three were arrested and imprisoned in a camp in March 1937. The Richters were executed the following year for belonging to an anti-Soviet organisation within the camp.[109] Bach died in prison later, on 10 February 1941.[110] When news of his and the Richter's trial appeared in South African newspapers, Marty wrote to Georgi Dimitrov, Comintern's general secretary, criticising the publicity that Comintern had given to Bach's and the Richters' punishment. His own feeling, he reminded Dimitrov, was that their treatment should have been more forgiving. Expulsion and repatriation to Latvia would have sufficed, and then 'we [should] see what they [were] to do by their own work'.[111] The Richters and Bach supplied a convenient scapegoat for the party's failures during the Comintern's 'new line' phase for criticism could be directed at individuals rather than Comintern policies. So, for example, in the party's own self-criticisms, the chief problem identified was 'mistakes made in the correct application of the line', not the line itself.[112]

GEORGE HARDY'S VISIT to South Africa would last nearly a year. His autobiography supplies a short but revealing outline of his efforts 'to help our South African comrades in working out a number of questions of organisation and programme that had arisen in acute form'.[113] Hardy had no special knowledge of South Africa, as he himself admitted; he spent the first few weeks after his arrival in Johannesburg, reading up the country's history in the public library. His selection for this mission by the British party was expedient; he'd been involved in a love affair with the wife of a comrade and his temporary removal from Britain on party duties would help prevent a scandal.[114] Hardy spent time with Bill Andrews in Cape Town, and much of his understanding of South African political dynamics appears to have been shaped by his encounter with the veteran trade unionist. Andrews at that stage was still outside the party, and only rejoined it in 1938, though, as we have seen, by 1936 he was no longer estranged from CPSA leadership.[115] In 1937 he accepted an all-expenses-paid visit to Moscow, staying at the Hotel Lux, Comintern's favoured venue for entertaining senior foreign party officials. He kept a diary during his visit, which seems to have been taken up mainly with an officially arranged sight-seeing tour; he thought the Lenin Museum was 'disappointing to anyone interested in Lenin as an individual'. He managed to slip away from his guides on at least one occasion, to sell clothing purchased in London at thirty times its value at the official exchange rate.[116] Such street sales were a common feature in the experience of foreign visitors to the Soviet Union, though they were quite illegal. Andrews impressed his Comintern minders; he should have been a member of the party, they told Dimitrov, 'a good trade unionist, well known among the SA workers and natives'.[117] During his journey he met Harry Pollitt in London, who would urge him to 'resume his membership of the Party'. After his reinstatement, Pollitt advised the South Africans, they should make him the party's chairman.[118]

Most of the South African discussion in Hardy's book focuses on the party's early history, up to the 1922 strike. From his reading and conversations, Hardy became convinced that the main priority for South African communists was to convince 'organised' (white) workers 'that it was in their interests to put an end to segregation and help in organising African workers'.[119] After all, Hardy reasoned, 'Equal rights for African trade unions ... were a necessity too for the defence of workers of European descent.. to protect the skilled, higher paid workers ... against ... dilutees.'[120] While in Cape Town he told Ray Alexander, by then a key organiser of coloured and African trade unions, that he felt that local communists 'were too obsessed by colour'.[121] Hardy's understanding was his own, and he does not appear to have received a detailed briefing from

Comintern; later, in March 1937, he would be reprimanded by André Marty for, in Marty's words, 'pushing through a white line' in the party.[122]

All the evidence indicates that within the dominant group in the party's leadership, he did not have to push very hard. Under a leadership in which the authoritative personalities, Issy Wolfson and Willie Kalk, were both white trade unionists, communists would be assiduous in their efforts over the next four years to extend their influence within white organised labour and the white working class more generally. Edwin Mofutsanyana was the party's secretary but, as one of his African comrades commented, in this capacity he was 'only a figurehead'.[123] About Willie Kalk, both Roux and Solly Sachs use the expression 'plodding'; in Sachs's characterisation, 'without a great deal of glamour but plodding away tirelessly'.[124] Other views are more judgemental: several contemporaries refer to Kalk's laziness.[125] Though he was present at Young Communist League meetings that decided 'we should have no colour bar in the movement', Kalk retained inner reservations about the Native republic, which ostensibly, as we have seen, he supported. As he recollected fifty years later, he believed that 'historically speaking the black man wasn't ready'.[126] Once at a party meeting, probably in 1923 or 1924, he criticised Roux for saying in public that 'natives should walk on pavements'. That sort of sentiment provoked trouble for the party, he observed.[127] Black comrades seem to have sensed his reservations. Peter Ramutla in an unguarded moment, 'under the influence of liquor', accused Kalk at one meeting of treating Africans like servants and acting as a boss.[128] Kalk was close to the Jewish Workers: as a German speaker, he found it easy to learn Yiddish and was 'always welcome' at the Jewish Workers' Club.[129]

Issy Wolfson, born in 1906 near Krugersdorp, was a relatively recent recruit to the party, joining it in 1934, after a decade of trade union work among tailors, heading the craft workers' union that separated from the garment workers. He also helped to found the Transvaal Textile Workers' Union in 1934.[130] He and Kalk would find key support in their leadership of the party from the Joffe brothers, Louis and Max. Louis was the party's only paid white functionary; he served as the party's treasurer, a post he had held under Wolton's and Bach's leadership. He was by all accounts a persuasive fundraiser, bringing in a monthly income for the party of about £120, often from donations by local shopkeepers in Doornfontein and Fordsburg, which just about covered its printing costs. Louis, a small plump man who always carried a black briefcase reputedly filled with secret papers, was notable within the party for his doctrinal deference: in Roux's words, he 'accepted the Comintern line for ever and ever'.[131] Redeemingly, he also had a 'certain tough innocence' that rendered him 'immune to argument'.[132] Louis had considerable influence within the party not because of his intellectual authority but because he was the party's paymaster, maintaining a cohort of five African organisers whom he paid 30 shillings a week, a rate which by the late 1930s the party could only just afford. Apparently the organisers were not very effective; Joffe found jobs for unemployed African members chiefly for compassionate reasons; understandably, 'they thought the world of him'.[133] Aside from Louis Joffe himself, the party could not find any white organisers at that rate.[134]

Louis's brother, Max Joffe, earned his living as a doctor but often worked full-time for the party for free, being especially busy in its various anti-fascist front organisations, chairing the International Youth League for example. Rusty Bernstein's memoir includes an evocative picture of Joffe's surgery, opposite the City Hall, busy with comings and goings, 'one third medical and two thirds political'. A statuesque blonde receptionist would direct the traffic through various doors, from which 'a harassed looking Joffe' would from time to time emerge, 'stethoscope dangling from his neck, touching his temple with an elegant sigh of exhaustion and suffering before scuttling back out of sight'.[135] Meeting Joffe was Bernstein's first real contact with the Communist Party. The final influential personality in the party's leadership between 1937 and 1939 was Hyman Basner, who, like Wolfson, was a relatively recent recruit and hence relatively unaffected by the disputes of the Native republic era. Latvian-born Basner rather stood out from the tailors and shop assistants who mainly constituted the party's Doornfontein-based Jewish following. His parents, who managed a prosperous dairy next door to the Buntings, saved up enough to pay for their son to study law at the University of California. The money ran out rather quickly and Basner returned to Johannesburg to serve articles with a firm specialising in acting for Indian businessmen and African petty offenders. Opening his own practice in 1930, he became the party's favoured lawyer in taking briefs from *Ikaka la Basebenzi* and joined the party in 1933, being drawn initially by anti-fascist activism but quickly forming friendships with Edwin Mofutsanyana and John Marks. Just 30 when he joined the Politburo, he was intellectually self-possessed, energetic and irreverent, with interests and a lifestyle that by his own admission many of his comrades would have described as 'bourgeois'.[136]

With this new leadership established in Johannesburg, an 'activist plenum' meeting in April 1937 produced a set of resolutions. The omissions from these were as significant as what was included, and both illuminate the party leaders' understanding of the implications of Comintern's new policy. Absent was any direct reference to land confiscations; instead, peasants were enjoined to struggle against heavy taxation and the cancellation of debts. There was no mention of universal suffrage. 'No opportunity should be missed to enlist the sympathy and support of white toilers' and the party 'must be a means to bring about unity of struggle in the ranks of white toilers'. Communists should also support the white working class, poor farmers and 'struggling petty bourgeoisie', through the formation of a 'Farmer-Labour Party'.[137] A Farmers' and Workers' Party did lead an ephemeral existence for a year or so, a development welcomed by the communists though it had no connections with them, but, in other ways as well, party leaders would signal very clearly the fresh importance they were going to attach to attracting white workers and other white groups.[138] A lengthy piece in *Umsebenzi* (23 May 1936) referred to two different kinds of alliances the party should be striving to foster – a united front or fronts between groups with similar class interests: white and black workers; and landless white peasants who could struggle against big estate owners 'with the help of a native peasantry'. And then there was the 'people's front', a multi-class formation, but here 'it is ... evident that apart from help by the revolutionary conscious section of the Blacks whenever such help is required or useful, the part of the natives in this peoples' front must be limited for the time being'. So, notionally, communists would be working to foster class unity among workers but they would also be involved in wider political efforts that would remain racially separated. And with respect to workers, significant compromises were needed to build class unity. In the first of these, the party newspaper underwent another change, back to being titled *South African Worker* on 13 June. The change was not welcomed by everybody, as Hardy later reported. Roux called the alteration 'Jim Crowism'. However, Hardy observed: 'When we changed the paper one comrade alone got over 150 subscribers in Johannesburg and one report states that party membership has doubled.'[139] The *Umsebenzi* masthead would be reintroduced at the beginning of 1938, less than two years later. In fact, after Roux's departure, the newspaper's sales declined and in mid-1938 it ceased publication.

In any case, more was needed to make the party appealing to white workers than merely name changes. As Edwin Mofutsanyana pointed out at the party's long-delayed conference held in September, 'we have to consider the prejudices existing, which resists the question of unity'.[140] In line with this consideration, the party resolved itself in favour of an unskilled minimum daily wage for Europeans of ten shillings and five shillings for native workers. In future, it was decided the party would assume an active role in 'national reformist mass organisations' while simultaneously 'working consistently' within the European working class.[141] As Jonathan Grossman has observed, the resolutions did not appear to assign any particular political role to black workers. For black activists, the priority was to work with nationalist bodies; at this stage, when party leaders spoke about organised labour, they were mostly referring to registered unions.[142] The resolutions elicited mixed comments from André Marty in his report to the Anglo-American Secretariat; the general line they reflected was appropriate but they were far too wordy to be understood easily by the groups the communists were trying to appeal to: 'They are primitive people,' he reminded his colleagues.[143] A leaflet circulated shortly afterwards argued the case for 'defend[ing] the positions attained by skilled and high paid workers'. At the same time, it was 'imperative' to win over 'rank and file Afrikaners', particularly poor whites. In building alliances, the party should acknowledge the difference between fascism and 'ordinary colonial oppression'. At present, it was still possible that 'when a native suing the police for violence [they] can obtain a favourable verdict.[144] In fact, in the white-led 'People's Front' that was constituted in 1936, communists encountered considerable resistance from 'white men who answered a call to drive Greyshirts off the streets', to any appeal to oppose the police's enforcement of pass laws through raids and pick-up vans.[145] Quite what the party would mean by a united front was evident at a conference it helped to sponsor at the Trades and Labour Council, at the beginning of October. Despite representation from the Natives' Trade Union Coordinating Committee, a body led by Gana Makabeni, who had still not returned to the party,[146] not a single African, coloured or Indian trade unionist was chosen as an office-bearer or appointed to its national organising committee.[147] The following year, Willie Kalk took the step of proposing a racially differentiated minimum wage at a meeting of the Trades and Labour Council. Despite objections from other party members present, probably from the Cape, Kalk's suggestion was adopted;[148] it was, after all, in line with the party's own resolutions at its conference in 1936. In the manifesto which the party used to contest general elections in May 1938, it reproduced Kalk's proposal, calling for a minimum wage of ten shillings for European and five shillings for African workers.

Meanwhile, as Hardy noted in February 1937, 'it took considerable persuasion to convince Comrade Kotane as to the need to adopt a class attitude towards exclusion of Natives from the railways'; that is, to accept that for the time being employment on the railways would remain a preserve for unskilled white employment.[149] In the same conciliatory vein, a well-attended ('mostly natives') meeting of the Johannesburg district in April 1937 discussed preparations for May Day. The Labour Party, Willie Kalk reported, wanted a 'European Only' platform. It was necessary to compromise, he said. Kalk had to 'shout down their throats' when people disagreed with him, Wolfson reported, but he got his way: 'we decided to put forward two platforms'.[150] In November that year, Hyman Basner wrote to André Marty, expressing his concerns about the effects of Kalk's and Wolfson's leadership. It was necessary, Basner felt, 'for these two comrades to drop a certain attitude of bossism towards the native members of the party'. He was also worried by a resolution drafted for the party by its British communist supervisors, which 'seems to take South Africa out of the category of a colonial country and is formulated in such a way as to express that a fundamental change of conditions can be brought about without the native masses'.[151] The resolution's main focus was about the ways the party could oppose 'the war danger' and fascism, and it was indeed mainly concerned with how alliances embracing white workers might be constructed.[152] André Marty seems to have agreed with Basner, writing to Dimitrov that the Londoners 'had completely excluded the natives from the next election campaign for parliament'. George Hardy was exercising far too much influence 'because of his so-called "familiarity" with South Africa' and had completely subjected Issy Wolfson. The position of the London committee was 'completely wrong', he believed.[153]

How far the party had moved from the non-racial solidarities that it was beginning to achieve in the late 1920s is illustrated by the content of a party-published pamphlet, undated, but actually issued in 1938 by the Johannesburg District Committee. Moses Kotane made an angry reference to it at the party's conference at the end of that year.[154] Entitled *Communism and the Native Question*, the pamphlet was written in a way that suggested that the party could quite comfortably accommodate everyday racial prejudices. It seems to have been directed at organisers so that they could obtain insights on how to address such sentiments. They could start, the authors of the pamphlet advised, by pointing out that 'if you are drowning, you cannot stop to enquire whether your rescuer has a black skin or a sour smell'. But more careful arguments might need to be marshalled among more intransigent groups of white workers:

> If the 'Kafir Boetie' jibe doesn't get home, such people will follow up with the shameless assertion that it will end up with the races getting mixed up, and 'How would you like your sister to marry a native?' This sort of talk shows a great want of confidence in South African women and is a cheap

and unworthy insult to them. It overlooks the fact that neither race wants to mix up with the others. Where racial intermixture does take place, it is largely due to poverty and backwardness of native women which leaves them without self respect. If both races have the self respect that comes from a proper human status and a proper standard of living, mixing will be far less likely to take place [10–11] ... To many workers the barbarity, uncouthness and backwardness of the native is a serious deterrent. The individual worker may object to the native's colour or his smell and may start by shuddering at the idea of being his 'comrade' but the Communist Party knows that economics is not a parlour game ... The European worker must therefore help and teach the native to organise his labour. It matters not if to start with they are put into separate trade unions as long as the unions of the native workers affiliate to and act in conjunction with the European trade unions [12] ... He wants the European to help him and lead him.[155]

Did these efforts pay off? Is there any evidence that the party elicited fresh sympathy and support from white workers and other groups during this period? There are a few indications in party records that the communists may have been reaching new groups. Reporting to Comintern in mid-April 1937, Issy Wolfson mentioned 'good work' in Pretoria where George Findlay had constituted a trade union study group, 'teaching Marx to 60 European trade unionists'.[156] Party members were, arguably, extending their presence in leadership positions in white trade unions. In another of his reports, in October 1937, Issy Wolfson referred to 'a leading member of the Ironmoulders' Union' as a recent recruit to the party. In general, he thought, 'the relation of the Party to the trade unions' had improved recently in Johannesburg, especially with respect to the numbers of party members holding leading positions in the Trades and Labour Council.[157] How many of them made their party affiliations conspicuous or explicit he did not disclose. In Cape Town in 1937, James Emmerich was elected to the secretaryship of the Cape Tramways Union, though without revealing he was a communist;[158] in fact, in that year he stood unsuccessfully in a municipal election as a Labour Party candidate. Another left-winger, Betty Radford, did win a seat on the Cape Town City Council. Betty Radford would actually join the Communist Party only in 1941, but she was considered by party members as a sympathiser. In 1937, as well as winning her council seat, she would edit *The Guardian*, a new weekly newspaper which unofficially became the party's voice in Cape Town and, indeed, nationally. Radford was an experienced journalist, formerly the editor of the *Cape Times*'s social page. Married to a wealthy Dublin-trained surgeon, George Sacks, and with her cut-glass English accent and British 'county' background, she rather stood out among the comrades.[159] It was in fact George who founded *The Guardian*, probably using funds he had inherited from his father's tobacco factory.[160] *The Guardian* would become an influential and popular paper, by far the most professional of the journals associated with the party.[161]

In the same year, the party started producing an Afrikaans-language bulletin, *Die Ware Republikein*, paying the Afrikaner nationalist media house, Nasionale Pers, for its printing.[162] As noted above, winning over supporters of 'Malan's movement' was a key priority identified by the Marty Commission in 1936; even Kotane during this discussion had suggested that trying to find Afrikaner nationalist allies among the opponents of Fusion would be a worthwhile undertaking.[163] For the purpose of attracting working-class Afrikaners, Comintern officials as early as February 1932 prepared a resolution in which the party would offer support for 'the struggle of the Boer people' and 'for the creation of an independent Boer republic'. They had second thoughts about this, it seems, for the resolution remained a tentative draft and was taken no further.[164] Winning support from Afrikaner workers may appear retrospectively a hopelessly quixotic quest, but, as the case of the Garment Workers' Union (GWU) illustrates, in the 1930s unskilled or semi-skilled Afrikaner workers could respond to militant left-wing leadership and, in doing so, work collaboratively with black organised labour. Women members of the GWU often lived in households headed by unskilled railway workers, a group that was a principal target for Afrikaner nationalist trade unionism.[165] On the whole, the trade unions in the Transvaal, assembled under the Trades and Labour Council, which communists helped lead, were dominated by craft-based bodies that made no serious effort to organise unskilled Afrikaner workers, leaving the field open for Malan's wing of Afrikaner nationalism.[166] As with the textile workers, the white garment workers were fairly exceptional within the Trades and Labour Council fold in that they were at best semi-skilled and undertook productive work rather than exercising supervisory functions over Africans.[167] That and their composition from a relatively marginalised group, recently urbanised Afrikaans-speaking white women, help to explain their instances of solidarity with black workers. But with respect to Afrikaans-speaking workers, to draw them into the party's embrace, rather more would have been needed than republican bulletins or free trips to the USSR for union leaders. It would have needed a more systematic approach within high trade union politics as well as fresh organisational initiatives. In this period, communist pro-Afrikaner propaganda was belied by electoral support for the Labour Party and the Party's presence within the hierarchy at the Trades and Labour Council, a body that generally neglected the unskilled workforces composed mainly of white Afrikaans-speaking men.[168]

Be that as it may, in Johannesburg braver Youth League members were deployed to sell *Die Ware Republikein* at the fringes of Afrikaner nationalist gatherings held at Melville Koppies; one of them only escaped an almost certain beating after being rescued by a motherly group of Kappie Commandos.[169] Sellers of *Die Ware Republikein* encountered more receptive readers in the poorer parts of Cape Town apparently, and Ray Alexander remembered that at this time Afrikaner railway workers actually began to attend party meetings.[170] Issy Heymann, whose entry into the party in 1936 was preceded by Jewish Workers' Club activism, organised a party branch with 20 white and Indian members in Krugersdorp in 1939. Interviewed in 1987, he recalled an especially well-attended picnic in Emmarentia, near the Zoo, organised by the Young Communists in 1938; it drew more than a thousand visitors, he thought.[171] The occasion was in fact an event held under the auspices of the International Youth League, a party-led front with a membership of about 500. Louis Joffe, like his brother Max, was one of its main moving spirits and, according to Wolfson, he had 'put a lot of money in to the movement himself'.[172] Its membership overlapped considerably with that of the Jewish Workers' Club.[173]

Well-attended picnics or even communists holding senior positions in white trade unions did not generate a significant organised following among white South Africans. As Wolfson ruefully admitted in his reporting to the Comintern, the party had not even attempted 'to get a foothold … in any of the European working class suburbs in Johannesburg'. Anti-fascist agitation or even events associated with the Friends of the Soviet Union did not result in any significant extension of the party's organised base, even in those neighbourhoods or among those groups in which these bodies were active.[174] As Allison Drew has noticed, 'amongst white trade unionists, broad sympathy for the USSR could co-exist with dismissal of the CPSA as a significant political factor'.[175] Even Garment Workers' Union leaders like Anna Scheepers and Dulcie Hartwell, for whom the party arranged invitations to visit the Soviet Union, tended to remain within the Labour Party, holding back from joining the communists. In 1938, relations with the GWU, which had become warmer after 1935, once again deteriorated after communists who held official positions in the Trades and Labour Council became embroiled in a sharp dispute with Solly Sachs. Trades and Labour Council executive members had withheld their support from Sachs's efforts to secure employer recognition for the GWU branch in King Williamstown, and after he had accused them of betrayal, they expelled Sachs from the executive, an action that he successfully contested in court.[176] Communists in Cape Town rather tended to side with Sachs in this quarrel, for, as Eli Weinberg pointed out, 'if it had not been for Sachs in Cape Town we would not have been able to do much of what we have done'.[177] In Cape Town communists had organised their own 'fraction' within the GWU.

In general, between 1936 and 1939 the party's membership remained roughly the same and very small. The total figures in party reports in this period, which refer to the organisation's active following, fluctuated between 150 and 250. Moreover, as Wolfson commented in April 1937, any recruitment successes were hard to sustain, for organisers were finding it 'difficult to retain new members'.[178] The minutes of a Politburo meeting on 11 June 1937 contain a list of the party's active groups in the vicinity of Johannesburg: in all the places mentioned – Sophiatown, Ferreirastown, Doornfontein, Vrededorp, Benoni, Pimville, Eastern Native Township and Prospect – the names of the organisers for each group suggest they were composed mainly of Africans, with the exception of Doornfontein and Ferreirastown, in which the organisers were both activists with Jewish Workers' Club backgrounds.[179] The organiser for Pimville was listed as William Thibedi, now reinstated in the party and in fact employed to organise a steel workers' trade union, a body that he had helped start in Vereeniging in 1928.[180]

How busy were these groups is questionable. Wolfson, writing in October 1937, maintained that in the Transvaal 'the only place where there is some independent party activity is at V.', where apparently the party held regular meetings on Sundays at the town hall square. 'V' may have stood for Vereeniging, but this would be puzzling. In a pamphlet the party denied involvement in a riot in which two policemen were killed following liquor raids in Vereeniging's Topville location.[181] The party had no local presence, the authors of the pamphlet claimed. Wolfson's report would appear to contradict this, and indeed it would be strange if the party had no residual local support in Topville, which only a few years before had provided it with one of its largest local African followings. The commission of inquiry appointed to investigate the causes of the riots did in fact ask questions about whether communists had been engaged in any way and concluded in its report that they had not.[182] Tensions had been building up over police enforcement of local regulations, especially controls on lodgers or sub-tenants. One of the witnesses they interviewed, the manager of the main compound housing steel workers, did believe there was a 'certain amount' of communist activity in the district. But he did not think that communists had been involved in the riots. Another witness mentioned that in June two African workers had been dismissed from one of the local steelworks for inciting workers to strike, possibly evidence of activity by William Thibedi's revived steel workers' union.[183] Clearly, though, for the party leadership in Johannesburg, the Vereeniging riots were about local grievances that were not connected to their strategic priorities, though in the aftermath of the riots communists began selling their newspaper in the location.[184] In fact, the 1936 Urban Areas Amendment Act had introduced a fresh range of controls over African urban residents, including new powers to deport non-taxpayers, but the party's African-focused agenda at this point was directed at rather different concerns, in particular the formation of a people's front.

AMONGST AFRICAN COMMUNISTS, the party's strategic vision as expressed at its plenary meeting in April 1936 directed them into supporting a new body, the All African Convention (AAC). The AAC began as a conference called for by the ANC in May 1935 to oppose impending legislation that would have abolished the Cape franchise, replacing it with an advisory Native Representative Council and special (white) Native representatives in the House of Assembly and the Senate. A second draft Native Trust and Land Bill offered the prospect of more land for the reserves, in tacit compensation for the loss of the common roll voting rights, though the Land Bill also threatened further removals of Africans from white farms. The AAC would assemble in Bloemfontein between 15 and 18 December 1935, bringing together 400 delegates across the African organisational spectrum, including representatives of the Communist Party. Edwin Mofutsanyana was elected to the AAC's executive, which was otherwise dominated by ANC notables as well as ICU veterans. The Convention expressed outright opposition to the new arrangements for African political representation, though its response to the Land Bill was more ambiguous. The AAC did succeed in securing a meeting in February 1936 with Prime Minister JBM Hertzog, who offered the possibility of changes in the bills if African leaders were prepared to accept the loss of the common roll vote – a proposal that for a while succeeded in dividing the leadership that had gathered at Bloemfontein. By June, at its second conference AAC leaders were split on how to protest against the government's measures, which became law in April 1936. Subsequently most Convention leaders would support participation in the new electoral dispensation, though a minority held out for a boycott. In mid-1937 elections were held for the three House of Assembly representatives for the Cape Province and the four senators as well as the Native Representative Council (NRC).

The party's plenary meeting in April 1936 envisaged that the AAC would become a permanent body with an organised mass base constituted by 'peasant unions' and other grassroots formations that would mobilise in conjunction with a revived trade union movement. During the rest of 1936 and 1937, communists continued to argue in favour of the AAC becoming the main vehicle for African organised protest. In December, Moses Kotane wrote to Johnny Gomas to express his view that the ANC 'is today in its death pangs', though he held out the hope that with a change of leadership, that 'catastrophe might be averted'. An article in the *South African Worker* in September 1937 referred to the possibility of a revived ANC taking its place as a key force in a United African Front.[185] In reality, neither the AAC nor the ANC in those years had the kind of participatory organisational structure that might accommodate militant on-the-ground activism. Even so, Edwin Mofutsanyana joined the ANC's executive at the end of 1937.[186]

The party did contest the 1937 Native Representative elections, backing Edwin Mofutsanyana as a candidate for the NRC election and allowing Hyman Basner to contest the senatorial seat for the Transvaal and the Free State. Basner in fact proposed himself, though he was one of the few party members with the necessary freehold property ownership to stand. JB Marks offered to help him campaign and, as Edwin Mofutsanyana was contesting an NRC seat that represented the townships of the Transvaal and the Free State, he, Marks and Basner would tour the relevant locations as a team. For Basner, Marks – 'fond of lively parties, strong drink, and strong polemics'[187] – provided engaging company, but he was often distracted by other commitments, being compelled to work for the rich bus owner, Richard Baloyi, because he was always broke.[188] Because of his warmth and wit, Marks might have been a better choice for the NRC seat candidature, but Mofutsanyana was the party's general secretary and, unlike Marks, was (in the words of Eugene Dennis) 'dependable and politically consistent', though, writing in 1933, Dennis had noted Mofutsanyana's lack of self-confidence.[189] The elections were indirect: votes would be cast by a mixture of Advisory Boards, acting on the basis of a majority decision, and rural councils made up of headmen or, in certain districts, chiefs voting on behalf of the men in their reserves. All these agencies needed to be visited and persuaded, though, as Basner would discover, approaches to the chiefs were unrewarding. In the Free State, support from former ICU leaders was helpful and the team made more headway with Advisory Board members in the smaller centres, using as initial contacts lists supplied by Keable Mote, 'one of Kadalie's leading lieutenants' – lists of 'teachers, self-employed artisans, clergy, general labourers, hawkers ... the names ... of men and women who had been office bearers in the ICU'.[190] JB Marks helped to win Mote's confidence; he had known him 'very well' since the 1920s.[191] In Kroonstad, 'natives came from all over the surrounding farms to the main meeting', Basner told his fellow members of the Politburo – information that suggests that here at least, the Communist Party was once again benefiting from earlier networks established by the rural ICU.[192] The party did itself have party groups in Kroonstad at one stage, apparently.[193] Mote advised Basner to 'concentrate on the women ... they are the real fighters', an observation that may have reflected the ICU's own experience of the contribution women made to tax protests during the late 1920s and early 1930s.[194] Basner had one speech, 'which he was to repeat over and over', directed mainly at women, though there were plenty of men in his audiences:

> He told them that their children did not go to school because it was ordained that they should be menials when they grew up – in kitchens, on mealie fields, and deep beneath the ground. He scarcely needed to tell them that their infant sons would be humiliated and brutalised ... He told them that their husbands, fathers and grandfathers were called 'boys' because they were paid a boy's wages and not a man's. He told them they lived in municipal locations under permit so that when they and their men became too old to be of use as workers they could be sent away to die – anywhere ... it was time to stop crying and drive their men into Congress and trade unions and make them strong.[195]

There must have been other speeches, because the ever-vigilant Robert Naumann noticed various 'sectarian' references to 'good boys' with regard to 'native reformists', but in fact Basner had been quite conscientious in his efforts to obtain support from the less conservative ANC leaders.[196] On election day Basner polled 66,234 votes, against the total of 404,447 for the winning candidate, JD Rheinallt Jones, the director of the Institute of Race Relations. This was a creditable performance and a foundation for his later successful senatorial campaign in 1942 in which he benefited from the revitalisation of the ANC as a localised political presence. The totals were actually misleading because Basner's share was heavily made up by Advisory Board polling whereas Jones obtained all the bloc votes wielded by chiefs, so Basner claimed. In fact, the electoral colleges wielding bloc votes were elected committees constituted by taxpayers, but these were mainly located in the countryside and their make-up would have been strongly shaped by chiefly influence, so outside urban locations Basner would indeed have struggled to win them over.[197] Mofutsanyana fared worse, obtaining one of the lowest totals, possibly because his speeches were doctrinaire expressions of party orthodoxies delivered in a manner that 'lacked the common touch',[198] though Mofutsanyana complained later that the party's support for him was half-hearted. It was true that the party could not find funding to pay for his travel during the campaign.[199] Mofutsanyana campaigned in the name of the Communist Party, whereas Basner presented himself as the candidate of the African Unity Committee, a group of notables including the Transvaal and Orange Free State provincial ANC's office-holders.[200]

As one member of the British party's Colonial Committee pointed out subsequently, the party made no significant recruitment gains during its electoral campaigning.[201] But encouraged by Basner's performance, the party resolved in November 1937 to contest Advisory Board elections. In the same month, a party member, Gaur Radebe, would be elected as general secretary at a conference of Native Vigilance Associations, a sign of the new attention that African communists would begin paying to township-based associational life.[202] As Basner had pointed out, Advisory Boards had an important role as local gatekeepers; preparations for the All African Convention had alerted communists to the importance of winning allies in the Boards if they were to obtain official sanction to call meetings.[203] Basner also found during his campaigning that Vigilance Associations were 'universally militant and radical in temperament'.[204] Standing for the Vigilance Association, Radebe won a seat in the Advisory Board elections in Orlando in December 1937.[205] In the municipal elections held in June that year, Wolfson tried to secure an agreement with Labour in which both parties would support each other's candidates in wards they were not contesting. He was rebuffed, politely apparently, but even so the party urged its enfranchised followers to vote Labour. In Johannesburg a few party members also maintained a party group within the Labour Party.[206]

DESPITE THE PRIORITY ASSIGNED by party leaders to winning over white workers, in fact during this period, between 1936 and 1939, the main successes the party enjoyed in extending its influence were among other groups. Reporting to Comintern's executive in February 1937, George Hardy mentioned a member of the Central Committee who was 'living on a native reserve', working as a chief's secretary. This was Alpheus Maliba, who had joined the party the previous year after learning to read and write at its night school. He began publishing articles in Venda for party publications in July 1939 and two years later would form the Zoutpansberg Cultural Association, an innocuous title for a body that would engage with farmers in opposition to new agricultural regulations, dealing with erosion, that restricted ploughing.[207] Meanwhile, Edwin Mofutsanyana, writing in the party paper in June 1937, referred to a growth of membership in the Johannesburg district but complained about a lack of supportive action to complement this fresh recruitment. There was 'criminal negligence', he charged, among party workers, and group meeting attendance was irregular. With respect to the new members, it was 'mainly natives filling in forms', he maintained.[208] There is evidence that a branch of the Young Communists became active in Alexandra township in 1938. This was new territory for the party.[209] But internal party documents rather confirm Mofutsanyana's contention that party officials were uninterested in supporting efforts to mobilise Africans. Wolfson, writing to the Comintern in April 1937, mentioned Willie Kalk's failure to pay the levy that had been imposed on all members to support Basner's and Mofutsanyana's campaigning, an omission 'that brings about a feeling of disgust amongst the rank and file'.[210] And in Johannesburg, the party's own efforts to revive African trade unions were desultory. There were African communists working in Makabeni's Coordinating Committee, and on the whole the party would attempt to develop friendly relations with Makabeni's group. As Wolfson had informed a Politburo meeting in November 1936, on the Witwatersrand it was the Trotskyists who were taking the lead in organising laundry workers and the party's own employment of Thibedi as a full-time organiser for steel workers 'had not brought in a single penny'.[211] Writing to Harry Pollitt nearly a year later, Solly Sachs confirmed that in Johannesburg 'the few native unions that do exist are in the hands of the Trotskyists'. The local party's 'haphazard' attempts to set up African trade unions were 'childish and stupid'.[212]

In Durban, on the other hand, communist-aligned trade unionism was supplying a fresh focus for local activism. In 1934 or possibly earlier, Eddie Roux had recruited George Ponnen, one of the first Indian South Africans to join the party, probably during the time when he was visiting with Bettie du Toit, trying to persuade Indian textile workers to come out on a sympathy strike. Ponnen's first encounter with Roux was when he bought from him a copy of *Umsebenzi* outside the Durban City Hall. In the following decade Ponnen would help establish and lead 27 trade unions. Together with another recently joined Indian communist, HA Naidoo, Ponnen led an arguably successful strike for wage increases and reduced hours at Falkirk Foundry.[213] This involved 400 Indian, coloured and African workers organised by a new Iron and Steel Workers' Union, and it started on 26 May 1937, lasting 13 weeks. The workers received strike pay funded by the Natal Indian Congress though Champion's ICU instructed the Africans to renege and return to work.[214] Communist-led trade union struggles may not necessarily have extended the local party's membership. Writing to the British party in October 1937, Wolfson noted that though communists maintained an office in Durban, because of the restrictive local political climate they could not 'carry on active political work as a Communist Party ... in Durban last year the Party has not been able to hold a single independent meeting ... you cannot say that the party exists in Durban'.[215] Two months later, Edwin Mofutsanyana was telling the Central Committee about 'the terrible position' in Durban, where the 'Native' and white comrades were at odds with each other – the Africans, Mofutsanyana reported, were saying that the whites were chauvinists and Trotskyists. To be sure, the 'comrades did good work in the trade unions', but 'there was no party work, no meetings, no propaganda'.[216] Much the same point emerges from the most authoritative academic commentary on the communists' contribution to Indian trade unions in Durban: the party was too small to really shape the local labour movement despite so many unions being communist-led, and its local industrial secretariat was too short-staffed to perform its intended coordinating and liaison functions. Party night schools were directed at an elite group of union officials, not ordinary workers. In their public messaging Durban communists joined Natal Indian Congress activists in emphasising objections to segregation rather than stressing any specifically working-class issues.[217]

In Cape Town, the party was more visibly assertive. Ray Alexander worked for the party as a 'full-time functionary' from 1932. In this capacity she made a major contribution to the organisational effort that helped the local party to survive the thirties and, even towards the end of the decade, prosper. Alexander arrived in Cape Town already a communist, an immigrant from Latvia. While learning dressmaking at a technical school in Riga, she became involved in clandestine networks; she knew of Lazar Bach by reputation, though because he had not turned up for a prearranged meeting, she had not met him. She also encountered the future Czech president, Klement Gottwald, at a secret encampment organised by Young Communists.[218] Later in Cape Town she refused to work with Lazar Bach after he insisted on booking the two of them into a single hotel room while they were on a visit. But she was a firm supporter of the Native republic. She joined the CPSA as soon as she arrived in Cape Town, aged 16, attending its study classes and selling papers after her daily work at a dress shop. By 1933, when she helped Douglas Wolton in his attempt to win votes on the Cape Flats, she had made her first forays into trade unionism, organising African laundry workers and coloured bus and tram workers. In 1935 she helped set up a new union for shop workers and in the following year she was involved in the formation of a Non-European Railway and Harbour Workers' Union, launched in the same hall in which the ICU had held its foundation meeting. Altogether, between 1937 and 1939, Ray Alexander helped to establish 19 unions in and around Cape Town, many of them under communist leadership, mostly with coloured or African membership, often working through Wage Board investigations in order to obtain early gains for their members.[219] Coloured worker organisations were included in official industrial conciliation procedures, and this facilitated parallel unionism among Africans in the same workforces. In her autobiography, Alexander maintains that the local party's expanding following at this time was largely a result of members recruited from these new trade unions.[220] Communist recruitment of Africans in trade unions in the mid-to-late 1930s in Cape Town and Durban took place in conditions that had become more favourable for African industrial workers. This was a consequence of the expansion of manufacturing after 1933 and, most importantly, a new Wage Act in 1937 in which the Wage Board was reorganised so that it could more actively set African worker wages. Between 1933 and 1939 the annual number of Africans involved in strikes rose from 300 to 4,800 and the claimed membership of unregistered unions rose as well, as official figures indicate.[221]

The second channel for recruitment into the party in Cape Town, Alexander has suggested, was supplied by the National Liberation League. The League was formed in December 1935 with James La Guma elected as its organisational secretary. La Guma was at this stage again a party member, according to his son's biography of him, having been accepted back into its fold in 1935. La Guma was the main moving spirit behind the League's formation, composing its anthem, 'Arise, Ye Dark Folks', using his own savings to buy its office furniture, and corresponding with the League Against Imperialism in Brussels about the details of its constitution.[222] He also edited and produced its newspaper, borrowing much of its content from the Profintern journal, the *Negro Worker*. Despite the presence in its leadership of established working-class activists, including La Guma and Johnny Gomas, the League's constituency was rather different from the normal social milieu of Communist Party activism, for many of its adherents came from a 'closely-knit' coloured intelligentsia, well educated and middle class occupationally. The League's president was Cissie Gool, the daughter of Dr Abdullah Abdurahman. She had obtained an MA in psychology, the first black South African woman to hold such a qualification.[223] Their radicalisation, Gavin Lewis suggests, was a consequence of rising expectations among a new generation of university-educated coloured men and women, the first real graduate cohort in the coloured community, who were confronted with an increasingly segregatory political climate.[224] Schoolteachers were especially conspicuous in the National Liberation League,[225] and coloured high school students supplied a high proportion of the attendance at its meetings.[226] The League adopted a list of demands, including universal suffrage and equality for all South Africans as well as unity with oppressed peoples in a joint struggle against imperialist control.

Its day-to-day activities were less confrontational in tone. In 1936, for example, Cissie Gool led a deputation to the City Council to seek relief work for coloured unemployed people.[227] The League's most successful campaigning would be in 1938 and 1939, against proposals for stricter segregation in public transport and housing. Here it mobilised an alliance of 39 organisations coordinated by a Non-European United Front (NEUF), which could summon large crowds in its demonstrations. The Communist Party was an affiliate of the NEUF – indeed, communists held key positions in the Front's leadership, though the Front's affiliates also included the New Era Fellowship, a group heavily critical of 'Stalinists'.[228] Within the Front the party itself organised its own 'residential party group around the fight against segregation'.[229] Indeed, the scale of the Front's protests persuaded the government to rescind legislation recently enacted by the Cape Provincial Council. The success of this campaign was partly attributable to coloured trade union support. The League also benefited from sympathetic reportage in a new commercial newspaper, the *Cape Standard*, which employed Peter Abrahams as one of its journalists.[230] Though its appearance in 1935 fitted in nicely with the party's united front policy, neither the League nor the Front was a surrogate organisation, and throughout their history leadership would be contested between communist and Trotskyist-aligned factions. Trotskyists opposed what they perceived to be overly cautious pragmatism or 'collaborationism', which they attributed to the presence of white communists. The League's membership was open to all races from its inception, though its constitution stipulated that 'non-Europeans' should predominate in the movement's top echelon.[231] The conspicuous role played by Sam Kahn and Harry Snitcher in the League, both party members and close associates of Cissie Gool and, like her, active in earlier anti-fascist events, appeared to violate this provision. Cissie Gool lived with Sam Kahn and she herself would join the party, in the late 1930s: she became a Politburo member in 1939.[232] Cissie Gool and her husband used to hold 'open house' meetings every Saturday at their home in District Six. One visitor, a recent refugee from Nazi Germany, encountered 'a veritable League of Nations', with the company including Sam Kahn, 'a leading Stalinist Communist', the artists Gregoire Boonzaier and Frieda Locke and IB Tabata, 'prominent member of the Trotskyite Spartacus Club, in earnest conversation with Dr Eddie Roux'. On this occasion, Cissie Gool was 'sitting next to her father, busy berating him, calling him an Uncle Tom, for his lack of radical opposition to the prevailing political and social system'.[233]

Both Gomas and La Guma supported the group that tried to bar whites from holding office in the League in 1937. La Guma nevertheless maintained good relations with Cissie Gool, and worked as her election agent in Cape Town's municipal ward seven in September 1938, to good effect evidently, as she was elected. Alex La Guma's biography suggests that his father was not opposed to white communists playing an advisory role or influencing leadership 'behind the scenes'.[234] But he was expelled from the League and the party in mid-1939 for his continued opposition to the inclusion of whites on the National Liberation League executive. La Guma disputed his expulsion from the League and refused to hand over its record books until Cissie Gool obtained a court order. During 1939, after Cissie Gool's election as city councillor, the League would be increasingly directed into what Gool's more radical opponents would perceive as reformism and coloured sectionalism.[235] The League would also routinely supply canvassing for communist electoral candidates through the early 1940s and became increasingly focused around municipal concerns. Just how significant a party transmission belt the League would be is rather questionable. Peter Abrahams, a fairly impartial observer of the League in 1938, thought that most of the young teachers active in the League took their cues from the Trotskyist leadership rather than Cissie Gool and James La Guma.[236] In fact, though energetic and systematically organised, the party membership in Cape Town remained small. According to a report submitted to the British Communist Party, at the beginning of 1939 there were 42 active communists in Cape Town, 11 of them African and 18 coloured.[237] These were probably mostly trade unionists, not 'intellectuals'. Eli Weinberg, reporting to the British party's Colonial Committee in London in February 1939, confirmed that in Cape Town party membership was mainly composed of trade unionists.[238]

South African communists' readiness to build more affable external relationships after 1935 was not matched any inner harmony; the party remained a troubled and divided body. One particularly conspicuous feature of its continuing interior tensions was reprimands, disapproval and sanctions directed at several of the organisation's most effective personalities. United front politics did not have as a pre-requisite the ending of intolerance of any breaches of conformity within the party. On the contrary, as an editorial in the *South African Worker* (25 July 1937) declared, 'the purging of the party of opportunistic tendencies' was 'the necessary pre-requisite for the struggle against Fascism'. Left opposition was a particular preoccupation during this time, party leaders in Johannesburg taking their cues from the coded language and associated demonology emerging from the Moscow show trials. For example, George Hardy, writing to Comintern in February 1937, identified a group of 'bad elements' in the Johannesburg area, whom he perceived to be acting as a 'fraction'. They included the 'nationalist Kotane' (presumably a right-wing opportunist, to use the preferred terminology) and the 'Trotskyist Roux'. Hardy was also worried by what he took to be evidence of fractionalism in Cape Town, noting 'the tendency to intrigue' among a group headed by Eli Weinberg and Ray Alexander. His report resonated with perceptions in Moscow where officials recalled that both these individuals had a history of being 'in the background of factional struggle'.[239]

For Hardy, Roux's Trotskyist affiliations were openly evident in August 1936 when he called the Moscow trials 'Red Terror'.[240] At about the same time there was an exchange of letters in the *South African Worker* (8 August 1936), Roux writing on the need for a 'complete break with academic and sectarian nonsense' and Issy Wolfson alerting readers to the outstanding feature of Roux's letter, its 'fractional attitude'. Indeed, for this failing, the Politburo had 'instructed Comrade Kalk and myself to point out his mistakes'. Roux, writing in the 1960s, seemed then to think he was expelled in 1936,[241] but that was clearly not the case. Throughout much of 1937 he was active as a communist in Cape Town, co-editing with Moses Kotane the *African Defender*, the newspaper published by Ikaka la Basebenzi. In October 1937, Wolfson, reporting to the British party, complained about the continuing 'factionalist' activities of Kotane and Roux, joined now by Johnny Gomas. Dealing with Roux's objections to the trials in Moscow of Zinoviev and Kamenev was now an urgent imperative, he thought.[242] André Marty, too, expressed his alarm in a letter to Georgi Dimitrov at what he saw as 'a new revival of factional struggle' by Roux and Kotane. Apparently, their revival and production of the *African Defender* was in defiance of instructions from George Hardy,[243] and to one reader in Moscow, Robert Naumann, its content appeared 'very nationalistic'. Like Marty, Naumann perceived the *Defender*'s appearance as a 'new attempt to revive factional struggle'.[244] Even so, Wolfson was inclined to be conciliatory. Roux's case had been discussed by party leaders during 1937. He had in fact 'drifted away from the Party' but, while he appeared to share the errant views of his wife Winifred, as Issy Weinberg had observed 'he cannot be classified as a Trotskyite and that we must handle him very carefully ... not treat him very harshly'.[245] Winifred Roux had been a target of party disapproval for a long time. In fact, in 1932 Eddie had defied party orders when he married her; as a teacher at the genteel girls' school Roedean, she had the wrong sort of background for a good cadre.[246] Roux lost his seat on the Politburo in December 1938 as a consequence of a directive from Comintern, and it seems likely that he was expelled from the party at the same time, despite the perception among certain Johannesburg leaders that he had been their best organiser when he worked there.[247] The young writer Peter Abrahams met him at this time, in 1939. He describes Roux as 'tall and gaunt, not agreed with the new line, and broken'.[248]

The anxieties of Comintern officials were accentuated by some of the reports they were receiving from South African visitors. At one of his meetings with André Marty in Paris in October 1937, Hyman Basner told Marty in the presence of Hardy and Wolfson, in response to a question about his views on party personalities, that Moses Kotane and Johnny Gomas were 'strong nationalists'. But Kotane was a 'clever man' with a 'just understanding', and for him Basner professed 'respect'. Gomas, though, 'was the worst type, not so honest, and does not understand so much'. Eddie Roux was 'a typical chauvinist intellectual' and 'very emotional'. His wife, Winifred, was definitely a Trotskyist. As for John Marks, Basner's companion and friend during his election campaign just three months before, he 'was an enemy of the working class' who 'made open provocations'.[249] With some justification, Marty afterwards confided to one of the British communists involved in the South African section, that he thought Basner was dangerous.[250]

EVEN SO, MARTY WAS sufficiently concerned about the continuing South African factionalism to dispatch a final Comintern agent. Harry Pollitt had suggested sending back Hardy, who had returned to Britain in March, but Marty obviously believed that Hardy had been ineffective. Instead, Comintern's final ambassador would be Peter Kerrigan, another British Communist Party trade unionist, who had represented the party on Marty's inquiry into the South Africans. Kerrigan's short visit in early 1938 has left only a short and cryptic archival paper trail, and there is no evidence that he attempted to end the party's internal feuding.[251] He had conversations with Wolfson and Basner but did not encounter Kotane, it seems, who at this stage was completely at odds with the party's leadership in Johannesburg. In his most detailed report Kerrigan was critical of the extent to which the party's leadership overlapped with the Jewish Workers' Club; in general, he felt that 'foreign people not born in South Africa' enjoyed too much influence within the party. Among these he referred specifically to Willie Kalk, who, though South African-born, was 'of German extraction', and Basner, 'a lawyer of Russian extraction'. Despite the absence of people in leadership from the 'decisive strata' of workers, the party had nevertheless 'done a real effort on the Trade Union question'.[252] Kerrigan's visit seems to have brought to a close Andre Marty's engagement with the South African party. At this point, he had other more pressing concerns, being fully engaged in desperate efforts to stiffen the International Brigade's resistance to General Franco's spring offensive, beating exhausted soldiers over the head with his pistol butt.[253]

Kotane had incurred disapproval because, in Eli Weinberg's words, he had 'run away from Johannesburg', joining Eddie Roux in Cape Town in February 1937.[254] At the time of his departure from Johannesburg he had become increasingly disenchanted by what he perceived to be mismanagement and, in certain cases, to use his words, 'the rank dishonesty of some members' of the Politburo. He had arrived back from Moscow in 1936 to find 'the anti-united front section of the party at the head of affairs and pretending they had always been correct'. He wrote to Hardy after 'a little talk they had together', to remind him that the Comintern had asked for a complete change of leadership. He also repeated to Hardy Comintern's view that a tiny organisation such as the CPSA did not need a 'politburo', as an elected central committee should suffice. Not very surprisingly, he did not find a welcoming atmosphere when rejoining his South African comrades: rather, he recalled twenty years later, he was 'somehow treated with suspicion and a certain coolness'.[255] Co-opted onto the Politburo, he rapidly became alienated by its internal bickering as well as the growing hostility he encountered from George Hardy, who, as we have seen, perceived Kotane as a fractionalist. Another source of his unhappiness in Johannesburg was the racial condescension that he perceived in the party's everyday internal functioning. As he explained at the end of 1938, 'even in the Party office a European rank and file member is addressed in preference to the secretary of the party, an African' – he was referring to Edwin Mofutsanyana, nominally the senior office-holder in the Politburo.[256] His departure from Johannesburg was not sanctioned; in fact he was very close to leaving the party. He told the Politburo meeting on 26 January 1937 that he was not going to ask whether he could go. He was prepared to face the consequences but he 'was not going to listen to any discipline'. The condition of the party had brought him to this stage, he said; he needed a holiday.[257]

At this meeting, his former adversary from the time of Lazar Bach's ascendancy, John Marks, was especially unsympathetic. Comrade Kotane's remarks were 'very incorrect'. Indeed, Marks opined, 'I feel he is not a communist.'[258] JB Marks himself would shortly be in trouble with the Politburo. Marks's offence was not so much ideological; rather, it was felt that he had compromised the party's security by reporting to the police the theft of his baggage, which he had lost while travelling back from Paris; this indiscretion prompted the authorities to investigate his illegal departure from South Africa. He had already been censured by Comintern officials for not arriving in Moscow in 1935, a decision which in his letter back to them he explained was a consequence of 'recent disturbances in the Soviet Union' which would make his journey unsafe – an oblique but nevertheless tactless reference to the purges. French communists had in fact dissuaded him from extending his journey. In his letter he also referred to rumours within the South African party that Nzula had been liquidated because 'he did not see eye to eye with the C.I. on the Native question'.[259] Neither his excuses for his non-arrival nor this kind of observation would have reassured Comintern officials. They were already alarmed by earlier rumours that Marks was a spy. Marks had in fact been approached by the police to work for them in 1930; he agreed to do so, but then told his comrades about this invitation.[260] The reasons offered for his expulsion in the *South African Worker* were to do with failures of discipline (3 July 1937) and 'gross and criminal negligence'.[261] But he was back in the party by 1940.

There were other expulsions of lesser personalities. In mid-1938 *Umsebenzi* carried a report on the expulsion of J Kamudi and Edward Mokoena 'for refusing to work under the discipline of the party and attacking, slandering and trying to discredit the party in the eyes of the public'.[262] Roth, citing Comintern documentation, had Gomas expelled in August 1937 after he blamed the poor state of the party on white communists.[263] The final major excommunication was that of Hyman Basner. The Central Committee decided at the end of that year that through publishing in the party's name a pamphlet on the Czech crisis in which 'he slandered the Comintern and some of its leading parties', he had 'introduced his Trotskyite views'. In future, the committee decreed, he should hold no senior positions.[264] In the pamphlet Basner had attacked the British and the French parties for their failure to oppose the Munich agreement. In October 1939, Basner announced his departure from the party in a letter to *The Star*, a solitary protest against the Soviet invasion of Finland.[265]

By the end of 1938, the personal antipathies within the party's upper echelon had reached a stage at which leadership had ceased to exercise any effective authority. In the words of the British committee charged with the party's supervision, the party's organisation in Johannesburg was simply chaotic.[266] The quarrelsome atmosphere was evident even to newly recruited members experiencing their first 'aggregate' meetings in the Johannesburg district: 'Debate was fierce and adversarial. Speakers snapped at one another, attacked each other passionately and personally. The jargon flew – factional, sectarian, opportunist, revisionist ... The first aggregate meeting ended with a spiritless singing of the Internationale. The factions separated and left without much more than a curt "good-night".'[267] The difficulties were partly a consequence of personalised antipathies, but they were also the product of the way that Comintern's 'line' on united and popular fronts had been interpreted in South Africa. The minutes of a lengthy meeting of the Central Committee beginning on 29 January supply a detailed picture.[268] As was the accepted routine, the meeting opened with Willie Kalk's report on the political situation and the party's forthcoming tasks. Kalk reviewed the rift between the Trades and Labour Council with the Garment Workers' Union and explained his objections to Basner's pamphlet on Czechoslovakia. He then spoke about the relationship communists were trying to build with the Labour Party, referring to a meeting between the two youth organisations of both parties in which communists were 'concerned only in scoring debating points', a predisposition he attributed 'to the low political level of the party'. He was critical of the Cape Town communists, who were mainly confining their activity to trade union organisation, he contended. The problem, he said, was that the Politburo had failed to lead. 'At present', he admitted, 'we are functioning in groups here and there and cannot really call ourselves a party.' Mofutsanyana then read out his report on African struggles. He was despondent about the situation of Africans in the party. 'At party meetings they do not speak' and it was impossible to persuade them even to make the minimal commitment of paying their subscriptions. Perhaps the party would be better off if it functioned through two formally designated racial sections.

Moses Kotane led the open discussion. Communists 'hadn't done much in any sphere', he suggested. It was not just the case of the neglect of issues that might engage Africans. It had failed, for example, to take up concerns Indians had about their trading rights. Here was the weakness, he said: 'the Centre has not agreed on a number of questions.' People were put in positions 'they are not capable of fulfilling'. Africans filled functionary (paid) positions nominally but remained an 'ornament'. Africans, even in positions of authority, were kept uninformed, about money matters for example. This was dangerously demoralising: 'as long as you have native members [who] think you have control of the money, you will never have a healthy party.' And it was true, the Johannesburg centre was failing, it was not providing directives or even responding to letters. But racial sections would not solve the problem, he felt; indeed, 'if we have two sections I shall walk out of the Communist Party'. Kotane claimed he was speaking on behalf of his Cape Town comrades, and in general this seems to have been the case. But Mofutsanyana's argument appeared to be shared by Johannesburg-based Africans at the meeting. Sections would be a good idea, Gaur Radebe believed. Mofutsanyana in working with Kalk and Wolfson 'felt out of place'; 'he'd had a row' and he had not been paid; he did not even have the stamps in the office that he needed to answer letters.

The minutes of the meeting extended to 46 closely typed pages. They include sharp observations about the failings of particular individuals: 'Kalk does not do any work', for example, or 'Edwin doesn't give leads when he is asked to time and time again' or 'Basner does not know the first thing about organising'. Most of the dissatisfaction expressed was directed at the way the key office-holders had neglected certain concerns and prioritised others. As Josie Mpama noted, 'in practice the separate work actually exists ... Natives' questions are not discussed at [Johannesburg District] meetings.' It was not just neglect, as Nikin, also from the Johannesburg district, explained: 'we are told there is no money for native work and we have to accept this.' In fact, as Wolfson admitted, even in 1938, a bad year financially for the party, when it supposedly could no longer afford to publish its newspaper, it had succeeded in raising £700, but 'what can we show for it?' The problem was not just limited to Johannesburg, Durban's HA Naidoo believed, for 'the Communist Party has not taken the Indian question seriously'. In Natal, he continued, there was 'plenty of scope for organisation' but at present the party had too few members there. In Johannesburg, Ray Alexander observed, members of the secretariat failed to attend group meetings. In Cape Town, district leaders made weekly visits to the groups. In Johannesburg, the groups were chiefly located in African areas, and their neglect certainly would have encouraged the perception that the party's leaders were interested in concerns located elsewhere, that (in Mofutsanyana's words) 'Europeans are given preference in the party'.

At the end of this argumentative marathon there was general agreement with Moses Kotane's view that, at least temporarily, the Johannesburg group 'should be relieved of all national tasks' and that these should be transferred to an executive body located in Cape Town. It was resolved, then, that the party's new headquarters would be in Cape Town. Moses Kotane, Bill Andrews, Ray Alexander, Cissie Gool, Sam Kahn and Jack Simons, all Cape Town-based, would constitute the Politburo together with Willie Kalk and Issy Wolfson to represent the Johannesburg membership. Moses Kotane, Bill Andrews and Jack Simons would staff a new secretariat with Kotane serving as general secretary. Bill Andrews's presence notwithstanding, the Communist Party had engaged a new leadership composed of people who would shape its history for the next five decades.

AT THE BEGINNING OF this chapter, detailed exposition of the party's activities in Germiston in 1932, in drawing upon independent archival and press reportage, offers a reassuring confirmation of the veracity of memoirs by the activists, the main source of authoritative treatments of the events. The success the party enjoyed here in eliciting responses across local racial divisions was unusual, though not unique. There were occasions during the early episodes of its campaigning among the unemployed in 1932 when communists succeeded in attracting multiracial crowds at its meetings. From time to time during the early 1930s, party initiatives in particular settings tapped into already animated local struggles motivated by particular grievances, most notably with respect to a wave of angry reactions to additional taxes that the government struggled to impose on African communities from 1929. These communal insurgencies could provide resonant settings for the party's campaigning. But in the neighbourhoods in which party workers succeeded in connecting their concerns to local tumults, they were unable to convert such connections into long-term followings. This was not least because a key accompaniment of 'Bolshevisation' was leaders' eschewal of any effort to build mass membership.

This was just one way in which directives from Moscow that arose from doctrinaire shifts in the interpretation of the Native republic slogan inhibited South African party activists from responding to opportunities resulting from changing conditions. Indeed, it is quite striking how occasional defiance or ignorance of Comintern injunctions could reap rewards, as in the efforts by communists in Durban to obstruct the docking of Italian shipping. But so often when opportunities arose, the party no longer had the right people in place to exploit them. Nowhere was this more obvious than in the case of organising African trade unions. In place of communists at the helm, the lead role in building African labour organisation was assumed either by rival groups – 'Trotskyites' – or by people the party itself had expelled, such as Gana Makabeni.

The failure to build new bases among black workers during the post-1933 revival of the industrial economy was also an effect of the external strategic promptings that followed Comintern's repudiation of its former 'new line' and its advocacy instead of popular fronts against fascism. To be fair, part of the responsibility for the way Comintern's policies were interpreted is attributable to the views of British communists appointed to supervise the South African party. It is also the case that in concentrating their efforts on trying to secure leadership among registered white trade unions, the trade unionists in the South African party's leadership were working in their own comfort zone. Now they were free once again to use tactics and work with organisations hitherto denounced as reformist or 'social fascist'. So, in effect, Comintern's strategic direction after 1936 restored the pre-1927 primacy of white labour in the party's priorities. Arguably it also allowed space for party activists in Durban and Cape Town to extend the reach of party-influenced registered trade unions among the coloured and Indian workers who were increasingly employed in industrial work. In Cape Town, Ray Alexander was rather exceptional in her willingness to move beyond the base which her leadership of the registered unions provided, to extend the party's reach among black workers. Popular frontism, focused mainly on trying to build alliances among white South Africans against fascism, produced few durable gains with respect to organised white labour or, more surprisingly, among Indian workers in Natal. It may have enhanced the party's appeal among well-educated middle-class professionals, a group regarded by Comintern agents with disdain, particularly if they were Jewish. Communists were conspicuous within trade union leadership but their popularity among workers did not bring the party new followers, partly because they themselves did not project a communist identity to shop-floor trade union members. Meanwhile, the party's developing entanglement with the English-speaking white labour establishment seems to have checked its capacity to build a following among semi-skilled Afrikaner workers, or at least to deflect them from embracing racially sectional nationalism, a key strategic aim. After all, the most successful white trade unionist in drawing Afrikaner workers into a socialist community was another expellee, Solly Sachs, with whom the party leadership remained at odds.

At the same time, the cohort of talented black party leaders who had emerged and had been trained during the Native republic period were sidelined or, worse still, subjected to racist condescension. At a time when black workers were expanding their share of the industrial workforce, the party very nearly lost the affiliation of its remaining experienced black organisers. And notwithstanding the strategic imperative that required communists to try to build a broad cross-class alliance against fascism, any organisational coherence among themselves was undermined by a political culture nurtured by Comintern injunctions in which disagreement was perceived as treachery.

These experiences were not exceptional; indeed, the South African party survived its ten-year phase of subjugation to the Comintern rather better than some of its sister affiliates across the globe, a benign consequence of distance from Moscow and slow communications with Moscow, Paris and London. The most useful comparisons are with other parties either in other British Dominions or in more directly colonial settings. Two cases must suffice. The Communist Party of Australia was ordered after Comintern's seventh congress to rebuild relations with the local Labour Party (ALP) and support it in elections; this, after seven years of opposition to the ALP as an embodiment of social fascism. As in South Africa, Comintern's 'new line' in 1929 almost destroyed the Australian party, reducing its membership and removing its influence with organised labour: as its own subsequent reports indicate, most of its activism in the early 1930s was confined to the unemployed. Popular frontism enabled it to regain positions in trade union leadership, but it failed to attract significant membership among trade union rank and file. The party's failure to secure a working alliance with the ALP was the subject of a special investigation by André Marty and the Anglo–American Secretariat in 1937. At the beginning of the war, the party was banned, a move which elicited no significant protest within the labour movement.[269]

With its advocacy of popular fronts, Comintern's commitment to colonial issues declined because of the Soviet Union's efforts to secure alliances with Britain and France.[270] This was reflected in the case of the British party in its relegation of earlier commitments to anti-imperialist concerns.[271] The case of one British colonial party, the Malayan Communist Party, is interesting. Because of its relative isolation from Comintern, it seems that it functioned through the 1930s without the kind of external supervision and instruction experienced by the South Africans and the Australians and, in doing so, prospered. After 1936 it adopted a united front policy but interpreted this in the light of local conditions to build a substantial following within the labour movement, and in achieving this it became increasingly multi-ethnic and well organised. Entrenchment within organised labour brought with it a degree of security and even protection from colonial officials, who viewed trade unionists as negotiation partners rather than adversaries, in contrast to the Special Branch police officers who had harassed the same communist activists during the earlier pre-popular front era.[272] As with the South Africans, the Malayan case suggests that local revolutionaries fared better when using their own judgements and knowledge.

FIVE

Patriotic Unity: The Communist Party of South Africa during the 1940s

Edwin Mofutsanyana and Michael Harmel checking the damage in the Party offices in Johannesburg after an arson attack in 1943. By this stage the Party was enjoying unprecedented popularity as well as a degree of official approval (evident in its access to rationed newsprint) but it retained enemies on the Afrikaner nationalist far right.

The years of the Second World War witnessed a revival of the fortunes of the Communist Party of South Africa (CPSA). At the beginning of the war, the party's following numbered less than 300, its influence in the trade unions was negligible, it was isolated from other political organisations among black South Africans, while its efforts with whites had succeeded neither in checking the growth of fascism or Afrikaner nationalism nor in building class unity. By the end of the war and during the years that followed, the party could count its adherents in thousands rather than hundreds, it was capable of winning white local government elections, and its members presided over the largest-ever African trade union movement, as well as contributing significantly to the leadership of the African and Indian Congresses. From 1945, knowledge of the party's development becomes vital for any understanding of the mainstream of black politics in South Africa. Through the late 1940s it sustained its presence in black townships, though the support it had gathered among white South Africans would fall away. This chapter will initially examine and attempt to explain the wartime expansion in the Communist Party's influence, first by referring to the social and economic conditions as well as the overall political environment of the time, and then by discussing the party's policies and strategies. CPSA responses to several different sets of movements or organisations will be reviewed: white workers and servicemen and movements of the urban poor, of peasants and of labour. The second part of the chapter will consider the party's progress in the years after the war. This was a period in which the party was weakened by strategic disagreements, mainly over the issue of how any united front or any other kind of alliance should be constituted.

Economic and social conditions which helped to promote a fresh mood of popular political assertion and which facilitated the rise of the CPSA's popularity have been well documented, and here need only brief recapitulation. For economic historians the years between 1939 and 1945 represent the concluding phase of an industrial boom which began with South Africa's currency devaluation in 1932. The war itself promoted manufacturing as South Africa became a major provider of military supplies, from weaponry to the twelve million boots and two-and-a-half billion cigarettes that were dispatched to the soldiery fighting their way across North Africa and Southern Europe.[1] Between 1936 and 1951 the industrial workforce doubled at an annual growth rate of six per cent.[2] This growth had a particular impact on Africans during the war because of the diversion of a quarter of a million whites into military occupations.[3] Africans in substantial numbers began to fill semi-skilled positions in factories, and here the wartime increase in the number of black workers was three times that of whites.[4] Movement into semi-skilled positions was one factor contributing to the narrowing of the wage gap between white and black manufacturing workers which occurred during the war.[5] 'Non-white' wages in manufacturing rose by more than eight per cent a year between 1942 and 1946 compared with the annual four per cent rises for white workers.[6] However, the 100,000 extra African factory workers recruited during the war (a 40 per cent increase in the total African manufacturing labour force) only accounted for a small proportion of the growing urban African population.[7] Between 1936 and 1946 official statistics revealed a virtual doubling of Johannesburg's African population to almost 400,000, while in some smaller centres the rise was even more rapid: in Cape Town during the war, the number of African inhabitants grew from 15,000 to an estimated total of 60,000. During the war more than a million black South Africans moved into towns. Additional numbers put an overwhelming strain on the already inadequate provision of housing, and shanty settlements mushroomed on the fringes of every significant town. Many of the people who inhabited these settlements were refugees from the overcrowded and drought-stricken reserves where economic conditions at the beginning of the war were beginning to attract even government concern.[8] The towns provided harsh havens, for though there was work for some, all had to face spiralling food prices[9] (partly the consequence of heavy grain export commitments and feeding soldiers in North Africa) as well as shortages, and most lived in conditions of fearsome poverty often in the sprawling shanty settlements well beyond the reach of conventional policing. The war accelerated and deepened social and economic changes that had already been in progress for nearly a decade. But government policies and the wider political setting were in some respects importantly different from what preceded and followed the war. In several ways during the war, the labour requirements of rising industrial production 'burst the boundaries of segregationist controls'.[10]

During the early years of the war, the government displayed an uncharacteristic anxiety to secure the support and loyalty of Africans. This concern reached a climax in 1942 when the Minister of Native Affairs, Deneys

Reitz, criticised the pass laws and ordered a relaxation of their application in the main industrial centres of the Transvaal and Natal.[11] There were significant reductions in the numbers arrested for pass law offences, and, probably more importantly, the authorities relaxed the controls exercised over people migrating from the countryside to the cities.[12] The same year, the Smit Committee recommended their abolition while the Minister of Labour, Walter Madeley, promised in November that legal recognition of African trade unions was impending.[13] Even at this point, any hopeful expectations would have been qualified by War Measure 145, which prohibited all African strikes, and by Smuts's repudiation of the relevance to black South Africans of the Atlantic Charter.[14] In any case, Smuts tended to delegate the tasks of keeping the African population onside to his cabinet colleagues. One of his own rare interventions concerning Africans was to bar the inclusion in a set of commemorative postage stamps of a depiction of a serviceman in the Native Military Corps, one of the 133,000 Africans whom the Union Defence Force recruited.[15] Nevertheless, talk of some post-war black amelioration continued, stimulated partly by the energetic efforts of parliamentary Native representatives (who included after 1943 the former communist Hyman Basner) as well as a flurry of commission recommendations. The state's overtures to Africans were chiefly attributable to its resolve to maintain high levels of industrial production and, of course, the government's feeling of vulnerability at a time of widening polarisation in white politics.

War brought a change in white public perceptions of the Communist Party. From 1941, the Soviet Union was a glorious and respected ally[16] (diplomatic representation in South Africa began in the following year). Groups such as the Friends of the Soviet Union (FSU) and the party-sponsored Medical Aid for Russia could draw respectable audiences at their well-publicised events. Medical Aid for Russia raised £750,000 between 1942 and 1945.[17] The FSU, until 1941 a coterie of CPSA enthusiasts, included among its patrons by the end of the war the mayor of Johannesburg and Colin Steyn, the Minister of Justice, as well as the Rhodesian Prime Minister, Sir Godfrey Huggins.[18] Alan Paton joined its committee in 1944.[19] JH Hofmeyr, Smuts's deputy, opened the Southern African Soviet Friendship Congress at Wits University in 1944.[20] The election of Bill Andrews as party leader in 1943 meant that the CPSA's figurehead was a celebrated veteran of the white labour movement.[21] The party in 1942 became conspicuously patriotic: for several months it arranged 'Defend South Africa' rallies in town halls up and down the country; its newspaper columns gave prominence to war news from the Western Desert; while the editor, Edwin Mofutsanyana, donned an air-raid warden's uniform and conscientiously patrolled the streets of Orlando – in the first months of 1942 Johannesburgers still took seriously the possibility that Axis air forces might launch bombing fleets from Madagascar or, even less plausibly, Somalia.[22] White comrades in the army helped to found a Springbok Legion, which attracted 55,000 members by 1945. Even the South African Broadcasting Corporation (SABC) responded to the spirit of the times. A Yiddish choir drawn from the Jewish Workers' Club sang the 'Internationale' on the radio and Bill Andrews was requested in 1942 to broadcast a May Day message to workers in support of the war effort.[23] The party's fresh appeal among whites was also evident in its development during the war of an organised presence on university campuses, firstly through the Liberal Study Groups that assembled left-inclined students and then, at least at the University of the Witwatersrand, a fully fledged party group. The party's war-time following among white workers would prove mostly short-lived, but many of the students who joined its following in the early 1940s would remain active communists forty years later.[24]

IT WAS A COMPLICATED TIME for the Communist Party. At the war's beginning, in conformity with communist parties in other parts of the world, the CPSA was to declare the war to be a conflict between rival imperialisms and opposed it on that ground.[25] Although, 'in the interests of humanity' it was 'essential that Nazism be destroyed', for South Africans this could be done most effectively by confronting the domestic threat of fascism.[26] As one pamphlet, published just before the war began, noted: 'the fight against fascism must start in our own country', and in any case the government at that time still included Nazi sympathisers.[27] 'This is an unjust war in which we have no interest', *Inkululeko* insisted, and Africans should refrain from giving money to support the war.[28] 'While they call on us to die for freedom,' warned one leaflet, 'they steal our freedom from us.'[29] This view represented a shift from that expressed in an *Inkululeko* editorial a few weeks earlier, which suggested that the impending war might not just be 'a war between imperialists', because there was a significant difference between 'fascist countries and democratic [Western European] countries. This perception was influenced by the USSR's earlier efforts to secure an alliance with Britain against Germany.[30] For a while, disagreements – quite common within leaderships of English-speaking communist parties – persisted about whether any war against Germany prosecuted by Western European governments might be an effective and progressive action against fascism or merely an internecine struggle between rival imperialisms.[31] The

German–Soviet pact of August 1939 was also a source of disagreement: Ray Alexander refused to endorse a statement by Cape Town's District Committee justifying the pact.[32] A report submitted to the party's conference in March 1940 clarified matters. Written probably by Michael Harmel, it proposed that the party's involvement in 'the national struggle of Non-Europeans' was the essential element in any development of 'a mass movement to resist fascism'.

During the 1940s, Harmel would be a pivotal figure in urging that the party should embrace black South African political preoccupations, and in the Transvaal he would often be the keynote speaker at public meetings in locations and townships. In 1940 he was a fresh figure in the party, having joined the British party during a 15-month sojourn in London. He was the son of an Irish-Jewish chemist of Lithuanian descent, Arthur Harmel, who had emigrated to South Africa in 1910. Michael was born in 1915 and grew up in a middle-class household in the Eastern Cape. He spent five years as a student at Rhodes University, conspicuous not as a political activist but as an editor of literary magazines, which Arthur helped fund, and as the owner of a car, in those days a rare asset for a student. The party's commentary on the Vereeniging riots of 1937 elicited a well-informed contribution by Michael Harmel to a student magazine, which ended with an attack on what he perceived to be liberal sentimentality about black South Africans:

> The liberals would eliminate the 'prejudice' against the Native, they would have him looked on as a good fellow who really doesn't stink. For heaven's sake, let's stop being hypocrites. The Native does stink because he's stinking poor: his poverty and our injustice raise a stench that all our perfumes of hypocrisy and benevolent sentimentality cannot conceal. A clash like that at Vereeniging serves to bare the naked forces of greed and oppression and brutal exploitation underlying our 'protection' of our native 'children'.[33]

Harmel may have joined the Communist Party at Rhodes; his biographer Milan Oralek thinks not, but his fellow students believed he was a communist.[34] In any case, influenced initially by his father's youthful experiences of Irish Republican socialism, he became increasingly attracted to Marxist ideas and travelled to Britain with the aim of signing up with the *Daily Worker*. Like the other unpaid trainees at the *Worker*, Harmel spent more time selling the paper than contributing copy, but he did write on African events and, through this, may have attracted the attention of the British party's Colonial Committee. As his biographer has discovered, Michael Harmel's name appears in the transcripts of telephone conversations between members of the committee monitored by British intelligence. It is possible that when he turned up at the party's office in Johannesburg in November 1939, he arrived with a certain authority. With his experience as a journalist at the *Daily Worker*, he was the obvious choice to be appointed as *Inkululeko*'s full-time paid editor shortly afterwards.[35]

As Harmel reminded his new comrades, the main threats confronting South Africa were hardly external. Any further efforts at anti-fascist mobilisation among white South Africans would be quixotic. The Politburo agreed with this reasoning: it would be 'childishly absurd' to hope 'that out of a white population of two million, which is divided by a deep cleavage from top to bottom, forces can arise that will save South Africa from fascist onslaught whether from within or without'.[36] Hence the party's emphasis shifted from popular front activity among whites to efforts to mobilise large numbers of black people in anticipation of a wartime administration's repression of workers' and democratic organisations. The party's anti-war campaign was therefore most publicly evident in the activity of those of its members who were already busy in the Non-European United Front.[37] Opinion within the party was not unanimous. Johannesburg communists held the view that the party should support an effective prosecution of the war, before being overruled by the leadership in Cape Town.[38] There was little determined dissent, though an already disillusioned Hyman Basner chose the Soviet invasion of Finland in November as the occasion to make his break with the party, announcing his resignation in a letter to *The Star*.[39] Meanwhile, the unpredictable Jimmy La Guma decided to join up, explaining his decision by arguing that the Second World War was 'a continuation of the Spanish Civil War'. Hitler and Mussolini were attacking workers and 'Internationalism demanded that workers be defended'.[40] If others had private qualms about, for example, the Nazi–Soviet Pact, they kept them to themselves.[41] For while the party apparently took its cue on the issue of the war from Comintern directives.[42] Nevertheless, opposing the war was locally popular among certain groups. Following the precedent set by nationalists in India, radical South African Indians were to make opposition to the war their main plank in their effective opposition to the conservative leadership of the Indian Congresses. Indian communists were conspicuously involved in the Non-European United Front. In Cape Town, John Gomas, writing in *Freedom* in June 1940, reflected a common sentiment when he argued: 'I am satisfied with the statement of the famous British scientist Professor JBS Haldane, that he would rather be a Jew in Hitler's Berlin than a native in Johannesburg ... How can we be interested in fighting Nazism thousands of miles away, while in reality we have a similar monster devouring us here.'[43]

The party's Johannesburg-based newspaper was at this point a cyclostyled leaflet with a print run of 2,000,[44] and its limited reportage does not contain much information about the party's activity during most of its anti-war phase. There was probably not very much; after all, the Joffe brothers whose joint efforts had held the party's organisation together during the late 1930s, were swiftly interned as German nationals. As Willie Kalk was to complain at the party conference at the beginning of 1940, the party chiefly sought to build influence, indirectly, through front activity.[45] Here Yusuf Dadoo was a pivotal figure, publicly conspicuous as the main voice of the Non-European United Front. Aside from Bill Andrews, Dadoo was probably the party's most influential public personality. He was the son of Mahomed Dadoo, reputedly the 'wealthiest Indian in Krugersdorp', and owner of a clothing shop. In 1920, he was the winner of a famous court case, when the Krugersdorp municipality tried to obtain a judgment against Dadoo's use of a limited liability company to acquire freehold property.[46] Mahomed sent his son to India to be educated at Aligarh Muslim College between 1925 and 1927, and from there Yusuf travelled to Britain to train as a doctor at Edinburgh, joining the Independent Labour Party. Three years after his return to South Africa, where he established his medical practice in Krugersdorp, he became in 1939 a member of the Communist Party.[47]

The Non-European United Front organised a series of anti-war rallies, and Dadoo was imprisoned for four months after making an eloquent and powerful case against the war at his trial.[48] The Front's opposition to the war did not take it into the strikes and boycotts contemplated at its inception at the conference that formed the Front in April 1939. The African National Congress (ANC) also supplied a focus of activity for African communists: JB Marks first transferred most of his energies to ANC work after being expelled from the party in the late 1930s,[49] and Moses Kotane, general secretary and full-time party functionary from 1939 onwards, led a revival of the ANC in Cape Town. The Johannesburg District Committee in its review of the previous year's work acknowledged in March 1941 the 'great importance attached to helping the ANC lead the African people in their struggle',[50] though in the same year the party conference warned that commitments to other organisations were causing neglect of the party itself.[51]

In fact, it is difficult to discern a strong central impulse to the CPSA's development in this period. A modest and rather belated beginning was made in the field of African trade union organisation, and some support was given to Alpheus Maliba's pioneering efforts to mobilise peasant resistance to betterment schemes in the Northern Transvaal. African members contested and won two and then three seats on the Orlando Advisory Board, while in Johannesburg's city centre, communists continued their weekly public meetings on the City Hall steps. The party also sought to gain Afrikaner support with its anti-war stance through maintaining its Afrikaans-medium journal, *Die Ware Republikein*, though it continued to stress the reactionary character of Afrikaner nationalism.[52] A debate in early 1941 about a new 'People's Programme' registered disagreements about Afrikaner nationalism, with a minority predisposed to perceive in it a potentially progressive force in any struggle against imperialism. Communists also disagreed about whether their immediate aims should be anti-imperialist or fully socialist; the first would of course justify alliances with nationalists. A majority of Cape Town's and East London's communists favoured building 'a powerful and conscious workers' movement, directed towards socialism'. There were also divisions about the extent to which the party should champion equal political rights for Africans.[53] A modest growth in membership was recorded, from 280 to 400, and a new District Committee was elected in Johannesburg, composed largely of men and women who had joined the party quite recently and who were thus unaffected by the divisions and tensions of its sectarian history in the 1930s. A new constitution was drawn up in 1941. Reconstruction of the party after the debilitations of the previous decade seems to have been the main priority; anti-war activity did not extend beyond public meetings. This notwithstanding, three communists were interned: the Joffe brothers in Johannesburg and the trade unionist Arnold Latti from Port Elizabeth. It is possible that the anti-war line did not inspire much enthusiasm within the party. According to Edwin Mofutsanyana, this period '[was] the time when Africans began asking whether they [the communists] were supporters of Hitler. They had phrases like "wamphethu Hitler" – "Hitler has got them alright".'[54] Alan Paton, then running a reformatory outside Johannesburg, recalled much later that at staff meetings after the government's declaration of hostilities, his white colleagues, mostly Afrikaners, constituted a surly 'anti-war brigade', though this was more than compensated for by the black staff's 'unanimous' enthusiasm for the war's 'vigorous prosecution'.[55] Maybe Paton's African staffers were exceptionally patriotic; elsewhere, parliament's Native representatives encountered general indifference when they tried to solicit African endorsements for the war effort. Among the comrades, though, there was an essential ambivalence with respect to the party's anti-war position: even its most determined exponent, Yusuf Dadoo, qualified his opposition with the proviso that if 'unfettered democratic rights' were extended to black people, then the conflict could be transformed into a 'just war' which it would be possible to support.[56] In this context, one of the resolutions debated at the May 1941 conference, when the party was still opposing the war, concerned the rights of African servicemen; they should be entitled to bear arms and to gain promotion to all military ranks.[57]

All this would begin to change in June 1941 when the German army marched into Russia. Four days after the invasion, the Central Committee produced a statement arguing that the total character of the war had altered: 'The Soviet Union is not an imperialist power and is not waging an imperialist war.' This was not an immediate realisation and the party altered its course haltingly. In fact, on the day of the invasion, district secretary Michael Harmel told a public meeting, which communists had called to protest against police shootings in Sophiatown, that now that Hitler 'was trying to steal another country', British and German imperialism were 'going to help each other'. Communists in South Africa should continue to 'fight against our enemies the Imperialists'. As late as 7 July, party speakers at a meeting in Orlando were still insisting that 'we in Africa' should 'have nothing to do with Imperialist war'. However, 'we will help the government win the war against the Nazis ... if we can be given our rights today or tomorrow', the speaker, A Msitshana, conceded.[58]

Several weeks would pass before the Communist Party and the Non-European United Front entirely abandoned their opposition to the war to the Trotskyists whose position remained unaltered by the attack on Russia. By August, 'Hitlerism', according to *Inkululeko*, was an immediate 'threat to the very hope of advancement and freedom for all workers and oppressed peoples'.[59] South Africa should strengthen its contribution to the destruction of Nazism by arming black soldiers and giving black people the vote: 'Give the people democratic rights, give them a country and decent life, give them arms and there is nothing they will not do to defend their freedom and their rights,' urged *Inkululeko*.[60] "Bad as South Africa is,' wrote Moses Kotane in early 1942 in a pamphlet entitled *Japan: Friend or Foe*, 'she is as much our home as she is that of the Europeans ... South Africa is what we Non-Europeans allowed her to be ... in the future she will be what we ourselves make of her'.[61] With support for the war effort the Communist Party was once again prepared to consider constituencies which three years previously had appeared to be lost causes: 'Our experience has shown that our Party can gain support and goodwill of all sections. We must establish close relations with Afrikaners ... We must build the Party among skilled workers.'[62]

The party's attitude to the war would influence the most vital spheres of its activity. For example, in calling for opposition to the government's anti-strike War Measure 145, the Central Committee in December 1942 advocated that the 'trade union movement should get the Government to withdraw this measure' and 'demand' full recognition of African trade unions. Just how trade unions should add force to these demands was not spelled out, though the statement went on to suggest that 'in the interests of South Africa's well-being, particularly in these serious times, every effort should be made to avoid strikes'.[63] In 1942, the party's posture also seemed to shape the attitudes of the authorities towards it. As already mentioned, Bill Andrews was afforded time on the SABC to broadcast a May Day message calling for the solidarity of labour against Hitler, and a subversion charge was dropped against Kotane after the Minister of Justice was shown a copy of *Japan: Friend or Foe.*[64] The relevant officials were also generous in their allocations to the party of rationed paper and printing supplies.[65] By 1942, the party's press included *The Guardian*, a left-wing broadsheet newspaper published in Cape Town, which from its inception had been supportive towards the CPSA. By 1941 its editor, Betty Radford, was a party member. *The Guardian* had a broader readership than that enjoyed by any left-wing newspaper before then, with circulations of 8,000 in 1939, 22,000 by July 1941, and 42,000 one year later. Its circulation reached a peak during the 1943 election, at 55,000 sold copies a week. Most of its readers were black.[66] *Inkululeko*, properly printed by 1941 and very much directed at the party's African following, circulated 18,000 copies in January 1942.[67] From 1940 the party also published a monthly 'theoretical' journal, *Freedom*. A series of professionally produced posters began to appear, printed in several colours by the new party press, Stewart Printing, Cape Town: 'For VICTORY in 1942, Open up a Second Front in the West', the first of these exhorted. In Durban in late 1942, alarmed by the spread of leaflets that argued that if black South Africans wanted freedom they should support the Japanese, the police requested a meeting with communist organisers in the Indian residential district of Verulam, and at the meeting asked the party to hold a public meeting to explain 'why it was supporting the war and why it would be wrong to allow the Japanese to come into the country'. Local communists assented and held the meeting.[68]

The party's changed stance on the war appears to have engendered no internal disaffection though on its left flank there were some noisy objections to the party's rationalisations of its new position.[69] In April 1942, the communists launched its Defend South Africa campaign. This was to take the form of approximately 30 open-air or city hall meetings, pageants or processions held in every major town and in several smaller centres as well: Johannesburg, Durban, East London, Port Elizabeth, Cape Town, Kimberley, Bloemfontein, Pretoria, Pietermaritzburg, Ladysmith, Dundee and Roodepoort were all visited by leading party spokesmen, black and white, calling upon the government to 'Avenge Tobruk', by 'mobilising our people and our wealth'. The public intentions of the campaign were spelled out in a lengthy pamphlet, *Arm the People*, thousands of copies of which were distributed during the eight months of its duration. *Arm the People* opened with a reference to the threat of invasion from Vichy-controlled Madagascar: the 'Fascist Peril' was 'approaching ever closer to our shores' and South Africa was 'faced with a desperate struggle for our existence'. After criticising the government for its neglect of adequate military training for blacks, its tolerance of the Ossewa Brandwag and similar components of a 'Fifth Column', and its continued diversion of national resources into gold production, the pamphlet went on to outline 'A Policy for Victory'. Black soldiers should be armed and army conditions improved so as to encourage recruitment. Industry should be put on a war footing with the establishment of workers' production committees to increase output, protect workers' interests, and prevent sabotage. African trade unions should be recognised and African workers allowed to acquire skills. The pass laws and segregation laws should go, and voting rights should be extended to blacks. Adequate air-raid precautions were needed. Food supplies should be improved through aid to small farmers and through the abolition of control boards, which functioned to maintain high farm-gate prices.[70]

Meanwhile, a cohort of communists would join up, not just the distinctly over-age Jimmy La Guma, taking the injunction to Defend South Africa literally. Those who couldn't enlist signed up in auxiliary formations, as air-raid wardens for example: it was a communist 'duty' to work in the government's Civilian Protective Services, a party leaflet enjoined.[71] In 1941, the party helped to establish a progressive servicemen's organisation, the Springbok Legion, a 'trade union of the ranks'. With its wartime membership peaking at around 55,000, the Legion was hardly a party surrogate, but communists were prominent in its top echelon (Jock Isacowitz was chairman and Jack Hodgson secretary). Parallel to the Legion, a Home Front League appeared to comprise mainly CPSA members and sympathisers.[72] If the underlying motive of the Defend South Africa campaign was to broaden the party's appeal, then it can be judged a success. A recruiting drive for membership was mounted simultaneously and application forms were distributed at public meetings. Rules about recruiting changed twice in 1942 and 1944, each time abandoning selective considerations that had hitherto restricted recruitment.

Each district and branch was set recruiting quotas. Durban was apparently the most successful in bringing new people into the party.[73] By the end of the campaign membership had quadrupled, with 1,346 new adherents.[74] Moses Kotane expressed reservations about quality and felt the party should distinguish between full members and supporters.[75] Rising membership and well-attended meetings brought in more money. In 1943 £5,000 had been donated to party coffers, helping to fund the increasingly costly printing bill for *The Guardian* newspaper.[76] At the same time, *Inkululeko* was sold 'house to house, particularly in Orlando'.[77] Indeed, the party was able to establish a full branch in Orlando in 1939.[78] In 1943 new party offices were opened in Port Elizabeth, Pietermaritzburg and East London while the head office in Cape Town maintained a full-time staff of three employees, including Solly Sachs's former wife working as Moses Kotane's secretary.[79] Kotane shared a flat with Eddie Roux in Clifton, not far from where Mrs Sachs lived. Her son, Albie, remembers him calling most days with work for his mother, but he was a family friend as well, and Albie called him 'Uncle'.[80] The party now maintained a network of active branches and groups, some of them township-based. For example, from 1939 there were weekly group meetings in Orlando on Tuesday evenings. In November 1942, a district party conference in Cape Town attracted delegates from 37 branches.[81] Communists also had a presence once again in their historical heartland of the East Rand. Pretoria's George Findlay, one of the party's most prominent public figures, spoke at a City Hall meeting with Danie du Plessis, the building workers' trade union organiser. Findlay was disappointed that his audience was small, only 60, but, he reported, 'I got the impression that the Springs District, fifty Europeans and two hundred Africans is pretty lively.' This was, he believed, attributable mainly to the work of 'Archie Lewitton'.[82] Levitan was a key figure in the party's efforts to reach Afrikaners.[83]

In its public pronouncements the party provided no indication as to which sections of the population it was most successful in building a following within at this time. While city hall meetings would have been directed primarily at whites, many of the events were staged in locations habitually used by black people, and African speakers often provided keynote addresses, though (as noted above) Michael Harmel would often share their platforms. To judge from membership statistics, it seems likely that a large proportion of the new recruits were African or Indian.[84] African members of the party tended to be literate and urbanised, often in occupations that provided them with some mobility and freedom from direct supervision. But it does seem that Africans were drawn to the party because of its local presence and its activism around local concerns rather than because of any inherent appeal in its ideas or the wider causes that it championed. Hence good African turnouts at Defend South Africa meetings may have been an effect as much of the party's attention to local community issues and black trade unionism as of the specific content of the campaign itself. For example, Michael Harmel appeared as a speaker at a meeting in Vereeniging in late 1941, one of a series after the party began engaging with local protests against police raids for tax receipts and lodgers' permits. The party received so many membership applications during this episode that, Harmel believed, the people of Vereeniging should be accorded their own branch.[85] However, as Fred Carneson would recall many years later, the membership signed up at big open-air meetings was unstable; a large proportion would fall away and in a few weeks become inactive.[86]

Partly because of the character of the new 'mass' membership, this expanding black following did not result in an increasingly African-led party. Indeed, the party remained predominantly white-led through the decade, to judge from the composition of its district and central committees, despite the increasing presence of Africans as delegates at annual conferences.[87] Writing in late 1942, Moses Kotane was critical of shortcomings in the party's education and training programmes, observing 'a general tendency of non-European members to take back seats and leave leadership to Europeans', a predisposition he attributed to lack of confidence.[88] Party leadership as evident from the composition of the central and district committees remained mainly white.[89] New white members were often middle class, Brian Bunting recalled.[90] But not all were: Rusty Bernstein looked after a new group of Greek refugees who formed their own communist section at the steelworks in Vanderbijlpark. After being fired, they on their own initiative constituted a communist 'fraction' in the Pan Hellenic Progressive Union.[91] They returned home in 1945. The Greeks aside, branches functioned openly and were mainly based in residential areas, in a repetition of previous organisational geographical concentrations that had been evident during the party's first efforts to build an African membership at the end of the 1920s. And, once again, party organisers tried to correct this tendency. Ray Alexander urged that communists 'must concentrate on the factories as the most vital sector of our work and our mass basis ... Everything else in our work is secondary to the factories.'[92] Building factory based groups would remain a largely unfulfilled aspiration, even in enterprises in which the party led strong unions. A few industrial groups were established among the party's remaining white workers' supporters: Arnold Selby, for example, joined an 'engineers' group' on entering the CPSA in 1942; he remembered that a building workers' group also functioned at that time.[93] Generally, though, as the Johannesburg District Committee observed, 'Party members active in trade union work are so engrossed in this work they find little time for party work.'[94] They were not always interested in the party's preoccupations outside the workplace, and were rather resistant to attempts to indoctrinate their trade union following, as the Johannesburg district noted when it complained about the 'lack of support by Party members in linking up the unity of the working class movement'.[95] As Ray Alexander warned, 'it takes a great deal of time for the workers to realise the real differences between the socialist system of society and the system under which we live'.[96] Durban may have been an exception to the general absence of factory-based party groups. Iain Edwards's informants recalled that after 1942 'cells' were formed 'in all the factories where Communists were established'.[97] This may have been the case, but other researchers drawing upon a wider range of sources have concluded that many of the unions communists established in Durban, including those that enrolled Indian workers, had no shop-floor organisation and no shop stewards, who would in any case have been very vulnerable to dismissal. Organisation was undertaken at the factory gates.[98]

THE MOVE AWAY FROM a Bolshevik vanguardist organisational style to a more open, looser, mass-party approach may have been qualified. Later the police would cite correspondence from the files they confiscated after raiding party offices in 1946. They claimed that the party's internal documentation used coded euphemisms and acronyms, including initials which, they asserted, stood for 'secret branch' – party entities constituted by people who would not be drawn into public activity and would not participate in normal group work.[99] If this was the case, then the identity of such people remained a secret, for every important and active communist was quite visible. But if, as the Simonses claim, it is possible to discern in the Defend South Africa campaign a programme for 'complete liberation from national oppression',[100] this was not the main emphasis in the CPSA's appeals to voters in parliamentary and municipal elections the following year. The party's intention to contest white elections, something it had not done seriously since 1929,[101] was signalled by Kotane at the final Defend South Africa rally when he announced a forthcoming new initiative 'to increase our influence, to press forward with our demands'.[102] Another pamphlet was published. Entitled *We South Africans* and aimed at potential white voters in the 1943 general election, it was studiously vague in its treatment of the party's approach to African political aspirations. Referring to the Labour Party's 'total segregation' policy, it suggested, tactfully: 'Africans may prefer such a system under socialism: it bears some resemblance to the "autonomous national republics" that have been recognised in Soviet Russia and may be a progressive step under socialism. But it is a very long term policy; the practical question today is how to remove the disabilities imposed upon the non-white people.'[103]

The pamphlet also argued that to protect their own long-term interests, skilled white workers should set about removing racial job reservation; and it contended that socialism would benefit 'members of the professions, artists and scientists, shopkeepers and small farmers'.[104] The party's nine parliamentary candidates – four in the Transvaal, one in Durban and four in the Cape – garnered 7,000 votes between them, an average of 11 per cent of the poll. 'Communists are needed in parliament,' Betty Radford explained in *The Guardian*, 'both for winning the war against Fascism and for finding a progressive solution to the problems of the post-war world.'[105] The best performance in the parliamentary poll was that of Harry Snitcher, who took 27.7 per cent of the votes in Woodstock, benefiting from a substantially coloured electorate.[106] In the Cape Provincial Council elections, an East Londoner, Archie Muller, supported by African voters was narrowly defeated, losing by a margin of only 200 votes.[107] With respect to Cape Town, Albie Sachs can remember as an eight-year-old being taken to a meeting in 1943 in Gardens, the constituency that Harry Snitcher was contesting. He also went to the polling station. General Smuts was there. Albie booed him and was told off by his mother for being rude.[108] In the same year the party's electoral efforts were rewarded with two seats on the Cape Town City Council and one each on the City Council of East London and Port Elizabeth, where Mohamed Desai, an Indian party member and trade union organiser, won the seat.[109] In East London, Archie Muller campaigned as a candidate for the Workers' Civic League, effectively a united front between the CPSA and the Labour Party around worker demands.[110] It was an encouraging start. The other left-wing contender in the general election, the Independent Labour Party, despite its well-known leader, Solly Sachs, and a prudent 'bread and butter' manifesto, collected only two per cent of the votes in the three working-class constituencies it contested.[111] Heartened by its modest success, the party continued to fight elections. Between 1943 and 1951 the lawyer Sam Kahn held a Cape Town City Council seat from four successive elections which he contested as a communist in a ward that was 70 per cent white and 30 per cent coloured. A party member since 1930 when he joined as a teenager, Kahn did not always have an easy relationship with his comrades in the party: George Findlay on a visit in 1944 encountered tensions among Cape Town's communists: Kahn had been suspended, and Harry Snitcher, loyal to Kahn, was at odds with the District Committee. More research is needed to tell us why the CPSA was able to win elections as well as to indicate the full extent it tailored its messages to the prejudices and predispositions of white voters.

In October 1944 Hilda Watts won a council seat in Hillbrow–Berea, defeating a Labour Party candidate in a central Johannesburg neighbourhood of high-density apartment blocks; and communists captured two further seats in Cape Town in September 1945. Norman Levy grew up in the neighbourhood in which Hilda Watts won her seat and as a teenager he encountered one of her street-corner meetings; most of the people who stayed to listen to her were black, he remembers.[112] She may not have needed to do much to tailor her appeal to white voters in her ward; many of them were relatively recent British immigrants who might have responded to her North London accent; she had a British childhood until 1934. She also received contributions to her campaign fund from recently arrived Eastern European immigrants.[113] Watts believed later she may have benefited from the effect that the Soviet army's victory at Stalingrad had on public morale.[114] One of her leaflets was clearly targeted at the families of servicemen: 'A little home, some soldier dreamed about. There are a lot of people dreaming of homes. Who is preparing them for the boys when they come back? In 26 years the Council has built only 360 houses for Europeans. Plenty of promises – BUT NO HOMES.' This particular leaflet made no direct references to Johannesburg's black residents, and even the illustrations portrayed only white people.[115] A longer manifesto did refer to 'some of the worst non-European slums', such as in Pimville, that were owned by the City Council. It also drew attention to the fact that only one doctor served Orlando's 60,000 residents, noting that the council had failed to provide any facilities 'for the treatment and isolation of infectious diseases amongst non-Europeans'.[116] The risk posed to general public health by the municipality's neglect of hygiene in poorer locations, as in the non-supply of water-borne sewerage and clean water, would be a key argument in communist appeals to white voters. As Hilda Watts reminded ratepayers in a leaflet endorsing the party's candidates for the 1945 elections, 'white tiled bathrooms' and 'constant hot water' were no protection 'from germs brought in by servants'.[117]

Referring to the 1945 municipal elections in Johannesburg, an *Inkululeko* correspondent reported on the 'disappearance of the old prejudices against communists' and the shock he encountered among white suburban residents 'at the horror of non-European conditions … [they] nearly always agree that improvements should be made'. 'The voters are waking up,' he concluded, 'and we communists, by fighting the elections, are helping them see the truth.'[118] In this election, Michael Harmel wrote the party's manifesto: its municipal candidates campaigned on the basis of his 'master plan' for Johannesburg's reconstruction, to make it a city of 'green belts, parks and playgrounds' as well as community centres, clinics and nursery schools. Tellingly, the inspiration for this vision was not from the socialist world; rather, the pictures and plans in the booklet are from American New Deal urban planning, in particular a Harlem housing project by the American modernist pioneer architect, William Lescaze.[119] Yet Johannesburg would remain in certain respects the same city. 'Native hostels within easy reach of each European area are needed', the plan suggested. While the propaganda did not explicitly state that all Johannesburg's citizens would share the new recreational facilities, there was a reference to the need for 'proper recreational services for the neglected non-European servant'.[120] In Harmel's ward, the voters were unpersuaded and he failed to get elected. A contributor to *Freedom* in 1946 noted that in Hillbrow 'the petit-bourgeois flat dwelling community has shown in the past to be not unfavourable to the Communist Party'.[121] A new ward delimitation put paid to any prospect of Hilda Watts repeating her 1943 victory in Hillbrow, as it included the affluent neighbourhood of Parktown and took out half of Berea, reducing her core supporters, the Hillbrow apartment tenants, to an isolated minority.[122] She would fail in her bid for re-election in 1947.[123]

Though the CPSA electoral propaganda was phrased in a way that invited recognition of wider social responsibilities, the party in these appeals downplayed the political and social implications of its policies. Support for the 'national democratic revolution' was frequently presented as merely the extension of civil rights to black South Africans. As the party's thinkers explained to their followers: 'Comrades, there are times when to be ultra-revolutionary is to betray the cause for which we are working. Which is the more revolutionary today – to say you want to nationalise the banks, or to say you want the vote and equality of rights for the non-Europeans.'[124] In January 1944, the CPSA removed from its constitution the clause that since 1941 had determined, as one of the party's principal aims, 'the abolition of Imperialism and the establishment of an independent republic of the people'. Explicit commitments to land redistribution and the extension of voting rights also disappeared.[125] The alien-sounding Politburo was renamed the Central Executive Committee; it would meet every week and all its members had to live within 50 miles of Cape Town. At this meeting the Central Committee urged that establishing close contacts with Afrikaners and building the party among skilled workers should be priorities as well as recruitment of Africans,

Indians and coloureds, 'who are ready to enter a new phase of struggle for national liberation'.[126] 'South Africa's way forward', a resolution adopted by the Central Committee at its meeting in July 1945, while calling for the expansion of democracy, included language directed at reassuring any fears that universal enfranchisement might 'endanger civilisation' in South Africa. Indeed, 'civilised standards' would be protected through 'the raising of the whole population' as a consequence of 'education and technical training'.[127] During most of the war and afterwards, communists sought to reassure the white public. Social equality between black and white would not necessitate the abandonment of customary social segregation. A party pamphlet published in 1942 addressed a familiar preoccupation in white politics:

> And what about inter-marriage? What about the disappearance of the white race? Clearly there is no society in which you can force people to marry against their will. If there is an inherent force which makes the mixture of races between black and white abhorrent then surely the same force will continue to act even in a socialistic society. In other words, there is no reason why the white race should disappear into the black majority unless it wants to. And if our posterity seeks things differently, who are we to decide thing for them?[128]

This issue continued to preoccupy party publicists. In 1945, the party offered an (ostensibly) African perspective on the topic of racial 'intermarriage':

> One who thinks a black man is sorry and ashamed of his colour is stupid ... we love our colour and we would not want to decrease it by intermarriage; we like our black girls dearly and wish them to marry and increase the black race. One who says we blacks might take European girls for marriage if we were freed talks rubbish.[129]

As late as 1947, the lecture series offered at the 'People's College' in the party's office at 960 Arcadia Street in Pretoria would include a contribution from George Findlay on 'Race, Breeding and Factors regarding Miscegenation'.[130] Within the party's leadership and following, there would certainly have been misgivings about such protestations. Cissie Gool lived with Sam Kahn after leaving her husband in 1938, and several other communists lived in 'mixed' households and marriages. In London, Michael Harmel had a love affair with Noni Jabavu, the future writer and the daughter of Professor DDT Jabavu, then a music student. It is likely, though, that the party's efforts through the late 1930s and during the 1940s to win white support would have brought people into the party who genuinely disapproved of such unions. On more strategic issues, the party's relative success among white South Africans was reflected in disagreements about priorities. These surfaced in debates at the party's conference at the end of 1944. For Jack Simons, national liberation needed to become the 'central issue'. Harry Snitcher had a different view: unity with the Labour Party and white trade unions was essential in any effort to promote the prospects of 'an alternative post war government', though, in working for such a project, the party should not make any compromises about black rights. George Findlay rejected any proposal for a united front calling instead for an independent struggle. The Bundist veteran Solomon Buirski called for a strengthening of the united front approach, stressing it should be confined to the labour movement; he was sceptical about the merits of any alliance with African nationalists. In the end the relevant resolution called for a broad people's convention, embracing white labour as well as African national liberation.[131] Beliefs about the possibility of working through a workers' alliance based upon the Communist Party, the Labour Party and the trade unions continued to animate a segment of the party's membership. They were sustained after the war by the continuation of a range of semi-skilled jobs shared by blacks and whites as well as by the continuing existence of racially mixed unions, including the Garment Workers' Union. More broadly, wartime and post-war white politics seemed to party leaders fluid and open to fresh possibilities.[132]

In this atmosphere, for certain communists in South Africa the ideas of the American communist leader, Earl Browder, appeared persuasive. Inspired by the spectacle of inter-Allied cooperation as at the Teheran Conference, Browder proposed that, as in the war itself, collaboration afterwards with progressive sections of the bourgeoisie might achieve more lasting social advances than a return to pre-war class struggle. In the United States, the practical implication of this view was the party's dissolution and its replacement with an association. In Britain, supporters of Browderism sought to reorganise the party around electoral politics and reformist goals, abandoning factory-based groups.[133] In South Africa, Jack Cope supplied a critical summary of the Browder thesis in the party's journal, *Freedom*, but Jack Simons, Lionel Bernstein and Archie Levitan were more inclined to take its proposals seriously.[134] Bernstein, a veteran of the Sixth Division's Italian campaign, believed that the experience of fighting alongside communist partisans had helped to erode prejudices among 'thousands of Springboks here in Italy', and that the war's major lesson was that 'friendly cooperation and trust between the great powers is as great a weapon now, for peace and security as it was yesterday for victory'.[135] George Findlay in the Pretoria party was sufficiently worried by Browderism's local impact that he published a pamphlet refuting the main theoretical arguments.[136] Findlay was unusually combative. He was convinced that Browderism had made deep inroads into the party's following in Durban, noting in his diary that 'Rowley Arenstein is all Browderite, inactivity and pretences of work take the place of realities'.[137] On the whole, he thought most communists in Cape Town and Johannesburg opposed Browderism, despite Bernstein's criticism of a piece he had written in *Freedom*: 'too silly and confused for words ... part revolution and part Labour Party'.[138] Findlay also believed that Michael Harmel had 'partly bought into Browderism'. Harmel was emerging then as the party's theoretical authority, and Findlay had an angry altercation with him at a Central Committee meeting in Cape Town.[139] His understanding of the extent of Browder's influence was probably exaggerated, but the American communist's proposals evidently seemed to resonate in South Africa and may have added doctrinal support to any continuing aspirations to build a united front with white labour. In 1945, in its 'V-Day' special edition, *The Guardian* reproduced Earl Browder's tribute to Roosevelt, 'our commander-in-chief'.[140]

Browderite reasoning is certainly discernible in a pamphlet the party published in 1944, detailing the essentials of what its post-war policies might contain. This text noted 'certain advances' in the government's policies, for example in the provision of a measure of social security for all citizens as well as its endorsement of the Teheran Agreement. A 'concerted drive for a policy of raising the living and cultural standards of the whole people' and the removal of 'colour bar restrictions' in the labour market might well 'obtain the backing of progressive capitalist and middle class people'. Of course, such a struggle should also aim for 'democratic rights' for everybody, but all these reforms need not mean 'that various racial groups must lose their separate identity'.[141] In this vein, under socialism, 'Africans themselves' might prefer a system of 'autonomous national republics' on the Soviet model. But this would be in the long term; 'the practical question today is how to remove the disabilities imposed on the non-white peoples'.[142]

The party's moderation of its public stance did not immunise it from attack. In Johannesburg, the Labour Party, having refused on two occasions the communists' offer of an electoral pact, published a leaflet in the 1945 election on what the Communist Party stood for. The leaflet detailed the CPSA's advocacy of universal suffrage and its espousal of the right of blacks to stand for election in addition to its desire for 'natives and coloureds [to be allowed to] ride in the same buses and live in the same residential areas as Europeans'. As *Inkululeko* plaintively pointed out, the leaflet 'said nothing at all about the constructive municipal policy advanced by the Communists'.[143] That the Labour Party produced this leaflet suggests that they viewed the CPSA as a serious competitor and, indeed, when the communists in 1943 first offered an electoral alliance, Labour leaders accepted an invitation to attend a formal meeting at the Trades Hall.[144] However, in 1945 communists failed to win new council seats in the Johannesburg election, for, though it achieved a total of 4,000 votes overall, its candidates polled the lowest scores in each of the four wards it contested. A slight consolation may have been that the new mayor, the Labour Party's 'progressive' Jessie McPherson, remained the president of the Friends of the Soviet Union.[145] George Findlay's disillusionment with the communists' efforts to induce a united front, and his impatience with 'labourites' within the party, 'masquerading as Communists', probably represented more generally shared sentiments.[146] Findlay kept a diary through the war, and in his entry for 25 July 1944 he recorded his conviction that the party should drop united front policies now that fascism was virtually defeated.

WHILE TRYING TO WIN electoral support from whites, the CPSA was also systematically attempting to build its black following. In November 1943, following a vigorous return to pass law enforcement by the police on the Witwatersrand,[147] an Anti-Pass Conference was held in Johannesburg under the auspices of the CPSA. From a platform decorated with a huge portrait of Johannes Nkosi, the Durban communist martyr of the 1930 pass campaign, and festooned with 'Mayibuye iAfrika' banners, the assembly was opened by speeches from Yusuf Dadoo and Edwin Mofutsanyana. The time had come, said Dr Dadoo, 'for the non European people[148] to unite, to raise their voice and carry on a campaign against the pass laws, against this badge of slavery which humiliates the African people'. 'We are not alone', he continued: 'If we campaign properly and well, we will win the support of the Coloured and the Indian people, and of the progressive Europeans.' The time had come, exhorted Mofutsanyana, 'to fight the passes to the bitter end'. This should be done by employing 'every channel we have'. 'We must petition the government and tell them we can no longer tolerate their pass laws. We must tell our representatives in Parliament in the coming session they must move a bill to abolish the pass laws.'[149] After the chairman had enjoined 'those who had nothing special to say not to speak', a pledge of support was taken by the 153 delegates (from 112 bodies representing 80,796 people), who then resolved to set up local pass committees; to send resolutions to the Prime Minister, the Minister of Native Affairs, and the Native Representative Council; and, as well as requesting the parliamentary Native representatives to introduce anti-pass legislation, 'to undertake every possible form of activity which will bring pressure on the Government to abolish the pass laws'. A leading committee of 15 was then elected, composed largely of African communists and non-communist members of the Transvaal ANC.[150]

The formation of local anti-pass committees rapidly got under way. By May 1944, when an elaborate launching ceremony was held for the campaign in Johannesburg, anti-pass activity had spread to affect most substantial African communities in the Transvaal: Brakpan, Roodepoort, Randfontein, Middelburg, Witbank, Springs, Vereeniging, Meyerton, Klerksdorp, Ermelo and Pretoria. Anti-pass committees also existed in Pietersburg and Sibasa in the Northern Transvaal. Work had begun in Cape Town, where the anti-pass committee held meetings during January in Langa, Retreat, Kensington, Bellevue, Philippi and Stellenbosch. Meetings were usually arranged in conjunction with local bodies: vigilance associations, tenants' leagues, food clubs, ANC and CPSA branches, and trades unions. By April 1944, local efforts were focused on the circulation of a petition and the selling of green-, yellow-and-black anti-pass badges. A somewhat belated endorsement of the campaign came in March from Dr Xuma, president general of the ANC.[151]

The campaign was formally inaugurated in Johannesburg on the weekend of 20–21 May. Some 540 delegates attended a meeting in Gandhi Hall, representing a diversity of organisations: trade unions, vigilance associations, food clubs, ANC and CPSA branches, churches, student groups, Advisory Boards and ratepayers' associations. After addresses by Dr Xuma, the Rev. Michael Scott, Dr Ahmed Ismail of the Indian Congress and the Native Representative Council members, a National Anti-Pass Council was elected. The form of the campaign was confirmed: a million-signature petition for presentation to the government in August, fundraising and the distribution of publicity material. Trotskyist or more militant forms of resistance were rejected by delegates, and subsequently *Inkululeko*'s columnist Umlweli reproved those who were arguing in favour of civil disobedience by the anti-pass leadership: this was foolish, for the task of leadership was to assist and give advice.[152] The climax of the launch was supplied by a demonstration of 20,000 people through the streets of Johannesburg. Few people were there to witness it, though, for it took place on a Sunday. In June, a delegation of ANC and party notables arrived at the office of the acting Prime Minister (Smuts was abroad), but Jan Hofmeyr was 'too busy' to see them.[153]

In June and July, the campaign seemed to be progressing well, especially on the East Rand. In Brakpan, home of the ANC's secretary and party member, David Bopape, anti-pass campaign tables were set up in the streets and by the gates of the location with copies of the petition for people to sign. In Heidelberg in June, after the arrest of a leading local communist and member of the anti-pass committee, Dan Mokoena, for not having a lodger's permit, hundreds of women marched outside the courtroom while schools closed and no one went to work. After a parade through the centre of the town, the mayor listened to a list of complaints against the location superintendent and promised the release of Mokoena. The superintendent was arrested the following week under suspicion of attempting to elicit sympathy by placing a bomb in his own office.[154] Meanwhile, further meetings were reported in Durban, Boksburg, Cape Town and Springs. A thousand men and women gathered in Sibasa, their numbers including several local chiefs and indunas. A request for 200 petition forms arrived from the recently established committee in Bloemfontein.

In August, however, the tempo of the campaign appeared to slacken. While in Brakpan on 10 August there was a stay-away by 7,000 African location residents in protest against the dismissal from his teaching post of David Bopape,[155] there were no reports of activity connected with opposition to passes from anywhere else in the Transvaal. In September it was announced that the date for the presentation of the petition had been postponed.[156] The next public pronouncement of the National Anti-Pass Council did not come until February 1945. This was a statement by Bopape on the closure of the petition drive.[157] Angered by the silences in Bopape's statement, two communist members of the Council, Edwin Mofutsanyana and Josie Mpama, made public criticisms of its work. In the Transvaal, they noted, the campaign

> became inactive after the [May] conference. Badges were not sold, petitions were not signed, and even the local committees have gone to sleep ... something is radically wrong with the working committee. Most of the Council members at the centre failed to attend meetings. There has been an average attendance of from five to seven; the work being left to three members ... it must be pointed out that the chairman [Dadoo] and the Secretary [Bopape] have not been the live wires they should have been. They have rather expected local committees and others to take the initiative.[158]

What had gone wrong? At the beginning there seemed to be no shortage of public enthusiasm for the campaign. Large numbers of people participated in demonstrations, passes were actually burned on several occasions in local initiatives,[159] and in at least two centres, Brakpan and Heidelberg, the issue of pass laws fused with other sources of local discontent to provoke impressive displays of communal solidarity.[160] On the East Rand, women were noticeably engaged in the earlier stages of the campaign. In March 1944, at the instigation of Josie Mpama, a special women's conference was held in Johannesburg – the war years did witness an effort by certain municipalities to regulate the movement of African women into town. It is likely the form the campaign took did little to retain people's interest and active support. In contrast to earlier types of protesting against the pass laws, petitioning was rather a tame tactic, particularly in communities in which most people could not write. At this juncture, it was hardly the case that the campaign had attempted 'every possible form of activity which will bring pressure on the Government to abolish the pass laws', as the delegates had agreed at its inception.

Of course, it is possible, as critics suggested, that leaders could have been more energetic, though it should be acknowledged that both Dadoo and Bopape were harassed by the authorities as a result of their roles in the campaign, but that seems unsatisfactory by itself as an explanation. In fact, communists maintained an assertive presence on the East Rand, being the most likely organised political group to respond to localised collective action. Through early 1945 communists in Benoni joined forces with African tenants protesting against rent rises from Indian landlords, and held well-attended weekly meetings in Wattville location. A key leader was Arthur Damane, an Advisory Board member and a paid CPSA organiser for the African Mineworkers' Union. When evicted, tenants occupied freshly constructed municipal houses, and the party paid the rents.[161] In 1945, communists did well in East Rand Advisory Board elections, winning three seats in Springs, three in Brakpan, one in Benoni and two in Nigel.[162] With respect to the anti-pass campaign, contemporary commentators suggested that the CPSA deliberately confined the protest to legal forms of activity as a consequence of its war policy.[163] In addition, it may be that the communists themselves were influenced by government proposals for reform to the extent of believing that if they campaigned 'properly and well', the authorities would be suitably impressed.

These sorts of considerations were very evident in party engagements in communal insurgencies in two other geographical focuses in the Transvaal for communist activity among Africans: Orlando and Alexandra. In Orlando from 1934, communists had dominated Advisory Board elections, having organised support for their candidates through the Vigilance Association. The communists recognised from the beginning the limitations of the Boards,[164] but argued that they should be used as a platform for 'a mighty struggle for self government in the locations', to be conducted not only through the Boards but also outside them: 'If the municipality and the Government does not listen to the Advisory Board members when they put forward your just demands, the Advisory Board members must call meetings of residents, lead deputations and demonstrations and compel rulers to fulfil these demands. The Advisory Board members must be real leaders and fighters for your demands.'[165] After 1937, there was an additional dimension to the CPSA's view of Board politics, for the Boards themselves were vital constituents in the process of indirect election of representatives to the Native Representative Council (NRC). The CPSA's own NRC candidate, Edwin Mofutsanyana, was a leading personality in the Orlando Board. Ascetic and hardworking, 'loyal Edwin'[166] lacked the popular touch; communist influence in Orlando owed more to organisational proficiency than charismatic leadership.

Communists were also very active in Alexandra, the freehold township to the north of Johannesburg. In Bram Fischer, the party had a representative on the Health Committee, nominally the governing local authority in Alexandra, and a substantial local branch had been built up through the efforts of Max Joffe, who during the late 1930s was active in establishing a local tenants' league. Alexandra and Orlando provided the settings for two of the most dramatic assertions of popular discontent during the war, and ostensibly the CPSA might have appeared well placed in both cases to exercise leadership. In Alexandra between 1940 and 1945, there were four separate protests over rises in bus fares. They took the form of boycotts which climaxed in a seven-week protest in November and December 1944. Beginning with simple refusals to pay the extra fare, the forms of resistance became progressively more elaborate and militant. In 1943, 10,000 people marched in a long procession the 18 miles to town, and in the following year the movement looked at one moment as if it might develop into a township-wide general strike. Local leadership was supplied by a Transport Action Committee (later called a Workers' Transport Action Committee), and from 1943 local leadership was supported and advised by an Emergency Transport Committee, established and led by Senator Basner, who had won that year's elections for the Senate seat representing Africans in the Transvaal and the Free State. By 1943, the CPSA, weakened in Johannesburg the year before by the expulsion of the mercurial but organisationally effective Gaur Radebe for 'petty bourgeois behaviour' (money lending), was just one of several groups jostling acrimoniously with one another for influence over the boycotters. The genesis of these groups and the intricacies of their relationship with each other are matters that have only partly been uncovered by researchers, but it does appear that during the 1944 boycott the CPSA functioned to limit and define the course of the movement; in other words, its influence was a restraining one. It opposed, for example, on quite sensible grounds, the extension of the boycott movement to the south-western townships (later, Soweto) and pressed for the acceptance of a City Council-subsidised coupon scheme which guaranteed the retention of the old lower fare for three months;[167] and it may have, through its influence on trade unions, delayed the implementation of the general strike call. Hilda Watts played a mediating role between the City Council and the Transport Action Committee. Subsequently the party was critical of Trotskyists on the committee, who were predisposed to 'oppose every settlement', rejecting 'useful proposals more than once'.[168] In all this the CPSA may well have been correct in interpreting the popular mood in addition to assessing accurately the limits of what might have been gained. It is worth noting, however, that in doing so they were opposed by more radical voices calling for a socialised form of public transport.[169] Local communists probably considered such proposals wildly utopian; in the wake of the boycott, the Alexandra branch of the party immersed itself in the more everyday preoccupations of its constituents. In July its spokesman announced from the party's new office in the old Health Committee rooms their intention 'to organise people around the issue of drains and the risk of small pox'. Party officials also wanted to raise with the municipality the question of the Health Committee's legal status. They wanted the committee to acquire trading rights so that it could embark on a programme of bulk-buying for consumer cooperatives.[170]

But if communists accurately gauged the limits to popular militancy in the Alexandra bus boycott, this cannot be said in favour of their judgements concerning the Orlando squatters' movement. At the beginning of the war, each of Orlando's 5,000 houses accommodated seven people. This average nearly doubled between 1940 and 1944 as a consequence of a huge influx of migrants from the farms and the reserves, seeking jobs and food. Rather than building accommodation for these people, the City Council lifted restrictions on subletting and tolerated the subsequent overcrowding. After fruitless agitation against the housing shortage, a group of Orlando residents led by James Sofasonke Mpanza, an Advisory Board member, organised an exodus of subtenants out of the location to construct hessian shelters on the empty veld in March 1944. Before the subtenants moved, Mpanza approached the communists and asked them to join his committee. Mofutsanyana and his comrades held back, arguing that at the beginning of winter Mpanza's plan was irresponsible and would merely lead to greater privations than already existed. Orlando's communists distrusted Mpanza in any case, with his background as a convicted murderer, born-again evangelist and small-time huckster, and they had been energetically contesting his influence within the Advisory Board for nearly a decade. But municipal hostility and cold weather notwithstanding, Mpanza's movement grew and, grudgingly, the communists had to concede support while questioning Mpanza's personal motives and criticising his administration. Their initial abstention cost them dearly. Thereafter Mpanza ensured their exclusion from any active contribution to the leadership of his kingdom, and they were confined to organising soup kitchens on its fringes and lobbying the Council in concert with liberal pressure groups for a more generous policy towards the squatters. The extent of their estrangement from the Orlando squatters was embarrassingly evident when a leading party member, Advocate Franz Boshoff, appeared for the Native Affairs Department in its efforts to have Mpanza deported from Johannesburg. Boshoff was suspended from his membership.[171] In three successive Advisory Board elections, in 1944, 1945 and 1946, the communists failed to win any seats.[172]

At one level the failure can be explained with reference to the personalities involved. The autocratic Mpanza was indisposed to sharing decisions with any but the most sycophantic counsel, and in manner and style he was light years away from trained party functionaries like Mofutsanyana. But the problem was deeper than this, for the communists had underestimated the housing crisis[173] and the intensity of public feeling arising from it, and had allowed the initiative to pass from their hands. As the Johannesburg District Committee acknowledged in a bracingly self-critical report: 'We failed to recognise the deep desire and need of the people for vigorous and correct political leadership, we did not act as a vanguard of the struggle.'[174] Their characterisation of Mpanza as 'irresponsible' was symptomatic of their unwillingness at that time to contemplate initiating direct action. In Orlando, this may have been partly a consequence of participation in Advisory Board elections. While at the beginning the communists professed to be conscious of the limited utility of the Board, by the 1940s it is possible that for them 'control' of the Board had become an end in itself. Certainly, in Orlando in 1944 the communists demonstrated considerable insensitivity to the needs and aspirations of subtenants, who were not, it should be remembered, entitled to vote in Board elections. It is also conceivable that Johannesburg communists may have been influenced in their response to the squatters by their understanding of the local dynamics of white politics. As the report quoted above went on to suggest: 'There is a large and growing body of European opinion conscious of the oppression of the non-European people and sympathetic to their demands and aspirations. It is the special duty of every European Communist devotedly and energetically to spread and deepen this consciousness and sympathy.'[175]

Johannesburg communists would still then have been encouraged by their support from white municipal voters. Michael Harmel wrote to the Central Executive Committee on 7 March 1945 with the good news that the party's majority presence within the Jewish Board of Deputies was about to increase; his letter was probably only half serious but he received back a reprimand for sending information through the post.[176] Harmel was, of course, a dominant personality among the group that believed that Africans would and should constitute the party's main following; and by that time he was making a key contribution to the party night school held in the bleak premises of a disused shop in End Street, which served as the branch office.[177] The class included Nelson Mandela among its attendees. Harmel and Mandela would later become close friends. But optimism about the party's prospects for extending its white support may have explained the predisposition noted by one observer of some 'European members' of the party to believe 'it [was] wrong to work among Africans in African areas as the Africans must develop their own leaders ... another way of tacitly developing a segregated policy'.[178] In the same article, its author suggested that the party had tended to concentrate resources and efforts around the chimerical goals of winning more municipal seats and, in doing so, neglected what should have been its more realistic priority, extending the party's influence on Advisory Boards.

Fortunately the kind of local challenge to the party provided by Mpanza was exceptional. Elsewhere, communist participation in local bodies such as residents' associations and Advisory Boards provided useful vehicles for agitation over administrative injustices, food shortages and material hardships, and helped significantly to extend their influence.[179] In Western Native Township, adjacent to Sophiatown, for example, party members Gaur Radebe and Joseph Kumalo led the local Vigilance Association, and were arrested for inciting residents to refuse to pay rent.[180] By 1945 there were communist branches or groups within African communities in most of the industrial towns.[181] Both locally and nationally, African communists took pains to collaborate with the ANC, often serving as key officials. Here their tactical emphasis on reformist demands and their apparent concern to avoid confrontation with authority helped to foster the alliance with a still very cautious and conservative ANC leadership, and they may have also accorded with the predispositions of residents. As Johnny Gomas explained, people were most readily 'drawn into the struggle for their immediate needs',[182] or, less positively, in the words of an East London communist, for most people politics was circumscribed by the limitations imposed by a 'hand to hand existence'. At the same time, small-scale organisation around subsistence issues could also prompt the first steps in communal organisation. In this context, the food-buying cooperatives developed by the communists in Johannesburg, Durban and Pretoria in the course of 1943 and 1944 were imaginative responses to the deprivation and helplessness of the urban poor.[183]

In general, then, despite their setback in Orlando, the early 1940s were years in which the communists established themselves as a popular agency in local urban African politics.[184] The revival of the Young Communist League (YCL) in 1945 helped to supply fresh activist energy. Strongest in Johannesburg and Cape Town, it also had branches in Durban and Brandfort. In Johannesburg, the YCL attracted an assertively active following in Fordsburg: Ahmed Kathrada and Paul Joseph were key personalities here. The League was led nationally by Lucas Masebe and Ruth First and, with an average age of 19, its membership grew rapidly in the year following its re-establishment.[185] At that time Ruth First was one of a cluster of communist-affiliated students at Wits; her companion Ismail Meer was another, and, together with fellow student Harold Wolpe, they established on campus a Federation of Progressive Students.[186] Joe Slovo would join their circle after his return from army service in Italy. Ismail Meer's flat at 27 Market Street was a key assembly point for politically minded students, including Nelson Mandela, who was then enrolled at Wits for a law degree.[187]

THE PARTY'S RECORD OF activist commitment was more uncertain in the countryside. For in the reserves, the close of the 1930s and the beginning of the 1940s witnessed the inception of an extended and increasingly violent struggle as peasants attempted to resist the government's efforts to reorganise land usage and political institutions. Through the courageous efforts of Alpheus Maliba, the communists had first-hand knowledge of the most serious of these conflicts, that of the Northern Transvaal, and for a time the party helped Maliba's Zoutpansberg Cultural Association (ZCA), providing legal assistance, an office, and in 1939 publishing a pamphlet by him.[188] The ZCA, established in 1939, had an office in the same building as the CPSA district headquarters. Renaming itself the Zoutpansberg Balemi Association

(ZBA) in 1943, it opened a second office in 1944 in Louis Trichardt, where it organised a night school and maintained a roster of 3,000 members before declining in later years. The ZBA's main historian, Peter Delius, suggests that at best the CPSA's backing for the Association was half-hearted. Writing partly from his own recollections, Baruch Hirson noted that the party's involvement in peasant struggles was the subject of some debate in 1940; those who felt the party should not divert attention from its urban activities emerged paramount.[189] Despite lukewarm support from his comrades, Maliba influenced rural workers at Denver hostel in Johannesburg to join the CPSA and the ANC from 1948. These included three key personalities in later years: Elias Motsoaledi, Flag Boshielo and John Nkadimeng. Through the ZBA the party formed a group at Jeppe hostel as well.[190] There was also an active ZCA branch in Pretoria whose members included trade unionists and party members.[191] Alpheus Maliba and other members of the ZBA were arrested in November 1941 for incitement of unlawful ploughing. The opening of his trial was accompanied by a demonstration and an open-air meeting in Piesanghoek, near Louis Trichardt. Those in attendance sang 'bavenda military songs' and shouted slogans: 'We want more land; we want vhuswa [food]'.[192] The case was subsequently dismissed, in a decision *Inkululeko* reported as a 'people's victory'.[193] In the following year, the party nominated Maliba as their candidate for the Native Representative Council,[194] though he fared no better than Mofutsanyana, for none of the party's nominated candidates secured a seat. But despite resolutions and the adoption of an agrarian element in their programme,[195] Maliba's cause did not figure prominently in the party's wartime concerns, despite the violent disruption of the ZBA's night school in Louis Trichardt in 1944 and Maliba's efforts to try to persuade the party to take up the issue of ZBA members conscripted for forced labour on bridges and dams.[196] Indeed, when the CPSA in 1944 held its first 'rural conference', marking, according to Moses Kotane, a 'new stage' in the party's development, it held it in the Western Cape for the benefit of farm labourers, not peasants.[197] It was Ray Alexander who first explored the possibilities of drawing farm workers into the party's embrace, reaching them through the Food and Canning Workers' Union, for most of the union's members had families who lived and worked on farms. She maintained contact with Alpheus Maliba and called upon him whenever she visited Johannesburg; clearly she saw their projects as interrelated.[198]

Kotane's opening address at the party's annual conference in 1944 looked forward to 'the penetration of the Party on a large scale into the rural areas' through meetings and discussion groups that would supply 'a clear lead on how to organise to protect and better their conditions of life'. [199] There may have been some progress in fulfilling this aspiration because four years later, at the CPSA's conference in 1948, one of the resolutions referred to efforts that were needed 'to secure an appointment of an organiser for rural areas'. Apparently, 'the growth of the Party in certain areas' signalled 'the importance of rural organisation' as well as the possibility of establishing 'new provincial district committees'.[200] There is no evidence of any subsequent developments of this kind. Ray Alexander and several of her fellow trade unionists tried to set up a farm workers' union but this proved too difficult: 'the fear [among workers] was too great'.[201] Of course, reaching reserve communities was often very difficult, but it was also the case that leading Transvaal communists felt that the party's prime tasks should be different. As the Pretoria advocate and party member George Findlay observed after defending Maliba in Louis Trichardt in 1941: 'The Platteland Africans are a secondary area – mere propaganda is needed there, not peasant revolts.'[202] Basner, who worked with Maliba in early 1944, implies that Maliba's activities were conducted in increasing isolation from the party.[203] It may have been the case that CPSA support for peasant struggles slackened after 1941 as a consequence of its tactical abandonment of an anti-imperialist stance. From 1928 the 'national problem' in party theory had been understood to include an important agrarian dimension, yet, as we have seen, the party paid only occasional attention to rural issues.

THE FINAL DIMENSION of wartime CPSA activity was trade union organisation. While it also fought a rearguard action within the white trade union movement,[204] the most important activity was developing workers' organisations among Africans and, in the Cape and Natal, among coloured people and Indians. The Second World War supplied a favourable climate for the growth of black trade unionism. The development of manufacturing and the increasing employment of Africans in semi-skilled industrial positions provided one vital impetus for trade union organisation. The inclusion of unskilled workers, mainly Africans, in Wage Board determinations through the 1937 Wage Act gave to unions legal space for manoeuvre, enabling them to deliver substantial benefits to their new members without bringing them into risky confrontations with the state. A high level of spontaneous industrial militancy during the war years helped to encourage an official perception of African trade unions as a means through which conflict between employers and their workforce could be regulated.

Communists were not the first in the field in wartime African unionism (though they did pioneering work with Indian and coloured workers in Durban and the Boland). After the depredations of the purges and popular frontism of the 1930s, they had retained only a few members with any experience of African trade unionism. The two clusters of African trade unions which had developed by 1941, the Joint Committee of African Trade Unions and the Coordinating Committee, with 20,000 and nearly 3,000 affiliated members respectively, were led by men who were wary of involvement with the Communist Party. The first had been set up as a result of the work of Max Gordon, a radical socialist employed by the Institute of Race Relations, and the second was under the aegis of Gana Makabeni, expelled from the party in 1931.[205] In 1941 communists led just three African unions.[206] But they were active as members and office bearers in unions affiliated to these bodies, and their merger into a Council of Non-European Trade Unions (CNETU) at the end of 1941 took place at a meeting over which Moses Kotane presided. At least four of the seven men who composed the first CNETU executive were communists. Nevertheless, CNETU is best understood as an uneasy coalition rather than a body over which the Communist Party exercised real control. CNETU's first conference was opened in 1942 by the Minister of Labour, Walter Madeley; Madeley asked his audience for patience over the issue of official recognition of African unions.

However, in the same year War Measure 145 would impose new penalties for strikers, in reaction to a wave of stoppages in the second half of 1942. Notwithstanding the minister's conciliatory language, the government generally remained opposed to making any real concessions when Africans were on the offensive. In 1942 Communist Party trade union organisers supported strikes once they occurred, though they tried to discourage them. For them the priority was African trade union recognition, an issue that would be the focus of campaigning through 1943, which culminated in a rally in Port Elizabeth attended by 2,500 trade unionists. Communists were unable to secure full support from the Trades and Labour Council, which instead resolved itself in favour of Africans being represented by whites on industrial councils. The Trades and Labour Council remained, led by representatives of white craft unions, well-paid artisans generally unsympathetic to the concerns of unskilled and semi-skilled workers. Meanwhile, the government would shelve its earlier tentative plans for a qualified degree of African trade union recognition, as a result of pressure from the Chamber of Mines as well as a consequence of the changing fortunes of war. By the end of 1943, with an Allied victory looking more likely, placating African workers became less important.[207]

The main thrust of Communist Party trade union work lay in the expansion of organisation largely in the service sector and light industry, though there were efforts also to organise power workers, metal workers and mine labourers as well. These unions tended to be strongest in fields in which Africans performed skilled or semi-skilled work: this was the case of laundry workers, who constructed one of the most resilient and militant unions of the decade.[208] Much of the organisation was of a fairly superficial quality: African officials served as secretaries for several different organisations and offices were centralised on party premises in Johannesburg. For the purpose of representing workers at Wage Board inquiries, such arrangements were adequate, but they would have been severely put to the test in more militant forms of action. The party made it quite clear on several occasions, however, that it opposed the use of the strike weapon. As Ray Alexander reported to the 1944 CPSA conference: 'Our party's policy is directed towards a peaceful settlement of disputes and avoiding any strikes or any actions that will hinder the war effort.'[209] This policy was 're-affirmed' in a conference resolution, though qualified by a 'serious warning' to employers that workers would act against any efforts to 'increase exploitation'.[210] When interviewed in 1993, Ray Alexander recalled that though she supported the policy in public, she did not agree with it: 'it wasn't really a party decision – it was suggested by Michael Harmel. The issue came from Johannesburg,' she thought.[211] She also thought the anti-strike line may have followed the practice of the British party. Alexander was the author of a pamphlet published in 1944 by the party entitled *Trades Unions and You*, which included advice on when workers should use the strike weapon; it made no reference to any anti-strike policy.[212] Norman Levy argues that 'effectively, the Party left it to the judgement of workers and the discretion of trade unionists to decide whether or not to strike'.[213] This seems mostly right.

There were, of course, practical considerations as well. As a contemporary liberal commentary pointed out in 1941, 'unions have endeavoured to avoid strike action as far as possible. It is illegal for Natives to strike and there is therefore a need for a high degree of organisation.'[214] Not that workers were unwilling; on several occasions unions had to curb the militancy of members. For example, in the Non-European Federation of Iron and Steel Workers it was necessary in 1943 to pass two resolutions against 'hasty ill-considered action' and 'unnecessary stoppages' *after* the granting of a modest pay award, and reports of dissatisfaction among rank-and-file workers with leadership persisted to the end of the war.[215] The communist-led Gas and Power Workers' Union intervened in December 1942 to prevent a strike by workers at the

Victoria Falls Company's power stations which supplied electricity to the mines 'because we felt it was our duty to prevent trouble when the country was in the midst of a serious war crisis'.[216] Gana Makabeni spoke to the workers at a meeting arranged by Department of Labour officials; in return, he was promised, they would help to organise a conference with officials and employers to consider grievances. Ultimately this undertaking led to the appointment of the Lansdown Commission. At this stage Department of Labour bureaucrats tended to be relatively conciliatory compared with employers, especially those represented by the Chamber of Mines, though their attitude became progressively tougher during 1944; they arranged, for example, the recruitment of military strike-breakers from Zoutpansberg mid-year.[217] In at least three strikes in which trade unions were involved, the milling workers', timber workers' and coal deliverers' disputes, all in 1944, the communists were sharply critical, accusing their leaders of being a 'handful of wreckers', 'fifth columnists' and 'scoundrels'.[218] In turn, the union organisers accused communist trade union leaders of following an 'uncompromisingly reactionary policy of Stalinism' and, in doing so, bringing 'many a promising strike or trade union struggle to an ignominious end', as well as isolating and withholding any support even to the arrested and convicted mill workers.[219] More specifically, in each case communists argued that the strikes were based upon inadequate preparation. These unions were led by Trotskyists, who delighted in irritating the communists, as on the occasion in 1943 when the African Commercial and Distributive Workers attempted to persuade the Trades and Labour Council to resolve against a second front, contending that it would 'be used only for the imperialists' dream of crushing the people's movement'. Such a position, charged the communists, was clearly 'Fascist-inspired', raising the 'suspicion in the workers' minds that the Soviet Union's allies are really her enemies'.[220] In the cases of strikes which were not Trotskyist-led, the CPSA took a more sympathetic position: despite policy, party members appeared on picket lines,[221] and the party itself defended the strikers in its propaganda for trade union recognition.[222] Such cases were, however, of registered unions with legal protections, and the strikes were not wage-related; for these the embargo evidently did not apply. In Cape Town, the trade unionist Pauline Podbrey was among Albie Sachs's mother's friends. She visited them during a lorry drivers' strike in the mid-1940s; she and they joined the pickets.[223]

With respect to mine workers, the party could make strong claims to have pioneered their organisation. The African Mineworkers' Union (AMWU) was founded at a meeting on 3 August 1941, sponsored by the Transvaal

African National Congress (TANC) but actually organised as a consequence of a party decision four months earlier.[224] As we have seen, there had been previous unsuccessful efforts by communists since the early 1920s to set up a union for African mine workers,[225] but in this case the decision to work through the ANC was to prove decisive. Communists hoped this would help them recruit workers in rural areas before their travel to the Witwatersrand. A steering committee was set up, with half of its members from the party.[226] The committee included William Thibedi in its membership.[227] It also included Edwin Mofutsanyana's friend James Majoro, leader of the African Mine Clerks' Association, a white-collar body tolerated by the Chamber of Mines. Mofutsanyana was a former mine clerk, and it was he and Gaur Radebe who had proposed the formation of the union to the Transvaal provincial executive of the ANC.[228] Majoro and his colleagues supplied the critical intermediaries that enabled the union to obtain access to the workforce, and their cooperation was a consequence of the respectability conferred on the project by the TANC's sponsorship; otherwise the TANC/ANC supplied no real organisational backing. Originally, the AMWU elected as its president Gaur Radebe, the TANC's 'secretary for mines and propaganda', but he was replaced in 1942 by JB Marks, a veteran labour organiser, Moscow-trained, and by then back in the party after a brief expulsion in 1937.[229] Marks was a good choice, widely liked, easily approachable and a powerful orator.

The first phase of the AMWU's development was discouraging. Working secretively, it signed up just 1,800 members by the beginning of 1944. But at the beginning of that year leaders boldly decided to risk prosecution for trespass by holding meetings on mining ground, just outside the workers' compounds, and by adopting a more open and less selective approach to recruitment – a reflection of a shift the CPSA undertook at its December congress in favour of 'a new phase of liberation from the colour bar system'. For the next eight months, union officials organised what at times was a daily schedule of meetings up and down the Rand, meetings often attended by 2,000 to 3,000 workers ready to be entertained by Marks's insolent and witty invective directed at the mining authorities, which drew attention to the bad food, poor wages and harsh conditions in the compounds. The AMWU's prestige may have been boosted by a modest 5d per shift wage increase awarded after the publication on 24 March 1944 of an official report on wages by the Lansdown Commission, a body appointed at the urging of the AMWU, though Gana Makabeni's union also helped to secure its appointment. In any case, Marks claimed the credit for the increase. He was taking a chance in making such claims, for on 30 July 1944, when the AMWU held its annual conference, delegates had called for a strike, angered by the ungenerosity of the Lansdown Commission's recommendations; their leaders counselled against striking or any other action that would damage the war effort.[230] As officials conceded, Marks was careful in his speeches, despite his use of the language of militancy, to stop short of strike advocacy, which would have been illegal, of course, and in any case in conflict with party policy. Such efforts were rewarded, it seems, with a significant expansion of the union's influence, and its membership claims increased by August 1944 to around 25,000. If accurate, this enrolment would have followed a very rapid expansion. Writing earlier that year, Eli Weinberg referred to a total membership of 10,000. His report suggested that internal wrangling between officials, hostility from the Trades and Labour Council (SATLC) and fears of victimisation had slowed recruitment.[231] In any case, in August 1944 War Measure 1425 brought this open phase of organisation and the union's expansion to an end, as it explicitly banned public meetings on mining ground. It took the Gold Producers' Committee several months to secure the meeting's prohibition: initially both the Department of Justice and the Department of Labour opposed a ban.[232]

Dunbar Moodie's ethnographic research conducted in Mpondoland among strike veterans in the 1980s provides insights into the extent and location of the union's influence.[233] Its active membership, his sources suggested, did not extend deeply into the compounds. Here, leadership was customarily exercised by *isibondas* – elected room heads – who in the representation of their roommates' grievances would negotiate with *indunas*, management-appointed foremen. If grievances were ignored, then the *isibondas* would instruct their roommates to assemble outside the office of the compound manager and remain seated until they were noticed, an action that contained a tacit threat of some kind of direct action: a strike, a riot or some kind of destruction of mining property. Most serious disturbances on the gold mines – and there were around a hundred major 'riots' between 1939 and 1948 – began with such a procedure being ignored. Grievances in such protests would be limited in scope: they did not involve issues that might have raised questions about the compound system or the authority of managers. Normally, *isibondas* would probably resist the influence of a union driven by much wider concerns. But there was a group of workers who were less likely to accept the normal relations of production. These were the *tshipas* – literally absconders – those who, though they still worked underground, had managed to settle outside the compound, living with women in nearby shanty settlements, and no longer maintaining rural homesteads. It seems that it was among the *tshipas* that the AMWU recruited most of its adherents, though it also attracted very young men in the compounds. The *tshipas* were concentrated in the mines near Johannesburg, they were much less likely to be found in the East Rand, and the AMWU's organised following was strongest around Johannesburg and on the West Rand. So, the AMWU's organised following was socially concentrated and spatially uneven.

Even so, African trade unionism by 1945 represented a substantial achievement. Communists were in leadership positions in 34 new African trade unions and 62 new registered unions.[234] The 199 bodies with their alleged 150,000 membership represented an impressive total, particularly if the very small number of trade union organisers is recalled. What is arguable is that more could have been achieved, especially if the party had been more willing to employ strikes in its campaigns for trade union recognition. In 1945, its policy of industrial discipline appeared as if it might place in jeopardy its ascendancy within the African trade union movement. Accusing the 'Stalinists' of 'Trade Union Fetishism',[235] a Trotskyist Progressive Trade Union Group produced a catalogue of various wrongdoings and shortcoming of the CNETU executive. These included, it alleged, communist-inspired 'pacification' of workers, the establishment of rivals to unions which did not conform with communist policies, and failure to support strikes.[236] In August, communists needed the help of allies to retain their position at the CNETU conference: a well-organised effort by the Progressive Trade Unionists to pack the meeting was defeated with the help of Senator Basner, who had been invited to open the meeting. Though at odds with the party since 1939, Basner had retained his friendship with JB Marks who had helped him win his senatorship. Thereafter, the Trotskyists were expelled.[237] As they took with them some of the most militant and experienced trade unionists, their departure did not portend well for the new phase of working-class action which was to succeed the ending of the common front against fascism.

Splits and ideological factionalism left the African trade union movement severely depleted well before the end of the war. One contemporary observer suggested that in the six months before June 1945 there had been a 'catastrophic' collapse affecting 17 unions on the Witwatersrand alone.[238] Communist trade unionists also disagreed among themselves over strategic issues. For example, Ray Alexander in Cape Town favoured working with SATLC in 1945, as did HA Naidoo in Durban, whereas many of her comrades in Johannesburg preferred only affiliation with CNETU.[239] One important consideration was proposed legislation that would have banned any strike activity, resolved any disputes through a central mediation board, and excluded African mine workers even from this procedure. SATLC opposition helped to keep the bill unenacted through to the 1948 election, and later it would be withdrawn.

Where Indians or coloured workers belonged to registered unions, as in Cape Town or Durban, for communists the SATLC could be an ally. Communist trade unionists began to be active in Durban in 1936. Here the leading personalities were HA Naidoo and George Ponnen, who, as we have seen, between them helped to establish 27 unions in or around Durban between 1936 and 1945.[240] Both became communists in 1934, being recruited by Eddie Roux. Naidoo prioritised unionising Indian workers because Indians were easier to reach, but he and his comrades were also keen to organise Africans, as well as drawing into the local party branch the unionised workers that demonstrated capacity for leadership. Of these, Philemon Tsele, the railway workers' organiser, and Wilson Cele were among Naidoo's most talented recruits. But Indians most readily presented themselves for recruitment. In the words of Errol Shanley, the secretary of Durban's SATLC, union officials at the Council's headquarters every day encountered 'an endless stream of workers, mainly Indian, knocking on our door, wanting to be unionised'.[241] Naidoo directed much of his effort at enlisting field and mill workers on the sugar estates. The authorities actually facilitated his travels around Durban, allowing him extra petrol rations on the assumption he would be spreading a pro-war effort message – a particular concern in Durban because of lingering anti-war sentiment among Natal Indian Congress leaders.[242] Naidoo and Ponnen did remain active in Congress circles and helped the left-inclined National-Minded Bloc organise a reception for Indira Gandhi in 1941 on her way back home after her studies in Oxford.

Naidoo's experiences are recorded in a memoir written by his partner and later wife, Pauline Podbrey, who, having joined the party after induction through the campus-based Liberal Study Group, was assigned the task of setting up a union for shop workers. She became secretary of the African Commercial and Distributive Union in 1942; she had no qualms about using the threat of striking in her altercations with employers. Her union could not of course obtain registration but she was careful even so to conform with the bureaucratic requirements of the Act: 'we were not legal, so we had to be strong'.[243] Podbrey was arrested on the picket line of a rubber workers' strike for allegedly kicking a scab worker and was subsequently defended by Rowley Arenstein, secretary of the Durban District Committee.[244] The union itself defended its strike in a leaflet that explained that the strikers, in seeking a cost-of-living allowance for the families of Dunlop workers now serving in the army, were 'defending the rights of former workmates up North'.[245] In this case, the party was sufficiently concerned about the strike in what was a key sector for the war effort, to appoint its own 'commission of inquiry'.[246] Naidoo and Podbrey moved to Cape Town in 1944: the party found them both jobs to make it easier for them to set up a joint household, encouraging them, in Jack Simons's words, 'to marry and settle down'.[247] Naidoo was given a paid post at *The Guardian* while Pauline began work on setting up a union for coloured sweet workers, joining Ray Alexander and Nancy Dick at Union House in Mowbray, which accommodated the offices of most of the left-inclined labour groups.

THE PARTY'S FINAL five years of legal existence before its dissolution and prohibition in 1950 have not received much attention. The 1946 mine workers' strike is depicted as the climax of the decade, and its defeat and the subsequent decline of the African trade union movement that communists had helped to build during the war are described by the Simonses as causing the deflection of class struggle currents into nationalist channels, a process that was to bring the party before its banning into a closer relationship with the ANC.

Alan Brooks in his analysis of the CPSA's activities during the 1940s suggests that throughout the decade a dialectical relationship existed between the forces of class struggle and national consciousness. After all, in 1941 the party had to enlist the support of the ANC to construct one of its major agencies of class struggle, the African Mineworkers' Union. In Brooks's phraseology, having 'achieved take-off ... the forces of class struggle were able to generate their own momentum on a scale sufficient in 1946 to stage the biggest strike of the decade. This further development of class consciousness in turn reacted upon the growing national consciousness of Africans and raised it to a new pitch.' In this latter phase, that is, in the years following the 1946 strike, the party moved from pursuing a class struggle to the 'more fundamental issue of national liberation'. So, from 1946, there was a shift away from the wartime emphasis on building African trade unions to a preoccupation with broader concerns around which the party could mobilise public support and strengthen its relationship with the ANC. Hence, for example, in defining its policy in the context of the upcoming general election in 1948, the party proposed that its 'primary task [was] that of advancing the struggle for the universal franchise and for social democracy and for rallying the people against imperialism'. Brooks describes a slow, tortuous and complex process of convergence between the CPSA and the ANC, incomplete at the time of the party's banning in 1950.[248]

If this is a more or less accurate account of the direction in party policy during the post-war period, existing treatments, written from perspectives that closely reflected the party's own retrospective understandings, do not tell us very much about how this transition happened and what its internal implications were for the party's development. The impression that they create is of a linear process of evolution in which the party's expanding African membership increasingly shaped the course of policy and ideological formation. The party's dissolution and banning are represented as a momentary hiccup that only briefly interrupts the passage of working-class revolutionaries into the ranks of the national liberation movement. In fact, the reality was more complicated and more interesting. This was a period of considerable conflict and division within the party and a period in which it began to fragment into a series of localised clusters of activists with contrasting strategic preoccupations and tactical predispositions. It merits examination in more detail.

Let us begin with the trade unions, which, as we have seen, embodied one of the major spheres of party activity during the war. Communists by 1945 were strongly represented in the leadership of the African unions that had been fostered by the umbrella body, the Council of Non-European Trade Unions (CNETU), a body that coordinated the work of 119 individual unions, which together claimed an affiliation of 150,000. Much, though not all, of the work involved in constructing these unions had been undertaken by communists. Within CNETU, by the end of the war, as we have seen, there were deep tensions, arising partly from the party's reluctance to support strikes after the Soviet entry into the war. At the August 1945 conference of CNETU, these tensions came to a head in the Trotskyist challenge to communist leadership. Communist success in mustering support for the expulsion of the Trotskyists resulted in the departure of some of the more militant and experienced labour organisers. But the exit of the Trotskyist unionists can only be one part of the explanation for the subsequent disintegration of CNETU, which was to take place in the succeeding three years or so.

The defeat of the African mine workers' strike, and the subsequent destruction of the mine workers' union, formed one of the central episodes in the post-war decline of African labour organisation. For party historians, it has become an event invested with historic importance. It was, after all, at the time when it happened, the biggest strike ever to have occurred in South Africa. Between 12 and 16 August 1946, at least 75,000 African workers stopped work one week after a strike call from union leaders. Out of a total of 47 mines, 21 were affected, 11 totally. The workers were striking for a ten-shilling daily wage. During the strike at least nine workers died, 1,248 were injured, and more than a thousand were arrested. The government used soldiers as well as 1,600 police to break the strike.

The strike was not the outcome of a carefully plotted strategy by either party or union; indeed, the emergence of a strike movement caught both organisations badly unprepared. Members of the government may really have believed that the strike was the outcome of a conspiracy by the CPSA's Johannesburg District Committee; this was the argument proposed in court by the prosecutor, Percy Yutar. The subsequent sedition trial of the party's national leadership revealed the limitations of their engagement and the charges were withdrawn in October 1948, though in an earlier trial in 1946 the prosecution did secure convictions for Johannesburg-based leaders accused of assisting an illegal strike. They received suspended sentences, after plea-bargaining in which the prosecution withdrew a more serious charge.[249] In the trial the state proposed that the Communist Party was losing support and the strike was a desperate attempt to boost its following.[250] The pressure for a strike came from below, from the 2,000 delegates who attended an AMWU annual general meeting on 14 April 1946, when mine workers responded to sharply worsening conditions in the compounds, inflation, and drought in the countryside where their families lived. A particular grievance was the substitution of canned for fresh meat, first undertaken in 1944: it was this issue that provoked a sequence of riots and even a hunger strike at Crown Mines in June 1945. Food shortages due to poor harvests led to an actual reduction of maize orders for the mining workforce. Anger at the deterioration in compound provisions was accentuated by the adoption during the war of 'scientific management' principles which resulted in stricter supervision. As Bernstein puts it, 'by 1946, the Union was being bombarded with demands from the men for strike action'.[251]

The meeting on 14 April pledged itself in favour of a struggle for the wage rise. Union leaders JB Marks and James Majoro counselled patience and caution. Two Johannesburg CPSA District Committee members, Louis Joffe and Issy Wolfson, who attended the meeting, offered party support in the event of a strike, though they joined Marks and Majoro in counselling caution: any strike would need very careful preparation.[252] Marks had only joined the party's District Committee that month. In late April a rash of wildcat strikes broke out on the West Rand, led apparently by the *tshipas*. The strikes were preceded by open-air meetings at which strike leaders raised the AMWU's ten-shilling wage demand. In doing this, the *tshipas* were ignoring the old practice of protest in which no leaders would stand in front of any assembly offering themselves for identification. In the next month or so, many of these wildcat strike leaders were fired by managers, who succeeded in breaking up the AMWU's West Rand network.

In mid-May the AMWU had another meeting, this time very badly attended, and its executive was confronted with another strike motion from the floor. Marks insisted that a strike should wait until delegates had meetings in their compounds. A final meeting was held on 4 August and voted overwhelmingly to down tools on the 12th, leaving only a week for any preparation by union officials. In fact, most of the preparation for the strike was undertaken by members of informal networks that had existed on the mines well before the inception of the union – the networks headed by elected room heads, the *isibondas*.[253] Deprived of many of its *tshipa* organisers, the AMWU's coordinating activities mainly took the form of producing and distributing thousands of leaflets outside the main compounds and soliciting support from CNETU for a sympathy general strike. CNETU resolved in principle to offer support as early as June but held no meeting to plan such action in the week after 4 August. In fact, 'no one in the [union] office had a plan – everything was improvised'.[254] AMWU's leafleting was assisted by the Johannesburg district leadership of the party. The leaflets were important in ensuring a united response, but the assent of the *isibondas* was essential, and it seems from evidence that Dunbar Moodie collected in Mpondoland forty years later that their reaction was a consequence of an accumulated sense of outrage which the leaflets triggered. The deterioration of food and the alteration of supervision arrangements for them went beyond routine setbacks: they represented a violation of a tacitly understood social contract. In short, far from instigating the strike, both the party and the union leadership were compelled to act in response to pressure from below. In May 1946, Senator Hyman Basner received a letter from Marks warning that 'he could not hold the position any longer, that the African mineworkers were threatening a strike and they would do so if the union agreed or not'.[255]

The Communist Party was sharply divided about the extent to which it should support the AMWU. In May, when the prospect of the impending strike started looking likely, the District Committee in Johannesburg wrote to the party's headquarters in Cape Town. The letter informed the Cape Town leaders about the strike decision and warned them that the district had resolved to supply vigorous support and was forming subcommittees for this purpose. The Central Executive Committee was disconcerted by this news. In the words of one of its members, 'we believed that the Johannesburg District Committee had misrepresented the situation'.[256] The letter, they believed, 'was hysterical'. Moses Kotane wrote back to Johannesburg, disapproving

– by implication at least – of the strike decision itself, as well as of the party's contemplated support. No action should be taken until he arrived in Johannesburg to consult with the District Committee. Kotane then wrote a second letter, adopting a softer tone. The party did not disapprove of the strike itself, but the party should confine itself to agitational activity; any more active kinds of support should be undertaken by other trade unionists, not people acting on behalf of the party.[257] Kotane then visited Johannesburg in June. He left some days later after having formed the impression that there 'was nothing much in the talk of a strike [and] that there was no likelihood of a strike'.[258] Reassured, the Central Executive Committee took no further action, except to put a stop to the disobedience of the East Rand district officials who, in defiance of instructions, were paying the salary of an AMWU organiser.[259] The Johannesburg District Committee did its best to interpret the phrase 'agitational activity' as widely as possible and, during the week of the strike, worked hard to support it, but it felt proscribed from undertaking any elaborate preparations in advance. Without clear direction from the party, CNETU offered the most belated support, calling for a general strike on the 13th for the 15th, a call that evoked a very slight response indeed. There was an attempt to organise a stay-away from work in Pretoria's Lady Selborne township, but police forced workers out of Lady Selborne, though party-orchestrated pickets succeeded in compelling a suspension of the bus service.[260] The strike came as a complete surprise to the Cape Town leaders, for 'just prior to the outbreak of the strike we had not been expecting any such action from the workers'.[261]

How does one explain the CPSA leadership's attitude? Independent socialist historians have criticised the party and the trade union leadership for their caution and traced this back to the reflexes developed during the wartime abstention from instigating strikes. It is possible that the no-strike policy may have had a lingering effect. It was also the case that the leadership in Cape Town was too far away to be well informed about the mood of workers around Johannesburg. Moses Kotane, the party's general secretary, was himself not fundamentally interested in labour issues; in the words of his friend and biographer, Brian Bunting, he 'found the perspectives of trade unionism limiting', or, as he himself once explained, 'I am not by nature a trade unionist. I am more inclined to political things.'[262] Kotane had initially asked Ray Alexander to travel to Johannesburg to find out more about the proposed strike, but she was in the last stages of pregnancy and so, reluctantly, he made the visit himself.[263]

Might things have been different if the party had been more willing to organise concerted support or if its leadership had been less reluctant in sponsoring a mine workers' protest during the war? In retrospect it seems unlikely. When gold miners did go on strike, as in the case of 500 workers at Langlaagte outside Johannesburg in March 1944, they were arrested en masse and charged, though sentenced to quite mild penalties. On this occasion the AMWU arranged their defence in court; it was not involved in the strike.[264] Mine owners were confronted with increases in costs and reductions in profit margins: the wage increases at the end of 1944 that followed the recommendations of the Lansdown Commission, limited as they were, represented for them a substantial concession. In any case the impetus that determined the timing of the strike came from below. It was given form and purpose by the AMWU but the union functioned as a funnel, not a generator of grievances. At no time did the union or the party marshal the resources that would have been needed to mobilise an effective solidarity strike movement. These were migrant workers, isolated from the local communities, which were supported by jobs in manufacturing and other urban occupations. The strikers on the East Rand, the strongest area of strike participation (and where AMWU organisation was especially weak), on three occasions marched towards the towns and on each occasion were bloodily beaten back by police. But their motivation in marching was not aggressive. Their intention was to visit the Native Commissioners' offices to secure their passes, which were lodged there, so that they could legally make the journey back to their starving families in the countryside. At the time they marched, they were already in retreat. This was hardly the behaviour of a socially conscious proletariat equipped with the 'recognition for the need of independent class action', as has been suggested by one influential treatment of the strike.[265]

Nor did the Communist Party in 1946 resemble the kind of organisation that might have supplied such leadership. Writing in December 1945 in a party journal, George Findlay, reflecting on the party's wartime expansion, observed: 'Our party is a composite Party; it has its Mensheviks, its opportunist elements. It has its incredibly muddled, confused and reactionary thinkers.'[266] With respect to trade unions, the party was still divided between the position of people like JB Marks who maintained that the organisation of *African* trade unions should be the party's main priority and that they should be kept organisationally separate from white unions and those, on the other hand, who believed that the main white labour federation, the SATLC, might still be induced to play a supportive and coordinating role for African labour organisation. Ray Alexander took this view, influenced by her own experiences in Cape Town.[267] Marks insisted at the party's annual conference in December

1945 that Africans were ignored by the craft unions who predominated within the SATLC. Issy Wolfson led the argument against this contention. After all, in Cape Town SATLC had taken a leading role in the fight against the introduction of pass regulations.[268]

Marks's antipathy to the SATLC remained a minority view. In fact, in 1947 communists actually increased their influence with the Council when three party members were elected to its executive, though police claims that communists 'controlled' most white unions were very exaggerated.[269] By 1945, five out the SATLC's 36-person executive were communists.[270] It was also the case that the racially mixed union affiliates of the SATLC appeared to be prospering; as the continuing resilience of Sachs's Garment Workers' Union indicated, their Afrikaner members remained loyal. There were other considerations that influenced the party's trade union policies. White communist unionists still hoped to restrict the advance of Afrikaner nationalism within the ranks of white labour, and retained within their ranks white labourites who continued to hold views about black workers that were heavily paternal. A Pretoria trade unionist writing in the party journal in 1946 found it necessary to point out the dangers of 'overestimating the present role of Africans ... and their present condition too far'. 'I am', he went on to say, 'a worker in the steel industry, and if I cannot speak of raw workers ... then I am not entitled to speak at all ... If Africans are to improve their conditions, it is necessary for them to realise they are still raw, and if we are to give them guidance, it is necessary for us to realise it too.'[271] In 1948 the first major split in the SATLC, still then the main federation for white industrial unions, occurred in 1948 in Pretoria when several unions broke away in opposition to the affiliation of African unions.[272] Even so, as late as July 1949, a report on party organisation proposed that 'one of the most important tasks facing us is work among the European working class. There are many questions on which they will be ready to lend us their ear, provided we evolve the correct technique of reaching them.'[273]

Official policies also made life difficult for African unions in the Transvaal. After the war many municipalities tightened local influx control. Pretoria's post-war regime was especially severe. Here, workers now subject to the new pass regulations became very vulnerable to dismissal. In reaction, from 1945 onwards, trade unionists in Pretoria shifted their attention from wage issues to contesting the powers of the new municipal labour bureaux. As unions ceased to win concessions, members lost interest, and stopped paying the subscriptions that enabled unions to employ full-time officials and rent their offices. The party could provide no compensatory support. In 1949 the

Pretoria City Council announced the dismissal of large numbers of African workers purportedly as an economy measure. By this stage the tightening application of local pass laws on local work-seekers was causing the expulsion of between 3,000 and 4,000 a month.[274] The pattern in Pretoria is likely to have been more general. By 1948, African trade union affiliation in the Transvaal was down to a claimed 19,000, and that figure may have been optimistic.

IN PLACE OF FACTORY and workplace struggles, what were the prevailing preoccupations within the party after 1946? In the Transvaal, during the post-war period, the focus of party activism shifted towards the African townships. Though the party was confined to the margins of the Orlando squatter movement because of the tensions within the Advisory Board between Mpanza and local communists, this was not the case elsewhere with respect to other shanty settlements. African communists help to lead squatters and tenants[275] in Alexandra; and on the East Rand in 1946 and 1947 township-based party activists were conspicuous in the large crowds and demonstrations that assembled to protest against the extension of pass laws in the East Rand townships.[276] After the formation in 1947 of a Johannesburg Joint Shanty Towns Coordinating Committee presided over by communists, the District Committee offered an apology at its annual conference. Its original discouragement of the shanty movement was a mistake, its resolution conceded. The movement's challenge of 'the African ghetto laws' was an important step 'towards the struggle for national liberation of the African people'.[277]

Johannesburg and East Rand communists were also assertive in 'food raids' on trading stores suspected of hoarding rationed, price-controlled foodstuffs in short supply and selling them on the black market.[278] The project was especially well organised in western Johannesburg, and even tried to reach shopkeepers. The branch maintained an office in Ferreirastown. This published its own pamphlet, *Smash the Black Market*, which included a list of other demands: an unskilled minimum wage of ten shillings, housing, a national health service, and votes for all.[279] Transvaal branches were recruiting larger numbers of African members and party activities proliferated in smaller towns in the outer limits of the Witwatersrand. Agitation against the black market extended as far west as Mafeking, where a resident party member organised a series of meetings in late 1946 before his home was 'ransacked' by local police.[280] African township membership seemed to intersect with a range of other forms of organised social and political activity, not just the ANC, which remained in the 1940s quite a small organisation with only a patchy branch structure.

The 1947 conference of the Johannesburg district included a number of delegates from rural or out-of-town areas – Louis Trichardt, Middleton, Lichtenburg, Wolmaransstad, Winburg and Makapanstad – who met in a special commission on the countryside to discuss the concerns of peasants and how the party might work with them.[281] The Winburg delegates represented a rare incidence of party support in the Free State, as a communist had succeeded in winning an Advisory Board seat. Michael Harmel visited the branch in 1948 as a speaker.[282] The year before, a Pretoria annual general meeting of the District Committee adopted a resolution calling for land and state assistance for African farmers as well as the expropriation of under-farmed white land. The land expropriation call was echoed in the resolutions adopted in January 1947 at the party's annual conference, which endorsed the break-up of large landholdings and their redistribution to cultivators as well as the abolition of racial restrictions on landownership.[283] There was a resurgence of contact and communication between party activists and rural and rurally oriented migrant associations, including the Zoutpansberg Balemi and Lekhotla la Bafo.[284] The party's African-edited newspaper began to report on the government's deposition of uncooperative chiefs, for example in Rustenburg and Hammanskraal in 1947, and also carried much more frequent reportage of rural conditions. What is likely is that party recruitment in townships was drawing people from the organised networks that linked migrant worker communities in the cities with their rural hinterlands. Certainly, it is possible to trace a link between some of the African communists recruited during this period and the migrant networks that later in the 1950s were to play such a critical role in the Sekhukhuneland unrest. It is difficult, however, to discern any centralised direction in this. As they proliferated in the townships, branches became more independent of central party organisation and black township-based comrades acted more or less on their own. Weakening trade unions meant that a hitherto important forum for multiracial party activity was becoming much less significant in bringing together party members from different communities. And between communities, levels of activism were uneven. At a meeting of the Central Committee in mid-1949, Edwin Mofutsanyana and Arthur Damane complained about 'lack of work done among Europeans'.[285]

In the Western Cape, elections continued to constitute a major focus for local party activity. The Communist Party-led Women's Food Committee, which had developed in 1945 out of the group elected to maintain fair behaviour in the forty-odd food lines that 30,000 people formed at mobile food vans, was by 1947 shifting its emphasis from food to franchise issues.[286] In 1948 the Food Committee decided to establish a Non-European Women's League 'to fight for the vote for all black women'. The local committees supplied a network of activists who could canvass support for Sam Kahn's campaign that year in the Native representative elections. This underpinned the efforts of the CPSA's Cape Town branch, which constituted Kahn's and, later, Fred Carneson's campaign committee. Local party leadership also invested considerable effort in the Cape Town City Council election in which Cissie Gool and Sam Kahn represented wards with coloured voters during the 1940s. More militant initiatives were less successful. In September 1948 the party encouraged the formation of a Train Apartheid Resistance Committee (TARC). This inspired a very short-lived campaign to defy new train segregation regulations. TARC attracted 300 volunteers on its first day but the protest petered out within the next couple of days.[287] Communists resigned from the committee in October, criticising its other members for their reluctance to undertake any personal action.[288] TARC later succeeded in persuading the courts to overturn the regulations, which provided a brief respite.

With respect to Cape Town we have a particularly detailed picture of party organisation at the end of the decade because of the records preserved in the Simons papers. They include the District Committee's report on organisational matters compiled in April 1950. African membership had increased but new members were poorly organised. The quality of many recruits was poor because 'attempts have not been made to recruit the trusted people'. In effect, 'all those who apply to join the party have been accepted', and hence membership was unstable. In the smaller towns 'members are migrants with peasant outlooks'. In Langa, membership was more urbanised and the party appeared to be 'trusted by the people', to judge from the Advisory Board elections. Communists had contested Langa's Advisory Board elections annually from 1944, winning several seats and collecting a majority of the votes every time, significantly from the more urbanised 'married quarters' voters, not from the migrant worker 'bachelors' inhabiting the 'barracks': here the party had no presence. At one stage Langa party membership peaked at 260.[289] Led locally by Johnson Ngwevela, they constituted a political elite, prominent in the ANC and conspicuous in a range of other associations. Ngwevela was the chairman of the Langa Wesleyan church network and the township's Red Cross organisation, and was a moving spirit in the Vigilance Association, which for a decade had constituted itself as an unofficial oversight body, monitoring the Advisory Board. The party's influence in Langa was enhanced by its access to the City Council from 1943. Betty (Radford) Sacks and Sam Kahn in their capacities as municipal councillors were active in the City's Native Affairs Committee. A degree of success in inducing the authorities to address housing shortages as well as other incremental improvements may help to explain why the party was able to mobilise an unusually wide and assertive response to the anti-pass campaign in the township; in August 1946, Moses Kotane led a series of well-attended mass pass-burnings in Langa, the only expressions of such militancy nationwide.[290] But by 1950 the groups in Langa were in a 'deplorable state', not meeting regularly and failing to collect subscriptions. Elsewhere in Cape Town that year, there were five groups 'working almost entirely among coloured people', but even so the party really had not established a public following among coloured Capetonians. With respect to the 'European' members, 'our ... membership [was] almost entirely of the same origin', still influenced by the 'labour traditions of Europe'. As in other regions, in the area around Cape Town the party had failed 'to set up groups in factories'. Finally, 'most of our area groups are uni-racial and have tendencies to think along national lines'.[291]

In the Eastern Cape centre of Port Elizabeth, the picture was much more encouraging. In contrast to other centres, the late 1940s was a period of very rapid industrial growth, largely because of the construction of two new motor plants. Around these a variety of other new factories and workshops developed that recruited Africans for unskilled and semi-skilled work. This local demand for labour helped to dissuade the municipality from restricting African migration into the city: compared with the Transvaal, Port Elizabeth remained relatively free from restrictions on African labour mobility. This helps to explain why the trade unions established in Port Elizabeth among African workers during the war not only survived but actually became stronger during the late 1940s. The early wartime unions were set up not by communists but first by William Ballinger's Friends of Africa group and then by Max Gordon. By 1944 communists took over most of the African trade union leadership. A key personality was Mohamed Desai, who was the secretary of a cluster of CNETU affiliates as well as a city councillor, one of two communists on the City Council, the other being Gus Coe, secretary of the local branch of the white and coloured National Union of Distributive Workers. Desai was actively involved in supporting a rent strike in New Brighton, but as a union leader he was venal and ineffectual, living off the monthly payments of £129 he received from the CNETU affiliates and using Food and Canning Workers' Union (FCWU) money to buy a building in his own name for his own use. He was eventually ejected from his FCWU secretaryship by Ray Alexander.

Under his local leadership CNETU's claimed affiliation in 1945 was grossly exaggerated: projected at 30,000, it was three times Port Elizabeth's African workforce employed in local factories, commerce and transport.[292] African unions organised under a CNETU umbrella also received Trades and Labour Council (SATLC) support in a fiercely fought laundry workers' stoppage in which the strikers actually received strike pay from the union. SATLC support was an effect of the presence within the City Council of communist-led registered unions. The laundry workers' strike between April and June 1948 also drew upon extensive community support mobilised in weekly mass meetings in New Brighton, which were well reported in the local press.[293]

During this period a tightly interwoven relationship developed between Port Elizabeth's ANC township branches, trade unions and the Communist Party: leadership of each overlapped. For example, the laundry workers' union's organiser, Raymond Mhlaba, was also secretary of the New Brighton branch of the party as well as the local chairman of the ANC. Frances Baard, the secretary of the African branch of the Food and Canning Workers' Union, was also the secretary of the ANC Women's League; she was originally appointed as the union's secretary in 1948 by Ray Alexander. Gladstone Tshume, who led a dockers' strike in 1946, was another trade unionist conspicuous in the local party and ANC leadership, winning an Advisory Board seat in 1948, and Robert Matji, who became the ANC's provincial secretary in 1951, also led unions and was an active communist and an ANC branch leader in New Brighton. Matji was 'a genius at organisation', in the view of Govan Mbeki (who arrived in New Brighton in 1956).[294] The dockers' strike, fiercely contested, had also elicited SATLC intervention, and for a while employers appeared to favour a wage increase. Meanwhile, strikers depended upon donations and the leadership produced leaflets printed in English and isiXhosa, reminding residents that 'a victory for the stevedoring workers is a victory for the community'.[295] The combination of trade union and political and community leadership was especially effective in the three-month-long 1949 bus and train boycott led by a committee that brought together communists, ANC branch leaders and unionists and over which Raymond Mhlaba presided. After the party's banning in 1950, this alliance was carried over intact and helped to explain the ANC's subsequent strength in Port Elizabeth.[296] As Govan Mbeki noted, during the 1940s the members of the Communist Party who were in the ANC's Youth League started reorganising the ANC: 'working class leaders dominated African politics in a way that was not characteristic of other centres'.[297]

Natal's communists were concentrated in its two main towns. In Durban, the district party leadership elected in April 1945 was entirely white or Indian; it included no Africans.[298] This was probably true in Pietermaritzburg as well. When freshly trained schoolteacher Harry Gwala was recruited at a party night school in Pietermaritzburg in 1942, he became one of only two African communists in the city. The main officials in the local branch were white; they included an architect and a baker.[299] The absence of Africans in the party's leadership reflected a recent provincial history in which the Communist Party in the 1940s was mainly constructed around Indian unions: during the late 1930s and early 1940s Indian trade unionists held leadership positions in the local Communist Party and also played a conspicuous role in an increasingly radicalised Natal Indian Congress. But Indian trade union militancy didn't always translate into cross-racial common identification with Africans: in their labour actions Indians were often compelled to defend their relative privilege in the labour market.[300] In the late 1930s and up to 1941, if Africans belonged to trade unions they were members of Indian-led organisations and the party's African trade union organisers, whom Harry Gwala joined as a full-time party worker in Pietermaritzburg in 1944, often worked with Indian workers.[301] Between 1941 and 1943 there was a spate of African trade union organisation in Natal, including communist-led groups among African sugar and railway workers, but much of it was independent of the party's influence and, indeed, in certain classes hostile to it. These unions seem to have had limited impact and were mostly short-lived.[302]

In the main, in contrast to other provinces, the Communist Party in Durban neglected African worker organisation during the 1940s, concentrating rather on Indian workers. This was the case when rubber workers went on strike in 1943 and laundry workers in 1945 to oppose their replacement by cheaper African workers; in the defeat of both strikes, the employment of Africans as scabs was decisive.[303] The rubber workers' strike began as a protest against the company's dismissal of trade union organisers, Africans and Indians, but the way it ended accentuated divisions among Indian and African workers. Similarly, though Indian communists sincerely espoused non-racialism, their broader political engagements tended to 'reinforce Indianness'.[304] There was at least one occasion after the war when the Communist Party enjoyed some success in channelling and leading Indian and African collective action. This was the campaign in 1946 against 'black marketing' of food, in which activists 'seized' stockpiled items and sold them at low prices. Here organisers could draw upon generalised resentment of Indian shopkeepers, among Indians and Africans alike. The campaign has the additional attraction for the party leadership of targeting traders who tended to support more conservative strands in Indian communal politics. But the campaign's popularity would have been reinforced by more generalised anti–Indian sentiment among Africans.[305] More generally, David Hemson argues, confronted with increasingly repressive conditions after 1943, Indian communist labour organisers became more and more 'diverted' by efforts to defend the Indian community against tightening segregationist measures, playing leadership roles in the Natal Indian Congress.[306] In any case, African workers had not been a key focus for Indian trade union activists.

By the late 1940s African unions, though sharing offices with communists, tended to be 'apolitical'.[307] They would in any case have been very much on the defensive in a local setting in which industrial and commercial activity slackened: African real wages in Durban fell by 11 per cent between 1946 and 1949.[308] Harry Gwala moved to Durban in 1948 to work briefly as a party organiser; by his own admission he could not achieve much in a setting of escalating Afro-Indian communal tensions.[309] In 1949, in the aftermath of the Durban riots, communists opposed a general strike led by Zulu Phungula, the popular dock workers' leader. Phungula was a migrant worker, an elected leader, very different in manner and ethos from the 'urbanised intelligentsia' who tended to constitute communist trade union leadership.[310] By the early 1950s Indian unions were fully within the fold of the South African Trades and Labour Council (from 1954, TUCSA) and tended to eschew confrontation. In 1947 the Durban party lost one of its most active leaders, Rowley Arenstein, who became politically inactive in 1947 so that he could build up his legal practice.[311]

In one city, Pretoria, the sources allow quite a detailed reconstruction of a local party history during the decade. Through this microcosm, we can obtain insights into the sources of the party's strength during the 1940s as well as the features of its development that made it vulnerable. The Communist Party established a branch in Pretoria in 1940; before then, Pretoria-based members of the Johannesburg District Committee tried to create a local following through the establishment of a short-lived night school. The school was closed after losing its premises in 1936. The first attempts to set up African trade unions in Pretoria were not by communists at all; for a short period a branch of the Johannesburg-based African Commercial and Distributive Workers' Union (ACDWU) opened an office in Marabastad and collected subscriptions. Its local founder, Naboth Mokgatle, a shop delivery worker, had been inspired at a public meeting addressed by the ACDWU's Trotskyist leader, Max Gordon. The Pretoria branch did not prosper; shortly after its formation in 1939, Gordon was interned and the administration of its Johannesburg office, to which the Pretoria subscriptions were sent, ground to a halt. Mokgatle then set up his own independent Pretoria Non-European Distributive Workers' Union and shortly thereafter in 1941 joined the Communist Party, which had recently set up an area group in Marabastad. In the year that followed, Mokgatle and his comrades formed 11 more unions, including organisations for municipal, railway, cement, building, dairy, iron and steel, laundry, metal and match workers.[312] These were all affiliated to the Pretoria Council of Non-European Trade Unions (CNETU), presided over by Mike Muller, in 1943 a 20-year-old former student from Pretoria University. At its peak in 1943, the Pretoria CNETU boasted the affiliation of 17,000 workers in 17 unions,[313] and in March, Mike Muller led several thousand of these in a city-centre demonstration for trade union recognition.

For three years this trade union movement in Pretoria flourished, its popularity being strengthened by a series of minimum wage determinations made by the wartime Smuts government. The communists' and trade unionists' status was also enhanced by a commission of inquiry which exonerated them from responsibility for a riot in late 1942 in the Marabastad municipal compound. In the weeks following the riot, the membership of the Marabastad Workers' Union swelled from 600 to 900.[314] After the war, as we have noted above, African labour organisation in Pretoria went into decline. By 1948, six of the unions Mokgatle mentions in his autobiography had evidently ceased to exist and CNETU claimed only 3,300 Pretoria-based workers in its affiliated membership.[315] This decline reflected a deteriorating political climate as well as organisational weaknesses within the unions and the party. In 1945, influx control was vigorously tightened in Pretoria and this, together with the end of wartime industrial growth, increased worker vulnerability to dismissal. Mokgatle reports that in this year the emphasis of trade union work shifted from wages to contesting the powers of the new municipal labour bureaux.[316] In 1946, the unions lost the office they shared when they were evicted by the landlord. Falling membership and the loss of the office reduced the flow of subscriptions, and five out of six African secretaries (one for each two unions) lost their jobs. Mike Muller as secretary managed to organise support for a bus boycott by Atteridgeville residents, mobilising volunteer transport mainly from African- and Indian-owned lorries.[317] But Muller left the party in 1947 (after quarrelling with Mokgatle because of the latter's failure to secure the reinstatement of some Central News Agency strikers), and the administration of the unions then revolved around Mokgatle and Stephen Tefu, a resident of Lady Selborne who, before his expulsion, had been a member of the Communist Party in Johannesburg.

Though Mokgatle was on the District Committee (and from 1949 was its chairman), his trade union work was carried on at a distance from the party. He and Tefu hired premises independently in Marabastad and launched a General Workers' Union.[318]

That African trade union work, when it began, was entrusted to some of the least experienced and junior members was a symptom of the divided character of the Pretoria Communist Party. A diary kept by one of its more socially distinguished local members, the advocate George Findlay, helps us to identify some of the essential problems.[319] Writing in 1944, Findlay depicts a group whose white members were split between supporters of Browderism and those who believed in a more confrontational strategy. The Browderites included Muller whereas Findlay, with Naboth Mokgatle's support, was highly critical of the policy.[320] Ironically, Muller was one of the few white communists who were doing what the Pretoria anti-Browderites insisted was imperative: mobilising Africans. Findlay was unimpressed by and also suspicious of Muller's evident access to money, discussing his anxieties with Moses Kotane: 'Is it possible the bosses tipped him?' he asked in his diary.[321] The majority of the party's local white membership and leadership were instead concerned to combat the influence of Afrikaner nationalists in Pretoria's white unions (in which they were winning wide support).[322] Whites tended to meet separately from the Africans; 14 people attended a house meeting at Findlay's home, all white.[323] Some of the tensions are evident in the diary. Commenting on the 'poor quality of the European membership', Findlay complains of the 'unconscious spirit of evading mass contacts'[324] and also mentions one of the leading African members, Eliphas Ditsele, as 'letting rip, saying that the European comrades were largely indifferent and failing all around'.[325] In February 1945, white youths stoned the party's local headquarters while education and ballroom dancing classes ('very orderly, no mixed dancing, tap dancing, ballroom')[326] were in session. Police intervened but took the side of the insurgents, and many of the hundred or so African dancers were beaten up or arrested. The party normally organised evening classes 'in the three R's' four times a week for Africans.[327] In the following month the landlord withdrew the premises, and there were expulsions and resignations from the party.[328] Even so, the district was sufficiently active to hold an eighth annual general meeting in February 1946, electing Mike Muller as chairman and a white woman, Leskin Winton, as secretary, and adopting resolutions calling for land expropriations and help for African peasants and white poor farmers.[329] Two months later a new branch for Pretoria Central held its first public meeting at the Empire theatre.[330] In May 1946 Muller led a reportedly 2,000-strong procession through central Pretoria in support of the party's call for food rationing. Concerns about food shortages and food prices would be a continuing local preoccupation, and the party established food action committees in African townships.[331] Muller and Winton would later be charged with illegal entry into the townships amid reports of an intensification of police pass raids.[332] Muller was later fined £1.[333] By this stage *Guardian* press reportage suggests that tightening pass controls had become a main concern for Pretoria's communists. The 1947 district annual meeting noted a 'high level of activity' through the year; at that stage the party was helping to lead a local bus boycott.[334] The party began holding a 'People's College' with lectures every Thursday.[335] Mike Muller and his wife, Shulamith, recently qualified as an attorney, moved to Durban in 1948 and, perhaps not coincidentally, there are no *Guardian* press reports about Pretoria's communists during 1949. By 1950, when preparations were being made for Pretoria workers to be called out for the national May Day strike to protest against the banning of the Communist Party leaders, the organisation was apparently entirely in the hands of Mokgatle and Tefu.[336]

It would have taken considerable social sensitivity on both sides to bridge the gulf that existed in class and background between white and black members of the party in Pretoria. The white members were generally from a professional background (in certain cases quite wealthy) whereas the African communists listed for Pretoria in the *Government Gazette* included five shop workers, messengers or delivery men, three labourers, two bus conductors, one clinic worker and one carpenter as well as Ditsele, who served as Pretoria agent of *The Guardian*. Eleven lived in Atteridgeville and four in Lady Selborne.[337] With the exception of Ditsele, it is unlikely that any of them had an extensive formal education and, not surprisingly, Findlay's diary only rarely mentions Africans as playing a significant role in the discussions which took place at party meetings. Mokgatle may not have been typical, but despite his attendance at a party school in 1943, his understanding of the party's policies seems to have been limited to its advocacy of an ideal society 'in which all children would have free education and equal opportunities ... [and] all ... would have the right to vote'. This is not to disparage their courage and their achievements in their efforts to mobilise a working-class movement in the face of such fierce opposition, but whether Pretoria's communists shared a clear sense of purpose is unlikely.

So what we have emerging in the second half of the 1940s is a regionally and sometimes even locally fragmented organisation of varying effectiveness and social character. An overall membership of 2,482 was predominantly African (1,673), with 269 whites, 428 coloureds and 112 Indians making up the balance. Geographically, this membership was concentrated in and around Cape Town (1,062), with the 665 communists in Johannesburg embodying the second-largest district.[338] In mid-1950, at the time of the party's dissolution, other district committee still existed for Pretoria, Durban and the East Rand.[339] Mainly African industrial workers (1,341) constituted just over half the party's following and the membership also included 452 farm or estate workers, 200 professionals and 500 housewives or domestic workers. These are the last detailed membership statistics available. Moses Kotane's report to the 1950 conference contained no numbers, though it noted that in certain areas district organisations had 'shrunk to the status of groups'. Overall, however, 'the people' were 'turning up for the Party in greater numbers' and African membership was 'growing by leaps and bounds'.[340] As Bill Andrews had acknowledged in 1947, the Communist Party was 'increasingly looked upon by the downtrodden as "their party"'.[341] This may well have been the case, though often the party's followers in African townships were animated not so much by the prospect of a socialist alternative but rather by the party's record for 'trying to speak for the rights of the Bantu people'.[342]

Only in one centre, Port Elizabeth, is it really possible to discern any dialectic between class and national consciousness of the sort that is sometimes attributed to the party's development in this period. It is possible to speculate that even if the party had not been banned in 1950, something very akin to the selective reconstruction of 1953 would have been necessary if it was to develop a coherent identity and purpose. Up to the close of the decade, national leaders continued to direct effort and resources in elections as they had done since the middle of the war, and indeed they continued to prioritise white or racially mixed municipal or parliamentary elections over contests for Advisory Boards – a source of continuing frustration among African party members.[343] This was despite a trend of increasing success in winning seats on Boards in Cape Town, Johannesburg, East London and the East Rand. The party continued to contest Johannesburg City Council seats though it was never able to repeat Hilda Watts's success in 1944. It retained seats on the Cape Town municipality, benefiting there from the racially mixed electorate. Ward changes and changing voter requirements put paid to the party's municipal electoral chances in East London and Port Elizabeth.[344] Less successfully, the party also campaigned in Native Representative Council (NRC) elections, nominating Edwin Mofutsanyana and Alpheus Maliba as their candidates.

In this it followed the ANC's example, first endorsing and then withdrawing from a decision to boycott the elections in the wake of the adjournment of the NRC during the mine workers' strike. In 1947, the CPSA decided to nominate a slate of NRC candidates pledged to repeal the 1936 legislation that removed Africans from the common voters' roll and demand the introduction of universal franchise. The party's continuing predisposition to contest the NRC elections with its own candidates was significant: at this stage it was still ready to compete with the ANC for African political support, and the decision was taken after a sharp debate at the previous party conference.[345] In May 1948 the party sponsored a 'People's Assembly for Votes for All' in Johannesburg, which was attended by 800 delegates supposedly representing 750,000 people.

More tellingly, its candidate for the parliamentary Native representative for the Western Cape, Sam Kahn, was elected in 1948, followed by the election to the Cape Provincial Council of Fred Carneson in 1949. As noted above, both benefited from the organisation communists had set in place with the food committees, as well as from Kahn's own achievements as a city councillor. Kahn's following may also have been enhanced by his prescient record as *The Guardian*'s horseracing tipster. For mobilising the several thousand eligible African voters, Kahn relied on Johnson Ngwevela, the leader of the communist group in Langa, which allied with the ANC in Advisory Board politics. Unlike the arrangements for the Transvaal and the Free State created in the 1936 legislation for African representation, in which the senators were elected indirectly, in the Western Cape former common roll African electors chose their House of Assembly parliamentary representative in a direct election. This helped to explain Kahn's overwhelming victory – 3,780 votes compared with the 948 votes gathered by his opponents.[346] Kahn would hold his seat until his expulsion in 1952 under the terms of the Suppression of Communism Act. In 1949 he particularly enraged National Party MPs with his attack on the Prohibition of Mixed Marriages Bill, 'the immoral offspring of an illicit union between racial superstition and biological ignorance'.[347] Especially provocative was his citing of an estimate that around 600,000 white South Africans had black forebears, and several parliamentarians were among this group.[348] Communists would continue to win the contests for African votes in the Western Cape until they were prohibited from standing in such elections in 1954. It was still the case, though, that in 1948 the party's electoral preoccupations included efforts to influence the choices of white voters, if only indirectly. The Springbok Legion still survived, now an ex-servicemen's organisation. It had lost most of its membership, many scared away by claims made by the prosecution in 1947 during the trial of party leaders that the

Legion was the communists' armed wing. By 1948 the leadership of the Springboks was entirely in communist hands. Before the election the Legion refused to support the Labour Party exclusively, preferring to urge support for both Labour and the United Party – an electoral victory for Smuts was preferable to Afrikaner nationalist ascendancy. During the next few years Legionnaires, some of them ex-communists, would actively cooperate with United Party officials.[349] As late as 1949 Fred Carneson would argue at a Central Committee meeting that there remained 'issues among which a common struggle between Europeans and Non-Europeans was possible, as the Nationalists were beginning to expose themselves even to their followers'.[350]

But though the party continued to try to influence white voters, in the late 1940s national leaders were increasingly predisposed to address broader African political concerns, an emphasis evident in the party's call for a 'people's convention'.[351] This was partly an effect of more global considerations. From 1945, solidarity with anti-colonial movements became a central preoccupation for the British party, and for this purpose it invited 11 parties, including the CPSA, to a Conference of the Communist Parties of the British Empire. A South African delegate did attend.[352] The South African party had a recent record of practical support for other liberation movements. In November 1945 and in October 1946 the party tried to organise dockers to refuse to load any material on ships destined to supply the British and Dutch armies in Java.[353] For matters closer to home in 1945, the party adopted a new campaigning slogan, 'Votes for All', despite certain members' apprehensions; this might have been expected to improve further its relationship with the ANC.[354] It was still the case that key party personalities had doubts about the ANC's suitability as a prospective partner. The most enthusiastic advocacy for alliance came from Edwin Mofutsanyana, who, writing in 1949, suggested that, despite weaknesses, the evidence suggested 'forward movement' in the ANC: 'there is a demand among the rank and file members for an active and militant Congress. The reactionary elements are usually defeated in their resolutions.'[355] Not all communists shared his optimism. The authors of *The Non-European and the Vote*, while conceding that the party might find allies among African nationalists, stressed the weaknesses and divisions in the national movement and proposed that only the working class by itself was capable 'of shouldering the burden of fighting for the right to vote for all'.[356] A Central Committee policy review in 1949 was similarly critical of the national liberation movement's shortcomings.[357]

So, in the closing years of the decade, the issue of how the party might align itself with the ANC remained a question over which the party's senior echelon differed. However, the advocacy of a primarily cross-racial class struggle-based approach in which the party would work independently of nationalist groups had become a minority position in 1950. This was a consequence of the departure of certain key leaders such as George Findlay, who had opposed united front policies, the weakening of the SATLC after Afrikaner nationalist defections in 1948, the growing preponderance of African membership within the party (increasing as it did during 1949), and the engagement of Transvaal and Natal party leaders in Congress politics, African and Indian. At the party's conference in January 1950, the Central Committee adopted a view of South African society which would require a strategic shift from unmediated class struggle. South Africa's situation was characterised as 'colonialism of a special type', the committee agreed. The phrase itself was borrowed from the liberal historian Leo Marquard, who suggested it to his friend Jack Simons as a descriptive analogy for relationships between black and white South Africans. It would rapidly acquire explanatory or theoretical authority, as it became conceptually developed by Michael Harmel.[358] From this vantage point, South Africa appeared to possess 'the characteristics of both an imperialist state and a colony within a single, indivisible, geographical, political and economic entity ... The Non-European population, while reduced to the status of a colonial people, has no territory of its own, no independent existence, but is almost wholly integrated in the political and economic institutions of the ruling class.'[359] The strategic implications of this perception would be spelled out later, but in such a setting, for South Africa's communists, African nationalism would an indispensable force with which the party should ally itself unconditionally.

THE PARTY'S RETROSPECTIVE view of the 1940s generally stresses the broadening of public support for the organisation, the militancy of communist activities, and the development of mutual perception and understanding between it and the African National Congress. In one scholarly study of the CPSA's development during the decade, Alan Brooks reflects the party's own interpretation in his analysis of the CPSA's apparently smooth and logical progression from purist advocacy of 'class struggle' to a more pragmatic espousal of 'national liberation'.[360] The most critical comment in Michael Harmel's official history is the extent to which the party embraced a legal or open form of organisational activity, leaving it ill prepared for its suppression at the end of the decade. Even so, looking back upon this era, Harmel perceived a 'leftward shift among the people', attributing the party's growing influence to this development. As the evidence in this chapter indicates, things were more complicated. This period of the party's history was characterised by its lack of militancy. Its identification with African national aspirations was often based on a carefully qualified interpretation of what they should be. Among those of its white members influenced by Browderism at least, there was a measure of optimism about the willingness of white society to entertain seriously proposals for social reform, an optimism which incidentally went well beyond most liberal prognostications.[361]

Critics of the CPSA both at the time and more recently have suggested that by allegedly subordinating local interests to the dictates of international politics (and particularly the Soviet Union's role in them), important opportunities were squandered. Indeed, such criticism rather shares the premises of Earl Browder's contentions as they were applied to South Africa during the war. The reasoning suggests that important groups within ruling circles favoured reforms and, with more militant actions, these would have been secured.[362]

Support for the war effort certainly acted as a brake on the party's willingness to support or initiate workers' strike actions, and it may have circumscribed its tactical repertoire in anti-pass campaigning, for example in rejecting civil disobedience. It is also the case that the aim of gathering a white following diverted attention and resources from political projects directed at Africans: this was the case with Advisory Board elections, for example. It is possible, however, that popular militancy may have provoked only intransigence and fiercer repression from the authorities, particularly as the communists and other opposition groups were still very weak organisations. Even the new African labour movement was very vulnerable. It was composed mostly of unskilled workers, predominantly in non-strategic industries, internally divided, and operating in a context of high unemployment, and thus easy to replace. Was this labour movement really capable of delivering decisive blows against employers and the state? The CPSA's left-wing opponents in the trade union movement were contemptuous of the 'milk and water' methods employed by the party in its campaigns for African trade union recognition, but their own strike actions were entirely confined to wage-related issues.[363] In the Western and Eastern Cape at least, the party's presence in municipal governments and in local Trades and Labour Councils sometimes enabled it to lever a degree of external support for African labour struggles and community protests.

And would the party have found popular support for more militant campaigning outside the factories? As Moses Kotane once pointed out, 'among those of the ruled, suppressed and dependent, the tendency is to take things as they find them, to resign themselves to the existing state of affairs'.[364] Through abandoning their previous policy of selective recruitment, communists accepted their new supporters as they found them and, despite Kotane's reservations, in doing this they accumulated an enduring following. All the evidence reviewed in this chapter suggests that the party built its African support around campaigning on local issues and achieving incremental gains and modest victories rather than through mobilising around wider political objectives. It was through 'bread and butter' struggles that activists were succeeding in persuading African township residents that the communists were, in Bill Andrews's words 'their party'. On the ground, this often brought it closer to the ANC; local communist leaders such as Johnson Ngwevela or Raymond Mhlaba often doubled up as Congress notables. But during most of the decade, the party's relationship with the ANC was equivocal; indeed, its very success in building African support encouraged some communists to believe that the party, not Congress, could mobilise an African mass movement around a democratic programme. After all, in several local settings such as the East Rand townships, as well as Langa and Port Elizabeth, the party probably had a larger organised activist following than the ANC. It may not have been 'the powerful and conscious workers' movement directed at socialism' envisaged in 1941 in the People's Programme, but the networks it embodied would often survive intact into the 1950s, underpinning mass campaigning against apartheid. This was the party's most important and durable achievement from this era.

It does seem more tenable to argue that the CPSA's role in the war was as much a reflection of the experience and predisposition of its members as a consequence of externally derived imperatives. There were those, like the lawyer Franz Boshoff, suspended from the party for accepting a state brief against Mpanza, who were still captives of their professional and social background. Then there were others, such as the veterans of the Jewish Workers' Club, who were representatives of a stream of East European radicalism. For them, identification with the needs of the Soviet workers' state required no external directives.[365] Some black men joined the party because it stood for, in the words of Naboth Mokgatle, the Pretoria trade unionist, a society 'in which all children will have free education and equal opportunities ... [and] all would have the vote'.[366] Some of the party's wartime adherents would have joined from a humanitarian impulse towards justice and equity rather than a knowledgeable commitment to Marxism. Hilda Bernstein, for example, joined the CPSA just before the war because it was 'the only party that had no colour bar'.[367]

The CPSA of the 1940s contained a diverse composite of South African political traditions. The abandonment of vanguardism and the shift to a less selective membership brought with it fresh groups into the party, more rural people for example, the beginnings of a following among migrant workers, white servicemen, and university students, who joined its more customary following among unionised industrial workers, black, coloured, Indian and white. This diversity contained both strengths and vulnerabilities. Anti-racialism and New Deal-style social democracy as well as practical engagement with everyday 'bread and butter' politics probably helped to attract the wider following that the party succeeded in drawing. It was recruiting through the decade people who would not have initially been susceptible to the harder-edged doctrine that characterised the party's public discourses before the war. However, the strategic disagreements that had divided the party in the 1930s persisted, particularly over what its relationship should be with African nationalism and over whether it should continue to invest hope and effort in attempting to influence white workers. Meanwhile, functioning in an increasingly open style, and concentrating effort around electoral politics and local protests, rendered the party vulnerable to repression, its organisational networks public and exposed to a vigilant state, and many of its members unready for any kind of clandestine activism.

SIX

Secret Party: South African Communists between 1950 and 1965

Albie Sachs and Mary Butcher, both members of the Modern Youth Society and about to join the clandestine SACP at a Defiance Campaign meeting with Joseph Nkatlo. Nkatlo had belonged to the CPSA but did not join the SACP; later he became a leader in the distinctly anti-communist Liberal Party. Albie Sachs and Mary Butcher were two of a very small group of white South Africans who participated as volunteers in the Campaign's civil disobedience, using the African entrance to the main post in Cape Town.

In 1953, South African communists attended the first formal conference of their clandestine party, three years after the dissolution and legal prohibition of the former Communist Party of South Africa (CPSA). The establishment of the new formation, which its founders named the South African Communist Party (SACP), was preceded by the spread of clandestine networks constituted by former CPSA activists, beginning in the closing months of 1950. The new party's formation would remain secret and unannounced until 1960, despite its recruitment of several hundred members. Many of these would main visibly active in other organisations as well as the party itself until arrest and imprisonment or exile would lead to the final destruction of its organised structures in 1965. For the next ten years or so, until the mid-1970s, the SACP would have no durable networks inside South Africa.

For about the same period, information about the SACP's development during its clandestine history in the 1950s and early 1960s would remain very restricted, especially for the period up to 1960. The party's own disclosures about its development in this time supplied a most abrupt narrative. An authorised history by Michael Harmel, writing under the pseudonym A Lerumo, became the standard source after its first publication in 1971. Harmel supplied a critical explanation of the CPSA's dissolution in anticipation of the liquidation measures in the Suppression of Communism Act, suggesting that the impending legislation gave rise to a distinction between CPSA members who perceived dissolution to be a temporary expedient 'and those who had come to doubt the need for the very existence of the independent Marxist-Leninist Party of the working class'. The first group would establish a new party with its own programme and rules and a new name. Its members decided their main task would be to combine 'legal mass work with the illegal work of building the Marxist-Leninist Party'. Harmel's history tells us very little about the 'illegal work', emphasising instead the mass-based campaigning of the African National Congress (ANC) and its public allies in which 'the Communist Party and its members played a worthy role'. During the State of Emergency in 1960, communist and national liberation leaders both recognised that 'it was necessary to abandon non-violence' and afterwards they worked together in a new armed formation, Umkhonto we Sizwe. Meanwhile, the party's new programme, *The Road to South African Freedom*, supplied the strategic justification for this decision, marking 'a major advance in ... theoretical development'. The party began to recruit 'less selectively'.[1] In July 1963, a police raid on the party's headquarters at a farm in Rivonia on the outskirts of Johannesburg began the destruction of most of its own networks together with the uprooting of the ANC's own underground organisation.

Subsequently a little more information became available from other party publications. A volume of documents appeared that noted that the evolution of the 'party line' could be tracked through statements by key individuals published openly in the press during the 1950s.[2] Attentive readers of such materials could begin to map the party's doctrinal development during the period, and scholarship of this sort began to appear during the 1980s.[3] The SACP began publishing its own journal, the *African Communist*, in 1959. In exile, approved biographies of veteran members would appear occasionally and these could supply occasional insights into party-sponsored activities in the 1960s. Brian Bunting's biography of Moses Kotane suggests that by 1956 the party had 'made great advances', which included 'a machine and cadres to operate it more efficient and united than those at the disposal of the ANC'. Indeed, 'the nucleus of the M-Plan', the ANC's scheme to create cell-based street-level organisation in African townships', 'often consisted of members of the Communist Party', Bunting noted.[4] Otherwise, for most of the period of the party's illegality, the other main source of information about its development between 1950 and 1965 was from the trials of Communist Party activists between 1965 and 1966 as well as insider accounts by former party members who testified as state witnesses against them.[5] The reliability of such testimony was obviously questionable.

After legal restrictions on the party were lifted in 1990, its members began to speak more freely in interviews with researchers and to publish their memoirs; from these a prolific genre of life histories now embody a major resource for historians. A pioneering essay by Raymond Suttner has reconstructed the way the SACP established its 'underground' from such sources.[6] More recently, archival materials have become accessible mainly as a consequence of individual donations to university libraries. The party has yet to open its own records though researchers have found its documentation in Russian and East German repositories. The archival sources, combined with the insights available from memoirs, biographies and oral testimony, illuminate quite a rich picture of the party's clandestine activities inside South Africa, and they help us to understand much better the complexities of its relationship with the Congress Alliance, the larger movement in which its members were so busy. In this chapter we will sketch out the key features of this hidden history and assess its wider significance in the scholarly interpretation of anti-apartheid resistance in the 1950s and early 1960s.

A CONSIDERATION OF THE state of the Communist Party at the time of its banning is a useful starting point because the new party would initially recruit exclusively from the membership of the banned organisation. As noted in the last chapter, the final careful count of party membership in January 1949 recorded a total of 2,500 active communists, nearly two-thirds of them black and most of the party's following concentrated in and around Johannesburg and Cape Town. At the beginning of 1949 about half the membership was drawn from African 'industrial workers'. Less than a thousand members were paid up, a feature which for certain commentators has suggested that the party's committed following was declining;[7] the report itself noted sharp falls in 'orders of party literature by districts' and that the quality of district organisation outside Johannesburg, Cape Town and Durban had deteriorated.[8] During 1950, African membership both in townships and in hostels expanded.[9] The 1950 report admitted there was 'a big gap between the spread of our influence and our present organisational strength'. A district committee report from Cape Town confirms that 'mass recruiting' was beginning in African townships, mainly among the most settled urbanised residents, though local party groups 'were in a deplorable state', meeting irregularly and usually well behind in collecting subscriptions.[10]

The information contained in such documents tended to be shaped by the extent to which information was available to the Cape Town-based leadership. In the 1949 report, Port Elizabeth appears as a minor centre of party activity. In fact, as we have seen, from 1947 overlapping membership between the party and the ANC, in which party officials assumed leadership roles, helped to extend its influence here and to create a habit of localised ANC activism in rent strikes and bus fare protests. The party also encouraged trade union members to join and radicalise the ANC branches in their vicinity. In contrast to other regions, the normally anti-communist Congress Youth League here was 'leftist' in orientation well before 1950 and the New Brighton CPSA branch chairman, Raymond Mhlaba, himself served as its propaganda officer and in this capacity conducted Marxist study classes.[11] Also unnoticed in the party's reports at this time was the expansion of communist recruitment in Johannesburg's migrant worker communities, especially in the Denver and Jeppe hostels; and here too, in response to party policy, hostel-based communists, in addition to playing an animated role as trade unionists, also joined the ANC, bringing, in the words of one of the Johannesburg party leaders, 'a very particular style of work that wasn't indigenous to these organisations'.[12]

Despite the predominance of black membership and the movement of African party cadres into the ANC, the party was beset by disagreements over strategy. In January 1950, the Central Committee's report, after discussing organisational issues and noting the CPSA's expanding influence among Africans, addressed the issue of how the party should build its relationship with the ANC. The report was sharply critical of the ANC and its Youth League, arguing that the leadership of both were 'liberal capitalists' seeking only 'the freedom ... of squeezing profit out of the people'. Even so, the party should engage more closely with the national movement, with the objective of changing it 'into a revolutionary party ... distinct from the Communist Party but working closely with it'. In such a transformed party, ideological struggle promoted by the communists would help to ensure that 'class conscious workers and peasants would constitute the main leadership'.[13] Brian Bunting, one of the Cape Town-based leaders at that time, suggests that the report and its recommendations were accepted by the conference and, indeed, that 'the lines of struggle indicated in this ... statement [would] become guidelines for the entire South African liberation movement'.[14]

Michael Harmel, one of the party's key thinkers during the decade, disagreed with this view. In an unpublished set of notes on the party's history that he wrote in 1960, a copy of which he later gave to Ronnie Kasrils, Harmel maintained that the report 'was strongly criticised' because of its perceived departure 'from the established united front position' and was rejected by the conference. Harmel himself, writing in 1960, felt the report revealed a 'liquidationist' predisposition and attributed its authorship to Jack Simons, who later refused to join the SACP. According to Harmel, Simons was beginning to believe there was no need for an independent Marxist Party, given the possibilities of changing the ANC's orientation through individual communist engagements, as was happening in Port Elizabeth and in the migrant worker hostels around Johannesburg.[15] As we have seen, united fronts were prescribed Comintern policy from 1935 and they implied that the Communist Party should seek the broadest range of alliances with even bourgeois-led groups in the struggle against fascism. In the international communist movement this strategic line had been supplanted in 1947 by

Andrei Zhdanov's two-camp theory, in which the world was divided into mutually antagonistic capitalist and anti-capitalist forces; and from this perspective, communist parties were supposed to avoid alliances with any bourgeois-led groups, even in colonies.[16]

South African communists do not seem to have paid much attention to Zhdanov's ideas. Interviewed in 1984, Lionel Bernstein recalled that in the 1940s and early 1950s there were simply no communications from Moscow and, indeed, 'nobody was very keen on communication' because of the damage done to the party in the 1930s by the doctrinaire application of Comintern injunctions.[17] CPSA documentation from the late 1940s makes it quite clear that the CPSA was still trying to build a united front against what it perceived as 'fascist' Afrikaner nationalism, not just with black organisations but with white parliamentary parties as well and, of course, with white labour.[18] Simons's report was at odds with this policy because of its proposal that communists should work towards a proletarian takeover of the ANC. As we shall see, within the SACP, when it became constituted, there would be differences over the degree to which communists should seek to change the ANC. Michael Harmel was among those who believed that the ANC should still retain an African 'national' bourgeois element in its leadership and should therefore eschew explicitly socialist politics.

So, on the eve of its dissolution, the CPSA represented a small but quite effective political organisation, certainly the largest activist body at that time with an African following, and its African members in one centre at least, Port Elizabeth, were beginning to reorganise the ANC as a mass-based militant movement. Its leadership was divided by three different strategic orientations. Firstly, there was a group who saw the party's main future as working in alliance with the ANC. Within this group, as we have noted, there were disagreements about the degree to which the party should seek to transform the ANC ideologically and socially. Most African rank and file would have been within this group. Secondly, there was a small minority, especially in the Cape, who maintained reservations about the party allying itself with African nationalism and who argued that the party itself should build a mass African following as well as concentrating on extending the party's work in building African trade unions.[19] Finally, there was a small number who still believed that the party's main mission should be to retain influence within the officially recognised labour movement, that is, the registered unions, white, Indian and coloured, as well as still seeking to influence white politics. This did not seem as quixotic an aim as it might appear in retrospect. After all, in 1944 Hilda Bernstein had been elected by white voters in Hillbrow to the Johannesburg City Council.

In 1946 communists occupied leadership positions in 67 registered (non-African) trade unions.[20] During the war CPSA servicemen had helped lead a 55,000-strong Springbok Legion, which favoured racial unity and a 'society based upon the principles of Liberty, Equality and Fraternity'.[21] Half of the Legion's members were Afrikaners, according to Rica Hodgson, herself a Legionnaire and married to its national secretary.[22]

Who took the initiative to reorganise a communist party is an issue over which even insider accounts are in disagreement. Harmel refers to 'a group of comrades gathered around ... Moses Kotane ... [who] decided to build the Party up on new lines' in late 1950.[23] Not surprisingly, Bunting in his biography of Kotane also accords to the former CPSA's general secretary the decisive role,[24] and Raymond Mhlaba remembers Kotane at this time visiting Port Elizabeth to discuss the party's re-establishment.[25] Bernstein, however, refers to two small groups that 'started embryo parties' that subsequently merged; the more assertive of these, he believed, 'was composed of Wits students headed by Joe Slovo, Ruth First and Harold Wolpe'.[26] Fred Carneson, when interviewed by David Everatt, remembered a meeting in Cape Town of former Central Committee members in mid-1951 to address the possibility of reconstitution. On this occasion many of the old leaders opposed illegal activity: it was at this juncture that the initiative shifted to the Transvaal-based communists.[27] However, independently of the Transvaal groups, in Cape Town would-be underground communists, including Albie Sachs, Denis Goldberg and Ben Turok, assembled in a Modern Youth Society and attended what were intended to be Marxist study classes given by Jack Simons – though, in proceeding through a history of political thought up to Marx, the group ran aground on Hegel.[28] The Modern Youth Society was busier. They succeeded in renting a space in a warehouse in Bree Street, only to be evicted when their landlord discovered they had covered a wall with a Mexican-style mural, following a design provided by Lesley Cope, the wife of Bill Andrews's biographer.[29] A band of white Youth Society adherents, including Albie Sachs, took part in the ANC-led Defiance Campaign, courting arrest by using the non-white entrance to the main post office. Raymond Suttner has found evidence of African communists using their own initiative to build a new organisation in the Northern Transvaal and the Eastern Cape.[30] In Pretoria, Naboth Mokgatle and Stephen Tefu, both prominent in the old CPSA branch, used their leadership positions in an African General Workers' Union as a cover for independent political activity. Michael Harmel wrote a disapproving review of Mokgatle's autobiography twenty years later: Tefu was an 'incorrigible and unrepentant disrupter', he observed, and Mokgatle should have consulted with his old comrades in Johannesburg before acting and there was no evidence he did so.[31] Mokgatle would pay a price for this neglect, it seems.[32]

While it appears that the Johannesburg-based groups succeeded by late 1952 in bringing most of these networks together, the complexity of the process through which the new party became re-established merits emphasis because it helps to explain the continuation within it of divergent ideological beliefs and strategic predispositions. The party established district committees in 1952 before holding its first formal national conference in 1953, Michael Harmel's notes record, after a national meeting around Easter 1952 definitively undertook to form a new clandestine organisation. The early formation of separate district groups also helped to build doctrinal diversity into the new party.

The 1953 founding conference adopted the party's new name, endorsed a brief interim programme of aims, and instituted two key rules: members should maintain 'total silence' about the party until any decision to announce its existence publicly and any recruitments should be sanctioned by 'unanimous [district] committee decision'.[33] The conference, held on the premises of an Indian-owned trading store in a small town in the Eastern Transvaal, was attended by 25 delegates elected through a procedure in which members of the new organisation's base units, three- to four-member 'groups', would nominate one of themselves and one other person that they guessed might belong to the new party. The district committee would eliminate wrong guesses and provide a final list, adjusted to ensure racial, geographical and gender balance: 'not quite Western style democracy, but as far as we dared to go'.[34] Groups were linked to the committee by only one member and had no lateral contact with each other. The Central Committee elected at the conference was entrusted to co-opt additional members. The SACP maintained these organisational principles throughout the period reviewed here, and they ensured that lower-echelon members, even when elected or co-opted onto district committees, remained ignorant of the identities of all party leaders as well as members in other districts.[35]

Who joined the new party? Brian Bunting suggests that 'the majority' of the old CPSA 'remained loyal' though he also told Sylvia Neame that before its prohibition, the party 'was full of people who were totally unsuitable for illegal work'.[36] This may have been so emotionally, but in reality at most a fifth of the old membership was recruited into the clandestine units. Several people refused when they were approached, including Edwin Mofutsanyana, Sam Kahn, Jack Simons and Johnny Gomas as well as Jimmy and Alex La

Guma, though Jack Simons and Alex La Guma joined later, in exile.[37] In a report he delivered at a meeting of the Communist Party of the Soviet Union, Moses Kotane claimed that by 1961 the SACP had a membership of between 400 and 500, and this was after a recent phase of expansion.[38] Bernstein notes that a majority of the CPSA's 300–400 membership in Johannesburg were against reconstitution.[39] We know that recruitment was selective and vetted by party leadership, and at least one well-known Indian CPSA member, Ismail Meer, who wanted to join believed he had been deliberately 'discarded'.[40] In the process certain key constituencies of the old party were either to fall away altogether or would become more weakly present in the new organisation. It seems likely that, as with the CPSA by 1950, most of the SACP membership would be African. African recruitment efforts especially targeted individuals who held local leadership positions – organisers of residents' associations, for example, as well as trade union officials: as Turok noted, in the 1950s the party perceived its role as a vanguard organisation.[41] Bunting in his biography of Kotane suggests that during the 1960 State of Emergency 'the party had a team of several hundred activists in the Johannesburg townships' alone, though this team may have also included ANC sympathisers.[42]

The hostel-based migrant grouping in Johannesburg remained within the party – these were manufacturing workers – while the other township-based African members were likely to be engaged in either literate occupations or as small businessmen. Moses Kotane and Walter Sisulu, two of the most important African communists in the 1950s, maintained livelihoods as a furniture dealer and an estate agent respectively while Govan Mbeki, who joined the party in 1953, supplemented his salary from *New Age* by running a shop in Port Elizabeth. Sisulu joined the party in 1955 while serving as the ANC's secretary general after attending Michael Harmel's Marxist study group, and one year later he was co-opted onto the Central Committee.[43] Port Elizabeth's communists were led by Raymond Mhlaba, a dry-cleaning worker, who was as a secondary school graduate untypically well educated. Through the 1950s, a new emphasis in African recruitment would bring university graduates into the fold – what the party perceived to be a prestigious new intelligentsia: Joe Matthews and Duma Nokwe were early entrants in this group. It was a development that prompted some discomfort among the older African working-class membership in Johannesburg.[44] In the late 1950s, African party recruitment efforts also began to focus on high schools.[45] Success in enrolling African 'intellectuals' may have encouraged certain recruiters to become additionally restrictive in their selection. Natoo Babenia, who joined Umkhonto in 1962, was discouraged from joining the party, being told that he 'was not sufficiently intellectually adept'.[46] He joined the party later, in prison.

The CPSA's old presence in the white labour movement was not reproduced in the new party: the most conspicuous white trade unionist in the CPSA, Danie du Plessis, was among those who opposed reconstitution. More surprising was the cessation of party influence within Indian trade unions in Durban. Those white trade unionists who joined the new party, notably Arnold Selby and Vic Syfret from the old engineering group, concentrated on setting up organisations among black workers: Syfret worked with the Non-European Railway and Harbour Workers while Selby was national secretary of the African Textile Workers' Union.[47] Indian unions had been a major arena of CPSA activity, but 'during the 1950s', according to one veteran of the SACP's Durban base, Rowley Arenstein, 'Indian workers were left in the cold'.[48] This was partly because union officials engaged in this sector who were also CPSA members were among the group that felt that communists should retain a 'class-based' emphasis in organising and should concentrate on factory-based labour organisation. Bettie du Toit and Mike Muller, key textile worker organisers, were among those who remained at odds with the new party; Du Toit had been involved in disagreements with the Cape CPSA leadership over trade union strategy for much of the 1940s.[49] Pauline Podbrey was another key Indian labour organiser who became disaffected with the party in the early 1950s.[50] Indian workers in Durban were discouraged from undertaking politically motivated strikes by the threat of replacement with Africans, as indeed happened after the dismissal of 300 Indian workers following a local ANC-led stay-away in June 1953.[51] For the party, reaching the 'unorganised' was the key priority. Arnold Selby was actually told by Joe Slovo that he should put his commitment to setting up a Workers' Council of Action among unionists affiliated to the Trade Union Congress of South Africa (TUCSA), because 'this work was among existing unions'. The council, intended to mobilise trade union opposition to pending restrictive industrial legislation, 'would wither away', Selby recalled. Later in the decade, communists would call for a broad united front that would aim to embrace TUCSA affiliates,[52] but by then their presence in the white trade union movement was minimal.

Whites and Indians were not the only workers left out. In 1955, when busy as an organiser for the Congress of the People, Ben Turok encountered a group of coloured farm workers in Kraaifontein who had once constituted a CPSA branch and who had never been contacted by any political activists since the party's dissolution.[53] However, the Western Cape-based, mainly coloured Food and Canning Workers' Union and its African counterpart were important bases for SACP recruitment through the 1950s, though, rather oddly, Ray Alexander, its original secretary, was not on the initial list of former CPSA members asked to join the new party. She was invited and became a member in 1954.[54]

When interviewed in 1986, Arenstein maintained that in the early 1950s the new party leadership was rather inclined to be contemptuous of trade unionism, viewing it as economistic 'reformism', and that their overriding preoccupation with alliance with the national liberation movement meant that a low priority was accorded to labour organisation. This is quite likely. Moses Kotane, the dominant African communist and the SACP's general secretary, was, by his own admission, 'not by nature a trade unionist ... [and] more inclined to political things'.[55] The party's representation of the South African state as increasingly 'fascist' also encouraged scepticism about trade unionism, for in a fascist polity, labour organisation would become inevitably circumscribed or compromised. Not always, though. As Eli Weinberg argued at one of the Discussion Club sessions, the careful and increasingly risky effort required in building African unionism through establishing factory committees, 'concentrating for long periods on an important factory', would in the end yield dividends: 'it would ... open new avenues of attack on Fascism'. Weinberg remained hopeful that white workers sooner or later might join in such a struggle, given that 'as the general crisis of imperialism deepens, the status of the white workers will deteriorate'.[56]

While active white communists were, as they had been in the 1940s, mainly (though not exclusively) drawn from Baltic Jewish immigrants or their children, they were more likely to include well-educated middle-class professionals than had been the case with the CPSA's leadership: the white liberal universities supplied a steady stream of recruits during the 1950s.[57] Ben Turok would be a good example: his father worked in a Cape Town leather factory; before arriving in South Africa from Latvia, he had belonged to the Bund. Ben enrolled in the engineering faculty at the University of Cape Town, where he was known as 'Bennie the Bolshie'.[58] People from a British-descended working-class background, a prominent group in the CPSA's early history, were rarer in the SACP: Fred Carneson, who first became a communist while working in Pietermaritzburg's post office, was unusual in this respect. Another son of working-class English immigrants was Jack Hodgson, an ex-mine worker in both South Africa and Northern Rhodesia, where he helped Roy Welensky set up the mine workers' union.[59] Despite their mostly middle-class status, white members in Johannesburg usually lived in the comparatively modest suburbs, just adjacent to the city centre, in Hillbrow's apartment blocks, and in small cottages in Bellevue and Yeoville. The lawyers tended to live better and, indeed, the comparative affluence of Joe Slovo and Ruth First's household in Roosevelt Park apparently elicited a degree of resentment 'among the lesser mortals of the movement'.[60] Lithuanian-born Slovo in fact came from an impoverished background and originally left school in 1941 to become a shop assistant, joining the party as a probationer at the age of 15. Military service in Egypt and Italy entitled him to special entry into Wits: five years later, he graduated as best law student and joined the Johannesburg Bar a few months after marrying Ruth First.[61] Like Joe Slovo, the key personalities in the new party's white leadership group were comparatively young, in their late twenties or early thirties, and a significant number had served as soldiers in the Second World War. Several of these army veterans, including Brian Bunting, Joe Slovo, Wolfie Kodesh and Lionel Bernstein, had returned home deeply impressed by what they took to be insurrectionary takeovers of Italian towns by communist partisans.[62]

Regional variations in the party's sociology may help to explain the political differences between districts. In Cape Town, Ben Turok, who joined the SACP in 1954, found that in this centre the party 'tended to be sectarian' and 'work in the national movement was hampered by the insistence on class perspectives'. Here too, he thought, there was an especially 'uncritical identification with Soviet positions'.[63] In general, he thought, communists in Cape Town 'had a more leftist perspective' than elsewhere.[64] This may have been a consequence of the presence in Cape Town of an alternative Marxist tradition, at that time represented by Trotskyists in the Non-European Unity Movement.[65] A trained surveyor, Turok had belonged to the British party before joining the SACP as well as to the London-based South African group within it – an unhappy community, he remembered, 'divided by personality and party lines'.[66] It was initially constituted by South African communists who had arrived in London to undertake studies or for other reasons before 1948 and were dissuaded from going home by the advent of National Party rule and particularly by the prohibition of mixed marriages.[67] For example, the Immorality Act prompted the Indian student Vella Pillay and his English wife, Patsy, to make London their permanent home while remaining active in the South African party for the next three decades.[68] In Ben Turok's case, when he returned to South Africa he discovered that he was one of the few party members who had worked in another African country, in his case helping to run farms in Zimbabwe for both Ian Smith and Garfield Todd: Smith he found both 'dull and mean with food'.[69] One problem in Cape Town, Turok found, was that 'the ANC was a very low key affair', weakly led, he thought, though he admired ANC and fellow communist activist Greenwood

Ngotyana, a 'natural lawyer and relentless agitator' who otherwise worked as a petrol attendant.[70]

In Johannesburg, it is likely that 'cross pollination between the Communist Party and the national movement' (Bunting's phrase) was most developed, and Moses Kotane's local influence kept in check any propensities for 'seeing the party as a rival to the ANC'.[71] As we shall see, both Kotane and Michael Harmel, the party's key theorist who was also resident in Johannesburg, remained wary of any 'transformationist' approaches to the ANC. In Johannesburg, incidentally, the spatial features of racial segregation ensured that most party base units, the groups, were uniracial, whereas in Durban and Cape Town units were more likely to be racially mixed. African members on the Witwatersrand were especially likely to be fully absorbed in ANC-related activity.[72] In Durban, the SACP began with comparatively few African members, for locally they had been in a minority in the old CPSA, a residual consequence of concentrated police action against the party after the 1930 anti-pass campaign. The most assertive African communists were trade unionists, and Durban would emerge in the late 1950s with the strongest group of affiliates in the ANC-allied South African Congress of Trade Unions (SACTU). The dominant personality intellectually in the Durban SACP, Rowley Arenstein, would argue that the chief task for the party should be building a factory-based organisation.[73] These differences would affect the ways in which SACP members in each centre understood the overall purpose of their activities, and it is to strategic and ideological concerns that we will now turn.

As HARMEL NOTES, on its formation the SACP decided that its members should involve themselves in legal mass work, in effect working within the ANC or allied organisations – from 1953 these would include a South African Congress of Democrats which white communists would join. At the time of the CPSA's dissolution, as we have seen, there were disagreements among communists about the character of African nationalism, and if and how they should engage with it. The regional switch in the communist leadership from Cape Town to Johannesburg that accompanied the SACP's establishment ensured that advocates for a close relationship with the ANC would prevail. The doctrinal justification for such a move drew on two arguments. The first of these was that South Africa was a 'colony of a special type'. The second proposition was that given this characteristic, communists should embrace a programme of intermediate 'national democratic' aims as a stage that would precede the full development of a socialist society.

A version of colonialism of a special type was spelled out in the CPSA's Central Committee report of 1950, in which South Africa was depicted as containing 'the characteristics of both an imperialist state and a colony'. As the argument developed over the next few years, the dominant or 'determining' economic sectors, mining and agriculture, were perceived by Michael Harmel and others to depend upon an essentially colonial exploitation of rightless black workers from segregated reserves by a white 'imperialist' state – a racial form of exploitation that inhibited workers' development of class consciousness. What made South Africa singular was that the local presence of settlers from the 'dominant imperialist nationality' resulted in the exclusion of black people from the commercial opportunities normally available to privileged groups within the indigenous populations in other colonies. Hence proto-bourgeois elements within the ANC leadership, in comparison with anti-colonial movements in other settings, were especially weak, and therefore as the Congress movement developed a mass orientation, workers would increasingly constitute its leadership. The ANC was also different, Lionel Bernstein noted, because its demand was for equality rather than a more racially assertive self-determination.[74]

The second key idea, national democracy, was linked to this recognition of the ANC's singularity. For if the ANC's leadership was not constituted mainly by an existing or, indeed, an aspirant black bourgeoisie, then the national liberation that it sought to achieve would not be a bourgeois democracy, but something different. For what that something would be, by the early 1950s there was beginning to be available from Soviet authorities fresh perspectives about the kinds of societies that might emerge from anti-colonial movements in the developing world. Contrary to Zhdanov's two-camp theory, anti-colonial 'national bourgeoisies' did not necessarily defer to imperialist interests, and characterising them in this way had been a sectarian error, Soviet theorists were concluding by 1956. In newly independent countries there might be a 'non-capitalist road' to socialism in which liberal democracy and nationalisation of foreign 'monopoly' enterprises in a state-owned sector would allow room for domestic private undertakings. In seeking to achieve this kind of society, workers and black property owners had convergent interests.[75]

These ideas were developed in the Discussion Clubs or Study Circles that were composed mainly of white ex-CPSA and subsequently SACP members, between 1952 and 1954. The chief focus of these groups was the effort to reach a consensus on the 'national question'. The clubs sponsored a journal, *Viewpoints and Perspectives*, as well as several other publications. The main issue over which the participants at these encounters disagreed, evidently, was the ANC's class trajectory. Most of the people who would join the new party accepted that a black bourgeoisie was non-existent and the petty bourgeois groups were too weak to impose their own particular class interests on Congress. In the longer term, would workers predominate in the ANC and constitute its leadership? Was it becoming a workers' movement? Here there was uncertainty.[76] But not everybody agreed that the nationalist movement was so free from bourgeois predispositions that it embodied, in Jack Simons's words, a 'genuine, healthy and dynamic nationalism'.[77] Exponents of this view included Danie du Plessis, of the Building Workers' Union, who had been a party member in the 1940s but would not be invited into the new formation. He disliked the ANC's continuing racial exclusivity. The ANC's bourgeois orientation was evident, he thought, in the issues it had taken up in the Defiance Campaign.[78] Its leaders were 'bourgeois agents'. Better to have a single political movement, open to all, led by a strong trade union movement.[79] In response to this line of argument, Lionel Bernstein, another influential figure in the Johannesburg group, argued that at this stage a purely working-class struggle was unrealistic.

Analysts of the party's intellectual trajectory disagree about the degree to which its leaders kept themselves informed about theoretical developments within the international communist movement. Working primarily from Soviet sources, Irina Filatova maintains that the really decisive impact in South Africa of Soviet notions of national democracy followed the first formal contact between the SACP and the CPSU in 1960, when the Soviet party formally adopted the idea of a non-capitalist road. Only after then, she thinks, did South Africans begin to understand national democracy as the corollary of colonialism as a special type.[80] In fact, there was plenty of more informal contact between South African communists and Soviet and other Eastern European countries, including the self-styled people's democracies, during the 1950s. Indeed, Rowley Arenstein believes that for party ideologues, countries like Poland and Czechoslovakia represented models of national democracy.[81] Pre-Second World War and wartime Eastern European communist experience was also a source of models of underground organisation; in this respect Julius Fučik's *Notes from the Gallows* was a canonical text for South African party leaders.[82]

From the late 1940s onwards, a procession of South Africans would visit and even stay for periods in Eastern Europe. Advocate Harry Bloom, a close friend of Bram Fischer, though probably not a party member, lived in Czechoslovakia at the time of the communist takeover in 1948. He and his wife, Beryl, using pseudonyms, wrote a vigorous defence of the Czech communists' accession. Their aim was to 'pose simple truths' against the 'barrage of hatred and distortion against the Czechoslovak people ... the absurd and violent slanders' dispatched by American and British pressmen.[83] Working as journalists, the Blooms bought a small cottage in Zalov, a commuter village outside Prague, and, in engagements with their neighbours, learned to speak a little Czech. They joined the village brigade in which on weekends city workers undertook voluntary work on farms. Keenly sympathetic observers, they 'followed the statistics of the two-year plan as if they were football scores'.[84]

Ruth First and Harold Wolpe visited Prague as International Union of Students delegates just after the war, and Ruth subsequently travelled to Warsaw. Molly Fischer visited East Germany, Czechoslovakia and the Soviet Union while travelling to China in 1954.[85] Paul Joseph encountered Jules Fučik's widow, Gustava, on a tram journey; excited that he had read *Notes from the Gallows*, she invited him home to meet her friends. On a second visit, Joseph was 'taken around' by a group of trade unionists. He had the temerity to ask them about the Slansky trial; they 'seemed surprised' he had heard about it.[86] Leslie Massina, first general secretary of SACTU, visited Czechoslovakia for a short training course on trade unionism in 1954.[87] Brian and Sonia Bunting visited Czechoslovakia and the Soviet Union in 1954, recording their impressions of Russian factory tours, visits to collective farms and 'art for the people' in a pamphlet entitled *Life Is More Joyous*.[88] Ben Turok attended the World Youth Festival in Warsaw, also visiting Prague in 1953. Moses Kotane spent nearly a year outside South Africa in 1955, during which time he was hosted by members of the British Communist Party and attended an international youth festival in Warsaw. It seems he also visited East Germany in 1956. Ruth First published a booklet in 1955 containing testimonies from various visitors to the Soviet Union, including Sam Kahn, who was keen, 'as a Jew', to discover 'how Jews lived' in Russia. He returned, convinced by his encounters and experiences in Moscow, that 'Jews had the same contented, happy look, the same gay carefree bearing of the people everywhere in the People's democracies'.[89] Pauline Podbrey and the sugar estate workers' organiser, HA Naidoo, spent three years in Hungary between 1951 and 1954, working in Hungarian Radio's foreign language section. A report written by Moses Kotane in 1961 suggests that on several occasions 'in the past', the party dispatched several people 'to the GDR for technical training'.[90] Newspapers and journals edited by party members during the 1950s paid plenty of attention to international communist developments.

There is an abundance of contemporary evidence that suggests that South

African communists were well aware of the underpinning rationale for national democracy through the 1950s. For example, in 1956 the journalist Lionel Forman was making the case for non-revolutionary roads to socialism in an issue of *Fighting Talk*, the former journal of the Springbok Legion, now edited by Ruth First. [91] Two years earlier, in an article in the *Guardian*'s successor, the party-controlled weekly newspaper *Advance*, Forman had addressed what nationhood could be in South Africa, urging his readers to 'get over this weird idea that all national liberatory groups are "bourgeois national"'. [92] At a subsequent public symposium arising from his article, Forman proposed that the national liberation movement had the potential to become a true people's movement, 'one that will not allow a mere transfer from national oppression … but will push forward to people's democracy'. [93] So far, he was in step with the emerging party doctrine, though he began to push its boundaries when he suggested that national groups, speaking the same language, were 'aspirant nations' and might enjoy 'national autonomy' in a people's democracy. [94]

Lionel Forman was unusually well qualified to talk about people's democracy. In 1950 he was studying law at Wits. Like his fellow students and party members Ruth First and Harold Wolpe, he was the South African-born child of Baltic Jewish emigrants. As a teenager he joined the Communist Party, then enjoying a wartime resurgence in South Africa and beginning to establish a following on the main English-language university campuses. Forman edited *Wits Student*, opposing anti-communist calls for the National Union of South African Students to disaffiliate from the International Union of Students (IUS). By 1950 the IUS had clearly aligned itself with the Soviet Union-led 'Peace' camp, supporting the North Koreans at its congress. Lionel Forman attended the IUS conference in Warsaw in 1951 and helped to convince those Western European delegates present to remain within the organisation. After the Warsaw meeting, Forman took up a position as a NUSAS delegate at the IUC's secretariat in Prague, where he would remain for two years, joined by his wife, Sadie, whom he married in Prague's town hall. They lived in a student hostel in Smíchov. Lionel worked hard to learn Czech and, though he was never a fluent speaker, he could follow conversations and radio broadcasts, and he and Sadie made friends with local people.

South Africans coming back from Eastern Europe usually returned impressed by what they chose to see. For black visitors there was also the emotional impact of the hospitality and courtesy they received, especially empowering for people normally subjected in their home society to humiliating subordination. As the trade unionist Elizabeth Mafeking recalled after visiting Czechoslovakia in 1955 to attend a youth festival, the warmth of her reception enabled her to 'really forget she was black'.[95] But thinkers like Lionel Forman who experienced people's democracy for longer would have returned to South Africa with more qualified reactions. Shortly after his stay in Prague, Forman wrote an autobiography. It was turned down for publication by Harry Pollitt of the British Communist Party because of its criticisms of a 'brother party'. Pollitt himself was the beneficiary of several extended spells of Czech party hospitality at various spas and sanatoriums in 1950 and 1951. Forman recalled his impressions from Prague in the party's newspaper, *New Age*, when he wrote about the 'Lessons from Hungary'. In Prague, he often encountered among his Czech colleagues 'cynicism towards the things about us that was a nagging worry to every one of us'. How could it be, he asked, 'that years after the war one of Europe's great cities should suffer the humiliation of a real black-out for lack of generating plant?' And his concerns were not simply limited to inefficiencies. In the same article he was self-critical of his failure three years earlier to recognise 'the alarmingly large number of ordinary citizens' who opposed the government, and he concluded that 'the sacrifices called for were too great' and 'the limitations on freedom out of all proportion to the need'.[96] The manuscript Harry Pollitt read probably contained more detailed recollections, but unfortunately the only surviving fragments are not about Prague.

Sadie Forman later wrote a memoir about her husband. In Prague he was, she remembered, very disturbed by the Slansky show trial, listening closely to live broadcasts of the proceedings and finding them 'frightful, disappointing and largely incomprehensible, making a mockery of communism'.[97] When Stalin died, among their local friends – the Formans sensed – a 'veil of anxiety lifted'.[98] In the Slansky trial 14 senior members of the Czech Communist Party were convicted on espionage charges as agents of American imperialism and international Zionism. Eleven were Jewish and most of them had been key figures in the party's wartime underground; in this context they were accused also of becoming Gestapo informers. Several were Spanish Civil War veterans. An official inquiry would confirm in 1968 that the charges were invented.[99] The trial must have caused some unease within the South African left community as the party press printed a pamphlet under the auspices of the Progressive Community for Jewish Affairs, which uncritically reproduced all the implausible detail of the charges against the supposed 'conspirators' and insisted that the Jewish identity of so many of the accused was incidental: 'the trial record refers to men not as Jews but as adherents of an ideology [Zionism] held by some Jews and opposed by other Jews as well as many non-Jews.'[100] Even so, Forman remained a loyal Communist Party member.

Indeed, in 1956 he convinced himself that across the socialist bloc, the 'lessons of Hungary' had been learned and that 'a new future [had] dawn[ed] for the world'. Moreover, when living in 'one of the most advanced of the people's democracies', even among anti-government people he spoke to 'I never met a single one ... who wanted to return to the days of capitalism'.[101] Forman's stay in Prague coincided with the harshest phase of the party's rule, when a series of political trials convicted thousands of supposed class enemies, including top-echelon communists. One month before Lionel Forman's departure a steep monetary devaluation effectively nullifying people's savings engendered widespread riots.[102] The Formans were taken aback by the 'chaos' that resulted from the devaluation.[103]

But for those observers who wanted to see it, there was also evidence of regime support: apparently 'joyous' crowds of young people assembling in May Day parades and the solemn procession of 200,000 mourners at Klement Gottwald's funeral. Reacting to an earlier phase, before the communists' takeover, the Blooms were impressed by what they perceived to be 'the real mood of the Czechoslovak people, the feeling of confidence, optimism and verve, the spirit of liberation'.[104] English-speaking visitors familiar with the austerities of post-war Britain, including Forman, may have been less troubled by consumer shortages resulting from the authorities' strategic emphasis on heavy industry. Meanwhile, the Czechoslovak welfare state could point to genuine accomplishments in the provision of sophisticated and free health care as well as the expanding network of well-equipped nursery facilities. In the two years they stayed in Czechoslovakia, the Formans 'did not come across any sign of poverty' and, like the Blooms, they were impressed by what seemed to them very obvious social equality.[105] Forman's reservations about the repressive political climate were also tempered by the gratitude he felt to Czech doctors who had been able to treat a serious heart illness complaint that had stymied British specialists. As Sadie Forman remembered, 'life in Prague was gratifying at a basic level'.[106]

Forman's conviction that the Hungarian experience offered 'lessons' was not widely shared within the party. He had been in a small minority within Cape Town's communist community who readily accepted the disclosures supplied by Khrushchev at the CPSU twentieth congress. Initially, most of the Cape Town group rejected the reports as untrue, as fabrications from the CIA. Forman's editorial on Khrushchev's speech earned him a harsh reprimand from Govan Mbeki. Albie Sachs was exceptional in taking Forman's side. Sachs had visited Czechoslovakia in 1954. In Prague he met Jaroslav Bartošek, a diplomat posted to Cape Town; Sachs had taught Mrs Bartošek English and had made friends with the couple. A visit to Cape Town by the Janáček String Quartet had also enthralled Sachs, initiating his lifelong passion for chamber music. He joined the multiracial audiences at all their concerts and became familiar with each of the players as well as their managerial escort; this functionary seemed to him quite superfluous as the musicians were not predisposed to defect: 'they were very comfortable, they wanted to go back to Czechoslovakia, as far as I could see'. In Prague, though, the Bartošeks were unhappy. He had been sidelined in the foreign service and he offered his young visitor an exasperated commentary about a party hierarchy riven with rivalries and nepotism. Sachs himself was taken aback by what he saw in Prague; not the bright socialist metropolis he was expecting, but a shabby 'run-down city'.[107] For younger-generation communists like Lionel Forman and Albie Sachs, Khrushchev's repudiation of Stalinism represented fresh grounds for hope.

Prompted by their activism within the Congress Alliance, South African communists were thinking about how a transition to socialism could happen incrementally, constructed 'from above', as it were, after a socially emancipatory national liberation which could then, to use Forman's phraseology 'push forward to people's democracy.'[108] In using such language South African communists could take their cues from the Czech version of such a 'push forward'. Here, after all, was a national setting in which a Communist Party with significant popular support (38 per cent of the vote in 1946 and a million members) found its way to power through participation in an all-party National Front, the basis for a coalition government. A 'national and democratic revolution', Klement Gottwald called this phase. Communist power within this coalition was expressed in major nationalisations as well as radical land reform – achievements which, Harry Bloom claimed, 'won them the respect of most of the people'.[109] The party's seizure of power in 1948, enabled by its control of the police and defence ministries, was accompanied by impressive expressions of public acclamation; indeed, public support was the distinguishing feature of the Czech transition, a key ingredient in the subsequent regime's revolutionary credentials.[110] What followed was a regime that could be extremely repressive but one which nevertheless retained substantial legitimacy, and in which in restricted, localised contexts officials sometimes tolerated or ignored non-confrontational challenges to government policy. Not quite totalitarian, Czech politics was a 'participatory dictatorship' in which communists could make strong claims about delivering social justice.[111]

And just what a people's democracy might embody in South Africa was spelled out in the same year by Moses Kotane himself, in a pamphlet entitled *South Africa's Way Forward*. A people's democracy, Kotane explained, would have all the civic freedoms conventionally associated with democracy but it would be more egalitarian. Land would be shared 'among its rightful owners'; big mining and other monopoly concerns would become the property of the people; there would be good wages, social security and housing for the homeless.[112] As Ben Turok's autobiography makes clear, the notion of national democracy was in fairly general usage within the SACP by 1955, notwithstanding continuing disagreements about its programmatic implications.[113] Progression to national democracy was not taken as a predetermined given or an inevitable prospect; it would require conscious effort to bring it about. With respect to their 'legal' activism, the SACP's engagement with national liberation between 1953 and 1960 had three particular emphases.

Firstly, and most obviously, following on from its own project of promoting national democracy, there were the party's efforts to shape the ANC's ideological predisposition. In 1954, after ANC leadership decided to collect popular demands for a Freedom Charter, a National Working Committee assembled, composed of representatives from the ANC itself and its three allies, the Indian Congresses, the South African Congress of Trade Unions (SACTU) and the recently formed South African Coloured People's Organisation as well as the Congress of Democrats. Lionel Bernstein joined this committee, whose other members included Walter Sisulu for the ANC and Piet Beyleveld from SACTU, both of whom were shortly to join the party after a recruiting process that probably preceded their invitations onto the committee.[114] Rusty Bernstein drafted the preliminary 'Call' for demands to be submitted for consideration at a Congress of the People one year later, and a nationwide process of canvassing steered by provincial committees started. In his autobiography Bernstein describes in some detail the process through which demands were elicited. Until shortly before the Congress, these were stored in Johannesburg in an old cabin trunk. The committee decided that distilling from these a draft charter was 'just a writing job' and entrusted this task to Bernstein. Working his way through thousands of scraps of paper, Bernstein 'cobbled together a synthesis'. In doing this, he recalls, he 'had no more idea of where to start than anyone else' and he read through the materials 'to get the general flavour' and to identify general thematic categories, doing his best to 'read into' their contents a coherent 'compromise or a consensus'. As he admits, 'the most difficult part of the exercise was to keep my own opinions from influencing the draft', and he insists that even those clauses he wrote that caused most contention, on land reform, nationalisation and non-racialism, were 'everyday stuff' among Congress activists.[115] To help him, Bernstein could show his draft to Joe Slovo and Walter Sisulu, who, together with Bernstein, constituted a drafting group. But the document was really his own work, its phraseology characteristically 'poetic'; this was the way he wrote, Slovo recalled thirty years later, and its content 'really did reflect what came in'.[116]

This was probably true, but, even so, Bernstein's understanding of political common sense may well have been affected by the programmatic concepts that he had helped to develop within the SACP. It is certainly the case that the Charter conformed rather closely to Kotane's notion of a people's democracy which he had outlined in his pamphlet in May 1954. As Norman Levy points out, 'Bernstein could hardly have drafted the charter without reference to the seminal expectations of Kotane.'[117] On nationalisation, Bernstein suggests that what he had drafted was not intended as 'a gateway to socialism' but simply a means through which injustice and inequality could be addressed, as their legacy 'could not be corrected by simply ending race discrimination or liberalising markets'. Writing in 1960, Michael Harmel observed that the Freedom Charter was 'identical in all its main provisions to the demands set forth in the immediate programme of the SACP adopted in 1953'.[118] Moses Kotane, writing one year later, noted that 'all major policy decisions' undertaken by the liberation movement 'either emanate from or have the approval of our C[entral] C[ommittee]'.[119] Bernstein's insistence that he did not intend the Charter's provisions to be socialist is quite reconcilable with the way the Johannesburg communists understood national democracy. At the time, Moses Kotane also argued that the nationalisation advocated by the Charter was not a socialist measure.

Partly influenced by the more 'leftist' ethos of the Cape Town party, Ben Turok perceived things differently. From the beginning of the Congress of the People campaign, Cape Town-based communists, Turok thinks, were determined the party should ensure that the Charter was a reflection of the party's minimum programme, whereas Transvaal communists were less inclined to be so assertively prescriptive: 'the Party should lead but not drive.'[120] Turok, together with Greenwood Ngotyana, also an SACP member, led the Local Action Council which solicited demands, and he was invited to attend the Congress as one of the ten keynote speakers with the brief of introducing the economic clause. While staying with the Harmels, he was shown a draft of the Charter and he claims that he redrafted the clause, amending it to stress 'that the commanding heights should be in public ownership'.[121] At the

Congress itself in 1955, Turok supplied in his speech a much more radical interpretation of the nationalisation provisions than Bernstein intended, telling his audience that there would be 'a committee of the workers to run the Gold Mines ... [and] wherever there is a factory and where there are workers to be exploited, we say that the workers will take over the factories'. 'Let us have a people's committee to run the banks,' he added.[122]

Turok's account is at odds with Bernstein's memoir. Bernstein remembers that the draft that Congress Alliance joint executive leaders reviewed the day before the Congress of the People had already been printed and there were no changes to his original. But Turok has been very insistent he was 'the author of the economic clause in the Freedom Charter'.[123] In 1985 he told this author that the original version did not refer to the question of industrial ownership but just used vague language about the sharing of material resources. Bernstein himself and other senior communists could not attend this meeting because they were banned. When Turok told Harmel that night what he had done, his host was a 'little appalled', for, in calling for a 'people's democracy', 'we'd gone some way beyond where the movement wanted to be'. [124] Nelson Mandela's gloss on the Charter's provisions, published in 1956 in *Liberation*, the journal edited by Michael Harmel, was more likely in tune with party orthodoxy when he suggested the 'breakup' and 'democratisation' of monopolies would 'open fresh fields for the development of a non-European bourgeois class'. After this, 'private enterprise' would 'flourish as never before'.[125] In 1959, the party itself in an editorial (written by Harmel) in the first issue of its own journal, the *African Communist*, declared its continuing adherence to a 'United Front of National Liberation' composed of all classes, 'workers, peasants, intellectuals *and* businessmen' (my italics).[126]

The second way in which the party would shape the ANC during the 1950s was through its contributions to the ANC's organisational structure. In an organisation in which, after the Defiance Campaign, membership would reach around 100,000, a few hundred communists constituted a tiny minority. As Bunting suggests, African communists were concentrated among the ANC's more assertive followers, and 'when it came to implementation of decisions, to the house to house canvassing and day to day organising, it was more often than not the Communist Party groups that did the work'.[127] Port Elizabeth party activists also supplied the model for the ANC's ambitious scheme to establish a cell-based local organisation, drawing upon their own experiences of establishing party groups in New Brighton, and it was they who explained and proposed the scheme to Mandela during a visit he made to the Eastern Cape in 1953.[128] It was in Port Elizabeth, 'like nowhere else', that the M-Plan was implemented.[129] During the preparations for the Congress of the People, it was SACP members working within SACTU structures in several regions who, according to oral testimony collected in the 1980s, 'performed the lion's share of the work', particularly in organising the house-to-house collection of demands.[130] So communists played an important role in helping to mobilise and train the ANC's base-level activists through the 1950s, introducing to them, as Bernstein noted, their own particular style of work and, at least in Port Elizabeth where the ANC maintained local 'political study groups', their own view of the world. These ten-person groups drew upon local party experience and, meeting weekly, followed a reading curriculum devised by Govan Mbeki, who had arrived in Port Elizabeth in 1956 to manage the party-owned newspaper *New Age*'s local office. Mbeki wrote a booklet in isiXhosa for the groups, disregarding reservations other communists voiced about aspiring to 'talk Marxism in Xhosa'.[131] Mbeki had joined the party only in 1953, despite viewing himself as a Marxist and a socialist from the time he encountered Eddie Roux at Fort Hare in 1933. Friendly with communists and, indeed, married to a party member, Epainette, since 1938, he had held back from joining the party, mainly because at that time the communists he encountered were not interested in rural activism.[132]

In one area at least, organising independently from their ally, communists brought a key new following into the ANC. This happened when the hostel-based communists in Johannesburg, with Flag Boshielo and John Nkadimeng, created a body of migrant workers from Sekhukhuneland, Sebatakgomo, which they decided to 'locate within the ANC'.[133] Turok recalled that the migrant workers' group was neglected and treated 'shabbily' by the party, which remained, he thought, urban-oriented.[134] In Port Elizabeth, Govan Mbeki was singular among local activists in his determination to build an underground network among migrant worker hostel dwellers, though it is unclear whether he thought of his recruits here as prospective party members.

The communist press also supplied a key organisational resource for the ANC. This included the weekly newspaper, *New Age*, published under a succession of titles in response to government bannings, as well as the more occasional journals, *Liberation* and *Fighting Talk*. The party press was owned by a company headed by Isaac Horvitch, who had been the CPSA's chairman after Bill Andrews's death.[135] Aside from their propaganda functions, the newspapers and journals, particularly *New Age*, through its network of street sellers and corresponding reporters, supplied a national system of communication. With respect to resources as well, the party helped the ANC financially to maintain a small number of full-time workers, some of whom worked for *New Age*, as well as paying for or arranging office accommodation. The party taxed its own members, ten per cent of their salaries, thereby helping to keep it in funds.

Finally, and most importantly, with respect to organisation, the party provided a group of leaders, disciplined and trained and, despite their own internal disagreements, united by their vision of overall purpose. Kotane asserted in 1961 that communists effectively led the national liberation movement, though that statement may have been more true after the ANC's legal prohibition than before.[136] As he noted, from their inception, communists were in the majority in SACTU's executive as well as in the top echelons of the Congress of Democrats (in which white communists made up a greater share of the members)[137] and, less strongly, in the hierarchy of the Coloured People's Congress. Within the ANC, SACP members held key positions. In the leadership elected in 1958, a communist, Duma Nokwe, became secretary general in place of then-banned Walter Sisulu, also a party member from 1955; and of the ten other executive members, at least four (Alfred Nzo, Leslie Massina, Gladstone Tshume and Caleb Mayekiso) belonged to the party.[138] Another indication of the extent of the party's activism more generally within the ANC and the Congress movement was the number of its members who were charged in the marathon Treason Trial of 1956–61. Using evidence, including materials the police confiscated at the Congress of the People, the state would argue, ultimately unsuccessfully, that ANC leaders and their allies were seeking to overthrow the state and replace it with a communist system. Among the 156 people charged in the original indictment, at least 54 were active communists, including most, though not all, of the party's top echelon. Of the 30 who were among the final accused, acquitted in 1961, 18 were party members. The original indictment also included several people strongly opposed to communist influence in the ANC. At no stage during the proceedings did the prosecution indicate any real knowledge about the party or its networks.[139]

An especially decisive effect of the party's committed embrace of the national movement was the extent to which it directed the African trade union movement into a supportive role as an auxiliary formation. This was in direct contrast to the situation in the 1940s when many communist trade unionists maintained 'slender contact with the party itself' and held back from wider political commitments.[140] In contrast, in certain regions, according to the Natal trade unionist and SACP member Billy Nair, 'SACTU cadres were actually politicised, educated, in fact trained to staff Congress branches in the first place',[141] though in this respect Natal might have been rather exceptional.

Rowley Arenstein also suggests that SACTU's role was crucial in ensuring the party's influence over the ANC in Durban: between the two there was 'an easy relationship', he thought, though this would change after 1960. Oddly enough, the party did not enjoy the same favour with the Natal Indian Congress, in which there was during the 1950s, according to one Indian activist, 'virulent antagonism towards Communists'.[142]

In which respects did party influence make a difference to the ANC leadership's decision-making? To what extent did the party determine the choice of campaigning and the tactics that were employed? Joe Matthews told one researcher in 2003 that 'contrary to popular belief, every important decision was taken by the Party not the ANC',[143] but this was after he had spent more than a decade in Inkatha, actively opposing the party and the ANC. Perhaps, more tellingly, Brian Bunting, when interviewed by Sylvia Neame in 1986 and at that time not speaking for quotation, took the view that 'in the 50s ... practically every initiative came from the Party ... practically all the drive came from the Party. I can't think of one basic decision taken from 1950 until Rivonia or even beyond that didn't derive its authority from the party.'[144] Writing in the 1990s, Joe Slovo maintained that 'long before any of the campaigns waned, the question of "what next" had already been the subject matter for many [Central Committee] agendas'.[145] Moses Kotane's assertions in Moscow in 1961 suggest that essentially the party was in a commanding position, but it would be a simplification to conclude from this that ANC mass actions followed a preconceived party agenda. After all, in the document cited here, Kotane was seeking help from fraternal parties and he obviously needed to emphasise the decisive character of the party's role.

With respect to some of the major set pieces of the period, we can be fairly sure the party did not always make the initial campaigning decision. In the case of the Defiance Campaign, the SACP was still in the process of being constituted. Bunting notes that it was 'hard to say where the impetus ... for the campaign originated',[146] though he is careful to place Kotane and Harmel among the first defiers (for speaking at a proscribed meeting). In Cape Town a very similar programme to the Defiance Campaign was conceived by the ex-CPSA-dominated Franchise Action Committee in January 1951, but subsequent divisions within the committee forestalled whole-hearted local communist commitment to defiance.[147] The Congress of the People was originally proposed by ZK Matthews, Joe Matthews's father it is true, but hardly a communist. When in 1959 the ANC decided to plan an anti-pass campaign, according to Lionel Bernstein, he and other Johannesburg-based party members had strong reservations; they doubted that large masses of people would be willing to risk the penalties that the state would inflict on campaigners. The 'decision [was] not ours but that of the ANC'.[148] Ben Turok notes that party members were 'not allowed to form caucuses within committees of the mass movement' and they were able to disagree with each other at any debates within the Congresses. However, the Johannesburg District Committee 'met at least monthly to discuss various campaigns of the movement' and, in any case, party members, including Turok and Sisulu, predominated within the Congress Alliance secretariat, 'a kind of steering committee for the movement'.[149] And 'on difficult questions, Chief Lutuli bypassed his officials and sent for Moses' Kotane.[150] The ANC's choice of campaigning issues was often reactive and opportunistic rather than carefully premeditated – with respect to the anti-pass campaign, this was prompted by women's struggles against passes in 1958 and 1959 in which the party played a much less decisive role. What does seem to be the case is that once a decision was reached, communists both collectively and individually impacted tactically on the ways in which campaigns were conducted.

In particular, it is possible to trace a consistent adherence to united front politics in the kinds of influence that the party exerted over ANC campaigning. Two key examples help to underline this point. Moses Kotane, himself a resident in Alexandra, played an influential behind-the-scenes role in the Alexandra bus boycott, advising the local ANC leadership to include stand-holders (that is, the local landlords) in their committee, and even to back the stand-holders' association's leader, Mr Mahlangu, as chairman of the committee. It was a decision that helped the local ANC to lose control of the boycott in its final stages, as the stand-holders favoured an unpopular compromise settlement with the bus owners. ANC leaders in Alexandra, who included two new SACP recruits, Thomas Nkobi and Alfred Nzo, earned a rare rebuke from Michael Harmel in *New Age* for their 'failure ... to give positive leadership'.[151] Another communist, Moroka (Soweto) resident John Pule Motshabi, was the main organiser of a series of solidarity boycotts across the Witwatersrand.[152] But the most important way in which SACP strategic doctrines shaped campaigning was evident in the Congress Alliance's use of 'stay-at-homes'.

In the generalised calls for 'stay-at-homes' that both the party and the ANC directed at workers during this period, people were called upon to stay away from their work on specific days to support political demands. The tactic was adopted initially after advice from party lawyers that calling upon Africans to strike for reasons that had nothing to do with their terms of employments was legal, unlike strikes by Africans about wages or conditions.[153] Stay-aways differed also from normal or even general strikes, because their focus of organisation was residential townships, not workplaces, and residents could be discouraged from going to work with pickets and street canvassing. The party pioneered the use of stay-aways when, in conjunction with the Council of Non-European Trades Unions, it organised a protest against its banning on May Day in 1950. The tactic was revived in 1957 on 26 June when a Congress Alliance 'Day of Protest, Prayer and Demonstration' was linked to a SACTU call for a £1-a-day minimum wage. There were successful stay-aways by African workers in Johannesburg and Port Elizabeth – in Johannesburg mainly as a consequence of propaganda work outside factory gates. At the end of that year, Chief Luthuli, the ANC's president, called for another national protest, this time to coincide with the white elections, and to last three days. An ANC campaign directed at discouraging whites from voting for the National Party became merged with SACTU's continuing effort to achieve a minimum wage; indeed, ANC leaders discouraged any perceptions that this was to be a protest mainly about worker preoccupations. It should not, Luthuli decreed, be treated 'as though it were a trade union affair primarily … confined to delegates elected from factories'. Indeed, work in the factories should not be at the expense of work in the townships, 'where we are strong'. In fact, there would be very little factory-based preparation for the 1958 protest, and a weak turnout in Johannesburg on the first day convinced the ANC leadership to call off the protest, without consulting SACTU leaders. Meanwhile, Moses Kotane published another pamphlet in which he argued the case for drawing 'into the movement' the widest array of groups possible, including the parliamentary opposition. All the signals were present, Kotane maintained, 'of an ever-widening repudiation by Europeans of the Government's terror policy and Apartheid'.[154]

Contemporary left-wing critics of both the ANC and the party excoriated ANC leadership for 'transform[ing] an essentially working class campaign into a broad political front' and for substituting 'a false slogan … "The Nats must go"' for the original minimum wage demand. They were critical not only of ANC leaders but also of a 'group inside Congress who professed to be Marxists' for 'surrender[ing] the working class to the mercy of a middle class leadership'.[155] More recent recollections by party members do suggest that these criticisms had a degree of validity. When the tactic was first conceived within the Communist Party, it divided opinion. In particular, those members whose main organisational experience was in the union movement argued 'that strikes had to be organised at the place of work', not in townships.[156] Communists in Durban who, even in their

ANC activities, emphasised factory-based mobilisation,[157] disliked the tactic; as Rowley Arenstein put it, it was 'Johannesburg's theory, not ours'.[158] From the vantage point of the party's leadership, Ben Turok conceded that 'SACTU was often dissatisfied with the way worker issues were handled by us'. Trade unionists often felt that workers' interests were given insufficient recognition and that there was even a bias against trade unionists. Turok himself drafted one of the 1958 stay-away exhortations and he remembers 'Sisulu standing over my shoulder, monitoring the choice of language used'. Even SACP members, Turok recalled, were 'restrained in their choice of language ... about the political role of workers and the special class interests of workers'. [159] Turok and the other key communist engaged in leading the Johannesburg preparations, JB Marks, urged trade unionists 'to go into industrial areas of Johannesburg and create factory committees', as was happening around Durban if we are to believe Rowley Arenstein's and Billy Nair's testimonies. Turok thinks that in Johannesburg SACTU officials were 'economistic and workerist', and this may have been true.[160] In 1958 Bettie du Toit, an influential organiser among textile workers, was herself heavily critical of what she termed 'irresponsible strike actions', arguing that workers would be less vulnerable to sanctions and police action if they used 'alternative tactics, such as a go slow campaign at the workbench'.[161] On the whole, during the 1950s and early 1960s, the key decisions that resulted in the mobilisation of organised labour for political purposes were made by party leaders such as Moses Kotane and Walter Sisulu, who themselves were fairly disengaged from the trade unions. There were indications of continuing divisions within even the Johannesburg-based African party membership on how and when organised workers should be mobilised,[162] but top leaders' commitment to united front strategies did not waver.

RUNNING PARALLEL TO ITS Congress Alliance-directed activities, the party maintained its own separate undertakings. These included 'regular and formal meetings' by its central and district committees[163] and, between 1953 and 1962, six national delegate congresses. Congresses initially were attended by around 20 delegates but they became larger and more representative subsequently.[164] As Slovo told Sylvia Neame, 'By the time of the 5th Congress we had such an impressive network in all the main centres.' Turok attended a congress in 1954 in a deserted factory outside Johannesburg: it 'came to life when Harmel, the undoubted brain of the movement, took over'.[165] The factory was probably Julius First's Anglo Union Furniture in Industria, used at least twice for party conferences.[166] During the 1956–61 Treason Trial proceedings, Moses

Kotane was apparently attending Central Committee meetings three times a week. As noted above, those charged in the trial included a large proportion of the party's leadership, and their enforced assembly in Johannesburg facilitated such meetings, bringing together people who otherwise were restricted by bannings and other prohibitions from travelling and meeting; several autobiographies by party activists from this period make this point.[167] The Central Committee had between 12 and 15 members, with Michael Harmel, Moses Kotane and Rusty Bernstein acting as a secretariat.[168] Groups also maintained a regular schedule of at least monthly meetings, sometimes holding them in their cars if they included both African and white members.

Until 1959, aside from evaluating and planning the party's contributions to Congress campaigning, the main purposes of these meetings were to exercise oversight over recruitment and to discuss internal documents generated by the Central Committee. As noted above, recruitment was initially very cautious. There was a special 'D' category of members of people who had not been CPSA members, who had not been jailed for political offences and who did not engage with Congress bodies but whose function was to perform 'deep cover' tasks, including, later, the purchase of property for the party as well as providing safe accommodation.[169] Training and education of new members was a priority assigned to the groups. Ben Turok ran a study class with new Alexandra members, and he recollects coaching Thomas Nkobi and Alfred Nzo in dialectical materialism in his car. Fundraising was another task. None of the communists themselves had easy access to private fortunes though a few came from quite wealthy families.[170] In practice, the main source of party funding was sympathetic Indian traders.[171] Yusuf Dadoo's exalted social status within the Indian community as 'Gandhi's favourite son' (with his picture in every Indian home)[172] was particularly helpful in eliciting these donations.[173] Party members reciprocated this generosity as several of them for the first time became business proprietors, lending their names to serve as 'fronts' for Indian-run businesses threatened with closure under the Group Areas Act.[174] Indians in Natal also contributed most of the donations that helped to pay for printing *New Age* – a reward for the newspaper's defence of rights threatened by Group Areas.[175] A more surprising source of help was recent Yugoslav immigrants, who had cornered the wholesale meat trade in Johannesburg and who donated the meat used to feed delegates at the Congress of the People. Rica Hodgson made contact with this group through her brothers, who ran a grocery business in the Johannesburg produce market: to her delight she discovered that several of the Yugoslavs had retained communist affiliations from their old homeland.[176]

No copies of the documents circulated through the party's clandestine organisation for this period are available yet in any archive, but they would have included statements published by the party in the legal newspapers and journals, including Kotane's *South Africa's Way Forward* and Michael Harmel's cautious assessment of Khrushchev's revelations at the Soviet party's twentieth congress. Apparently the Central Committee devoted 'several meetings' to a consideration of the congress's proceedings,[177] before concluding that, despite the 'great accomplishments and achievements of Stalin, whose place in history is secure', communists needed to acknowledge 'mistakes', including 'violations of collective leadership' and the framing of innocent people. 'Violations of socialist law' were at least partly attributable to the 'incorrect theory of the intensification of class struggle after the defeat of capitalism'.[178] On the whole, this kind of rationalisation sufficed for most South African communists, though Hilda Bernstein much later told one researcher that '1956 was a key year for me ... because of the revelations of Khrushchev'.[179] That year, the Soviet invasion of Hungary set off 'another crisis of belief'.[180] Pauline Podbrey, who had returned from Hungary very disillusioned with her experiences and who refused to rejoin the party on her return, told one researcher that before the invasion but after the uprising, the Central Committee 'sent a delegate' to Durban, 'to ask us back'. 'All the things you criticised', she was assured, 'have been put right.'[181] In Johannesburg, Monty and Myrtle Berman protested against the invasion and were expelled, though they had a history of disaffection with the party line: they refused to join the Congress of Democrats, for example, because it was a whites-only organisation.[182] More typical among Johannesburg-based communists was Bram Fischer's reaction to Khrushchev's revelations. He once asked Bob Hepple if there was any authority that refuted the reports about Stalin's crimes. Hepple told him the case against Stalin was unchallengeable. On hearing this, Bram Fischer shrugged his shoulders and said, 'Well, we now know what to avoid when we establish communism here.'[183]

In Cape Town, there was sufficient disquiet over the Hungarian events for Fred Carneson to summon a meeting of group leaders at which he explained that the country had been a home of reaction for decades,[184] an argument that was subsequently reproduced in *New Age*. Hilda Bernstein when interviewed in 1984 suggested that the invasion did not really disturb the party's composure, though 'there were a few people ... white intellectuals, who were very upset'.[185] These intellectuals may have included Bernstein herself as well as Ruth First, whose political differences over communist orthodoxy were a continual source of domestic tension with Joe Slovo.[186] Bob Hepple attributes what he thinks was a spread of ideological disaffection to the absence of any real independent activity by the party during the mid-1950s. In certain areas, he reports, party units, including his own, 'had fallen apart well before 1960 because they found their meetings a waste of time'.[187]

Aside from such external sources of dissension, the issue that party members most frequently mention as a matter over which they disagreed was secrecy. Clandestine operational rules were not the problem and the use of false names, coded communications, discreet venues and an organisational structure that kept the identity of party membership even internally hidden were accepted as common sense, even within families. But there were arguments at all the early congresses over whether the party should publicise its existence. At the end of 1955 there seems to have been an early decision to do so because Bob Hepple was given a party 'manifesto' to take with him on a trip to London for printing, but then the operation was halted because Moses Kotane had received advice against it while visiting East Germany.[188] Generally, Moses Kotane and other party leaders who worked most closely with non-communist ANC principals favoured silence in any case, fearing that an open announcement would alienate tacit allies, as did trade unionists. In October 1959, after the fourth congress held on the premises of the furniture factory owned by Ruth First's father, the launch of *African Communist* (though not initially identified as a party journal) was the consequence of a compromise suggested by Bernstein after a debate in which Joe Slovo had proposed the party's 'emergence'.[189] The first issue was cyclostyled in a thousand copies and from then onwards the distribution of party propaganda would become a main function of the groups. The British Communist Party arranged and paid for the printing of the next few editions of the journal after being asked to by South Africans living in London.[190] Secrecy about the party's existence was an issue connected to the way its leaders understood their relationship with the ANC, and there is at least one significant indication that this too remained contentious. John Pule Motshabi much later suggested that the admission into the party's top leadership of African 'intellectuals' was opposed by African workers in the party, including himself, David Bopape and JB Marks, and that it was prompted partly by party leaders trying to reduce potential support for Marks's bid for the party chairmanship. 'There 'then came a major reconciliation', he conceded.[191] Motshabi did not supply a full explanation for why there needed to be a reconciliation, but Turok's autobiography implies that Marks had become disenchanted with the downgrading of 'purely worker issues during the One Pound a Day campaign'.[192] If this was the case, then JB Marks's election as party chairman at the 1962 conference would have been the reconciliation to which Motshabi refers, an effort by the leadership to bring back into the fold advocates of a stronger 'class-based' line.

AFTER THE ANC'S BANNING at the outset of the State of Emergency on 31 March 1960, the distinction for party activists between 'legal' undertakings conducted within the Congress Alliance and illegal party work disappeared. In contrast to its development in the 1950s, this phase of the Communist Party's development has been the focus of recent scholarship, centred especially on its role in the decisions which led to the ANC's embrace of armed insurgency. In particular, Stephen Ellis's work has offered major revisions in what had been the general understanding of how this happened.

The party's own historians and older scholarship projected the adoption of violence as a consequence of the banning of mass campaigning and a process in which, simultaneously during 1961, non-communist ANC leaders and Communist Party strategists started questioning the utility of the tactics they had employed through the 1950s. South African researchers assembled in the SADET project, drawing upon oral testimonies from Umkhonto veterans they collected in the late 1990s and early 2000s, were the first to encounter evidence that the Communist Party had made a collective decision to take up arms before the end of 1960, though individuals in both organisations had begun to consider the use of violence much earlier.[193] Ellis's research exploits fresh testimony and draws upon additional archival sources to confirm that both among Communist Party and ANC rank and file, some people were ready to used armed action well before 1960, especially in the Eastern Cape. When it came to systematic organisation of urban guerrilla warfare, the party made the key decisions well before the ANC was able to, and it was to predominate within Umkhonto's command structure.[194]

In the standard historiography about this period, the period between the Sharpeville Massacre and the Stay-at-Home called in May 1961 in protest against South Africa's declaration of a Republic is presented as the time when it became clear to 'the leaders of the Liberation movement and the Communist Party', in Michael Harmel's words, that 'it was necessary to abandon "non-violence"' as impractical, a recognition that was 'strengthened by the temper of the masses'.[195] In reality, the party's own expansion of organised activity during the Emergency as well as the survival of ANC activist networks in certain areas suggests that there remained scope for non-violent kinds of militant opposition.

Johannesburg-based party leaders heard rumours that the police were about to arrest Congress supporters en masse just before the Emergency came into force. Even so, most of the party's leadership in its main centres were detained, and 150 or so communists were arrested altogether. Moses Kotane and Michael Harmel were among those who evaded arrest to live in nine 'safe houses', some of them supplied by 'D category' party adherents. Ben Turok, who shared various cramped quarters with them for several months, claims that these refuges became hubs 'of campaigning and planning'.[196] A small group of members including Ruth First spent the months of the Emergency in Swaziland: 'it soon became a typical exile community, fraught with tensions, real and imagined', as Norman Levy recalls.[197] On several occasions Kotane travelled around Johannesburg in a car driven by Wolfie Kodesh, making contact with any party and ANC network whose members remained at liberty.[198] Re-establishing the party's networks was made more difficult, apparently, because Michael Harmel had mislaid a secret list of contacts, one of a series of breaches of security procedures for which he would acquire a reputation.[199] Late in the Emergency, Ben Turok was able to visit Port Elizabeth to discuss the 'rebuilding' of organisation with Raymond Mhlaba. In June, what Harmel termed an 'enlarged Central Committee meeting', and what Bernstein suggests was a 'rump' of the Central Committee, decided, despite objections from Kotane, that the party should announce its existence, a decision that was publicised by a leaflet. Bunting notes that ANC people in townships helped to distribute this leaflet and that by the end of the Emergency 'the party had a team of several hundred activists at its disposal in the Johannesburg townships'.[200] A visitor from the Communist Party of Great Britain brought £1,000 in response to an appeal sent by the South Africans in April.[201] This helped to pay for printing and the cost of renting flats for hideouts. Harmel's memo, written in 1961, suggested that the party became stronger during the Emergency, and in Johannesburg at least, Bernstein thinks, the Emergency made relations with the ANC easier. The party recruited more members from among the detainees, which helped to expand its reach among ANC followers who remained committed to activism. At the same time, because of the end of open Congress Alliance campaigning, it became possible 'to allocate more cadres to purely party work'.[202]

Such claims about organisational resilience need to be treated with circumspection. But it does seem quite plausible that a body which over the preceding decade had made a point of recruiting people who were already leaders of other groups might well have expanded its influence within the wider movement. And where non-banned Alliance partners had a well-organised local presence, activist campaigning remained possible. In Durban, the Natal Indian Congress supplied offices and networks through which it was still possible to mobilise mass protest during the Emergency: Babenia, who worked as the Natal Indian Congress's district organiser, supplies examples of such protests. He also shows how leaders and members of ANC branches were in certain areas able to regroup around the residents' associations, which, in any case, were often led by Congress activists: the KwaMashu residents' association was a case in point, being led by Curnick Ndhlovu, a party member. Here, partly because of the survival of active ANC networks with a popular following, the party's influence came under stronger challenge: Babenia identifies a group of vigorous ANC leaders who were to become increasingly hostile to the party in Durban.[203]

During the Emergency, the party's organisational structure became more elaborate. A subgroup of the Central Committee, a working committee, was assembling for weekly meetings by the end of the Emergency. There are references in memoirs of this period to the functioning of area committees, which may have been a consequence of the growth in the number of groups, though it would have also helped to increase security, as groups would cease having direct representation on the district bodies. Several sources indicate that the pace of recruitment increased and that it became less selective. Jean Middleton joined in late 1960 after becoming friends with Hilda Bernstein, whom she knew from their shared activities on the Peace Council. She had 'heard of only two potential recruits who refused to join, and both promised to keep the secret'. In the 1950s, the party would only recruit people after its leaders were quite certain about their motivations. Her all-white unit or group 'focused on contact with young people', concentrating on recent entrants to the Congress of Democrats, whom they mentored through a series of activities that tested commitment and courage, such as night-time spray-painting of ANC slogans.[204] More than a decade later, it was still possible to make out the text of one of their exhortations in a run-down park on Yeoville's Rockey Street: 'An attack on communism is an attack on you'.[205] In general, in the cases of Jean Middleton and her closest comrades, their work emphasised propaganda circulation and one of their tasks was the compilation of mailing lists for Hilda Bernstein. As the vetting and criteria for selection of new members loosened, the party became more vulnerable. One of the recruits to Jean Middleton's group in late 1962 was Gerard Ludi, the first policeman to infiltrate the party.[206] He would later complain that following his entry into the party, 'in reality there was little action beyond manufacturing and distributing vast quantities of posters and leaflets'.[207] In general, party leaders now favoured evidence of commitment over doctrinal preparedness:

recruiters were enjoined to 'discard the conservative approach[es]' that had prevailed earlier.[208] Jean Middleton later joined an area committee, also all-white, and here she became more familiar with the party's overall structure. Habitually, area committee members used code names in speaking with and about each other, as had been the case with the group, where individuals used different names in the different organisational echelons.[209]

The party's propaganda capacity was considerably strengthened by the return from London of Mac Maharaj, who spent a year in East Germany, starting in March 1961, undergoing a printing apprenticeship and learning sabotage techniques during the second half of his stay. He joined an SACP unit in Johannesburg and repaired two old lithograph machines that the East Germans had donated to the party in 1958 and a second-hand linotype press purchased locally. He took over the editorship of *Sports Parade*, a fortnightly legal title the party had bought to replace the now-banned *New Age*. He joined a propaganda committee otherwise composed of Ruth First, Duma Nokwe and Dan Thloome.[210] Maharaj's skills were badly needed, for before his arrival one party unit had been reduced to reproducing stickers with a child's toy printing set.[211]

The party's decision to organise armed groups was probably encouraged by the reports it was receiving of rural rebellion. Moses Kotane, writing in 1961, claimed the 'Party could report successes of the peasants in Pondoland, Sekhukhuniland, Zululand and W Transvaal'.[212] Ben Turok visited the leaders of the Mpondo Mountain Committee in November 1960 on behalf of the ANC and was asked when Congress was going to supply them with weapons. There were earlier contacts, before the Emergency, between the Mpondos and the Port Elizabeth SACP–ANC principals after requests 'for assistance against government troops'.[213] The Port Elizabeth leaders were divided, with Govan Mbeki favouring helping the Mpondos and Raymond Mhlaba against this because he was convinced the revolt would fail.[214] As we have seen, Mbeki was atypical among the local ANC leadership for his interest in extending the ANC's reach into the countryside, working with migrant worker hostel dwellers in New Brighton.[215] Mhlaba himself had no objections to using violence; indeed, he recalls, he had suggested that 'we should fight the Boers' several times at SACP meetings and discussed the issue in some depth with Rusty Bernstein in 1959.[216] Certain narratives emphasise discussions among the Emergency detainees as the main generator of the party's policy turn on violence,[217] though, interestingly, Bernstein, who with Slovo was the last of the detainees to be released, tells us that on the last few days of their detention 'we [had] run out of things to talk about'.[218] Ben Turok maintains that the key agency was supplied by Michael Harmel, who wrote a strategic reassessment during the Emergency, which he presented to Kotane.

Yusuf Dadoo seems to have taken part in discussions of Harmel's paper because by the time he left South Africa in June he had become an advocate of 'a radical departure in tactics and strategy ... for a turn to armed struggle'. While visiting Peking in October, Dadoo explained to Mao that 'South Africa's armed struggle could not follow China's strategy of a long march' – an argument that implies that he too, as in the case of Raymond Mhlaba, had reservations about an initially peasant-based insurgency. Mao listened politely but was non-committal apparently, though the Chinese did provide military training the following year. For the Chinese, their priority in receiving their South African visitors was to lecture them about the pitfalls of Soviet revisionism.[219] In the 1990s Joe Matthews told researchers that he and Michael Harmel discussed the proposed policy switch with Soviet officials in November 1960 as members of a delegation that the SACP sent to attend an international conference of communist parties,[220] but Russian sources working with archival materials believe that this happened later, in 1961. This seems more likely, as the documents that survive from 1960 in which party leaders are obviously describing their organisation to close 'fraternal' allies do not refer to violence. Soviet officials did agree to provide money, $30,000,[221] which probably explains how the party was able to buy a farm in Rivonia on the outskirts of Johannesburg in mid-1961 to serve as its headquarters as well as renting another rural property nearby, Trevallyn.[222]

Formal acceptance of violent tactics took place at a conference held on 16 December 1960. Before this meeting, a version of Harmel's paper evocatively entitled 'What Is to Be Done' was circulated to party groups as a 'study document'.[223] In Bernstein's memoir the resolution on violence was 'squeezed into the agenda at the tail end of the conference' and was discussed cursorily.[224] The conference had a formal agenda, which even included greetings from 'fraternal parties' in China, Algeria, Britain, Tunisia, Sudan, Morocco, France, the Netherlands, Réunion and Martinique.[225] The Central Committee's report noted a 25 per cent membership increase during the Emergency and improvements in morale and subscriptions and the production of 'a regular organ in the African language, *Inkululeko*'.[226] The report also described 'profoundly revolutionary actions of the Pondo people', which had 'raised sharply the role and usefulness of armed force in the course of the South African People's struggle'.[227] Over a three-day meeting most of the time was taken up by Michael Harmel's report on the events at the international communist meeting he had recently returned from, which itself had been preoccupied with the Sino–Soviet dispute. His description of this part of the proceedings was a revelation for his listeners because until then 'we did not appreciate the depth of bitterness'.[228] Indeed, the year before, a *New Age* report had quoted Chou En-lai reassuring the Soviet party that 'Bonds between China and the USSR [were] unbreakable'.[229] All accounts of the meeting concur that the discussion of the resolution was abrupt and there was no real disagreement. Turok has Bernstein reading the resolution and, after its adoption, burning the document, but in fact a text has survived. The wording of the resolution is reproduced in a typed internal memorandum probably written in late 1962 or early 1963. The resolution first acknowledged that 'the people's movement could no longer' maintain 'exclusively non-violent forms of political struggle' given 'new government tactics' and the risks of 'disillusionment and spread of defeatism'. Therefore, it urged, activists should undertake 'a campaign of education and explanation be carried out within the movement to prepare for forcible forms of struggle when these became necessary or desirable'. In the meanwhile, 'the Party CC should take steps to initiate the training and equipping of selected personnel in new methods of struggle, and thus prepare the nucleus of an adequate apparatus to lead struggles of a more forcible and violent character'.[230] This wording stops short of an immediate and unequivocal commitment to armed action. Bernstein's memory was that 'we took what was no more than an interim decision. The Central Committee would consider the matter further', though in the meantime small units would be established 'to familiarise themselves with the practice and techniques of forms of armed struggle'.[231]

Reporting in Moscow in November 1961, Moses Kotane told Soviet party officials that at the conference, they had agreed that in future they would 'employ some elements of violence during our mass struggles, such as picketing and disruption of communications' and a subcommittee of the Central Committee would consider any further steps 'to be taken in anticipation of armed struggle'. This subcommittee would obtain small arms and organise training in the use of home-made explosives.[232] Bob Hepple, who helped organise the conference and attended it as a member of the Johannesburg District Committee, is emphatic that there was 'no suggestion at this time of full-scale guerrilla war'.[233] According to Turok, Kotane remained critical of the decision to use violence for the next couple of years at least, though he later told Bunting that he had thought 'the resort to violence was unavoidable'.[234] At the time, Hepple recalls Kotane as arguing that 'there [was] still room for their old methods if we are imaginative and determined enough'.[235] Perhaps reluctantly, Kotane nevertheless played a crucial intermediary role in persuading Chief Luthuli to accede in June 1961 to the establishment of Umkhonto we Sizwe, though Mandela's voice was also very important in this. In fact, Luthuli remained apprehensive about the embrace of even limited violence and was explicitly critical of the ANC's apparent abandonment of 'the militant non-violent techniques' of its former mass campaigning.[236] Govan Mbeki attended one meeting at which Luthuli 'wanted to know why the decision had been taken without him'. Luthuli was angry, and 'threatened to resign as president'.[237] More widely within the Natal provincial ANC leadership there was unease about Umkhonto's activities, if Bruno Mtolo's account is to be trusted.[238] While African communists remained deferential to the Chief, their comrades were less polite. When Mandela announced his intention to visit Luthuli after returning from Ethiopia, Joe Slovo's reaction was derisive: 'Why report to that old buffer?' he was reported to have said.[239]

December's decision was opposed in Durban by at least one locally influential personality who had not attended the meeting. Rowley Arenstein felt that the move was premature and unnecessary and that the party should instead 'emphasise building organisation in the factories'. In Durban, SACTU was still capable of maintaining robust industrial militancy, Arenstein believed. He was also critical of what he perceived to be 'the undermining of the ANC leadership with establishment of ad hoc committees that left out the leaders of the ANC'.[240] Arenstein was also predisposed to side with China in the Sino-Soviet rift at a time when the party was still undecided on the issue, and was called to a meeting in Johannesburg and reproved sharply by Kotane. Every time the party made a decision to which Arenstein was in opposition, he scolded: 'You are standing alone. Why is this?'[241] Arenstein recalled that after the December conference the Central Committee had circulated a statement condemning Mao's position as unMarxist, but no such attack appeared in *African Communist* during 1961; and in October 1961, after receiving an unsolicited invitation from the Chinese, the party would send six of its members, including Raymond Mhlaba, to China for military training. How much influence Arenstein's views had is questionable, even among SACP members who were close friends of his such as the trade unionists George and Vera Ponnen and Ronnie Kasrils, a cousin of his wife. Kasrils joined the party in 1961 and was inducted into Arenstein's group; shortly afterwards he became a resourceful regional commander for Umkhonto in Durban.[242]

No time was lost in recruiting 'proto armed units' in each of the party's districts. Bernstein notes that by June 1961 these had 'been running for some time'. The party's small group of ex-servicemen were conspicuous in the leadership of the earliest units: Wolfie Kodesh remembers former soldiers were given area command roles.[243] Bernstein also refers to a separate force into which Nelson Mandela was enrolling ANC volunteers, 'outside ANC structures'. Hepple remembers that Mandela was present at the meeting on 16 December, sitting next to Sisulu in a back seat and saying little: Joe Slovo told him then that Mandela was attending as an observer.[244] He accepted that explanation at the time and, writing more than fifty years later, Hepple still believed that it was 'entirely credible that Mandela was co-opted onto the Central Committee', but as an individual, not a communist.[245] Slovo offered a similar explanation to Stephanie Kemp some years later: Mandela's membership was only a 'constitutional technicality' so that he could attend the party's committee meetings: he wasn't a communist.[246] But other people who were present that day would recall that Mandela had joined the party by then.[247] John Pule Motshabi's observations about Mandela's recruitment well before 1960 seem to have gone unchallenged when he made them in 1980. In an internal memo he wrote for his party group, he noted that Mandela had joined the party together with Sisulu as early as 1954 or thereabouts. He referred again to Mandela's membership at a party gathering in Lusaka in 1982.[248] Two decades later Motshabi remained aggrieved that, immediately on joining, both Mandela and Sisulu had been co-opted onto the Central Committee: 'why do they not begin [by] being ordinary members before they are elevated to such positions'.[249] Brian Bunting told Sylvia Neame in 1986 that Mandela was at the meeting 'as a member of the CC ... the only time I met him in that capacity'.[250] In 1962 Hilda Bernstein knew that Mandela was a member of the party.[251] John Motshabi may have been confusing Mandela's recruitment with Sisulu's, for there is no corroborative evidence or testimony to suggest that Mandela joined the party before 1960. He was, however, on easy and familiar terms with party leaders. His friendship with Michael Harmel dated from his attendance at the CPSA night school in Johannesburg's Fox Street in the 1940s.[252]

Even so, given the secrecy even among members about who belonged to the party and its committees, the evidence for Mandela's membership is not quite definite. In 1967, in litigation to get his name removed from the liquidator's list of party members, Mandela insisted he had never been a member of either the CPSA or 'of its successor, the South African Communist Party'.[253] The memorandum cited above containing the 1960 resolution, written probably at the end of 1962, refers to Umkhonto we Sizwe's command as constituted by six men, five of whom were communists and one other a person 'who we regard as a close party supporter on the verge of party membership'.[254] By that stage Mandela was in prison, but there is no record of Umkhonto's command having been reconstituted at that time and it is possible that this sixth person might have been Mandela. But whatever Mandela's ideological political convictions may have been then, Hepple's impression was that he was certainly one of the keener supporters of the policy shift, prepared to take violence much further towards a fully militarised conflict than is suggested in the qualified wording of the resolution.

There is another way of thinking about Mandela's SACP membership. If we accept that the larger proportion of evidence suggests that he was a member, or was at least looked upon by other party supporters as someone who was in the process of becoming a member, questions can still be asked about his loyalties and commitments. For white SACP members and, probably, the older African SACP members of Kotane's generation, the party, or 'family' as they called it, was their primary political affiliation. For Mandela – and possibly Sisulu – joining the party may have been an engagement they welcomed, but their first emotional and moral affiliation may have remained with the ANC. Mandela's main reason for joining the party may have been simply instrumental; its leadership was willing to use violence at a time when the ANC was still divided on the issue and its surviving structures could not immediately be drawn into an armed formation.[255] Bob Hepple discussed political issues with Mandela during his trial and he concluded then, and still believed many years later, that Mandela remained a nationalist, 'never committed to the CP's aim of a socialist South Africa'.[256] And even after joining the party – the most likely date for this was at some point in 1960 – Mandela may have still been quite capable of undertaking actions independently of it, such as setting up under his own command a separate armed force, as Bernstein observed.

The scholarship on the subsequent establishment of Umkhonto we Sizwe is well developed. The freshly available archival evidence confirms the degree to which party members controlled its command structure and shaped operational decisions. In Durban, Umkhonto's first Regional Command was composed of SACP members entirely, all of whom, except for Ronnie Kasrils, were trade unionists and certain of them senior SACTU officials. Here, none of the local ANC notables who were not trade unionists belonged to Natal Umkhonto structures – a reflection of continuing political disagreements in the provincial ANC over the decision to use violence.[257] In Cape Town, Fred Carneson joined Umkhonto as regional political commissar and played a key role in early recruitments, for this purpose concentrating on left-wing groups among university students, white and black, and fellow servicemen veterans.[258] One of Carneson's recruits was Chris Hani. A training camp conducted by Denis Goldberg at Mamre, 30 miles north of Cape Town, assembled 27 young men, drawn mainly from the Nyanga Cultural and Social Organisation, a front for the Youth League. The proceedings were to constitute a key component in the prosecution's case against Denis Goldberg in the Rivonia Trial two years later, and there are different versions of what actually happened at the camp, but it seems likely that the purpose was to introduce participants to ideas about guerrilla warfare even if not all of them were aware of the programme's purpose. Albie Sachs visited on the second day, contributing talks on political economy and legal rights before the police arrived, having been summoned by the owner of the property that Goldberg had hired. Before leaving, the police ordered all present to report to Caledon Square police headquarters for further questioning.[259]

By late 1962 South African communists were ready to claim that 'the overall strategy and direction of policy of Umkhonto we Sizwe at all times remains in the hands of the leadership of the party'.[260] But this may have been a limitation. If it is true that during the Emergency the party's own organisational network strengthened, as its leaders claimed retrospectively, its networks were still insufficiently developed to supply good intelligence for on-the-spot decision-making. As Bernstein concedes, Mandela's decision to call off the anti-Republic stay-away after the first day was based on faulty information about the scale of its response outside Johannesburg. As Stephen Ellis has argued, it is quite probable that for Mandela himself and the others directly involved in setting up Umkhonto, the main purpose of the stay-away was to elicit the kind of repressive response from the state that would demonstrate to their own constituency that the days of non-violence were over.[261]

Umkhonto's command was preoccupied with initial training, the production of home-made explosives,[262] and the planning of the first sabotage operations[263] through the remainder of 1961. But planning for more ambitious guerrilla warfare began in early 1962, shortly after Mandela's departure on his African tour. One purpose of Mandela's tour was to secure support for an expansion of armed operations. Subsequently, as is now well known, in mid-1962, after touring Africa and meeting Kaunda and other continental statesmen, Mandela realised that an armed force in which command was formally shared by the SACP and the ANC as alliance partners would engender opposition from potentially sympathetic African governments. In various meetings with communists he argued that the future insurgency would have to be under ANC and African leadership. It is possible at this stage that he may have reconsidered his own membership of the Party. Paul Landau's very thorough exploration of Mandela's thinking at this time does suggest that he had a very different view of the party's leadership role in national leadership from that of his comrades in the SACP. He was ready, for example, in a reflective commentary he wrote at the time, to consider the possibility that the 'working cooperation between a non-Marxist political organisation and the CP ceases because policy differences emerge'.[264] Taken together, the SACP's reliance on Mandela's stature and power in influencing the wider movement, and Mandela's own willingness to downgrade the party's role in Umkhonto's command, are reasons to be sceptical about the party's own claims of being able to 'direct' the insurgency. In any case, as we shall see, the party itself was divided about the merits of the strategic vision embraced by Joe Slovo and other Umkhonto commanders.

After the December conference, or the fifth party congress as it became known within SACP history, Michael Harmel and Moses Kotane were tasked with drafting a party programme. The product of their efforts, *The Road to South African Freedom*, was adopted at the party's sixth congress, in October 1962.[265]

The *Road* opened by explaining that in an era in which capitalism had lost its creative function, it was a 'dogmatic distortion' to insist that African countries in a pre-capitalist stage of development must necessarily pass through a period of capitalism before achieving socialism', and that with external support 'young African states' could follow non-capitalist paths of development. National democracies could then supply transitional incubators for socialism. A substantial section followed that elaborated the argument that South African experience embodied a colonialism of a special type against which the 'forces for change' struggled to achieve a national democratic revolution. This revolution was defined in the Freedom Charter, which would 'lay the indispensable basis for the advance of our country on non-capitalist lines'. Within the black population there were no 'acute or antagonistic class divisions' because white monopolisation of economic and political power had 'strangled the development of African capitalists'. In this struggle every channel of legal protest was undergoing closure and, in such a setting, patriots and democrats would need to 'organise guerrilla armies and undertake various acts of armed resistance, culminating in a mass insurrection'. However, the party would continue to use all forms of struggle available, not just violent actions. It was possible that 'contradictions within the ruling class' induced by the activities of 'revolutionary and militant people's forces' might open the way for a peaceful and negotiated transfer of power before an insurrection The struggle for national liberation would be 'headed' by the ANC, but even so, for the Communist Party, its 'immediate task' would be to 'lead the fight for the national liberation of the non-White people'. The distinction between 'heading' and 'leading' is left unclear, an omission that has invited surprisingly little attention from the party's critics.[266] The final part of the document spelled out immediate programmatic aims for a people's democratic state, which would still allow scope for 'the interests of private business when these are not incompatible with the public interest'.[267]

Drafts of the document were circulated to groups before the congress and a committee led by Harmel and Kotane met at Bob Hepple's house in August and September to review 'hundreds' of suggestions for changes.[268] Hepple acknowledges that the document borrowed quite heavily from the phraseology used at the international meeting Michael Harmel had attended in November 1960, and Irina Filatova has found that the *Road* 'reproduces' that meeting's usage of 'national democracy'.[269] According to Bob Hepple, the references to post-apartheid South Africa were deliberately ambiguous, to 'bridge the gap between those who envisaged a rapid transition to socialism and those who did not'.[270] One earlier draft spelled out the party's 'supreme aims', including a proletarian dictatorship; this does not appear in the final document. It also suggested that the achievement of national democracy 'on the basis of a lasting alliance between workers and rural people' would facilitate 'change along non-capitalist lines to socialism'. The same document cited Ghana, Guinea and Mali as existing African national democracies.[271] Vagueness about final goals probably helped to build a broad agreement around the programme's underpinning arguments, though at least one SACP member who would play a key role in Umkhonto, David Kitson, remained critical of the internal colonialism argument. He led a faction still influenced by Andrei Zhdanov's arguments that maintained that the South African setting required an 'anti-imperialist programme' led by a working-class movement.[272] The implication of this view would be that the party itself should recruit a mass membership rather than functioning as a vanguard within the Congress Alliance – an option that was rejected at the meeting in May 1960, when the party decided to proclaim its existence.[273]

The flexible language about violence probably had the same consensual purpose. For by the date of the party's sixth congress, the communists who were directing Umkhonto had already developed an outline conception of how they would conduct guerrilla warfare. Joe Slovo, Govan Mbeki and Arthur Goldreich were the main authors of this plan and they began work on their draft during the first half of 1962. Goldreich was the named purchaser of Lilliesleaf farm at Rivonia and posed as its proprietor while maintaining his livelihood as the designer of window displays for one of Johannesburg's smartest department stores. Like Slovo, he was a military veteran, though, unlike Slovo, he had real combat experience in the Israeli Palmach. To help Goldreich maintain appearances, a group of migrant workers from Sekhukhuneland were brought in as farmhands; 'a gardener for every weed', as Norma Kitson sardonically noted.[274] The party's Sekhukhuneland networks were also to generate some of the early Umkhonto recruits. After leaving Port Elizabeth in late 1962 when the enforced closure of *New Age* ended his employment as a reporter, Govan Mbeki began living at Rivonia full-time.[275] At this juncture the farm at Rivonia had become the de facto base both for the party's and Umkhonto's leadership. Party leaders also used the farm as a site for short-wave radio transmissions and sending morse code messages, enabling the police to identify the location with direction-finding equipment supplied by British intelligence. The police were also alerted to the presence of Walter Sisulu and other party or Umkhonto principals through reports from neighbours: police records confirm that the farm was under observation from the end of 1962.[276] Trevallyn was not. The police only discovered its existence some weeks after the Rivonia operation when the landlord of the now deserted property reported a burglary. The police searched the empty house and found documents describing plans for manufacturing explosives.[277]

In 'Operation Mayibuye', the title Umkhonto's planners accorded to the envisaged campaign, 'armed resistance leading to victory by military means' would become the 'main content' of mass revolutionary action. Undertakings by the 'political wing' of the movement would be relegated to an auxiliary function. Cuba supplied the inspiration for believing that small guerrilla bands could serve as detonators for a general uprising. Support from African and socialist governments would significantly alter the balance of forces and, given such help, the state's structure might 'collapse far sooner than we envisage'. Operation Mayibuye would begin with the establishment of sea-borne supply lines at four points along South Africa's coast and border to sustain the landings and subsequent activities of four bands of trained fighters. These would have sufficient weaponry at their disposal to arm several thousand local recruits. The offensive would begin with attacks on strategic targets in four rural theatres.[278] Encouraged by the development of its own rural following in Sekhukhuneland, the party's strategists were increasingly convinced that 'rural areas are no longer placid backwaters' and that local struggles in rural settings were the 'starting point that can ignite the South African revolution'.[279] This was a contention that Mbeki had been proposing for years, an argument that would reach its most developed form in his book on peasant revolt, written in 1960 though only appearing in print in London four years later.[280]

Debate about the merits of this scheme helped to preoccupy the party's leadership for almost a year before Joe Slovo's departure from South Africa at the beginning of June 1963. A Central Committee meeting first considered the plan in detail in November 1962, shortly after the sixth congress.[281] One of Slovo's purposes in leaving was to obtain support from the ANC's exiled leadership for the plan, but he left behind him strong disagreements about its viability. Already in early 1962, a Central Committee document was expressing concerns 'that in our recent activities, our whole organisation has tended to focus too much of its attention on discussion of political sabotage, and too little on the development of mass political work'.[282] SACP principals who were not involved in Umkhonto's command would find additional sources of such worries in Operation Mayibuye's 'main content'. Rusty Bernstein thought the plan's foundations were set in 'military thinking at its worst' and he believed that it was premised on a 'wholly inadequate analysis of the balance of power'.[283] He maintained his objections after Slovo's departure and prepared a careful critique that he brought with him to Rivonia on 11 July, the day of the police raid on Lilliesleaf farm, where most of the South African-based Central Committee members were arrested. He remembers that Bram Fischer disliked the plan, as did Ahmed Kathrada. Bob Hepple, co-opted onto the Central Committee, was against its adoption and he remembers Walter Sisulu and Ruth First 'equivocating'.[284] Bram Fischer later testified in his trial that when the document was first reviewed by the party's Central Committee, it was rejected with 'complete disapproval'.[285] Sisulu later testified in court that his own feeling was that the Operation failed to 'correctly outline the tasks before the national movement' and that it was impractical.[286] Ben Turok was in prison by the time of Slovo's departure, though retrospectively he thought it was 'incredibly unrealistic and ambitious'. He notes that Ivan Schermbrucker 'condemned the exercise unreservedly'.[287] Bram Fischer explained his views at his trial in 1966. He thought the plan was 'wholly impractical' and 'wholly unsuited to the situation in South Africa' given the 'prevailing conditions'. One of his more specific objections, which he didn't elaborate in his trial statement, was the plan's reliance on external direction and supply.

None of these issues were resolved by the time the police arrived at Lilliesleaf farm on 11 July. Here they found and arrested Raymond Mhlaba, Govan Mbeki, Ahmed Kathrada, Lionel Bernstein, Walter Sisulu, Bob Hepple and Denis Goldberg. Goldberg had left Cape Town, intending to cross the Bechuanaland border, but he was persuaded to prolong his stay in Johannesburg so that he could use his expertise as an engineer and advise Umkhonto's commanders on how to make explosive bombs and landmines.

Among the documentation the police found later at Trevallyn was the report he had written for this purpose. Arthur Goldreich was away from Lilliesleaf when the police arrived and they arrested him on his return later in the evening. The police also took away with them a hoard of documentation including incriminating materials left behind by Nelson Mandela, more than a hundred maps detailing sabotage targets, and a copy of 'Operation Mayibuye', which they discovered hidden behind one of the hubcaps on Arthur Goldreich's car. After the Rivonia arrests, Bram Fischer advised Wilton Mkwayi that Umkhonto should revert to simple operations using home-made materials. Fischer viewed the exodus of party leadership into exile as unnecessary and a dereliction of responsibility, a feeling that was shared quite widely among communists who remained inside South Africa.[288]

Despite their critics, Slovo and Mbeki seemed to believe that by the time of Slovo's departure, the proposal had been sanctioned by the party's internal leadership.[289] That seems to have been the impression further down Umkhonto's command structure, for Babenia remembers that by mid-1963 he and his comrades were experiencing 'pressure on us from within the movement to move in a more insurrectionist direction'.[290] In April 1963, Jack and Rica Hodgson were told to leave South Africa and use their more protected status as British citizens to lease a farm on the Bechuanaland border that would serve as a crossing point for guerrilla recruits. However, they had just time to harvest a crop of carrots before they were compelled by the colonial authorities to depart.[291] Bruno Mtolo claims that he was summoned to Rivonia from Natal in May 1963 and told by Walter Sisulu and Govan Mbeki to relay a demand to the Durban leadership to supply 200 urban and 2,000 rural recruits for local military training.[292] In Cape Town, after the arrests at Rivonia, Fred Carneson was scathing about Umkhonto's activities at a District Committee meeting. In his view the Communist Party shouldn't be involved in sabotage even; such tactics were for adventurists and romantics.[293] His attitude may have been coloured by the difficulties he encountered in trying to remove the explosives Denis Goldberg had cached in a hired storage unit at Pickford's.

Disapproval of Mayibuye may have gathered momentum inside South Africa subsequently. After completing his prison sentence, Ben Turok left South Africa but not before meeting Bram Fischer. In Nairobi he repeated to Yusuf Dadoo the messages he had been asked to convey, and first among these was that back home among those struggling to maintain the party's structures 'there was universal criticism of Operation Mayibuye'.[294] This may have been an exaggeration. Jean Middleton, arrested in 1964 after her involvement in non-violent SACP activities in Johannesburg, could not recall anyone on her area committee 'question[ing] the need for armed struggle'.[295] Indeed, members of her local group helped to edit and write Umkhonto's cyclostyled newssheet, *Freedom Fighter*.[296] If we are to believe Gerard Ludi, she also told members of her unit, in breach of the party's own security rules, 'that one of the white Communist Party cells had been given the task for looking for targets' for Umkhonto.[297]

By then many of the personalities who had shaped the party's strategy during the previous decade had left South Africa. Michael Harmel was the probably the decisive influence in the party's embrace of military action. He left South Africa in April 1963 together with the Hodgsons, wearing a wig, 'looking exactly like Michael Harmel in a wig'.[298] He was facing a court summons for violating his house arrest provisions. He hoped to make a speedy return with the help of a more thoroughgoing disguise. In the Czech national archives there is a record of a meeting between Michael Harmel and the chair of the Czechoslovak parliament's international affairs committee on 12 July 1963. Harmel's main purpose was to object to the maintenance of trade and diplomatic links between Czechoslovakia and South Africa, but he also wanted to know if he, Joe Slovo and Moses Mabhida might undergo plastic surgery so that they could return undetected to South Africa.[299] This was not the first contact between South African communists and the Czechs. In Johannesburg, in 1962, Joe Slovo had a discreet meeting with the Czech consul, Tomáš Lahoda. Slovo's single purpose in visiting the consulate was to demand its closure and to request Czech compliance with the United Nations' boycott resolution. Lahoda was unimpressed, explaining to Slovo 'that the existence of a general consulate as the only point of contact was immensely important'. As he recalled, forty years later, 'I told him that while the Consulate could not do much for them, it was the only means through which the socialist countries could obtain day-to-day information about South Africa.'[300] In a more cordial encounter in February 1963, Arthur Goldreich and Ivan Pillay in London asked Czech diplomats if they could help with the provision of a formidable list of munitions: three tonnes of plastic explosives, 10,000 detonators, 500 machine guns, 2,000 automatic rifles and military training.[301] Raymond Mhlaba asked for plastic explosives during an earlier visit as well.[302] Initial responses were encouraging, apparently, and the Czechs did indeed train a few Umkhonto soldiers. With what seemed then to be real possibilities of external help, Mayibuye's progenitors were becoming increasingly impatient with more cautious counsels. As Bernstein complained later: 'we were being bounced into a *fait accompli*.'[303]

The party's internal organisation survived the Rivonia arrests for more than two years. New people needed to be brought onto the Central Committee, which, with arrests and departures into exile, was reduced to Bram Fischer and Ruth First in Johannesburg and Fred Carneson in Cape Town: they were to be joined by Hilda Bernstein and Piet Beyleveld.[304] Beyleveld, formerly the chair of the Congress of Democrats, had never been very active in the party and, when he joined the Central Committee, he had misgivings about using violence, he claimed later.[305] A document, 'A Time for Reassessment', which was circulated to all the party's units, set out new security precautions that should accompany any further activity and warned about the likelihood of the police using torture during interrogations of ninety day detainees.[306] According to Gerard Ludi, though arrests had depleted party leadership severely at its centre and in the districts, 'the lower echelons at area and cell level were, however, still functioning fairly well'.[307] Bartholomew Hlapane, co-opted onto the Central Committee in May 1964, served as the party's treasurer until his arrest in September, and he was instructed to pay full-time party officials, including Wilton Mkwayi, Duma Nokwe's wife, Tiny, and Michael Dingaka. He was supposed to receive for this purpose sums from Mac Maharaj, who in turn obtained the money from Piet Beyleveld. Hlapane was told to buy a car. At a Central Committee meeting he learned that Hilda Bernstein was in charge of communications with London, using a book code. Hlapane also handled funds for 'wages and transport' for ANC and Umkhonto personnel; for this Issy Heymann gave him R2,450.[308]

A second High Command replaced the original Umkhonto leadership, but sabotage operations were put on hold for the duration of the trial of the Rivonia leadership, that is, until 11 June 1964. David Kitson later claimed that the second Command had 600 members in the Transvaal.[309] The SACP's propaganda committee had been mostly depleted as well, but under Ruth First's direction, until her detention in August, Mac Maharaj continued to print leaflets and organise their distribution. He also served as 'paymaster', distributing living allowances to the party's underground operatives who had given up their jobs and were in hiding to avoid arrest: he received money and lists for this purpose. In between these tasks, Maharaj manufactured pipe bombs, 'sacks of them',[310] in anticipation of the resumption of guerrilla activity. In the second half of June 1964, together with members of the successor Command, Maharaj organised a series of sabotage attacks on commuter rail lines around Johannesburg. Umkhonto commanders and party leaders considered and then rejected a proposal to organise assassinations of state witnesses.[311] Remaining Central Committee members and Umkhonto leaders were arrested on 2 July

1964. Through their own infiltrator, Gerard Ludi, police had monitored the activities of Jean Middleton's group since 1962.[312] Police raided a party safe house at which members of the 'D group' were staying; here they were able to find address lists.[313] In detention, Piet Beyleveld provided the police with more names of party functionaries and information about the party's internal structure.[314] Mac Maharaj was captured five days later.

In Durban, most of Umkhonto's regional command, itself constituted by much of the SACP district leadership, was arrested in May 1963. Undeterred, Ronnie Kasrils and other survivors, including his future wife Eleanor and Bruno Mtolo, assembled a fresh regional command and established an operational base outside Durban, in Kloof, on a smallholding owned by Eleanor's parents. From here members of his group made journeys into Zululand to recruit new members for MK: 'we began to sense the possibilities of establishing a rural network'.[315] They also maintained contact with Harry Gwala, the Communist Party personality in Pietermaritzburg who had set up his own team of saboteurs.[316] One of the Durban commanders, Bruno Mtolo, was arrested in August and he quickly turned informer. Eleanor was detained but succeeded in convincing her captors that she was undergoing a nervous breakdown and was transferred to an asylum, from which she escaped. She and Ronnie crossed the Bechuanaland border with Ruth First's father, Julius First, with support from the 'underground pipeline' established by Joe Modise.[317] A National Command also functioned for a year from October 1963: all its known members were communists, including Wilton Mkwayi, David Kitson, Laloo Chiba and Lionel Gay. Kitson formally represented the party on the Command, working with Fischer for this purpose.[318] Under its direction, recruitment continued and nearly 60 sabotage operations were undertaken before being halted at the opening of the Rivonia trial.

That the party now depended upon a cross-border operation controlled by the non-communist Modise is a sign of how attenuated its networks had become, though it did establish an Escape Committee after the Rivonia arrests.[319] Bram Fischer set up the committee to arrange for the departure of a key D-list member, Vivian Ezra, who had previously been given the task of memorising all other D-list members.[320] Joe Modise seems to have been a key agent in otherwise party-sponsored escape activity: he worked with Harold Wolpe and Joe Slovo in an earlier effort to free Nelson Mandela from police custody, drawing upon his 'ex-Sophiatown network' which extended 'right into the police force'.[321] Later, much of the support for people who succeeded in escaping from or evading police capture indicates the pivotal role of Bram Fischer in holding and coordinating what remained of the party's networks.[322]

That he was able to stay out of police hands after jumping bail in January 1965 for nearly a year reflected the party's success in maintaining the security of at least a section of its members who were able to help him.[323] Fischer's arrest in November 1965 closed down the party's remaining active networks.[324]

Most of the available information about the closing phases of the SACP's activities before Fischer's second arrest comes from the evidence provided by state witnesses as well as party documents presented by the prosecution in two trials. From late 1963, Bram Fischer led a reconstituted Central Committee, which initially also included Mac Maharaj, Dan Thloome, Ivan Schermbrucker, Hilda Bernstein, Piet Beyleveld, Hilda Bernstein, Eli Weinberg and, until his arrest, Bartholomew Hlapane. Gertrude Shope distributed money from the party leadership across a surviving ANC network in Soweto: here Violet Weinberg was the main intermediary.[325] It was a secretariat of this committee that drafted the document 'A Time for Reassessment' at the end of 1963. This reviewed a series of careless practices that had made the party vulnerable: holding meetings in the same venues; keeping written documents in places where they could be found; allowing too many people to know about each other's party activities; and so on. More encouragingly, in the Transvaal at least, organisation was still quite robust, despite losing many African members, with area committees still functional and a network of SACTU office-holders remaining in place. This was thanks partly to Bob Hepple, who had protested against the deployment of trade union officials in Umkhonto.[326] The loss of African members was an effect of arrests, of course, but also of their dispersal: between mid-1961 and mid-1963, according to South African military intelligence, Umkhonto's commanders had succeeded in dispatching more than 400 recruits, mainly African, across the border for training.[327] The party was still receiving funding from outside as well as tithing those of its members who still had jobs.

The arrest of Bram Fischer and 13 other Johannesburg-based communists in mid-1964 removed the most active leadership group. Fischer himself obtained bail to appear as counsel in a civil case in London and one month after his return, in January 1965, he estreated bail and went into hiding. For this move, his comrades had prepared quite elaborately with their renting of safe accommodation, forging of identity documents, and opening of various bank accounts. Fischer remained at liberty until his rearrest in November, though the police later claimed they had him under observation for several months while they identified the individuals who were helping him. This claim was probably exaggerated, as the police made at least one arrest of someone they mistakenly thought was Fischer at the end of October. Initially he stayed at a farm cottage in Rustenburg where he experimented with disguises, including removing part of his hair with an electric needle, but he moved back to Johannesburg in July. Under his leadership during most of 1965 the party retained at least a semblance of organised activity inside South Africa, with the appointment of another ad hoc Central Committee and its successful reconnection with remnant networks in Cape Town and Durban. In Cape Town during 1965, Fred Carneson maintained an increasingly diminishing network until his arrest on 8 December.[328] Contrary to the intentions stated in 'A Time for Reassessment', most of the people who remained actively engaged in Johannesburg were very much party veterans, mostly from Bram Fischer's closest circle of friends.[329]

Fischer was able to keep in contact with Joe Slovo and Yusuf Dadoo, who had established a secretariat and an office in Goodge Street in London, writing to them using book code once a week, but his letters didn't always engender helpful or prompt responses.[330] As late as 13 August 1965 he was complaining about their failure to respond to earlier requests for funds to support underground workers to whom payments were due.[331] While he was in London, Slovo, Dadoo and Michael Harmel had tried to persuade him to remain outside.[332] A full Central Committee was held in London in May 1965 and, with Fischer's endorsement, work began on setting up leadership structures for the external party.[333] The trial supplied details of money transfers during this period from London, and prosecution evidence also suggested that South African-based communists had attended an SACP meeting in London. A forged passport was sent from London for Fischer's use: the plan was that he should take 'leave' from the stress and isolation of underground existence, but he stayed in South Africa. Fischer remained convinced that opportunities for continued activism existed inside South Africa. Ben Turok, released from prison after serving his sentence for sabotage, was contacted by a member of Fischer's circle, 'a very, very small group', he thought, and careless about their security. He exchanged messages with Bram Fischer, for he felt he needed his permission before leaving South Africa. Fischer assented, but conditionally: leave illegally and, after undertaking plastic surgery, return quickly.[334] A draft 'discussion document', probably written by Fischer, acknowledged that, for the time being, sabotage actions were impossible, and that the party's priority should be its reorganisation along the clandestine model supplied by the experiences of Portuguese communists. The other main political task should be the rebuilding of SACTU, still in theory a legal formation.[335] Implicit in the document is criticism of the movement of the party's leadership outside South Africa. Scope still existed, the document proposed, for 'internal mass political work' given a sensible combination of legal and illegal activities. If parties with well-organised clandestine networks could exist in Spain and Portugal, the document's author continued, 'then there is every reason to think they could be far more effective in South Africa, where fascism has not developed to its full extent'.[336] It does seem that Fischer was able to maintain contact through 1965 with a few remaining Umkhonto and ANC groups, possibly supplying money for full-time organisers.[337] After Fischer's rearrest, the police would make no further claims in uncovering any SACP organisation for the remainder of the decade. For the next ten years or so, subsequent SACP-sponsored activity inside South Africa would be directed from outside, with no indications of active support from any surviving internal networks.[338]

AS WILL BE EVIDENT, with the sources that are now available, it is now possible to undertake a detailed reconstruction of a narrative that used to be well hidden. But why does this story matter? During this period the Communist Party remained a very small organisation. Did it have a wider importance?

This question has divided historians and political scientists who have addressed the development of anti-apartheid resistance in South Africa. The most authoritative early treatments of the ANC during the 1950s and 1960s were those of the team originally led by Gwendolen Carter and Thomas Karis. Their six-volume documentary survey of black resistance tended to discount communist influence within African nationalist organisations. The omission of references to Communist Party activism was especially noticeable in their fourth volume, which was made up of biographies. Writing in 1986, Thomas Karis conceded that the influence of communists within the wider movement in which they worked in the 1950s was 'to an extent greater than their numbers', but, he insisted, they were never in a position to dominate or control. More specifically he noted the absence of communists among the ANC's top office-holders during the 1950s.[339] To an extent Karis's observations were guided by the limitations of reliable information available at the time, but they also reflected the predispositions of liberal sympathisers of the ANC who maintained that the 'independently minded African patriots' who led the ANC were more than capable of prevailing in any collaboration they might undertake with communists.[340]

To a degree, the localised and bottom-up analyses of township-based resistance in the 1950s, which the Wits social history school published through the 1980s, represented a revision of this view. For example, my own investigation of the local activist trajectories that helped to explain the level of participation in the Defiance Campaign in Port Elizabeth stressed the role CPSA branches played in the preceding decade in creating the networks that sustained the ANC's following there in the 1950s.[341] On the whole, however, because of the emphasis in this kind of work on local settings, it did not directly challenge the earlier contention that when it came to leadership, communists played a subsidiary role. Communist influence at leadership level during this period did receive more attention from historians of trade unionism, who were arguing by the 1980s that the subordination of SACTU's class preoccupations to the imperatives of national liberation was indeed a consequence of union leaders' embrace of the SACP's notion of a revolution in two stages.[342] But the real challenge to the argument that the communists were just one contending influence among many came much later. For Stephen Ellis, the ANC's banning and its turn to armed struggle were the key developments through which the Communist Party arrived at the point at which it could exercise real authority over the ANC.[343]

Ostensibly, the history surveyed in this chapter would appear to offer confirmation of Ellis's depiction of communists as holding command positions in the ANC. If anything, the narrative recounted above might suggest this development happened earlier than in Ellis's account and that the movement's organisational changes which accompanied the transition to guerrilla warfare were less decisive. After all, from the mid-1950s onwards, SACP members were already well established in the ANC's top echelon and, indeed, held several of the important offices. In certain locations, the party's earlier activist traditions shaped the ANC's transformation into a mass movement. During the 1950s, the party's influence within the ANC was consolidated through a vanguardist recruitment strategy that emphasised in local settings the enlistment of community leaders and, nationally, the drawing into the party's embrace of members of the university-educated African 'intelligentsia'. SACP ideologues succeeded in shaping the ANC's programmatic orientation, especially in the central role they played in projecting their vision of a people's democracy into the Freedom Charter. This programmatic vision helped to determine the ANC's key strategic and campaigning decisions. The party added critically useful techniques, resources and skills to the ANC's organisational capacity.

Contemporary archival materials – documents written by party members at the time – indicate that they understood their role as much more than just influence. In describing the party's relationship with the ANC, Moses Kotane and Michael Harmel used the language of direction and control, not merely prompting and persuasion. But this picture of the party in command is too simple. Firstly, the ANC's organisational structure during the 1950s did not lend itself to centralised leadership, and certain important campaigning developments happened autonomously. Opposition to women's passes was a case in point and, significantly, the SACP's influence over women's organisations was limited. Moreover, not all strong local centres of ANC activity were animated by communists. Secondly, the party was internally divided over strategic issues and even over the meaning of key ideological concepts. For instance, there were wide differences over what a national democracy might look like. Party principals who were closest to the ANC favoured the establishment of the kind of post-apartheid social order which many non-communists within the ANC might also have welcomed, and it is arguable that without the party the ANC might have adopted a very similar set of aims and objectives. Thirdly, the party's progress towards embracing violent tactics was certainly quicker than the ANC's, for, after all, it was a much smaller and more disciplined formation, but was it really so decisive? There is plenty of evidence of willingness to use violence within the ANC during the 1950s campaigns, and this was not confined to ANC members who were also communists. As we have seen, within the party an important section of its leadership retained reservations about the strategic emphasis on guerrilla warfare, and right until the SACP's final suppression communists remaining inside South Africa were committed to building political – that is, non-military – organisation. Even so, despite these qualifications, the secret history reviewed in this chapter is not the story of a sideshow. It played a central role in the unfolding of popular opposition to apartheid between 1950 and 1965.

SEVEN

Out of Africa, 1965–1977

Zeleni Mkhonzo, Umkhonto we Sizwe recruit, enjoying a day off during his training in Brno military academy, Czechoslovakia in 1963. Mkhonzo would be killed by Rhodesian soldiers while fighting in 1968.

Bram Fischer's arrest in December 1965 removed the Communist Party's last major personality active inside South Africa; as the party's London-based leadership admitted, 'we are no longer in touch with any member at home'.[1] For the next two and a half decades most of the people who had led the party since its reconstruction in 1953 would be confined in prison or living in exile. Communists would have no underground organisation inside South Africa for the rest of the 1960s, and, even 25 years later, the party's internal records suggest that it still functioned mainly outside the country's borders. But the extent to which the party retained a presence and wider influence inside South Africa may have been greater than is suggested by its own membership calculations, as will become clear in this chapter. Even so, the history of the party in this period is a story in which the South African diaspora supplies the main setting.

As we have seen, party leaders reporting on developments in the 1950s claimed that communists had become decisive agents in shaping the broader struggles around them, determining the ANC leaders' strategic choices and influencing their longer goals. Hostile perceptions of the party's history in exile have suggested that it retained and even increased its dominant presence within the ANC's leadership. Arguably, the exile community that the ANC embodied was an easier organisation to discipline and influence than the sprawling movement that the ANC presided over inside South Africa in the 1950s. The understanding that communists were ascendant in the liberation movement during their exile is also premised on the view that the party's membership of an international communist movement brought it powerful allies and consequent leverage. At least one former communist has observed that compared with the South African Communist Party (SACP), no other communist party 'managed to insinuate its presence and influence [in a national liberation movement] on such a scale'.[2] Stephen Ellis's analysis of the exile movement suggests that by 1968 the party had re-established the guiding role within the ANC's diaspora it once enjoyed inside South Africa, 'but now on a higher level of sophistication'.[3]

This view of a party-dominated exile liberation movement is contested, however. Joe Slovo, for example, by claiming that in 'no other period in our history [did] the Party [play] such a seminal role in the unfolding of the struggle as in the years between 1960 and 1963' implied that in exile it would lose influence.[4] As Raymond Suttner points out, 'having the presence of large numbers of SACP members in leadership structures of the ANC does not mean the SACP was necessarily giving strategic direction'.[5] After all, with its leadership dispersed and often quite distant from the ANC's headquarters, the party units at best could hope to function as 'a sort of informal left-wing caucus within a wider clandestine ANC exile milieu'.[6] The more intimate the relationship became between the two organisations, the bigger the risk for the party of losing any political base for an independent existence.[7] In Eddy Maloka's history of the party abroad – a treatment that appears to have enjoyed the sanction of the party's leadership – rather than being in the ascendancy for much of its exile, South African communism was 'struggling' as much for 'its own survival as a political force' as for its position 'within the liberation movement'.[8] The secrecy under which it was compelled to function in most parts of Africa also inhibited its capacity to orchestrate or coordinate its own activities, let alone those of its allies; for most of its exile in Africa, it was impossible for the party to assemble more than a few people for meetings.[9]

One key change that resulted from exile was that for two and a half decades the party would lose its former self-sufficiency, becoming dependent almost entirely upon externally sourced finance as well as upon the goodwill of governments and officials, inside and outside Africa. It also became increasingly open to externally derived ideas, possibly more so than in the era of Comintern's promptings, though during this phase the external sources of strategic thinking would diversify. Certainly, the party's affiliation to an international community was a key factor in its resilience and progress in exile. But, as would quickly become evident, in contrast to the 'Native republic' era, Soviet Union strategic thinking was more stable and much more broadly sympathetic to anti-colonial nationalist movements and far less predisposed to accord any privileged status to communists in colonial or post-colonial settings.

The party's history between the destruction of its clandestine organisation inside South Africa in 1965 and its public re-establishment in 1990 can be divided into two phases. In its first phase, from the early 1960s to 1977, leadership and leadership structures were located mainly in London, though from 1972 the party began to establish units among the ANC's exile communities in East Africa. Of course, key communists were present throughout this period within the ANC leadership in Dar es Salaam, holding senior positions, but in this setting they worked as ANC officials, not as communists – not collectively, anyway. In the 1960s, most white and Indian communists were based in London or other European centres. During this time senior African and African-based communists within the ANC leadership opposed the party having any organised presence in Africa, partly because they were anxious that the ANC should not attract hostility from African host governments. This chapter focuses on this first period, when the party was based mainly in London.

AS WE HAVE SEEN, DURING the 1950s a small group of South African communists assembled in London, several of them Indian South Africans, for a while encountering each other in a special section of the Communist Party of Great Britain.[10] From 1960, and throughout the decade, the British party paid for the printing of the *African Communist*: the journal was printed and published in Britain and distributed through its London agent, Ellis Bowles, a British party official. For this and other reasons, London was the obvious refuge in exile for white and Indian South African communists, even though they were not usually of British descent. Yusuf Dadoo, when he left South Africa in June 1960, travelled first to London, where he would work closely with Vella Pillay. Michael Harmel arrived in April 1963 and Joe Slovo a little later, both at that stage hoping to return to South Africa shortly. Brian, Sonia and Rebecca Bunting also made their home in London in 1963, and for the next three decades Brian would work in London as the correspondent for the Soviet news agency TASS. Lionel and Hilda Bernstein arrived after Lionel's acquittal at the Rivonia trial. Harold Wolpe and his wife, AnnMarie, also travelled to London after his dramatic escape from prison with Arthur Goldreich, though it required an intervention from the Labour MP Barbara Castle before the British were persuaded to grant him asylum. Both Harold and AnnMarie found new careers as academic sociologists, enrolling as PhD students – in Harold's case, with the support of a Nuffield fellowship.[11] Within a year most of the key party personalities who remained at liberty were living in London. In certain cases, they had been able to transfer money when they left South Africa and could purchase houses or apartments, mainly in what were then modest middle-class neighbourhoods around Highgate and Muswell Hill. For even leading personalities, living conditions could be quite austere; when Jack and Rica Hodgson arrived in London in mid-1963, they shared a damp basement flat, hosted by Yusuf Dadoo and his wife, Winnie. It proved too uncomfortable for Jack, by now ill with phthisis, and so they moved in with the Buntings and their three children, who were then living in a more spacious and comfortable apartment near the Finchley Road underground station.[12]

The party's Central Committee held its first meeting in exile in Prague in December 1963, with hospitality negotiated from the Czechoslovaks by Vella Pillay.[13] Czech generosity had its limits. The Czechs warned Pillay, when he asked if they would host the meeting, that they could provide only for local expenses 'not in excess of Kčs 6,000' and not for anything such as air tickets that needed payment in hard currency.[14] The committee used the occasion to draft a lengthy statement about the Sino-Soviet dispute, calling for an end to the 'all-in controversy we have been witnessing'.[15] Though the party viewed the Soviet side in the dispute sympathetically, in 1963 *African Communist* still carried advertisements for Mao's writings on guerrilla warfare and for the *Peking Review*, and the meeting drafted a conciliatory letter to the Chinese party. At this stage, leading South African communists perceived the Chinese as 'fraternal' allies. After all, Yusuf Dadoo and Vella Pillay had negotiated Chinese training for Umkhonto in 1961 (without Oliver Tambo's knowledge). Pillay maintained friendly relations with Chinese officials and would continue to work for the Bank of China, despite later pressure from his South African comrades. Pillay stopped being active in the party in 1964.[16] Vladimir Shubin, later the Soviet Communist Party (CPSU) official who was the main point of liaison between the Soviet party and the South African exiles, ANC and SACP alike, suggests that the South African party 'was not in a hurry to take sides in the Sino-Soviet dispute', supporting Tambo in trying to keep the ANC non-committal until the rift hardened into a split.[17]

In this early phase the Czechoslovaks were a key source of 'fraternal' assistance for the London communists. From the beginning of 1962, SACP leaders had been engaged in negotiations with the Czechoslovaks, initially over the continuing diplomatic and trading links between Czechoslovakia and South Africa. In Prague in February 1962, at the first party-to-party meeting, Moses Kotane raised the issue of sanctions but decided against any formal objection to the Czechs' continuation of their South African diplomacy and trade, but the issue remained the subject of increasingly bad-tempered exchanges until the Czechs were persuaded by the Soviet party to change course in mid-1963.[18] By then, exploiting their moral advantage, London-based South African communists were negotiating arms shipments from the Czechs, weaponry for the trainee guerrillas in the ANC's Tanzanian military encampment at the old groundnut scheme settlement of Kongwa, and plastic explosives for the Umkhonto command still functioning in South

Africa. The Czechs also agreed to supply military training. For this purpose, SACP activists in Fordsburg dispatched across the border ten recruits, mainly Indian and coloured young men, several of them communists; they included Moses Kotane's son, Joseph Cotton. The training took place at the Czechoslovak army's military academy near Brno and included instruction in guerrilla tactics from wartime partisans. Three of the graduates from the Brno programme would participate in the Umkhonto operations in Rhodesia in 1967 and 1968.[19]

The Czech training programme was a party initiative, initially conducted without the knowledge of the ANC leadership in Dar es Salaam. At about the same time, quite separately, Oliver Tambo had persuaded the Soviet authorities to train a much larger number of Umkhonto recruits from Tanzania.[20] There were other signals at that time that London party leaders were inclined to assert their own authority. For example, in late 1962 ANC representatives visited the Czechoslovak embassy to request scholarships for 100 students needing placements at schools and universities. Before passing on the request, Czechoslovak diplomats sought the advice of 'local friends', that is, SACP people. They in turn told the Czechoslovaks they could 'not guarantee the reliability of students nominated by this organisation'.[21] Clearly at this juncture, party leaders in London were rather inclined to take a territorial approach, viewing the ANC's independent contacts with the Czechoslovaks as infringing on their domain. In Prague, officials recommended the award of two scholarships to South Africans so they could attend the University of November 17th, the special institution established to host students from Africa.

During 1964, the party established its own London office, one room in 'a poky building' furnished with three desks and a battered filing cabinet, in Goodge Street. It was used mainly by Yusuf Dadoo and Joe Slovo, with Stephanie Kemp helping with secretarial tasks. Ronnie Kasrils provides an engaging description of the daily office routine, which was taken up with deciphering and compiling invisible texts and with conversations in coded expressions accompanied by hand gestures, to stymie any unwelcome listeners.[22] For refreshment and more frank exchanges, the comrades would repair to Dadoo's favourite pub, the Valiant Trooper. In mid-1965, at its third meeting in exile, held again in Prague, the Central Committee formalised London's status as the party's headquarters: here a secretariat as well as a Central Executive Committee would base itself. Dadoo was appointed as deputy general secretary with the authority to negotiate help from fraternal parties. The party's senior office-holders, Moses Kotane and JB Marks, who had left South Africa in 1963, would remain in Dar es Salaam in their posts as key ANC leaders. Kotane became the exile ANC's treasurer. Duma Nokwe had accompanied Kotane in his journey into exile; remaining a top-echelon communist, he resumed his role in Dar es Salaam as the ANC's secretary general. In Oliver Tambo's words, 'among the people of South Africa' JB Marks had been 'known mainly as an ANC leader rather than a Communist Party leader'. On his arrival he 'fitted perfectly' into the 'ANC machinery in Tanzania'.[23]

At the SACP's Prague meeting, concerns were raised about the need to improve what were evidently poor communications between London and Dar es Salaam as well as about the fact that in Britain the SACP's exile community was mainly white: 'leading African comrades' were needed in both the party's and the ANC's London offices, it was felt.[24] To complete the administrative arrangements, Yusuf Dadoo and Julius First set up a charitable foundation, the London Aid Committee, which would serve as a conduit for party financing; the Aid Committee would establish bank accounts and lease buildings for the party.[25] From 1960, following a visit to Moscow in July by Dadoo and Joe Matthews, the CPSU would provide funding for the party annually – the major part of the South Africa party's income. At the same time the Soviet party's annual subventions to the ANC were often ten times larger, having been negotiated quite separately during a visit by Oliver Tambo to Moscow in 1963.[26] This visit would trigger the major cooperation between the Soviet Union and the ANC, and Shubin suggests that the SACP did not play a role in these negotiations.[27] CPSU financial support for the SACP fluctuated. In 1960 the SACP received $30,000. With the onset of armed struggle the allocation increased, up to $112,000 in 1961 and then down to $56,000 the following year. The South Africans informed the CPSU about plans for the sabotage campaign in 1961. The Russians' response was encouraging though they also advised that one form of struggle should not entirely replace another – a sensible caution.[28] During the rest of the decade the party allocation was usually $30,000 a year.[29] The party also received funding from the 'International Trade Union Fund for Assistance to Left Workers' Organisations at the Romanian Council of Trade Unions', a facility supported by all the Eastern bloc countries.[30]

During the course of 1966, in London – then the only centre in which the party had a fully organised presence – its members would join three task groups, focusing on solidarity and anti-apartheid work, political education within the broader liberation movement, and 'technical work' for the party itself.[31] From 1967 Yusuf Dadoo, Joe Slovo and Michael Harmel, already the party's day-to-day leadership, constituted a secretariat, publishing and circulating an *Inner Party Bulletin*, which is today the best archival record of the exile party's inner life. A meeting of the Central Committee in Moscow in 1967 decided that all the party's London-based membership would constitute an executive group to support the secretariat, thereby effectively confirming London as the party's geographic base.[32]

DURING THIS TIME, the London communists had two chief preoccupations. The first of these was to achieve a closer and better recognised status in its relationship within the ANC. Secondly, the party sought to revive its own presence within South Africa. In the background of both these concerns was a view, quite widely shared within the party apparently, that the time of the party needing an autonomous organisational structure was over, that communists should simply work within the ANC – an option that Jack Simons had proposed in 1950. It was certainly a course ANC principals would have preferred. As the party's secretariat noted after a meeting of the Central Committee in 1975, '[Oliver Tambo's] attitude remains an extremely complex one. At the [Revolutionary Council] meeting itself he paid tribute to the Party but in his own rather complicated way, he emphasized the need for the Party to work in the tradition of Malume [Moses Kotane] by which he understands it should not really be organized as an independent force.'[33] This was a view that top ANC leadership on Robben Island shared. At one stage Harry Gwala was told to refrain from setting up party cells on the island; Mandela and other ANC principals, including communists, were worried about risking any divisions within the ANC community on the Island.[34] In February 1968, at a Central Committee meeting, London-based members referred disapprovingly to 'reports circulating about the liquidationist tendencies that existed in the Party from about 1964 to 1968'.[35] At least one major African communist party had recently experienced 'liquidationism'. In Egypt in 1964, on the eve of Nikita Khrushchev's visit to Cairo, General Nasser released hundreds of imprisoned communists, compelling them at the same time to dissolve their organisation and instead take up senior positions in the Arab Socialist Union and ministries.[36] In Africa, during this time, Soviet policy tended to favour 'progressive' non-capitalist regimes even if these were at odds with local communist parties. This predisposition would remain throughout the decade and beyond, evident in 1971 in Sudan where the 'national democratic' Nimeiri regime was suppressing the Communist Party. In an exceptional expression of interest of African events, in 1971 Vasil Bil'ak, at that time the party leader influential in determining Czech foreign policy, which closely followed Moscow's line, condemned Sudanese communists as irresponsible after their attempt to seize power from Nimeiri through a trade union-supported military coup.[37] For South African communists, their Sudanese counterparts were familiar personalities; the two parties were on friendly terms.[38] But the implications of the Sudanese events were clear enough; when it came to the broader strategy of the international communist movement in Africa, this was the era in which communists should work within national democratic movements, not against them. Global great power rivalries tended to predispose the Soviet Union to support allied Third World governments even when they persecuted local communists.

One initial difficulty in the SACP's relationship with the ANC was that during the 1950s its influence within the Congress Alliance was exercised through trade unions and those organisations representing minority racial communities in which communists had played a leading role: the Congress of Democrats and the South African Coloured People's Organisation. So, in the first years of its exile there was no formal structure helping to embody its de facto alliance with the ANC or the initial collaboration in setting up Umkhonto we Sizwe and sharing its command. The issue was initially raised at a gathering at Joe Slovo's house in late 1965, which Oliver Tambo attended.[39] The London communists also hoped that the party could establish its own cells in Umkhonto, an option that at this stage ANC leaders (including Moses Kotane) rejected.[40] A subsequent 'London Memorandum' proposed a Council of War that would represent the groups that included white, Indian and coloured exiles, one of which was the SACP – the language was reportedly Joe Matthews's. The ANC responded with the appointment of a subcommittee of its National Executive to consider the memorandum. Duma Nokwe, JB Marks and Moses Kotane met for this purpose. They noted that in the exile setting, any public alliance might detract from the 'image of the ANC as the leading organ of the liberation movement'. However, as a compromise, in November 1966 the ANC established a Consultative Congress Committee to coordinate activity between the ANC and former Alliance partners. At no stage did the subcommittee refer to the SACP explicitly in its reported deliberations, and indeed at its inception the SACP was not invited to join the Consultative group. At its first meeting there was apparently a contentious exchange between Michael Harmel and Moses Kotane over the role which white democrats or communists could play at that stage in the struggle.[41] A subsequent resolution from the SACP Central Committee at the beginning of 1967 calling for its inclusion within the Consultative group did result in an invitation for the party to send a representative to subsequent meetings.[42]

Secondly, there was the problem that in Tanzania the SACP could not have an officially sanctioned presence, and the Tanzanian authorities were unwilling to host South African exiles who were not members of the ANC or the PAC. It wasn't a rigid embargo: Eleanor Kasrils worked for a while in the ANC's office in late 1963, driving Moses Kotane around the city and being trusted by him to deposit and withdraw money from the ANC's bank account. Meanwhile, her husband, Ronnie, accompanied Joe Modise and Moses Mabhida to Odessa for military training. Later Ben Turok obtained a job as a surveyor employed by the Tanzanian government; he secured a job offer before entering Tanzania from Kenya in 1965.[43] The Kasrils stayed in Dar es Salaam until 1965, leaving only after Eleanor, who was pregnant, contracted malaria. In 1965, Jack Simons and Ray Alexander would set up home in Lusaka, where he had been offered a post at the University of Zambia; they were allowed to make Lusaka their home after influential local friends lobbied on their behalf.[44] But, on the whole, when white South African exiles arrived in Dar es Salaam, they were encouraged to move on. Joe Slovo was actually designated as a prohibited immigrant by the Tanzanian authorities, and was allowed to return for visits only in 1977.[45]

ANC members in Tanzania who were communists were rather inclined to support the Tanzanian government position. Moses Kotane himself was worried about drawing any attention in Dar es Salaam or, more widely, in Africa to the presence of communists within the ANC or to the ANC's collaboration with the SACP; both would have been more obvious with the local presence of a significant group of white communists. In any case, he did not think the party should organise any units locally, not in Africa. In Joe Slovo's words, 'Moses seemed to think that his presence [in Dar es Salaam] was sufficient; if he was there, then the Party was there, so to say.'[46] He discouraged Kongwa camp political commissars from teaching Marxism; instead they should instruct their charges in the 'African image' emphasised at the ANC's conference in Lobatsi in 1962.[47] As late as 1975, Kotane was suggesting that Umkhonto might best be an 'all-African' body.[48] Kotane was also against opening up the ANC's racial restrictions on membership because he believed this would elicit a resentful African 'nationalist' reaction within the ANC. So, at least until 1968, and possibly after that, the party had no organised presence in Africa.[49] Even certain African communists felt apparently that 'Africa is ours. Others must stay in Britain' (Tennyson Makiwane's phraseology), but the sentiment was shared by others.[50] In taking up this position, they may have been reacting against the way that senior white communists still predominated in the party's strategic and doctrinal thinking: John Pule Motshabi, for example, disliked the way, in his perception, leadership roles within the party were 'always entrusted with white intellectuals'.[51] Such resentments did not necessarily affect African party members' self-identification as communists. Ambrose Makiwane, Tennyson's cousin, was commander of the ANC military camp at Kongwa in 1965. He had joined the party at Fort Hare, at the same time as Chris Hani, then the political commissar at the camp. Makiwane liked to describe himself by saying, 'Ndibomvu, ndibomvu, nomnqundu lo' (I'm red, red, even my arse is red).[52] He may indeed have been sincere in such professions but he also had a reputation for venality and for being abusive, though veterans remember a good camp commander who was 'politically strong'.[53] He was in fact removed from his post at Kongwa in 1966 after an investigation into triple billing for camp supplies.[54] Ronnie Kasrils encountered him in Odessa; he found him 'ultra-conspiratorial' and 'otherwise unpleasant'.[55] So, geographically divided in itself and hence unable or unwilling to caucus effectively, and with its leaders denied a corporate status in the ANC's decision-making, the party depended on personal relationships rather than institutional channels in its efforts to influence the ANC – very much the way that both Oliver Tambo and Moses Kotane preferred in working with each other.

Proponents of the view that the party during its exile was the dominant partner in its relationship with the ANC suggest that its exclusion from formal channels of influence was quite short-lived. Stephen Ellis, for example, maintains that after the ANC's consultative conference in 1969, the party once again became the guiding force within the wider movement and, indeed, was able to exercise influence 'on a higher level of sophistication'.[56] Kotane's hospitalisation in Moscow in November 1968 after a cerebral haemorrhage also helped to improve the London-based SACP leadership's access to the ANC, Ellis suggested, as he had been a strong opponent of the party having any organisational presence in Africa. Probably as important in broadening opportunities for the party were the rank-and-file criticisms directed at the Dar es Salaam-based ANC leadership, both military and political, after the failures of Umkhonto's first major military operation in exile. Here some background about wider developments within the exile movement may be helpful.

In the mid-1960s 'Operation Mayibuye' remained the ANC's strategic blueprint. Umkhonto first made a series of efforts to re-establish transit routes through Botswana during 1966 and early 1967, which could be used to infiltrate nuclei of trained personnel to the insurgent starting points identified in the document. These were checked by local police. Then, after heavy pressure from an increasingly impatient OAU Liberation Committee, Joe Modise, working with Zimbabwe African People's Union (ZAPU) officials, dispatched three groups into Rhodesia from August 1967 through to 1968. The intention behind the Rhodesian missions was that the South Africans would first help ZAPU soldiers establish their own base facilities before using them as springboards for infiltration into South Africa. Much the same kind of thinking as in Mayibuye seems to have inspired the sense of purpose in this: the South African expeditions would be undertaken by small groups directed at four regions.[57] The idea may have been originally inspired by advice Che Guevara had given in a talk he delivered at the Cuban embassy in Dar es Salaam. He suggested that the southern African movements should join forces and collaborate in freeing each settler-dominated territory in turn, working their way southwards. At the time the South Africans in his audience, who included Ronnie Kasrils and Chris Hani, were unenthusiastic, for, of course, in this scheme they 'would be last in the queue'.[58] But Hani evidently changed his mind; according to his biographers, he began arguing the case for 'opening a route to South Africa through the wild open bushland of Rhodesia' as early as 1964.[59]

The Rhodesian expeditions involved a total of about 240 fighters, consisting of roughly equal shares of ZAPU and Umkhonto personnel. The first incursion wasted no time in any preparatory work, attacking a Rhodesian army patrol 11 days after crossing the Zambezi on 2 August 1967. Nearly two weeks of subsequent clashes with the Rhodesians in the Wankie game park supplied plenty of evidence of the guerrillas' military capabilities and their courage, but they were heavily outgunned and the Rhodesians had either captured or killed all the guerrillas who had not escaped across the Botswana border one month after their arrival. The Rhodesians lost eight men, according to their records. The two subsequent expeditions the following year were no more successful, though in the case of the second venture (the 'Sipolilo' campaign), the guerrillas managed to remain undetected for six weeks before encountering Rhodesian soldiery, though as soon as they began trying to obtain food from the local population, their presence was reported to the Rhodesian army. Umkhonto guerrillas had been led to believe that local people would be supportive and that this had been established through reconnaissance; if there had been any earlier exploration of the territory, it was clearly inadequate. The bands were issued with school maps that showed no topographical detail. These kinds of undertakings were too costly to be sustained: of the 240 or so insurgents crossing the Zambezi, nearly 80 were killed and about the same number captured, a casualty rate that provoked angry rank-and-file criticism of Umkhonto command. A much smaller group that attempted to cross into Mozambique in the company of FRELIMO soldiers was ambushed and dispersed by Portuguese troops after a few days in Niassa. In a memorandum they composed afterwards, survivors of this group compared the high-handed behaviour of Umkhonto's upper echelons with the egalitarian relationships they had encountered within FRELIMO.[60]

Planning the Wankie and Sipolilo expeditions was confined to the ANC's top echelon in Dar es Salaam. Members of the party's secretariat in London claimed later that they first learned about the operations from press reports.[61] Ellis is dismissive, suggesting 'it would be absurd to pretend that the [SACP's] leadership was not fully aware of that initiative'; after all, among the National Executive members who sanctioned the operation were a substantial number of veteran communists.[62] Ronnie Kasrils's memoir, however, recalls learning about 'MK's incursions' only after they happened.[63] This is probably true. As we shall see, the party prepared pamphlets for circulation inside South Africa at the time of the Wankie campaign, and couriers carried them through Rhodesian customs as the offensive began – a coincidence party planners would have avoided if they had known about the military operations in advance.[64] The pamphlets were in the name of the party and did not mention Umkhonto. Certainly, the London party leaders were left out of the important decision-making. Joe Slovo, who was by then replacing Michael Harmel as the party's key strategic authority, was openly critical of the Cuban-derived thinking that had helped to inspire Operation Mayibuye, condemning as a 'dangerous delusion' the proposal that 'the injection of armed groups into a country in which there is severe repression will of itself "slowly spread like an oil patch"'.[65] As a subsequent SACP 'plenary meeting' warned, guerrilla warfare might serve as a powerful stimulus to a revival of political struggle, but 'this [would] not come of its own accord'.[66]

Crucially, criticism within the exile movement of the strategic conception of the campaign was not limited to oblique commentary in London. Even before the guerrillas crossed the Zambezi, there were disagreements over basic strategy. This may have started with the return to Africa of the graduates from the Czech training programme. As members of this group discovered when they joined the ANC's army at Kongwa, their training seemed to compare rather favourably with the courses undertaken by those who had attended programmes in the Soviet Union. Soviet trainees at Kongwa apparently demonstrated no evidence of any intensive preparation for guerrilla warfare

– just basic grounding in weapons handling and conventional military manoeuvres, as Amin Cajee recalled. Josiah Jele, one of the Mozambican campaigners who had undergone training in Russia, remembered that the emphasis in his classes was on preparation for regular warfare rather than guerrilla tactics.[67] Other Umkhonto veterans have suggested that at that stage Soviet training at Odessa mainly emphasised 'mobile warfare', a more advanced form of operations than light-armed guerilla units could undertake.[68] Soviet courses did include at least theoretical instruction in guerrilla warfare; Chris Hani, for example, who was trained in Odessa, thought 'it was well suited to their needs'.[69] Be that as it may, the 'Czech group' at Kongwa became heavily critical of the prevalent strategic line maintained by the external Umkhonto command. Commander-in-chief Joe Modise favoured a militarist approach: large formations and sophisticated weaponry. The Czech-trained group began to propose a more protracted kind of struggle in which small-scale infiltration and political preparation of host communities would precede any ambitious military operation – quite the opposite of what happened in the Rhodesian expeditions, which involved quite large bodies of men (up to 100 in a single detachment) with no preliminary political preparation or reconnaissance.

According to Amin Cajee, the Czech trainees won over the camp's commissar, Chris Hani, to their point of view, and the training offered in Kongwa camp shifted away from basic drill and weapons handling. Hani would leave for Lusaka in 1965, to lead an ANC committee charged with returning trained Umkhonto personnel to South Africa.[70] We must take Cajee's word for all this, but there is a definite indication of the effectiveness of the Czech training in equipping Umkhonto's men with the skills they needed as field commanders. Of the nine men who completed their training in Brno, three, each of them SACP members incidentally, played key roles in Umkhonto's Rhodesian operations. Basil February and Zeleni Mkhonzo were killed by Rhodesian security forces; James April participated in successive Rhodesian expeditions and managed to reach South Africa in 1971 before being arrested and imprisoned – one of a tiny number of Umkhonto soldiers before 1977 to succeed in returning home. Cajee himself left Kongwa in early 1967 and became a refugee after being accused of treason by Joe Modise. The charges were spurious; he was accused of siding with a pro-Chinese faction to overthrow the existing leadership. In fact, Cajee and other members of the Czech group had offended the top military echelon with their strategic criticisms, especially when their views began to be echoed by other people.[71] Cajee suggests that when it came to selection of the men who would make up the Umkhonto detachments in the missions, 'all seemed to be comrades from Kongwa who were considered by leadership to be dissidents', several of them communists.[72] This may have been true, though both at that time and later, operational deployments were sought after, and the comrades who were fetched from the camp in Zambia-bound Land Rovers were called 'the Chinamen', lucky winners in a fah-fee lottery. Hani was an eager participant in the expedition and at that stage the most senior camp official – hardly a dissident – though he had his own reservations about the planning of the expedition: he thought it was seriously under-armed.

After their two fierce encounters with Rhodesian soldiers, Hani and the other survivors crossed the Botswana border and were then arrested and imprisoned. On their release in December 1969 and return to Zambia, Hani and his comrades became increasingly disenchanted by the failure of the ANC leadership and the Umkhonto command to invite them for a debriefing and, more generally, by the absence of any indications of follow-up operational planning. They wrote and circulated a memorandum that criticised a 'Leadership-in-Exile' that had 'created a machinery which [had] become an end in itself'. The memo also targeted individual ANC notables. Joe Modise spent more time supervising the various 'mysterious business enterprises' that the ANC had originally established as fronts in Lusaka than he spent with his soldiers. Duma Nokwe was 'indifferent and cynical'. Various other principals such as ex-Czech trainee Joseph Cotton (Kotane's son) and Duma Nokwe's wife, Vuyiswa, had made local friendships that compromised security, such as with Peace Corps personnel and Israeli businessmen.[73] Too many people with leadership connections enjoyed relatively privileged lives in exile, notably Thabo Mbeki, Govan's son, who had studied at the University of Sussex, and whose liberation credentials were limited to leading a 'bogus' student organisation in South Africa: 'they will just come home when everything has been made secure and comfortable for them'.[74] The document called for a conference that would bring together leadership and Umkhonto's rank and file, 'not just handpicked individuals'.[75] Attacking individuals by name was especially provocative and risky. Thabo Mbeki, whom Hani had known at school, had indeed benefited from favoured treatment. In Johannesburg, where he studied for British A-levels in 1962 with the help of a SACHED grant,[76] he was also 'under the tutelage' of Duma Nokwe and Walter Sisulu.[77] Duma Nokwe recruited Mbeki into the party in 1961 and he received his instruction in the Marxist canon from Bram Fischer: 'A lovely old fellow. Very good man. Very good teacher,' Mbeki told his biographer fifty years later.[78] Hani's recruiter had been Thabo's father, Govan, always on the look-out for promising potential cadres on the Fort Hare campus; as Mbeki's biographer notes, Mbeki's and Hani's future rivalry had a sibling quality to it.[79] As well as his year's training in the Soviet Union, Hani's education included his Fort Hare degree in classics and English. Initially Hani and the seven other men who had put their names to the memorandum were arrested by ANC security officials, and they were to be subjected to a disciplinary tribunal. Rumours that the tribunal was considering executing the men elicited a dismayed protest from Hani's parents and an angry reproof from Ray Simons: the Simonses had organised a welcome party at their home in Lusaka for Chris Hani on his return from Botswana. At Tambo's behest and also as a consequence of arguments from Mzwai Piliso, the tribunal limited itself to expulsions, which the ANC leadership confirmed at the end of March.[80] Jack Simons would help Hani write an appeal against this decision. The memo nevertheless succeeded in its immediate objective; together with other signals of discontent among the guerrillas, it helped to convince ANC leaders to summon delegates to a conference, to be held in Morogoro, Tanzania, on 25 April 1969.

Seventy delegates assembled at Morogoro, 12 of them invited to represent the SACP, SACTU, and the Coloured and Indian Congresses – among these delegates, three were white. The decisions at this meeting certainly enhanced the party's position within the ANC, as was noted afterwards in an East German intelligence report.[81] The party itself had decided at a meeting before Morogoro that it favoured the opening up of ANC membership, though Brian Bunting, Joe Slovo and Ray Simons argued against such a move.[82] A new nine-person National Executive was elected; with five communist members, the party's share of the top-echelon positions increased significantly. The meeting compromised on the issue of non-African membership despite pressure from Umkhonto delegates in favour of opening up completely.[83] Flag Boshielo, one of the party's Sekhukhuneland recruits in the 1940s, made a telling speech in favour. In future the ANC would sign up non-Africans into its external mission (leaving open the issue of whether whites could belong to the ANC until after its return to South Africa), but for the time being its executive would remain racially exclusive. However, non-Africans could belong to the Revolutionary Council, a new body expected to supply Umkhonto with strategic leadership: initially it would be constituted by Oliver Tambo, Joe Modise, Yusuf Dadoo, Reg September, Joe Slovo and Joe Matthews. Modise lost his former title of 'commander-in-chief' though he remained Umkhonto's commander – an alteration understood at the time as a demotion.[84] The conference adopted a new programme, *The Strategy and Tactics of the South African Revolution*, a text originally written by Slovo at Oliver Tambo's request and then redrafted after modifications by Matthews and Nokwe.[85] The meeting also agreed to an amnesty and the readmission of Chris Hani and his comrades. Hani was restored to his position as a commissar in June 1969. Veteran communist and trade unionist Moses Mabhida was entrusted with the task of setting up a new body to look after intelligence and security; the old arrangements had been discredited by the harsh behaviour of security officials at Kongwa and elsewhere. Meanwhile, Thabo Mbeki's continuing political ascendancy was evident in June 1969 when he joined an SACP delegation (using the pseudonym J Jabulani) in Moscow with Yusuf Dadoo, Michael Harmel and JB Marks to attend the International Meeting of Communist and Workers' Parties.[86] Mbeki was already in Moscow, undergoing ideological training at the Lenin School. Mbeki's strained relationship with Slovo dates from this period. His hosts had complained about his behaviour and Slovo had tried to warn him; Mbeki resented what he perceived to be unwarranted interference.[87]

Shortly after the conference, Oliver Tambo met communist leaders. A compromise was reached about organising in Africa. The party should still refrain from recruiting units within Umkhonto, but in Lusaka and in Dar es Salaam a designated member of the Central Committee could have meetings with soldiers while another committee functionary would be responsible for better liaison with the ANC. This was needed, it was agreed, for, as Tambo observed, previously he had been 'unaware of the gap that appears to have existed'. Also at this meeting, JB Marks complained that 'the isolation [in London] of some of our members ... had created wrong attitudes ... even questioning of the wisdom of the present democratic phase of our revolution led by the ANC'. Apparently some London communists were rather prone to 'confuse' the party's professed function as a working-class vanguard with the role of leading the liberation movement. A more structured relationship with the ANC and a better presence in Africa might help put an end to such presumptions.[88] As a Central Committee report in 1970 noted, for much of the previous decade 'the absence of proper institutional links with the ANC ... [was] an obstacle to the ability of the Party to exercise its vanguard role'.[89] However, functioning as a vanguard was not the same thing as leading, senior communists would add. Shortly after this encounter, two of the major opponents of the ANC opening up its membership to whites and Indians, Ambrose Makiwane and Alfred Kgokong (both whom had been party members), were demoted. Kgokong had fallen out with the party for quite different reasons in 1968 when he emerged as a critic of the Soviet invasion of Czechoslovakia, which the party supported. He was suspended from his position as director of publicity, and replaced by MP Naicker.

The Morogoro decisions appeared to confirm the restoration of the party's influence within the ANC. This was most evidently the case with respect to programmatic issues. As the authors of *Strategy and Tactics* explained, any efforts to achieve South African national freedom were happening during a global era 'of transition to the Socialist system'. In the 'zone' in which South Africa was situated, national liberation was the 'main content' of this process. The implementation of the Freedom Charter would complete the 'first phase' of transition to South African socialism. The document began with a review of the earlier history of the ANC to explain the timing of its decision to embark on military action. Joe Slovo and his collaborators then prefaced their strategic prescriptions with a warning about 'the danger of the thesis that regards the creation of military areas as the generator of mass resistance'.[90] 'All-round' political mobilisation should accompany armed action, they insisted. In South Africa, revolutionary political leadership would need to be present within and outside the 'actual areas of combat'. Armed action in the first phases would be outside 'the enemy strongholds in the cities, in the vast stretches of our countryside'. In the longer term, though, a mobilised industrial African working class would be a key to victory. Meanwhile, despite the resources that South Africa's minority rulers could command and the loyalties they could depend upon among white citizens as a consequence of their colonial relationship with black South African subjects, the regime had its vulnerabilities. A vast territory offered geographical challenges in any efforts to maintain ubiquitous supervision. For a determined force of guerrillas the 'early development of a relatively safe (though shifting) rear is not beyond the realm of practicality'. At some stage, a 'substantial section' of the white working class might defect from the settler community. 'Our nationalism' should avoid 'the chauvinism or narrow nationalism of a previous epoch', while acknowledging that African liberation should be the 'main content … of the present stage of the South African revolution' – a 'national democratic' stage. Hence, whites willing to make common cause with this movement and members of 'other oppressed groups' needed to be integrated within it 'on the basis of individual equality'. There should be no 'second class participants'.

This was a very generalised strategic blueprint, much less detailed than 'Operation Mayibuye'; it was, after all, a public document. Its most important prescription was that though guerrilla action should remain mainly rural for the time being, armed activities in themselves would be insufficient, and there needed to be simultaneous political mobilisation to build support, not just in operational areas but everywhere. Up to the mid-1970s, communist propaganda circulated inside South Africa would continue to suggest that the guerrilla war 'would begin in the countryside' and that besides the 'freedom fighters with guns', there would need to be 'freedom fighters of the village, the farm, the reserve'. Only later would people in 'even the town' join and strengthen 'the men with the guns', though here they would use 'their own methods'.[91]

An accompanying codicil offered a fresh reading of the Freedom Charter. This sketched out the kind of society that would emerge during national democracy. Its political provisions remained quite cryptic. Parliament would become an Assembly of the People for which everyone could vote or stand as a candidate. There would also be provincial and local 'democratic organs of self-government'. Africans, Indians, coloured and white people would have equal status with respect to language use and development of their 'folk cultures' – the terminology here may have drawn inspiration from Soviet conceptions of 'national rights' within multi–ethnic states. On economic issues, the commentary was more specific. Major or 'monopoly' industries, including vineyards and sugar plantations as well as mining and banking, would be nationalised, and other industries and trades would 'be allowed' under private ownership, but 'with controls'. Land would be confiscated from corporate owners and redistributed: all land would be open to 'ownership and use' by all people, subject to limitations on the size of holdings. Free medical care, education, rent controls and a huge expansion of state welfare would ensure 'houses, security and comfort'.[92] To be sure, all this closely conformed to communist notions of national democracy, and suggested a more confined space for private ownership than in the Charter itself, but there was really little here to which non-communists within the ANC's exile leaders would have objected. After all, many of them were living in Dar es Salaam, hosted by a friendly government that had recently embarked upon a much more radical programme of social and economic transformation. A 'communist analysis' of the Charter that appeared in 1974 conceded that its economic clauses '*may* give scope' for the 'emergence on a wider scale' of a black 'petit bourgeoisie', but such a development would be quite different from any black ascent 'into the ranks of the bourgeois class proper'; that would not happen.[93] As communists recalled three decades later, this was a time when within the top ANC echelon there was apparent 'consensus' about 'the ultimate need to continue our revolution towards a socialist order', a general agreement that the national democratic revolution would be only 'the beginning of a process' through which any kind of capitalist exploitation would end.[94]

That may have been so, but party leaders could still feel they were being sidelined. For example, in 1971 the ANC's National Executive assembled in Lusaka to consider apparently important 'strategic questions connected to new developments inside country'.[95] Communists were present, of course, as members of the executive, but this was, according to a report prepared for the upcoming Central Committee, the first occasion 'of its kind since 1966 in which brother organizations, including the Party, were not asked to send a participant or an observer'.[96] But the problems about the party's status as a partner ran deeper than the occasional snub of this sort. As Joe Slovo observed in 1972,

> A pattern has been set that the Party has call only on its white, Indian and coloured members – and that Africans are the almost exclusive property of the ANC ... the impression has become even more entrenched that we are a minority organization ... no public African figure of stature seen to be at the top ... we have only a qualified right at home to mobilise people under the Party's banner ... In other words we are expected to accept a position which makes a complete mockery of our independence.[97]

It was still the case, Slovo confirmed, that communists were encountering difficulties in their efforts to establish an organised presence within the South African exile community in Africa. And while Morogoro delegates had supported the integration of non-Africans into the ANC's rank and file, important personalities remained ready to contest the decision. Ambrose and Tennyson Makiwane as well as Alfred Kgokong lost their positions on the National Executive in 1969 and around them would gather a disaffected faction. This group may have included Robert Resha, who died in 1973; certainly some of the other members of the 'Gang of Eight', who were expelled from the ANC in 1975, were also influential figures, and Stephen Ellis cites sources that suggest they had considerable support among members of the ANC's rank and file in Zambia and Tanzania as well as in East Germany and London who agreed that 'African nationalism' had been 'hi-jacked' by the 'white SACP'.[98] The evident support this disaffected group could apparently attract even within the ANC community in London would have heightened SACP leaders' perceptions of the vulnerability of the party's terms of engagement with its ally. In London some ANC exiles were unhappy about the replacement of Mazisi Kunene as the organisation's representative by Reg September – a withdrawal, they felt, from the older policy of the ANC stressing its 'African image', which had been decided at Lobatsi in 1962.[99] Initially Oliver Tambo tried to avoid any confrontation with these dissidents, sharply reproving the party for circulating written instructions to its own cadres to refrain from cooperating with eight named individuals.[100] However, Ambrose Makiwane condemned the 'non-African clique' in the SACP for 'manipulating' the ANC, at a ceremony for the unveiling of Robert Resha's headstone in 1975.[101] His audience included Duma Nokwe as well as a sprinkling of diplomats and in response, despite Oliver Tambo's misgivings, the ANC's National Executive agreed with Nokwe's urgings to expel from the organisation eight people involved in this event.[102] Given what he knew about the divisions within his organisation, it was not so surprising that Tambo was inclined to question the need for party leaders to meet as a caucus before any sessions of the Revolutionary Council. In any case the Revolutionary Council was less influential than party leaders hoped; Duma Nokwe – himself a communist – played an obstructive role in 'vitiating' its powers and questioning its relative independence.[103] The expulsion of the Gang of Eight may have decided Tambo to assert himself in future more vigorously, checking the influence of 'the ANC's aggressive left wing', as Karis and Gerhart have suggested.[104]

WITH THESE CONSIDERATIONS in mind and against this backdrop of events, the Central Committee decided to strengthen its presence in Africa. An extended meeting in Moscow in June 1970 had already introduced fresh leadership to the party's top echelon, including Josiah Jele, Chris Hani, Moses Mabhida and Thabo Mbeki. From 1972, the party's African-based leadership assumed fresh responsibilities for the party. Chris Hani would be appointed as assistant secretary in 1972; the party asked for him to be released from his responsibilities in Umkhonto, a request that the ANC leadership declined. At that time, he claimed later, Hani himself was making 'a serious effort to organize party life'.[105] Instead, Eric Mtshali would be supported for a while as a full-time party organiser in Dar es Salaam, after being summoned from his post at the World Federation of Trade Unions in Prague for this purpose. SACTU would be re-established as an exile formation, and headquartered in Lusaka, effectively providing another organisational arena for party activity.

But if the party was to extract from the ANC leadership the kind of recognition it wanted as an independent formation, it needed to build its own capacity for independent action by reviving its own organisational networks inside South Africa. And, indeed, it started trying to do this in 1967. Here the pivotal personality in organising for this purpose was Ronnie Kasrils. With support from a United Nations scholarship, he signed up for a BSc in Sociology at the London School of Economics in 1966. His motivations certainly included a lively intellectual interest in his subject, though he hardly could be said to have approached it with an open mind.

'Why do we have to bother with this rubbish,' he reportedly remarked to one of his classmates after his first encounter with the work of Max Weber.[106] But Kasrils had other reasons for enrolling at the LSE. In his first term he began looking for recruits among his fellow sociologists, personalities who were committed, disciplined and brave enough to open up new lines of communication for the party and the ANC into South Africa. Anti-apartheid was beginning to be a major cause for student activism, especially at the LSE. Here by 1967 students were particularly animated by the appointment of a new principal, Dr Walter Adams, formerly Principal at University College Rhodesia, who was perceived by the students to have collaborated with the Rhodesian authorities.[107] During 1966 at least 40 per cent of LSE's student population would be involved at one time or another in anti-Adams protests, which would continue through the next two years; and in 1968 this movement would fuse with tumultuous demonstrations against the Vietnam War, in which 800 students staged a sit-in. But Kasrils did not confine himself to the activist student community. He also sought the help of acquaintances in the British Communist Party and, through two London-based office-holders in the Young Communist League, George Bridges and Bob Allen, the students Ronnie Kasrils approached directly would be supplemented by a larger group of British communist activists.

Having confirmed their willingness, and after warning them of the risks they might face, Kasrils would teach his new adherents how to handle timing devices and explosives for 'bucket bombs' used for distributing leaflets and how to assemble loudspeakers that would broadcast tape-recorded speeches. The technology used in these devices was the work of Ronnie Press, an industrial chemist who had joined the party in the 1950s and emigrated to Britain in 1961. At Joe Slovo's behest he had visited East Germany to acquire the expertise needed to make 'leaflet throwers' from everyday, easily obtainable components; his Stasi instructors used techniques inherited from clandestine communist activity during the Nazi era.[108] This was in the era before cassette recorders became easily available, and the volunteers would need to solder amplifiers to specially adapted portable reel-to-reel recorders. As in the case of the bucket bombs, it took 'considerable skill' to assemble the equipment.[109] The volunteers would test out the more dangerous devices they assembled on Hampstead Heath. When his pupils were ready, Kasrils would provide them with money for fares and expenses, and false-bottomed suitcases pre-packed with leaflets and the egg-timers or parking-meter alarms needed for the bucket bombs. The 'London recruits' would then travel to South Africa, normally by air, but sometimes making the sea journey on the

Union-Castle line if they had particularly large consignments of leaflets, which were packed into tea chests. They would pose as tourists or would-be immigrants, book themselves into modest hotels – they were told which ones to use – and then begin familiarising themselves with their new urban surroundings, identifying suitable landmarks and places where large numbers of people might be present to read their leaflets; places used by black people, their main target audience. On certain occasions the recruits would undertake mass postings, buying the required quantities of stamps and envelopes for their pre-prepared sticky labels, and then distributing their mailings among different letter boxes.

Between 1967 and 1974, at least 44 of these non-South African, mainly British volunteers would engage themselves in these missions, nine of them women. On the whole, Kasrils was looking for people who already had a history of political commitment and experience of working on the margins of institutional politics; this made people with a Communist Party background obviously attractive, quite aside from any philosophical affinity they may have shared with their new mentor. But Kasrils was not dogmatic in his choices: among the group were three Trotskyists, members of the International Socialists (later the Socialist Workers' Party) with whom Kasrils enjoyed arguing. In the recollections of John Rose, later a lifelong friend, Ronnie was the only person he had met who 'not only owned Stalin's *Collected Works*, but would quote directly from them' after reaching for the appropriate volume on his bookshelves.[110] Intellectual independence and assertiveness seem to have been one of the key attributes that Kasrils was looking for. Several of the people he brought into the groups would later in their lives become distinguished academic authorities.[111] At least 26 of the London recruits were Young Communists, often with several years' membership. Several were second-generation communists; one of them, Sean Edwards, was the son of an International Brigader, a Spanish Civil War veteran. In the cases in which we have detail about their backgrounds, they were mainly working class and, while the group included 12 who were university-educated at the time of their first encounter with Kasrils, others had left school at 15 to become apprentices, train guards, shop workers, telephonists or clerks. There was also a separate group of seamen, recruited through the Communist Party in Liverpool, and brought in, as we will see, for a particular purpose.[112]

The routine assignments for the London recruits were directed at demonstrative displays of leafleting, accompanied by banners and loudspeaker-relayed messages, usually activated on symbolic anniversaries. Their progress can be tracked by following local press reports, for the fireworks that released the leaflets attracted considerable publicity. Each year, from 1967 to 1971, between six and eight of Ronnie Kasrils's trainees would travel to one or other of the main towns – Johannesburg, Cape Town, Durban, Port Elizabeth and East London, but not Pretoria – to explode their devices or undertake mass mailings. The leaflets were mainly in the name of the ANC, and more occasionally from the SACP. In 1968, an ANC leaflet reported on the Wankie operations; a leaflet in 1970 had a message from Mandela on one side and a recipe for making a Molotov cocktail on the other. The timing devices were parking-meter alarms, adapted for their new purpose by Jack Hodgson.[113] Mailings were more focused on the party's revival. For example, working from his dingy hotel bedroom in Hillbrow, Daniel Ahern addressed and then posted 1,200 printed letters from Yusuf Dadoo in his capacity as chairman of the South African Indian Congress – an initial move in an SACP effort to resurrect the Indian Congresses, which had been virtually front organisations for the party in the late 1950s and which had never been banned. Alice McCarthy posted SACP leaflets in Cape Town after disembarking from her Union-Castle liner in 1970. Mary Chamberlain also took a Union-Castle sea voyage to Cape Town so she could bring with her 5,000 closely printed booklets, miniature versions of Michael Harmel's short party history, packed in London into tea chests after their delivery from East Germany. Travelling with her boyfriend, they arrived as prospective immigrants, so that they could explain the quantity of their baggage. Learning from the experience of earlier visitors, they rented an apartment in Cape Town to give them the privacy they needed to unpack and prepare their mailings.

In most cases, volunteers confined themselves to leafleting; they were not expected to engage with local people politically. Their purpose was simply to signal to ANC and party supporters that the movement was once again present inside South Africa; to supply, in Ronnie Kasrils's phrase, a 'visible expression that we survived the terror and continued to grow'.[114] A few were deployed as couriers or, more ambitiously, in reconnaissance activity. For example, in 1967 Daniel Ahern, one of those involved in leafleting, was also asked to take a train from Johannesburg to the Beit Bridge border post so that he could watch the routines used by customs officials, whether they checked all the incoming cars and lorries, and whether the drivers who were checked were mainly black or white. The task does rather suggest that Kasrils may have been aware about the planning of Rhodesian-based infiltration, despite his disavowals. Ahern made his observations, then travelled across Rhodesia by bus, and later gave his report to Oliver Tambo. Several of the other volunteers were asked to leave packages in dead letter boxes, after being prepared in the appropriate 'tradecraft' techniques on Hampstead Heath; Kasrils himself as well as two of the recruits attended intelligence courses in the Soviet Union. Katherine Levine and Lawrence Harris – who were rather exceptional in that they were Cambridge-trained social anthropologists who first encountered ANC people during their Tanzanian fieldwork – were entrusted with one of the first efforts to smuggle weapons into South Africa. Using a specially equipped Land Rover, they crossed the Zambezi several times during 1971, burying the munitions they brought with them under a bridge just outside Gaborone. Harris had been a lecturer at LSE; he crossed the line and supported the student sit-in in 1968 and was dismissed. Levine's background was unconventionally comfortable. She was brought up in a wealthy secular Jewish family in Newcastle, and educated at the progressive co-educational boarding school Bedales, where she was impressed by a visit from the headmaster at Waterford, Michael Stern. Waterford was a non-racial private school in Swaziland; it would count among its pupils Nelson Mandela's daughters. Levine began her African odyssey by spending her gap year at Waterford, working as a teaching assistant. Finally and most ambitiously, several of the London-based recruits as well as the sailors whom the British communists selected in Liverpool were engaged in 'Operation J', an effort to land Umkhonto we Sizwe cadres on the South African coastline in the *Aventura*, a vessel specially purchased for this objective.

Operation J was very much a party-sponsored undertaking, though coordinated carefully with the ANC: the ANC records contain an enthusiastic correspondence between Slovo and Tambo during the planning phase of the mission. The mission's timing was fortuitous; for in 1970, in reaction to a series of clashes in Kongwa by rival groups as well as in response to the Lusaka Manifesto, Julius Nyerere asked the ANC in 1969 to remove its soldiers from the camp, giving them 14 days to leave the country or face disarmament and confinement in a guarded refugee camp. The Umkhonto men were airlifted to the Soviet Union for three years for 'refresher courses' before being allowed to return to Kongwa.[115] In making his demand, Nyerere was also prompted by diplomatic considerations; that year he had signed the Lusaka Manifesto, which appeared to reverse previous unqualified support across Africa for armed struggle against apartheid. Referring to possible 'changed circumstances' that might affect progress in the emancipation of black South Africans – an oblique reference to Prime Minister Vorster's new 'outward policy' of détente – the manifesto suggested that African governments might in future 'urge our brothers in South Africa to use peaceful methods of struggle even at the cost of some compromise'.[116] Relations between Nyerere and the ANC leadership were also damaged by the evidence that emerged in an investigation and subsequent trial of coup plotters. The coup attempt implicated Oscar Kambona, Tanzania's former Foreign Minister, himself friendly with the ANC leadership and also considered to be pro-Soviet. In 1968, he had approached leaders of both the South African liberation movements during preparations for the coup, hoping to enlist their guerrilla forces. The ANC's Tambo had rejected Kambona's request but held back from warning the Tanzanian authorities, who instead learned about the coup from the leader of the Pan Africanist Congress, Potlako Leballo. During the trial in 1970 ANC leaders were asked to leave the country.[117] At this juncture, Oliver Tambo badly needed fresh evidence of his movement's ability to re-establish itself as a fighting force back home. In August 1970, Flag Boshielo and three other men tried to cross the Caprivi Strip into Botswana; they were intercepted by the South African police and killed. Their intention may have been to establish a foothold in Sekhukhuneland, for Boshielo had been involved in the Sebatakgomo resistance network there during the 1950s.[118] The venture was Boshielo's idea, reluctantly sanctioned by Oliver Tambo. Boshielo was a veteran communist and the most senior ANC personality killed in action, the first member of the National Executive to try to re-enter South Africa. Poignantly, in the months before his death he had undergone preparation as an *ngaka*, a diviner.[119]

Joe Slovo first asked Soviet officials for help for a seaborne landing in 1967. They seem to have been receptive. Among the instructions handed to Yuri Loginov, a KGB agent who was arrested in Johannesburg in July 1967, was the injunction that he should find suitable landing places along the South African coastline 'for terrorists and saboteurs'. He was also asked to ascertain the 'present strength and activities of the African National Congress'.[120] The idea that Umkhonto could return its trainees to South Africa in ships first appeared in Operation Mayibuye, and in 1969 Ben Turok had arranged with Oliver Tambo that in his ocean journey from Dar es Salaam to Southampton he should make a point of using his skills as a surveyor to 'examin[e] the terrain', using the ship's equipment to 'inspect the coastline of Pondoland and the Transkei'. The captain of the East German vessel agreed to allow Turok access to the ship's charts. Subsequently he composed a report for Joe Slovo.[121] In October 1970, shortly after an 'augmented' Central Committee meeting in Moscow, the party was informed that the Soviet authorities would support a landing of Umkhonto soldiers on the Transkeian coast and would provide £75,000 for buying a boat. 'Operation J' was code-named after Slovo, and he, together with Ronnie Kasrils and Yusuf Dadoo, provided the planning: Turok was left out despite his reconnaissance contribution and the early research using topographical maps was undertaken by Stephanie Kemp.[122] In fact, the task of establishing exactly where the landing or landings should take place was entrusted to several of the London recruits, Alex Moumbaris, Bill McCaig and Bob Newland. Moumbaris was an Alexandria-born Greek, employed in London at Reuters, who had relatives in the Johannesburg expatriate Greek community. He was originally recruited for one of the first letter-posting expeditions. He received training in the Soviet Union in 1969 and 1971, and made two journeys to South Africa to explore the Wild Coast in 1970 and 1971 and photograph and film suitable locations. For the photography he needed special lessons, and a party member also helped him learn to drive. 'Plucky, taciturn and stubborn',[123] Moumbaris's commitment to the South African cause went well beyond anti-apartheid solidarity: as he explained later, 'the object of my struggle was the struggle of the workers'.[124] A member of the British Communist Party, he also joined the SACP. Bill McCaig was recruited in Liverpool. He was a marine engineer and in 1970 would obtain a job at the Durban docks, and for the next two years he would work with Moumbaris, helping to prepare for the landing. In 1971 he was joined by Bob Newland, who had arrived in Cape Town after travelling on a Union-Castle liner so he could bring in the radio equipment they needed. Other preparations for the landing included opening up communications with Transkeian-based 'contacts' in West and East Pondoland as well as Matatiele: these 'were ready to receive our men' by January 1971.[125]

In the end the vessel Joe Slovo had purchased broke down in March 1972 after the first stage in its journey from Mogadishu to Mombasa. The engines seized up, probably because of sand in the fuel – possibly an intentional sabotage. In this first phase of the *Aventura*'s voyage the crew was Greek, recruited by the Greek party.[126] These sailors were then replaced by the six seamen enlisted by British party officials in Liverpool. They tried to set sail again but the mechanical difficulties persisted. The Liverpool recruits had to travel home after efforts to obtain replacement parts failed; the ship had originally been built as an ocean-going yacht in the United States and has been used by President Roosevelt, but, notwithstanding this illustrious provenance, spares were unavailable. Soviet disappointment at this disheartening episode was signalled by a reduction of funding for the party.[127] Alex Moumbaris was then deployed in a hastily planned effort to infiltrate Umkhonto men recruited for the *Aventura* expedition across the Swazi and Botswana borders. Sean Hosey, another Irish second-generation communist, was sent to support this operation, bringing in money and forged identity documents, after receiving a request from one of the men who had crossed the Swazi border. The documents were probably the work of Jack Hodgson, who had installed himself in a workshop in London in which he forged passports and immigration stamps.[128] Hosey was arrested shortly after his arrival in October 1972; his intended contact had already been turned by the police when he'd written asking London for help. Moumbaris and his wife would be arrested shortly afterwards while organising the Botswana crossing, for which the police were fully prepared, using knowledge from another defector from the Swazi group. Hosey would spend the next five years in prison; Moumbaris was sentenced to 12 years.

From 1969, the SACP's London-based secretariat began to dispatch its own South African members, returning young recent recruits to the party who had joined while staying in London and hence who could be reasonably expected to make their return to South Africa without attracting police attention. Though they were asked to undertake the same sorts of propaganda tasks as the British volunteers, they were also meant to constitute the beginnings of an organisational base inside South Africa. The Central Committee meeting in Moscow in 1970 made the party's political reconstruction inside South Africa a priority, sanctioning the revival of the newspaper *Inkululeko* for this purpose.[129] Even so, the party's new cadres were urged to be very careful; unlike the visiting British volunteers, they were returning to South Africa as their home, and survival was a key imperative. Once back in South Africa, they were expected to operate as disciplined party functionaries and even, occasionally, recruit people, though any candidate for such recruitment needed approval from London.[130] As Raymond Suttner recalled, 'expansion was discouraged' and the mostly white clandestine operators were told to hold back from political contacts with black people.[131] Communication was conducted through ordinary letters overwritten with home-made invisible inks; Ronnie Kasrils and Jack Hodgson provided the training for this purpose and the instructions for assembling bucket bombs. These became more sophisticated after Ronnie Press was taught by Stasi tradesmen in 1974 how to improvise a home-made mortar with a 40-metre 'throw', using easily obtainable chemicals for the explosive charges.[132] The first South Africans prepared for these missions left London in 1969; in one case, David Rabkin, he was to remain at liberty and politically active with his wife, Sue, while working as a reporter for the *Cape Argus* until his capture in 1976.[133] Anthony Holiday also succeeded in avoiding arrest for seven years between 1969 and 1976. Holiday recruited three local helpers and set up a propaganda unit in a rented office in Loveday Street in Johannesburg, producing a journal, *Revolt*, and undertaking mass mailings.

Holiday's duties included intelligence gathering.[134] One of Holiday's recruits was Jeremy Cronin, then a first year student at the university. Later Jeremy Cronin would work with the Rabkins, constituting a party cell.. Cronin's background was unusual among the party's recruits. He was the son of a South African naval officer who had served on the wartime Arctic convoys to Murmansk and Archangel, a facet of his biography, as Jeremy recalled in his haunting poetic memoir of his childhood, that would have to stand as 'slender evidence ... as I search now for retrospective conciliation'.[135] His 'path into politics' was 'wholly intellectual', and was initially stimulated by the Parisian student revolt and a spell at the Sorbonne.[136]

High school teacher Ahmed Timol, visiting London from December 1966, was recruited into the party by Yusuf Dadoo. In South Africa he had been a boyhood friend of Essop and Aziz Pahad, key personalities among the younger generation of South African communists, and fellow students with Thabo Mbeki at the University of Sussex. Timol would train at the Lenin School between February and October 1968, at the same time as Thabo Mbeki, and then returned to Johannesburg in February 1970, with the direction to 'target the Indian community'.[137] Timol compiled an 8,000-name mailing list and began planning a monthly student newsletter. He also recruited people, as many as 25, some of them possibly as party members.[138] Before constituting his cells, he consulted with London; from the correspondence that the police produced later, it is clear that he intended for the time being only to engage these people in helping him with propaganda activity, though he did identify in his letters personalities who might 'have potential to embrace our Communist ideology and not merely stop at liberal or petty-bourgeois politics'. He was arrested more than 18 months later at a routine roadblock, in October 1971, when the police searched his car and discovered leaflets, including 757 copies of a message addressed to 'Sons and Daughters of Africa', *Inkululeko* stencils, and his correspondence with London, which he had unwisely kept. He died five days later after continuous interrogation – a suicide, the police claimed; they maintained he had thrown himself out of a tenth-floor window in their new headquarters building at John Vorster Square. Forty-six years later, a reopened inquest, drawing upon forensic evidence disregarded in the first investigation, confirmed that Timol had either been pushed out of the window or had been dropped from the roof. Fellow detainees who saw him a few hours before his death testified that he could not walk. A post-mortem found that his body was severely bruised by beatings; the scars were clearly the result of injuries inflicted before his fall from the tenth floor. Several of his fellow detainees were tortured by the same officers present during his detention. At the original inquest the police produced a forged version of *Inkululeko* with additions to suggest that the SACP instructed its members to commit suicide if detained. The text contained elementary errors including spelling mistakes and the misnaming of the party.[139]

Raymond Suttner was born in 1945 into a 'liberal Jewish family'; his parents supported Helen Suzman's Progressive Party. He was brought up in Cape Town and studied law before becoming a junior lecturer at the University of Cape Town. As a student he engaged in protest activism, but by the end of the 1960s he became disaffected: 'Liberalism was getting us nowhere.' Marxism appeared to offer an attractive alternative; his first reading in this vein was a second-hand primer by Emile Burns, with Bram Fischer's signature on the flyleaf: 'it delivered a blow to my conceit'. Travelling to Britain to take up a place at Oxford, he gave up his doctoral studies after six months and supported himself with various odd jobs, while 'nagging and pestering the cadres for months'. A series of meetings with Joe Slovo led to his induction into the SACP and a course of doctrinal instruction from Rusty Bernstein. Meanwhile, Ronnie Kasrils showed him how to assemble bucket bombs, manufacture invisible ink, and avoid being followed. As importantly, he prepared himself morally; he spoke to people who had been captured by the police and who had been tortured during their confinement, trying 'to find out how they had been able to withstand the pressures'. He received training for this purpose, which he thinks helped develop his 'confidence and determination'. Returning in 1971 to South Africa to take up a post at the University of Natal in Durban, he began a double life, teaching his students in the daytime and spending nights typing stencils and reproducing the leaflets he was sent from London. He worked by himself for three years, for 'there were no groups or structures into which I could be integrated'. As a loner he was advised not to use bucket bombs; instead, he would post his leaflets, dividing the batches between as many places as possible. 'I gradually came to know the whereabouts of every postbox in Durban and Pietermaritzburg.' Only in 1974, when he again met Joe Slovo and Ronnie Kasrils during a visit to London, was he given permission to recruit helpers. The collapse of Portuguese rule in Angola and Mozambique had convinced the London secretariat that it was time to step up operations inside South Africa. Raymond was to produce a newsletter, *Vukani/Awake*, writing it himself. Like his other productions, it was to be directed primarily at an African readership. His final issue, 10,000 copies of which he posted with his two recruits just before his arrest, included an 'isiZulu translation of the Freedom Charter'. He was arrested by the police on the evening of 17 June 1975. Two days later the police apprehended his two assistants, though he had held out, refusing to offer his captors their names. This was despite assaults that included two several-hours-long sessions of electric shocks; for this purpose a telephone dynamo was wired to his penis, as one of the policemen concerned admitted two decades later. His recruits subsequently testified against him in court as state witnesses, and Suttner would spend the next eight years in prison.[140]

Raymond Suttner has provided the richest testimony about his experiences as a clandestine activist. Other stories have yet to be recounted in such vivid detail, though Jeremy Cronin's poetry also offers sharply rendered experience, especially from the prison term he served alongside Raymond between 1976 and 1983. Houston and Magubane suggest that Suttner replaced James April as head of an ANC–SACP propaganda unit. April, one of the survivors of the Wankie campaign and a graduate of the Czech military training which the SACP had arranged in 1963, arrived in Durban in 1970 after further training in East Germany and instruction from Slovo and Hodgson.[141] He had taken a flight to Johannesburg and used a false passport. As with Timol, his purpose was to make connections with the Indian community, this time in Durban. He was arrested in early 1971. At his trial the police evidence included invisible ink messages he sent to London.

Tim Jenkin and Stephen Lee, recruited after they visited the ANC offices in London, would establish themselves in Cape Town in 1975: they remained at liberty until March 1978, detonating as many as 50 leaflet bombs during this period, including copies of *Inkululeko*.[142] They worked quite separately from the Rabkins and Jeremy Cronin, and were in fact unaware of their activities. Lee and Jenkin had become friends as students at the University of Cape Town and they left South Africa to join the ANC. At the time of his arrest in 1978, Lee was enrolled in a master's programme. A dual British–South African national, he was recruited while working in London as a bus conductor. Jenkin and Lee would escape from their captivity the following year, in December, together with Moumbaris, using duplicate keys made in the prison workshop at Pretoria Central. The escape took nearly a year to plan. Contact between Denis Goldberg in the prison and Baruch Hirson, by then in London, elicited initial expectations that, once out of prison, the escapees could rely on help organised by Joe Slovo from Maputo. These plans fell through, and the trio would make their way to Swaziland, using taxis, hitched lifts and a short train journey as well as walking for much of the distance: they crossed the unfenced frontier on foot.[143]

Retrospectively, Ronnie Kasrils suggests that 'many of the 1976 generation were influenced by our propaganda actions'.[144] This is very optimistic and

Kasrils cites no evidence to support his contention. It is true that the leaflet 'bombings' attracted considerable publicity; as Jenkin notes, in the mid-1970s 'small things like leaflet bombs made big news'.[145] In researching her popular account of anti-apartheid resistance, Julie Frederickse found one informant, the Rev. Fumanekile Qqiba, who witnessed a bucket bomb exploding at Mowbray police station in Cape Town in 1975. He recollected that the event had a considerable impact locally: people were impressed with its relative sophistication: 'People said, "Ah, our boys have come back."'[146] Joe Slovo told Sylvia Neame in 1986 that the work of the London recruits 'made the name of our movement re-emerge' and that people started to 'come back to the Party'.[147] Mac Maharaj was evidently on one of the mailing lists, and his recollection was that after he received in the post a copy of *Inkululeko*, shortly after his release from prison and while he was staying in Durban, it was a real morale booster: 'it made me feel that the Communist Party was present.'[148] One can only guess at the reactions of workers at the Ford Factory in Port Elizabeth when in 1971 two of the London recruits set off a bucket bomb at its entrance.

Possibly the most long-lasting contribution during this time to reviving the party's presence in South Africa was the work of Chris Hani. Accompanied by 'Thomas', another communist, Hani climbed across the Botswana border post in 1974 and walked to Zeerust, then travelled by bus and train to Johannesburg; their infiltration depended on no reception committee or special transport arrangements, and was probably safer for this reason. Hani received three months' training in East Germany before his infiltration and, while he was there, Joe Slovo taught him to ride a bicycle. He also received instruction in the Soviet Union 'on the principles of forming an underground organization'.[149] Before leaving London, he and Stephanie Kemp agreed to use Gabriel Garcia Márquez's *One Hundred Years of Solitude* as the text for their book code; it was her favourite novel but, to her disappointment, Hani didn't like the book at all,[150] which is unsurprising given that Jane Austen was his favourite author. Equipped only with cash, Chris Hani spent four months in Johannesburg possibly setting up a network of cells, relying initially on hospitality and shelter from old friends and family members. He then travelled to Maseru to establish himself there as a local resident, remaining in Lesotho until the end of 1982, and visiting the Transkei, the Eastern Cape and the Free State to set up fresh three-person cells, connected vertically to Maseru; 'We never allowed any horizontal communication ... We didn't allow for a coordinated system of structures inside the country.'[151] His father, Gilbert, lived in Lesotho, running a trading store in Mafeteng, and sharing a home with Elizabeth Mafeking, a veteran unionist and party member and an old associate of Ray Alexander. Gilbert Hani could supply knowledge about the frontier geography as well as contacts with sympathetic Basotho politicians.[152] Two of the SACP's British volunteers, 'Jack' and 'Jill', would work as teachers in Lesotho, travelling there in 1974, after their recruitment by Joe Slovo, especially so that they could provide safe houses and other kinds of support for Hani and his confederates.

Hani's 'deployment' in Maseru was ANC sanctioned. His intended role was to establish infiltration and supply routes for Umkhonto as well as to recruit and train, but it seems that he also saw himself as a party organiser. Maloka's history suggests that Hani was organising an 'underground presence' for the party and SACTU, particularly in the Eastern Cape. After the Durban strike movement in 1973 signalled a new African labour militancy, the party was particularly keen to restore SACTU's authority over any emerging trade union revival inside South Africa, and it included SACTU's resurrection among Hani's new organisational tasks.[153] Raymond Suttner thinks that Chris Hani did build party units inside South Africa during this time, though he concedes that 'Hani's activities are one of many cases where the line between ANC and SACP underground organization was blurred'.[154] Hani's own testimony, in an interview in 1990, suggests that the main purpose of the organisation he was setting up was for military recruitment for Umkhonto. As escorts for the recruits, he employed couriers resident in Transkei districts bordering Lesotho, who were familiar with pathways across the mountainous frontier. However, Hugh Macmillan in his biography of Jack Simons cites Simons as an authoritative source for maintaining that Hani's main role in Lesotho was 'not military' and that he and the people he was recruiting were interested in 'the organization mainly of civic associations and trade unions'.[155] Trial evidence from the 1980s does confirm that among the people with whom Hani was in contact were four men who were engaged in SACTU networking in and around Mdantsane outside East London.[156] The appearance of Communist Party leaflets in Umtata in 1981 could have been the work of one of the party units that Hani may have established.[157]

WHAT IS STRIKING IS that activists better placed to do so than Hani were not instructed to make any contact with the labour movement that was beginning to construct itself in the wake of the 1973 strikes. While he was preparing and posting his leaflets, Raymond Suttner was working on a university campus in

Durban at which white student activists were actively engaged in the strike movement, supplying advice and other kinds of support. At roughly the same time as his arrival in Durban, SACTU actually opened an office in Durban in 1972 – the organisation had never been prohibited legally. The initiative seems to have been local, not directed from outside; it was only in the following year, 1973, that SACTU set up an organisational headquarters in Lusaka together with various 'internal committees' in Front Line states tasked with establishing SACTU groups within the emerging African labour movement inside South Africa.[158] In Botswana, John Gaetsewe bought an old mining property on SACTU's behalf, using donor money and a bank loan. The idea was that it might accommodate a stopover cafe for South African truck drivers, though whether it was ever used as an operational base as opposed to a money-earning venture is unclear.[159] In Mozambique, a SACTU group based itself in a building in the industrial suburb of Matola, on the outskirts of Maputo, in 1975.[160] William Khanyile, Harry Gwala's cousin, who had joined the party in the early 1960s before serving eight years on Robben Island, was 'brought out of the country in 1977' to help run the SACTU office in Maputo.[161]

In Durban, Harold Nxasana was the main personality in the effort to open the SACTU office; then in his late thirties, he was a veteran SACTU organiser who had spent a year in prison for ANC activities. He and his collaborator, Joseph Mdluli, issued a pamphlet announcing SACTU's revival, and, according to his testimony, 'workers started flocking into the offices'.[162] A residual memory of the earlier generation of trade union activity in Durban may have helped elicit this response. A survey conducted in 1973 among unregistered trade unionists in Durban asked if they could 'think of a leader present or past who can or could improve the position of African workers'. The four most frequently mentioned names were Albert Luthuli, Chief Buthelezi, Nelson Mandela and Moses Mabhida.[163] Nxasana and Mdluli brought the old SACTU president, Stephen Dlamini, into this undertaking, naming him chairman, though Dlamini was restricted by a banning order and was effectively under house arrest. They had no material resources to help them, and had to shut up shop. Nxasana went on to contribute to the building of two new industrial unions, for textile workers and metal workers, while at the same time he and Mdluli as well as a recently released Harry Gwala started building an underground SACTU network. Jacob Zuma may also have been involved in this network from 1974 after his return from Robben Island; his biographer repeats a claim that 'he was active behind the scenes of industrial unrest'.[164] It is most likely that he was in touch with the people involved in the efforts to revive SACTU. Mdluli and Dlamini were old comrades with whom he had worked closely as a SACTU organiser in the 1950s and early 1960s. Phyllis Naidoo, Zuma's attorney, sent him to a friend of hers who might have been willing to offer him a job. Her friend was impressed: Zuma, he said, 'was very articulate; very aware of workers' rights. He probably will bring my workforce out on strikes, but equally I think I could talk to him.'[165] In Zuma's case, his prime interest in engagement with any underground networks, SACTU, ANC or SACP, was to enlist any 'potential information-gatherers and soldiers for the struggle'.[166] Zuma himself was the main figure in building new Umkhonto recruitment lines across the Swazi frontier, liaising for this purpose with Thabo Mbeki, who was by then established in Swaziland. And, indeed, evidence from Harry Gwala's subsequent trial suggests that as a trade unionist, Harold Nxasana would experience heavy pressure from Gwala, 'not for the purpose of building trade unionism but to act as a recruiter for MK'.

On the basis of this sort of evidence, Martin Legassick has argued that, on the whole where a SACTU underground succeeded in establishing itself in the 1970s, it mainly 'attempt[ed] to recruit workers and youth to leave the country, where they would join MK'. In effect, he maintains, SACTU continued to function 'as a signpost to MK', as it had done in the early 1960s.[167] However, correspondence that has survived in Mark Shope's papers suggests that around Johannesburg at least, SACTU's Transvaal underground really existed and it was trying to establish a factory-based presence in newly established industrial unions in the early 1970s, though with very little success.[168] While he was in Swaziland in 1975, Mbeki received reports on individual SACTU members working through legal trade union centres, including the Institute for Industrial Education and the Industrial Aid Society (IAS).[169] Ray Alexander also kept in touch with veteran unionists in the Cape, and she, John Gaetsewe and Dan Thloome in their capacities as SACTU leaders attended a discreet meeting in 1975 with IAS organisers Phindile Mfeti (a nephew of Govan Mbeki) and Gavin Andersson in Botswana – at this juncture Mfeti had already joined the ANC and Andersson was to become a member during this trip.[170] The IAS included SACTU activists but it was not a SACTU front; Mfeti would often warn Andersson that they should 'resist simply following instructions from outside', for 'these folks' – ill-informed about local conditions – 'could make severe miscalculations'.[171] Later, the IAS would become increasingly opposed to unions making political alliances, especially with underground formations. In 1975, apparently, SACTU attempted to assemble South African-based union leaders 'to establish a broad trade union centre' among metal and transport workers, but the initiative foundered, 'due to interference by some academics'.[172] SACTU's main office was in London, where it rented premises in Flowers Mews, Archway. It was under the direction of Zola Zembe (Archie Sibeko), the ex-railway workers' union leader. In 1976 it started publishing *Workers' Unity*. Tensions would develop between the newsletter's editorial board, constituted by Rob Petersen, Paula Ensor and David Hemson, three white activists who had been involved in the trade union revival in 1973 and 1974 in Durban and Cape Town. After being banned and leaving South Africa in 1976, they had been invited by John Gaetsewe to help edit *Workers' Unity*. Through the agency of Ted Grant, originally a South African, they also connected up with Militant, a Trostkyist entryist faction within the British Labour Party. They would be suspended from the ANC and SACTU in 1979 after advocating British trade union support for the emerging 'independent unions', a position at odds with the traditional insistence by both the party and many SACTU veterans that the British labour movement should have no direct dealings with South African-based organisations and that any contact would be a violation of sanctions.[173]

The group associated with *Workers' Unity* were exceptional in taking their cues from New Left Marxism. On the whole SACTU activity involved people who were active party members or, at least, party veterans, including Chris Hani, Harry Gwala, Joseph Mdluli and Stephen Dlamini, as well as the key figures in the SACTU headquarters in Lusaka, such as Eric Mtshali and Mark Shope. Whether there was a concerted and systematically organised party initiative to revive a party-aligned workers' movement remains questionable. Hani's own testimony, recorded in 1990, rather suggests that for him, the main priority in his work in Lesotho and the Eastern Cape was Umkhonto recruitment; that he mentions nothing else in this interview is surely significant. In any case, whatever SACTU's leadership was trying to accomplish when it set up its southern African infrastructure in 1973, it was a long way from London where the key SACP decision-makers were still located. In at least one instance, the London SACP leadership actively discouraged an effort by one of their own comrades to support the reconstruction of workers' organisation by a party veteran in Durban.

Ben Turok, excluded it seems from the circle managing the London recruitment, received a letter in 1973 from Harold Strachan, a convicted Umkhonto saboteur who had joined the SACP in 1961 and with whom Turok had become friends while serving his own prison sentence at Pretoria Central. Strachan was then trying to raise support for trade unionists in Durban, working with MD Naidoo, an old CPSA activist who had built Indian unions in the 1940s. When Turok approached Joe Slovo on Strachan's behalf, Slovo treated him dismissively, telling him that 'structures were in place and that all was being taken care of'. Turok told him he needed a more reassuring response to give to Strachan's wife, who was in London at the time. Slovo then suggested that perhaps Harold Strachan's problem was that he was not working within 'movement structures'. At this stage, Turok lost his temper and the meeting ended angrily. Subsequently Turok arranged for money he obtained from Canadian Oxfam to be sent to Harold through the International University Exchange Fund (IEUF); another former fellow prisoner, Hugh Lewin, organised the details. At this stage neither Turok, nor Lewin, nor indeed the SACP leadership knew about the IEUF's infiltration by the South African security police agent Craig Williamson. The financial transfers were successful: Naidoo received the money, as he confirmed later when he encountered Ben Turok in London. Turok then received a visit at his home from Rusty Bernstein and Barry Feinberg, calling on him in their capacities as members of the London Central Committee. They had heard from Canada that he, Turok, was raising money for trade unions in South Africa. What could he tell them about it? Turok confirmed that he had been sending money to South Africa but refused to name Strachan or Naidoo as recipients. He was then warned that his reluctance might be perceived as a 'breach of Communist discipline', but Turok remained adamant that he would not give them any names. Subsequently, in February 1976, Turok was expelled from the SACP, for assisting groups that had no connection with either the party or the ANC and that might actually be opposed to them.[174] Turok's expulsion was at the time decided by the secretariat; the broader Central Committee had favoured a milder sanction.[175]

In LONDON, THE NUMBER of London-based communists who were involved in the efforts to re-establish a party presence inside South Africa in the early 1970s was very small indeed, a sensible enough security precaution.[176] Turok's experience suggests they guarded the boundaries of their jurisdiction very zealously. For most of the London-based South African communist community, party work was directed chiefly at supporting the British Anti-Apartheid Movement. For many, in any case, full-time activism was precluded by the need to make a living. Rica Hodgson, Jack's wife, was able to combine both vocations, working as Canon Collins's secretary for Defence and Aid, the organisation that channelled more than £100 million to South Africa to support detainees, political prisoners and their families.[177] Joel Joffe, a member of the defence team at the Rivonia trial, after travelling to Britain on an exit visa, had established the Abbey Life Insurance Company. Joffe was not a communist, but Abbey Life supplied livelihoods for a significant number of the South African comrades, including, briefly, Thabo Mbeki: as Joffe himself once observed wryly to a visitor, 'some of our best workers are communists'.[178] Paul Joseph became a manager of Abbey Life's post room. Rather oddly, despite his track record as a key organiser for Umkhonto and the party in Fordsburg, he was not drawn into the efforts to prepare the London recruits; perhaps this was because by the time of his arrival, his main London contact, Vella Pillay, was out of favour on account of his refusal to give up working for the Bank of China. On arriving in London in 1965, Joseph joined a large party group with 17 members. Meetings were mainly taken up with discussions of articles in *African Communist*. Joseph's memoir suggests that such sessions could be quite lively and even contentious, though too often 'we sat through boring and tedious speeches by Soviet leaders'.[179] Ronnie Kasrils was rather unusual among the South African communists in his willingness to engage with a cross-section of British Marxism. On the whole, though, the party's senior leadership in London remained well insulated from any wider intellectual currents generated by the emergence of the New Left on university campuses, though, as we shall see, this was not true with respect to its wider exile community.

As noted above, in 1968 the SACP and, indeed, the ANC both published statements on the Warsaw Pact invasion of Czechoslovakia, justifying it with reference to 'reactionary, anti-socialist forces in the country, based on remnants of the former exploiting classes'. The party's Central Committee in fact published two declarations on the subject, one three weeks before the invasion, praising the internationalism of the Soviet Union and other Warsaw Pact leaders. It was 'false and slanderous', the Central Committee maintained, 'to paint the situation as if the Soviet Union were resisting the process of "democratisation" in Czechoslovakia'.[180] The ANC's statement was signed by Duma Nokwe.[181] Oliver Tambo, apparently, expressed polite disquiet about the ANC's support for the Soviet invasion; he did not sanction the ANC's statement and he felt, personally, 'the ANC ought not to meddle in Cold War inter-state conflicts', he told Sobizana Mngqikana at the time.[182] Alfred Kgokong was one senior leader who at the time expressed reservations about the invasion and was suspended from his position as director of publicity. In Dar es Salaam, Duma Nokwe's endorsement of the Soviet action on the ANC's behalf probably caused wider unease among the ANC's following in Tanzania, as the Tanzanian authorities encouraged students to demonstrate against the invasion and then suspended diplomatic relations with the Czechs. Meanwhile, the ANC's rival, the Pan Africanist

Congress, condemned the invasion.

Of course, the SACP depended upon financial support from the Soviet Party, and the German Democratic Republic had been a key source of support of one kind or another since the 1950s. Within the international communist family, the South Africans would be among the most vigorous defenders of the Warsaw Pact's action, even rebuking the Romanian leader, Nicolae Ceauşescu, for criticising the invasion at a conference.[183] It is likely that the South Africans' support for the suppression of the Czech reform movement reflected deeply held convictions, not just pragmatic considerations. In a lengthy editorial the party's theoretical journal supplied an explanation of the party's decision – probably the work of Michael Harmel. The democratisation under way in the Prague Spring would have destroyed socialism, *African Communist*'s editors insisted. The kind of democracy that communists should fight for was not a capitalist democracy: 'democracy is not merely a formal question of allowing many parties to function'. Quoting Lenin, the editorial went on to argue that any socialist society of necessity is a dictatorship, as long as it requires 'the forcible suppression of exploiters as a class'.[184] In the case of South Africa, after all, the party's own programme since 1992 had proposed that a national democracy, while guaranteeing civil liberties, would also maintain 'a vigorous dictatorship ... by the people against former dominating and exploiting classes'. This suggests a rather different kind of political order from the parliamentary democracy cited by Kotane in his pamphlet in 1954.[185]

Michael Harmel worked for a year in Prague at the *World Marxist Review* before his death in June 1974. Aside from Moscow, Prague was the metropolitan centre for communist internationalism, accommodating the headquarters of a panoply of global institutions. Harmel was the chief architect of the party's vision of national democracy. He was a conventional Marxist-Leninist. As one of his friends noted, he 'never deviated' and certainly 'he was never deceived by Czechoslovakia and Hungary'.[186] Indeed, Yusuf Dadoo observed in his funeral oration that Harmel was 'steadfast in his support for the Czechoslovak people during the 1968 crisis'.[187] Harmel was sent to Prague partly because of his authority as a theorist, though it was also a compassionate decision by the SACP leadership, for by that time Harmel was seriously unwell. Harmel's surviving correspondence from Prague includes approving references to Czech high culture and praise for what he believed to be decent housing and efficient public services.[188] Aside from his work at the *Review*, he seems to have been chiefly active within the still-substantial African student community, though he mentions a few Czech friends.

In his interpretation of the Czech reform movement, Harmel relied on the official justifications for the invasion. We do not know whether he consulted any South African communists who were there at the time. There were at least two, Mark and Gertrude Shope, who might have offered a different perspective. Mark Shope was one of a succession of South Africans representing SACTU at the World Federation of Trade Unions' Prague headquarters; others included, from 1963, Wilton Mkwayi, Moses Mabhida, Eric 'Comrade Stalin' Mtshali and Joe Molokeng. Mark Shope's daughter, Lyndall, and his wife, Gertrude, accompanied him during his five-year posting between 1963 and 1969. Lyndall attended primary school in Prague; she can still remember the stories she was told about Prague's liberation by the Red Army. She won a Czech national flag as a prize on one occasion, a poignant award as she, as a black South African, had no flag for her own country.[189] Gertrude Shope reminisced about her time in Prague for a commemorative World Federation of Trade Unions (WFTU) publication; in her life it was an unusually happy period, the only time in her long exile when she and her husband and children could live together as a family.[190] She was shocked and bewildered by Jan Palach's suicide in January 1969, one of the few political events in Prague she recalled when interviewed in 2015, but she could offer no firm views about the Soviet invasion. As guests, the South Africans at the WFTU believed they should hold back from any local political engagement.[191] This may have been true of Gertrude's immediate circle, but in fact the WFTU's secretariat condemned the invasion, by seven votes to one, responding to an appeal from Czechoslovak trade unions.[192] Peter Waterman, a British communist attached to the WFTU at the time, recalled later that during the preceding 'Spring', his Czech colleagues, at least the 'younger and more open' among them, 'had not abandoned the hope', after witnessing 'Czechoslovak society gradually coming to life again'.[193] Waterman worked in Prague with African trade unionists, and was himself an enthusiastic supporter of the Czech reform movement and a critic of its suppression.

Michael Harmel's views of the Prague Spring and its suppression were probably shared quite widely within the party's few hundred members, though not by all of them. Joe Slovo and Ruth First disagreed about the events of 1968 and apparently had lengthy arguments about it, though these never surfaced in public.[194] Hilda Bernstein objected to the invasion, again like First, arguing with her husband, Rusty. She resigned from the party.[195] Ruth First remained in the party but would question doctrinal orthodoxies; in fact she was allowed unusual licence to do so.[196] Norman Levy, then a fresh immigrant in London after serving his prison sentence for party activities alongside Bram Fischer, was also dismayed by the invasion. He rather thought

Dubček's aim of 'socialism with a human face' was 'quite appropriate' and expressed this view to his 'fellow expatriates'. Brian Bunting would 'overlook' asking him to join a party group in London for ten years; for the time being, former comrades maintained an 'enigmatic silence'. In his own mind, Levy 'never separated from the organization'.[197] For Albie Sachs, the invasion was 'an extremely bitter moment'. The spectacle of 'a Socialist country attacking another socialist country' could not be rationalised away. Albie's father, Solly, expelled from the party nearly four decades before, was unsympathetic: 'Albie,' he said, 'you'll never be a Bolshevik.'[198] By this time, Albie Sachs was no longer active in the party.[199] For the older Lenin School-trained veterans, such as Solly Sachs, Moses Kotane or JB Marks, the Warsaw Pact's suppression of 'counter-revolutionaries' was no occasion for soul searching. Ronnie Kasrils, whose own intellectual trajectory had taken him through Sartre's existentialism before he encountered Marxism, later remembered other exchanges between South African communists on the topic, but 'in the debates that took place I found all the older comrades, as well as my peers, disappointingly closed-minded about the developments.' He allowed himself to be persuaded, finally, that 'the Soviet Union had no option', a judgement that later he 'came to regret'.[200]

Even the British Communist Party, with which the South African exiles were so closely aligned, divided quite sharply and publicly over Czech events, and, on the whole, leading South African communists remained close to the faction that endorsed the invasion. But it would be too simple to characterise the London exiles as an intellectually enclosed group, unaffected by the ideas and thinking of the communities that hosted them. Harold Wolpe is an especially arresting example of a South African communist whose thinking would be shaped by fresh analytical approaches he encountered in his new career as an academic sociologist, a following he took completely seriously. Wolpe's most influential academic work would distance him from SACP doctrinal orthodoxies. This is evident in two of his early papers, one, published in 1972, that considered the class interests served by apartheid, and the other, written a couple of years later, that took issue with the party's argument that South Africa's political economy was shaped by a form of 'internal colonialism'.

Wolpe's efforts to recast the theoretical base for Marxist and, more specifically, communist understandings of modern South African history were shaped by the French anthropologist Claude Meillassoux, from whom he drew the idea that within a single economic system there could exist two interrelated modes of production. Before 1948, Wolpe proposed, non-capitalist farming in the reserves had helped to maintain capitalism, through its provision of social security, enabling especially low wages. By the time of the National Party's electoral victory, non-capitalist farming in the reserves had almost ended, having been undermined by a range of factors, including inefficient cultivation. The 1948 election pitted against each other capitalist factions that had different proposals to address a crisis that was expressed in the rising militancy of black migrant workers. In the new dispensation, favoured by the growing 'Afrikaner industrial and financial capitalist class', the ethnic homelands would retain key systemic functions. Though they had lost the productive capacity to support the workers' social security that capitalists in a low-wage economy were disinclined to pay for, tribal authorities with their continuing ideological authority would exercise crucial control procedures over workers, who would increasingly find their livelihoods in relocated factories adjacent to homeland borders in which employers could pay even lower wages than those prevalent in the cities. Under apartheid, race relations had become integrated with capitalist relations 'to such a degree that the challenge to the one becomes of necessity a challenge to the other'.

In this analysis of 'Capitalism and Cheap Labour Power', Wolpe refrained from any direct criticism of Communist Party theory.[201] It was probably not his intention, but certain readers took his analysis of the way in which modern capitalism in South Africa was systemically interwoven with racial oppression as a rationale for rejecting strategic approaches that emphasised 'national' mobilisation ahead of class struggle. But in his subsequent writing, Wolpe was more explicit in contesting party orthodoxies, opening up the possibility that there might exist among and between black South Africans exploitative class-based relationships. Too often, Wolpe suggested, in the party's programmatic writing, including its *Road to South African Freedom*, 'class relations are simply assimilated to race relations'.[202] It was not an argument he carried through to any detailed conclusion; instead, he used his cheap labour analysis to defend the party's view of South Africa as embodying a 'colonialism of a special type'. The editors of *African Communist* were evidently unappreciative; Michael Harmel rejected an early draft of Wolpe's 1972 article, without explaining why.[203] Wolpe's friend Joe Slovo seems have been more open-minded, echoing much of the argument in Wolpe's cheap labour power thesis in his own elaboration of the party's theory of internal colonialism. Wolpe's influence is especially evident in Slovo's discussion of the 'real function of the Reserve system'.[204] In his contribution to a volume in the Penguin African Library series, Slovo's preoccupation was not so much with apartheid's formation but rather with its future destruction and what might follow, but, here too, Wolpe's analysis helped to underpin his own argument.[205]

In a wider setting, Harold Wolpe's work would help trigger important academic debates; there is no question about its importance in shaping South African historiography. In this story, its significance has to do with its unintended activist influence. For by the mid-1970s in South Africa, ostensibly arcane scholarly discussions among historians and social scientists were beginning to shape public events. Wolpe's writings enjoyed a wide circulation in South Africa, being facilitated by the advent of cheap and accessible reproduction that enabled 'a photocopying culture ... in which tatty British seminar papers were widely circulated among student activists'.[206] The ambiguities in Wolpe's arguments meant that they had quite different effects. For some of his white student readers, the centrality of capitalism and class in his explanation of apartheid's genesis supplied a rationale for their engagement in struggles that challenged economic exploitation and acted quite independently of African nationalist movements. For students at the University of Natal beginning to engage in supportive work with trade unions, Wolpe's papers became foundational texts, supplying 'a theoretical basis to their socialism', and helping to establish a freshly compelling Marxism, 'stripped of its Stalinist accretions', which would achieve an almost hegemonic authority on English-language university campuses in the next decade.[207] For other readers in South Africa, Wolpe's academic writing, increasingly prescribed as it was in university classrooms during the decade, was a key contribution in 'facilitating the political shift among many black students from Black Consciousness to the ANC and the SACP'.[208] Among this group, Wolpe's reputation was doubtless buttressed by his heroic status as a Rivonia escapee. But it was Wolpe's academic authority which would really be important, for, as we shall see, during the late 1970s and 1980s campus-based activism would become a major arena in struggle politics and the party's gathering influence.

During the 1970s university students had acquired a fresh political importance; together with black factory workers, they became key drivers of extra-parliamentary opposition to apartheid. Social and economic changes over the previous decade help to explain these developments. Two key changes in the 1960s were politically transformative. The first was happening in the factories. Partly because of a doubling of foreign direct investment between 1960 and 1972, the South African economy grew by more than five per cent a year. Much of this economic expansion was in manufacturing; here black, mainly African, employment rose by 75 per cent between 1958 and 1968. The tasks that Africans were performing in factories were increasingly likely to be skilled or semi-skilled. For example, by 1973 in Durban textile workshops, 90 per cent of the workforce was African, and only 10 per cent was unskilled; nearly half were trained machine operators, factory clerks or needle setters. Africans moved onto the auto assembly lines in Port Elizabeth in 1960; by 1970 they predominated there. Secondly, to support this economic expansion, a massive increase in schooling was both needed and achieved. By the 1970s, literacy and high school enrolment were normal experiences in urban working-class families; in the 1950s they had been exceptional. Overall, school enrolment between 1960 and 1976 expanded from 1.5 million to 3.7 million students. Working-class Africans were increasingly newspaper readers: in 1975 in Soweto, three out of four adult residents read a daily newspaper, usually the tabloid *World*, which enjoyed a six-fold readership increase between 1962 and 1975. Educational expansion included higher education: new segregated universities for black students as well as teacher training colleges and seminaries. Historically white universities, some of which still enrolled a few black students, also expanded and proliferated.

On white English-speaking university campuses, the authorities tolerated white student activism up to a point as long as they perceived the students as socially liminal. From 1963, as Julian Brown argues, the National Union of South African Students (NUSAS) had become 'by default' the 'principal face of opposition to the government', perceiving itself as such and being increasingly viewed in this way by the authorities. NUSAS incubated the generation of black students who went on to establish the Black Consciousness Movement; and when black students set up their racially exclusive organisation, relations between black and white student leaders – contrary to conventional depictions, as Brown shows – remained cordial. In the late 1960s, white students drew upon external sources of inspiration to experiment with new protest tactics, experiments which were then taken up and developed on blacks-only campuses from 1971. Through the early 1960s the activism of both black and white students was competitive and at the same time mutually reinforcing, in an 'implicit dialogue' with each other. Arguably, student organisations, black and white, supplied models and inspirations to each other and 'to other groups and communities'. As importantly, by becoming targets of state repression against 'agitators' and 'outside influences', the students distracted the state's attention from the local arenas of workers' protest. Subsequently, with the authorities' acceptance of the view of the Durban strike movement as 'apolitical' and hence 'outside the realm of political contest', a new, relatively protected space opened up for student activism, black and white, to build new working-class networks of communal solidarity.[209] The authorities' toleration of campus-based support for activism would end in late 1976 in the wake of the Soweto uprising, when the Minister of Justice banned 26 union officials as well as several academics.

Exile communists were aware of shifts in the make-up of the industrial workforce, though they paid much less attention to anything happening in high schools or on college campuses. Joe Slovo in his 1976 essay suggested that 'class-based action' would play a central role in apartheid's overthrow; moreover, this fact would minimise any prospect 'for the national struggle to fall under bourgeois hegemony'. In the South African setting, Slovo explained, 'national liberation' had to imply 'expropriation of the means of production'. It would be most unlikely in the coming phases, he reasoned, that a black bourgeoisie could emerge with the capacity or the will to 'stop the revolution in its tracks'.[210] Though the concluding sections of Slovo's essay chiefly made the case for 'armed tactics' as 'one of the main foundations ... in South Africa's future liberation struggle', his description of how the future struggle for national democracy might develop emphasised a combination of all methods: 'legal, semi-legal and clandestine'. In particular, 'the muscle power' of black labour needed to find 'organizational expression'.[211] So, in Slovo's formulation, the national democratic revolution would depend heavily, if not primarily, upon worker and peasant 'class action'. Even so, party strategists still maintained that the revolution would be embodied in a broader alliance. As one of the cyclostyled leaflets that Raymond Suttner so painstakingly retyped on his stencils explained, the 'middle and upper classes amongst the black groups' remained affected by apartheid's humiliations. Hence:

> It is both necessary and possible, therefore, to retain a broad section of this group in the liberation struggle, as long as the necessary vigilance is maintained against the importance of counter-revolutionary ideology into the national movement. The petty bourgeoisie naturally vacillates between oppressors and oppressed, depending partly upon the strategy of the main antagonists in the struggle. This, the effective heightening of our liberation front of confrontation with the racist state, will win over the broadest sections of the black majority including sections of the middle class.[212]

So just at the time, in the early 1970s, when the party and the ANC were beginning in very tentative ways to rebuild networks inside South Africa, there were fresh constituencies available for mobilisation, in schools, on higher-education campuses and in factories. And, to be sure, with the British London recruits and most of their South African counterparts, they found their target audiences in the urban transport hubs used by black commuters, probably as often as not factory workers who lived in hostels near their workplaces. Timol seems to have been exceptional in preparing a leaflet directed at high school students. They were also communicating with the people on their mailing lists, generally older-generation former activists. But to judge from the content of the leaflets that have survived, both from the bucket bombs and the mailing lists, their messages did not refer to what was happening in the workplace; they were about the armed struggle.[213] And even when clandestine propagandists such as Raymond Suttner or Stephen Lee worked on university campuses, they held back from any political engagement with students. Harold Wolpe's participation in a new wave of Marxist 'revisionist' scholarship was singular in its effect of helping to open up campus-based communities to the party's influence, even if this was more accidental than intentional.

Meanwhile, it seems, the SACTU networks being resurrected by Jacob Zuma, Harry Gwala and Chris Hani only occasionally intersected with the new trade unionism emerging in the Durban factories. As we have seen, Chris Hani's and Jacob Zuma's main preoccupations were to re-establish lines of communication that could enable the onset of recruitment and the dispatch of new recruits for training outside South Africa, just in time before the exodus from South Africa of activist refugees who began arriving in Botswana and Swaziland in the wake of the Soweto uprising of 1976. Setting up logistical lines would be much easier from 1975 onwards, because Mozambique's new FRELIMO government would provide the ANC and 'non-African' SACP activists with a welcoming environment. Moreover, Angola was willing to allow the ANC to establish training camps for Umkhonto on a much larger scale, and the accession of a series of Marxist-Leninist regimes across Africa would help induce fresh Soviet commitments of military support for the ANC. A shift in the SACP's new acceptability in certain African vicinities was evident that year in November when officials in the ruling party and government leaders in Congo-Brazzaville received an SACP delegation for 'militantly frank' discussions.[214] In 1977, the party would appoint a new executive group at a Central Committee meeting in East Germany, calling it the Politburo – its three active members, Joe Slovo, Moses Mabhida and Thabo Mbeki, would be based in Africa.[215] By this stage Thabo Mbeki was Oliver Tambo's 'political secretary' – essentially 'Tambo's gatekeeper'.[216] Assertive party leadership was no longer confined to London.

AT THE OPENING OF its exile history, the party's prospects must have seemed bleak. Its networks inside South Africa had been destroyed and much of its leadership was denied residence in the other parts of Africa where the ANC had established bases. Black South African communists who were active within the ANC in East Africa often held senior positions but they did not act collectively as communists and they did not actively recruit within the ANC on the party's behalf. Individual communists contributed to key decision-making if they held ANC office; otherwise, they were excluded through most of the 1960s. Communication between the party's secretariat in London and top-echelon communists in Dar es Salaam was intermittent. In the case of the most significant ANC operations, the two Rhodesian expeditions and the attempt to send guerrillas back to South Africa through Mozambique, although in each case communists were engaged as field commanders, the party was not consulted beforehand and was not involved in any of the strategic planning. To be sure, the failure of these initiatives caused a shift in ANC policy and the construction of a strategic planning body on which London-based communists were appointed, and arguably the party began as well to actively shape the ANC programmatically from 1969 onwards. Even so, 'non-African' communists continued to feel that they were kept at a distance through the opening years of the 1970s. The reality was that they were unable to join ANC leaders in Dar es Salaam on a long-term basis or live anywhere else in sub-Saharan Africa until 1975.

Critical perceptions of the party's survival and its capacity to maintain its identity and influence in this period sometimes stress the importance of its role as a broker between the broader liberation movement and the Eastern bloc countries that supplied the ANC with resources. In fact, from 1963 the ANC negotiated its own financial support from the Soviet Union. The presence of communists within the ANC leadership was probably helpful for this, but an alliance with the party was hardly a condition for obtaining Soviet funding. Soviet foreign policy sometimes supported African governments that suppressed their own communist parties; the Egyptians in 1964 were a case in point, and the Sudanese in 1971 would be another. Stephen Ellis views Moses Kotane's illness and death as a key development in enabling the party once again to exert an active corporate presence within the ANC's hierarchy. This argument seems overstated, not least because the limitations on the party's formal presence continued after Kotane's departure for hospital in Moscow.

What the narrative traced in this chapter shows is that the party's survival during this phase of its history was not so much a consequence of its ability to sway the leadership of the larger exile community or spread its influence within the ANC's rank and file. Rather, it was the result of its own independent cultural life and its own activism. The detailed history of its early engagement with the Czechs suggests that it was able and willing to follow its own independent initiatives. The recruitment of couriers and agit-prop carriers in London, and their successful dispatch to South Africa from 1967 onwards, are evidence of this. From 1972 the party began attracting fresh enrolments mainly, though not exclusively, among white South African students, several of whom were able to build their own cells inside South Africa and reproduce and circulate party propaganda. They also began to reconstruct a presence within the Indian communities around Johannesburg. From 1974 Chris Hani, based in Lesotho, also began building a party presence in townships in the Eastern Cape, which would endure into the next decade. London, Dar es Salaam and Lusaka-based communists were active in SACTU, which began its attempt to rebuild an organised labour following in Durban, Johannesburg and Cape Town from 1972, though its influence would be resisted or, at least, contested by the new generation of trade union leaders emerging inside South Africa. SACTU's presence within the wider labour movement was, however, probably more an effect of locally based veterans such as Harold Nxasana becoming active again than a consequence of external direction. Finally, and at least as importantly, Harold Wolpe's efforts to recast the theoretical foundations of the party's analysis of South Africa's 'internal colonial' status helped bring SACP ideas back onto South African university campuses during a crucial time of student ferment.

EIGHT

Mayibuye iAfrika, 1977–1990

A banner for the Communist Party was held up by activists in Cradock at the funeral of Matthew Goniwe and his three murdered comrades on 20 July 1985. It was brought from Johannesburg by Obed Bapela and Maurice Smithers who made in in their screen-printing workshop.

In the second phase of its exile, after 1977, party units began to function more widely within the ANC's pan-African following and the party established its own organised presence within Umkhonto we Sizwe's training camps in Angola; by this stage communists predominated within Umkhonto command structures. The first part of this chapter will follow the party leadership as it relocated from Europe to Africa to entrench itself in the ANC's military organisation. As will become clear, despite the heavy presence of party members within the ANC's senior echelons, especially within the military organisation, its influence over ANC strategic thinking would remain limited, not least because communists themselves disagreed with one another strategically.

The remainder of this chapter will address three questions. Firstly, to what extent did the Communist Party 'own' the ANC's war effort and its instrument, Umkhonto we Sizwe? Secondly, aside from the ANC's army, where else was the party active? And, finally, what was the extent of the party's influence during its exile?

IN CONTRAST TO OTHER African states up till then, both Mozambique and Angola were willing to host white South African communists as long-term residents. In the case of the Mozambicans, there were friendships between SACP and FRELIMO leaders that dated back to the 1950s. For example, Pamela Beira, Ronnie Kasrils's school friend, had married Marcelino dos Santos, FRELIMO's deputy president and by 1977 Minister for Economic Development.[1] In 1962, Samora Machel had obtained a lift on an SACP-chartered flight from Botswana to Dar es Salaam, so that he could join FRELIMO; JB Marks gave up his seat for him.[2] Professedly Marxist-Leninist from the mid-1970s, both Angola's MPLA and FRELIMO included white and *mestizo* (mixed race) people in their leadership echelons. The relationship between the SACP and FRELIMO was particularly close at this point. When FRELIMO was excluded from a 'summit' of workers and communist parties in Moscow in 1978, Sérgio Vieira of FRELIMO asked Yusuf Dadoo to ensure that in future they would be included in such undertakings; Dadoo was evidently successful in his lobbying.[3] Several South African communists would make Maputo their home. Albie Sachs began working at Eduardo Mondlane University in 1977 and would remain in Mozambique for 11 years. In 1976, Ruth First would be invited to conduct research at the university in Maputo; she made the city her home from 1977. Her husband, Joe Slovo, would also leave their daughters behind in London to work full-time in Africa. Appointed by Oliver Tambo to Umkhonto's command as deputy chief of operations in 1976, Slovo would establish himself in Luanda, where he opened the ANC office in April 1977.

From 1979, Slovo would manage the Special Operations Unit, an elite group that carried out especially elaborate and ambitious sabotage attacks, such as the rocket attacks on the Sasolburg oil refineries and the Voortrekkerhoogte military base – key operations in Umkhonto's campaign of armed propaganda. For this purpose he joined Ruth in Maputo, where they lived among the FRELIMO elite in the smart middle-class neighbourhood of Sommerschield, though the unit was based at Matola, an industrial quarter 22 miles from Maputo's centre. As its main leadership was increasingly concentrated in Africa, the party's headquarters would shift in 1977, from London to Luanda, and a mainly African-based Central Committee began meeting more regularly. At another 'augmented' Central Committee meeting held in Berlin in 1979, Moses Mabhida would be chosen to succeed Moses Kotane as general secretary; Kotane had died in Moscow in 1978. The meeting would set up a 'permanent secretariat' in Luanda. The party's regional committees were instructed to 'devote uninterrupted attention to the task of creating internal Party units and contacts'.[4] In 1982, the party's headquarters relocated to Maputo, and Slovo, Josiah Jele and Chris Hani would constitute a three-person secretariat.[5] They remained there until the Nkomati Accord between South Africa and Mozambique in 1984, when most of the ANC community that had established themselves in Maputo were compelled to leave, in most cases relocating to Lusaka.

In 1977, the ANC set up the first of its four Angolan guerrilla encampments, at Novo Catengue, next to the Benguela railway line. Quibaxe, a former coffee estate, provided the setting for a second camp, and here Ronnie Kasrils spent three months between October and December 1977. Mark Shope moved from the WFTU offices in Prague to become Novo Catengue's political commissar. Stephen Ellis has argued that in the camps political commissars were 'invariably party members',[6] a view with which Eddy Maloka, working from official party records, seems to agree; this ensured, Maloka suggests, that 'trainees' political education and orientation was 'communist'[7]. Ronnie

Kasrils and Jack Simons assembled a training manual for political instructors. Simons made his first visit to Nova Catengue in September 1977, having been invited by Joe Modise at Oliver Tambo's behest to 'take charge' of political classes at the camp, thereby replacing Francis Meli (Allan Madolwana), who was apparently ineffectual as a teacher. Leipzig-trained Meli would travel to London to become editor of *Sechaba*, the ANC's quarterly journal. Ellis's informants remember both Simons and Shope with 'real affection'; Simons seems to have projected infectious enthusiasm in his classes.[8] Simons was impressed with his students, noting in the diary he kept during his second visit that 'sound Marxists are coming up – not concerned with hair-splitting or abstractions – and able to apply concepts – also to South Africa'.[9] Simons made two visits to the camp, staying there for five months between February 1977 and March 1978 and between December 1978 and March 1979. He may well have had a ready audience.[10] In engaging with his students at Quibaxe, Kasrils discovered that 'the topic they were most interested to learn about was communism'.[11] Simons rejoined the party in the course of 1978. His views could sometimes challenge orthodoxies, which was maybe one reason why the party hesitated for so long to welcome him back into its fold. To Kasrils's surprise, his fellow instructor was willing to express sympathy with 'Eastern European dissidents', observing that 'unconventional thought' could be 'a force for development' that ought to be encouraged, not suppressed. Apparently, on this topic he made little headway, for 'many black comrades, particularly workers, continued to sympathise with Stalin's tough practices'.[12] In the camps, Ellis suggests, the party commissars functioned as 'talent scouts'; this may be an exaggeration but we do know that the party began to set up units inside the Angolan camps. This information comes from one of the most detailed accounts of life in Quibaxe in this early period of the camps' history, written by Barry Gilder, the first white South African to undergo Umkhonto training.

Brought up in a middle-class Johannesburg household, Barry Gilder joined the ANC in 1976 after leaving South Africa to evade military call-up. He was politically active as a NUSAS leader and had already developed an engagement with Marxism through reading Lukács at Wits. After an encounter with Ronnie Kasrils at an anti-apartheid conference in Amsterdam, he joined the ANC in June 1976 in London. For the next two years Gilder supported himself in Britain as a musician in a travelling theatre group while undertaking research on the South African Defence Force for the ANC; here his experiences during his pre-university military service gave him unusual capabilities among South African expatriates in London. In 1979 he succeeded in persuading the ANC to send him to Angola for military training, its first post-1976 white recruit to undergo such an experience, spending a year in Quibaxe. Gilder himself was recruited into 'the family', that is, the party, in 1979 in the toilets at Quibaxe by one of his instructors. 'Party membership is reserved for the most advanced cadres. It is the vanguard,' he was told, but Gilder needed no persuasion; indeed, he had assumed that because he had had no such approach until then, he 'hadn't made the grade'.[13] Gilder's recruitment took place three years before the ANC agreed to allow the party to set up units inside Umkhonto, a decision taken in 1982.[14]

By the time Gilder received his military training, the routines in the Angolan camps were beginning to be established. What is striking from his account is the extent to which they were constituted around Soviet-derived programmes. Umkhonto even borrowed from the Russian military lexicon, calling its recruits 'kursants' and using Russian expressions in its parade ground commands, for instance 'smirno' for 'attention'. Food supplies when not obtained locally were often Russian imports, tinned *slava* pork stew being an especial favourite.[15] In 1979, during Jack Simons's visit, a holiday from classes was held at Novo Catengue to honour 'Red Army Day'.[16] Russian instructors themselves supplied the advanced training; they were deployed for the first time in Africa with the Angolans, Shubin suggests, from 1979 and numbered about 200 through the 1980s.[17] Company commissars often cited Russian experiences in their lessons. Kasrils refers to one of Jack Simons's protégés, 'Che O'Gara', a 'young man with an engaging smile', who referred to episodes from Alexander Bek's wartime novel, *Volokolamsk Highway*, in his address on discipline as 'the mother of victory'. Political lessons were usually more home-grown, but as well as ANC history these included the essentials of Marx, Engels and Lenin. Gilder received the Simons–Kasrils curriculum through Che O'Gara, his recruiter into the 'family'. By the time he arrived at Quibaxe, there was a 'well stocked camp library'.[18] Discipline at this stage in the camps' history, Kasrils insists, was 'mild'; minor infringements were punished with additional light duties, and more serious offenders were subjected to short assignments of more laborious tasks and night-time detention in a basement, used as a 'lock-up' in colonial times, but with the door kept open, and the prisoners were given airbeds and bedclothes.[19] A tougher and, indeed, harsher regime would develop later, but even at this early stage, in 1978, ANC security chiefs were worried about the risks of their camps being infiltrated by South African spies masquerading as refugees. Taking their cue from Quibaxe, camp commanders constructed detention cellars at all the encampments.[20]

By May 1978 Kasrils had been appointed as regional commissar, responsible for the functioning of the Angolan commissariat. Helping him as the commissariat's secretary was Jabulani Nxumalo or 'Mzala' ('cousin'), his favoured Umkhonto *nom de guerre*; he was a graduate of Jack Simons's classes, and a man whom his classmates remember as often to be seen 'sitting on the stoep ... consumed by a book'.[21] The son of teachers, Mzala had a background as a Black Consciousness activist, like most of the young men in Novo Catengue, though he had also been involved, it seems, as a schoolboy in KwaDlangezwa in the 'workers' struggles for decent wages' that grew out of the 1973 Durban strikes.[22] In 1980 Mzala, 'the cream of the crop' among the young commissars that Jack Simons and Ronnie Kasrils taught, would depart from Angola for 'advanced' ideological instruction in East Germany.[23] He was most likely by this time a party member.[24]

Quite evidently communists functioned as a key leadership group within the camps. But how influential or pervasive within the camps' wider population were the ideas and beliefs that communist instructors attempted to instil through their classes and the other kinds of training they supplied? Certainly, party education was prestigious and an important source of 'derived' ideology. But the descriptions of camp life supplied by Ronnie Kasrils or even by Barry Gilder may have unintentionally exaggerated the extent to which communist ideas and the training supplied by external agencies impacted on the camps' cultural climate. They were certainly not the sole agency in constructing the moral framework governing daily routines. Young recruits from the townships – some of them very young – would be initiated into adulthood when they arrived in the camps through locally adapted versions of the Tswana *bogwera* ceremony associated with circumcision. Paul Landau finds other traces of both 'traditional' and Christian assumptions in the way camp social structure was organised around patriarchy and age sets.[25] Joe Slovo's nickname in the camps, 'Ijuda', again suggests a cultural fusion.[26] Slovo was admired as the leader 'who listened and who made sense', but the affectionate though hardly respectful soubriquet derived from rural isiXhosa slang for Jewish shopkeepers and traders; it was a term that Eddie Roux excised from the translations he used in *Umsebenzi* in the 1930s. There were other belief systems animating Umkhonto's community aside from the structured logic offered by dialectical materialism; they persisted and interacted with the ideas brought in from outside, and even communists could straddle them, as Flag Boshielo's training as a herbalist suggests.

Another more damaging kind of fusion was the way that beliefs about witchcraft reinforced or even underlaid convictions and accusations that setbacks of one kind or another were the result of malign conspiracies. Many recruits would certainly have brought such beliefs with them even if they came from highly urbanised settings. As quite recent ethnography suggests, in Soweto people often lived in 'a world with witches' in which everyday life was conducted 'on the presumption of malice' and in which suffering or misfortune was seldom perceived as accidental.[27] So, for example, in 1977 members of the Novo Catengue community were very willing to blame an outbreak of food poisoning on the work of enemy infiltrators rather than poor sanitation and dirty kitchens – the more plausible explanation favoured both by the Cuban trainers present and by Jack Simons in his diary. This willingness might well have been shaped by the rationality of witchcraft accusations with which Umkhonto's new recruits would have had a ready familiarity. To be sure, people fell ill from poison in the food, but who put it there? Stephen Ellis explains the inclination of ANC security officials in the camps to find sinister conspiratorial reasons for accidental events as a product of their East German training – and this may be true – but beliefs about the presence of infiltrators were not confined to security specialists. They were quite prevalent and were not wholly misconceived: there *were* police agents in Umkhonto's camps – if not in Novo Catengue in 1977, then later. But such beliefs could also feed off a folk culture that explained misfortunes with reference to sorcery – beliefs that have an especial resonance in social settings characterised by uncertainty and insecurity. Significantly, in his diary Simons calls the search for infiltrators a 'witch-hunt': as an African law specialist with anthropological training, this is not a term he would have used carelessly.[28]

But despite the continuing imaginative hold of alternative ways of understanding the world (without their exercising an uncontested cultural hegemony within the various exile encampments), by the time the ANC's armed struggle gained impetus, communists were well represented within Umkhonto we Sizwe's command echelons and they predominated within the commissariat in the Angolan camps. They also took the lead in setting up the communication lines along which recruits would travel to reach the ANC's camps, through Lesotho and Swaziland. The ANC's guerrilla warfare supplied the backdrop to the party's development over the next decade. To understand the party's role within the large movement in which its members worked as soldiers or activists, an outline of Umkhonto's campaigning inside South Africa between 1976 and 1990 may be helpful.

THE FIRST UMKHONTO operations inside South Africa since its suppression in the mid-1960s began in the months following the Soweto uprising. Combatants operated in small two- to three-person units. Though there were early efforts to establish local – that is, internally based – military command structures, these were usually short-lived, and most of the direction of guerrilla activity would be in the hands of various regionally focused 'machineries' located in neighbouring territories. At this early stage, keeping units supplied was especially difficult. In London, in June 1976, Jack Hodgson and Aziz Pahad commissioned Ronnie Press to buy and adapt a Fortnum & Mason hamper and its contents so that detonators and grenades could be hidden in the tins of various delicacies. These would be smuggled into South Africa on the Nairobi-to-Johannesburg flight by an appropriately well-dressed courier with the purpose of supplying Soweto-based Umkhonto units.[29] But it was only in 1979 that the ANC's leadership would adopt a broadly conceived plan which would bring to this activity a more defined sense of strategic purpose. In 1978 a group of National Executive leaders, together with Joe Slovo, visited Vietnam on a 'study tour' between 11 and 26 October, where they met, among other people, General Giap, the victor at Dien Bien Phu. In March 1979, after a series of meetings and drafting sessions, including an encounter between the ANC's leadership and the SACP's Politburo, the ANC would adopt what was nicknamed 'The Green Book', a set of recommendations by a Politico-Military Strategy Commission, composed of Oliver Tambo, Joe Modise, Thabo Mbeki, Moses Mabhida, Joe Gqabi and Joe Slovo.

The key lesson that the visitors had taken away from their trip to Vietnam and their conversations with General Giap was that 'the political struggle' had to be 'primary' during all the revolution's 'phases'. Operations should develop 'out of political activity'. Armed struggle had to 'grow out of … mass political support'. A national liberation army would need 'popularly rooted internal rear bases'. So, with respect to the current South African situation, the main task would be 'to concentrate on political mobilisation', with the aim of constructing these internal political revolutionary bases that would sustain the military effort. At this stage the armed struggle should be 'secondary'. Its functions would be to 'keep alive' the prospect of 'people's revolutionary violence' as the ultimate weapon for the seizure of power. For the time being, armed action should have a propaganda function – 'armed propaganda' that would 'support and stimulate' political activity.[30] So the first task was the construction of the political bases. These would sustain 'a protracted people's war in which partial and general uprisings' would later play a 'vital' role, leading to a 'seizure of power'. Essentially, serious guerrilla warfare directed at military targets should only begin once the ANC had the kind of organisational and political 'underground presence' in which it could count on supportive civilians. For this purpose, the ANC should still retain its broad social appeal; it should not tie itself to the ideology of Marxism-Leninism, for example, though 'it should be emphasized that no member of the Commission had any doubts about the ultimate need to continue our revolution to a socialist order'. Apparently, during the preceding discussions, it was Joe Slovo who raised the possibility of the ANC declaring itself a Marxist-Leninist party. Thabo Mbeki pointed out that the logical corollary of such a move would be the SACP's dissolution, and Moses Mabhida, shortly to be elevated to the position of the party's secretary general, vetoed the idea.[31] Slovo had taken his cues from General Giap's insistence that Communist Party leadership was the key factor in North Vietnam's victory. The issue took two days to resolve, and the time was taken up mainly with Mbeki arguing with Slovo.[32] Slovo didn't drop the idea completely. In 1981, writing under his preferred pseudonym, he speculated about 'the emergence of a single organization out of the various strands of the liberation front'. Perhaps, after achieving the first objectives of liberation, the needs of any 'continuing revolution' might, 'as in Cuba', require a 'unified political force'.[33]

The Green Book was not specific about the geographic location of armed propaganda, but the implication in much of the text was that a large part of the initial political activity would be directed at urban people, factory workers; indeed, the document emphasised the build-up of SACTU as the key agency for securing the loyalty of organised labour. This was very different from what happened in South Vietnam. In the Vietnam War, the National Liberation Front had initiated its efforts to build all-encompassing functional organisations in the countryside, not the cities; its Farmers' Liberation Association would remain the largest of the Viet Cong's mass organisations.[34] Whether North Vietnam's victory was attributable to such politically led mobilisation was in fact questionable; in the final military confrontations, they were putting into the field battalion-strength formations.[35] In Vietnam political mobilisation failed to engender the intended insurrectionary uprisings in 1968 and 1972. In 1975 the outcome of Vietnam's war was determined by the actions of conventional military force, and General Giap had by then long been sidelined when it came to strategic decisions. But the South Africans were not trying to replicate every facet of Vietnam's experiences, and the lesson they understood from what they were told was that political organisation should precede and accompany military action, and that political considerations should always prevail. In any case, more study was needed, the Green Book's authors conceded, to work out a detailed programme 'for the mobilisation of the masses in the countryside'.

In the next few years, Umkhonto's commanders would indeed prioritise urban focused missions: the rural orientation of the ANC's earlier Cuban-inspired strategic perspective was dropped. Umkhonto trainees who underwent Soviet training courses were by 1976 learning 'tactics of urban guerrilla warfare',[36] using a manual based on a Soviet strategic conception derived from Second World War partisan operations.[37] Joe Slovo would lead the establishment of a Special Operations Unit for armed propaganda; its activities would be mainly urban-centred. In 1978, ANC enlisted the help of the Irish Republican Army, the world's most sophisticated urban guerrilla force. In Dublin, Kader Asmal made contact with the Provisional IRA, approaching Gerry Adams through acquaintances in the Irish Communist Party, which, surprisingly, was rather more sympathetic to the nationalist Provisionals than the Moscow-aligned (Marxist) Workers' Party, successor to the Official IRA.[38] In due course IRA men set up a bomb-making school in Luanda, though it was Ron Press who made the remote control ignition that Umkhonto guerrillas used in detonating a car bomb outside Pretoria's air force headquarters.[39]

Meanwhile, ex-Robben Islander Mac Maharaj was charged with responsibility for constructing the ANC's internal political network. He turned down an offer from Joe Slovo to pick his recruits from the Angolan camp population – not the sort of people he was looking for, he said. The problem was that people with the skills and predispositions he was looking for were in short supply in a movement in which 'everybody seems to be going for military training'.[40]

As Umkhonto's own analysts noted, the frequency of betrayals of its cadres to the police by ordinary township residents suggested that MK remained well short of achieving local safe zones during the early 1980s.[41] This was notwithstanding increasingly tactically sophisticated and politically visible military operations by specialist units directed by Joe Slovo, working out of Mozambique, including a sequence of attacks on military bases, police stations and important industrial infrastructure. One key defector to South Africa claimed in 1983 that even after the Matola 'transit camp' was attacked by the South African army on 21 January 1981, Mozambican security officials remained willing to work closely with Joe Slovo and even provide money because they hoped that attacks on South African power installations would increase South African dependence on hydroelectricity from Cahora Bassa and compel them to discourage any attacks on the dam by RENAMO rebels.[42]

Again and again, internal reports noted, ambitions to build non-military ANC 'area political committees' remained unfulfilled.[43] As a party bulletin pointed out, 'Our military underground is still way ahead of the political underground.'[44] This was at least partly because senior Umkhonto commanders had other priorities. For example, in 1982, Joe Modise was telling Botswana-based infiltrators that rural guerrilla warfare in the Western Transvaal could begin without any locally supportive networks in place. Modise was unconvinced by the new strategy – in his view, armed struggle would prevail. Predictably enough, Botswana-based incursions appeared to have little impact. Meanwhile, most Umkhonto cadres remained in their Angolan camps, leaving them only to join Angolan army units in anti-UNITA counterinsurgency operations. These were generally unpopular and, indeed, dangerous undertakings, which by the end of 1983 engaged 450 of the ANC's soldiers and helped provoke a violent camp rebellion during 1984. Umkhonto cadres may have disliked service against UNITA, but Soviet officers who served with the counterinsurgency groups remember that they were rather effective.[45]

By the end of 1984, independently of the ANC's own underground organisation, the United Democratic Front's emergence at the head of an insurrectionary rebellion in the South African townships arguably supplied a substitute for the task of the ANC's internal reconstruction. The Green Book itself had proposed the combination of legal and semi-legal political struggles as well as the organisation of front-like formations. Indeed, one reading of its contents has suggested that the Green Book projected a 'blueprint for ... a mass-based movement along the lines of the United Democratic Front'.[46] As was clear from the tumultuous assaults on the elected Black Local Authorities recently established by the government, the Politico-Military Council noted in November 1983, 'mass receptivity to violence is becoming more and more evident' even though the 'objective of creating political revolutionary bases had not been met'.[47] In any case, given the public expectations aroused by the UDF inside South Africa, the confined objectives of armed propaganda seemed for ANC leaders too modest. Merely signalling the ANC's presence and its support for local community-based struggles was insufficient. It was time to start preparing 'guerrilla zones' in which Angolan-trained insurgents would establish permanent bases in select locations and start training people locally.[48] In the model brought back from Vietnam, locally based guerrilla units with the capacity to engage with regime soldiers could 'initiate a stage of armed struggle where you have contested areas that the enemy control by day and the revolutionaries at night'.[49] In such areas, the enemy would be unable to move small units safely, and it would have to deploy soldiers in large groups. ANC leaders started using the phraseology of 'people's war' in 1984 to imply their strategic shift in this direction, though they acknowledged at their consultative conference in Kabwe in 1985 that for the moment their operations remained 'aimed at registering our presence rather than [at] serious military conflict'. Umkhonto was still failing to actively 'draw in the masses' and still lacked an 'organised ... presence in the country', being too reliant on rear bases and a geographically distant command 'from the rear'.[50] Once inside South Africa, its soldiers usually returned to familiar neighbourhoods in which they were immediately vulnerable to gossip and informers. One technique Umkhonto borrowed from the Vietnamese was digging tunnels to create subterranean hideouts, for, as one of the fighters explained, 'the people were intimidated and not ready to support freedom fighters'.[51] The challenges posed by distance were amplified after the 1984 accord which the Mozambicans agreed with the South Africans at Nkomati in March. The Mozambique government expelled most of the ANC community in Maputo, and Slovo's Special Operations Unit's command centre had to relocate to Lusaka. Ronnie Kasrils was in Swaziland when the accord was signed and was prevented entry at Maputo's airport.[52]

Was Umkhonto able to overcome these shortcomings? There were tactical shifts after 1985: more operations in 'white areas'; less hesitation about hurting civilians, including a few undertakings in which civilian casualties appeared to be the main objective; and a two-year period, from 1985 to 1987, in which white farmers along the northern border were targeted with landmines, because of their role as military auxiliaries in the rural commando system. In a dozen or so landmine blasts, no farmers were killed; the main fatalities were children and farm workers riding in the backs of pick-up trucks. The frequency of Umkhonto operations increased: in September and October 1988, more than 50 limpet mine blasts were set off with the intention of supporting a boycott of municipal elections, a total that represented an all-time high. Most attacks took the form of limpet mine detonations though a mortar shelling of a military encampment near Mafikeng by a 25-man group in May 1989 was an exception to this generalisation; directed by Joe Modise, this was the most ambitious Umkhonto operation to date. By this stage, Modise's enthusiasm for such relatively ambitious undertakings may have been informed by a sense of strategic purpose quite different from the Green Book. Exhibitions of military 'professionalism' made good sense if ultimately the expectation was that a political settlement would have to be negotiated with adversaries.[53] In any case, given the difficulties that Umkhonto commanders were encountering in Front Line states ever more reluctant to allow the transit of South African guerrillas and especially the Angolans' agreement to close the ANC camps, the fact that Umkhonto was able to expand its South African presence was impressive. Even so, the largest active deployments of Umkhonto personnel during the decade were made in defending their Angolan encampments against UNITA in 1987–8, a campaign that cost them another 80 lives. The increasing difficulty in infiltrating trainees back into South Africa led to the build-up of an undisciplined and sometimes mutinous body of around a thousand armed personnel in and around Lusaka in 1988–9 as well as a growing rate of desertions from the new camps in Tanzania.

During the wave of limpet mine explosions in the run-up to the municipal elections in September and October 1988, South African police claimed the arrest of 50 Umkhonto cadres;[54] if true, this would have been a record rate of attrition. Police successes were mainly intelligence-led; informers, infiltration, torture and cross-border assaults and murders enabled the police to effectively destroy the Swazi-based command 'machinery'. It is true that by 1989 the ANC had taken the first steps in constructing an internal command structure with the undetected infiltration of key political and military leaders, including Mac Maharaj and Siphiwe Nyanda, the fourth most senior Umkhonto official, in what was known as Operation Vula. But it was still the case that Umkhonto's campaign in late 1989 remained for the South African authorities a policing concern, not a serious military challenge; essentially it was still, as it had been five years earlier, a propaganda operation rather than 'a serious military conflict'.[55] Between 1976 and April 1994 the police counted 1,400 'acts of terrorism', attributing 90 per cent of them to the ANC. In 1988 there were 222 Umkhonto infiltrators inside South Africa, according to the ANC's own records.[56] Ronnie Kasrils believes that the number of attacks rose in 1987 and 1988, in each year exceeding 300 operations, a rise that he explains as a consequence of a new method of travelling across South Africa by foot: the guerrillas picked their route through disused farms mapped by his military intelligence section. In this way it was possible virtually to reach Pretoria by 'sticking to the bush'. Captures were declining too, he thinks. He remains certain that Umkhonto 'was promising to become more effective in the 1990s'.[57] Other ANC leaders evidently disagreed. In an unguarded statement at the end of that year, the ANC's secretary general, Alfred Nzo, admitted that the organisation lacked 'the capacity to intensify the struggle in any meaningful way'.[58] As things turned out, it didn't have to; two weeks after Nzo's admission, the ANC was unbanned and from the mid-1990s the ANC's army started returning home.

The remainder of this chapter will address three questions. Firstly, to what extent did the Communist Party 'own' the ANC's war effort and its

instrument, Umkhonto we Sizwe? Did the party as a whole share the Green
Book's strategic vision of how revolutionary change might happen, that is,
starting with the construction of political bases, which would then sustain
'a protracted people's war in which partial and general uprisings' would
later play a 'vital' role, leading eventually to a 'seizure of power'?[59] Secondly,
aside from the ANC's army, where else was the party active? How successful,
for example, was it in its efforts to influence the labour movement or, more
broadly, in shaping legal and quasi-legal political life inside South Africa?
What else did the party do? And then, finally, did the party really determine
the ANC's strategic choices during the 1980s? To return to the question posed
at the beginning of this chapter, what was the extent of the party's influence
during its exile?

SO, FIRST, DID THE party own Umkhonto's war? It is very likely that party
members wrote most of its strategic blueprint. Oliver Tambo joined the
Politico-Military Strategy Commission, but it seems improbable that he was
its main author: according to one source, the particular feature of Vietnam's
experience that impressed him especially deeply was the apparent freedom
of churches in a unified Vietnam.[60] Joe Modise, as noted above, did not take
the Green Book's prescriptions seriously. His view was that military action
would be decisive – ultimately, 'all the political 'stuff' was mere trimming',
he would opine.[61] In fact, in its predictions of how a South African guerrilla
war might take shape, Joe Slovo's 1976 essay anticipates much of the
Green Book's content particularly with its reference to the mass political
mobilisation, legal, semi-legal and clandestine, that would need to precede
and accompany military engagements.[62] Slovo's biographer cites the usually
well-informed Luli Callinicos as believing that Slovo was the Green Book's
author, and certainly his voice is unmistakable in certain sections.[63] We know
that the party's programmatic statements continually suggested that national
liberation would be brought about by an armed seizure of power. In 1968,
the party was projecting 'the winning of the national liberation war' as the
condition for any 'future advance to socialism'.[64] It was certainly a view
shared by many of Umkhonto's political commissars, who were so often party
members. The phraseology used by Khumalo Migwe in a contribution to
African Communist would have been fairly typical: the 'final objective' in any
'arming of the masses' should be 'the unconditional surrender of the Pretoria
Boer to the armed people'.[65] There should be no compromising: 'Our strategy
emphatically calls for the seizure of power in contrast to the reformist call

for power-sharing,' Mzala noted in 1986. Indeed, he continued, there was no need to wait for the ANC to build its own revolutionary committees, because these already existed in the various township-based organisations affiliated to the UDF. As with the Paris Commune, many of these embodied 'a new type of government ... ready to serve as organs of people's war and insurrection'.[66] As another commentator noted, 'it is the masses, not a politically conscious minority who begin to create the structure of the new democratic state'.[67] To enable such a moment, military supremacy would be decisive, Mzala insisted, for 'the passage of political power from the racist minority to the democratic majority will ultimately be decided by material strength and military force is the key element of that strength'.[68] As late as 1989, the authors of the programme which the party adopted at its seventh congress in Havana were maintaining that within South Africa at that time there existed 'the potential for a relatively rapid emergence of conditions which make possible seizure of power'. The most likely path to power, the programme argued, would be an insurrection, that is, 'a mass revolutionary upsurge', itself generated by an escalation of both 'political and military struggle'. Of course, not every successful insurrectionary movement has to include organised armed activity, the *Path to Power*'s authors conceded, but in South Africa the movement's 'factory, urban and rurally based combat groups' would form a key set of agencies among many contributories to the 'revolutionary moment'.[69] *The Path to Power* was the product of a participatory drafting process that had proceeded over several years, incorporating 1,250 amendments, not to mention a last-minute addition by Thabo Mbeki.[70]

The party's commitment to a vision in which national democracy would happen through an armed victory was certainly bolstered through the 1970s by the support it received from the Soviet Union and other socialist countries. Soviet motivations in providing help for the party and the ANC during the 1970s and 1980s were primarily 'ideological' rather than 'strategic', as former officials and specialists who engaged with the South Africans insist retrospectively. From the 1950s, Soviet theorists had looked forward to the possibility that in Africa decolonisation might well open up the possibility of a non-revolutionary path to socialism.[71] Of course, if decolonisation came about through the agency of a violent rebellion, then so much the better. A revolutionary national liberation could offer even more likely prospects for non-capitalist territorial paths to socialism, given help from outside, from the socialist world.[72] To be sure, in the everyday world of geopolitics, South Africa was not especially important for Soviet leaders, not as far as 'the real national interests' of the USSR were concerned. But if a measure of help to sympathetic allies could bring closer the end of 'global imperialism', then well and good. It was also the case that from 1970 Soviet leaders perceived both China and the United States as having become increasingly interested in building influence in Africa for strategic purposes. All the more reason, then, to take up any opportunities that presented themselves for building or strengthening alliances with liberation movements or left-aligned governments, if in so doing American interests could be 'squeezed'.[73] The United States was the 'principal enemy', as his KGB mentors had told the spy Yuri Loginov.[74] Sub-Saharan Africa was a region in which American influence could be contested cheaply at relatively low risk, without endangering global 'détente', and in which Moscow could orchestrate periodic 'shows and positions of strength'.[75] The Vietnamese victory, the Ethiopian Revolution, and the accession to power of avowedly Marxist-Leninist governments in Angola and Mozambique added impetus to this approach – signals that 'the world was going our way', to quote Karen Brutents, deputy head of the CPSU's International Department.[76] Angola in particular was perceived optimistically in 1975 as presenting the prospect for a 'model of an African socialist state', and the MPLA as an 'initiator of Marxist-Leninist parties on the African continent'.[77] More widely, there was an expansion of the group of countries that Soviet Africanists regarded as 'states of socialist orientation', and during the 1970s these would become major recipients of Soviet arms transfers.[78] In Africa, great power rivalry could become more martial without risking nuclear conflagration – a second Cold War, in effect.[79]

This did not mean that the SACP and the ANC's Soviet and Eastern supporters completely shared the South Africans' vision of how liberation might actually happen. As the German Democratic Republic's espionage head, Markus Wolf, later admitted, the East Germans at least did not regard the ANC 'as a force that could take power', a view that was echoed by many (though not all) Soviet officials who engaged with the South Africans.[80] On the whole, Russian military leaders were sceptical about the chances of the ANC achieving a militarised seizure of power, though the officials in the CPSU's International Department who worked with the ANC most closely may have been more sanguine, and their influence was often decisive. Indeed, the relationship between departmental officials such as Vladimir Shubin and the South Africans, both communists and non-communist ANC leaders, sustained as it was between the same individuals over decades, developed into friendship, commitment and camaraderie. But, as Irina Filatova and Apollon Davidson note, Soviet leaders were generally wary of any prospect of full-scale military confrontation with South Africa. They did not wish to become committed to supporting the ANC–SACP in a full-scale civil war.[81] Their material support for Umkhonto was carefully calibrated, 'conservatively calculated'.[82] The weaponry the ANC's allies supplied was mainly light firearms and easily carried explosives, 'largely … surplus supplies of outdated Soviet and East European munitions'. This was the kind of arsenal best suited to the principal Umkhonto combat tactics involved in 'self-protected assaults on stationary targets'.[83] The munitions matched the sorts of instruction provided on Soviet training programmes during the 1980s and particularly after 1985, being very much oriented to the kind of revolutionary insurrectionary transition envisaged in the Green Book. They supplied training for people's war and the preparation of cadres to join an underground military that could inspire, support and possibly even direct wider, more spontaneous 'mass action'.[84]

Soviet military support to the ANC was generous, certainly more than adequate for the size and nature of the military force that the ANC could deploy in the field. In total it was worth more than $40 million. Its scale expanded steadily through the 1980s, peaking in 1989–90.[85] Financial support during the 1980s was also considerable; figures for transfers to the ANC are not available, but we know that by the end of the decade the party was receiving $100,000 every year from the CPSU, though this was more than matched by the Swedish government, which from 1973 was contributing annual sums that would range between $200,000 and $1 million.[86] Certainly, the warmth of the relationship between the ANC and the Soviet Communist Party was quite exceptional, and partly a consequence of the South Africans' history of active cooperation with a local communist party. After all, the first financial help the Soviet Union directed at the South African armed struggle came in response to requests from the party: $50,000 in 1960 and $112,000 in 1961.[87] At times in the early 1960s, the party's endorsement was a critical consideration in determining the outcome of particular ANC requests for help.

As we have seen, the Czechs were early suppliers of military training, and they would revive their support after the Soweto uprising, dispatching weaponry for '2,000 combatants', including Scorpion machine pistols. This was despite objections from the Czechoslovak Department of Defence, for Scorpion exports were an important source of hard currency.[88] The following year, Foreign Minister Vasil Bil'ak commissioned an assessment of South African anti-apartheid organisations. The resulting report included warm commentary about the SACP's ideological role, both in 'setting the line' within the ANC and shaping people's beliefs more widely. Among black workers, 'the ideas of Marxism-Leninism are spreading'.[89] But Bil'ak's presentation to his colleagues suggested that neither the party nor the ANC had been able to build an effective organisational presence throughout the country. This was a reasonable assessment; at that stage, the Czechs were well informed by their own African-based intelligence officials.[90] Subsequent Czech help would be less generous; aid to the ANC would be limited to scholarships and medical treatment, they decided, and for the SACP two places at spa resorts every year.[91] The Politburo also decided to host an ANC delegation. As might be expected, in 1979 Oliver Tambo brought with him a list of items that the South Africans hoped the Czechs could donate. Mostly, they were materials in short supply or items that 'could not be tropicalized'. The Czechs did dispatch consignments of non-military supplies worth Kčs 1.5 million, including tinned food, toiletries, cigarettes, wristwatches and 2,000 bags of cement for the construction of the ANC's secondary school in Tanzania.[92] The Czechs' parsimony reflected an order of priorities, for at that time Czech military support for African liberation movements was focused on the Namibians. The comparative standing of the South Africans was rather evident when the party once again requested Czech hospitality for a plenary meeting in 1983: they would be made welcome, but, as the Czechs told their South African supplicants, in line with previous practice they couldn't pay for the tickets.[93]

East German help was more readily available during the decade. The SACP formalised party-to party relations with the Socialist Unity Party in 1980, though in fact East German material support for both the party and the ANC dated from the 1950s. A few South African communists would make their home in Berlin, most notably the trade unionist Arnold Selby, who joined Radio Berlin as editor of its African service for more than twenty years.[94] From 1970, the East Germans provided free printing services for the *African Communist* as well as the ANC's *Sechaba*, importing paper from Finland for the purpose.[95] The East German Solidarity Committee, drawing on monthly citizen donations, raised 4 million marks for the equipment that was shipped to the ANC.[96] Anti-apartheid activity was for the East German leadership a source of domestic regime legitimation, in line with its 'anti-fascist' ideology, and considerable effort was invested in mobilising ostensibly voluntary activity, much of it genuinely willing.[97] About a thousand Umkhonto personnel travelled to East Germany for training, about 80 a year from 1976 onwards.[98] They were chosen carefully, for the training was prestigious[99] and, apparently, more practical and creative than the programmes offered in the Soviet Union. For example, at Teterow, trainees excavated Vietnamese-type tunnels and bunkers.[100] The East Germans also supplied training for a considerable number of ANC security officials, a field in which in other African settings they were often the major influence. As we shall see, Soviet views of South Africa's future became more complicated and more qualified by the end of the decade. Whatever Markus Wolf's private thoughts about the likely outcome of the South Africans' struggle might have been, East Germany after 1986 increasingly found itself at odds with the Soviet Union over Soviet support for political and military solutions to African regional conflicts. The East Germans remained loyal supporters of the 'barracks-style socialism' of African Afro-Marxist regimes at a time when Moscow policy increasingly favoured 'national capital' governments.[101] In any case, given the flow of resources that continued through the decade, SACP leaders had good reasons to believe that their allies regarded their strategic planning as plausible and were willing to support them.

ALL THE MORE SURPRISING, then, was the slow progress that would be made in constructing the political bases that were needed before the onset of a full-scale guerrilla war. The area political committees that were meant to play such a vital coordinating role within the country were never put in place. The task of setting these up was assigned to the Internal Political and Reconstruction Department (IPRD), established in 1969 by the Revolutionary Council. Mac Maharaj became its main organiser – officially its secretary – at the end of 1977. Maharaj had emerged from prison in December 1976, bringing out with him the manuscript of an autobiography Mandela had written. He stayed under house arrest at his sister's flat in Merebank in Durban, putting the handwritten text into order and working as a clerk in a hotel. He was able to make contact with the emerging leaders of the reconstituted Indian Congress, including Pravin Gordhan, before smuggling himself across the Swazi border fence. Maharaj mentions briefly meeting Gordhan. At the time Gordhan was one of a group of students, critical of the older Indian Congress leadership, and animated by the SACP's materials that had reached them. They would become, according to Howard Barrell, one of the ANC's 'more significant underground units'.[102] At the time he met Maharaj, Gordhan already considered himself to be a member of the SACP as well as of the ANC.[103] On reaching Lusaka, Maharaj began working with John Motshabi, chair of the IPRD, who was apparently not just an ineffectual figure but increasingly obstructive because of his anxieties about white and Indians assuming leadership positions.[104] Motshabi turned down his suggestion that the department should promote a Release Mandela campaign. Motshabi was worried about rumours that Mandela was 'selling out' and, in any case, 'we don't want to feature an individual'.[105] Maharaj would spend most of the rest of the year in London, attempting to reconstruct his marriage, and dictating Mandela's manuscript to Sue Rabkin, herself recently released from prison. He rejoined the party. Yusuf Dadoo had initially been helpful with the Mandela manuscript, commissioning Sue Rabkin's services as a typist, but after he and Joe Slovo read the typed-up text, they decided against publication. Joe Slovo, Maharaj thinks, was affronted because Mandela's narrative did not acknowledge Slovo's role as a co-founder of Umkhonto. Back in Lusaka, Maharaj began work on the task of internal reconstruction. He asked to see the department's records and was handed a single folder. It was empty, he discovered: it appeared little had been done with respect to political mobilisation within South Africa, and for what had been done, 'there were no records'.[106]

The absence of the paperwork may have been a bit misleading. We know that in the case of one of the 'forward areas', Swaziland, Thabo Mbeki and Jacob Zuma had worked hard together in 1975 and early 1976 to draw key personalities into a clandestine ANC network functioning inside the country: among their recruits was Nkosazana Dlamini.[107] She was a distant kinswoman of Mbeki's wife and at that stage a medical student in Durban and vice president of the South African Students' Organisation. Mbeki kept records, but they had disappeared by the time Maharaj assumed his role at the IPRD two years later. A 5,000-word report, written by Mbeki in June 1975, that listed contacts with ANC groups led by recently released prisoners survives today in the ANC's archives.[108] The first action Maharaj took on his return from London in 1978 was to set up or reinvigorate political committees in Lesotho, Botswana, Mozambique and Swaziland – the 'forward areas'. In Botswana, for example, he put Marius Schoon in charge. John Nkadimeng would direct internal political organisational building from Mozambique. The regional political committees would attempt to coordinate their work with regional military leaders in the same countries through 'senior organs'; in Mozambique this body was functioning by 1980, chaired by John Nkadimeng with Jacob Zuma as secretary. Ronnie Kasrils joined them.

Existing members of the IPRD whom Maharaj encountered believed 'that a political underground should facilitate the military and not the other way around'.[109] Military command echelons were sometimes obstructive, unwilling to contemplate coordinating their operations with non-military projects. The real problem was that the soldiers did not take the IPRD and its mandate seriously. As Maharaj points out, of ten departments reporting to the Revolutionary Council, nine were there to support the armed struggle. Joe Slovo should have been an ally, given his authorship of the Green Book strategy. But after the Green Book recommendations had become policy,

Slovo 'reverted to form', Maharaj maintains, placing 'full throttle on the armed struggle'. Here one should treat Maharaj's account with caution. He and Joe Slovo found it difficult to work together, and their relationship was tense throughout the decade. It got off to a bad start when Maharaj asked Slovo for the transfer to his department of Slovo's third-ranking commander in his Special Operations Unit, Aboobaker Ismail ('Rashid'). Slovo refused; Rashid was indispensable in training and preparing his own cadres.[110] Finding people willing to return to South Africa to undertake political work was also difficult; so many of the younger men and women who had left since the Soweto uprising wanted to become soldiers, they wanted to join Umkhonto, and, after reading Slovo's 'No Middle Road' in the camps, they hero-worshipped the Umkhonto commander.[111] As Thenjiwe Mtintso remembered twenty years later, in the camps 'there were three comrade leaders who were most trusted; number one Oliver Tambo, number two Joe Slovo; and number three Chris Hani, and in that order ... When he came, he listened, he made sense'.[112]

And when the political committees in the forward areas did succeed in recruiting people with the appropriate attitudes and skills, and began to 'groom' them, regional military commanders would too often 'poach' them, Maharaj complains. This may have been true generally, though in Maputo, in the early 1980s at least, Ronnie Kasrils did try to bring in 'some promising cadres' he 'had spotted in Angola' to deploy as political organisers. He concedes, though, that until his intervention 'the political structures had been acting as second cousins to the military'. He also admits that right up to 1990 they had never really succeeded in 'politicizing rural people', not in KwaZulu-Natal anyway.[113] The regional committees enjoyed some success in sending people back into the country, but all the available evidence from relevant security trials suggests that networking remained at a very embryonic stage. Barbara Hogan, recruited as an ANC member in 1977 and operating under the direction of Marius Schoon in Botswana, seems to have worked most closely with white left-wingers, several of whom were engaged in trade union activity. A list of contacts she composed in 1981, in response to what she took to be an instruction from Lusaka, named just eight people who knew she was an ANC member, though only three of them were similarly 'under discipline'.[114] As Maharaj notes, despite several years of effort, the area political committees, first mooted in 1981, 'did not take root', though the ANC was claiming by 1985 to be deploying 790 underground organisers inside South Africa.[115] By the time of the 1984 Vaal uprising – the rebellion against the rent rises imposed by the new Black Local Authorities – whatever ANC-directed political networks existed were unable to shape events. As

Maharaj puts it, the localised insurrections triggered by the Vaal tumult 'took place in a vacuum'.[116] This was despite the efforts of a considerable number of people in Lusaka whose work was directed at establishing a 'home front', apparently around 100 by 1985.[117]

Certainly, much of the difficulty in creating durable networks had to do with the nature of the task. An extensive system of police informers made any clandestine work in townships very risky. Even the military, with more people and probably more resources, found it very challenging to establish a permanent and networked internal presence. During the decade, most Umkhonto units worked in isolation from each other and more often than not were captured or killed after a few weeks. Even so, the infiltration routes and the intelligence collection that guided guerrilla operations did depend on increasingly complicated and resilient organisational arrangements inside South Africa, and these were in place by mid-decade, if not earlier. Here Barry Gilder's experience is illuminating. After attending a brigade commander's course in Moscow, Barry Gilder's main task in Botswana between 1983 and 1989 was establishing and running an intelligence operation constituted, firstly, by white South Africans recruited outside and inside South Africa when opportunities arose and, later, by cadres selected from the camps, working quite separately from the 'senior organ' that supposedly coordinated the work of the Botswana-based political and military committees. Gilder's network was evidently effective, for he was able to dispatch to Lusaka photographs taken by one of his agents of UNITA's base in southern Angola. From information supplied by white national servicemen, Gilder's unit 'pieced together' the South African Police's and the South African Defence Force's 'orders of battle'.[118] White conscripts also warned ANC intelligence officers about an impending air attack on Angolan camps in February 1979.[119] Gilder's agents undertook reconnaissance of Umkhonto targets and checked the life histories that recruits supplied at the time of their induction into MK. It is obvious that 'intelligence' in this setting was essentially information that could guide and safeguard military undertakings. Gilder and his operatives appear to have had no interaction with other kinds of 'struggle' activity – no contact with the United Democratic Front and its formations, for example, of which, Stephen Ellis suggests, Gilder's intelligence boss, Mzwai Piliso, was especially dismissive.[120] At the peak of military operations, Gilder managed the main conduit through which trained guerrillas would enter South Africa. Their dispatch rate rose to ten armed men a week; this was in 1986. They were also sending in the graduates of a specially instituted intelligence course; these people started arriving in groups of two from November 1987.

Gilder's infiltration routes were entirely controlled by his own organisation until the guerrillas crossed the border. Thereafter, he suggests, they relied on public transport, walking to Mafikeng and then taking combi taxis and trains to Johannesburg. Weapons were driven into South Africa: an ANC Intelligence Department agent specialised in hiding weapons in vehicles and running a music bar in Gaborone as cover. The Botswana-based organisation was never busier than in its final year of operation, 1989, Gilder insists, and communications between them and their internal network had improved to the extent that it began to be possible, albeit 'with difficulty', to recruit new members of the Communist Party inside South Africa.

It seems that much earlier than in 1989, the party was actively engaged in trying to set up its own internal organisation, separate from the area political committees that were becoming the focus of Mac Maharaj's efforts in his work for the ANC's IPRD. As we have seen, Chris Hani may have attempted to rebuild Communist Party organisation in the Eastern Cape when he was based in Maseru in the mid-1970s, though this was not evidently his main preoccupation. Pravin Gordhan claims he joined the party in or around Durban in the early 1970s, though this may have been affiliation with a self-constituted group of people who were animated by party propaganda – self-professedly communists when they met Mac Maharaj in 1977. In the Simonses' papers there is more definite evidence that at least as early as 1980 the party was beginning to rebuild an internal presence. A letter from Ray Alexander to Moses Kotane, dated 31 August 1980, claimed that a process of 'identifying and regrouping' members in Cape Town was under way, and that a 'new recruit', active in the Western Province General Workers' Union, had established a 'new unit'. Another party member was organising dock workers.[121] A report written two years later supplies a less positive picture. This is a record of exchanges in August 1982 involving John Nkadimeng, who was visiting SACP leaders in Botswana on behalf of the Politburo. The discussion focused on 'the cause of organizational stagnation inside the country'. The Botswana group had organised a courier 'to act as a go-between' between them and internal units. They had yet to receive a report-back. At the meeting it was agreed that in future it would be better to have 'direct contact machinery with individual cell leaders'.[122] Not an altogether encouraging picture, then, but unless the Botswana-based party members were misrepresenting the situation completely, the report does suggest that by 1982 embryonic internal party formations were in existence, albeit only in intermittent contact with external leadership. From the mid-1980s there was an SACP unit active in Alexandra, which drew into its membership Paul

Mashatile and other members of the Alexandra Youth Congress leadership – key activists in one of the most vigorous local insurrectionary movements. Raymond Suttner's research has also uncovered liaison and communication between members of the party in Zimbabwe and a group drawn from Catholic Youth, though it is not clear whether its adherents joined the SACP.[123]

So, it remains a puzzle why the political 'reconstruction' envisaged in the Green Book was so halting. Slovo and his comrades acknowledged the importance of the political work that Maharaj's committees were trying to do, and, indeed, members of his Special Operations Unit worked closely at times with Maharaj. Communists were conspicuous in command echelons and in key parts of the ANC's organisation: Slovo's two confederates in running Special Operations, Rashid and Montsho Mokgabudi ('Obadi'), both belonged to the same SACP cell as Ruth First. Together with several other party comrades, including Mduduzi Guma, translator of the party's manifesto into isiZulu, Obadi would die in a South African army raid on Matola in January 1981 and Ruth First was assassinated on 17 August 1982, killed by a letter bomb sent to her office by the South African security police.[124] At her cell meetings with Obadi and Rashid, Ruth First was gently critical of the way the two would 'just think of military operations'. She also spoke to them about what she saw as the lack of 'interface between the military operations and the political'.[125] The IPRD was replaced with a Political Committee after Kabwe, and the Revolutionary Council was renamed the Politico-Military Council, in recognition of the priority that rebuilding the ANC's underground political organisation represented. Replacing Motshabi as chair of this Political Committee was a Lenin School-trained party member, Josiah Jele, veteran of the Mozambican expedition in 1968.

Commentary on the character of the exile ANC as a movement suggests that it was culturally 'militarist'. This may be overstated. In leadership echelons, military orientation may not have been the consequence of deliberate or misconceived intentions but rather an effect of the strategic distraction arising from the operational tasks in which so many of the most energetic and forceful of the ANC's and SACP's strategic architects were engaged. For Joe Slovo, running the Special Operations Unit and plotting its 'armed propaganda' expeditions, each the product of careful reconnaissance, was a commitment that 'consumed [his] world throughout the early 1980s'.[126] Even Maharaj allowed himself to get diverted into engaging with a military project, working with Special Operations Unit people for over a year, in planning the derailment of a troop train. Oliver Tambo called off this scheme, to Maharaj's secret relief. In fact, 'militarist' diversions from the strategic agenda could simply be the result of becoming focused on immediate problem-solving. For Joe Slovo and his colleagues, the key issues that required concentrated attention were often tactical, technical and logistical; how to move a Grad-P rocket launcher across the Swazi border, for example. There were also pragmatic considerations that may help explain the party's determination to put itself at the helm of the ANC's military. South African communists drew lessons from the historical experiences of communist parties in Egypt and Algeria, countries in which nationalist uprisings put the military in the ascendancy and former communist allies were suppressed. 'The Party should ... work within the army,' Jack Simons was arguing as late as 1980.[127] It was also the case, though, that during the 1980s important ANC leaders, including communists, were drawn into the kinds of preliminary negotiations with 'the enemy' that would begin a trajectory towards a very different sort of political transition from any insurrectionary seizure of power. This raises questions about whether all leading communists actually believed in their own party's strategic doctrine.

FROM AS EARLY AS 1984 there were signals of an ostensible willingness among ANC leaders to consider a negotiated political settlement. As Ray Alexander observed in her contribution to a 1984 Central Committee meeting, 'at least certain ANC members believe they could achieve "victory" through merely a continuation of the sabotage campaign' and through exerting 'pressure on world imperialism in the framework of the sanctions issue'. Even the party's statements could reflect such thinking. Any outcome of such a course 'wouldn't come anywhere near conquering state power' and would certainly 'involve a most decisive restriction of the power of the masses'.[128] In September 1985, the ANC hosted a delegation of South African businessmen at President Kenneth Kaunda's game lodge: the nationalisation envisaged in the Freedom Charter might leave privately owned companies with a 49 per cent stake in the mining industry, as was the case in Zambia, the ANC's guests learned.[129] Chris Hani was present at this meeting but apparently said very little.[130] At the end of 1985 Nelson Mandela, through his lawyer George Bizos, sent a letter to Oliver Tambo, telling him about his intention to meet members of the South African government. The first of several meetings between Mandela and the Minister of Justice, Kobie Coetsee, would begin one year later. In early 1986, the British Commonwealth's Eminent Persons Group (EPG) nearly obtained the ANC's acceptance of its proposals in which the ANC would agree to a cessation of hostilities in return for the lifting of its legal prohibition as a precondition for the start of negotiations, before the South African government ended the initiative with raids on Umkhonto bases.[131] The EPG met Mandela. In October 1987, the ANC's National Executive adopted a statement on negotiations: the ANC would be willing to participate in 'genuine negotiations'. Any such process should have 'only' one objective, though: 'transformation of our country into a united and non-racial democracy'. During 1988 Nelson Mandela, using his own initiative and only occasionally able to communicate with Lusaka, would have 47 meetings with members of a committee set up by Minister Coetsee. In mid-1988, Thabo Mbeki met Richard Rosenthal, a human rights lawyer who had obtained authority from Stoffel van der Merwe, the Information Minister, to act as an intermediary to 'narrow the talking distance between the government and the ANC'.[132] On this occasion, Mbeki told Rosenthal that in any negotiations the ANC would be 'absolutely pragmatic, and would not make unreasonable demands'. The ANC 'understood the reality of whites' fears' and their need to be reassured about the future. Government would often quote the ANC as saying it was interested only in 'a transfer of power'. But, 'to his knowledge', Mbeki said, 'such a statement had never been made'.[133]

If Richard Rosenthal's reportage of this conversation is accurate, Thabo Mbeki was being disingenuous. In May 1986, the SACP's Politburo circulated its own uncompromising reaction to any prospect of negotiations that might lead to a bargained transition as opposed to a transfer of power. At that time an 'immeasurable strengthening of the revolutionary forces' was 'creating a situation in which the white power bloc is beginning to lose control'. Recognising that change was becoming inevitable, 'sectors of the white power bloc and some imperialistic strata' were starting to 'seek a transformation' that would involve the extension of varying forms of democracy within the framework of capitalism'. These groups could be expected to try 'to push the revolutionary forces into negotiation before they [were] strong enough to achieve their objectives'. The revolutionary movement should 'resist any confusion between the national democratic revolution ... and the classical corrupt constituents of bourgeois democratic revolutions'. Of course, participating in talks might have the merit of 'breaking the cohesion and unity of the ruling class', but the movement should refrain from participating in any efforts to 'work out compromises ... for some hypothetical negotiating table'. Certainly, most post-war revolutionary struggles 'reached their climax' at the negotiation table; this had been the case with Algeria, Vietnam, Angola and others. 'But the question of negotiation usually arises at a time of a major revolutionary climax involving the transfer of power based on the massive strength of the people's offensive'. No talks or talks about talks should be allowed to 'defuse' or check 'the rising momentum of the people's offensive'; indeed, 'politico–military struggle' should become even more vigorous. In other words, a negotiated settlement might feature in the final stages of the conflict, but only at a point where revolutionary forces had become so strong that they would have an overwhelming advantage in any bargaining. At this stage, the 'broad strategy' was unaltered: mobilising the masses 'for a seizure of power through a combination of political action and armed struggle in which partial and general uprisings will play a vital role'.[134]

In an interview the following year, Joe Slovo offered a vivid picture of just how an insurrectionary overthrow of the regime might happen:

> If all the occurrences that have created the crisis for the other side escalated throughout the country and you had a sort of massive refusal by the people to collaborate with some of the major laws, complete resistance, civil disobedience growing in all kinds of areas, combined with the growing power of the workers, a general strike combined with increased blows by the combat units, combined with external sanctions … it seems possible there could be a moment – because that is what an insurrection is, an historic moment – where the situation is transformed. I don't mean by insurrection that we can envisage in any near future the liberation forces meeting and defeating, on a frontal basis, the military force on the other side. It will be a combination of mass political activism on such a scale that the regime is unable to survive.[135]

Significantly, in this kind of conception of an insurrectionary uprising, the organised guerrilla forces are just one element among many, possibly still fulfilling mainly an armed propaganda function. The previous ANC sources in press interviews had cited the Iranian Revolution as a transition that happened in a setting analogous to contemporary South Africa.[136] Within the party leadership, though, there were different ideas about the extent to which an insurrection might involve armed forces. In August 1985, for example, Politburo members drew a distinction between an insurrection of the kind Slovo described in the passage quoted above and a more militarised national uprising that would require massive increase in Umkhonto deployments.[137] But, in any case, before any insurrectionary moment or national uprising, in the party's view, it was too early for the liberation movement to make a serious commitment to engage in negotiations. The view expressed at a Central Committee meeting that 'we are not strong enough to impose our will or enter into negotiations from a position of strength' was widely shared in 1986.[138] Moreover, SACP leaders maintained, under the present balance of forces, in any negotiations South Africa's ruling groups would be most unlikely to concede even the basic features of liberal democracy. As Joe Slovo would insist as late as 1988, 'our capitalist ruling class in general continues to be opposed to the universal extension of democracy (as normally understood)'.[139] Even so, in that year, the ANC drew up a set of Constitutional Guidelines. The preparatory work for these had been carried out by a three-person Constitutional Committee that Oliver Tambo had appointed: Kader Asmal, Albie Sachs and Jack Simons, each of them SACP members, at least nominally. As finally adopted, the Guidelines prescribed the establishment of a multi-party democracy and a regulated economy in which the state would 'have the right to determine the general context in which economic life takes place' – careful phraseology that omitted any direct reference to nationalisation.[140] The Guidelines were the product of a four-day seminar held in Lusaka in March which addressed, often in considerable detail, the issues that would arise in any post-apartheid institutional reconstruction. Kader Asmal, for example, supplied a survey of electoral systems, arguing in favour of a first-past-the-post plurality ballot, because of its tendency to ensure 'effective government'.[141] Thabo Mbeki contributed a paper that offered 'broad perspectives' on South Africa's future economy; it included, surprisingly, critical references to the 'deficiencies' of the countries of 'realized socialism'. Their positive achievements were balanced by 'repression, cultural stagnation, repudiation of individual rights and civil liberties'. Certainly 'central planning can be highly efficient'; this was a key 'historic lesson', Mbeki acknowledged. However, he continued, socialist countries today offered less attractive models than they had thirty years ago: necessary reforms were blocked by 'great centralisation of power'.[142]

Albie Sachs, speaking about the Guidelines at New York University in May 1989, maintained that while the liberation movement was often perceived to favour 'a planned economy, socialization of the means of production and so on', in the circumstances 'we don't feel this is or ought to be the key question on the agenda right now'.[143] The qualified language in the Guidelines, which was echoed in Albie Sachs's address, was strikingly different in tone from the forecasts about a post-apartheid South Africa that SACP members had made earlier in the decade. 'Any programme to end racial oppression in South Africa has to be anti-capitalist', Raymond Suttner proposed in a lecture he delivered in September 1984, though even in a fully liberated South Africa, he suggested, 'there [were] some types of work, such as those of barbers, that are performed most efficiently on an independent basis'.[144] Albie Sachs, in his talk in New York, spoke about the possibility that in the event of a negotiated 'process of change', a 'multipronged approach to the land' was possible in which individual white farmers might remain in managerial roles, collaborating in more equitable relationships with their workers. More generally, he thought, the ANC in power would show some sympathy for the position of those 'white farmers with a deep attachment to and love for the land'. Again, this kind of speculation implies a very different scenario from Mzala's suggestion in 1985 that 'if our national democratic revolution is not aborted', then 'we have reason to believe' that land would be distributed 'in such a way that collective farms are created to exist side by side with state farms'.[145]

Of course, in the late 1980s, commitments to flexible pragmatism may simply have been expedient. In an international setting in which the ANC was beginning to enjoy success in diplomatically isolating Pretoria in Western Europe and North America, professions of 'reasonable' moderation would have been sensible enough, but they may not have reflected convictions and principles; an insurrectionary moment might be all the more likely to arise in a setting in which the regime lost its external support. In an unusually revelatory interview, though, Thabo Mbeki seemed to be suggesting that the dynamics between the diplomatic and the insurrectionary struggles might be rather different: that the armed insurgent 'offensive' might create the conditions for a bargained settlement. As he explained to the London *Observer*'s correspondent in March 1986:

> The call you must make to the people is the same, saying you are not prepared to negotiate, that you must intensify the offensive. But, in the course of that offensive it is clear that one of the most important things is breaking up the power structure ... Out of this you will get a re-alignment of forces. We are not talking of overthrowing the government but of turning so many people against it that it would be forced to do what Ian Smith did.

What Ian Smith did, of course, was to sign off on the Lancaster House settlement, a British-sponsored decolonisation that resulted in a quite limited political transformation, well short of the SACP's conception of 'national democracy'. Here Thabo Mbeki was using very much the same kind of language as Oliver Tambo, who was reported that year in the *Financial Mail* as explaining that the ANC's aim was not 'a military victory but to force Pretoria to the negotiating table'.[146] Thabo Mbeki, at that time director of the ANC's Information and Publicity Department, was the assertive personality in the various encounters during the 1980s between the ANC and white South African officials and businessmen. These developed their own strategic momentum; indeed, Mark Gevisser believes that Mbeki deserves much of the credit for 'the negotiated settlement that spared South Africa a descent into bloody civil war'.[147] Of course, a cynical explanation of the language that he was using in his interview with *The Observer* would be that he was merely trying to project the kind of reassuring representation of the ANC that he knew would appeal to his liberal middle-class British readers. After all, they were the sorts of people with whom he had become friendly when living in England in the 1960s. At this time he took to wearing English tweed jackets and smoking a pipe as well as acquiring a liking for cricket.[148] While a student at Sussex, he undertook door-to-door canvassing for the Labour Party; one view of Mbeki is that this experience was formative for him and that Eastern European socialism 'never again held attraction for Mbeki'.[149] That may have been the case, but, if so, it is likely that at that time Mbeki kept any such reservations to himself, for in 1967 he was invited to join the editorial board of *African Communist* – an unusual expression of confidence in one of the party's youngest members.[150]

Thabo Mbeki's biographers do rather confirm that by at least 1985, and probably earlier, he had recognised that an armed insurrectionary seizure of power was 'a pipe dream'.[151] In the mid-1980s he began confiding to friends that in the event of an ANC accession to power, the alliance with the party would probably end – at that stage a heretical sentiment.[152] It seems likely that Mbeki's attachment to the Communist Party was a complicated and even qualified adherence, not a rigid or doctrinaire affiliation; by the 1980s it certainly did not translate into uncritical admiration for Eastern Europe. Friendships with Swedish diplomats and aid workers in Lusaka also helped to elicit his interest in Scandinavian social democracy: Sweden had become a major ANC funder. As Barry Gilder ruefully acknowledged, Scandinavian support induced the 'development of a social democratic ideology amongst some ANC members'.[153] Much later, Mbeki told his biographer that a holiday visit to East Germany in the early 1980s was revelatory; a key moment was when their guide began complaining about the ruling party's leadership.[154] As noted above, Mbeki had joined the party when staying with Duma Nokwe in 1961 and enjoyed a rapid ascent through its hierarchy. In his early phases he was not especially critical of the repressive character of Eastern European regimes, differing from his British left-wing friends at Sussex, for example, in his ready approval of the Warsaw Pact invasion of Czechoslovakia. Two decades later, to judge from his contribution to the ANC's constitutional seminar, it was the economic malfunctioning of existing socialism that he found really disillusioning. In 1982, Mbeki was dropped for two years from the Politburo, a consequence of tensions with Joe Slovo, and, though restored to the party leadership in 1984, he became an increasingly 'passive' participant.[155] Disagreements with Slovo persisted: Stephanie Kemp refers to 'unresolved and heated debates' between the two men at Central Committee meetings in the late 1980s.[156] All the evidence, then, suggests that Mbeki did not believe that a seizure of power was a likely outcome, a conviction which his biographer thinks he arrived at early in the decade. Mbeki was a major personality in the party leadership, and it is likely that he influenced other party members, especially those of his own generation. In the various encounters that he had with delegates and delegations from different South African groups during the 1980s, he was not acting alone. His closer associates included other party members, such as Aziz Pahad and Jacob Zuma, who joined Mbeki in a discreet meeting with key Broederbonders in London in late 1986, as well as Joel Netshitenzhe ('Peter Mayibuye') and Joe Nhlanhla.[157]

What possibly helped to strengthen any strategic scepticism that individual South African communists may have had were discernible shifts in Soviet African policy. The hopes that avowedly Marxist-Leninist regimes in Africa might open up fresh paths towards modernisation and socialism had faded by the 1980s. One telling signal was the decision in 1981 to reject Mozambique's application for COMECON membership.[158] More widely, Soviet and Eastern European Third World specialists were all too conscious of failures in the application of Marxist-Leninist models of development, especially with respect to agriculture.[159] They were beginning to argue in favour of mixed economies in which the Soviet Union would engage in 'trilateral cooperation' with Western firms in working on tenders from developing countries' governments.[160] The East Germans also adopted a comparable policy shift in 1988 towards cooperation with Western governments in development.[161] This did not mean any lessening of support for the South Africans: in fact, the quantities of money and military material that the Soviet Union donated peaked in 1988 and continued thereafter. This was an expression of Gorbachev's own version of 'socialist internationalism' in which Soviet aid to a range of 'leftist' groups, including both the ANC and the Sandinistas, increased while support for Third World authoritarian regimes dropped.[162] Significantly, military training, while emphasising the 'military combat' tactics that would be used by urban guerrilla units through the 1980s, also offered for a select group a second stream providing advanced training for pilots and artillery officers. These were the kinds of preparation that would be urgently needed if Umkhonto was to be reconstituted as a conventional army – a likely consequence of any negotiated settlement.

In an increasingly open intellectual atmosphere in Moscow, Gleb Starushenko, deputy director of the Africa Institute, suggested there might be 'real possibilities' for a negotiated constitutional compromise that could include guarantees to the white population and a two-chamber parliament, one constituted by universal suffrage and the other 'possessing the right of veto on the basis of equal representation of the four communities'.[163] Starushenko was not an authoritative figure politically, and perhaps not too much should be made of his views; they evoked a tactful rejoinder from Joe Slovo. Dr Starushenko's pro-liberation credentials were indisputable, but any kind of 'multi-nationalism' would be 'an unacceptable starting point'; in any case, 'we cannot, at this stage, allow ourselves to be diverted by speculation about future justifiable compromises in the interests of revolutionary advance'.[164] In the following year, 1987, Starushenko's colleague Victor Goncharov told South African journalists that the Soviet government was prepared to act 'more realistically, more flexibly, with the participation of all sides'.[165] He also expressed misgivings about certain ANC members who 'put out before the national liberation movement the tasks of the socialist revolution', a predisposition that in his view risked the ANC 'los[ing] allies in the population'.[166] As in the case of Starushenko, Joe Slovo was unimpressed; Goncharov was looking at the first stage of the South African revolution, 'through bourgeois democratic spectacles', confusing radical but essential changes with socialist transformations.[167]

In Prague, at about the same time, four Soviet scholars presented their ideas about South Africa at the offices of the *World Marxist Review*. Among other things, they suggested that armed force should not be used in class struggle. They failed to persuade their audience. Bert Ramelson of the British Communist Party was especially critical, even though he came from that party's Eurocommunist wing. Essop Pahad, then visiting Prague to attend an editorial board meeting of the *World Marxist Review*, pointed out that even the World Council of Churches supported the ANC's armed campaigning.[168] These revisionist perspectives would have been opposed by the key people, closer to policy-makers, who had direct dealings with the South Africans, such as Vladimir Shubin or Vasily Solodovnikov, the ambassador in Lusaka. In November 1986 the Soviet authorities arranged a public meeting between Tambo and Gorbachev, a significant recognition, and also promised an increase in military supplies.[169] Even so, among Soviet Africanist specialists and possibly among policy-makers as well, there were clearly disagreements.

When he visited Moscow in 1988 for talks with the CPSU leadership, Slovo felt he needed to emphasise that 'attempts at securing negotiations at this point in time would not bear any fruit except to assist the regime in breaking out of international isolation'. He may not have been altogether reassured by Politburo member Ligachev's qualified agreement that 'while communists would prefer a peaceful solution, that time had not yet come'.[170]

WHATEVER DIFFERENCES THERE may have been among ANC and SACP leaders about the way any political transition might ultimately happen, there was broad agreement over the need to pursue the intermediate goals of the Green Book, that is, to establish an organised political presence for the ANC inside the country and build internal bases for military operations that could elicit more generalised armed rebellions – 'people's war' – which would help to generate what Mbeki had called in his *Observer* interview the necessary 'realignment of forces'. In 1985, at the ANC's second consultative conference held in Kabwe in Zambia between 16 and 23 June, the political resolutions adopted by 250 delegates were worded to make it quite clear that victory could only be the outcome of a 'seizure of power'. Delegates agreed they would not 'even consider' negotiations so long as ANC leaders were in prison. But as Oliver Tambo noted in his report, drafted for him by Thabo Mbeki, 'we cannot be seen to be rejecting a negotiated settlement in principle'. In any encounters with 'sections of the white population', including officials of the 'ruling fascist party', it was nevertheless 'vital' that 'any contact that may be established does not have any negative effects on the development of our struggle'.[171] Among the strategic decisions, tougher language on guerrilla tactics appeared to rescind Umkhonto's traditional embargo on attacking soft (civilian) targets. The delegates also voted in favour of moving the military campaign into a 'people's war' phase, that is, broadening the base of guerrilla operations through the enlistment of auxiliary groups of local and locally trained part-time combatants – the 'people in arms' – who would use 'simple basic equipment' to attack the police and any government institutions within their own communities. The ANC needed to build up stores of the necessary supplies in the main urban centres.[172] The Commission on Cadre Policy, Ideological and Political Work reported that 'the development of our underground', which was crucial if the ANC was to lead an all-round people's war, 'has matured where the possibilities for the creation of this underground have never been as favourable as they are now'.[173] In other words, the underground structures that were needed were still largely absent. What was required by 'military combat work', the combined work of 'advanced combat formations', the 'people in arms', and whatever groups of the 'enemy forces' that could be subverted,[174] was a centralised command structure reaching district level: this, too, still needed to be 'attended to'.[175]

So, the prerequisite organisation for people's war still needed to be put in place. But just how military combat work might fuse with other kinds of resistance, and what sorts of scenarios might lead to an insurrectionary takeover, were not spelled out in any detail. Thabo Mbeki had been charged with drafting a new strategy document, but his formulaic efforts were apparently unconvincing, confined to 'well-worn homilies', and they elicited a scornful reaction from Joe Slovo. Mark Gevisser's explanation is that Mbeki knew that his own strategic views would be rejected, and so he had taken 'the path of least resistance' to the insurrectionists. Oliver Tambo asked Pallo Jordan to rewrite the document, but it wasn't ready in time for the conference.[176] The final key decision at the Kabwe meeting was the opening up of leadership elections to 'non-Africans', a decision opposed by Brian Bunting, editor of the *African Communist*, and equally vigorously supported by Jack Simons.[177] Delegates chose a 26-person National Executive Committee (NEC), which included Mac Maharaj, Aziz Pahad, Reg September, Joe Slovo and James Stuart. Eighteen members of this enlarged body were SACP members, including all but one of its Politburo members, though Josiah Jele, not elected to the NEC at Kabwe, would become a co-opted member in the following year. In another way, too, the Kabwe meeting appeared to result in the upgrading of the party's status: the movement started using the phrase 'tripartite alliance' to describe the formal relationship between the SACP, the ANC and the trade union movement, and in the next four years, between 1986 and 1989, there would be eight Tripartite Alliance meetings.

Conspicuously absent in the agenda at Kabwe was any serious consideration of the issues that had arisen in the mutiny that disrupted Umkhonto's Angolan camps in 1984, except that a new code of conduct explicitly forbade the use of torture. In Stephen Ellis's critical treatment of the party's role within the ANC's exile communities, the Angolan mutinies and their suppression constitute defining events. He suggests that the party's control over the ANC's security department and its subsequent influence in the guerrilla training camps caused the grievances that helped provoke rebellion. In his account of the mutiny, the party's contribution to its gestation was not simply the effects of actions by different people appointed to key positions who happened to be communists, but, rather, that SACP strategic priorities and its ideological predispositions shaped events. Was this true?

Shortly after the Angolan camps were established, the ANC leadership started a process of reorganising its Department of Intelligence and Security, informally known as NAT (short for 'national') and nicknamed 'Mbokodo' (grinding stone). This body screened incoming recruits, asking them to write multiple autobiographies that would be checked for inconsistencies.[178] NAT's evolution would be shaped by training supplied by the East Germans after an agreement between the ANC and the Socialist Unity Party. Trainees undertook a Stasi course, in which, among other things, they learned about the behavioural traits that might signal the presence of infiltrators and spies. Even before the first graduates of these programmes returned to Angola, camp administrators and (as we have noted) even the ANC's leadership often interpreted accidental setbacks, such as a case of food poisoning at Novo Catengue, as evidence of the presence of 'enemy agents'; Stasi's instructions may have helped reinforce such predispositions. In reaction to complaints about deteriorating discipline through the movement in 1979, the mild disciplinary measures that Ronnie Kasrils had helped put in place at Quibaxe in 1978 were replaced by a harsher regime, and NAT was given fresh powers. In 1980 its new head, Mzwai Piliso, was accorded full authority over all the Angolan camps. A counter-espionage campaign, enforced through arrests, detention and beatings, gathered impetus after the South African army attacked Umkhonto and SACTU offices in Matola, Maputo. The ANC's leadership believed that the South African military's choice of targets was guided by informers within the ANC.[179] A new campaign, 'Shishita' (Bemba for 'sweep'), intended to identify traitors, was launched with a speech by Moses Mabhida, one-time head of NAT and now the SACP's general secretary. Mabhida has just returned from a tour of the Angolan camps and was taken aback by the reports of indiscipline he had received. Among other measures, Mabhida suggested that dagga smokers should be shot. The discovery of a supposed spy ring in Lusaka also helped raise alarms about security. On 5 March 1981 ANC leaders formally sanctioned the use of corporal punishment in the camps. A special 'correctional facility' was established at Quatro, a short distance from Quibaxe, to detain NAT's suspects. In the Shishita drive, several hundred people would undergo detention and various kinds of ill-treatment, mainly beatings, from which at least six people would die during 1981. Only a minority of the 60 or so people who confessed were likely to have been hostile infiltrators, Ellis argues,[180] though this minority may have included people in key positions.[181] Certainly, NAT's tendency to attribute conspiratorial intentions to any kind of disaffection resulted in the imprisonment of many innocent people and also created a climate in which members of the camp hierarchy could ignore complaints and abuse their own positions.

In late 1983 there was a fresh source of demoralisation in the camps when Umkhonto soldiers began counterinsurgency operations against UNITA; in Ellis's narrative, this was initially a popular deployment, but dearth of supplies and high casualties changed rank-and-file perceptions.[182] On 12 January 1984 these soldiers sent a list of demands to the ANC's executive, then visiting the main Umkhonto base camp. They called for NAT's suspension, the ending of the deployments against UNITA, an inquiry into the conditions at Quatro, and a national consultative conference. After eliciting no reaction, the soldiers assembled at Viana transit camp, 15 miles from Luanda. In response to advice from Umkhonto's regional commander, the 300 or so mutineers elected a ten-person committee. The Angolan presidential guard laid siege to the camp on 7 February and, after a brief skirmish, the mutineers agreed to give up their arms. On 13 February a specially appointed ANC commission of inquiry, chaired by James Stuart, began its work, interviewing almost everybody at Viana. The Angolans arrested the leaders and eventually handed them over to NAT officials, who dispatched them to Quatro. A second, more violent rebellion took place in May when a group of dispersed Viana mutineers held at Pango camp succeeded in taking over guard posts, arming themselves and distributing weapons. In seizing control of the camp, they killed its commander and seven other people. One week later, on 18 May, Umkhonto's regional command organised an assault on the camp, in which 16 mutineers died. In its immediate aftermath, a military tribunal executed seven of the leaders, and several others would remain imprisoned during the decade. The ANC would shoot another eleven mutineers later.

Stephen Ellis's argument is that NAT's accumulation of authority followed urgings by 'leading Party members' for the ANC to establish an efficient security apparatus and that the party itself was determined 'to keep a grip on the security organ', as part of its more general aim of securing its position within the ANC. The party as well as its East German allies was also responsible for the 'highly ideological view of what constituted disloyalty'.[183] In Ellis's book, communists constituted an SACP–Mbokodo 'senior command' that sought to impose a 'Stalinist' conformity within Umkhonto.[184] If this was the case, then the assessment of the first mutiny conducted by an inquiry, led as it was by senior SACP members James Stuart, Aziz Pahad and Sizakele Sigxashe, was quite surprising. They presented their report after four weeks' investigation, on 14 March, two months before the second, more serious camp revolt. Disaffection in the camps, they concluded, was not the work of enemy agents but rather a consequence of deteriorating material conditions – particularly shortages of fresh food and medicines – neglect of recreational facilities by the camp's leadership, and evident inequities in access to better rations, cigarettes and liquor between rank and file and officials. The behaviour of NAT administrators posted to the camps amplified discontent. Too often NAT used 'the methods of the Boers'. The inquiry was especially critical of NAT's head, Mzwai Piliso, as well as of the national commissar, Andrew Masondo, himself a party member and one of Govan Mbeki's recruits at Fort Hare. Moreover, regional Umkhonto commanders ignored 'abnormal' conditions and, in any case, they spent too much time in Luanda. The Commission recommended amnesties and echoed the mutineers' call for a consultative conference. In subsequent discussions within the ANC leadership, Joe Slovo and Mac Maharaj supported the commission's findings.[185] Both Piliso and Masondo would lose their positions in reassignments later in the decade, Mzwai being replaced by Joe Nhlanhla, a party member.

Even under fresh leadership NAT's excesses would continue. What would become increasingly evident was that the Department of Intelligence and Security was very much its own agency, an autonomous fiefdom, not subject to any corporate grip, not by the party leadership or any other authority. Its use of torture continued, to the dismay of at least one East German official, who compared NAT's methods to those used by the Gestapo.[186] In Ronnie Kasrils's own encounters with Stasi instructors, he was told that physical torture was ineffectual and misleading. This was in line with the Stasi's internally instituted operational procedures. On the whole, in East Germany Stasi interrogators did not torture detainees, not in the sense of subjecting them to physical pain, though they did use sleep deprivation and various carefully calculated psychological abuses which are defined as torture in the 1984 UN Convention.[187]

In mid-1988, NAT officials arrested Thami Zulu (Muziwakhe Ngwenya), who was then head of Umkhonto's Natal 'machinery' in Swaziland. Recruited into the ANC by Thabo Mbeki in Swaziland in 1975, Zulu had joined the party at Novo Catengue and attended its Central Committee meeting in Berlin in 1979. Kasrils met him at the camp and his memoir includes a warm recollection of Thami Zulu's personality. NAT suspected him of being a police agent; it was certainly the case that the South Africans had an extensive presence within the ANC's Swazi-based structures. Despite prolonged detention and possibly repeated torture, Zulu made no confession.[188] Five days after his release in November 1989 he was dead, from poison. He was cleared of any treachery and received a graveside tribute from Hani. For Hani, Thami Zulu was a victim of hysterical paranoia within ANC's security. Zulu was very much his protégé and, indeed, his appointment in command of the Natal machinery had been resisted by Jacob Zuma and Moses Mabhida, who were building their own faction, Ellis suggests. This kind of factionalism was not new, Ellis argues. Communists within Umkhonto were active participants in factional ethnic rivalries between a 'Tswana' group assembled under Modise's patronage and Hani's 'Xhosa' supporters. More prosaically, Gavin Evans, a member of the party's clandestine network in Johannesburg and a visitor to Lusaka at the time of Zulu's death, observed that 'the underground and the Party hated' the security officials.[189]

Be that as it may, Thami Zulu's treatment suggests limits to party influence within Mbokodo as well as ways in which the party itself could be divided by factional loyalties resulting from the compartmentalised nature of the ANC's bureaucracy. It was certainly the case that there were a significant number of party members in the ANC's security hierarchy, though Ellis's suggestion that Piliso was the party's man seems unlikely.[190] But the reactions and responses of senior leaders in the party to Mbokodo's operation rather undercuts the argument that the growing influence of the ANC's security establishment was the outcome of any SACP-sponsored grand design. Party leaders could themselves be very critical of NAT's conflation of any disaffection with treachery. As early as 1981, the Politburo had warned against any 'groundless witch-hunt against innocent members' and also expressed concern about interrogations that used methods that 'undermine[d] revolutionary morality'.[191] In 1986, a Central Committee meeting acknowledged 'defects in the work of many comrades connected with security and intelligence structures'.[192] As we have seen, the propensity to attribute any setback to the agency of hostile forces was an early feature of camp life; it didn't need to be the outcome of an ideologically programmed set of responses fostered by SACP doctrines.

So DID THE PARTY predominate in the ANC's war effort, and were its leading members animated by a shared conception of strategic purpose which they succeeded in imposing onto the wider movement? Certainly, with the acceptance of the Green Book's strategic recommendations, the ANC adopted the party's insurrectionary conception of a seizure of power that would be followed by the installation of a socialist-oriented national democracy. This project was made all the more plausible by the kind and scale of material support and training that the ANC and the SACP received from its principal East European allies, the Soviet Union and the German Democratic

Republic, even if their Russian and German sponsors did not altogether share their certainty about the kind of power transfer that would take place. But the ANC's military command itself did not wholly share the presumptions in the Green Book, and even among communist advocates of people's war different priorities and different operational requirements in their day-to-day work help explain the failure for most of the 1980s to make substantial progress in building the political infrastructure needed to coordinate and direct an insurrectionary movement inside South Africa. During the decade, all communists would refer to a seizure of power as the desirable outcome of their efforts, especially at formal occasions such as major in-house meetings and conferences. However, influential communists began engaging in the opening moves towards a negotiated political settlement, which implied a quite different trajectory to power and subsequent reconstruction from that envisaged in the Green Book. In 1989 the party's new programme, *The Path to Power*, though continuing to hold out the prospect of a seizure of power, conceded that 'liberation struggles have rarely ended with the unconditional surrender of the enemy's military forces'. Armed struggle should not be 'counterpoised with dialogue, negotiation and justifiable compromise, as if they were mutually exclusive categories'.[193] The language was added to the draft during discussions at Havana, 'skilfully steered' by Thabo Mbeki for this purpose, though Joe Slovo too apparently helped to 'put negotiations on the agenda'.[194] Oliver Tambo's message to the congress (written probably by Thabo Mbeki) had made much the same point: there was a 'new climate of hope' and 'our friends will see in this climate the possibility of a compromise solution'. All the more important to maintain the pressures that had brought about these new possibilities, 'including the intensification of armed struggle.'[195] Finally, communist influence over the military could be checked by bureaucratic factionalism as well as by the disruptive actions of the ANC's security department, in which party members were certainly present but often acting against their comrades in military command positions.

Aside from 'armed propaganda' and the more diplomatic efforts to explore the possibilities of negotiation, in which other domains were key party personalities busy and driven by a sense of strategic purpose? After Kabwe, Mac Maharaj's efforts to build a disciplined internal presence for the ANC would receive fresh encouragement. Operation Vula (short for 'Vulindlela' – as in 'open the door') was a final sustained effort to build the kind of organisational structure inside South Africa, led by senior people, that would be needed to coordinate political and armed activities. Its primary mission, according to Maharaj, was to 'build capability' for a 'protracted people's war'.[196] It was especially secret: knowledge about this undertaking was very restricted. For example, Joe Modise was not informed about Vula's conception or progress, and most members of the ANC's National Working Committee were kept ignorant. On the other hand, to Maharaj's annoyance, Joe Slovo insisted in July 1988 that the party's Politburo should learn about Maharaj's mission, just before his departure. This meant that aside from Tambo and Slovo, other top leaders in the know would include John Nkadimeng, Jacob Zuma, Thabo Mbeki, Chris Hani and Sizakele Sigxashe.

Operation Vula would have several purposes, including the infiltration of authoritative figures into the country and the establishment of a reliable and quick channel of communication between Vula's leadership as well as other leaders inside the country and Oliver Tambo's office in Lusaka. In addition, Vula would set up fresh supply lines for weapons and money and conduct ambitious intelligence and infiltration undertakings. The weapons would be brought in from Botswana, using specially adapted cars – Toyota Cressidas hired in Johannesburg. Ten AK-47s could fit into welded secret compartments. Larger quantities of one tonne at a time would be imported into South Africa in a Bedford truck, ostensibly fitted out for tourist safaris and driven between Nairobi, Lusaka and Cape Town by a new set of London recruits, sought as in the past from British Young Communist networks. 'Africa Hinterlands' was organised in London at Joe Slovo's behest by an old friend and SACP comrade of his from the 1950s, Mannie Brown, now prospering in exile as a businessman.[197] Later, the police intelligence chief, Hermann Stadler, would concede that in Vula the ANC would 'come closer to the actual implementation of proper guerrilla war strategies'.[198] Stephen Ellis maintains that Vula was 'almost entirely a party affair', intended to 'further its agenda'.[199] This may not have been the case, but Vula certainly used the same organisational networks and methods that the party had employed in the late 1960s, updated, as we shall see, to engage with more modern communication techniques. It was true that Vula was initially driven by beliefs about the viability of an insurrectionary path that Maharaj shared with Joe Slovo and Chris Hani. Ultimately, however, its effects would help to sustain ANC commitment to a settlement agenda.

Operation Vula was sanctioned by Oliver Tambo at the beginning of 1986, initially as an effort to install key ANC and Umkhonto leaders inside the country, who could then work with the internal 'mass democratic movement'. Mac Maharaj was asked by Tambo and Slovo to work up a blueprint. Maharaj's scheme was for separate regional groups that would communicate with Lusaka separately, using computers. To keep the plan under wraps, no money from the ANC budget would be used and, instead, Maharaj raised the necessary funding in London from Joel Joffe. Planning took two years. Maharaj was chosen to lead the organisation's Transvaal and Natal networks, and a separate group would undertake preparatory work in the Western and Eastern Cape, where the intention was that Chris Hani would eventually supply the decisive leadership. Cradock-born Charles Nqakula ran Vula's Cape Town-based activities. Maharaj undertook various kinds of training in the Soviet Union, East Germany and Cuba, in the last case so that he could learn more about the historical relationship between Fidel Castro's July 26 Movement and the Cuban communists; he believed that insights he might gain from Cuba's experiences could have 'a bearing on both the way COSATU and the UDF worked together and how we worked with them'.[200] In London, Ronnie Press and Tim Jenkin helped him design techniques of 'computerized encryption' of messages that could then be instantly transmitted on the public telephone system.[201] Tim Jenkin had made his way to London after escaping from Pretoria Central in 1979. Conny Braam of the Dutch Anti-Apartheid Movement supplied state-of-the-art coding equipment, drawing upon her extraordinary range of well-qualified specialists with the sorts of technical skills needed for clandestine organisation. Maharaj's biographer refers to a band of 'sleepers' recruited from the German and Canadian communist parties who would travel to South Africa to set up secure accommodation. We have more detail about the Dutch citizens that Conny Braam coordinated; during 1987 they found work in Swaziland, Botswana and Cape Town, living in carefully selected houses so that they could be 'fronts for comrades'.[202] As she notes, between 70 and 80 Nederlanders in one or way or another contributed to Operation Vula.[203] One of Braam's Dutch helpers, a telephone engineer, visited Johannesburg to take photographs of South African call boxes, mapping their locations and checking their wiring systems. Braam also mobilised couriers – KLM air hostesses – and people with the necessary expertise for making disguises – cosmetic artists, wigmakers and dentists – who turned Mac Maharaj, for instance, into 'a chic businessman, an affluent older gentleman', with moulded denture covers changing the shape of his face.[204] The Dutch disguise specialists equipped Charles Nqakula with horn-rimmed spectacles and a hearing aid, ageing him by twenty years and pushing out his ears. Before travelling to South Africa, Maharaj met Yusuf Vawda in Mauritius; he belonged to Pravin Gordhan's communist unit in Durban. Then on 31 July 1988 Maharaj with his four wigs from Conny Braam and his assigned deputy, Siphiwe Nyanda ('Gebuza'), crossed the Swazi frontier, helped by a Swazi-based 'infrastructure' that was coordinated by Ivan Pillay, and drove to Johannesburg where he would be looked after by Ismail Momoniat, a member of an SACP district committee that had established itself.

Vula's strongest presence would be in Durban. Here Maharaj worked closely with Moe Shaik, who was directing a quite separate clandestine ANC network coordinated by NAT's counterintelligence section, directed by Jacob Zuma in Lusaka. Originally a member of the clandestine networks that assembled around Pravin Gordhan during the early 1980s,[205] Shaik's major preoccupation was Operation Bible, an enterprise established to build up a picture of the Security Police's penetration of the ANC's structures in the forward areas as well as in the UDF's and COSATU's leadership. A cooperative police officer who had befriended Shaik during his detention in 1985 supplied him with files for overnight photocopying. Shaik set up a network to analyse the material and to communicate with Lusaka; in 1987 he'd obtained received two months' intelligence training from Stasi tutors in Berlin specially for these purposes.[206] Steering clear of the people Moe Shaik identified in these files, Maharaj would enlist a coordinating network of around 20 people. They would supervise units in 16 out of 24 districts in Durban, engaging around altogether 100 activists, most of whom would not be aware of Vula's existence. Maharaj's chief communication officer was Janet Love, the daughter of a concentration camp survivor from Lithuania, whom the SACP infiltrated into the country in 1987.[207] Every fortnight Conny Braam's air hostesses would bring computer disks with fresh codes that Tim Jenkin had devised with the help of Dutch expertise. Similar but not as elaborate organisational underpinnings for Vula existed in the Western Cape and Johannesburg. By 1989, Maharaj was able to maintain frequent contact with the UDF leadership – mainly the trade unionists, including Sydney Mufamadi, Cyril Ramaphosa and Jay Naidoo. Contact with Lusaka and London was 'almost daily'.[208] One sphere of Vula activity was propaganda: for example, in Durban Maharaj oversaw the production of a local edition of the SACP newsletter *Umsebenzi*, with a circulation of around 5,000. Weapons stockpiling and military recruitment were separate concerns, being mainly Siphiwe Nyanda's responsibilities. What Vula was unable to build or set in place was any network that could support lateral communication or coordination between Umkhonto units inside South Africa. As Ronnie Kasrils told Howard Barrell shortly before his deployment by Vula into South Africa, Umkhonto still did not have 'city underground committees' that could enable this.[209]

Vula's most important tasks were political. By the end of April 1989, Maharaj had established a line of communication between Nelson Mandela and Lusaka, working with Mandela's lawyer Ismail Ayob. Informed about the content and progress of Mandela's talks with government, he would work hard to successfully counter the suspicions among UDF leaders that Mandela was 'selling out'.[210] He also tried to restrain the efforts by the recently released Harry Gwala and Govan Mbeki to act as local warlords commanding their own military operations, while resisting their demands for arms supplies for the impromptu Umkhonto armies they were setting up. Govan Mbeki's unconditional release in November 1987 was a concession urged by Mandela in his talks with the Minister of Justice, Kobie Coetsee.[211] Maharaj left South Africa for a debriefing with Oliver Tambo in Moscow on 12 July 1989. By then, Vula was a vigorous and purposeful collective entity and its networks were still flourishing when he returned in February 1990, though, by this stage, both the ANC and the party had been unbanned. The weapons smuggling continued; by 1994 the 'Africa Hinterlands' Bedford had shifted 40 tonnes since its first journey in 1987.[212] As Kasrils explained, negotiations might have begun, but that didn't rule out the need for the ANC to maintain 'an insurance policy'.[213]

Was Operation Vula a 'party affair', to use Stephen Ellis's phraseology? Virtually all the key South African personalities mentioned in this brief history were communists, though their personal loyalties and their political intentions were probably more complicated. As with the earlier party-sponsored propaganda campaign undertaken by the London recruits, Vula would draw support from international communist solidarity networks, their political empathy imbued with older European lineages of resistance. For example, Conny Braam recruited her first safe-house occupant from the Nieuwmarkt area, a scruffy Amsterdam neighbourhood populated by 'all the old Spanish civil war fighters and Spanish workers'.[214] Many of her volunteers were born in 'Red nests', she recalls; children of wartime resistance activists. Within South Africa, Maharaj would initially depend on the skeletal networks that the party had succeeded in building by the time of his arrival: Ismail Momoniat's committee in Johannesburg, and Pravin Gordhan's unit in Durban. He reported separately on specifically party-related issues to Slovo. Later, after February 1990, the party used the networks embodied in Vula's machinery to 'convene' its new following.[215] But to characterise Vula as a 'hard-line' insurrectionary project ignores its key role in establishing communications between Oliver Tambo and Nelson Mandela as well as Mac Maharaj's efforts to deflect local criticism of Mandela's talks. Vula helped ensure that the different ANC negotiators kept in step with one another. For Oliver Tambo, Vula's importance was its success in opening up communications with the ANC's internal leaders and supporters: that was its main purpose. The rest, even the gun-running, was secondary – 'insurance', so to speak.

Vula was a significant organisational advance. In the networks Mac

Maharaj had constructed by 1989, both the party and the ANC established within the country the political command centre that their strategic plan had perceived as a prerequisite for any serious insurgency. Its achievement was too late, though, to check the dynamic towards a quite different sort of outcome from the insurrectionary climax envisaged by Joe Slovo and the other writers of the Green Book. But did they need such a command? After all, as 'Mzala' had argued, there already existed in the local associations affiliated to the UDF organisations very willing 'to serve as organs of people's power and insurrection', and so there was no need for the ANC to build its own revolutionary committees. Mzala was partly right: within the UDF's popular following there were plenty of would-be insurrectionists, though since the time he was writing two successive States of Emergency had supplied fairly telling evidence of the state's capacity to contain, if not suppress, localised tumult. In any case, not all UDF leaders supported the ANC's strategic plans; most of them, including communists, were not, in Jeremy Seekings's words, 'committed insurrectionists'.[216] Increasingly, however, the UDF would echo the ANC's strategic formulations, although for the UDF, as Pravin Gordhan noted, in its contacts with the ANC leadership 'it was more a question of reporting than receiving'.[217] Gordhan himself tended to be one of the more cautious UDF principals. But the UDF itself was a complicated organisation, and people working under SACP or ANC discipline were unevenly and intermittently present in its hierarchy and its affiliates. In any case, it was not an easy organisation to direct, not least because many of its affiliates insisted on retaining their decision-making autonomy.[218] In 1985 the ANC claimed to its Swedish funders that it was supporting nearly 800 underground organisers inside South Africa, working mainly in legal organisations.[219] This was probably an exaggeration, but in any case it is probably unlikely that they functioned as a collective, capable of steering as large and as decentralised a formation as the UDF. One year earlier, apparently, the UDF's formation 'came as a shock' to Thabo Mbeki, and the ANC was startled too by the evidence of its ideological authority within the UDF, so at this stage its own communications with its clandestine cadres were obviously restricted.[220] When senior UDF leaders (including party members) sought advice from the ANC, they preferred to travel out of the country; as the UDF's historian has noted, at the time of the declaration of the State of Emergency in mid-1986 they 'did not have sufficiently good links with the ANC underground to ensure reliable communication'.[221]

The party's own records suggest a very limited communist internal presence: 99 full members and 19 probationers by 1989, organised in 35 units and supervised by regional and district committees, with the main groupings in Cape Town, on the Witwatersrand and in the Border area. The records kept by the leadership may have been misleading, as internal supporters may have considered themselves members even if they had not been recruited formally. As a report would acknowledge later: 'In July 1990, as we emerged from 40 years of illegality, our party had just over 2000 members' – a figure well in excess of the total cited in internal documentation at the end of 1989.[222] Raymond Suttner with his first-hand knowledge suggests that internal groups 'engaged in underground struggle for the SACP' in the 1980s totalled significantly more than the few hundred members that existed in the 1950s.[223] Around Johannesburg and in the Eastern Cape the party's recruitment was factory-focused, with key people active in legal trade unions.[224] Not all of them would have been active inside the UDF; trade unionists tended to refrain from direct engagement with the Front. In the Border region, the UDF convenor was Charles Nqakula – in 1983, a party member.[225] Nqakula's approach was non-sectarian, for in the East London area many of the UDF's affiliates would maintain 'nationalist anti-communist' predispositions while remaining within the 'Charterist' fold.[226] We know from Mac Maharaj's testimony that the SACP's Johannesburg District Committee, led by the Wits mathematics lecturer and Lenasia activist Ismail Momoniat, was sufficiently well established to accommodate and protect him on his arrival back in South Africa in July 1988 and that he would work very closely with Pravin Gordhan's party group, which had existed in Durban since the mid-1970s. Gordhan was a key figure in reviving the Natal Indian Congress and was influential within the UDF. Momoniat and Gordhan were conspicuous in the early 1980s in bringing together Freedom Charter supporters at a key conference in Durban in 1981.[227] There was an influential SACP presence in the Alexandra Youth Congress from at least as early as 1985: Paul Mashatile, a party member, was one of its founders and he later joined the UDF hierarchy, becoming secretary general in 1989. Party units were active in Cape Town's emerging trade unions from the early 1980s as well as being busy among trade unionists in East London and Mdantsane. David Rabkin had been enlisting supporters for the party in Cape Town from the late 1960s, chiefly targeting the university community, it seems, to judge by his best-known recruits, Jeremy Cronin and Rob Davies. Jeremy Cronin was a philosophy lecturer when he joined the party. Between 1984 and 1987 he was political education officer for the UDF in the Western Cape, editing its national theoretical journal, *Isizwe*. Working from Botswana, Barry Gilder had been able to support party-recruiting efforts inside South Africa, probably focusing on Johannesburg townships, particularly Alexandra with its combi taxi traffic with the Botswana border towns.

A very small number of communists held a few key positions in the UDF. As a Politburo meeting noted in January 1988, there was then 'encouraging evidence of Party leadership work by internally based structures'.[228] There was little evidence of party members acting as a collective, except perhaps in the case of the closely knit group assembled around Pravin Gordhan in the Natal Indian Congress, which dominated the provincial UDF leadership. By this stage Gordhan was considered an authoritative figure by his associates, in Moe Shaik's words 'an active and respected comrade, who excelled in Marxist thinking and methodology'.[229] Members of Pravin Gordhan's network often arrived at national meetings 'with prepared papers and cogent arguments'.[230] That did not mean that their views prevailed, not least because among influential African township-based leaders and activists there was resentment of what they took to be the excessive influence within the UDF of a largely Indian 'cabal'. Communist activists were influential in shaping the UDF's 'political education' programmes – both Raymond Suttner and Jeremy Cronin were important in this respect. Jeremy Cronin's poetry, widely read by students, helped to express and sharpen awareness of political continuities with earlier struggles. A powerful example in this vein was his tribute to his fellow prisoner John Matthews, one-time *Inkululeko* street seller in the 1930s, whose father 'came home blacklisted from the 1922 Rand Revolt'.[231] The almost hegemonic position on English-language university campuses of a left politics that often echoed SACP positions and in which the party's history was a major source of reference was evident in a range of student publications. Campus-generated pamphlets and newspapers also took their cues from UDF propaganda or, indeed, functioned themselves as media for the broader movement. The extent to which university students supplied a key social base for party activism remains underexplored. There were certainly important figures in the white student movement whom the party recruited: an example would be Gavin Evans, who helped found the End Conscription Campaign and who by the mid-1980s belonged to a three-person party cell in Johannesburg, communicating with the party leadership through Garth Strachan in Harare. Later he belonged to Vula's Johannesburg-based leadership: he was unimpressed with Maharaj, not least because he disagreed with Maharaj's 'expectations of an insurrectionary seizure of power'.[232]

Recruitment on campuses was not a party priority, except perhaps at the University of the North (Turfloop), close to one of the party's historical areas of rural influence. As Moses Mabhida noted at the party's sixth congress in 1984, communists had 'no organized presence amongst the youth'.[233] But in the early 1970s, independently of whatever rudimentary organisational networks the SACP had begun to build in Durban, Cape Town and Johannesburg, a new Marxist-influenced historiography was beginning to affect sister disciplines in the social sciences, transforming academic activity on certain campuses. Inspired by the British History Workshop movement and pioneered by British-trained returning South African postgraduates, it helped reinforce and shape the democratic socialism that informed students who were beginning to engage with the embryonic workers' movement emerging from the Durban strikes. In this milieu certain party-affiliated intellectuals emerged as key authorities, especially, as we have seen, Harold Wolpe; and, more widely, communist activists both in exile and inside South Africa began contributing to the journals and other publications that helped to animate political life at the universities of Wits, Cape Town and Natal. In general, while white campus activists may have occasionally included members of clandestine networks, both SACP and ANC, many members of the 'white left' navigated their own political pathways. As Gavin Andersson, the founder of the Wits-based student journal *Africa Perspective*, explained much later: 'At times we tended to define ourselves as communists outside the SACP, i.e. not Stalinists, but more in the vein of Gramscian communists. We read Capital as just one of the many Marxist texts and were schooled in most of the "classics" – Marx, Engels, Lenin, Luxemburg, Gramsci etc. through to more recent writers.'[234]

Internal party support could also be the effect of residual or historical networks, surviving from the 1940s and 1950s. After all, Peter Nchabeleng had remained busy trying to maintain party networks as late as 1967. In that same year, the veteran rural organiser Alpheus Maliba was arrested up by police at his home near Louis Trichardt, was charged under the Terrorism Act and died two weeks later in a police cell – suicide by hanging, the police claimed. The clearest evidence of this sort of communist agency at work inside South Africa was in Sekhukhuneland. As noted in the previous chapter, during the 1950s Sebatakgomo, an organisation of Bapedi migrant workers, was founded and led by SACP members, a group based in hostels in Johannesburg, who included John Nkadimeng and Flag Boshielo. Several of the Sebatakgomo leaders, SACP and ANC members, would become important Umkhonto organisers. John Nkadimeng began reconstructing ANC organisation in Soweto in early 1970s. He would leave South Africa to join the exile leadership in Lusaka, but not before making contact with his old party comrade Peter Nchabeleng, once the leader of the Pretoria Sebatakgomo group and a SACTU organiser who, after serving an eight-year term on Robben Island, returned to live in his birthplace in Abel, Sekhukhuneland. Prompted by the arrival in Abel of an Umkhonto group led by Tokyo Sexwale in 1976, Nchabeleng would revive his old network and begin training new fighters. After skirmishing with police, members of the group were captured and put on trial, though Nchabeleng was acquitted. In 1984, while continuing to work in clandestine ANC formations (the ANC came closest to setting up an area political-military committee in this part of the Northern Transvaal), Nchabeleng emerged as the regional chairperson of the UDF. Within two months of his election, he would die from beatings in police detention. His funeral, on 5 May, attracted a crowd of 20,000. Young mourners carried a huge hammer-and-sickle flag, one of several banners on display.[235] Clearly, Nchabeleng's political affiliations were no secret locally; after all, for decades local police had warned villagers to keep away from this dangerous communist. At this stage Communist Party insignia were unusual at rallies, unlike the ANC's colours, which had become commonplace. The only previous occasion nationally recorded by the press was at the funeral of the murdered Cradock Four, at least one of whom, Matthew Goniwe, belonged to a party unit in Cradock set up by Chris Hani.[236]

One of Nchabeleng's co-organisers twenty years before, both in Sebatakgomo and in SACTU, Nelson Diale, ran an advice office in Jane Furse: this would become a hub of local UDF organisation. In this region, then, the UDF acquired its most impressive rural following, partly a consequence of the maintenance of the historical networks established by Peter Nchabeleng and his comrades. But the support for the UDF was of a quite different social character from the migrant worker formations that had mobilised peasant disaffection in the 1950s. Here the UDF would be a youth movement, reflecting regional demography; more than 70 per cent of the population was aged under 20, and unemployment was officially at 37 per cent and certainly affecting school-leavers more heavily. And unlike the migrants of the 1950s, this was a literate population; indeed, secondary school enrolment, standing at 80 per cent of the relevant age cohort, had doubled in the previous ten years. This generational rebellion would be as likely to take its cues from the Marxist texts circulated by student organisations based at the University of Turfloop as it would draw upon older, more local belief systems. A party cell existed at the university at least as early as the late 1980s, when it was joined by pharmacy student Sello Moloto, later a provincial Premier of Limpopo. University students conducted workshops for village-based youth group leaders; as a consequence, 'a highly formal brand of Marxist-Leninist discourse' would shape the phraseology used by activists in Sekhukhune villages.[237] For the

Turfloop students, a favourite authority was Maurice Cornforth, the British author of *Materialism and the Dialectical Method*, a staple text for SACP probationers in the 1950s. But in this rural setting the class dynamics were very different from the revolutionary seedbed envisaged in Marxist orthodoxies. But this was a generational movement in an impoverished rural setting in which peasant farming had long since collapsed and adult workers were absent, away in the cities. In their mobilisation, the Sekhukhune youngsters, mostly male, were repudiating the authority of their compliant parents as much as they were opposing local structures of political authority, for in a patrimonial and gerontocratic political environment both were interwoven. And the rebellion's teenage constituents adopted as their icons not the grey-haired prisoners on Robben Island, but Chris Hani and Joe Slovo, the generals of Umkhonto.[238] However, to make things more complicated, though the local activists objected to the customary rituals and conventions that sustained patrimonial village leadership, their rebellion was also coloured by the local moral universe. In particular, setbacks and misfortunes would be blamed on witchcraft and the identified scapegoats, usually elderly widowed pensioners, were burned to death.[239] The witch burnings that scarred the movement and led to its repression were themselves an innovation. In condemning the witches, the young activists usurped the customary functions of the chiefs' and elders' courts, and the terrible penalties they imposed imitated the necklace burnings of the cities: burning witches was not conventional in Sekhukhuneland.[240] The persecution of supposed witches was discouraged ineffectually by Youth Congress leaders; it was 'nothing to do with the ANC', they insisted.[241]

Aside from the organisational network that he revived, which supplied the initial basis for insurgent organisation, did Peter Nchabeleng shape in other ways the regional political uprising that was consolidating at the time of his death? The most militant formations among the UDF's local affiliate structure were the Youth Congresses. One of the earliest of these was the Seshego Youth Congress, formed in the township outside Pietersburg in 1984, one of whose office-holders in 1988 was Polly Boshielo, who, on the party's unbanning, would become a key figure in its regional leadership. So, it is conceivable that there may have been a dynastic element in the revival of a Communist Party network here, and it is possible that memories of an older set of external radical ideas that shaped an earlier rebellion may have helped create a receptive audience for the Leninist cadences introduced to village assemblies by the student activists. One key transmitter of such ideas was Elleck Nchabeleng, Peter's son, released from Robben Island in 1986 and subsequently employed by the Community Resource Information Centre (CRIC) in Johannesburg as an emissary for its rural outreach programmes. Elleck was a frequent traveller to his home village, bringing with him propaganda materials and money for organisers. CRIC, set up by former NUSAS activists in a Braamfontein office block adjacent to Wits University, was a key provider of the agitational materials that helped give expression to this Sekhukhune uprising, working closely with local Youth Congress leaders.[242] NUSAS itself was an important propagator of argumentative texts that interpreted South African politics through Marxian analytical frameworks, and two Wits-based student journals, *Africa Perspective* and *Work in Progress*, found ready readerships in Sekhukhuneland, being disseminated through CRIC's network.[243]

MORE INTENTIONALLY, COMMUNISTS hoped to establish a leadership role among organised workers in the cities. In 1980, party leadership resolved that trade union work should receive priority status in 'forward areas', each of which should host a SACTU 'collective'. South African communists were still predisposed to take a Leninist view of trade unions and their limitations, politically. They could not generate the kind of consciousness needed for a revolutionary movement. The party's role was critical, for 'workers [could] acquire class consciousness only from without, from outside the sphere of their immediate economic struggle'.[244] At that stage, the Politburo was still hoping that SACTU would become the 'prime mass instrument' for ensuring 'the emergence of a strong and independent trade union movement', though it acknowledged that the emerging black labour movement was already constituted by 'genuine' trade unions. In the long term, party leaders agreed, SACTU should aim to win their affiliation, though at present 'internal conditions make this aim extremely difficult'. Instead, SACTU organisers should encourage unions to organise along industrial lines and affiliate to the new Federation of South African Trade Unions (FOSATU). Ideally there should be a 'national SACTU underground' present in 'every national union'.[245] As we have seen, by 1980 party members were active in the Western Cape, reporting to Ray Alexander on their efforts to organise dock workers, and were also busy in the Western Province General Workers' Union. We know from trial evidence that SACTU had some influence around East London, becoming the stronghold for another general union, the South African Allied Workers' Union (SAAWU).

On the whole, the single-industry unions that had emerged from the 1973 strike movement and that were supported initially by white student activists were less amenable to SACTU promptings. The group that would unite in the new federation, FOSATU, in 1979 explicitly rejected political connections, not just for practical reasons but also because of their leaders' conviction that trade unions should be working class-led and politically independent. Party statements about the Polish Solidarity movement would have done little to shift such beliefs. There was 'no absolute right to "free" trade unions to exist', *African Communist* editorialised in 1982, for 'all rights and freedoms must be interpreted and applied in their class context: do they promote or hinder the development of socialism?'[246] The Cape Town-based Food and Canning Workers' Union (FCWU) was an exception among industrial unions in its political predispositions and in working closely with SAAWU, but the union was a survivor from Ray Alexander's work in the 1940s, and its African parallel body was led by 70-year-old party veteran Oscar Mpetha, though it too kept well clear of any 'underground' trade union networks. However, FCWU leaders exchanged weekly letters with Ray Alexander via a London forwarding address from the time of her departure from South Africa in 1965 until her return 25 years later.[247] Neither Jan Theron nor Neil Aggett, the FCWU's main organisers in Cape Town and Johannesburg respectively, were communists nor did they engage with SACTU. Increasingly, black union leadership would be divided into two factions, each characterised by the other as 'workerist' and 'populist', disagreeing over whether or not to form political alliances and also at odds over the government's new labour reforms: SAAWU and the general workers' unions opposed registration and the FCWU itself for a while considered de-registration. But even the trade union officials more sympathetic to SACTU would resist external promptings, as on the occasion when the Botswana 'forward area' instructed Gavin Andersson to issue pamphlets calling for a general strike in June 1981, an idea that even Andersson's 'key comrades' rejected. Outside South Africa, within the party and the ANC as well as SACTU there were different views about registration, though by 1982 FOSATU was no longer perceived as the 'ideal umbrella' for the new unions.[248] In a speech on JB Marks's birthday, Joe Slovo attacked Joe Foster, FOSATU's general secretary, as well as 'university students trying to use trade unions to build a workers' party'.[249] In an assessment written probably in 1982, its authors admitted that there had been little progress in following up the Politburo's decisions two years before. In 1983 Ray Alexander, writing under her pseudonym RS Nyameko, suggested that general workers' unions should 'phase themselves out' and that registration should not be an issue of principle to hold up trade union unity, a view reiterated in a Central Committee statement.[250] In three years the line had shifted; in 1980 the Central Committee had condemned the government's reformist 'Wiehahn scheme' as a 'bosses' charter' that would deal a 'death blow' to independent black unions.[251] In the end SACTU had to work hard to persuade SAAWU and other general workers' unions to join COSATU, a body that would certainly be dominated by their rivals from the 'workerist' group.[252]

There was, to be sure, a sprinkling of party members taking up influential positions in the trade union movement during the 1980s, but they seem to have worked quite independently from each other. Through the decade SACTU, led as it was almost exclusively by party members, appeared to lose what little traction that it may have exercised within the South African labour movement in 1980. Just how out of touch the external trade unionist leadership had become was evident at the beginning of 1986 when SACTU leaders in London and Lusaka were apparently planning to organise or revive their own South African mine workers' union. They were overruled by the SACP Politburo after objections from the ANC's Politico-Military Council. From now on, there would be 'unanimity' that 'the unity of mineworkers' would be built around the National Union of Mineworkers, which was originally a project of the Black Consciousness-affiliated CUSA but was by 1986 the largest constituent of the new Congress of South African Trade Unions (COSATU).[253] In March that year, a COSATU delegation, which included Jay Naidoo, Chris Dlamini and Cyril Ramaphosa, met the ANC's leadership in Lusaka; John Nkadimeng represented SACTU at this encounter. The delegates' self-confidence apparently disconcerted their hosts. They were emphatic that in any relationship that developed, COSATU would not be a subordinate partner and nor should any external funding for South African trade unions be channelled through the exile formation.[254] At this point, COSATU's signed-up affiliate strength was 500,000 members, mostly in key heavy industries, many of whom paid their dues to COSATU through employers' check-off agreements. Ron Press, who was invited to join SACTU's executive in 1973 by John Gaetsewe and who later worked at its London office in Archway, attended an 'enlarged' Politburo meeting in Lusaka after COSATU's formation, held to address the question of what SACTU's future should be. During a break in the discussion, he chatted with Joe Slovo. Slovo confided that in his view SACTU's value was in its past achievements, but he was not going push that argument because many people at the meeting would have disagreed.[255] As Press explained in his autobiography, 'many comrades had a stake in SACTU – offices that came with certain advantages and a sense of purpose'.[256] He attended at least one more meeting with top SACTU and party comrades, 'but this was a weak affair with nothing to fix it in memory'.[257] Of course, in the London office, much of the activity in which

Press was engaged was to do with eliciting British trade union solidarity while discouraging direct contacts between British unions and their South African-based counterparts.[258] It is possible that the Lusaka SACTU-based officials may have continued to try to influence internal developments, but Slovo's remark suggests this was not the case. For the time being, it was agreed there were still certain functions that SACTU could perform, 'certain vital areas of work (by their very nature given the fascist conditions) which require input from a revolutionary trade union movement'.[259]

To judge from later developments, it does seem likely that the SACP enjoyed some success in recruitment in certain COSATU affiliates in the later 1980s.[260] In 1986, the Politburo called for 'selective recruitment of suitable trade union militants' while also observing that its Industrial Subcommittee needed to be more effective.[261] That year, a Department of Industrial Work was established under Joe Slovo's supervision as general secretary.[262] Before the end of the decade, several senior COSATU trade union leaders would join the SACP, including Moses Mayekiso (metal workers), John Gomomo and Alec Erwin, the former FOSATU general secretary, though Erwin later maintained that he was 'never very active in its structures'.[263] Cyril Ramaphosa may have joined at this time.[264] He had met Slovo in Lusaka in 1986 and agreed to Slovo's suggestion that his union should distribute copies of the party's commemorative pamphlet on the 1946 strike. Slovo asked if they would manage to distribute 2,000 copies and Ramaphosa told him they would take 10,000. The pamphlets arrived in Johannesburg thereafter, and Ramaphosa was duly impressed: 'We knew then that we were dealing with an efficient and effective revolutionary who could keep his word.'[265] The party would build an especially strong presence within the National Union of Mineworkers.

Whether the party's new recruits within the trade union movement inside South Africa shared the insurrectionary visions that had animated party leadership at the beginning of the decade is questionable. It is most unlikely that they all would have agreed with the conception that 'every political unit in the country must be oriented and transformed into an armed wing within the political structure'.[266] Some of the exemplary testimony from the party's recruits in the labour movement does rather suggest that some of them did, with one party operative suggesting that his comrades should prioritise establishing a presence in factories producing strategic supplies for the military: 'How possible would it be to barricade the whole zone with delivery lorries?'[267] In *The Path to Power*, however, the conception of insurrection had shifted; organised labour would supply its main force while the guerrilla units played a support role.[268] In fact, a fresh strategic rationale for building influence in the unions was very evident in 1988 when Joe Slovo wrote a 'discussion pamphlet' addressed to the party's new trade union following. Here Slovo's main message was to reassure workers that 'class struggle does not fade into the background when workers forge alliances with other classes'. A purely working-class struggle, such as 'workerists' had advocated, was a mistake, for 'we would in fact be surrendering the leadership of the national struggle to the upper and middle strata'. Liberation would necessarily involve radical transformations, for 'no significant national demand can be completely fulfilled without the eventual destruction of the existing capitalist structure'. No 'Chinese wall' separated the different stages in South Africa's revolution.[269] Slovo and other communists had been making much the same point for at least a couple of decades. But his emphasis on the class struggle dimension of national democracy was quite fresh. Only three years before, *African Communist* published an attack on 'workerists', which noted that 'the problem with people advocating "socialism now" is that they expect those blacks who cannot read or write to run socialist industries and mines'.[270] Whatever the merits of such observations, this was not the kind of public language that party members would now employ in defending national democracy. Communists would also shift in their attitude to a workers' charter, an undertaking that hitherto they had considered unnecessary.[271]

ONE REASON WHY THE party's presence within South Africa was so limited and scattered was because its own corporate existence outside South Africa was so intermittent and perfunctory. Barry Gilder recalls that 'it was impossible to tell much difference in the content of discussions between a party committee meeting and that of the ANC's regional politico-military committee or any other ANC collective'.[272] His contention is supported by available archival evidence. The Simonses' papers contain minutes of a sequence of meetings for unit seven, the party cell that Ray Alexander belonged to in Lusaka. As was noted on 14 November 1980, 'A problem that most comrades seem to have is to find time to do their Communist Party work as well as their ANC work.' But time wasn't the only problem, the minutes acknowledged: 'The unit is of the opinion that there is a strong wish among Party members to make its presence felt and to act openly as members of the Party. However, this feeling is frustrated by the failure of the Party to take the plunge and create the necessary conditions for the Party's emergence.' An earlier meeting listened to a report of a visit to the Botswana 'forward area'. Here, apparently the 'party's presence' was 'not felt', and political education among freshly arrived exiles was neglected. On a more upbeat note, the visitors returned to Lusaka with a list of five members of SACTU who might prove to be 'likely recruits'. Several of the other meetings evidently focused on movement-wide shortcomings of morale and indiscipline rather than on specifically party concerns, though one meeting on 23 January 1980 referred to worrying lapses of conduct by party members who had become involved in the smuggling of stolen cars for use by ANC leaders.[273]

More widely, secrecy about membership inhibited the development of a strong consciousness of community among party members. Ron Press's autobiography describes the practical difficulties South African communists in London encountered in nominating and electing a district committee in a secretive setting in which they could only guess who was likely to be a communist.[274] Even outside South Africa, the party remained a small organisation, its recruitment very selective. Maloka's history refers to the party's own statistics in April 1989: 340 members in eight regions, not counting South Africa. Of these, 67 members lived and worked in Lusaka, constituting a total of ten units. In addition, at that time probationers numbered 66, signalling an upsurge in recruitment, a development which worried the Politburo, which was concerned about too rapid an expansion.[275] As well as the army units, by 1989 transferred from their Angolan bases to Tanzania and Uganda, there was a small group at Mazimbu, the ANC's educational centre where a unit was established in 1980 by Rica Hodgson;[276] a larger community in London; and about 20 party members who at any one time were attending the Lenin School or other European training schemes.

By 1980 there was a generally shared perception expressed in a Central Committee discussion document that in 'holding its face', the party had been 'too timid'. There needed to be more open recognition that 'ANC leaders are also party leaders'. In effect, the party's restraint was 'a form of liquidationism', which had allowed 'a position to develop in which work in party structures and collectives is completely neglected.'[277] The following year, the Central Committee in a statement about 'accountability' needed to remind members that 'every Party cadre who is active at any level of a fraternal organization is accountable to the Party executive' and that it was the 'duty of each Party comrade to seek guidance from his or her collective on all new policy decisions'.[278] Obviously this was not happening, not least because it was also party policy that its members should not act as a clique or a caucus when working within allied formations. Central Committee meetings themselves were in fact rather occasional during the early 1980s. Between 1979 and 1983 the committee convened itself just three times.

Organisationally for the party, it was an 'untenable situation', the Central Committee agreed, when after a two-year interval it assembled in late 1983. There were still no full-time party officials. There was no programme or plan 'for the building of the Party inside the country'. Internal propaganda work was limited to the dispatch and circulation of the illegal miniaturised edition of *African Communist*, itself written mainly by people living outside Africa. It was still the case apparently that the London District Committee was chiefly responsible for 'internal work',[279] and even in forward areas 'our units ... depend upon spasmodic contact to receive directions and give reports'.[280] In Lusaka and elsewhere, party members working in the wider liberation movement tended 'to do so as individuals', rather than in any way that was shaped by awareness of obligations to the party. The 1981 resolution on accountability was 'more honoured in the breach'. For example, no party group or 'collective' had discussed the recent reorganisation within the ANC of 'its apparatus responsible for internal military and political work'. It was quite wrong that there should be more members outside South Africa than inside. Part of the difficulty stemmed from the rule that 'only the Politburo' had 'the power to admit new members', and all too often Politburo members were fully preoccupied with non-party responsibilities.[281]

A party congress held in Moscow in early 1984, and 'attended by tens of delegates',[282] acknowledged these shortcomings. This was the first such meeting for more than three decades and, in future, delegates decided, congresses would be held every four years, and in-between congresses party bodies should meet more regularly and frequently. The Politburo would in fact meet 76 times before the next congress in 1989.[283] A new system of recruitment and probation was adopted. Delegates reviewed a new constitution, though the party would retain its adherence to democratic centralism and other features of Leninism, 'despite the fact that the term is somewhat out of fashion in large parts of western Europe'.[284] Once again, the distinction between vanguardism and leadership was spelled out: communists should act as the 'leading political force of the SA working class', though remaining loyal members of a 'liberation front headed by the ANC'.[285] The carefully balanced position on caucusing and accountability with respect to work in the ANC was reiterated. It apparently needed to be, for, as Moses Mabhida pointed out, 'Members working in other organisations are no longer being given tasks by the Party and hence meetings of party units have become nothing more than discussion clubs.'[286] Part of the purpose of the meeting – originally conceived of as an extended Central Committee assembly[287] – was to prepare for the ANC conference to be held in Kabwe; in a discussion on 'people's war', one

442

delegate suggested recruitment of gangsters.[288] As we have seen, communist delegates at the Kabwe meeting would disagree over whether the ANC should open up its leadership to non-Africans.

Despite more frequent leadership gatherings, the internal documentation indicates that for many members, ANC commitments left little time for party work. 'We need our members, even in senior ANC positions, to attend more to Party work', a Central Committee meeting minuted in January 1986.[289] It was a 'problem which continue[d] to plague us', that is, the 'small number of party members who devote their time to direct party work'.[290] Two years later, it was still the case that 'Party members have failed to attend or to participate in the work of units for long periods', and indeed 'some of the units are not functioning regularly'.[291] And while it was true that 'our party's prestige at home is growing visibly', the party itself remained too self-effacing; 'we face the risk of being regarded more as an adjunct of the liberation alliance than as an independent force'.[292] There was, however, by 1986 'a noticeable improvement in our political work in the army'.[293] But, 'especially inside the country', the party's organised presence was 'weak'.[294] By 1988, internal members actually attended a Central Committee 'plenary'. Even so, 'much more' was needed 'to strengthen our organisational presence inside our country', notwithstanding 'encouraging evidence of Party leadership work by internally based structures'. One of the South African-based delegates confirmed that in the mass organisation in which he held a leadership position, there were plenty of signals of party influence, not least because so much party literature was in circulation.[295] Since 1985, the party had begun to direct its propaganda at a wider internal readership, with quarterly issues of *Umsebenzi* (a name change from *Inkululeko*) and a pamphlet, *Conversations with a Communist*, in both English and isiZulu versions.[296] Its text, ostensibly addressed to the mother of a young party recruit now on Robben Island, projected the life of a rank-and-file Umkhonto soldier, and its specifically communist message was limited to underlining the solidarity role undertaken by socialist countries: 'Your first born ... he uses a Soviet made gun. He is fed while he trains on food made in the GDR. He is clothed in trousers from Czechoslovakia, shoes from Hungary, shirts from Cuba. He lives in Angola. These are the countries that help the ANC. It is because these countries are Communist that they help oppressed peoples all over the world.'[297]

Towards the end of the decade South African communists were beginning to enjoy a political revival inside South Africa, with increasing recognition at least among trade unionists of their role as an 'independent force', not just an 'adjunct' to the liberation movement. In the South African political diaspora, though, their influence remained more subject than ever to the limits of working as an entryist formation in a much larger organisation that itself was discovering new partners and engaging in a major strategic redirection. In an international setting in which the ANC was increasingly attracting sympathetic consideration in Western Europe and North America, the SACP was just one ally among many. An open meeting in London to celebrate the party's 65th anniversary on 30 July 1986 reflected this shifting perspective. Alfred Nzo was on the platform wearing his ANC hat. His address was friendly enough, but, to one observer at least, its chief effect was to 'squeeze the SACP on to the sidelines'.[298] To be sure, in a democratic South Africa, Nzo told his audience, the ANC would 'continue to defend the right of any South African who so chooses to belong to the SACP', just as it would 'respect the right of any of our compatriots to belong to any party of their choice'. The ANC was also keen to 'ensure that the capitalist, as well, acts against the apartheid regime'. Of course, the ANC was 'happy' that 'communists in our country are to be found amongst these millions' mobilising against the apartheid regime, 'side by side with the religious people, with people of other religious persuasions'. The socialist bloc received a brief mention for its support for the liberation struggle together with careful acknowledgement of the aid the ANC had received from the 'non-aligned' states of Western Europe. Joe Slovo was present in his new capacity as general secretary; he had just succeeded Moses Mabhida, who had died in Maputo in March. His speech was 'muted, theoretical and cautious' rather than celebratory, seemingly calculated to call off 'the hot heads'.[299] It clearly had in mind a different audience from the party faithful assembled that evening, with its references to a post-apartheid future in which there would be partial measures to redistribute wealth … [that] do not in themselves point in a socialist direction', and in which a mixed economy would provide plenty of room 'for managers and businessmen and people of good will who have or are prepared to end racism'. An edited version would subsequently appear in the London *Guardian* newspaper.[300]

JUST AS WAS THE CASE at the time of its exile, the party would return to South Africa with its members occupying key positions at the helm of the wider liberation movement to which it belonged. Yet its presence within the ANC's leadership did not really result in control at any stage during the 30 years of the external mission. During the 1960s, party leaders were split between London and Dar es Salaam, and the key African leaders in Dar es Salaam, such as Moses Kotane or Duma Nokwe, did not usually function in a separate collective entity from their non-communist comrades in the ANC's leadership structures. The party's de facto alliance with the ANC took nearly a decade to become more formally institutionalised. The establishment of an organised Communist Party presence within the ANC's African diaspora community began only in the 1970s, gathering impetus in 1977 when the ANC moved its guerrillas into Angolan camps. Here, it is true, the party's members acted decisively to shape the ways in which the soldiers were instructed and indoctrinated; they almost always filled the positions of camp commissars, for example, and later predominated in Umkhonto's elite formations. Overall discipline was nevertheless in the hands of separately organised security officials; party members were present in NAT but exercised no corporate influence and often took actions that put them at odds with other communists. Certainly, the party made a significant impact upon the ANC's intellectual life, with communists writing the ANC's most important strategic and programmatic statements from 1969 onwards, modelling them around their own collectively shared trajectories of revolutionary change. However, as we have seen, despite any formal resolutions to which they signed up, party members had their own different understandings of how their struggle might play out. Key personalities among them, such as Thabo Mbeki, were sceptical about the prospects for any 'seizure of power', working to secure the kind of negotiated transition that the party itself either believed could not happen or, later, warned against. Even within the 'insurrectionist' encampment there were different conceptions about how an insurrection might or should happen. Within the ANC's army, party strategists were unable to predominate completely, and the organisational steps needed before any serious escalation of military activity remained incomplete, partly because of competing strategic visons within Umkhonto's command. At no stage, even after the inception of Operation Vula, did Umkhonto or the ANC as a political movement develop a leadership network inside the country capable of coordinating its cadres under discipline, including the armed units.

The party itself distinguished between the leadership role that the ANC was supposed to perform in directing national liberation and its own purpose as the vanguard formation of the South African working class. However, its own internal networks and contacts within the trade union movement as it developed in the 1980s were too limited to determine trade union leaders' decision-making, and during the decade the party would increasingly shift its policies about trade unionism in deference to organised labour. It retained influence within the labour movement, to be sure, but as a respected ally and a sympathetic partner, not as a decision-maker. More generally, through its entryist relationship with the ANC in which the party's few hundred members often occupied important and demanding ANC posts, engagement in ANC work left little time for specifically party-related activity – a degree of engagement and immersion in a larger organisation that inhibited any capacity for autonomous action. And though the party's fraternal allies in Eastern Europe and the Soviet Union, through their support and hospitality, helped ensure wide admiration for existing socialist models throughout the liberation movement, increasingly communist governments would deal with the ANC directly, acknowledging its senior status. Here, in this relationship, the party held no real leverage, though its presence probably influenced the scale and duration of Soviet, East German and Czechoslovak generosity to the ANC.

That the party could not control the ANC is plain enough, but a more difficult and contentious question is about the ways in which the party shaped the larger organisation's history during this period as well as the nature of its contribution to the broader course of anti-apartheid resistance inside South Africa. How did it make a difference? There are at least three answers to this question.

First of all, although in retrospect it is easy enough to identify flaws and mistakes in the party's strategic understandings, at the time they were developed they served as sources of hope and moral certainty, not just for party ideologues but among the ANC's own rank and file, helping to sustain the movement and ensure its survival. The party's own textual analyses of the political economy of liberation would accumulate canonical authority during the 1980s within South Africa. This was the case especially within the student movement and among many trade unionists, reinforcing their conviction and determination.

Secondly, the party brought with it a range of helpful resources to the larger organisation: technical and professional skills, organisational habits, a diversity of social contacts in host societies, and skilful managers – 'cadres' as the party liked to call them – renewing these successively through selective recruitment and careful preparation. The extent to which Umkhonto's armed struggle was politically successful in building the ANC's prestige and authority inside South Africa was at least partly attributable to the energy and dedication invested in sustaining operations dependent on very extended supply lines. Most of the logistical staff-work and intelligence-based planning for these operations as well as much of the field command was in the hands of communists. The party's membership of an international communist family enabled it to draw upon and enlist sympathisers from European communist traditions, who could bring their own skills, resources and idealism.

Thirdly, inside South Africa the party installed its own remarkably resilient networks that helped underpin wider political formations and bring to them a perception of inclusive loyalty. Using its own resources, the party succeeded in re-establishing its own internal presence within South Africa either through its dispatch of recruits from London in the late 1960s onwards or through the self-assembly of would-be communist groups such as Pravin Gordhan's cluster in Natal in the mid-1970s as well as through the reactivation of historical bases such as in Sekhukhuneland. All these networks, often functioning in crucial sites of leadership, helped ensure that the massive resistance movement that consolidated itself in the 1980s shared a consciousness of historical succession, an adherence to non-racialism, and a common iconography.

Significantly, when the ANC finally succeeded in establishing a clandestine leadership structure inside South Africa in Operation Vula, already-existing communist networks would supply the organisational underpinnings. Paradoxically, this very achievement would work against any fulfilment of the party's strategic vision. In establishing secure lines of communication between external and internal ANC leaders, Vula would help to cement Nelson Mandela's authority and support a very different route to government from the party's envisaged pathway to power.

NINE

Post-Communism and the South African Communist Party

Chris Hani, Jacob Zuma and Joe Slovo enter the arena at the SACP's first return home rally, 1990.

In 1990 South African communists would return to South Africa to begin the work of reconstructing their party as a legal organisation. This was a year in which global politics would change fundamentally. Throughout its history, the party had been inspired and supported by the reality of existing socialism, state systems embracing half of Europe and Asia, in which the ruling group was at least notionally committed to the building of communist societies. With the fall of Eastern European regimes and the fragmentation of the Soviet Union, one key set of material foundations for the party's programmatic beliefs crumbled and its most important international alliances would end. Certainly, East Asian models of socialism or, rather, state-managed capitalism were to endure and Cuba would survive as a lonely base of communist practice in the West, but, as we have seen, the party's closest affiliations in the global socialist community were located in Eastern Europe and Russia. In many ways, the international order which would help shape the party's new history was a post-communist world.

Former ruling communist parties in Eastern Europe have had mixed fortunes since 1990. In Poland and Hungary, for almost two decades, they prospered as relatively significant parliamentary parties, after 'rebranding' themselves as social democrats favouring market reform, before losing support to the populist right.[1] In these two countries, they enjoyed some success in winning over younger, urban (and urbane) and middle-class supporters. By contrast, while the relatively ideologically untransformed 'neo-communist' Czech Communist Party of Bohemia and Moravia actually gained electoral support, slightly, from its 13 per cent share in the 1990 poll, its core adherents tend to be male, pensioned, working class, and living in deindustrialised rust-belt regions. The average age of its 200,000 membership is 70.[2] In Western Europe, in the case of Italy, with its history of a relatively popular communism, the party has been supplanted by a differently named centre-left formation that retains electoral vigour particularly in municipal politics, organised around charismatic leadership and retaining many former communists in its party membership. In France, the Communist Party maintains a vestigial parliamentary presence with eight deputies; its electoral support has dwindled in every contest despite its abandonment of Leninism and its sporadic efforts to tap anti-immigrant sentiment, and its increasingly elderly supporters are, if not pensioners, most likely in public employment.[3]

In which ways does the trajectory of the South African Communist Party correspond with the experience of other communist parties in this fresh environment? Has it reinvented itself as a social democratic electoral force along the lines of the 'rebranded' Eastern European groups? Has it succeeded in finding fresh support and new causes? Or is it, as in the case of the Czechs and the French communists, confined by its history, a prisoner of its past?

As will become evident, the South African Communist Party remains far from reconstituted as a post-communist formation. The party's leadership remains inspired by Leninist precepts and its own historical strategic perspectives. It also draws its sense of purpose from its proximity to power. This last point indicates that its situation in 1990 was fundamentally different from the European communist parties, both Eastern and Western. The party's long-standing relationship with an overwhelmingly popular national liberation movement brought it a particular resilience compared with other communist parties in the post-communist setting. After all, its leaders in the 1950s and in exile were important figures in the ANC, professedly committed to the democratic goals of a movement with a very broad social following. In any case, in 1990 communists in South Africa could anticipate very real prospects of themselves soon holding government office, prospects that would have made the collapse of 'existing communism' in Eastern Europe much less discouraging than it would have been for communists in other places. Indeed, since 1994 several of its members have served as cabinet ministers in every administration. Its members have also continued to hold key positions in the largest trade union confederation, the Congress of South African Trade Unions (COSATU). Just as before 1990, communists would continue to hold senior positions in South Africa's continuously ruling party, the African National Congress, and indeed four out of five of South Africa's post-apartheid presidents, Nelson Mandela, Thabo Mbeki, Kgalema Motlanthe and Jacob Zuma, at one time or another belonged to the party. As the history unfolded in this book has shown, the Communist Party helped shape the ANC's programmatic development well before its election into government, especially during its exile. It was influential even before then, particularly during the popular resistance to apartheid during the 1950s, which was underpinned by the party's systematic organisation in the localities that supplied the ANC with its strongest bases.

But in the fresh setting of a democratic South Africa, the nature of the party's relationship with the ANC would alter. In exile and inside South Africa under the conditions of illegality, the ANC's influence depended not so much on disciplined organisation but rather upon loyalties and camaraderie among activists in a range of different bodies, ranging from township street committees to foreign solidarity associations that considered themselves members of a movement. Within the most organised parts of the ANC, as we have seen, the party could exercise considerable influence. From 1990, though, the ANC began reconstituting itself as a structured mass party with a presence in every location and a bureaucracy of full-time officials. Once in power, especially with its command of electoral support confirmed for the second time in 1999, ANC leaders looked to construct a modern political machine, moving away from the social movement politics that had accompanied their ascent to office. Depending less and less on the mobilisation of activist support, the organisation increasingly relied on a politics of patronage facilitated by the systematic 'deployment' of its cadres (often themselves SACP members) into the public administration and the parastatal corporations. And, as the ANC has evolved into a 'party-state', its engagement with its former allies has become increasingly perfunctory.

In Eastern Europe and the former Soviet Union, 'post-communism' brought changes in the wider political environment that were particularly challenging for organisations that based their ideological appeal around class solidarity and sought to root themselves in an industrial society. It might seem perverse to include South Africa in this kind of consideration of post-communist experience. Before the transition to democracy, South Africa's governing politicians were neither communists nor self-professed African socialists. And it is not really the case that there were significant similarities between South Africa's racially exclusive order and Eastern European communist regimes, as free-marketeer critics of apartheid used to suggest, notwithstanding restrictions on labour markets and property ownership.[4]

Nor did South Africa's progress from authoritarian rule involve a 'triple transition' of the kind generally characteristic of the replacement of the communist order by political pluralism. Certainly, during the 1990s South Africa underwent political democratisation and economic liberalisation. But the third dimension of post-communist transition, nation-building, was absent, for in South Africa this task was already complete. South African nationalism and national identity are inclusive and civic rather than ascriptive and cultural, partly a consequence of the party's ideological impact on high politics. Opinion polling indicates widespread acceptance of the state's legitimacy across historical communal divisions, though other aspects of cross-communal solidarity are weaker.[5] In particular, social inequality has restricted normative consensus about the values that might underpin both democratisation and marketisation – as has been the case with many post-Soviet states. But whereas in post-communist settings, states have divested themselves of responsibility for providing basic social services, in South Africa, far from contracting, welfare provisions and social services have expanded and proliferated and the public service has become bigger and better paid – again, to an extent, an effect of the party's presence in government. So, in certain respects, in 1990 South African communists would appear to have been advantageously placed compared with their former fraternal allies in Eastern Europe. But in the open politics of a democratic South Africa, the party would struggle to maintain, let alone increase, its ideological authority. In particular, challenges would arise from a political economy in which the industrial working class would weaken, a black middle-class salariat would expand, and the party's own mass membership would become increasingly recruited from a growing population of unemployed rural youngsters.

This chapter will first focus on the party's situation in the early days of South Africa's transition when it moved away from vanguardism. We will then move forward three decades to outline its present profile and orientation so that we can identify the most important changes as well as the similarities that still exist between its modern or contemporary characteristics and its salient features at the beginning of the 1990s. The chapter will explore changes in the party's membership and social location, as well as shifts and continuities in its programmatic predisposition. It will assess the extent and quality of its contribution to the ANC's and the government's leadership and its impact on policy as well as its wider influence. The party's history and its historical impact will be the focus of the final pages of this chapter. Arguably, communists at different times have shaped South Africa's politics decisively and, in doing so, they reshaped the communities in which they were active. Here, in the final pages of this book we will identify the moments and the ways in which the party's course had its most profound and long-lasting effects.

IN 1989, AT ITS SEVENTH congress in Havana, SACP membership was estimated at two thousand, a doubling of its size during the decade. The growth reflected efforts to cultivate within South Africa a more assertive public presence, which was signalled by the appearance of SACP flags and propaganda at rallies and funerals. In Havana in 1989, officials supplied a breakdown of membership. Among the exiles, three-quarters of the party's adherents were ex-students, professionals or intellectuals and only a minority were workers. Within the country, the party was largely proletarian and African. Cursory as it was, this information was far more detailed than anything the SACP had chosen to disclose about its membership since the suppression of the Communist Party of South Africa, its legal predecessor, in 1950. Apart from naming its most senior office-bearers, however, the identity of even the other members elected onto the Central Committee remained secret.

The Havana meeting included other innovations. It adopted its new programme, *The Path to Power*, to replace the by-then decidedly venerable *Road to South African Freedom*, the party's canonical text since 1962. After noting the resilient quality of modern capitalism, the *Path* turned to more pressing concerns. In tune with previous advocacy by the general secretary Joe Slovo of a gradual pace for any transition to socialism, the programme drew upon continental African experience to warn against 'the drive to move ahead of objective conditions', for example through the 'premature' elimination of private property. *The Path to Power* maintained the party's view of South Africa as characterised by a 'colonialism of a special type', an essential formulation in its justification of its alliance with a multi-class nationalist movement. Even so, the struggle remained revolutionary, for its goals 'cannot be merely for civil rights within the framework of the existing system', but were rather for 'fundamental change' that could only follow 'a seizure of power'. As noted in the last chapter, the party reaffirmed its commitment in its strategy to armed insurgency and, indeed, its 'escalation'. To expand 'organised combat activity', cadres should prioritise enlisting 'factory, urban and rurally based' guerrilla units. More conciliatorily, the programme conceded that the party's custodianship of Marxism-Leninism did not give it 'a monopoly of political wisdom or a natural right to exclusive control of the struggle'. Elsewhere ideologues also emphasised that the programme 'clearly implied' that a multi-party system should characterise post-apartheid politics. Among other decisions publicised after the congress was the rehabilitation of four members expelled in the 1930s and the admission that three of them had died in Soviet labour camps.

From this testimony, then, it was possible to learn that the SACP was already expanding its active membership inside South Africa after lengthy abstention from any serious internal recruitment, and that, while it remained committed to armed victory, it foresaw a rather long period of 'national democracy' before the arrival of socialism. Also in conformity with *perestroika*, it was more discriminating about its own history and that of other constituents of the socialist world.

Later revelations about the identities of the party's leadership echelon would also supply indications of the extent of its influence within the exile ANC. Of the 35 members of the ANC's National Executive elected in 1985, 21 belonged to the party. Party members were entrenched in the command of Umkhonto we Sizwe, the ANC's army. As was clear in the developments described in the last chapter, leading communists played a central role in defining the ANC's strategy in the mid-1980s, in particular in determining its military dimensions. We also know that towards the end of the 1980s, the party began to emphasise recruitment of key trade unionists. But there were limits to its influence. The ANC's diplomatic initiatives were led by non-communists or communists such as Thabo Mbeki who were sceptical about the practicality of the insurrectionary course.

The terms of settlement suggested by the ANC's 1988 Constitutional Guidelines, partly drafted by communists, did not suggest the 'fundamental' transformation that might be expected to occur after any 'seizure of power'. Indeed, they fell well short of the kind of changes anticipated in the SACP's understanding of 'national democracy'. Occupying commanding positions within the ANC's exile superstructure was no guarantee that the party could impose its view on the larger organisation, even if it had wanted to. In any case, the party itself was not monolithic in the 1980s and its members sometimes disagreed publicly. Though they appeared united in their antipathy to 'compromises ... which constitute a retreat from the main aims of the national democratic revolution',[6] communists differed over the necessity for negotiations, the choice of guerrilla tactics, and the likelihood of a popular insurrection. And certain communists were even doubtful that any transition would be revolutionary at all and believed 'that a compromise solution would have to be found'.[7]

Taken by surprise by South Africa's sudden democratisation, communists adapted quickly to the political opportunities that followed their legalisation, while they maintained a residual commitment to armed activity. Although Operation Vula was, strictly speaking, an ANC undertaking, under Oliver Tambo's personal supervision, it was communists who made the key contribution, stockpiling the weaponry imported into the country that would arm 'mass combat units' defending local ANC territory against incursions by rival organisations.[8] Vula came to an end with a series of arrests by the police between 12 and 18 July 1990. Mac Maharaj, Pravin Gordhan and several others would be held on terrorism charges before their eventual release a few months later. Disclosures by the police identified five safe houses in Johannesburg and ten in Durban that Vula had rented. In these places they found explosives and arms, including ground-to-air missiles as well as computers and modems used for communication with London and a quantity of print-outs detailing weapon deliveries.[9]

By the end of 1991 the party had experienced a fivefold expansion of its membership to 25,000 since its assembly in Havana. This was modest compared with the ANC's following of 750,000, but the party was not aiming to compete. It needed recruits who would enlist effort into its work, not 'bystanders'.[10] A 22-person Internal Leadership Group, though predominantly constituted by returning exiles, included four very senior COSATU leaders, Chris Dlamini, John Gomomo, Moses Mayekiso and Sydney Mufamadi. Their presence was crucial, for, as Jeremy Cronin recalled, much of the initial organisational work would be undertaken 'through union structures'. Membership assembled in 250 branches distributed fairly evenly across the country's main urban centres.[11] Branches were supposed to have 25 to 50 members and were generally located in residential areas though factory groups also existed 'with special tasks'.[12] Thirty 'factory cores', for example were established during 1990 in Port Elizabeth, the historical centre of the auto industry. Communists were also busy recruiting mine workers – Welkom boasted no less than ten SACP branches, each launched at a different mine shaft.[13] Another source suggests that Welkom at this time had 24 branches based at mine worker hostels. More generally, mining regions in the Transvaal and the Free State became 'a bastion of Communist influence'.[14] In smaller towns in the Border region, where the party had 30 branches by the close of 1991, most of this new following was young, under 30, drawn from the street Jacobins of the 1980s township revolts – the unemployed school-leavers and classroom activists who constituted the rebellion's vanguard. Around Johannesburg and in the Transvaal and the northern Free State mining regions, trade union members constituted the party's most active following.[15] In its Johannesburg headquarters and its five regional offices, the SACP maintained a modest bureaucracy – not more than a dozen paid staff in Johannesburg.

To judge from the tumultuous crowds that assembled at its launching rallies, the party enjoyed rather wider appeal than these details suggest. But its expansion was constrained by shortages. According to an internal document leaked to *The Citizen* on 28 December 1991, in the 16 months since its launch, the party's income totalled just under R2 million, mostly from donations from local benefactors; help from fraternal foreign organisations had dwindled. For a long time after 1990, a major source of party financing would be COSATU's 'political fund'. In 1991, half this income went on salaries and printing. Cash shortages compelled the shelving of plans to print the party's newsletter

Umsebenzi as a monthly tabloid, and regional offices had to do without vehicles and computers. Poor circulation of party publications hampered the training of new members. Through much of the 1990s, the party relied on monthly private donations from Nelson Mandela to balance its books, donations that totalled several million.[16]

The party's strength was not just the sum of its membership, even though this had grown as a consequence of its aiming to constitute, to use Jeremy Cronin's felicitous phrase, a 'fairly mass party',[17] for the SACP remained committed to vanguardist conceptions of its purpose. Party leaders were ready to concede that in the past communists internationally had misinterpreted this function as a presumption to lead 'society at large' and ignored the necessity for 'a renewable mandate'.[18] Historically, the SACP's opposition status and its relationship with the ANC had helped it avoid these pitfalls. Now, its goal should be to win its place at the head of the working class 'by its superior efforts of leadership'. Despite some internal misgivings, SACP leadership generally felt that this superiority could become evident through the role of individual communists within the ANC and, of course, in the trade unions. Consequently, in the early 1990s, its political weight was of a different order from the scale suggested by its disciplined following. In any case, outside the cells and networks that actually constituted the party's organisation, there were other groups, acting independently, who looked to the SACP for inspiration and moral authority and who would claim to act in the party's name.[19]

After the ANC's 1991 conference, 19 communists were elected onto its National Executive, nearly half the elected places, with Chris Hani receiving most votes and Joe Slovo and Ronnie Kasrils in the third and seventh polling rankings respectively. Eleven out of 26 members of the ANC's National Working Committee belonged to the party, though the top senior positions included no active communists. Communists were also conspicuous in the ANC's regional echelons. As might be expected, communists featured heavily in trade union hierarchies, especially around Johannesburg. For instance, when the SACP's Transvaal internal leadership announced its existence, 13 of its 23 members were senior trade union officials.

Ostensibly, the party acknowledged limitations to its influence. As early as 1989, prompted by its alliance with COSATU, it published a workers' charter that insisted that trade unions should be independent and that 'no political party ... [should] directly or indirectly interfere with that independence'.[20] This was a commitment it had initially resisted. Certain unions, notably the National Union of Metalworkers (NUMSA), prohibited the formation of 'party political blocs'. Similarly, ANC leaders felt they 'should not tolerate the formation of factions within the movement'. For both – the unions concerned and the ANC – merely belonging to the SACP did not conflict with this principle as long as communists were not perceived to be functioning as a caucus. Party spokesmen were reassuring on this score. As Joe Slovo observed, 'If you have ever been to an ANC conference, you would have seen how communists argue in completely different directions on ANC policy.'[21]

The party's critics were sceptical about such protestations. A group of communists within the ANC's executive and working committees were alleged to have rearranged portfolios in August 1991 during Nelson Mandela's absence overseas so as to ensure that 'hardliners' shaped negotiations with the government. In March 1991, *The Citizen* published extracts of what it claimed to be minutes of a meeting of SACP representatives from greater Johannesburg. If these are to be believed, discussion centred on 'how could the SACP ... prevent a bourgeois element from taking the upper hand in the liberation movement'. It could be argued that there was nothing reprehensible about party members promoting a common agenda within other organisations so long as they did this openly. And, indeed, the South African communists had no hesitation about defining their own political priorities and pursuing them publicly. Throughout the 1990–4 transition, leading communists were consistent and unabashed advocates of a negotiation strategy in which mass action was 'strategic' and not merely 'tactical', believing that without popular pressure negotiations would extract few gains, and they were often critical of any deviations from such a course by ANC leaders.[22] 'We must avoid the danger of suffocating the mass struggle,' a 'consultative' party meeting agreed.[23] Occasionally during these years mass action was decisive in shaping developments, as in the 1994 Bophuthatswana uprising, which displaced a homeland leader. Here in Mafikeng 400 or so local communists busy in civil service workplace crisis committees helped organise a strike that precipitated a more generalised insurrection.[24]

One key limitation in its ability to influence the outlook of its allies was that as the party expanded and became more intellectually open, it became more internally argumentative. Not all the old guard were pleased with Joe Slovo's efforts to distance the SACP from its Stalinist lineage. In 1990, Slovo published his critique of 'alienation in existing socialism'.[25] Though Slovo's contentions were well within the boundaries of what had become customary in other communist parties, no other South African communist had before produced such an unqualified denunciation of Stalin's 'socialism without democracy'. Slovo's analysis included the admission that 'we kept silent for too long after the 1956 Khrushchev revelations'.[26] Harry Gwala, an austere

Bolshevik from Robben Island, and a pioneer of Natal trade unionism in the 1950s, could not share Slovo's enthusiasm for Gorbachev's prescriptions. Gwala and the party's strong Pietermaritzburg branch, which he led, welcomed the August 1991 coup against Gorbachev. The 'excesses' of Soviet history should be understood in their context and, in any case, 'Who is not wiser after the event?' Gwala asked. Gwala himself remained loyal to older icons, keeping a complete set of Stalin's collected works in a bookshelf above his bed's headboard.[27] But certain new members, especially those the party was gathering at universities, welcomed Slovo's analysis of the roots of 'socialism without democracy'. In Graeme Bloch's view, Lenin's deployment of the slogan 'dictatorship of the proletariat' had been 'the source of a permanent blind spot in Marxist thought'. Slovo's pamphlet in fact argued that Lenin's argument had been abused and that it had an 'intrinsic democratic content'. He did concede, though, that 'the choice of the word dictatorship' to describe a society in which power was exercised in the interests of the majority 'open[ed] 'the way to ambiguities and distortions'. In effect, the party's course to power would be very different from Lenin's; it would happen through 'democratic persuasion and ideological contest'.[28] Even under socialism, competitive multi-party elections would be indispensable, Slovo insisted.

For most communists, these debates were arcane, well removed from the teleological beliefs that still animated most of the party's followers. In 1992, at the SACP's eighth congress, they prevailed with a series of amendments to the draft constitution that were up for adoption. A series of references to 'democratic 'socialism were deleted: as Harry Gwala commented, how could socialism not be democratic? This was a 'firm' rejection, Gwala's protégé Blade Nzimande noted approvingly, though the party would no longer retain Leninist language about a proletarian dictatorship.[29] Delegates also insisted on the reinstatement of 'Marxism-Leninism' in the 'guiding principles' listed in the constitution. In the same spirit, the section on organisational principles was altered. Out went a sentence which read, 'Members who have a minority view shall not be compelled to pronounce support for majority policy.'[30] The party leadership accepted defeat on these issues good-naturedly enough, choosing to interpret the rank-and-file triumph as evidence of the party's abandonment of oligarchy.

As fissures within the party opened up, its relationship with the ANC began shifting. Legalisation had accentuated differences. In 1992, the 'new' ANC with its burgeoning bureaucracy, its R90 million budget and its policy-making departments represented a massive contrast to the small, impoverished party. It was not just the disparity of scale, but it was also a question of relative power. In exile, very selective SACP recruitment was a key stage in individuals' upward mobility within the ANC's hierarchy. But by 1992 it was possible to be openly critical of the SACP without jeopardising one's position in the ANC. Allan Boesak's election to the Western Cape presidency of the ANC was a case in point; it occurred only months after he had urged the ANC to sever its links with the party, arguing that the alliance alienated potential supporters who were Christians. Certainly, from the moment of its re-entry into legal politics, the ANC recognised that creating a distance between itself and its old ally was expedient. The ANC's top office-holders included people who in 1990–1 renounced their party membership. These included Thabo Mbeki, Aziz Pahad and Jacob Zuma. Despite these shifts, the party's leadership took it for granted that they would stay within the organisational configurations of alliance politics; before 1994 communists did not consider seriously any prospect of contesting elections independently of the ANC. As Jeremy Cronin admitted when interviewed, they would be unlikely to obtain as much as five per cent of the vote.[31]

What sort of people were leading the party at the inception of its trajectory into the territory of liberal democratic politics? The eighth congress's Central Committee elections did indicate a renewal of its upper ranks. It still included a few survivors from the cohort that had matured in the 1950s and that had led the party for most of its clandestine existence. Occupying the honorific position of chairperson was one of these remaining stalwarts, Joe Slovo, then the party's dominant thinker. Recently, Slovo had worked hard to foster 'a new perception of social democracy', drawing upon 'the democratic spirit which dominated the re-emerged trade union movement'. Probably the party's most enthusiastic admirer of Gorbachev's *perestroika*, Slovo was by this stage ready to call for a reappraisal of South African communist attitudes to the market – in his view, not 'necessarily a purely capitalist institution'. This was hardly a fresh view: Czech economists had experimented with notions about market socialism in the mid-1960s before the Prague Spring, but this was an innovation in South African Marxism. In his red socks, floral ties and loudly checked jackets, Slovo was a picturesque platform performer and his acclaim extended well beyond his party comrades. In 1991 he obtained the third-highest number of votes in the poll for the ANC's National Executive. Between 1992 and 1994 he assumed a decisive role in negotiations, championing the necessity to offer and accept a transitional regime through 'sunset clauses' in the constitution, which would enable the ANC's adversaries to retain a share of executive authority, and using his very considerable moral authority to build consensus within the ANC on such concessions.[32] On market socialism, however, even among his comrades there seem to have been few takers for Slovo's call for a reappraisal: as Jeremy Cronin conceded ten years later, the party in the early 1990s was 'not so well positioned, theoretically, in terms of policy formation', for communists simply hadn't 'profoundly' thought about 'the socio-economic terrain'.[33] As one usually sympathetic critic of the party wrote at the time, intellectually it was locked in a state of 'theoretical immobility'.[34]

Replacing Slovo as general secretary was Chris Hani, though his term would end tragically with his assassination in the driveway of his home by a Polish immigrant, Janusz Waluś, one year later, in 1993. Chris Hani lived with his family unguarded in the modest, mainly Afrikaans-speaking suburb of Dawn Park in Boksburg.[35] In contrast to Slovo, Hani was not a theoretician. His intellectual enthusiasms were for the Roman and Greek classics he first encountered at Fort Hare, rather than doctrinal dissection of Lenin or Gramsci.[36] To judge from his laconic forays into the trickier conceptual issues in the Marxist catechism, theoretical questions bored him. His courage and his charm were two ingredients in his personality that made him hugely popular within the ANC. Hani had joined the party in 1961. He was one of a cluster of talented men whom the SACP recruited at the University of Fort Hare. He was the most conspicuous survivor of the ANC's first guerrilla campaign in Rhodesia in 1967–8. Hani's decision to accept the SACP's highest executive office ostensibly put him out of the running for the ANC's presidential succession stakes, in which he was widely considered to be an effective rival to Thabo Mbeki. He explained this choice as springing from his emotional empathy with the poor, a feeling derived from his own harsh childhood. His view of the party's destiny was that in future it would serve as a tribune for the poor – 'the poorest people in our country need the Communist Party' – and function as the ANC's 'conscience' on 'radical ideas on socio-economic issues'.

The remainder of the Central Committee could be categorised into four groups, each characterised by different types of experience. The older age set, including Joe Slovo, Govan Mbeki, Billy Nair, Stephen Dlamini, Brian Bunting and John Nkadimeng, formed the last of the group who presided over the party's clandestine reconstruction in the 1950s and the cementing of its alliance with the ANC. Then there was the group which received most of its political schooling in the liberation diaspora, such as Hani, who were recruited on university campuses at the beginning of the 1960s and who acquired senior status in the ANC's bureaucracy in the 1970s, especially in Umkhonto. Their number included Ronnie Kasrils, one of the managers of the ANC's 'people's war' strategy. An experienced guerrilla, with strong reservations about the merits of a negotiated settlement, Kasrils's uncompromising romanticism was evident in his heroic poetry published under his pen name, ANC Khumalo.

As might be expected, COSATU trade unionists constituted the third category of leadership, being usually younger men and women than those in the first two groups. Both the 'populist' and 'workerist' strains of the labour movement were represented, a significant inclusiveness, because in the 1980s these factions had been adversaries over whether they should defer to the ANC's (and the SACP's) leadership. Finally, there were the 1980s internal political activists, in some cases, for instance Jeremy Cronin (another poet) and Raymond Suttner, strongly associated with the 'above-ground' United Democratic Front (UDF) leadership, and in the case of others, such as Jenny Schreiner and Tony Yengeni, men and women who worked in subterranean ANC formations inside South Africa. Blade Nzimande, general secretary of the party today, also belonged to this category. Mentored by Harry Gwala before becoming active in the UDF and the trade unions, Nzimande worked as a lecturer at the University of Zululand, where he joined the clandestine party in 1988. In all, by 1991, a rather impressive group was at the party's helm, combining a range of skills. It was fairly youthful, and, though predominantly working class in origin, it included a number of university graduates.

IF WE CONSIDER THE backgrounds of the party's office-holders elected most recently in 2017 at its fourteenth congress the most obvious contrast with the 1992 group is how much younger they are. The oldest member of the Central Committee was born in 1947, and most are much younger, joining the party after initial political engagements during the 1980s. At least one, Joyce Moloi (national treasurer), is young enough to attribute her politicisation to post-apartheid 1990s campus activism. More are women, 13 out of 40 Central Committee members. Four are white: SACP leadership is today overwhelmingly African. Fourteen have held senior positions in trade unions, especially in the National Union of Mineworkers (NUM). A significant number, five, were imprisoned for activity in Umkhonto. For others, their 'struggle' credentials were obtained through leading township-based civic organisations. The group most under-represented compared with the earlier leadership is that of people whose political formation took place mainly in the exile movement. The two most senior office-holders are Blade Nzimande, general secretary since 1998, who belongs to the party's intelligentsia, and the chairperson, Senzeni Zokwana, ex-president of NUM. Other top officials include Solly Mapaila, dubbed by the press 'Comrade Crackdown' for his role as Nzimande's 'enforcer', an ex-Umkhonto soldier and subsequently a member of the Defence Force; and two ex-teachers, both also trade unionists, Thulas Nxesi and Joyce Moloi. Former teachers, after mine workers, embody the largest occupational grouping within the SACP leadership. Twelve Central Committee members have advanced academic qualifications and most at least have completed high school; this is a strikingly well-educated leadership.

So, the party's leadership has become younger and, if anything, has become more strongly rooted in the trade unions. A share of leaders with higher academic qualifications gained after their entry into government, usually in administrative specialisms. As we will see, key decision-making office-holders are trade unionists, and this is in contrast to the party's pre-1990 history. In exile and before, trade unionists, though conspicuous, were in fact kept in check by party leaders suspicious of trade union 'economism'.

What about the party's following? Membership has expanded, many times over the 1992 level, and in particular, in the last decade, growth has accelerated. Membership totals moved from 50,000 in 2007 to 150,000 in 2012 and to 284,000 in 2017, in effect making the SACP, with respect to membership, South Africa's second-largest political party.[37] The latest figure was a total of 319,108, reported at the special national conference in December 2019.[38] The steepest surge was between 2008 and 2009 when membership doubled. In 2005, the party had deliberately set itself a goal of recruiting one per cent of the national population, 400,000,[39] a target driven by the recognition that 'the SACP's influence within the ANC has diminished over the last fifteen years' and, moreover, that 'between 1996 and 2002 a relatively coordinated offensive' had been launched against the party by key ANC officials seeking to marginalise the left.[40] Under President Mbeki, party leaders believed, the dominant group within the ANC were seeking to promote 'a socio-economic project based around modernising the dominant capitalist accumulation path'.[41] Recruiting a mass membership, then, was primarily a way to expand the left's influence within the ANC or, as one authoritative statement put it, 'to build working class influence … in all key sites of struggle and significant centres of power'.[42]

Whether as a consequence of deliberate effort or more involuntary sources of attraction, the party now has a mass base. Reporting to a Central Committee meeting in 2015, deputy general secretary Solly Mapaila profiled this membership. About half was aged above 40, and ten per cent were over 60. He also mentioned 147,949 students and pensioners. Given the age demographics just cited, this suggests that the larger proportion within this group consists of students – in South African terminology, anyone in full-time education. About 5,000 specifically university students belong to the SACP – too few, Mapaila acknowledged. On campuses, the party struggled to compete with the Economic Freedom Fighters, the ANC break-away group which supplied much of the leadership in protests over fee increases. Up to 2017 Blade Nzimande was Minister of Higher Education (he was reappointed to the post in 2019), an appointment which rather aligned him with university authorities, despite his sometimes abrasive encounters with university vice-chancellors. Roughly as many women as men belonged to the party. Though most members were working class, 'the majority of workers joining the SACP are unemployed'; as Mapaila noted, the party also needed to make an effort 'to increase membership among unionised workers'. Finally, just over a quarter of the membership lived in KwaZulu-Natal, a disproportionate share.[43] The party's following also included the 90,000-strong Young Communist League, revived in 2003, not all of whose adherents were full party members. Organisational reports of the League indicated that the Young Communists had an especial concentration in Limpopo province, in its smaller towns and villages – 16,611 members out of a total national membership of 53,794 in 2010.[44] As an earlier report observed, 'the YCL is mainly based in the countryside, or is weak in the urban areas, and this our membership is mainly impoverished, excluded from socio-economic activities, and mainly unemployed'.[45] From its formation, the YCL was well placed to help swing ANC Youth League branches leftwards and behind Zuma. Under Blade Nzimande's general secretaryship, the SACP and YCL were to undergo a considerable expansion of membership, especially in the KwaZulu-Natal countryside. Rural recruits to the Young Communists may well have reinforced any existing patriarchal dispositions in the party: Stephanie Kemp, provincial gender coordinator in KwaZulu-Natal in 2006, was taken aback when 'one young male comrade', responding to her efforts to persuade women to speak at meetings, protested 'that women are not allowed to speak at izimbizo'.[46]

Clearly, Zuma's accession to the presidency of the ANC in 2007 and the perception that the SACP was a key agency in this encouraged a groundswell of recruitment; the growth in KwaZulu, Zuma's heartland, of the party's membership dates from this time. Kotze has suggested that since 2008 people have been drawn once again to the SACP because 'the party retains a cachet' and enjoys prestige as a 'thought leader' within the Alliance, and because, more fundamentally, after Zuma's accession it was perceived as an 'access point to government'.[47] This explanation makes sense, given the increasing tendency for the party to be especially entrenched among unemployed school-leavers in rural areas; for them, the party may well represent a rare channel for social mobility. This is confirmed by earlier observations by party officials.

Well before Zuma's accession, with the government under an ANC leadership less evidently sympathetic to the SACP, internal reports suggested that 'people join the party branches to gain position on election lists'.[48] After elections as well, there would be a 'periodic influx of those unable to gain position in government'.[49] Gauteng's provincial SACP organiser noted in 1999, 'we need to guard against those who join the Party in order to put forward their own interest, e.g., the Local Government positions'.[50] Such warnings evidently went unheeded. SACP engagement in the rent-seeking factionalism associated with local government office-holding seems widespread. A recent government investigation found Communist Party officials in control of the 'Stalini' faction in Port Elizabeth, which succeeded in siphoning off R300 million from a public transport renewal project to reward its followers.[51]

In 2001, Gauteng officials noted that most members in the province had belonged to the party for less than a year and were, moreover, very young.[52] Significantly, and discouragingly, in South Africa's most industrialised province of Gauteng, the party had failed to build a single 'industrial unit', notwithstanding earlier resolutions to build factory-based branches.[53] Nor, it seems, had party organisers succeeded in extending their support among mine workers from the bases they had constructed in the early 1990s. Changes in the industry supply part of the explanation. As a report in 1998 noted, at Leeudoorn mine on the West Rand, SACP recruitment began but 'retrenchments facing the gold mines' distracted organisers from 'party building activities around Westonaria'. In several instances, branch decline was a consequence of developments similar to those at Leeudoorn. In Mohlakeng, 'the departure of some of the active workers from the area' weakened the branch at the mine, whereas at Kloof 'the active members' were focusing 'their attention on union work and not providing us with alternates'. Meanwhile, in Bekkersdal, 'we have a serious problem of constancy of contacts which affect communication and overall coordination of party work at the mine'. What is clear from these reports from West Rand branches is that most members were non-miners. Mostly, members were living in the main urban centres and were often engaged in municipal politics, in which factionalism could paralyse party functioning.[54] There is another way in which the party's expansion has loosened its relationship with the earlier union base: now with a substantial flow of membership subscriptions, it can afford to become less reliant on COSATU's funds; indeed, regular donations from COSATU ceased in 2010.[55] The relationship with COSATU remains close, with the party occupying a rented office suite in the federation's headquarters in Braamfontein, Johannesburg.

If today the party's following is less industrial, the leadership remains representative of the groups that joined the party just after its unbanning: employed workers especially in the mining industry as well as the soldiers, technocrats and intellectuals who predominated in the liberation movement. Developments preceding the 2012 Marikana massacre highlighted the fissure within the labour movement on the mines, a key SACP constituency, when a break-away union, the Association of Mineworkers and Construction Union (AMCU), enlisted underground workers at the Marikana platinum mine. Over two decades, the communist-led NUM became dominated by surface workers, mostly white-collar workers and local residents, who were separated from the experience of the migrant rock drillers and who became, at Marikana, targets of their anger. Responding to the massacre at Marikana, when on 16 August 2012 police fired into two groups of striking miners, killing 34, SACP leaders were quick to absolve the authorities of any blame. The strikers were manipulated by 'dark forces' who were able to exploit 'backward beliefs and practices amongst sections of the working class'.[56] Certain party members were even readier than Blade Nzimande to exculpate the police. Dominic Tweedie, who at the time worked in COSATU's press section, opined that 'the police used their weapons in exactly the way they were supposed to … The people they shot didn't look like workers to me. We should be happy. The police were admirable.' Not to be outdone, the North West's provincial party took it upon itself to recommend the arrest of AMCU officials.[57] In fact, video film of the shootings showed police firing into a retreating crowd, and later an official inquiry censured police conduct.

In South Africa's first democratic decade, the NUM in particular was widely viewed as a key guarantor that politics would deliver substantive gains for ordinary South Africans. As Michelle Williams notes, the union enjoyed a 'centrality in movement history', and ascent through its echelons has 'served as a pathway into political leadership',[58] as is evident from the succession of top ANC leaders whose initial ascent was made through NUM ranks. Political influence within the ruling party and organisational muscle at the workplace generated impressive benefits for its members: steady wage rises as well as the union's own pension and social security provisions. In the process, however, the gap between the union's leadership echelons and its rank-and-file membership widened as the organisation's administration consolidated itself. In a key study, Raphaël Botiveau's account of bureaucratisation in the union emphasises strategic choices as well as derived ideas.[59] In particular, he identifies the imprint of the Communist Party in the union's oligarchy. His argument begins with the union's formation and its early development. Unlike the unions that evolved in the 1970s, the NUM was constructed very quickly in the mid-1980s from the top down; initially its branch-level structures were weak. It was always a centralised organisation with tenuous downward accountability. Sketchy organisation at the base was compensated for by energetic and assertive headquarters staff as well as full-time paid regional organisers, principally responsible for recruitment. By the late 1980s the NUM was the country's largest union. It exploited 'recent openings in South African labour law' and concentrated initial mobilisation in enterprises in which employers were relatively conciliatory. A 'remarkably legalistic approach' distinguished the NUM's early operations.[60]

The union's local dependence on clerical workers employed in pithead offices helped to consolidate a comparatively sophisticated administrative architecture, staffed often by academically well-qualified cadres. Tough bargaining tactics, wage gains, and willingness to use the strike weapon as well as a combination of emphatic charismatic leadership and principals embodying managerial efficiency helped maintain the union's vitality and its popularity during South Africa's democratic transition. Since then, oligarchical reflexes have hardened and have become institutionalised, and the social distance between leaders and rank-and-file membership has expanded. As bureaucratic kinds of leadership authority have become more pronounced, the union has in the process lost prestige and support among underground workers, including the rock-drill operators who led the strikers at Marikana. Oligarchical leadership is legitimated in the prevalent rhetoric of worker control. In practice, this does not mean rank-and-file control but rather selective recruitment of workers – usually white-collar workers – into full-time official positions. It is strengthened in a leadership selection process which, though formally subject to election, discourages competition and stresses prerequisite skills acquisition. It is consolidated in educational programmes funded by check-off revenues that are selective and confined mainly to secondary-educated workers, still a small minority – in essence, cadre development programmes. It is evident in the use of externally commissioned surveys as a means of assessing rank-and-file morale rather than leaders making themselves accessible and directly accountable. Finally, Botiveau argues, oligarchy was reinforced by political procedures borrowed from the SACP's democratic centralist catechism: three-yearly congresses, discouragement of debate, controlled succession, command-style discipline, and demonisation of critics as enemies, traitors and, as in the case of the

Marikana strikers, 'dark forces'. The NUM is not unique in its experience of these trends. More generally, the social character of organised labour has changed, moving from its older bases in mining and manufacturing, as its main constituents have increasingly become public sector unions and as its leadership has become professionalised and less altruistic.[61] In any case, within industry, new labour practices involving contracting out and casualisation confront trade union organisers, as workers become more vulnerable and harder to reach.

SHIFTS IN THE CHARACTER of the party's social following need to be understood against the background of broader developments in South Africa's political economy. Here, for a few pages, we shall widen the focus from the party to take in broader national developments.

After 1994, ANC governments maintained and expanded the liberal economic policies initiated in the late-apartheid era, despite trade union opposition, especially from COSATU, and despite the presence of communists in all ANC cabinets. Though encouraged by World Bank advisors, the new administration held back from foreign borrowing, instead seeking additional funding by making taxation more efficient and aiming to entice fresh foreign investment. The World Trade Organisation imposed 'developed country' conditions for entry; this required swift tariff reductions, which the government hoped would make local firms more competitive.[62] Between 1993 and 2004 protection rates in manufacturing would drop from 48 per cent to 12.7 per cent.[63] In 1997, industries stopped receiving export incentive subsidies. Clothing and textile factories lost hundreds of thousands of jobs. Especially vulnerable were the light manufacturing enterprises situated on homeland borders, which up to 1994 had been encouraged with tax holidays and other incentives. Few of these would survive the decade.[64] A key dimension of economic liberalisation was privatisation policies. These have had their most profound effect on municipal administration, an area of policy determined by a ministry headed by ex-trade unionist and party member Sydney Mufamadi from 1999 until 2008. Heavily indebted local authorities now contract out basic services, such as water supply and garbage collection, to private companies. To put the railroad network on a commercial footing, many smaller rural stations were closed. Effectively, the state mostly abandoned its former provision of cheap, subsidised public transport. Even so, the transport corporation remains wholly state-owned after successive failures to attract foreign investors and local black empowerment groups. Indeed, since 2004, government has stopped selling public assets partly because of difficulties in finding a buyer for the telephone utility. In that year Telkom's partial sale to a Malaysian consortium made it obvious that black South Africans would not be the main beneficiaries of any further 'core' privatisation. Black businessmen cannot mobilise sufficient capital by themselves to purchase major stakes, and in most of the privatisations up to 2004, they assumed a junior partnership.

Liberalisation brought only modest rewards. The South African economy grew at an average rate of 2.3 per cent through the 1990s. It then quickened, peaking at 5 per cent annually between 2005 and 2008, an upsurge that added two million jobs to the labour market, mainly as a consequence of Chinese trade in mining commodities, and then falling to 2.5 per cent and 3.5 per cent a year until 2016, when contraction reduced the rate to 1 per cent, an effect of drought as well as power shortages (the latter a consequence of two decades of under-investment in power stations). The 2009 global financial crisis reduced demand for mining products and most of the job gains of the preceding decade were lost. Growth was stimulated by rising foreign direct investment after 1994, at an annual average of $1.8 billion up to 2002, but slackened thereafter – these are unimpressive figures compared with many lower-middle-income countries.[65] In 2014, Nigeria received three times as much foreign investment as South Africa – a striking reversal in their comparative economic status.[66]

Since 1994, South African attempts to draw investment towards heavy industry have failed, and meanwhile there has been very little fresh funding for light manufacturing. Efforts to 'reindustrialise' through the provision of publicly funded infrastructure have been one aspect of government policy enthusiastically supported by the party and, indeed, led by the relevant communist ministers. Disappointingly, most foreign investment has been made into previously existing South African-owned firms rather than starting up new branches of production or new enterprises. In addition, official policy has tended to eschew any references to 'labour-intensive' industrialisation, preferring to emphasise the enlargement of a 'high wage, high productivity' workforce – an approach that invites capital-intensive manufacturing investment, though investors have generally held back.[67] This is partly because the government's efforts to promote skills development have been very ineffectual indeed. South African firms have increasingly exported their own investments, chiefly to other African countries and, more recently, to China, facilitated by the relaxation of currency controls, which was intended to promote foreign investment. In general, for investors, manufacturing became less profitable in comparison with services.[68]

At the same time, redistributive policies attempted to expand the social scope of private ownership rather than broaden the public sector. For instance, between 1994 and 2013, the government helped to finance the construction of more than 3.3 million low-cost houses through grants to impoverished families that enable them to buy their own houses, and through negotiating guaranteed mortgages with banks. This vast number of homes was built by private contractors on cheap public land with the state supplying water, sanitation and electrical connections. For many township residents, home ownership was more expensive than rented housing or the payments they had made to 'shacklords' in squatter camps; the housing subsidies usually did not altogether cover construction costs, and poor families who moved into the houses often ended up paying more on mortgage repayments than they had on rents. Moreover, rural–urban migration and demographic pressure combined to increase the figures for the 'housing backlog'; in 2016, at least another 2.2 million houses were needed to meet the needs of shanty dwellers. At the present rate of construction of government-subsidised low-cost houses –140,000 a year – many of the shanty settlements that surround South African cities will remain for at least another decade.[69]

Today the most politically contentious arena for redistributive policies is land reform, briefly the preoccupation of a communist-led ministry during Mandela's government. At present, two-thirds of South African land is owned privately, mainly by corporations or by white farmers. Of the remainder, 15 per cent is under communal tenure, 10 per cent is public, and the remainder is urban land accommodating 60 per cent of the population. Agriculture contributes 2 per cent of GDP and 10 per cent of exports, and employs 5 per cent of the workforce, including 700,000 workers on commercial farms. Since 1994, farmers have evicted a million labour tenants in anticipation of reforms to improve their status. Of around two million African small-scale farmers, only a minority of these derive a full-time income from farming. Under its land restitution programme, the government awarded most of the mainly urban claimants with R40,000 compensation grants. Rural claims were more costly and complex and those that received land were unable to farm their new properties successfully, needing capital and other kinds of support. Between 1994 and 2013 nearly 5,000 farms bought at market prices were transferred to 250,000 aspirant farmers. The Minister of Rural Development and Land Reform suggested that most of these undertakings were failing, though academic researchers disagree.[70] In 2004 communal land rights legislation strengthened the power of traditional leaders, and despite a successful Constitutional Court challenge to the new law, chiefs continue to erode customary access to communal land.[71] In general, then, the record is of fairly desultory progress. Through all the ANC administrations, government budgets for land reform have been modest, roughly equal to expenditure by the Department of Transport, or less than 0.5 per cent of public expenditure. As Communist Party leaders conceded in 2018, 'we have been very weak and confused about our objectives in land reform'.[72] Today the party favours socialised ownership, through cooperatives and the leasing of publicly owned land to individual farmers as well as the expropriation without compensation of absentee landlords – positions that put it well to the left of government policy.[73]

In contrast to land reform, enlarging the share of black ownership in the economy remains a policy priority. A series of laws enacted since 1999 promote black business. For example, the Preferential Procurement Act, which regulates the awarding of government contracts, requires winning companies to allocate shares to 'previously disadvantaged' people. In mining and energy, which are traditionally reliant on public subsidies, the government has extracted corporate commitments to black empowerment, and it has also provided black entrepreneurs about R2 billion a year of start-up capital. On the whole, empowerment has enabled black businessmen to buy into existing sectors rather than set up new concerns; unsurprisingly, therefore, it has tended to reinforce existing paths of 'jobless growth'.[74] Meanwhile, the share of the economy owned by the 'black bourgeoisie' remains quite modest. In 2013, 23 per cent of the shares of the top 100 companies traded on the Johannesburg Stock Exchange were held by black South Africans, mainly through pension funds – roughly the same proportion as that owned by white South Africans (the rest are owned by foreign investors), according to the JSE's own research. Black-controlled companies – that is, companies in which most shares are black-owned and the company is managed mainly by black South Africans – represent a much smaller percentage, around 3 per cent.[75] Even so, now that there has been a rise in the black share of economic ownership, the government certainly has stronger incentives to maintain business-friendly policies. Business has acquired new kinds of political influence and, given the pattern of black entry into its executive echelon, new black capitalists are likely to defend existing kinds of commercial and industrial activity and to resist any effort by the state to reorient them. Many who have benefited most from these measures have been and have remained politically well-connected, especially former activists.[76] Party spokesmen have become increasingly critical of what they call 'parasitic' black businessmen; empowerment policies, they maintain, should be directed at a more 'productive' group.[77] It is also true that political pressure has induced companies to promote black managers, and this has helped fuel the rapid expansion of a black middle class.

Black empowerment by itself has not reduced black poverty; what reduction has occurred has been an effect of extending social welfare. South Africa remains one of the most unequal societies in the world despite efforts to alleviate poverty. Measured by the Gini coefficient statistical measure of income inequality, in which 0 is 'perfectly equal' income and 1 is 'perfectly unequal', South Africa's inequality in 2015 was a disturbingly high 0.63, the highest in the world, only slightly lower than the coefficient of 0.65 recorded in 1993.[78] Since then, real wages of the bottom 10 per cent of earners have fallen.[79] To be sure, large numbers of Africans have been joining the richer population: those in the top fifth of income-earners rose from 400,000 in 1994 to 1.9 million in 2008, although this also means that income inequality among Africans has increased dramatically. Unemployment, chiefly affecting Africans, remains very high; the official figure was at more than 29 per cent in mid-2019, compared with 23.4 per cent in 1996.[80] School-leaver or youth unemployment is much higher, at 54 per cent in 2016. Youth unemployment, at 50 per cent, is the worst in the developing world.[81]

To be sure, after 1994, public policies attempted to equalise entitlements and allocations as well as broaden access to public goods. In its election campaigning the ANC had promised low-cost housing, better health care, extension of pension access (many black South Africans were omitted from the existing system), domestic electrification, jobs through public works, land redistribution, clean water and compulsory education – modest enough pledges from a movement once committed to revolutionary transformation, but in line with the expectations that its own market research had encountered.[82] In power, the ruling party would honour these pledges. The pensions, grants and expanded public services were funded through taxation, in effect an annual redistribution of as much as 10 per cent of GDP.[83] More people than ever receive welfare grants, 16 million today, up from 3 million in 1994. Measures to alleviate poverty include providing running water for about a third of the rural population. In 1999, municipalities began to implement free water and electricity allowances. During the 1990s, the electricity network expanded massively to embrace poorer rural communities. In addition, 1,300 new clinics have supplied free health care to millions of pregnant women and children.[84]

Have these efforts resulted in less poverty? Certainly, since 1994, poor people have benefited from government services and public support. However, their absolute numbers have not been reduced: in 1993 the poverty rate was 56 per cent and it has since then remained at around 54 per cent. The poorest 60 per cent of the earning population receive 10 per cent of total income.[85]

In 1993, a fifth of households were grants beneficiaries and in 2010 a half. Expanding the provision of welfare grants certainly alleviated poverty.[86] But a really dramatic increase in economic growth is needed to reduce poverty significantly. Unemployment prevents poverty reduction on a significant scale. The manufacturing workforce shrank by 400,000 in ten years after 1988, a 25 per cent fall. At the same time 500,000 workers left farms. Public sector employment has shrunk only slightly – a reflection of the leverage exercised by public sector trade unions. By the late 1990s, they were the major players in the still-powerful union movement. Despite unemployment, union membership has expanded. In 2015, overall union membership was 3.7 million. Unemployment is concentrated among school dropouts.

In short, South Africa's democratic transition was accompanied by reintegration into the global trading system and a mild economic revival which quickened in the first decade of the new century. However, the national economy retained its vulnerabilities, being heavily dependent on extractive industries, short of foreign and domestic investment, and with the most growth in service and finance sectors as well as construction – growth that generated few employment gains to compensate for industrial and farming job losses. A sophisticated and powerful financial sector facilitates capital export. On the other hand, vigorous government spending on primary health care, housing, domestic electrification, water provision, and social grants and pensions checked poverty and child mortality. But South Africa remains as socially unequal as it was during apartheid, and unemployment, which was already severe in 1994, has increased.

How much of this record is attributable to the presence of communists in government or the influence of the party over policy? As we have noted, communists have been conspicuous in every administration since the ANC's accession in 1994, holding half a dozen or so cabinet positions as well as taking up regional premierships. Until recently, communists have been well represented on the ANC's electoral lists. But communists were in executive positions and parliament by virtue of their standing within the ANC, and they regularly disavowed any intention to function as a caucus – behaviour which the ANC's own rules prohibit. And by all the available evidence, such disavowals were truthful. Indeed, researchers conducting interviews with ordinary party members during both the Mandela and the Mbeki presidencies encountered 'a groundswell of frustration' at the failure of communists in government 'to display ideological cohesion'[87] and their evident lack of interest in promoting party policies. Several communists were key figures in economic liberalisation – what the party would call the '1996 class project'. Sydney Mufamadi in Local Government and Alec Erwin in Trade and Industry would be cases in point: both in fact ceased to be active in the party after joining government. More generally, communist ministers themselves admit they are not in government 'with a party mandate'.[88] In any case, they continue, their own policy ruled out any possibility of their performing an 'entryist' role.[89] However, they maintain, it was still possible to work in a way that was informed by the party's 'culture' and its 'perspectives', functioning as the ANC's conscience, as it were; indeed, Jeremy Cronin himself habitually borrows Chris Hani's evocative phrase. In 2001 Cronin himself was a member of the parliamentary transport portfolio committee at the time efforts were undertaken to privatise Transnet. As he told Helena Sheehan, it was his 'responsibility as a Communist Party person who is an ANC MP involved with transport, to engage with [the proposal] and not to assume that it will be privatised'. But as he noted, the 'ANC ministers responsible ... happen to be also SACP members' and 'they [were] doing it because they think it is the best thing'. 'There is space for dialogue,' he concluded, and 'they are not by definition the enemy.'[90] In 2007, though, the twelfth congress noted that the party had been too ready to give a 'blank cheque' to comrades in government to pursue policies that conflicted with party aims: 'this must come to an end'.[91]

Given the ANC's own efforts to alleviate poverty through the extension of public goods and services, communist ministers could find a measure of justification for arguing that both the ANC and the party had identical short-term and medium-term goals. Communists often held positions in which it might have been possible to be active agents in addressing basic needs of the poor, as was the case when Mandela assigned the Housing portfolio to Joe Slovo and put Derek Hanekom in charge of land reform. In both cases, as we have just seen, they promoted policies in tune with market principles. For example, Slovo's main efforts after 1994 and until his death from cancer in 1995 were directed at persuading banks to underwrite the construction of low-cost freehold housing in which the state's role would be confined to the provision of subsidies and serviced plots. Certain communist ministers had to implement policies inimical to the party's traditional stance and disliked by the unions, for instance the commodification of service provision in local government. And Mandela was quick to react angrily to any party criticism, calling in personally at the party offices in Johannesburg in June 1996 after the Central Committee had had the temerity to suggest that the government's 1996 Growth, Employment and Redistribution strategy 'had failed to deliver jobs'.[92] It was a reasonable complaint given that one of GEAR's objectives was to encourage private-sector job creation through a mixture of measures intended to promote growth: more rapid tariff reduction, deficit reduction, civil service 'right-sizing', privatisation, and holding wage rises below productivity increases. In 1998, the SACP adopted a restrained repudiation of the GEAR plan: 'it was not the appropriate macro-economic framework for our society ... and this overall thrust must be rejected'.[93] This was a clear shift. When GEAR was first published, as one contributor to the *African Communist* recalled, 'so firm was the ANC's hold over SACP leaders at the time that the SACP issued a disordered media release validating the objectives of the programme'.[94] Indeed, the party's first response to GEAR in 1996 praised its 'consistent endeavour to integrate different elements of policy', suggesting that in particular it provided a 'clear framework within which market policy and internal reserve policy work'.[95]

Rank-and-file displeasure with communist ministerial performance was especially evident during the Mbeki administration; indeed, in 2002 Jeffrey Radebe, then Minister of Public Enterprises, and Essop Pahad, Minister in the Presidency, lost their positions on the party's Central Committee at its eleventh congress. This was an occasion at which Mbeki broke existing fraternal protocol by refusing to attend as the ANC's president, sending in his place Mosiuoa Lekota, who was greeted by delegates singing, '*Makuliwewu Mbeki ahafun sithethatthethane*' (Let us fight because Mbeki does not want to talk). Relations with Thabo Mbeki had worsened after Jeremy Cronin and Blade Nzimande wrote a critique of a key strategy paper drawn up by members of Mbeki's staff. The paper, entitled 'State and Transformation', released at the end of 1996, had made the case for the 'democratic state' establishing 'a dialectical relationship with private capital as a social partner for development and social progress'. 'We need transformation, not a balancing act,' Cronin and Nzimande retorted. 'How does one reconcile the notion of a golden triangle, of both labour and capital standing equally, with the leadership of the working class?' they asked. An ANC-governed state could not and should not be class neutral, they added.[96] The deterioration of relations between the party and Thabo Mbeki's supporters probably reached its nadir in 2001–2. Party support for a COSATU-led strike against privatisation in August 2001 prompted allegations in a draft ANC 'briefing document' about a 'left conspiracy', and even calls from certain ANC National Executive members for expulsions. Another paper, this time signed off by Jabu Moleketi and Josiah Jele, both working in the President's Office, referred to a 'left sectarian faction which has placed itself in the liberation movement', ready to act 'as the decisive army of counter-revolution'.[97]

In 2007, communist support for Jacob Zuma's replacement of Mbeki, though generalised, was not unanimous, and several key communists perceived as Mbeki's allies lost their posts in government and subsequently disengaged with the party. Those so displaced included Essop Pahad and Ronnie Kasrils. A less conspicuous leaver was Stephanie Kemp, then active in the KwaZulu-Natal provincial leadership. She suggests that any 'intelligent voices' who 'dared question the unthinking and dangerous support for Zuma' were hounded out of the party.[98] In particular, the Young Communist League championed Zuma's ascendancy, and its leaders opposed the re-election of five of Zuma's communist critics at the party's congress in 2006.[99] The party's role in mobilising delegates to vote for Zuma in 2007 at the Polokwane conference was amply rewarded after the 2009 elections. Given Zuma's own efforts since 2001 to adopt a friendly stance to the party and his favoured consensual style of cabinet management, in which in practice ministers were to be accorded much more autonomy than under Mbeki, prospects for the party exercising its 'conscience' role seemed brighter with his accession. Blade Nzimande remained committed to continued 'deployment' of communists in the cabinet, resisting trade union pressure to end the practice,[100] and sending Solly Mapaila to tour the provinces before the thirteenth congress, to ensure that supporters of the Nzimande line were elected to key positions.[101] After all, as a Central Committee report noted, the outcome of the ANC's conference had 'created space for a reconfigured alliance', for with Zuma's victory the neo-liberal '1996 class project' had been 'somewhat defeated'.[102] And one year later, with the publication of the government's National Development Plan (NDP), the parameters of that space were defined. As a 'discussion document' at the time noted, the plan, despite its shortcomings, did 'mark a key shift away from the 1996 neo-liberal package' and, while the party should make the 'necessary criticisms', it should also engage with the plan, not totally reject it.[103]

Communist presence in government remained at roughly the same level as earlier, but under Zuma committed SACP members were ostensibly in a stronger position to determine economic policy. Jeff Radebe as Minister in the Presidency, together with his party comrade Buti Manamela as his deputy, coordinated the implementation of the 'generally reasonable' NDP and also headed up the cabinet's economic 'cluster'. In fact, Radebe was not one of the party's left-wingers, and hitherto had demonstrated no explicit interest in macroeconomic concerns, despite his wealthy family connections. In his earlier incarnation as the Minister of Justice, he had loyally tried to limit any official investigations of various scandals implicating Jacob Zuma. Probably more significant in respect of policy direction was the appointment of ex-trade unionist Ebrahim Patel in Economic Development and the retention of Rob Davies, Erwin's successor at the Department of Trade and Industry, both keen advocates of more regulation of mining and local 'beneficiation'. Initially Zuma's government provided openings for policies that party principals helped to shape, especially with respect to trade and industry and state-led infrastructural investment.[104] As regards foreign trade, one of Davies's preoccupations, South Africa did benefit from belonging to the BRICS group. BRICS stands for Brazil, Russia, India, China and South Africa, an alliance of the world's largest developing economies, which South Africa joined in 2010. In 2018 South African trade with the BRICS group was five times larger since 2005, and China had become the biggest export market for South Africa and its fastest-growing investor, especially in banking and mining as well as manufacturing – the Chinese established a $750 million automobile plant in 2017. Earnings from Chinese exports were crucial in helping South Africa weather the 2008–9 global recession.

A final area of policy which the party helped influence was the new land reform legislation giving the government more powers of expropriation, passed in 2014. Here the driving personality was a non-communist minister, ex-UDF leader Gugile Nkwinti, but communist MPs played an important role in defending the bill at the portfolio committee stage, which was chaired by a party member. However, fiscal and Treasury policy remained a domain from which assertive communists continued to be excluded, and budgetary restraint continued to ensure that a 'pragmatic' vein predominated in NDP implementation. Even so, party strategists in 2014 could still believe that 'policy fundamentals for [the] programmatic priorities to place our society on a new growth and development path are already basically in place'.[105]

Despite this conviction, and in contrast to their caution during the Mbeki administration, communists in Jacob Zuma's government were much readier to criticise. As Nzimande pointed out in announcing the SACP's 'Red October' campaign in 2009, 'being [in] a multiclass movement is not the same thing as being class neutral'. In the campaign, communists were called upon to demonstrate their support for a National Health Insurance scheme, something that the ANC had already committed itself to establishing in its manifesto and so a safe area for the party to engage in militant-appearing street activity. This conformed to earlier politically uncontentious emphases in party campaigning, such as sponsoring producer cooperatives, [106] or organising demonstrations in support of 'people's demands' with respect to banks.[107] A rather more risky venture was launched in 'Red October' in

2009. Here the party's annual activist initiative would seek to 'disrupt the intersection between business and public service interests',[108] and, more generally, to protest against corruption. Nzimande himself claims to have invented the term 'tenderpreneur'; certainly he popularised its usage in South African political life.[109] In 2010, a communist Central Committee member and the Sports Minister in the North West administration, Grace Bothman, lost her job after calling for the resignation of the provincial premier, who, she said, was protecting a venal official. In parliament, communist portfolio committee chairpersons became much more willing to confront senior ANC ministers.

From 2015 party propaganda became sharply critical of 'state capture' by President Zuma's businessmen cronies. A party 'discussion document' also suggested that the struggle against the '1966 class project' had become 'overly personalised', and the communists and trade unionists had invested 'undue expectations' in Zuma's ascendancy.[110] This represented a quite sudden change of course. In 2012, Jeremy Cronin criticised 'left-leaning NGOs and social movements' opposing proposed secrecy legislation that in effect would have protected venal officials from press investigation. In joining forces on this issue with the Democratic Alliance, he argued, they had allowed themselves to become 'swept up into what is, fundamentally, a conservative anti-majoritarian agenda'.[111] Earlier, in 2010 the Western Cape's provincial Communist Party explicitly supported the legislation and characterised its critics as 'foreign-sponsored NGOs'. As late as 2014, Blade Nzimande criticised an investigation by the Public Protector into the misuse of public funds expended on Zuma's rural estate, Nkandla, suggesting that the Protector was 'wittingly or unwittingly' helping to promote 'an anti-democratic regime change agenda'.[112] In 2017, though, Zuma was not invited to the fourteenth congress, an unprecedented snub to an ANC president. And, as we have seen, Nzimande lost his cabinet post shortly afterwards. However, other communist ministers remained in cabinet despite earlier intimations from party spokesmen that they would resign if Zuma dismissed his Finance Minister, former party member Pravin Gordhan, who was a key figure in attempting to limit the venality around the presidency. Estimates of the cost of public corruption during Jacob Zuma's presidency suggest a total of R500 billion, or around R60 billion a year, much of it through procurements in which politically well-connected suppliers cooperated with officials in charging inflated prices; this severely weakened the impact of investment in infrastructure that communist ministers had promoted.[113] For example, a R27 billion invoice was presented for work on two new power stations, but was reduced after investigation to

R2 billion.[114] The estimate for the costs of rent-seeking during the Zuma presidency would represent a sharp increase: in the first ten years of ANC government, the cost of corruption amounted to about R1 billion a year.[115] The party's turnaround on the issue was quite late in the day.

In the succession contest at the ANC's elective conference outside Johannesburg in December 2017, the party's leadership supported Cyril Ramaphosa. In doing, communist or even trade union support was not a decisive factor in Ramaphosa's quite narrow victory, in contrast to Zuma's ascendancy ten years earlier. The conference was disheartening for another reason: not a single one of the party's own senior officials obtained a seat on the ANC's National Executive. Communists would fare badly as well in the procedures that generated the parliamentary electoral lists.[116] Given the party's claimed membership of around 300,000, this might seem surprising: nominally at least, communists constituted a sizeable proportion of the ANC's claimed million-strong organised following at the time of the conference. But the party's mass membership is likely to be as factionalised as the ANC's, and is hardly susceptible to directed bloc voting. Indeed, party officials themselves distinguish between mass members and a 'much narrower' group of disciplined 'leading cadres'. In fact, at the 2017 conference the king-makers were the Mpumalanga delegates loyal to provincial premier David Mabuza – and very much at odds with provincial Communist Party leaders who had repeatedly called for his dismissal because of corruption allegations.[117] In selecting his cabinets, both in the interim period between Zuma's removal from the state presidency in February 2018 and after the 2019 election, Ramaphosa was compelled to maintain the factional alliances that had secured his accession. The communists' presence in today's administration is similar to their role in that of his predecessors. Four leading party members hold ministerial portfolios: Blade Nzimande (Higher Education), Ebrahim Patel (Trade and Industry), Thulas Nxesi (Employment and Labour) and Gwede Mantashe (Minerals and Energy). David Masondo, a former Young Communist president (and a holder of a New York PhD after writing a dissertation about the car industry), became deputy Finance Minister. A prominent critic of venal officials during the Zuma era, Masondo himself faced, and survived, calls to step down in 2020 after reports that he had arranged for the police anti-corruption agency to arrest a former mistress. Despite Masondo's presence at the ministry, the party would be heavily critical of Treasury policy: a strategy paper released in September 2019 was, it said, 'embedded in the private sector' with its 'offensive on wages'.[118]

Communists, then, continue to have a presence in government, in some cases holding key posts that might in future influence the definition of macroeconomic policy. For nearly a decade now, at least within the party, there has been the expectation that its leaders' participation in government should bring progress towards 'national democracy'. For at its twelfth congress in July 2007 the party adopted a fresh political programme. This new *South African Road to Socialism* contained both continuities and breaks with the party's earlier strategic trajectories. Absent is any prospect of an insurrectionary seizure of power. However, this document maintains the party's commitment to the analysis of South Africa's political economy as embodying a 'colonialism of a special type' (CST) and the continuing relevance of a struggle to achieve 'national democracy' – the kernel concepts of its 1962 formulation.[119]

The most recent version of the programme was adopted in 2012, at the fourteenth congress, substantially the same text as in 2007. Two decades after apartheid, South Africa's political economy remains shaped by colonial features of its past. But the notion of 'colonialism of a special type' has been updated and reinterpreted and, interestingly, substantially deracialised. Modern global capitalism, the *Road*'s authors suggest, was 'beginning to approach absolute limits' and, in its efforts to survive, a 'restructuring of the working class [was] leaving billions more unemployed'. Despite what communists call 1994's 'democratic breakthrough', South Africa was still a colonial society because of its situation within the international capitalist economy, in which 'the dependent-development path of our society and the reproduction of underdevelopment persist'. The economy remained export-oriented and reliant still on imports for capital goods; and within the workplace workers were losing rights and security through 'casualisation'. Neither in 1994 nor today had South Africa achieved a national democratic revolution, nor should national democracy be perceived as a 'stage' in which communists should await the advent of mature capitalism before beginning the struggle for socialism. Indeed, achieving national democracy will 'require an increasingly decisive advance towards socialism'.

References to 'colonialism of a special type' had continued to be a staple of party programmes, but here the effort to redefine the concept was significant, signalling a distinct shift to the left. This shift has been observable in the party's adoption of more radical policies, for example, with respect to land reform. More broadly, party strategists believe that communists should push for 'the decommodification of basic needs' (health and housing) as immediate imperatives, not long-term aims, as well as 'rolling back' the market in other ways.[120] They should also work to build 'working class hegemony in key sites of power', a phrase used in its 2007 programme.[121] But the party's historical relationship with its allies, especially with the ANC, could no longer be seen as an unproblematic fusion of short-term and medium-term interests, as earlier observations by party personalities had suggested. For in building working-class power, the party would be challenging what its leaders saw as a 'strategic alliance between monopoly capital and an emergent fraction of capital linked closely to elements in the ANC/state leadership'.[122] Yes, the alliance with the ANC was still relevant and the SACP could not afford its rupture, for it still represented the best 'way of maximising the size and coherence of a popular camp', but keeping that camp popularly oriented was becoming more difficult. To be sure, individual SACP members' participation in the ANC's and the government's leadership positions still allowed the party to shape important areas of public policy. This was the case especially with respect to state support for local industrialisation and through licensing and other kinds of regulation to 'roll back' the influence of the dominant 'mineral-energy-finance' complex. More than ever, though, the ANC was 'contested space', a phrase used by Jeremy Cronin in 2004.[123] For within the ANC, the SACP had to confront a 'technocratic class project' being undertaken by representatives of an emerging black bourgeoisie, who were only supposedly 'patriotic' but were in fact comprador allies of neo-liberal finance capital. Abandoning the alliance and surrendering its constituents to 'narrow black bourgeoisie tendencies' and 'big man messiah politics' would be irresponsible.

Today, the SACP's commitment to its historical alliance with African nationalism is quite delicately poised, in what it now calls the 'radical, second phase of the national democratic revolution'.[124] In this phase the party aims to 're-surface more clearly the imperialist dimension of our persisting structural problems', through 'de-linking from the imperialist north'.[125] Other kinds of uncoupling are also under consideration in certain quarters. Since at least 2004, there has been an assertive minority proposing that the party should contest elections separately. The first public suggestion from within the party of such a course of action came from Anthony Holiday, a lecturer at the University of the Western Cape, in 1996.[126] Those in favour of such a course were particularly vocal in the Johannesburg Central branch, though newspaper reports suggested that strong sentiment favouring such a move was expressed at six of the party's provincial conferences in 2004, especially from Young Communist League members.[127] The Johannesburg branch submitted resolutions to the provincial congress calling for separately elected communists, who would then 'entrench revolutionary parliamentarianism'.[128] The resolutions failed to garner support, though research conducted at the time indicated that party leaders were not fiercely opposed to such a prospect.

Blade Nzimande, for example, told David Thomas that 'maybe we [should] be looking at a coalition',[129] in which the party could extract concessions for its support in government. But most of Thomas's interviewees were doubtful that the party would win much support as an independent electoral competitor nor were they inclined to take the risk that such a move would certainly entail, that is, allowing the ANC to become more susceptible to right-wing influences. In any case, the SACP had no money to fight elections, and even some kind of compromise position, such as a pre-agreed pact or coalition, might be difficult after fighting the same turf in a contest 'in which victory means a paid position', the Central Committee explained.[130]

Such arguments prevailed up to 2017. In 2012 COSATU surveyed its membership to assess the extent of support for independent SACP electioneering and discovered only six per cent favouring such an option.[131] On the other hand, the Young Communist League favoured separate electioneering – possibly a reflection of the lethal rivalry that can exist at branch level between the Young Communists and ANC Youth Leaguers. In 2016, in Mpumalanga, a provincial resolution calling for the SACP to field its own electoral candidates followed a succession of murderous attacks directed against Young Communists during contested nominations for the 2014 local government poll.[132] At the fourteenth congress in July 2017, in response to membership pressure, the party did resolve that, in future, it would 'certainly contest elections', though the 'exact modality' of how it would do this would 'need to be determined'. It might, for example, be through a 'reconfigured alliance' or through an agreement about 'post-electoral' coalitions with the ANC.[133] The party's leadership appeared still to be hedging their bets, but in November 2017 they allowed local branches to contest a municipal by-election in Metsimaholo (Sasolburg) in the Free State. The decision was opposed by COSATU, and so party campaigners had to do without trade union support. They contested all 21 wards, winning none but securing about eight per cent of the vote, sufficient to be allocated three of the proportional representation council seats. They took their votes from the ANC, eroding its support especially among young voters. The experience seems to have had chastening effects. Present policy is that the party should continue to abstain from independent electioneering, but the ANC in constituting its candidate lists should 'reflect the composition of the alliance'; in other words, the party and COSATU should have a say.[134]

Counterbalancing any pressure from younger communists to oppose the ANC in elections, at least since 2009, was the continuing appointment of communists to ministries and to other important positions, including that of former NUM leader and party chairperson, Gwede Mantashe, to the ANC secretary-generalship. Mantashe was elected alongside Jacob Zuma as one of his principal allies at the ANC's Polokwane conference in 2007 and he continued to defend Zuma's presidency against party critics until his removal in 2018.[135] Mantashe opposed the party's decision to contest the Metsimaholo by-election; and party thinkers continued to believe that their comrades 'deployed' into influential positions since Zuma's ascent could 'drive important advances in the key economic-infrastructure and related sectors'.[136] In 2017, Zuma removed Blade Nzimande from his cabinet in a reshuffle in October, an action that Solly Mapaila interpreted as an 'act of war', though he also conceded that the five other party members holding cabinet positions would remain 'to serve the interests of society'.[137] Disagreements about the issue are likely to continue. Provincial party leaders in Natal regard proponents of the argument that communists should stand against the ANC in elections as 'the biggest threat to the Party'. In particular, they are critical of Young Communists, opaquely attributing their 'stand-alone regime change predisposition' to a 'petty bourgeois mode of thinking'.[138]

Is the party's debate about electoral participation an indication of the vigour of its internal democracy? Party officials are ready to speak about the issue in public; indeed, it is the main inner disagreement that surfaces in the party's public reports. The issue has been on the agenda of the last four party conferences and has been resolved in a similar fashion every time. The Johannesburg Central branch, which played a key role in incubating the debate, was at odds with national leadership from the late 1990s onwards. Its officials complained in 2001 that 'de-Stalinization of the SACP has only begun in theory and has not taken root in practice'.[139] The branch was excluded from the party's provincial council held on 6 February 2000 after being accused of maintaining 'a secret agenda' to undermine the provincial party leadership.[140] Disaffection in the Johannesburg Central branch has continued to represent a challenge for party leadership, it seems; the branch, the largest in Gauteng, was the target of disapproving commentary in a Central Committee statement in 2014. Certainly, the party is less predisposed to publicly discuss any internal differences over doctrinal issues than it was in the early 1990s, and it continues to insist on the disciplinary tenets of democratic centralism, though this emphasis suggests they are often in practice breached by unruly rank-and-file membership.[141] As is evident from the electoral issue, important disagreements can be debated quite openly over major strategic decisions. Since the early 2000s, however, expulsions and suspensions for public criticism of party decisions have become more frequent. In 2006, for example, a former YCL national secretary, Mazibuko Jara, was expelled for questioning the party's support at that time for Jacob Zuma, following Zuma's dismissal from the deputy presidency after his implication in a corruption trial.[142] One-time Gauteng SACP's provincial secretary Vishwas Satgar also had his membership ended in 2009 after questioning the SACP's alignment with Zuma. Seemingly, then, there are key issues over which the party curtails debate and other areas in which dissent is tolerated. Another signal that the party's internal life may be becoming more authoritarian is the way it fills its leadership positions. Internal elections for top office-holders, not contested in 1995, had become vigorously competitive by 2002. Most recently, as at the 2017 fourteenth congress, the party made a virtue of filling its top offices without contested elections, and, indeed, it re-elected virtually all serving Central Committee members.

THIS YEAR, 2021, THE PARTY commemorates its hundredth anniversary. Far from becoming a post-communist formation, it remains very much a product of its long history, continuing to be invigorated and animated by its organisational memory. The party still views itself as guided by Leninist organisational and programmatic principles, possibly rather more so recently. At its special conference in 2015, it adopted a statement, 'Towards an Organisational Renewal', which emphasised the need 'to strike a balance between ensuring an unstifled democratic process without undermining democratic centralism', and it was quite clear that, at least in its formalised procedures, 'centralism' remains dominant.[143] In its view, the world's existing communist parties fell into two groups: 'adherents of the democratic centralism system' and followers of 'the notion of the party mass line'.[144] The SACP views itself as belonging to the first camp, in which it includes the Czech, Cuban, North Korean and Chinese parties, each of which routinely sends greetings or even representatives to party conferences. Indeed, the party would like to become more 'vanguardist'. In practice, however, in a setting in which the party itself has become large and in which it is seeking to assume a much more critical 'conscience' role in its alliance with the ANC, maintaining discipline is considerably more difficult than in the era when the ANC's leadership status was unquestioned and unproblematic. Ironically, the party's newest recruits seem to have a keener appetite for conceptual phraseology of the Marxist canon than was the case in 1990 with the veteran architects of the party's alliance with the ANC. When the Young Communist League was re-established in 2003, delegates attending its national consultative conference insisted that it should resurrect the aim of seeking to establish a dictatorship of the proletariat, a goal dropped from the parent organisation's agenda in 1992.[145] Today, as in the early 1990s, Leninist 'orthodoxy' within the party's rank and file can be an expression of rebellion against leaders too eager to conciliate non-communist allies.

For, generally speaking, despite the party's revisions of its analysis of colonialism of a special type, its strategic approach remains rooted in the concept of national democracy, the concept developed by party theorists in the 1950s from then-existing models supplied by post-war people's democracies to justify its alliance with African nationalism. Even so, the party has moved a long distance from the elitist character it maintained up to 1990. Its organisation is now based largely on the support of unemployed school-leavers whose major preoccupations are to do with the day-to-day insecurities that resemble rather closely ordinary life in post-communist settings in other parts of the world.[146] In the meantime, the labour movement, which used to supply its main source of leverage for political influence, has become increasingly factionalised and oligarchical. Among rank-and-file trade unionists, though class solidarities may persist, as internal party commentaries suggest, many of the party's new members may be primarily motivated by hopes of individual fulfilment rather than egalitarian camaraderie.

This is where we will leave the modern party, struggling to reassert an independant identity that can set it apart from the wider nationalist movement it joined more than seven decades ago. It seeks to do this without disengaging from its alliance and from what it continues to perceive as the main sites of struggle and the chief centres of power, remaining within the wider movement it joined in the 1950s, not outside it. South African communists' reluctance to abandon their alliance is not just strategic. It is influenced by a history in which communists have played such a central role in the evolution of organised political activities that have sought to engage all South Africans as citizens. It is not a history they can forsake easily, for it includes significant achievements, developments and moments when communists shaped the wider political area decisively and helped initiate and consolidate important social changes.

Even in the first stages of their protracted journey to public office and political power, in the early decades of the last century, communists helped introduce and foster new kinds of solidarity and fresh ways of understanding the world – innovations that had enduring effects. Even before the party's formation in 1921, the men and women who would be its founders, through their engagement with syndicalism, introduced a vision of a socialist commonwealth brought about through industrial action. A legacy of this vision was a strategic imprint that would shape South African politics for decades, long after the specific injunctions of Daniel De Leon had been forgotten. Moreover, a distinctive characteristic of revolutionary sects that preceded the Communist Party's formation was their fluidity on the issues of race and cross-communal solidarity. In both Johannesburg and Cape Town, De Leonite syndicalism induced socialist organisers to start building wider class-based fraternities and syndicalist groups, enrolling black workers in both cities. Arguably in each case, they helped incubate much larger movements of workers' insurgency among African mine workers in the one city and dock workers in the other.

Jewish Bundist immigrants would also bring a reflexive set of political practices that shaped South Africa's wider oppositional politics profoundly, making a lasting contribution to the evolution of South Africa's revolutionary socialism, while initially reinforcing its predisposition to extend organisation beyond white workers. These people sometimes arrived in South Africa ready to replicate the organisational formations in which they had been engaged in Lithuania, formations in which Bundists had played the pioneering role. Finally, South Africa's embryonic socialism was also shaped by black people. Men like William Thibedi and Hamilton Kraai began adapting and domesticating imported utopian thinking and applying an exotic lexicon to their own everyday needs as well as their more idealistic imaginings and, in doing so, they assertively established their active agency in indigenising a South African socialist lineage. And after the party's formation, black South African communists would help organise the massive following accumulated by Clement Kadalie's ICU and make their first efforts to enrol mass membership in certain African townships, in Bloemfontein, in and around Durban, and in several centres in the Transvaal. Here they would absorb former ICU branches as Kadalie's movement foundered. At the beginning of the 1930s, prompted by Comintern injunctions, party activists tapped into already animated local struggles motivated by particular grievances, most notably with respect to a wave of angry reactions to additional taxes that the government struggled and, in the end, failed to impose on African communities from 1929. These communal insurgencies could provide resonant settings for the party's campaigning, though organisers were unable to convert loose followings into enduring disciplined membership.

To judge from official commentaries at the end of the 1920s, they were for a while more successful in building early industrial unions among African workers. Here, though, Comintern disdain for pragmatic 'economistic' workplace struggles as well as expulsions in 1931 of the party's most experienced trade unionists nearly destroyed this embryonic labour movement. Even so, communist-trained labour organisers such as Gana Makabeni continued to be active. Later in the decade communists would build unions among both coloured and African workers in and around Cape Town with more enduring effect: the successors to the organisations that Ray Alexander helped construct nearly 90 years ago are still active today. That a young immigrant woman from the Russian Pale could assume such a determining role in the party's early history is noteworthy. In the 1930s and later, a significant number of women were conspicuous in the party as effective leaders or energetic community organisers: Rebecca Bunting, Josie Mpama, Molly Wolton and, a little later, Dora Tamana, Pauline Podbrey and Bettie du Toit and, later still, Ruth First are all key personalities in the stories recounted in this book. From the 1930s onwards, the party created more space for women to assume active and assertive roles in its thinking and campaigning than existed in other South African political movements.

It was during the 1940s that the party really began to impress its ideas and methods on wider social movements in a way that was historically decisive. Without its agency, things might have been very different. During the decade the party recruited Africans in campaigns about local issues and through achieving incremental gains and modest victories rather than by mobilising around wider political objectives. It was through 'bread and butter' struggles that activists succeeded in persuading African township residents that the communists were, in Bill Andrews's words, 'their party'. On the ground, this often brought the party closer to the ANC, with local communist leaders such as Johnson Ngwevela or Raymond Mhlaba often doubling up as Congress notables. In several local settings, such as in the East Rand townships, as well as in Langa and Port Elizabeth, the party probably had a larger organised activist following than the ANC. The networks it embodied would often survive intact into the 1950s and even beyond, underpinning the mass campaigning against apartheid. This was the party's most important and durable achievement from this era. Forced to function clandestinely from 1950, the party's African support base remained mobilised in the vicinities in which the ANC would find its strongest and most methodically constituted following.

And, as we have seen, communists continued to provide crucial training and ideological inspiration for fresh generations of Congress leadership. Here, party night schools performed a crucial function, nowhere more so than in Port Elizabeth where Govan Mbeki would invest so much effort in educational programmes to achieve political development. As Elias Motsoaledi, one graduate of Michael Harmel's evening classes for African workers in Johannesburg, recalled after his release from his life sentence imposed at the Rivonia trial: 'The Party taught me the struggle ... To me the ANC did not interpret the aspirations of the masses. But the Party taught me that it was my responsibility to tell the ANC about our aspirations.'[147] There is a wealth of similar testimony about the formative effects of the party night schools: Naboth Mokgatle supplies rich insights into the classes the communists started holding in Pretoria in 1935. For Mokgatle, the climactic moment of his political education was a 30-day course of 'intensive training' held at the Johannesburg Left Club in Commissioner Street in 1943.[148] It is possible that this kind of experience had wider developmental effects than simply fostering effective political leadership at the time. The anthropologist Gill Hart, while undertaking her fieldwork in Ladysmith in 2000, encountered young activists who could 'recall stories told by their elders of regular meetings that came to be known as "Oom Gov's University"'. In her book Hart suggests that the myths and memories about Govan Mbeki's presence in Ladysmith between 1953 and 1955 were one key source of inspiration in the post-apartheid era for officials and leaders in one of KwaZulu-Natal's more effective municipal governments. The forms of resistance he helped to engender 70 years ago are a distinguishing feature for the locality, today still helping to shape a developmental trajectory that made the town very different from its neighbours.[149]

In different black residential neighbourhoods at the beginning of the 1950s, the networks the party had built during the 1940s supported the ANC's transformation into a mass movement: without their presence, the ANC would have been more inchoate and less effective. Meanwhile, during the decade the party's African leadership gained influence within the ANC's top echelon. This was achieved partly through drawing into the party's embrace members of the university-educated African 'intelligentsia'. SACP ideologues succeeded in shaping the ANC's programmatic orientation, especially in the central role they played in projecting their vision of a 'people's democracy' in the Freedom Charter. This programmatic vision helped determine the ANC's key strategic and campaigning decisions. The party added critically useful techniques, resources and skills to the ANC's organisational capacity, including a popular press. It also strengthened the ANC's commitment to a civic pluralist nationalism, though the party's non-racialism was only one factor in this. Here the party was important in the way it conducted its own social life. Raymond Mhlaba's recollections acknowledge the formative impact on his own perceptions of experiencing 'Whites, Coloureds, Indians and Africans sitting together discussing problems'. As we have seen, reaching the point where this could be a routine feature of the party's internal life was a difficult journey, but it was a route the party travelled long before any other South African political organisation. At the end of the 1950s, the communists were influential both in promoting and in enabling the ANC's engagement with armed opposition to apartheid; it may well have happened without their contribution, but it would likely have been less sustained and less coordinated.

In its first phase of exile the party's survival was substantially the effect of its own more or less independent efforts to rebuild a presence in South Africa: this is a rather different view from historical treatments that suggest its growing influence was the effect of a parasitic and surreptitious presence within the ANC. Before the establishment of the Angolan training camps in 1977 allowed the party to recruit systematically within Umkhonto's commissariat, it had already begun to build its own networks inside South Africa, drawing in people who still occupy leadership positions today. Moreover, its thinkers were making key contributions to the ANC's strategic and programmatic thinking. In the final decade of the ANC's war against apartheid, as we argued at the close of the last chapter, the party's presence and its contribution made a difference in at least three ways. Firstly, the party's strategic understandings served as sources of hope and moral certainty, not just for party ideologues but among the ANC's own rank and file, helping to sustain the movement and ensure its survival. Secondly, the party brought with it a range of helpful resources to the larger organisation. The party's membership of an international communist family enabled it to draw upon and enlist sympathisers from European communist traditions, who could bring their own skills, resources and idealism. Thirdly, inside South Africa the party installed its own remarkably resilient networks that helped underpin wider political formations and fostered a consciousness within them of historical succession, an adherence to non-racialism, and a common iconography.

As blueprints, the party's ideas about insurrectionary revolution and post-apartheid national democracy were chiefly important as armed propaganda and articles of faith rather than as effective and fully implemented strategies. Militarily speaking, the armed struggle did not, as we have seen, represent a serious challenge to the South African authorities. But by the 1980s, the party's narratives helped bind together a massive movement inside the country, giving it a sense of purpose and a confidence about its ultimate ascendancy – a morale-building teleology, as it were. And still today, the party's ideas, including its projection of a future national democracy, continue to shape wider South African political life.[150] Even an increasingly non-communist ANC leadership still routinely claims in its programmatic statements to be committed to the goals of a national democratic revolution, even if in everyday policy-making government decisions are shaped by quite different imperatives. That the ANC relies on such a key party doctrine in legitimating its performance among its own active following suggests that communists following their red road still belong to South Africa's political mainstream. Their hundred-year history remains unfinished.

Notes

Preface

1   Tom Lodge, *Black South African Politics since 1945*, Longman, London, 1983.

2   Edward Roux, *Time Longer than Rope*, Victor Gollancz, London, 1948.

3   HJ and RE Simons, *Class and Colour in South Africa, 1850–1950*, Penguin, Harmondsworth, 1969.

4   Bill Freund, 'Labour Studies and Labour History in South Africa: Perspectives from the Apartheid Era and After', *International Review of Social History*, 58, 2013, p. 496.

5   See especially Baruch Hirson, *Yours for the Union: Class and Community Struggles in South Africa*, Zed Press, London, 1989.

6   Sheridan Johns, 'Marxism-Leninism in a Multi-racial Environment: The Origins and Early History of the Communist Party of South Africa, 1914–1932', PhD dissertation, Department of Government, Harvard University, 1965. Its long overdue publication came in 1995 under the title *Raising the Red Flag*, Mayibuye Books, Bellville, 1995.

7   See especially Irina Filatova and Apollon Davidson, *The Hidden Thread: Russia and South Africa in the Soviet Era*, Jonathan Ball, Cape Town, 2013.

8   AB Lerumo, *Fifty Fighting Years: The South African Communist Party, 1921–1971*, 3rd edn, Inkululeko Publications, London, 1987.

9   AB Lerumo, 'A Century of Oppression: Review of Class and Colour in South Africa', *African Communist*, 40, 1970, pp. 82–6.

10 Robert H Davies, *Capital, State and White Labour in South Africa, 1900–1960*, Harvester Press, Brighton, 1979.

11 FA Johnston, 'The IWA on the Rand', in Belinda Bozzoli (ed.), *Labour, Townships and Protest*, Ravan Press, Johannesburg, 1979.

12 FA Johnston, *Class, Race and Gold: A Study of Class Relations and Racial Discrimination in South Africa*, Routledge and Kegan Paul, London, 1976.

13 Jonathan Hyslop, *The Notorious Syndicalist: JT Bain – A Scottish Rebel in Colonial South Africa*, Jacana Media, Johannesburg, 2004; Lucien van der Walt, 'Anarchism and Syndicalism in South Africa, 1904–1921: Rethinking the History of Labour and the Left', PhD dissertation, Department of Sociology, University of the

Witwatersrand, 2007.

14 Allison Drew, *Between Empire and Revolution: A Life of Sidney Bunting, 1873–1936*, Pickering and Chatto, London, 2007.

15 David Everatt, *The Roots of Non-Racialism: White Opposition to Apartheid in the 1950s*, Wits University Press, Johannesburg, 2009.

16 Mia Roth, *The Communist Party in South Africa, Racism, Eurocentrism and Moscow, 1921–1950*, Partridge, Johannesburg, 2016.

17 Stephen Ellis, *External Mission: The ANC in Exile, 1960–1990*, Hurst and Company, London, 2012.

18 Eddy Maloka, *The South African Communist Party: Exile and after Apartheid*, Jacana Media, Johannesburg, 2014.

Chapter 1

1 'Proletarian Dictatorship', *The International*, 7 February 1921.

2 Apollon Davidson, Irina Filatova, Valentin Gorodnov and Sheridan Johns (eds), *South Africa and the Communist International*, volume 1: *Socialist Pilgrims to Bolshevik Footsoldiers, 1919–1930*, Frank Cass, London, 2003, p. 60.

3 'The ISL Phoenix', *The International*, 2 November 1917, p. 1

4 'Johannesburg White Guards Organising', *The International*, 4 June 1920.

5 James Gibson, 'The Russian Revolution', *The International*, 23 March 1917, p. 1

6 'Our Motley Proletariat', *The International*, 15 November 1918, p. 1.

7 Lucien van der Walt, 'Anarchism and Syndicalism in South Africa, 1904–1921: Rethinking the History of Labour and the Left', PhD dissertation, Department of Sociology, University of the Witwatersrand, 2007, p. 181.

8 Irina Filatova and Apollon Davidson, *The Hidden Thread: Russia and South Africa in the Soviet Era*, Jonathan Ball, Johannesburg and Cape Town, 2013, p. 17.

9 Allison Drew, *Between Empire and Revolution: A Life of Sidney Bunting*, Pickering and Chatto, London, 2007, pp. 48–9.

10 Filatova and Davidson, *The Hidden Thread*, p. 64.

11 WH Andrews, 'A Glimpse of Southern Russia', *The International*, 14 Dec 1923.

12 Basil Davidson, *Report on South Africa*, Jonathan Cape, London, 1952, pp. 102 and 92.

13 Tom Mann, *Tom Mann's Memoirs*, Spokesman, Nottingham, 2008, pp. 198–9.

14 Mann, *Tom Mann's Memoirs*, p. 199.

15 Norman Herd, *1922: The Revolt on the Rand*, Blue Crane Books, Johannesburg, 1966, p. 11.

16 Van der Walt, 'Anarchism and Syndicalism', 181.

17 Van der Walt, 'Anarchism and Syndicalism', 182.

18 Van der Walt, 'Anarchism and Syndicalism', 182.

19 A Henry Glass appears in the left-wing newspaper *The International* in 1916, writing on behalf of the then defunct Germiston Socialist Society, proposing the donation of its bank balance to the recently formed International Socialist League. Might this have been the same person as the Henry Glasse living in Port Elizabeth three decades earlier? A letter from a Henry Glass survives in the papers of Bill Andrews, an important leader of the Communist Party; the letter was written in 1949, with birthday greetings for Andrews, signed 'yours fraternally'. The note paper is printed with the address of H Glass, General Merchant, Port Karee, Orange Free State; if this was the same person as Henry Glasse, he would have been aged about 90 (Henry Glass to WH Andrews, 16 April 1949, WH Andrews Papers, Mayibuye Archives, University of the Western Cape, MCH06 2-6-209).

20 Mark Israel and Simon Adams, '"That Spells Trouble": Jews and the Communist Party of South Africa', *Journal of Southern African Studies*, 26, 1, 2000, p. 148.

21 Jonathan Hyslop, *The Notorious Syndicalist: JT Bain – A Scottish Rebel in Colonial*

South Africa, Jacana Media, Johannesburg, 2004, p. 82.

22   Sheridan Johns, 'Marxism-Leninism in a Multi-racial Environment: The Origins and Early History of the Communist Party of South Africa, 1914–1932', PhD dissertation, Department of Government, Harvard University, 1965, p. 22.

23   Hyslop, *The Notorious Syndicalist*, p. 132.

24   Hyslop, *The Notorious Syndicalist*, pp. 96–102.

25   HJ Simons and RE Simons, *Class and Colour in South Africa, 1850–1950*, Penguin, Harmondsworth, 1969, p. 45.

26   Van der Walt, 'Anarchism and Syndicalism', p. 184.

27   Rob Davies, *Capital, State and White Labour in South Africa*, Harvester Press, Brighton, 1979, p. 53.

28   Philip Bonner, 'South African Society and Culture, 1910–1948', in Robert Ross, Anne Kelk Mager and Bill Nasson (eds), *The Cambridge History of South Africa*, volume 2: *1885–1994*, Cambridge University Press, New York, 2011, p. 263.

29   Shula Marks, 'War and Union, 1899–1910', in Robert Ross, Anne Kelk Mager and Bill Nasson (eds), *The Cambridge History of South Africa*, volume 2: *1885–1994*, Cambridge University Press, New York, 2011, pp. 163–9.

30   Van der Walt, 'Anarchism and Syndicalism', p. 204.

31   Davies, *Capital, State and White Labour*, p. 59.

32   Baruch Hirson and Gwyn A Williams, *The Delegate for Africa: David Ivon Jones, 1883–1924*, Core Publications, London, 1995, p. 106.

33   Gavin Lewis, *Between the Wire and the Wall: A History of South African 'Coloured' Politics*, St. Martin's Press, New York, 1987, p. 16; Van der Walt, 'Anarchism and Syndicalism', p. 194.

34   Johns, 'Marxism-Leninism', p. 38.

35   Bill Freund, *Insiders and Outsiders: The Indian Working Class of Durban, 1910–1990*, James Currey, Oxford, 1995, pp. 46–7.

36   Johns, 'Marxism-Leninism', p. 32.

37   RK Cope, *Comrade Bill: The Life and Times of WH Andrews*, Workers' Leader, Stewart Printing Company, Cape Town, 1944, p. 193. Even so, Matthews told a subsequent official investigation into poverty that though he believed in treating Africans decently, he would rather have a white youth working under him than 'a kaffir, or two kaffirs for that matter' (Simons and Simons, *Class and Colour*, p. 88).

38   Edward Roux, *SP Bunting: A Political Biography*, Mayibuye Books, Bellville, 1993, p. 105.

39   Hyslop, *The Notorious Syndicalist*, pp. 6–7.

40   'Recollections', WH Andrews Papers, MCH06 4-4-452.

41   Simons and Simons, 'Recollections', WH Andrews Papers, MCH06 4-4-452s; Simons and Simons, *Class and Colour*, p. 89.

42   Van der Walt, 'Anarchism and Syndicalism', p. 202.

43   Van der Walt, 'Anarchism and Syndicalism', p. 203; Simons and Simons, *Class and Colour*, pp. 152–3.

44   Jonathan Hyslop, 'The Imperial Working Class Makes Itself "White": White Labourism in Britain, Australia and South Africa before the First World War', *Journal of Historical Sociology*, 12, 4, 1999, pp. 398–417.

45   Van der Walt, 'Anarchism and Syndicalism', pp. 203–4; Simons and Simons, *Class and Colour*, 1968, p. 80.

46   Johns, *Marxism-Leninism*, p. 28; Cope, *Comrade Bill*, p. 82.

47   See Henry Tobias and Charles Woodhouse, 'Revolutionary Optimism and the Practice of Revolution: The Jewish Bund in 1905', *Jewish Social Studies*, 47, 2, 1985, pp. 135–50; Henry J Tobias, 'The Bund and Lenin until 1903', *Russian Review*, 20, 4, October 1961, pp. 344–57. Founded in Vilna, a leading

industrial centre in the Russian Pale (the region in which Jewish settlement was permitted), the Bund or League of Jewish Workers functioned as a group within the Russian Social Democratic Party. Marxist and committed to a revolutionary socialist programme, it would side with the Mensheviks in the split with Lenin in 1903. The Bund, though secular and indeed anti-religious, looked forward to a federalised political system in which Jews would enjoy a degree of cultural autonomy, especially with respect to the stratus and usage of Yiddish. The Bund was anti-Zionist; in its view, Jewish workers should fight for civic rights in the places in which they lived. They were focused on workers; there were no Jewish peasants in the Pale, for Jews could not own land and in Russia revolutionary peasant movements were often anti-Semitic.

48 Marcia Gitlin, *The Vision Amazing: The Story of South African Zionism*, Menorah Book Club, Johannesburg, 1950, pp. 136–8.

49 At the 1907 conference of the Second International, Bund representatives would reject proposals from Australian, Dutch and American delegates that referred to 'backward' nationalities (Ezra Mendelsohn, 'The Jewish Socialist Movement and the Second International, 1869–1914', *Jewish Social Studies*, 26, 3, July 1964, pp. 131–45).

50 Van der Walt, 'Anarchism and Socialism', p. 205.

51 Hyslop (*The Notorious Syndicalist*, pp. 167–75) supplies a brief history of the Transvaal Independent Labour Party formed by JT Bain in Pretoria in 1906 with which Bill Andrews's Johannesburg-based ILP group merged.

52 Simons and Simons, *Class and Colour*, p. 107.

53 Coloured ratepayers could vote in municipal elections and coloured people could vote in parliamentary elections provided they were literate and earned more than £75 annually. In the Cape there were nearly 15,000 coloured voters, less than four per cent of the white electorate, but they constituted a much larger share of the voters in certain Cape Town districts (Lewis, *Between the Wire and the Wall*, p. 21).

54 Johns, *Marxism-Leninism*, p. 42.

55 Hirson and Williams, *The Delegate for Africa*, p. 102.

56 Jon Lewis, *Industrialisation and Trade Union Organisation in South Africa, 1924–55*, Cambridge University Press, Cambridge, 1984.

57 Johns, 'Marxism-Leninism', pp. 38–40.

58 Paul Buhle, 'Daniel DeLeon', in Mari Jo Buhle, Paul Buhle and Dan Georgakas (eds), *The Encyclopedia of the American Left*, Garland Publishing, New York, 1990, pp. 188–90.

59 Cope, *Comrade Bill*, p. 98.

60 Drew, *Between Empire and Revolution*, p. 118.

61 Van der Walt, 'Anarchism and Socialism', pp. 186–7 and 234.

62 Van der Walt, 'Anarchism and Socialism', p. 189.

63 Leibl Feldman, *The Jews of Johannesburg*, Isaac and Jessie Kaplan Centre, University of Cape Town, Cape Town, 2007, p. 112.

64 Van der Walt, 'Anarchism and Socialism', p. 198. Meanwhile, the (coloured) African People's Organisation led a delegation to Britain to object to the legislation, joining the South African Native Convention in its protest.

65 Wilfrid Harrison, *Memoirs of a Socialist in South Africa, 1905–1947*, Stewart Printing Company, Cape Town, 1948, p. 19.

66 Allison Drew, *South Africa's Radical Tradition*, volume 1: *1907–1950*, University of Cape Town Press, Cape Town, 1996, p. 42.

67 Van der Walt suggests that at the time of his election in 1906, Alexander was associated with the SDF ('Anarchism and Syndicalism', p. 195). Morris Alexander was a lawyer, well known for his lobbying against anti-Jewish immigration

restrictions. At that stage he was a Zionist and chairman of the Imperial Union Club. His political connections were eclectic, though, and he corresponded with Olive Schreiner (Baruch Hirson, *The Cape Town Intellectuals*, Wits University Press, Johannesburg, 2001, pp. 28–9). He kept up his friendships formed during this period: nearly twenty years later, a report in the Communist Party's newspaper referred to his successful defence of communist leaders of a local unemployed workers' movement charged with unlawful parading in Adderley Street ('Leaders Summoned', *The International*, 25 July 1924, p. 8).

68 Lewis, *Between the Wire and the Wall*, p. 21.

69 Van der Walt, 'Anarchism and Syndicalism', pp. 194–5.

70 Harrison, *Memoirs of a Socialist*, p. 65; Gitlin, *The Vision Amazing*, p. 140.

71 Ruth First and Ann Scott, *Olive Schreiner*, André Deutsch, London, 1980, p. 253. For a canonical treatment of Schreiner by a leading party thinker in the 1950s, see Michael Harmel, *Olive Schreiner, 1855–1955*, Real Printing and Publishing, Cape Town, 1955.

72 Feldman, *The Jews of Johannesburg*, p. 133. The Friends of Russian Freedom lasted until 1909 and then closed down, weakened by its constant efforts to raise funds to defend Jews in Russia.

73 Alex La Guma, *Jimmy La Guma: A Biography*, Friends of the South African Library, Cape Town, 1997, p. 18.

74 Van der Walt, 'Anarchism and Syndicalism', p. 191.

75 Hirson and Williams, *The Delegate for Africa*, p. 45.

76 Van der Walt, 'Anarchism and Socialism', p. 219.

77 Quoted in Simons and Simons, *Class and Colour*, p. 155.

78 Van der Walt, 'Anarchism and Syndicalism', p. 218. Davidoff moved to Cape Town later and was active in the SDF there in 1916.

79 Simons and Simons, *Class and Colour*, p. 142.

80 Hyslop, *The Notorious Syndicalist*, p. 190.

81 Simons and Simons, *Class and Colour*, p. 128. He had originally stood in 1910, in Fordsburg, narrowly losing by 590 votes to Patrick Duncan ('Recollections', WH Andrews Papers, MCH06 4-4-452).

82 Cope, *Comrade Bill*, pp. 98 and 129.

83 Notebook entitled 'Personal Reminiscences', p. 21, RK Cope Papers, Wits Historical Papers, A 953.

84 Simons and Simons, *Class and Colour*, p. 129.

85 Hyslop, 'The Imperial Working Class', p. 415.

86 Simons and Simons, *Class and Colour*, p. 166.

87 Van der Walt, 'Anarchism and Syndicalism', p. 227.

88 Van der Walt, 'Anarchism and Syndicalism', pp. 245–6.

89 Secretary of Mines Annual Report, 1913, quoted in Davies, *Capital, State and White Labour*, p. 121.

90 Hyslop, *The Notorious Syndicalist*, p. 200.

91 Hyslop, *The Notorious Syndicalist*, p. 207

92 Hyslop, *The Notorious Syndicalist*, p. 202.

93 George Mason recalled later that during the strike he appealed to African workers at the mine for support: 'they responded almost to a man and the mine was stopped' ('Call to Native Workers', *The International*, 7 April 1916, p. 2).

94 Visser Wessels, 'The South African Labour Movement's Response to Declarations of Martial Law, 1913–1922', *Scientia Militaria: South African Journal of Military History*, 2003, pp. 142–57.

95 Hyslop, *The Notorious Syndicalist*, p. 2.

96 Elaine N Katz, *A Trade Union Aristocracy: A History of White Workers in the*

Transvaal and the General Strike of 1913, African Studies Institute, University of the Witwatersrand, Johannesburg, 1976, pp. 217 and 457–67.

97   Hyslop, *The Notorious Syndicalist*, p. 220.

98   Hyslop, *The Notorious Syndicalist*, p. 210.

99   Hirson and Williams, *The Delegate for Africa*, p. 120.

100 Simons and Simons, *Class and Colour*, p. 153.

101 EA Mantzaris, 'Radical Community: The Yiddish-Speaking Branch of the International Socialist League, 1818–1920', in Belinda Bozzoli (ed.), *Class, Community and Conflict: South African Perspectives*, Ravan Press, Johannesburg, 1987, pp. 160–73.

102 Eddie Roux and Win Roux, *Rebel Pity*, Rex Collings, London, 1970, p. 7; Van der Walt, 'Anarchism and Syndicalism', p. 273.

103 Johns, 'Marxism-Leninism', p. 42.

104 'Call to Native Workers', *The International*, 7 April 1916, p. 2.

105 Van der Walt, 'Anarchism and Syndicalism', p. 293.

106 Drew, *Between Empire and Revolution*, p. 85.

107 Drew, *Between Empire and Revolution*, p. 88.

108 Drew, *Between Empire and Revolution*, p. 85.

109 Drew, *South Africa's Radical Tradition*, p. 44.

110 Jonathan Hyslop, 'The War on War League: A South African Pacifist Movement', *Scientia Militaria*, 44, 1, 2016, pp. 25–7.

111 Hyslop, 'The War on War League', p. 26.

112 Notebook entitled 'Personal Reminiscences', p. 53, Cope Papers.

113 Hirson and Williams, *The Delegate for Africa*, p. 132.

114 Notebook entitled 'Personal Reminiscences', p. 16, Cope Papers.

115 Hirson and Williams, *The Delegate for Africa*, p. 95.

116 Israel and Adams, '"That Spells Trouble"', p. 149.

117 Cope, *Comrade Bill*, p. 169.

118 Hirson and Williams, *The Delegate for Africa*, p. 153.

119 Simons and Simons, *Class and Colour*, pp. 164–5.

120 Johns, 'Marxism-Leninism', p. 82.

121 Van der Walt, 'Anarchism and Syndicalism', p. 349.

122 'Call to the Native Workers', *The International*, 7 April 1916, p. 1.

123 Simons and Simons, *Class and Colour*, p. 196.

124 A statement drafted by the ISL's management committee shortly before the conference suggested that abolition of the pass laws should be 'gradual' ('The League Conference', *The International*, 10 December 1915, p. 2). Between 1915 and 1918, the ISL's newspaper published at least 20 statements including election manifestos calling for solidarity between white and black workers. They were all reproduced in 'Irrespective of Colour', *International*, 9 August 1918, p. 4.

125 See commentary in 'Conference Jottings', *The International*, 14 January 1916, p. 3.

126 Brian Bunting, *South African Communists Speak*, Inkululeko Publications, London, 1981, p. 26.

127 'The Segregational Socialist', *The International*, 19 May 1916, p. 1.

128 WH Andrews, 'Position of the Native and Coloured Workers', *The International*, 20 July 1917, p. 4.

129 Drew, *Between Empire and Revolution*, p. 96.

130 *The International*, 9 February 1917, quoted in David J Mason, 'Race, Class and National Liberation: Some Implications of the Policy Dilemmas of the International Socialist League and the Communist Party of South Africa', MSc dissertation, Social Sciences, University of Bristol, 1971, p. 12.

131 Hirson and Williams, *The Delegate for Africa*, p. 152.

132   For reports on Bunting's contributions to TPC debates, see *The International*, 30 March 1917, p. 3; 13 April 1917.

133   'The League's Municipal Manifesto', *The International*, 29 October 1915, p. 1.

134   He was expelled from the League after introducing a draft ordinance on behalf of shopkeepers that would have extended trading hours ('Councillor Clark's Expulsion from the League', *The International*, 13 April 1917, p. 3).

135   An article on racial differences in *The International* (JM Gibson, 'The Bantu Race', *The International*, 31 May 1918, p. 2) probably represented widely shared views. It argued that 'the biological evidence is that there is not on average any degree of difference between [Bantu language speakers] and the white races', adding that 'they [were] learning fast' as a consequence of entering an 'industrial arena' that was 'instilling ideas of the economic injustice of our so called civilisation'.

136   'The "White Soviet" and the Red Herring', *The International*, 4 April 1919, p. 2.

137   'The Class War on the Rand', *The International*, 16 February 1917, p. 4.

138   'International May Day', *The International*, 27 April 1917, p. 1.

139   Hirson and Williams, *The Delegate for Africa*, p. 148.

140   Van der Walt, 'Anarchism and Syndicalism', p. 15.

141   Van der Walt, 'Anarchism and Syndicalism', p. 324.

142   Van der Walt, 'Anarchism and Syndicalism', p. 329.

143   Van der Walt, 'Anarchism and Syndicalism', pp. 331–2.

144   Johns, 'Marxism-Leninism', p. 107.

145   Hirson and Williams, *The Delegate for Africa*, p. 157.

146   Hirson and Williams, *The Delegate from Africa*, pp. 242–6; D Ivon Jones, 'Lenin's First Book', *Communist Review*, 4, 11, 1924, https://www.marxists.org/archive/jones/1924/03/x01.htm.

147   Cope, *Comrade Bill*, p. 98.

148   Notebook entitled 'Personal Reminiscences', p. 24, Cope Papers.

149   Cope, *Comrade Bill*, p. 178

150   *The International*, 15 October 1916, p. 1. At that time it was a reasonable comparison. Karl Liebknecht was the only German parliamentarian to vote against the war. His subsequent treatment by the authorities was very different from Andrews's experiences during the war. Despite Liebknecht's theoretical immunity as an MP, he was conscripted and then subsequently imprisoned for the rest of the war. Shortly after helping to form the German Communist Party, and in the aftermath of the failed Spartacus uprising in Berlin, he and Rosa Luxemburg were abducted and murdered by the Freikorps on 15 January 1919.

151   Hirson and Williams, *The Delegate for Africa*, p. 149.

152   Roux and Roux, *Rebel Pity*, p. 10.

153   Letter from Sidney to Rebecca Bunting, 24 February 1918, in Brian Bunting, *Letters to Rebecca: South African Communist Leader SP Bunting to His Wife, 1917–1934*, Mayibuye Books, Bellville, 1996.

154   Rosa Luxemburg, *The Accumulation of Capital*, 1913, chapter XXIX.

155   To judge from his later observations about the absence of African peasants in South Africa in the 1920s.

156   JM Gibson, 'Political Action', *The International*, 20 September 1918, p. 4.

157   'Manifesto, Troyeville By-election', *The International*, 19 January 1917, p. 1.

158   '"Labour" and the Black Worker', *The International*, 29 June 1917, p. 4.

159   WH Andrews, 'The Position of the Native and Coloured Workers', *The International*, 20 July 1917, p. 4.

160   Hirson and Williams, *The Delegate for Africa*, p. 167.

161   'The Socialist Sunday School', *The International*, 28 April 1916, p. 4.

162   'Branch Notes', *The International*, 30 June 1916.

163   'A League Census', *The International*, 7 July 1916, p. 3.
164   WH Andrews, Obituary CB Tyler, *The Guardian*, 22 July 1944 (cutting in the WH Andrews Papers, MCH06 4-2-378).
165   Johns, 'Marxism-Leninism', pp. 112–16.
166   Johns, 'Marxism-Leninism', p. 118.
167   Sylvia Neame, *The Congress Movement: The Unfolding of the Congress Alliance, 1912–1961*, volume 1, Human Sciences Research Council Press, Pretoria and Cape Town, 2015, p. 49.
168   'Call to Native Workers', *The International*, 7 April 1917, p. 2.
169   'Workers of the World Unite', *The International*, 16 March 1917, p. 1.
170   FA Johnston, 'The IWA on the Rand', in Belinda Bozzoli (ed.), *Labour, Townships and Protest*, Ravan Press, Johannesburg, 1979.
171   Johnston, 'The IWA on the Rand', p. 250.
172   Johnston, 'The IWA on the Rand', p. 251.
173   Johnston, 'The IWA on the Rand', p. 255.
174   Roux, *SP Bunting*, p. 77.
175   Johnston, 'The IWA on the Rand', p. 132.
176   Johnston, 'The IWA on the Rand', p. 261.
177   Bunting, *Letters to Rebecca*, p. 25.
178   Johnston, 'The IWA on the Rand', p. 263.
179   Hirson and Williams, *The Delegate for Africa*, p. 174.
180   'The Native Boycott', *The International*, 13 February 1918, p. 1.
181   Bunting, *Letters to Rebecca*, p. 23.
182   Bunting, *South African Communists Speak*, p. 30.
183   '170 Million Recruits', *The International*, 23 March 1917, p. 1.
184   Irina Filatova and Apollon Davidson, '"We, the South African Bolsheviks": The Russian Revolution and South Africa', *Journal of Contemporary History*, 52, 4, 2017, p. 941.
185   'Report of WHA as Delegate to the International for the ISL', WH Andrews Papers, MCH06 6-4-38. Unfortunately Andrews's report contains no details of what he and Litvinov said to each other.
186   Ivon Jones to WH Andrews, 21 January 1918, WH Andrews Papers, MCH06 3-4-270.
187   Filatova and Davidson, *The Hidden Thread*, pp. 59–66. The most detailed treatment of early exchanges between South African communists and Comintern is Apollon Davidson's 'Komintern i rozhdenie pervoi kompartii v Afrika', in LP Deliusin, MA Persits, AB Reznikov, and RA Ul'ianovskii (eds), *Komintern i Vostok*, Nauka, Moscow, 1969, pp. 448–507.
188   Cope, *Comrade Bill*, p. 194.
189   'Report of WHA as Delegate to the International for the ISL', WH Andrews Papers, MCH06 6-4-38.
190   'The Maximalist Programme', *The International*, 30 November 1917, p. 3.
191   *The International*, 15 June 1917, p. 2.
192   'Lenin's Career', *The International*, 15 February, 1918, p. 3.
193   Van der Walt, 'Anarchism and Syndicalism', pp. 357–64.
194   'The Word Becomes Flesh', *The International*, 30 November 1917, p. 1.
195   See Van der Walt for quotation from *The International*, 3 August 1917 ('Anarchism and Socialism', p. 357).
196   'Russian Workmen Vindicate Marx', *The International*, 18 May 1917, p. 1
197   Lars T Lih, 'Lenin and Bolshevism', in Stephen A. Smith (ed.), *The Oxford Handbook of the History of Communism*, Oxford University Press, Oxford, 2017, p. 66.
198   Arthur Ransome, 'Conversations with Lenin', *The International*, 10 October 1919, p. 6.

199   Hirson and Williams, *The Delegate for Africa*, p. 166.

200   Israel and Adams, '"That Spells Trouble"', p. 148.

201   Bernard Sachs, *Multitude of Dreams*, Kayor Publishing House, Johannesburg, 1949, p. 132.

202   Mantzaris, 'Radical Community', p. 169.

203   The section probably facilitated the absorption of the Bund into the Communist Party, a process completed in 1921. By this stage the Bolsheviks were ready to sanction certain 'national' rights and, for a period, in Minsk, encouraged the formation of separate Jewish schools supplying instruction in Yiddish. See Yitzhak Arad, *The Holocaust in the Soviet Union*, University of Nebraska Press, Lincoln, 2009, p. 17.

204   Mantzaris, 'Radical Community', p. 168.

205   Mantzaris, 'Radical Community', p. 170.

206   Feldman, *The Jews of Johannesburg*, p. 50. The term was taken from 'PERUV', an abbreviation of 'Polnischer und Russischer Yiddische Verein', the name of a mutual support organisation formed by the first group of Baltic immigrants to reach Johannesburg. Yiddish speakers were despised by the more middle-class and more assimilated German-descended Jews who were anxious to dissociate themselves from the new 'uncultured' arrivals. The expression was in general usage by the time that John Buchan, a former Johannesburg resident, was writing his novel *Greenmantle* in 1916 (John Buchan, *Greenmantle*, Penguin, Harmondsworth, 1956, p. 114). See also Sydney Brenner, 'Where Did the Insult Peruvian Jew Come from', https://www.youtube.com/watch?v=IU9jKTplxZw.

207   A profile of Israelstam appears in Feldman's *The Jews of Johannesburg*, pp. 110–13. Born in 1870, he arrived in South Africa in 1900 after working as a coal miner in the United States where he first became a De Leonite socialist. He was among the speakers who addressed the South African Native National Congress at its opening conference in 1912.

208   Bunting, *South African Communists Speak*, p. 27.

209   Hirson and Williams, *A Delegate for Africa*, p. 168.

210   Cope, *Comrade Bill*, p. 195.

211   'International May Day in Johannesburg', *The International*, 3 May 1918, p. 3.

212   The quotation is from a description of a meeting attended by 'perhaps a thousand native men' and addressed by Thibedi; see Ray E. Phillips, *The Bantu Are Coming: Phases of South Africa's Race Problem*, Student Christian Movement Press, London, 1930, pp. 45–6.

213   Neame, *The Congress Movement*, volume 1, p. 37.

214   Report of the Interdepartmental Committee on the Native Pass Laws, UG 41, 22, 5, quoted by Philip Bonner in 'The Transvaal Native Congress, 1917–1920: The Radicalisation of the Black Petty Bourgeoisie on the Rand', African Studies seminar paper no. 89, African Studies Institute, University of the Witwatersrand, March 1980, p. 3.

215   Bonner, 'The Transvaal Native Congress', p. 10.

216   Bonner, 'The Transvaal Native Congress', p. 15.

217   Bonner, 'The Transvaal Native Congress', p. 9.

218   Cope, *Comrade Bill*, p. 197.

219   'Iconoclasm', *The International*, 8 November 1918, p. 3.

220   Bonner, 'The Transvaal Native Congress', p. 170.

221   Ivon Jones's phrase reprinted by Bunting (*South African Communists Speak*, p. 53).

222   Neame, *The Congress Movement*, volume 1, p. 67.

223   Cope, *Comrade Bill*, p. 197.

224   John Higginson, *Collective Violence and the Agrarian Origins of South African*

Apartheid, Cambridge University Press, New York, 2015, p. 196.

225 Simons and Simons, *Class and Colour*, p. 209.

226 'No Socialism for Natives', *The International*, 26 July 2926, pp. 1–2.

227 An article in *The International* on 4 October 1918 ('A Framework Fiasco', p. 3) hinted that Luke Massina was more than a police spy. For later revelations, see Hirson and Williams, *The Delegate for Africa*, p. 212.

228 'Socialism and Violence', *The International*, 6 September 1918, p. 2.

229 Roux, *SP Bunting*, p. 78.

230 'Black Crawfords', *The International*, 14 June 1918, p. 2; see also 'Native Unrest', *The International*, 21 June 1918, p. 4.

231 Moses Kotane quoted by Allison Drew, *Discordant Comrades: Identities and Loyalties on the South African Left*, Ashgate, Aldershot, 2000, p. 78.

232 'International May Day in Johannesburg', *The International*, 3 May 1918, p. 3.

233 Bonner, 'The Transvaal Native Congress', p. 35.

234 Hirson and Williams, *The Delegate for Africa*, p. 183.

235 Drew, *Between Empire and Revolution*, p. 112.

236 Simons and Simons, *Class and Colour*, p. 210.

237 *The International*, 21 December 1918.

238 Bonner, 'The Transvaal Native Congress', p. 38.

239 Neame, *The Congress Movement*, volume 1, p. 81.

240 Van der Walt, 'Anarchism and Syndicalism', p. 472.

241 Cope, *Comrade Bill*, p. 181.

242 '1919 Annual Conference', *The International*, 10 January 1919, p. 2.

243 Cope, *Comrade Bill*, p. 206.

244 Van der Walt, 'Anarchism and Syndicalism', pp. 418 and 422.

245 Filatova and Davidson, '"We, the South African Bolsheviks"', p. 943.

246 Johns, 'Marxism-Leninism', p. 172.

247 Bunting, *Letters to Rebecca*, p. 27.

248 'Preparing for Action', *The International*, 29 November 1918, p. 3.

249 'The Strike Situation on the Rand', *The International*, 6 February 1920, p. 2.

250 'League Notes', *The International*, 6 December 1918.

251 Van der Walt, 'Anarchism and Syndicalism', p. 505; Hyslop, *The Notorious Syndicalist*, p. 287.

252 Roux, *SP Bunting*, p. 83. The story originally appeared in *The Star*, 31 March 1919.

253 Van der Walt, 'Anarchism and Syndicalism', p. 426.

254 SP Bunting, 'The "White Soviet" and the Red Herring', *The International*, 4 April 1919, pp. 1–2.

255 WH Andrews, *Class Struggles in South Africa*, Stewart Printing Company, Cape Town, 1941, p. 30.

256 The organisers themselves used the term 'Soviet'.

257 WH Andrews, 'The Durban Soviet', *The International*, 16 January 1920, p. 4; Harry Haynes, 'What Are the Results', *The International*, 16 January, 1920, p. 2. Haynes was a member of the ISL but in Durban he was working with a smaller group, the Durban Marxist Club, which the ISL leaders perceived as an allied group.

258 David Ivon Jones, 'The White Workers' Burden', *The International*, 11 April 1919, p. 3

259 David Ivon Jones, 'Syndicalism in Action', *The International*, 25 April 1919, p. 7.

260 'The League's Election Manifesto', *The International*, 30 January 1920, p. 5.

261 'The Soviet and the Native', *The International*, 13 February 1920, p. 3.

262 Hirson and Williams, *The Delegate for Africa*, p. 213.

263 Figures cited in 'Development of Trade Unions in South Africa', *Social and*

Industrial Review, 1926, pp. 45–8, an anonymous article in Ambrose Lynn Saffery Papers, Wits Historical Papers, AD 1178, A1.

264   Bunting, *South African Communists Speak*, pp. 37–8.

265   'Emancipation', *The International*, 25 July 1919, p. 3.

266   Van der Walt, 'Anarchism and Socialism', p. 447.

267   Most eligible local residents disagreed, though the SDF found favour with a substantial share of the electorate. Abdurahman won a clear majority with 542 votes to Harrison's tally of 212. See Harrison, *Memoirs of a Socialist in South Africa*, p. 23.

268   AB Lerumo, *Fifty Fighting Years: A Short History of the South African Communist Party*, Inkululeko Publications, London, 1980, p. 37.

269   Harrison, *Memoirs of a Socialist in South Africa*, p. 64.

270   'Cape Notes', *The International*, 24 January 1919, p. 2.

271   'Cape Notes', *The International*, 1 August 1919, p. 4.

272   Just why the ISL's Yiddish-speaking branch was so adamantly opposed to electoral action is puzzling. After all, the Russian Bundists by 1920 were moving closer to the Bolsheviks and from 1918 the Russian Bundists merged with the Bolsheviks, dissolving their organisation in 1921. The Bolsheviks' punishment of anti-Semitic pogromists was one reason for this (Sai Englert, 'The Rise and the Fall of the Jewish labour Bund', *International Socialism*, 135, 2012). In any case, they had shifted at various points in their earlier history over the issue of electoral participation. What seems likely is that the branch's delegates at the conference were indeed syndicalist purists, but this was probably not true of all the branch's members, especially those who had arrived in Johannesburg quite recently.

273   David Ivon Jones, 'The League and Political Action', *The International*, 5 December 1919, p. 4.

274   Van der Walt, 'Anarchism and Syndicalism', pp. 460–78.

275   Van der Walt, 'Anarchism and Syndicalism', p. 480. For the relatively equal followings which the ICU and the IWA enjoyed among Cape Town's dock workers at this point, see Henry Dee, 'Clements Kadalie, Trade Unionism, Migration and Race in Southern Africa', PhD dissertation, University of Edinburgh, 2019, p. 115.

276   Cope, *Comrade Bill*, p. 213.

277   Dee, 'Clements Kadalie', p. 139.

278   Van der Walt, 'Anarchism and Syndicalism', p. 473.

279   'Emancipation', *The International*, 25 July 1919, p. 3.

280   'The Native Workers' Purgatory', *The International*, 2 May 1919, p. 1.

281   VL Allen, *The History of Black Mineworkers in South Africa*, volume 1, Moor Press, Keighley, 1992, p. 291.

282   Philip Bonner, 'The African Mineworkers' Strike', in Belinda Bozzoli (ed.), *Labour, Townships and Protest*, Ravan Press, Johannesburg, 1979, p. 282. Hirson and Williams suggest that the ISL may have played a more active role in the mine workers' strike but cite no evidence (*The Delegate for Africa*, p. 186).

283   Phillips, *The Bantu Are Coming*, p. 47.

284   75,000 mine workers participated in the 1946 strike.

285   Bonner, 'The African Mineworkers' Strike', p. 281.

286   Allen, *The History of Black Mineworkers*, p. 294.

287   Bonner, 'The African Mineworkers' Strike', p. 284.

288   'Don't Scab', *The International*, 27 February 1920, p. 1.

289   Allen, *The History of Black Mineworkers*, p. 290.

290   'To Scab or Not to Scab', *The International*, 27 February 1920, p. 8.

291   Bunting, *South African Communists Speak*, p. 53.

292   In 1918 *The International* did publish a letter from a 'native correspondent', in

May, which described the tough labour regime experienced by 'boys employed in the mines on hand drilling or hammers' ('Worthy of His Hire', *The International*, 17 May 1918). This does suggest that League propaganda was at least reaching educated African men employed as clerical workers on the mines.

293 'The Darkest Blot of All', *The International*, 5 July 1918, p. 1.
294 'Kimberley Workers Awake!', *The International*, 12 December 1919, p. 5; Doreen Musson, *Johnny Gomas: Voice of the Working Class – A Political Biography*, Buchu Books, Cape Town, 1989, pp. 17–18.
295 Musson, *Johnny Gomas*, p. 21.
296 'Kimberley Strikes', *The International*, 2 January 1920, p. 3.
297 'Our Kimberley Delegates', *The International*, 9 January 1920, p. 5.
298 Van der Walt, 'Anarchism and Syndicalism', p. 467.
299 'Johannesburg Notes', *The International*, 3 September 1920, p. 4.
300 'The Indian Strike', *The International*, 5 December 1919, p. 7.
301 See reports in *The International*, 21 November 1919, p. 6 and *The International*, 28 November 1919, p. 5.
302 Van der Walt, 'Anarchism and Syndicalism', pp. 409–13.
303 'League Notes', *The International*, 15 March 1918, p. 4.
304 Hirson and Williams, *The Delegate for Africa*, p. 195.
305 Trial record in *Natal Law Reports*, XL, 1919, pp. 266–76, cited in CM Gorham, 'Keeping the Red Flag Flying: The International Socialist League of South Africa and the "Bolshevik Pamphlet" Case', BA Honours dissertation, History Department, Rhodes University, October 1990, p. 36.
306 'Bolshevism on Its Trial', *The International*, 16 May 1919, p. 4.
307 'Judgement in the Maritzburg Case', *The International*, 29 August 1919, p. 1.
308 Simons and Simons, *Class and Colour*, p. 230.
309 Davidson et al., *South Africa and the Communist International*, volume 1, pp. 58–9.
310 Filatova and Davidson, *The Hidden Thread*, p. 47.
311 Whether they were committed Bolsheviks seems unlikely; they told quite different stories to the British authorities in Baghdad before travelling to South Africa. When they arrived, they had plenty of money apparently, though they told Wolberg they were destitute. They showed officials letters of recommendation to a list of respectable people in Johannesburg (Filatova and Davidson, *The Hidden Thread*, p. 46).
312 Davidson et al., *South Africa and the Communist International*, volume I, pp. 35–58.
313 Davidson et al., *South Africa and the Communist International*, volume I, p. 38.
314 Apollon Davidson, 'Lenin on South Africa', *African Communist*, 91, 1982, p. 77.
315 Simons and Simons, *Class and Colour*, p. 257.
316 'Communist Exploitation', *The International*, 23 January 1919, p. 3.
317 JM Gibson, *The International*, 24 January 1919, p. 4. Gibson is profiled briefly in Lucien van der Walt, 'The First Globalisation and Transnational Labour Activism in Southern Africa', *African Studies*, 66, 2–3, 2007, p. 232.
318 'Lenin on the Soviets', *The International*, 27 September 1917, p. 3.
319 Cope, *Comrade Bill*, p. 208.

Chapter 2

1 HJ and RE Simons, *Class and Colour in South Africa, 1850–1950*, Penguin, Harmondsworth, 1969, p. 256.
2 Allison Drew, *Between Empire and Revolution: A Life of Sidney Bunting, 1873–1936*, Pickering and Chatto, London, 2007, p. 117.
3 VI Lenin, *Collected Works*, volume 32, Progress Publishers, Moscow, 1977, p. 482.
4 Simons and Simons, *Class and Colour*, pp. 259–60.

5 'The 1910 Offensive', *The International*, 31 January 1919, p. 2.

6 Sheridan Johns, 'Marxism-Leninism in a Multi-racial Environment: The Origins and Early History of the Communist Party of South Africa, 1914–1932', PhD dissertation, Department of Government, Harvard University, 1965, p. 235.

7 Lucien van der Walt, 'Anarchism and Syndicalism in South Africa, 1904–1921: Rethinking the History of Labour and the Left', PhD dissertation, Department of Sociology, University of the Witwatersrand, 2007, p. 518.

8 Apollon Davidson, Irina Filatova, Valentin Gorodnov and Sheridan Johns, *South Africa and the Communist International: A Documentary History*, volume 1: *Socialist Pilgrims to Bolshevik Footsoldiers, 1919–1930*, Frank Cass, London, 2003, p. 67.

9 Andrews's comment may have been prompted by the League's recent experience with police informers; its announcement of its first night school included a sardonic welcome to any Africans in government service present including CID agents; they along with everyone else in attendance would be quite eligible as class members ('League Notes', *The International*, 12 April 1918, p. 4).

10 Brian Bunting (ed.), *South African Communists Speak: Documents from the History of the South African Communist Party, 1915–1980*, Inkululeko Publications, London, pp. 41–55.

11 Davidson et al., *South Africa and the Communist International*, volume 1, p. 73.

12 Baruch Hirson and Gwyn A Williams, *The Delegate for Africa: David Ivon Jones, 1883–1924*, Core Publications, London, 1995, p. 215. Apollon Davidson notes that Jones was called 'member of the Comintern Executive from Africa' (Apollon Davidson, 'Lenin on South Africa', *African Communist*, 91, 1982, p. 78).

13 Davidson et al., *South Africa and the Communist International*, volume 1, p. 62.

14 Allison Drew, *Discordant Comrades: Identities and Loyalties on the South African Left*, Ashgate, Aldershot, 2000, p. 68.

15 Davidson et al., *South Africa and the Communist International*, volume 1, p. 75.

16 'Labour's Hymn of Hate', *The International*, 12 September 1919, p. 3.

17 In the end Poalei Zion would decline to join the communists.

18 Bunting, *South African Communists Speak*, 1981; Van der Walt, 'Anarchists and Syndicalists', p. 521.

19 Simons and Simons, *Class and Colour*, p. 257.

20 Davidson et al., *South Africa and the Communist International*, volume 1, p. 83.

21 Brian Bunting (ed.), *Letters to Rebecca: South African Communist Leader SP Bunting to His Wife, 1917–1934*, Mayibuye Books, Bellville, 1996, p. 38.

22 Davidson et al., *South Africa and the Communist International*, volume 1, p. 80.

23 See 'Branch Notes', *The International*, 2 September 1918, p. 4. The reference is an 'adjourned debate' on 'the decision of natives in branch membership' but the report offers no additional information.

24 No reports suggest that any other of the IWA members had belonged to the ISL. In 1918 a report ('A Members Pow-Wow', *The International*, 5 April 1918) mentions that about a dozen IWA members were present at an industrial conference organised by the League but these 'have so far not become members'.

25 Simons and Simons, *Class and Colour*, p. 268.

26 These characteristics seem to have been stable features of the League at that time. In its issue of 19 January 1917, *The International* contained an occupational analysis of the League's leadership that had just been elected: three carpenters, two fitters, an electrician, a sampler, a cabinet maker, a pipe fitter, a bricklayer, a blacksmith, and, finally, a bookkeeper (David Ivon Jones). The names suggest a mainly British immigrant leadership though the executive included one Afrikaner and three names that may have been Jewish.

27 Davidson et al., *South Africa and the Communist International*, volume 1, pp. 85–7.

28 Alexander Vatlin and Stephen A Smith, 'The Comintern', in Stephen A Smith (ed.), *The Oxford Handbook of the History of Communism*, Oxford University Press, Oxford, 2014, pp. 188–9.

29 Henry Pelling, *A Short History of the Labour Party*, London, Macmillan, 1961, p. 54.

30 'The Third International: Report of the South African Delegates', *The International*, 2 September 1921, p. 2.

31 Edward Roux, *SP Bunting: A Political Biography*, African Bookman, Cape Town, 1944, p. 90.

32 Bunting, *Letters to Rebecca*, p. 59.

33 See comment by David Dryburgh in *The International*, 11 May 1923, quoted in Bunting, *Letters to Rebecca*, p. 39.

34 Jon Lewis, *Industrialisation and Trade Union Organisation in South Africa, 1924–55*, Cambridge University Press, Cambridge, 1984, p. 17.

35 'Is the White Miner a Miner?', *The International*, 25 May 1917, p. 3.

36 Jeremy Krikler, *White Rising: The 1922 Insurrection and Racial Killing in South Africa*, Manchester University Press, Manchester, 2005, p. 29.

37 Krikler, *White Rising*, p. 30.

38 Krikler, *White Rising*, pp. 164–5.

39 A Lerumo, *Fifty Fighting Years: The South African Communist Party, 1921–1971*, 3rd edn, Inkululeko Publications, London, 1987, p. 45; Van der Walt, 'Anarchism and Syndicalism', p. 541.

40 Hirson and Williams, *The Delegate for Africa*, p. 230; Simons and Simons, *Class and Colour*, p. 276.

41 Simons and Simons, *Class and Colour*, p. 270.

42 Van der Walt, 'Anarchism and Syndicalism', pp. 541–4.

43 RK Cope, *Comrade Bill: The Life and Times of WH Andrews, Workers' Leader*, Stewart Printing Company, Cape Town, 1944, p. 225.

44 *The International*, 18 November 1921, cited by Simons and Simons, *Class and Colour*, p. 276.

45 *The International*, 27 January 1922, quoted in Allison Drew, *South Africa's Radical Tradition: A Documentary History*, volume 1: *1907–1950*, University of Cape Town Press, Cape Town, 1996, p. 49.

46 *The International*, 3 February 1922, cited in Johns, *Marxism-Leninism*, p. 277.

47 Roux, *SP Bunting*, p. 91.

48 Simons and Simons, *Class and Colour*, p. 286.

49 Cope, *Comrade Bill*, p. 21.

50 Hirson and Williams, *The Delegate for Africa*, p. 230.

51 Cope, *Comrade Bill*, p. 244.

52 Report of EC to 2nd Congress CPSA, 28 April 1923, cited in Davidson et al., *South Africa and the Communist International*, volume 1, p. 127.

53 Davidson et al., *South Africa and the Communist International*, volume 1, 127.

54 'The Native Scare: Who Raised It?', *The International*, 16 February, 1923, p. 4.

55 Andrews, cited in Krikler, *White Rising*, pp. 327–8.

56 Davidson et al., *South Africa and the Communist International*, volume 1, p. 98.

57 Henry Dee, 'Clements Kadalie, Trade Unionism, Migration and Race in Southern Africa', PhD dissertation, University of Edinburgh, 2019, p. 30.

58 *The International*, 17 February 1922, cited in Hirson and Williams, *The Delegate for Africa*, p. 234.

59 Irina Filatova and Apollon Davidson, *The Hidden Thread: Russia and South Africa in the Soviet Era*, Jonathan Ball, Johannesburg and Cape Town, 2013, p. 503.

60 See Davidson et al., *South Africa and the Communist International*, volume 1, pp.

102–3 and 108–9. Also, Irina Filatova and Apollon Davidson, '"We, the South African Bolsheviks": The Russian Revolution and South Africa', *Journal of Contemporary History*, 52, 4, 2017, pp. 935–58; Apollon Davidson, 'Lenin on South Africa', *African Communist*, 91, 1982, pp. 73–9.

61 Cope, *Comrade Bill*, p. 232.
62 For more in this vein, see Cope, *Comrade Bill*, p. 233; Simons and Simons, *Class and Colour*, p. 281.
63 Simons and Simons, *Class and Colour*, p. 285.
64 Krikler, *White Rising*, pp. 124–5.
65 Drew, *South Africa's Radical Tradition*, p. 50.
66 *The International*, 10 February 1922, cited in Hirson and Williams, *The Delegate for Africa*, p. 228.
67 Krikler, *White Rising*, p. 51.
68 Macmillan, cited by Drew, *Discordant Comrades*, p. 62.
69 Eddie Roux, *Time Longer than Rope*, Victor Gollancz, London, 1948, p. 156.
70 Hirson and Williams, *The Delegate for Africa*, pp. 228–64.
71 Krikler, *White Rising*, p. 79.
72 Van der Walt, 'Anarchism and Syndicalism', p. 539. Though Boer commandos also elected their officers during the first stages of South African War (Fransjohan Pretorius, 'Life on Commando', in Peter Warwick (ed.), *The South African War: The Anglo-Boer War of 1899–1902*, Longman, London, 1980, p. 108).
73 Edward Johanningsmeier, 'Communists and Black Freedom Movements in South Africa and the United States, 1919–1950', *Journal of Southern African Studies*, 30, 1, 2004, p. 161.
74 Hirson and Williams, *The Delegate for Africa*, p. 230.
75 CF Glass, 'March, 1922: Its Place in Working Class History', *The International*, 14 March 1924, p. 5.
76 Krikler, *White Rising*, p. 112.
77 Krikler, *White Rising*, p. 113.
78 Krikler, *White Rising*, p. 110.
79 Krikler, *White Rising*, p. 52.
80 Willie Kalk, interviewed by David Everatt, Orange Grove, 19 March 1987, David Everatt Papers, Wits Historical Papers, A 2521, Aa8.
81 Bernard Sachs, *Multitude of Dreams*, Kayor Publishing House, Johannesburg, 1949, p. 120.
82 For another example , this time of African leather workers striking in East London for the reinstatement of a white employee, see DH, 'Class Solidarity in East London', *The International*, 2 April 1920, p. 3.
83 Roux, *SP Bunting*, p. 91; Krikler, *White Rising*, p. 115.
84 See, for example, Harry Haynes, 'Straight Tip to the Sjambok Men', *The International*, 20 February 1920.
85 Hirson and Williams, *The Delegate for Africa*, p. 235.
86 Krikler, *White Rising*, p. 145.
87 Keith Breckenridge, 'Fighting for White South Africa: White Working Class Racism and the 1922 Rand Revolt', *South African Historical Journal*, 57, 2007, pp. 228–43; see also Drew, *Discordant Comrades*, p. 62.
88 Davidson et al., *South Africa and the Communist International*, volume 1, p. 97.
89 Yann Beliard, 'A "Labour War" in South Africa: The 1922 Rand Revolution in Sylvia Pankhurst's Workers' Dreadnought', *Labor History*, 57, 1, 2016, p. 23.
90 'The Rand Revolt: Causes and Effects', p. 10, typescript, RK Cope Papers, Wits Historical Papers, A 953/6a.
91 Cope, *Comrade Bill*, p. 279.

92   Union of South Africa, *Report of the Martial Law Inquiry Judicial Commission*, Pretoria, 1922.
93   Johns, 'Marxism-Leninism', p. 283.
94   Eddie Roux and Win Roux, *Rebel Pity*, Rex Collings, London, 1970, pp. 24–5.
95   Memorialised in *The International* as 'the first judicial victim of the murderers of the working-class of South Africa' (*The International*, 12 October 1923, p. 1).
96   Bunting, *South African Communists Speak*, p. 69.
97   Sidney Bunting, 'The Rand Revolt: Causes and Effects', Cope Papers, A 953/6a.
98   Sidney Bunting, 'The "Colonial" Labour Front', 23 October 1922, reprinted in Drew, *South Africa's Radical Tradition*, p. 53.
99   DI Jones 'Further Statement on the South African Situation', 25 March 1922, in Davidson et al., *South Africa and the Comintern*, volume 1, p. 98.
100 Davidson, 'Lenin on South Africa', p. 78.
101 Drew, *Between Empire and Revolution*, 127. Wilfrid Harrison recollected that Ivon Jones wrote to Bunting after his arrival in Berlin on the way to Moscow, telling him that he, Jones, himself wanted to 'represent South Africa in proxy' (Wilfrid H Harrison, *Memoirs of a Socialist in South Africa, 1903–1947*, Stewart Printing Company, Cape Town, 1947, p. 82).
102 Sheridan Johns, 'Imperial Preferences: The Case of the Comintern and South Africa', Western Australian African Studies Seminar, Perth, 7 August 1993, p. 4.
103 SP Bunting to General Secretary, Comintern, 1 January 1923, in Davidson et al., *South Africa and the Communist International*, volume 1, p. 113.
104 Drew, *Discordant Comrades*, p. 67.
105 JT Campbell, 'Romantic Revolutionaries: David Ivon Jones, SP Bunting and the Origins of Non-racial Politics in South Africa', *Journal of African History*, 39, 2, 1998, p. 322.
106 Davidson et al., *South Africa and the Communist International*, volume 1, p. 107.
107 Davidson et al., *South Africa and the Communist International*, volume 1, p. 120.
108 DI Jones to Comintern Executive, 23 March 1823, in Davidson et al., *South Africa and the Communist International*, volume 1, p. 121
109 Report by SPB on the 4th Congress of the Comintern, 29 April 1923, in Davidson et al., *South Africa and the Communist International*, volume 1, p. 130.
110 Oscar Berland, 'The Emergence of the Communist Perspective on the "Negro Question" in America: 1919–1931, Part One', *Science and Society*, 63, 4, 1999–2000, p. 422.
111 Drew, *Discordant Comrades*, p. 69.
112 Bunting, *Letters to Rebecca*, p. 47.
113 Bunting, *Letters to Rebecca*, p. 50; Davidson et al., *South Africa and the Communist International*, volume 1, p. 113.
114 Bunting, *Letters to Rebecca*, p. 49.
115 'It has always been understood to be a principle of real Labour politics … that Labour representatives should in no circumstances join in a government with any other party' ('Portfolios for the SALP', *The International*, 11 May 1923, p. 3). The communists' application for affiliation was in the form of a letter by Sidney Bunting. This was written in a manner hardly calculated to elicit a welcoming response. In applying for affiliation, Bunting noted that the Labour Party would have to change its rules and at the same time, he warned, the communists had no intention of surrendering any of their principles or, indeed, their freedom to be critical (SP Bunting, 'Affiliation to the Labour Party', *The International*, 25 May 1923, p. 2).
116 Bunting, *Letters to Rebecca*, p. 56.
117 Bunting, *Letters to Rebecca*, p. 59.

118 In a letter Bill Andrews wrote to Ivon Jones on 17 December 1918 he confided: 'Bunting I don't think altogether likes me.' Quoted in Bunting, *Letters to Rebecca*, p. 51.

119 See for example, CF Glass, 'The Solution of the Native Problem', *The International*, 11 January 1924, p. 1, where Glass wrote, approvingly, about the evidence of cross-racial class solidarity in Cape Town , and how in the Transvaal, sooner or later, 'constant increasing contact in industry ... will result in breaking down the mutual prejudice'.

120 Roux, *SP Bunting*, p. 102.

121 Roux and Roux, *Rebel Pity*, p. 36.

122 Sachs was born 'in a working class family' in Lithuania; his mother had worked in a match factory from the age of seven. The family emigrated to South Africa when Solly was 14. He left school two years later and worked in mining concession stores, joining his first trade union for shop assistants in 1919. He studied at night, and succeeded in matriculating but lack of funds ended his studies at Wits after a year. ES Sachs, *An Open Letter to Garment Workers*, Pacific Press, Johannesburg, 1948, Garment Workers' Union Papers, Wits Historical Papers, AH 1092, Bce 2.1.

123 This is rather confirmed by the reportage in *The International* on YCL solidarity activity. For example, 'Young Workers of the Rand', *The International*, 2 March 1923, p. 4. Other YCL activities at the time included distributing an anti-militarist leaflet in Johannesburg high schools ('The R-r-r-r-ed Plot', *The International*, 2 February 1923, p. 2).

124 'The Boy Scout Movement', *The International*, 22 June 1923, p. 2.

125 CF Glass, 'Organiser's Report', *The International*, p. 3; 'Young Workers' Sporting Association', *The International*, 24 August 1924, p. 4.

126 'Com. Mrs J Chapman's Election Address', *The International*, 25 October 1923, p. 2.

127 In Cape Town's ward six, contested by a communist representing the Unemployment Committee, the candidate, William Green, obtained 311 'single votes' compared to the winner's 411. He failed to secure many 'plural votes', that is, the multiple votes landlords cast for tenants ('The Cape Municipal Elections', *The International*, 14 September 1923, p. 1). *The International* reprinted Wilfrid Harrison's electoral appeal in Cape Town, which included primary compulsory education for 'all children including native and coloured' and the immediate opening of existing high schools and universities to black students' (25 October 1923, p. 2).

128 'May Day and the Cape Unemployed' and 'Unemployed Movement', *The International*, 11 May 1923.

129 Bunting, *Letters to Rebecca*, pp. 71–4.

130 'The Writing on the Wall', *The Torch*, July 1923, p. 2.

131 Dee, 'Clements Kadalie', p. 141.

132 'A Helots' Bill of Rights', *The International*, 1 June 1923, p. 2

133 'Nationalism and War', *The International*, 21 September 1923, p. 2.

134 'Communists in Conference', *The International*, 4 May 1923, p. 4.

135 'The Peep of Day', *The International*, 5 October 1923, p. 1; 'The SAMWU and Native Mine Workers', *The International*, 12 October 1923. International reporting rather suggests this was a leadership-initiated discussion.

136 Editorial, 'Getting the Black Workers', *The International*, 28 December 1923, p. 2.

137 WA Andrews, 'A Letter to a South African in Russia', *The International*, 14 March 1924, p. 3.

138 WH Andrews, 'The South African Trades Union Congress and the Industrial Organization of the Non-European Workers', p. 10, WH Andrews Papers,

Mayibuye Archive, University of the Western Cape, MCH06 3-3-265.

139　Bunting, *Letters to Rebecca*, p. 69.

140　Bunting, *Letters to Rebecca*, p. 63.

141　For Bunting's defences of the Comintern's position on the United Front, see SP
Bunting, 'An Open Letter', *The International*, 30 March 1923, p. 4. Cape Town's
objections were expressed in a second Open Letter by William Harrison (*The
International*, 13 April 1923, p. 4), who argued that Comintern policy was being
determined by short-term Russian foreign policy interests rather than communist
principles.

142　'Turffontein', *The International*, 3 August 1923.

143　'SP Bunting, Trade Unions and the SALP', *The International*, 4 April 1924.

144　Cope, *Comrade Bill*, p. 289.

145　WH Andrews, 'How It Is Done', *The International*, 27 June 1924.

146　'News from Comrade Andrews', *The International*, 24 August 1923, p. 3.

147　Davidson et al., *South Africa and the Communist International*, volume 1, p. 131.

148　Davidson et al., *South Africa and the Communist International*, volume 1, p. 133.

149　Drew, *Discordant Comrades*, p. 71.

150　National Archives document sent by Bob Edgar to Baruch Hirson, of a letter
written by Mbeki as an informer to D/H/C Boy, dated 20 January 1930. I am
grateful to Baruch Hirson for sending a copy to me.

151　Briefly, when it looked likely that the South African Party would stand unopposed
in the elite Parktown neighbourhood of Johannesburg, the communists nominated
Frank Glass, but then withdrew their nomination after the Labour Party
hurriedly decided they would contest the seat after all ('The Parktown Seat', *The
International*, 23 May 1924).

152　Not Wanted', *The International*, 30 May 1924, p. 1.

153　'Election Manifesto', *The International*, 16 May 1924.

154　'The Pact', *The International*, 13 June 1924, p. 7

155　'Free Speech', *The International*, 13 June 1918, p. 1.

156　'Fads and Fancies', *The International*, 4 July 1924, p. 5.

157　SP Bunting, 'A Mess of Pottage', *The International*, 4 July 1924, p. 6.

158　Breckenridge, 'Fighting for a White South Africa', p. 243.

159　David Yudelman, *The Emergence of Modern South Africa: State, Capital and the
Incorporation of Organized Labour on the South African Gold Fields, 1924-1933*,
Greenwood Press, Westport, 1983, pp. 223–9.

160　'Communist Councillors', *The International*, 15 August 1924, p. 4. See *The
International*, 29 August 1924, p. 3 for profiles of candidates.

161　Roux and Roux, *Rebel Pity*, p. 46.

162　Campbell, 'Romantic Revolutionaries', p. 322.

163　Roux, *Time Longer than Rope*, p. 201.

164　'Young Communist Notes', *The International*, 1 February 1924, p. 8.

165　'Black and White', *The Young Worker*, January 1924, p. 2.

166　'Young Communist Notes', *The International*, 25 April 1924, p. 8

167　Davidson et al., *South Africa and the Communist International*, volume 1, p. 137.

168　'Votes for (Native) Women', *The International*, 22 February 1924, p. 2.

169　Bunting, *South African Communists Speak*, p. 80; Simons and Simons, *Class and
Colour*, p. 326.

170　Lerumo, *Fifty Fighting Years*, p. 52.

171　Cutting from the *Rand Daily Mail*, 18 August 1925, WH Andrews Papers, MCH06
6-3-409.

172　Cope, *Comrade Bill*, p. 301.

173　Roux, *Time Longer than Rope*, p. 69.

174   Roux, *Time Longer than Rope*, p. 197.
175   Helen Bradford, *A Taste of Freedom: The ICU in Rural South Africa, 1924–1930*, Yale University Press, New Haven, 1987, p. 78.
176   Drew, *Discordant Comrades*, p. 78.
177   See JN (from Nancefield), 'Slavery in South Africa' and Kaffir Boy, 'Labour vs. Labour', *The International*, 22 February 1924, p. 3. See also A Native, 'The Curse', *The International*, 7 March 1924; Kaffir Boy, 'Is the Frying-Pan Better than the Fire?', *The International*, 16 May 1924, p. 3.
178   'Native Views of Coalition', *The International*, 11 July 1924, p. 3.
179   Jonathan Grossman, 'Class Relations and the Communist Party of South Africa 1921–1950', PhD dissertation, University of Warwick, 1985, p. 119.
180   Grossman, 'Class Relations', p. 120.
181   Melanie Yap and Dianne Leong Man, *Colour, Confusion and Concessions: The History of the Chinese in South Africa*, Hong Kong University Press, Hong Kong, 1996, pp. 240–4.
182   La Guma to Anglo-American Secretariat, ECCI, 10 March 1927, in Davidson et al., *South Africa and the Communist International*, volume 1, p. 150.
183   'Natives Urged to Organise', *The Star*, 7 September 1925 (cutting in Lionel Forman Papers, UCT Manuscripts and Archives, BC 581, B1.3). Andrews appeared at the meeting in his capacity as secretary of the South African Association of Employees' Organisations.
184   Bunting to Roux, 15 December 1926, quoted in Sheridan Johns, 'Marxism-Leninism', p. 355.
185   Dee, 'Clements Kadalie', p. 195.
186   Harrison, *Memoirs of a Socialist*, p. 103.
187   Bradford, *A Taste of Freedom*, p. 78.
188   Peter Wickens, *The Industrial and Commercial Workers' Union of South Africa*, Oxford University Press, Cape Town, 1978, pp. 97–9.
189   Dee, 'Clements Kadalie', pp. 151–2.
190   Sylvia Neame, *The Congress Movement: The Unfolding of the Congress Alliance, 1912–1961*, HSRC Press, Cape Town, 2015, volume 2, p. 315.
191   Sylvia Neame, *The Congress Movement*, volume 2, p. 205.
192   Wickens, *The Industrial and Commercial Workers' Union of South Africa*, pp. 83–4.
193   Allison Drew cites documentation in the Comintern files in *Discordant Comrades*, p. 77.
194   Wickens, *Industrial and Commercial Workers' Union*, p. 104.
195   Simons and Simons, *Class and Colour*, pp. 269–71.
196   J La Guma, General Secretary's Report on Inspection of the Branches, 6 March 1926, Lionel Forman Papers, BC 581, B.2.7.
197   Laurie Greene, *The International*, 6 August 1926; *The International*, 13 August 1926. See Neame, *The Congress Movement*, volume 2, pp. 185–6.
198   Neame, *The Congress Movement*, volume 2, pp. 207–8.
199   Dee, 'Clements Kadalie', p. 199.
200   Neame, *The Congress Movement*, volume 3, p. 212.
201   Simons and Simons, *Class and Colour*, p. 356.
202   Wickens, *The Industrial and Commercial Workers' Union*, p. 108.
203   Wickens, *The Industrial and Commercial Workers' Union*, p. 106.
204   Wickens, citing a report in the ICU's newspaper (*The Industrial and Commercial Workers' Union*, p. 111).
205   As reported in *The Star* on 21 January 1927, cited in Neame, *The Congress Movement*, volume 2, p. 219.
206   Wickens, *The Industrial and Commercial Workers' Union*, p. 131.

207   Wickens, *The Industrial and Commercial Workers' Union*, p. 136.
208   Creech Jones to Kadalie, 15 September 1927, Lionel Forman Papers, BC 581, B3.87.
209   Ethelreda Lewis to Winifred Holtby, 4 February 1928, Industrial and Commercial Union Records, 1925–1947, Wits Historical Papers, A 924, A6.1.
210   'Natives Urged to Organise', *The Star*, 7 September 1925.
211   Kadalie was very critical of La Guma's administration of the headquarters; he felt the general secretary was too office-bound and overly bureaucratic (Neame, *The Congress Movement*, volume 2, pp. 214–15).
212   WH Andrews, 'The South African Trades Union Congress and the Industrial Organization of the Non-European Workers', p. 5.
213   Wickens, *The Industrial and Commercial Workers' Union*, p. 129.
214   Wickens, *The Industrial and Commercial Workers' Union*, pp. 131–2. See also Neame, *The Congress Movement*, volume 2, p. 249.
215   Neame, *The Congress Movement*, volume 2, p. 226.
216   Drew, *Discordant Comrades*, p. 82; Neame, *The Congress Movement*, volume 2, p. 225.
217   James La Guma, Statement to Praesidium, ECCI, 16 March 1927, in Davidson et al., *South Africa and the Communist International*, volume 1, p. 151.
218   SP Bunting at the Fourth National Conference, 16 December 1925, in Davidson et al., *South Africa and the Communist International*, volume 1, p. 141.
219   Davidson et al., *South Africa and the Communist International*, volume 1, p. 60.
220   Report of J den Bekker and S Barlin to ECCI, 25 January 1921, in Davidson et al., *South Africa and the Communist International*, volume 1, p. 60.
221   'Young Communist Notes', *The International*, 24 April 1923, p. 8.
222   Drew, *Discordant Comrades*, p. 77; Drew, *Between Empire and Revolution*, p. 142.
223   Davidson et al., *South Africa and the Communist International*, volume 1, pp. 143–4.
224   Davidson et al., *South Africa and the Communist International*, volume 1, p. 146.
225   J den Bakker to M Kobetsky, March 1921, in Davidson et al., *South Africa and the Communist International*, volume 1, p. 65.
226   DI Jones to ECCI, 15 March 1922, in Davidson et al., *South Africa and the Communist International*, volume 1, p. 91.
227   DI Jones to M Rakosi, 23 May 1922, in Davidson et al., *South Africa and the Communist International*, volume 1, p. 110.
228   Bunting, *Letters to Rebecca*, p. 72.
229   Davidson et al., *South Africa and the Communist International*, volume 1, p. 142.
230   Sachs to Comintern, January 1926, in Davidson et al., *South Africa and the Communist International*, volume 1, p. 144.
231   Bunting to Secretary, ECCI, 3 November 1926, in Davidson et al., *South Africa and the Communist International*, volume 1, pp. 146–8.
232   Mia Roth, *The Communist Party of South Africa: Racism, Eurocentricity and Moscow, 1921–1950*, Partridge, Johannesburg, 2016, pp. 72–7.
233   Johnny Gomas, interviewed by Sylvia Neame, 1962, transcript, p. 10, Sylvia Neame Papers, Wits Historical Papers, A 2729.
234   Edward R Roux Papers, Wits Historical Papers, A 2667, B1. 8.
235   Cited in Drew, *Discordant Comrades*, p. 79.
236   Rebecca Bunting, interviewed by Sylvia Neame, transcript, p. 32, Sylvia Neame Papers.
237   Andrew Thorpe, 'Comintern "Control" of the Communist Party of Great Britain', *English Historical Review*, 113, 452, 1998, pp. 649–50.
238   Statement showing ICU head office income and expenditure, 1 May to 31 October 1927, Lionel Forman Papers, BC 581, B2.143.

239 ICU National Council Meeting Minutes, 18–25 November 1927, Lionel Forman Papers, BC 581, B3.168.
240 Henri Danielle Tyamzashe, 'Summarised History of the ICU', typescript, p. 21, Ambrose Lynn Saffery Papers, Wits Historical Papers, AD 1178, B5.1941.
241 Neame, *The Congress Movement*, volume 2, p. 105.
242 Sheridan Johns, 'The Birth of the Communist Party of South Africa', *International Journal of African Historical Studies*, 9, 3, 1976, p. 360.
243 Johanningsmeier, 'Communists and Black Freedom Movements in South Africa and the United States, 1919-1950', p. 177.
244 For a discussion of the relationship between Jewish traders and black South Africans in shops used by black workers, see Leibl Feldman, *The Jews of Johannesburg*, Isaac and Jessie Kaplan Centre, University of Cape Town, Cape Town, 2007, p. 192.
245 And not just in South Africa. In Limerick, in Western Ireland, two weeks after the appearance of the Johannesburg Soviet a syndicalist strike movement seized control of the municipal administration and the Strike Committee's leaders happily agreed with journalists in characterising their local regime as a 'Soviet'. See DR O'Connor Lysaght, *The Story of the Limerick Soviet: The 1919 General Strike against British Militarism*, Limerick Soviet Commemoration Committee, Limerick, 2009, pp. 6–11. The Johannesburg events were reported only cursorily in the Irish press, in a brief Reuters dispatch, for example, published in the *Irish Times* ('Labour Settlement in Johannesburg', 7 April 1919), and not mentioned at all in the *Limerick Leader*. It is unlikely, then, that the Limerick strikers were taking any cues from Johannesburg.
246 From his report on the tactics of the Russian Communist Party, 5 July 1921 (VI Lenin, *Collected Works*, volume 32, Progress Publishers, Moscow, 1977, p. 482). Jones did concede at the time that the ANC might have the potential to be a revolutionary movement.
247 Quotations and citations in David J Mason, 'Race, Class and National Liberation: Some Implications of the Policy Dilemmas of the International Socialist League and the Communist Party of South Africa', MSc dissertation, Social Sciences, University of Bristol, 1971, pp. 12–13.
248 Davidson et al., *South Africa and the Communist International*, volume 1, p. 143.
249 Bryan D Palmer, 'Rethinking the Historiography of United States Communism', *American Communist History*, 2, 2, 2003, p. 171.

Chapter 3

1 For a short period from March 1926 until the end of 1927, a British Secretariat at Comintern's headquarters oversaw the activities of the British, Irish, Dutch, Australian and South African affiliates. In December 1927, this body was replaced with the Anglo-American Secretariat, which exercised its jurisdiction over the American parties together with the British and British Dominion parties (Sheridan Johns, 'Imperial Preference: The Case of the Comintern and South Africa', Western Australian African Studies Seminar, Perth, 7 August 1993, p. 5).
2 Allison Drew, *Between Empire and Revolution: A Life of Sidney Bunting, 1873– 1936*, Pickering and Chatto, London, 2007, p. 150.
3 Johnny Gomas, interviewed by Sylvia Neame, 1962, transcript, p. 12, Sylvia Neame Papers, Wits Historical Papers.
4 Jimmy La Guma was born in Bloemfontein in 1894. His French and Madagascan parents died when he was in his infancy and he was fostered by a washerwoman who sent him to work in a bakery. Running away from a subsequent apprenticeship as a leather worker, he accepted a labour contract to work in South West Africa,

the first indication of a restlessness which would become a key feature in his personality and politics. During the First World War he found employment in the diamond fields, forming a workers' committee in 1918, and leading a strike in Pomona. In 1919 he learned about the ICU and, after contacting Kadalie, set up a branch in Lüderitz. Two years later Kadalie asked him to help organise the ICU in Cape Town. He joined the Communist Party in 1925, first working with party members during a seamen's strike. He moved to Johannesburg when the ICU established its headquarters there; by this stage he was assistant general secretary of the union. He was forced out of the ICU at the end of 1926 together with other communists; he had been the main instigator of an investigation into corruption in the organisation's leadership.

5   The text of this document is not included in the Davidson volume, nor is it included in the documents available online. Its reference number is RGASPI, 495/2/71/175-80. For the content of the resolution, see Oleksa Drachewych, 'The Comintern and the Communist Parties of South Africa, Canada and Australia on the Questions of Imperialism, Nationalism and Race', PhD dissertation, McMaster University, July 2017 (/drachewych_oleksa_m_2017september_PhD.pdf), p. 142.

6   Apollon Davidson, Irina Filatova, Valentin Gorodnov and Sheridan Johns, *South Africa and the Communist International: A Documentary History*, volume 1: *Socialist Pilgrims to Bolshevik Footsoldiers, 1919–1930*, Frank Cass, London, 2003, p. 153.

7   Davidson et al., *South Africa and the Communist International*, volume 1, pp. 154–5.

8   Allison Drew, *Discordant Comrades: Identities and Loyalties on the South African Left*, Ashgate, Aldershot, 2000, p. 20.

9   Alex La Guma, *Jimmy La Guma: A Biography*, Friends of the South African Library, Cape Town, 1997, p. 35; Doreen Musson, *Johnny Gomas: Voice of the Working Class*, Buchu Books, Cape Town, 1987, p. 48.

10 La Guma, *Jimmy La Guma*, p. 35.

11 HJ and RE Simons, *Class and Colour in South Africa, 1850–1950*, Penguin, Harmondsworth, 1969, p. 405; Edward Roux, *SP Bunting: A Political Biography*, 2nd edn, Mayibuye Books, Cape Town, 1993.

12 Douglas Wolton, letter to Jack Simons, 23 August 1967, Simons Papers, UCT Manuscripts and Archives, BC 1081.

13 Brian Bunting, *Moses Kotane: South African Revolutionary*, Inkululeko Publications, London, 1975, p. 57. Douglas Wolton attributed to La Guma the main role in writing the slogan and its justification when I interviewed him on 12 September 1984.

14 *International Press Correspondence*, 53, 23 August 1928, p. 943.

15 Roux, *SP Bunting*, p. 122.

16 La Guma, *Jimmy La Guma*, pp. 31–2.

17 Sheridan Johns III, 'Marxism-Leninism in a Multi-racial Environment: The Origins and Early History of the Communist Party of South Africa, 1914–1932', PhD dissertation, Department of Government, Harvard University, 1965.

18 Wilson Record, *The Negro and the Communist Party*, University of North Carolina Press, Chapel Hill, 1951, p. 55.

19 Record, *The Negro and the Communist Party*, p. 59.

20 Johns, 'Marxism-Leninism', p. 432.

21 Drachewych, 'The Comintern and Anti-Imperialism', pp. 143–5.

22 Stephen F Cohen, *Bukharin and the Bolshevik Revolution: A Political Biography, 1888–1938*, Oxford University Press, Oxford, 1980, p. 257.

23 Roux, *SP Bunting*, p. 125.

24 Johns, 'Marxism-Leninism', p. 433.

25 Davidson et al., *South Africa and the Communist International*, volume 1, p. 161.

26   Allison Drew, *South Africa's Radical Tradition: A Documentary History*, volume 1: *1907–1950*, UCT Press, Cape Town, 1996, p. 20.

27   Jonathan Grossman, 'Class Relations and the Communist Party of South Africa, 1921–1950', PhD dissertation, Department of Sociology, University of Warwick, 1985, p. 152.

28   Robert H Davies, *Capital, State and White Labour in South Africa, 1900–1960*, Harvester Press, Brighton, 1979, p. 195.

29   Grossman, 'Class Relations', p. 105.

30   Clements Kadalie, *My Life and the ICU: The Autobiography of a Black Trade Unionist in South Africa*, Frank Cass, London, 1970, p. 196.

31   Johns, 'Marxism-Leninism', p. 375.

32   Brian Bunting, *South African Communists Speak*, Inkululeko Publications, London, 1981, p. 74.

33   Sylvia Neame, *The Congress Movement: The Unfolding of the Congress Alliance, 1912–1961*, HSRC Press, Cape Town, 2015, volume 2, p. 225; Davidson et al., *South Africa and the Communist International*, volume 1, pp. 153–4.

34   Edward Roux, *Time Longer than Rope*, University of Wisconsin Press, Madison, 1964, p. 172.

35   Roux, *Time Longer than Rope*, p. 210.

36   Miriam Basner, *Am I an African? The Political Memoirs of HM Basner*, Witwatersrand University Press, Johannesburg, 1993, p. 36.

37   In 1931, the Buntings in fact moved to a modest house in more comfortable Kensington, a change they could afford from Rebecca's earnings as a dressmaker (Drew, *Between Empire and Revolution*, 191). Miriam Roth suggests that Bunting could afford a middle-class lifestyle because Comintern paid him a generous salary but she cites no evidence (Mia Roth, *The Communist Party in South Africa: Racism, Eurocentrism and Moscow, 1921–1950*, Partridge, Johannesburg, 2016, p. 28).

38   Drew, *Between Empire and Revolution*, p. 139.

39   Harry Haywood, *Black Bolshevik: The Autobiography of an African American Communist*, Liberation Press, Chicago, 1978, p. 270.

40   Roux, *SP Bunting*, p. 124.

41   Eddie and Win Roux, *Rebel Pity*, Rex Collings, London, 1970, p. 34.

42   Roux and Roux, *Rebel Pity*, p. 5.

43   Roux was not the only communist who was susceptible to Kadalie's charm. When interviewed in 1964, Rebecca Bunting remembered that she and her husband liked Kadalie; indeed, she once told Sidney that 'if I was wasn't married, I would fall in love with him' (Rebecca Bunting, interviewed by Sylvia Neame, 1964, transcript, p. 49, Sylvia Neame Papers).

44   Roux, *Time Longer than Rope*, pp. 210–23.

45   Neame, *The Congress Movement*, volume 2, p. 208.

46   Neame, *The Congress Movement*, volume 2, p. 320.

47   Roux, *SP Bunting*, p. 102.

48   Roux and Roux, *Rebel Pity*, p. 38.

49   Neame, *The Congress Movement*, volume 2, p. 206.

50   Musson, *Johnny Gomas*, p. 49.

51   Davidson et al., *South Africa and the Communist International*, volume 1, p. 166.

52   Drew, *South Africa's Radical Tradition*, p. 89.

53   Bernard Sachs, *Multitude of Dreams*, Kayor Publishing House, Johannesburg, 1949, p. 136.

54   National Archive document sent by Bob Edgar to Baruch Hirson, of a letter written by Mbeki as an informer to D/H/C Boy, dated 20 January 1930.

55   Davidson et al., *South Africa and the Communist International*, volume 1, p. 166.

56   Davidson et al., *South Africa and the Communist International*, volume 1, p. 170.
57   Davidson et al., *South Africa and the Communist International*, volume 1, pp. 172 and 178.
58   Johns, 'Marxism-Leninism', p. 417.
59   Haywood, *Black Bolshevik*, p. 235.
60   Bunting, *Moses Kotane*, p. 33.
61   Bunting, *Moses Kotane*, p. 31.
62   Roger Field, Martin Klammer and Blanche La Guma, *In the Dark with My Dress on Fire: My Life in Cape Town, London, Havana and Home Again*, Jacana Media, Johannesburg, 2011, pp. 16–20.
63   Davidson et al., *South Africa and the Communist International*, volume 1, p. 178.
64   Davidson et al., *South Africa and the Communist International*, volume 1, p. 178.
65   Douglas Wolton, interviewed by Sylvia Neame, 13 May 1960, p. 1, Sylvia Neame Papers.
66   Davidson et al., *South Africa and the Communist International*, volume 1, 179
67   Davidson et al., *South Africa and the Communist International*, volume 1, p. 179.
68   Davidson et al., *South Africa and the Communist International*, volume 1, p. 178.
69   Secretary of Interior to Secretary of Native Affairs, South African National Archives, NTS 2707, 185-301, p. 28.
70   Davidson et al., *South Africa and the Communist International*, volume 1, p. 182
71   Davidson et al., *South Africa and the Communist International*, volume 1, p. 173.
72   Rebecca Bunting, interviewed by Sylvia Neame, 1968, transcript, p. 32, Sylvia Neame Papers.
73   Haywood, *Black Bolshevik*, pp. 215–16.
74   Johns, 'Marxism-Leninism', p. 392.
75   Drew, *Discordant Comrades*, p. 99.
76   Simons and Simons, *Class and Colour*, p. 391.
77   Drew, *South Africa's Radical Tradition*, p. 60.
78   *South African Worker*, 25 February 1927.
79   *Umsebenzi*, 28 February 1929 and 10 October 1930.
80   Secretary of Interior to Secretary of Native Affairs, 19 February, 1929, South African National Archives, NTS 181-301, p. 28.
81   Robert Edgar, *The Making of an African Communist: Edwin Thabo Mofutsanyana and the CPSA, 1927–1939*, University of South Africa, Pretoria, 2005, p. 9.
82   Julie Wells, 'The Day the Town Stood Still: Women in Resistance in Potchefstroom, 1912–1930', in Belinda Bozzoli (ed.), *Town and Countryside in the Transvaal*, Ravan Press, Johannesburg, 1983, p. 286.
83   Drew, *Discordant Comrades*, p. 85.
84   Edgar, *The Making of an African Communist*, pp. 11–12; Robin D Kelley, 'The Religious Odyssey of Black Communists in South Africa and the US South: Observations from the 1920s and 1930s', paper given at ASA annual conference, Atlanta, 2–5 November 1989, p. 3.
85   Johns, 'Marxism-Leninism', p. 399.
86   Roth, *The Communist Party in South Africa*, pp. 94–5.
87   Edgar, *The Making of an African Communist*, p. 10.
88   Roth, *The Communist Party in South Africa*, p. 81.
89   Memo on the Federation of Non-European Trade Unions, 7 February 1929, South African National Archives, ARB 3608, 1103, 1.2.
90   'Natives and the Red International', letter from William Ballinger to *The Star*, 19 February 1929, press cutting in South African National Archives, ARB 3608, 1103, 1.2.
91   CW Cousins to the Minister, 10 January 1929, South African National Archives, ARB 3608, 1103, 1.2.

92 Chief Inspector Ivan Walker to the Under-Secretary, 'Communist Propaganda among the Natives', 8 May 1929, South African National Archives, ARB 3071, 1103, p. 1.

93 Davidson et al., *South Africa and the Communist International*, volume 1, p. 200. ES Sachs, writing in 1953, claimed that at its peak the Federation had an affiliate strength of 3,000 (ES Sachs, *The Choice before South Africa*, self-published, London, 1953, p. 159).

94 Grossman, 'Class Relations', p. 197.

95 Ivan Walker to the Secretary, 10 August 1929, File on Native Labour Organization: Correspondence, South African National Archives, ARB 3608, 1103, 1.2.

96 David Duncan, *The Mills of God: The State and African Labour in South Africa, 1918–1948*, Witwatersrand University Press, Johannesburg, 1995, pp. 155 and 187.

97 Jon Lewis, *Industrialisation and Trade Union Organisation in South Africa, 1924–55*, Cambridge University Press, Cambridge, 1984, pp. 56–62.

98 Iris Berger, 'Solidarity Fragmented: Garment Workers of the Transvaal', in Shula Marks and Stanley Trapido (eds), *Class, Race and Nationalism in Twentieth Century South Africa*, Longman, London, 1987, p. 129.

99 Sidney Bunting, 'Recent Trade Unionism in South Africa', document submitted to the Sixth Congress of the Communist International, ER Roux Papers, Wits Historical Papers, A 2667, A3.

100 Roux and Roux, *Rebel Pity*, p. 62.

101 Roux and Roux, *Rebel Pity*, p. 63.

102 Roux, *SP Bunting*, p. 122.

103 Haywood, *Black Bolshevik*, p. 240.

104 Drew, *Between Empire and Revolution*, p. 159.

105 Speech by Rebecca Bunting, ER Roux Papers, A 2667, A4.

106 Davidson et al., *South Africa and the Communist International*, volume 1, p. 186.

107 Roux, *SP Bunting*, p. 129.

108 Davidson et al., *South Africa and the Communist International*, volume 1, p. 185.

109 Drew, *South Africa's Radical Tradition*, pp. 95–7.

110 Drew, *South Africa's Radical Tradition*, p. 93.

111 ER Roux to Douglas Wolton, 22 November 1928, ER Roux Papers, A 2667, B1.

112 Davidson et al., *South Africa and the Communist International*, volume 1, p. 186.

113 Drew, *South Africa's Radical Tradition*, pp. 87–93.

114 Davidson et al., *South Africa and the Communist International*, volume 1, pp. 188–90.

115 Musson, *Johnny Gomas*, p. 48; Haywood, *Black Bolshevik*, p. 272.

116 Drew, *South Africa's Radical Tradition*, p. 95.

117 Roux, *SP Bunting*, p. 129.

118 Bunting, *South African Communists Speak*, pp. 91–7.

119 Allison Drew, *Between Empire and Revolution*, pp. 162–3.

120 RK Cope, *Comrade Bill: The Life and Times of WH Andrews, Worker's Leader*, Stewart Printing Company, Cape Town, 1944, p. 312.

121 Johns, 'Marxism-Leninism', pp. 472–3.

122 Allison Drew, *Between Empire and Revolution*, p. 165.

123 Bunting, *South African Communists Speak*, p. 106.

124 Bunting, *Moses Kotane*, p. 40.

125 Wilfrid H Harrison, *Memoirs of a Socialist in South Africa, 1903–1947*, Stewart Printing Company, Cape Town, 1947, p. 103.

126 Harrison, *Memoirs of a Socialist*, p. 103.

127 Harrison, *Memoirs of a Socialist*, p. 104.

128 Harrison, *Memoirs of a Socialist*, p. 106.

129 Simons and Simons, *Class and Colour in South Africa*, p. 410.

130 Grossman, 'Class Relations', p. 137.
131 Drew, *Discordant Comrades*, p. 102.
132 Johns, 'Marxism-Leninism', p. 500.
133 Davidson et al., *South Africa and the Communist International*, volume 1, p. 188.
134 Davidson et al., *South Africa and the Communist International*, volume 1, pp. 157–8.
135 Bunting and Kadalie kept in touch. Kadalie on at least one occasion after 1927 approached Bunting, then still the party's treasurer, for money to support his organisation, writing at the end of 1928 to request £8 for paying the ICU's telephone account (Bennie Weinbren, interviewed by Sylvia Neame, 1962, Sylvia Neame Papers).
136 Drew, *South Africa's Radical Tradition*, p. 101; Davidson et al., *South Africa and the Communist International*, volume 1, p. 198.
137 Bunting, *Moses Kotane*, p. 41.
138 Drew, *Discordant Comrades*, p. 103.
139 Bunting, *South African Communists Speak*, p. 102.
140 Drew, *Between Empire and Revolution*, p. 171.
141 Rebecca Bunting, interviewed by Sylvia Neame, 1968, Sylvia Neame Papers.
142 Roux, *SP Bunting*, p. 136; Sachs, *Multitude of Dreams*, p. 163.
143 Rebecca Bunting, interviewed by Sylvia Neame, 1968, transcript, p. 15, Sylvia Neame Papers; Drew, *Between Empire and Revolution*, p. 172.
144 The text is included in the transcript of Sylvia Neame's interview with Rebecca Bunting, 1968, p. 15, Sylvia Neame Papers.
145 Rebecca Bunting, interviewed by Sylvia Neame, 1968, transcript, p. 27, Sylvia Neame Papers.
146 Drew, *Between Empire and Revolution*, p. 179.
147 Drew, *Between Empire and Revolution*, p. 173.
148 Drew, *Between Empire and Revolution*, p. 176.
149 Roux, *SP Bunting*, p. 138.
150 Rebecca Bunting, interviewed by Sylvia Neame, 1968, transcript, p. 17, Sylvia Neame Papers.
151 Drew, *Between Empire and Revolution*, p. 180.
152 Wolton might have expected to do better. He was familiar with the Cape Flats as he'd been an energetic district secretary in Cape Town between 1925 and 1927, working hard to build an African following for the party, and finding a group of fresh recruits in Ndabeni location. During the 1929 campaign he had a party group to help in in Ndabeni and he also held meetings in Langa, then under construction (Douglas Wolton, interviewed by Sylvia Neame, 13 May 1960, transcript, pp. 5–6, Sylvia Neame Papers). The constituency included Salt River, inhabited by white workers, many employed on the railway; here Wolton was helped by Gomas and La Guma, both of whom were 'received well' at meetings (Douglas Wolton, interviewed by Sylvia Neame, 13 May 1960, transcript, p. 14). Wolton himself, reporting to Comintern, claimed that other communist leaders had been unsupportive though he also acknowledged insufficient party work in the constituency before the electoral season (Drew, *Discordant Comrades*, p. 106).
153 Sachs, *Multitude of Dreams*, p. 163.
154 Davidson et al., *South Africa and the Communist International*, volume 1, p. 227.
155 Simons and Simons, *Class and Colour in South Africa*, p. 418.
156 Roux, *SP Bunting*, pp. 141–2.
157 Roux, *SP Bunting*, p. 142.
158 Davidson et al., *South Africa and the Communist International*, volume 1, p. 226.
159 Drew, *South Africa's Radical Tradition*, p. 106.
160 There is a flyer for a meeting to consider the formation of the League dated 25

August 1929 in the SP Bunting Papers (Wits Historical Papers, A 949, A1.4), which refers to the aim of the 'extension of the native franchise to the other provinces'.

161   Drew, *Between Empire and Revolution*, p. 190.

162   G Makabeni to SP Bunting, 4 October 1929, ER Roux Papers, A 2667, B2.

163   Roth, *The Communist Party in South Africa*, p. 88.

164   Sergeant WJ Markman to Divisional CI Officer, CID, Kimberley, 4 October 1929, 'League of African Rights', South African National Archives, JUS 1193 1/400/29.

165   Davidson et al., *South Africa and the Communist International*, volume 1, pp. 218–19.

166   Sheridan Johns, 'Internationalism, Intervention, or Irrelevance? Comintern Emissaries from Moscow to the Communist Party of South Africa, 1929–1937', Canadian African Studies Association, Ottawa, 2–5 June 1998, pp. 3–4.

167   Allison Drew, 'The New Line in South Africa: Ideology and Perception in a Very Small Communist Party', in Matthew Worley (ed.), *In Search of Revolution: International Communist Parties in the Third Period*, IB Tauris, London, 2004, p. 343.

168   Davidson et al., *South Africa and the Communist International*, volume 1, p. 119.

169   Davidson et al., *South Africa and the Communist International*, volume 1, pp. 225–7.

170   Richard Weisfelder, 'Early Voices of Protest in Basutoland', *African Studies Review*, 17, 2, 1974, p. 403.

171   Roux, *Time Longer than Rope*, p. 220.

172   GM Haliburton, 'Walter Matitta and Josiel Lefela: A Prophet and a Politician in Lesotho', *Journal of Religion in Africa*, 7, 2, 1975, p. 125.

173   See Edgar, *The Making of an African Communist*, p. 32. In early 1938, Lekhotla applied for affiliation to the party ('On the Situation of the CPSA', 4 April 1938, Comintern Archives Online, 495/20/666).

174   Drew, *South Africa's Radical Tradition*, p. 117

175   Neame, *The Congress Tradition*, volume 2, p. 185.

176   LH Greene to Douglas Wolton, 2 January 1929, ER Roux Papers, A 2667, B2. See also Gilbert Coka, 'The Story of Gilbert Coka', in Margery Perham (ed.), *Ten Africans*, Faber and Faber, London, 1963, p. 313.

177   On Champion's intentions in dealing with communists: letter to Howard Pim, [1929], Ballinger Papers, Wits Historical Papers, AD 1178, B4. On the marches: Tim Nuttall, 'Class, Race and Nation: African Politics in Durban, 1929–1949', DPhil dissertation, University of Oxford, 1991, p. 83.

178   Drew, *South Africa's Radical Tradition*, pp. 22–3; Drew, *Discordant Comrades*, pp. 112–15.

179   Haywood, *Black Bolshevik*, pp. 257–8.

180   Cohen, *Bukharin and the Bolshevik Revolution*, p. 291.

181   Johns, 'Marxism-Leninism', p. 491.

182   Davidson et al., *South Africa and the Communist International*, volume 1, pp. 292–3.

183   'To the CPSA. Basic Organisational Tasks', letter from the Comintern Executive, 2 September 1930, Online Comintern Archives, 425/4/399/1-10.

184   Davidson et al., *South Africa and the Communist International*, volume 1, p. 14.

185   Drew, *Between Empire and Revolution*, pp. 194–7.

186   Davidson et al., *South Africa and the Communist International*, volume 1, p. 234.

187   *Rand Daily Mail*, 17 December 1929; Philip Bonner, 'South African Society and Culture, 1910–1948', in Robert Ross, Anne Kelk Mager and Bill Nasson, *The Cambridge History of South Africa*, volume 2, Cambridge University Press, New York, 2011, p. 302.

188   Drew, *Discordant Comrades*, p. 117.

189   Bunting was running the Johannesburg party office during 1930 though the party secretary was Johnny Gomas, based in Cape Town. His relations with William

Thibedi deteriorated after Thibedi's temporary restoration to the Federation's secretaryship. Bunting wrote to Gomas on 22 September 1930, complaining about Thibedi's 'serious mischiefmaking' and on 29 November Bunting in a letter to Eddie Roux made an exasperated reference to Thibedi using 'the cry of white domination to cover peculation' (SP Bunting Papers, A 949, A4.2).

190   Bunting, *Moses Kotane*, p. 57.

191   Douglas G Wolton, *Whither South Africa?*, Lawrence and Wishart, London, 1947, p. 68.

192   Roux and Roux, *Rebel Pity*, p. 112.

193   Historicus, 'Albert Nzula: Our First African General Secretary', *African Communist*, 65, 1976, p. 93.

194   Robin Cohen, 'Introduction', in AT Nzula, II Potekhin and AZ Zusmanovich, *Forced Labour in Colonial Africa*, reprint, Zed Press, London, 1979, p. 9.

195   Davidson et al., *South Africa and the Communist International*, volume 1, p. 218.

196   Sylvia Neame, *The Congress Movement*, volume 3, p. 18.

197   Bunting, *South African Communists Speak*, p. 108.

198   VL Allen, *The History of Black Mineworkers in South Africa*, volume I, Moor Press, Keighley, 1992, pp. 331–3.

199   Johns, 'Marxism-Leninism', p. 497.

200   Ray Alexander Simons, *All My Life and All My Strength*, STE Publishers, Johannesburg, 2004, p. 57.

201   Davidson et al., *South Africa and the Communist International*, volume 1, p. 235.

202   Drew, *South Africa's Radical Tradition*, p. 113.

203   Roux and Roux, *Rebel Pity*, p. 85.

204   Roux and Roux, *Rebel Pity*, p. 89.

205   Roux and Roux, *Rebel Pity*, p. 90.

206   Grossman, 'Class Relations', p. 210.

207   Willie Hofmeyr, 'Rural Popular Organisation and Its Problems: Struggles in the Western Cape, 1929–1930', *Africa Perspective*, 22, 1983, pp. 28–9; Gavin Lewis, *Between the Wire and the Wall: A History of South African 'Coloured' Politics*, St. Martin's Press, New York, 1987, p. 113.

208   Davidson et al., *South Africa and the Communist International*, volume 1, p. 219.

209   Lewis, *Between the Wire and the Wall*, pp. 108–10.

210   Colin Bundy, 'Land and Liberation: Popular Protest and the National Liberation Movements in South Africa, 1920–1960', in Shula Marks and Stanley Trapido (eds), *Class, Race and Nationalism in Twentieth Century South Africa*, Longman, London, 1987, p. 265; Musson, *Johnny Gomas*, p. 64.

211   Apollon Davidson, Irina Filatova, Valentin Gorodnov and Sheridan Johns, *South Africa and the Communist International: A Documentary History*, volume 2: *Bolshevik Footsoldiers to Victims of Bolshevisation, 1931–1939*, Frank Cass, London, 2003, p. 82.

212   On Pettersen, see Davidson et al., *South Africa and the Communist International*, volume 1, 44. Pettersen owned a chandler's business in Durban and was also the proprietor of a whaling station, Lina Linga, that employed a sizeable African workforce of 200, harshly supervised according to eyewitness reports from Norwegian sailors (Kirsten Alsaker Kjerland and Bjørn Enge Bertelsen, *Navigating Colonial Orders: Norwegian Entrepreneurship in Africa and Oceania*, Berghahn Books, Oxford and New York, 2015, p. 131). Bunting described him to Gomas as 'one of those who can be used in so far as they can be made useful, but not to be treated as a thick or thin reliable and staunch comrade' (Bunting Papers, A 949, A4.A2).

213   Pettersen would eventually win a municipal election in Durban on his sixth

attempt, in 1935. From 1932 he campaigned on an anti-Indian platform. His biographer suggests that his hostility to Indians was a consequence of the Natal Indian Congress's decision in 1930 to recommend voters to support the Labour Party. In the 1929 election, Pettersen had published a leaflet in which he recalled his support for Gandhi and strikes by Indian plantation workers in 1913. In 1948 Pettersen joined the Senate as a member of the National Party (FA Mouton, 'Van matroos tot senator: Die kleuryke en stormagtige politieke loopbaan van SM Pettersen', *Kleio*, 19,1, 1987, pp. 37–9).

214   SP Bunting to CPSA Secretary (Johnny Gomas), 20 July 1929, Bunting Papers, A 949, A4.2.

215   Drew, *South Africa's Radical Tradition*, p. 113; Grossman, 'Class Relations', p. 182.

216   Paul La Hausse, 'The Dispersal of the Regiments: African Popular Protest in Durban, 1930', *Journal of Natal and Zulu History*, 10, 1987.

217   Neame, *The Congress Movement*, volume 3, p. 17

218   Naboth Mokgatle, *The Autobiography of an Unknown South African*, University of California Press, Berkeley, 1971, pp. 174–80.

219   Sifiso Ndlovu, 'Johannes Nkosi and the Communist Party of South Africa: Images of Blood River and King Dingaan, 1920s–1930', *History and Theory*, 39, 4, 2000, p. 121. Ndlovu also cites reportage in the *Natal Advertiser* suggesting that at least 3,000 people gave up their passes for burning.

220   Ndlovu, 'Johannes Nkosi', pp. 127–8.

221   Sachs, *Multitude of Dreams*, p. 155. For doubt as to whether the police killed Nkosi, see Roth, *The Communist Party of South Africa*, p. 182. Sifiso Ndlovu cites testimony from the inquest report suggesting that Nkosi was shot after being taken into custody unconscious; other contemporary reports accused police of stabbing him, At the inquest black police were blamed by white witnesses for the violence used against demonstrators (Ndlovu, 'Johannes Nkosi', p. 123).

222   Grossman, 'Class Relations', p. 193, citing *Umsebenzi*, 6 February 1931.

223   Roux, *Time Longer than Rope*, pp. 260–1.

224   Davidson et al., *South Africa and the Communist International*, volume 1, p. 239.

225   Bundy, 'Land and Liberation', p. 261.

226   Davidson et al., *South Africa and the Communist International*, volume 1, p. 242.

227   'To the CPSA: Basic Organisational Tasks', letter from the Comintern Executive, 2 September 1930, Online Comintern Archives, 425/4/399/1-10.

228   JB Marks, interviewed by Sylvia Neame, August 1969, p. 11, Sylvia Neame Papers.

229   JB Marks, interviewed by Sylvia Neame, August 1969, p. 1, Sylvia Neame Papers.

230   Wolton used the phrase 'liberal paternalism' to describe Bunting's relationship with Africans (Douglas Wolton, interviewed by Sylvia Neame, 13 May 1960, p. 6, Sylvia Neame Papers).

231   Drew, *Between Empire and Revolution*, p. 200.

232   Roux and Roux, *Rebel Pity*, p. 128.

233   Davidson et al., *South Africa and the Communist International*, volume 2, pp. 19–20. Later Kotane would make amends; he wrote a generous tribute to Bunting suggesting that he had been recruited by him in a letter to Rebecca on her 80th birthday. 'If it weren't for you many of us would not have joined the party, you and Sidney' and she herself was 'the mother of all of us', he wrote (Rebecca Bunting, interviewed by Sylvia Neame, 1968, pp. 8 and 50, Sylvia Neame Papers).

234   Drew, *Between Empire and Revolution*, p. 200.

235   Roux, *SP Bunting*, p. 26.

236   Davidson et al., *South Africa and the Communist International*, volume 1, pp. 247–8.

237   Drew, *South Africa's Radical Tradition*, p. 111.

238   Johns, 'Marxism-Leninism', p. 535.

239 Drew, *South Africa's Radical Tradition*, pp. 114–19.
240 A Lerumo, *Fifty Fighting Years: The Communist Party of South Africa, 1921–1971*, Inkululeko Publications, London, 1980, p. 64.
241 Johns, 'Marxism-Leninism', p. 541.
242 According to his statement written in Moscow in 1937, Back joined the Latvian party in 1929, shortly before his departure to South Africa, though before then he had also been involved in a communist student group at the University of Riga.
243 Roux, *Time Longer than Rope*, p. 46. Lazar Bach was born in Latvia in 1906, the son of a then-prosperous leather factory owner. During the Russian Revolution, in 1920, his father was arrested by the Soviet authorities in Rostov for speculation, and narrowly escaped shooting. According to his NKVD file, Lazar attended university in Riga but had to stop attending after his father's business failed. He joined the Latvian Communist Party in 1929 after becoming a member of a leather workers' union and being involved in a communist group at the University in Riga. His experience in the Latvian party, brief as it may have been, provided him with familiarity with illegal activism which would have been exceptional in the South African party (Handwritten statement, translated from Russian, 1937, Lazar Bach Papers, Wits Historical Papers, A 3381f). Without warning his party comrades, Lazar Bach accompanied his father and three brothers to South Africa and the family bought a tannery in Paarl. He left home after joining the South African party in Cape Town, though he maintained close connections with his family, as one Comintern official noted disapprovingly (Davidson et al., *South Africa and the Communist International*, volume 2, p. 72).
244 Davidson et al., *South Africa and the Communist International*, volume 1, pp. 251–7.
245 Drew, *Between Empire and Revolution*, pp. 203–4.
246 Johns, 'Marxism-Leninism', pp. 553–5.
247 'Imprecor' was the abbreviation used to refer to the Comintern's journal, *International Press Correspondence*, essentially a record of all important statements, speeches and documents released by Comintern's headquarters.
248 Drew, *Discordant Comrades*, p. 121; Bunting, *Moses Kotane*, p. 61.
249 Bunting, *Moses Kotane*, p. 55.
250 Johns, 'Marxism-Leninism', p. 555.
251 Roux and Roux, *Rebel Pity*, p. 99.
252 Drew, *Discordant Comrades*, pp. 123–4.
253 Roux and Roux, *Rebel Pity*, p. 115.
254 Grossman, 'Class Relations', p. 200.
255 Davies, *Capital, State and White Labour in South Africa*, p. 247.
256 The picture is reproduced in Henry R Pike, *A History of Communism in South Africa*, Christian Mission International of South Africa, Germiston, 1988, p. 175.
257 Pike, *A History of Communism*, p. 158.
258 Roux, *Rebel Pity*, p. 43; Sachs, *Multitude of Dreams*, p. 144.
259 Eugene Dennis also recognised her gifts as an 'effective mass agitator', though he had reservations about her 'strong petty-bourgeois individualistic traits' and her tendency to swing from 'strong sectarian tendencies, to right opportunistic capitulatory policies' (Davidson et al., *South African and the Communist International*, volume 2, p. 72). He may have been influenced in his views of her by an occasion when she failed to keep a secret appointment with him in Joubert Park at which she was meant to introduce him to Eddie Roux. Roux had to find Dennis by himself, leaving Molly sitting in the party office nursing her feet which were sore from shoes she had bought at least a half-size too small (Roux and Roux, *Rebel Pity*, p. 96). She was born in 1906 as Molly Selikowitz in Lithuania and joined the South African party in 1922, two years after her arrival in South Africa. She

married Douglas in 1925.

260   Roux and Roux, *Rebel Pity*, p. 115.

261   Baruch Hirson, 'The Black Republic Slogan, Part II', *Searchlight South Africa*, 4, February 1990, p. 46.

262   Drew, *Discordant Comrades*, p. 131.

263   Ray Adler interviewed by C Purkey and Les Witz, 8–10 May 1990, Johannesburg, transcript, Colin Purkey Papers, Wits Historical Papers, A 1984.

264   Taffy Adler, 'The History of the Jewish Workers' Club', paper presented at the African Studies Institute, Wits, 1977, p. 91.

265   Matya Ozinsky, interviewed by C Purkey, Les Witz and S Ozinsky, 21 February 1988, Johannesburg, E21, p. 1, transcript, Colin Purkey Papers, A 1984.

266   Dora Alexander, 12 April 1989, interviewed by Colin Purkey and Les Witz, E29, p. 4, transcript, Colin Purkey Papers, A 1984.

267   Paul Trewhela to Naidoo, 1 December 2004. See also handwritten note from Naidoo, 20 November 2004, Naidoo Papers, University of Durban-Westville.

268   Dora Alexander, 12 April 1989, interviewed by Colin Purkey and Les Witz, E29, p. 1, transcript, Colin Purkey Papers, A 1984.

269   Roux and Roux, *Rebel Pity*, pp. 103–4.

270   Basner, *Am I an African?*, p. 48. Roth cites a Comintern instruction that in 1935 ordered Inkaka to stop defending 'apolitical' cases involving passes and liquor offences. Roth suggests that once Ikaka stopped defending such cases, it lost support (Roth, *The Communist Party of South Africa*, p. 55).

271   Simons and Simons, *Class and Colour in South Africa*, p. 471.

272   Central Committee meeting minutes, 31 December 1937 – 3 January 1938, Comintern Archives Online, 495/14/355. Shortly after his return from the commission, Moses Kotane told a Politburo meeting on 24 August 1936 that in Moscow, the South Africans had been told that 'the Jewish elements must not infiltrate too much into the Party' (Politburo meeting minutes, 24 August 1936, Comintern Archives Online, 495/14/350).

273   Dora Alexander, 12 April 1989, interviewed by Colin Purkey and Les Witz, E29, p. 5.

274   Issy Heymann, interviewed by Luli Callinicos, 31 May 1987, transcript, Colin Purkey Papers, A 1984.

275   Drew, *Discordant Comrades*, p. 126.

276   Davidson et al., *South Africa and the Communist International*, volume 2, p. 16.

277   Roth, *The Communist Party of South Africa*, p. 90.

278   Rebecca Bunting, interviewed by Sylvia Neame, p. 52, Sylvia Neame Papers.

279   Davidson et al., *South Africa and the Communist International*, volume 2, p. 75.

280   Martin Nicol, 'The Transvaal GWU's Assault on Low Wages in Cape Town', in Belinda Bozzoli (ed.), *Class, Community and Conflict*, Ravan Press, Johannesburg, 1987, p. 219.

281   Drew, *Discordant Comrades*, p. 126

282   Nicol, 'The Transvaal GWU's Assault', p. 225; La Guma, *Jimmy La Guma*, p. 57.

283   Field, Klammer and Guma, *In the Dark with My Dress on Fire*, p. 17. La Guma's estrangement from the party in 1929 began with his abrupt departure from Johannesburg to return to his home in Cape Town where he took over the running of a tea room that he'd inherited from his aunt. Johnny Gomas persuaded him to rejoin and himself supported La Guma's family from the money he was getting as a full-time party organiser (Johnny Gomas, interviewed by Sylvia Neame, Cape Town, September, 1962, p. 13, Sylvia Neame Papers).

284   Musson, *Johnny Gomas*, p. 67.

285   Nicol, 'The Transvaal GWU's Assault'; Musson, *Johnny Gomas*, p, 67.

286   Simons, *All My Life and All My Strength*, p. 64.

287 La Guma, *Jimmy La Guma*, p. 57.
288 ES Sachs, *Rebels' Daughters*, MacGibbon and Kee, London, 1957.
289 Drew, *Between Empire and Revolution*, p. 208.
290 Sachs, *Multitude of Dreams*, p. 164.
291 Rebecca Bunting, interviewed by Sylvia Neame, Sylvia Neame Papers.
292 Roux and Roux, *Rebel Pity*, pp. 102–3.
293 Simons Papers, BC 1081, 08.1. The Simonses obtained the document from the 'Russian state archive of socio-political history', Moscow, and an archival reference number appears on it in Ray Alexander's handwriting: 495/64/122/2-7.
294 Roux and Roux, *Rebel Pity*, p. 98.
295 Sam Malkinson, interviewed by Sylvia Neame, 1964, transcript, p. 6, Sylvia Neame Papers.
296 Henry Dee, 'Clements Kadalie, Trade Unionism, Migration and Race in Southern Africa', PhD dissertation, University of Edinburgh, 2019, pp. 181–4.
297 Sam Malkinson to SP Bunting, 30 November 1929, ER Roux Papers, A 2667, B2.
298 Sam Malkinson, interviewed by Sylvia Neame, 1964, transcript, p. 7, Sylvia Neame Papers.
299 Drew, *Between Empire and Revolution*, p. 205.
300 Drew, *Discordant Comrades*, p. 122.
301 Roux and Roux, *Rebel Pity*, p. 98.
302 Letter from Comintern Executive reprinted in *Umsebenzi*, December 1931, quoted in Grossman, 'Class Relations', pp. 191–2.
303 Davidson et al., *South Africa and the Communist International*, volume 2, pp. 9–11.
304 Davidson et al., *South Africa and the Communist International*, volume 2, pp. 16–17.
305 Nzula, Potekhin and Zusmanovich, *Forced Labour in Colonial Africa*, p.138.
306 Nzula, Potekhin and Zusmanovich, *Forced Labour in Colonial Africa*, p. 151.
307 Historicus, 'Albert Nzula', p. 101.
308 Robert Edgar, 'Notes on the Life and Death of Albert Nzula', *International Journal of African Historical Studies*, 16, 4, 1983, pp. 675–9.
309 Cohen, 'Introduction', p. 15. Cohen obtained this information when he interviewed James.
310 Roux and Roux, *Rebel Pity*, pp. 203–4.
311 Drew, *Between Empire and Revolution*, p. 211; Davidson et al., *South Africa and the Communist International*, volume 2, pp. 22–5 and 46.
312 Drew, *Discordant Comrades*, p. 127.
313 Davidson et al., *South Africa and the Communist International*, volume 2, p. 61.
314 And indeed as Bernard Sachs asserted in his *Multitude of Dreams*.
315 Drew, *Between Empire and Revolution*, p. 223.
316 Drew, *Between Empire and Revolution*, p. 223.
317 Davidson et al., *South Africa and the Communist International*, volume 2, p. 18.
318 Drew, *South Africa's Radical Tradition*, p. 129.
319 Martin Legassick, 'Class and Nationalism in South African Protest: The South African Communist Party and the "Native Republic", 1928–1934', Eastern African Studies Program, Syracuse University, July 1973, pp. 50–1; Bunting, *Moses Kotane*, p. 62.
320 Bunting, *Moses Kotane*, p. 61.
321 Davidson et al., *South Africa and the Communist International*, volume 2, p. 29.
322 Roth, *The Communist Party of South Africa*, p. 94.
323 Bunting, *Moses Kotane*, p. 61.
324 Davidson et al., *South Africa and the Communist International*, volume 2, p. 63.
325 Davidson et al., *South Africa and the Communist International*, volume 2, p. 23.
326 Elizabeth Gurley Flynn, 'The Life of Eugene Dennis', *Political Affairs*, 11, 3,

1961, p. 9.

327 South African Commission, 1936, transcript, Comintern Archives Online, 495.14.20a/80.

328 Roux, *SP Bunting*, p. 168.

329 Davidson et al., *South Africa and the Communist International*, volume 2, p. 21.

330 Flynn, 'The Life of Eugene Dennis', p. 5.

331 Davidson et al., *South Africa and the Communist International*, volume 2, pp. 36–46.

332 Davidson et al., *South Africa and the Communist International*, volume 2, p. 33.

333 Roth, *The Communist Party of South Africa*, p. 53.

334 Harry Pollitt, 'The Work of the Communists of South Africa in the Trade Unions', *Communist Review*, December 1932, p. 588. See also 'Urgent Questions on the Work of the South African CP', *Communist Review*, IV, 8, August 1932, pp. 391–8.

335 Pollitt, 'The Work of the Communists of South Africa in the Trade Unions', p. 589.

336 Pollitt, 'The Work of the Communists of South Africa in the Trade Unions', p. 590.

337 Pollitt, 'The Work of the Communists of South Africa in the Trade Unions', p. 598.

338 Davidson et al., *South Africa and the Communist International*, volume 2, p. 83. Pollitt's report may also have used information from Otto Huisgood, a delegate from Profintern, charged with investigating the African Federation of Trade Unions. He visited South Africa in the second half of 1932 and was in contact mainly with La Guma, Gomas and Ray Alexander. Born in Surinam, Huisgood was a CPUSA member, though a Dutch national (Johns, 'Internationalism, Intervention, or Irrelevance?', pp. 8–9). As the first black communist functionary to visit South Africa, it is a little surprising that his visit elicited so little local comment. When I interviewed him in 1984, Douglas Wolton remembered 'Bennett' as another Comintern visitor with whom he had discussions, though confusingly he thought he was an American. Bennett was a name used by Max Petrovsky, probably the originator of the Native republic slogan (Douglas Wolton, interviewed by Tom Lodge, 12 September 1984).

339 This was a view of the AFTU, which was shared by people still inside the party. Kotane in 1935 told André Marty in Moscow, 'There is no AFTU, we cannot kid ourselves, there is no such union' (Online Comintern Archives, 495/14/20/73).

340 Davidson et al., *South Africa and the Communist International*, volume 2, p. 52.

341 Johns, 'Marxism-Leninism', p. 433.

342 Roux, *Time Longer than Rope*, p. 569.

343 Johns, 'Marxism-Leninism', p. 431 ; Roth, *The Communist Party of South Africa*, p. 34.

344 Davidson et al., *South Africa and the Communist International*, volume 1, pp. 12–13.

345 Hirson, 'The Black Republic Slogan', p. 44.

346 Roux, *Time Longer than Rope*, p. 256.

347 Lerumo, *Fifty Fighting Years*, p. 65.

348 Allison Drew, 'Urban Activists and Rural Movements: Communists in South Africa and Algeria', *African Studies*, 66, 2–3, 2007, p. 314.

349 Simons and Simons, *Class and Colour*, p. 405.

350 Edward Johanningsmeier, 'Communists and Black Freedom Movements in South Africa and the United States, 1919–1950', *Journal of Southern African Studies*, 30, 1, 2004, p. 179.

351 Drew, 'Urban Activists and Rural Movements', p. 301.

352 Andrew Thorpe, 'Comintern "Control" of the Communist Party of Great Britain', *English Historical Review*, 113, 452, 1998, p. 641.

353 Drachewych, 'The Comintern and Anti-Imperialism', p. 275.

354 Drew, *Discordant Comrades*, p. 108.

355 Simons and Simons, *Class and Colour*, p. 408.

356 Legassick, 'Class and Nationalism in South African Protest', p. 36.

357   For more commentary on whether Comintern was right in trying to close down the League, see especially Sylvia Neame's *The Congress Movement*. She suggests that Bunting's attempt to set up an organisation to rival 'the genuine, if embryonic, African nationalist movement' was unrealistic. But Comintern was wrong, she thinks, to propose that the ANC could be transformed into a 'full scale revolutionary movement' (Neame, *The Congress Movement*, volume 3, pp. 21–2).

Chapter 4

1   Mia Roth, *The Communist Party in South Africa: Racism, Eurocentrism and Moscow, 1921–1950*, Partridge, Johannesburg, 2016, p. 112. See pp. 8–9 for commentary on the reliability of *Umsebenzi* between 1931 and 1938, which, she maintains, under Roux's editorship, reported events that never happened and included articles purportedly by Africans which were not in fact by Africans. Roth thinks that Roux edited *Umsebenzi* between 1930 and 1938 but in fact his editorship ended in 1936. She claims that African members referred to reports that did not happen. It was certainly the case that Roux wrote much of *Umsebenzi* by himself, if we are to believe Richter's testimony at the Marty Commission (Comintern Archives Online, 495/14/20a/261). But Josie Mpama's statement at the commission suggests that because Roux did not often accept unsolicited submissions from African party members, *Umsebenzi* actually *under-reported* local African party activism, rather than exaggerating it (Apollon Davidson, Irina Filatova, Valentin Gorodnov and Sheridan Johns, *South Africa and the Communist International: A Documentary History*, volume 2: *Bolshevik Footsoldiers to Victims of Bolshevisation, 1931–1939*, Frank Cass, London, 2003, p. 193). For a positive contemporary view of *Umsebenzi*'s impact and its success in projecting the Communist Party's message even among rural Africans, see the report written in 1932 by the African American missionary Max Yergan (David Anthony, 'Max Yergan in South Africa', *African Studies Review*, 34, 2, 1991, p. 42).

2   Davidson et al., *South Africa and the Communist International*, volume 2, p. 71.

3   Miriam Basner, *Am I an African? The Political Memoirs of Hyman Basner*, Witwatersrand University Press, Johannesburg, 1993, p. 55.

4   Eddie Roux, *Time Longer than Rope*, Victor Gollancz, London, 1948.

5   Jon Lewis, 'The Germiston By-election of 1932', in P. Bonner (ed.), *Working Papers in Southern African Studies*, Ravan Press, Johannesburg, 1981, p. 106.

6   HJ and RE Simons, *Class and Colour in South Africa, 1850–1950*, Penguin, Harmondsworth, 1969, p. 460.

7   Brian Bunting (ed.), *South African Communists Speak: Documents from the History of the South African Communist Party, 1915–1980*, Inkululeko Publications, London, 1981, p. 116.

8   Eddie Roux and Win Roux, *Rebel Pity*, Rex Collings, London, 1970, p. 117.

9   Roux and Roux, *Rebel Pity*, p. 118.

10   Davidson et al., *South Africa and the Communist International*, volume 2, p. 84.

11   Roux, *Time Longer than Rope*, p. 271.

12   Roux, *Time Longer than Rope*, p. 268.

13   Roux, *Time Longer than Rope*, pp. 272–3.

14   Roux and Roux, *Rebel Pity*, p. 126.

15   Bunting, *South African Communists Speak*, p. 118.

16   Ray Adler, interviewed by Colin Purkey and Leslie Witz, Johannesburg, 1990, Colin Purkey Papers, Wits Historical Papers, A 1984.

17   Bernard Sachs, *Multitude of Dreams*, Kayor Publishing House, Johannesburg, 1949, pp. 152–3. He also recalled them quite vividly when I interviewed him in 1984.

18   Eli Weinberg, 'Why I Am a Member of the Communist Party', *African Communist*,

87, 1981, p. 54.

19   The coverage was noticeably uneven between different newspapers. As the references cited here indicate, the *Rand Daily Mail* referred to the party's Germiston campaign quite frequently. The earliest mention in the Johannesburg *Star* of Marks's candidature was as an aside in a report on a Communist Party meeting on the Johannesburg City Hall steps ('Protest Meeting City Hall Steps, *The Star*, 7 November 1932, p. 5). The *Star*'s reporting about polling day in Germiston makes no reference to the communists' activities that day.

20   WA Poulton, 'Communists in a Riot', *Rand Daily Mail*, 11 October 1932, p. 8.

21   WA Poulton, 'Effort to Nominate a Native Communist', *Rand Daily Mail*, 3 November 1932, pp. 4 and 10.

22   GH van L Ribbink, 'Banishment of the Reds', *Rand Daily Mail*, 7 November 1932, p. 9.

23   'Elusive Mr Roux', *Rand Daily Mail*, 14 November 1932, p. 8; 'No Trace of Mr Roux', *Rand Daily Mail*, 17 November 1932, p. 10; 'Elusive Mr Roux: Police Search', *Rand Daily Mail*, 19 November 1932, p. 10.

24   'Elusive Mr Roux: Police Search', *Rand Daily Mail*, 19 November 1932, p. 10.

25   'Roux Arrested at Last', *Rand Daily Mail*, 28 November 1932, p. 7.

26   Arthur G Barlow, 'The Germiston Election', *Rand Daily Mail*, 1 December 1932.

27   'Germiston Riot: Trouble at Location', *Rand Daily Mail*, 14 November 1936.

28   Sub-inspector Fourie to District Commandant, South African Police, Boksburg, 22 August 1922, File: Strike of Garment Workers, Germiston, 1932, South African National Archives, JUS 593 2024/32.

29   Deputy Commissioner Commanding Witwatersrand Division to Commandant of the South African Police, 6 September 1932, File: Strike of Garment Workers, Germiston, 1932, South African National Archives, JUS 593 2024/32.

30   The most detailed analysis of the strike is in BM Touyz, 'White Politics and the Garment Workers' Union, 1930–1953', MA dissertation, Comparative African Government and Law, University of Cape Town, 1979, pp. 60–4.

31   R White, Sub-inspector Germiston to the Commissioner of the SAP, 25 August 1932, File: Strike of Garment Workers, Germiston, 1932, South African National Archives, JUS 593 2024/32.

32   'Railwaymen Protest Banishment Order', *Rand Daily Mail*, 17 November 1932, p. 10.

33   Touyz, 'White Politics and the Garment Workers' Union', p. 63; ES Sachs, *Rebels' Daughters*, MacGibbon and Kee, London, 1957, p. 91.

34   Roux, *Time Longer than Rope*, p. 273.

35   Roux, *Time Longer than Rope*, p. 275.

36   Douglas G Wolton, *Whither South Africa?*, Lawrence and Wishart, London, 1947, p. 80.

37   Davidson et al., *South Africa and the Communist International*, volume 2, p. 72.

38   Bettie du Toit, *Ukubamba Amadolo: Workers' Struggles in the South African Textile Industry*, Onyx Press, London, 1978, pp. 25–9.

39   Roux, *Time Longer than Rope*, p. 279.

40   Issy Diamond had been or was about to be expelled.

41   ENW Tucker, 'May Day Clash', *Rand Daily Mail*, 2 May 1933, p. 8. The *Mail*'s report also estimated the crowd size at 2,000 and named Josie Mpama correctly. The Communist Party meeting was followed by the event organised by white labour leaders. The communists had apparently agreed to a timetable for their demonstration so that it would not clash with the Trades and Labour Council's gathering.

42   Roux, *Time Longer than Rope*, p. 282.

43   Davidson et al., *South Africa and the Communist International*, volume 2, p. 88.

44   Ray Alexander Simons, *All My Life and All My Strength*, STE Publishers,

Johannesburg, 2004, p. 76.

45 Davidson et al., *South Africa and the Communist International*, volume 2, p. 92. It seems that his defence of his South African record was successful, for he and Molly remained politically active in the British party and later in the decade he was offered the position of business manager at the *Daily Worker*. The letter arrived at his home when he was abroad, in Moscow, and the post eventually was filled by somebody else. The British party's press published his memoirs in 1948 so he evidently retained influence (Douglas Wolton, interviewed by Tom Lodge, 12 September 1984).

46 Roux, *Time Longer than Rope*, pp. 283–4. See also Anthony, 'Max Yergan in South Africa', p. 43. Anthony cites a 1987 press interview with the then veteran communist, Govan Mbeki, who had attended Roux's talks shortly after arriving as a student at Fort Hare.

47 Roux and Roux, *Rebel Pity*, 132.

48 Davidson et al., *South Africa and the Communist International*, volume 2, p. 67.

49 Davidson et al., *South Africa and the Communist International*, volume 2, p. 69.

50 Davidson et al., *South Africa and the Communist International*, volume 2, p. 75.

51 Davidson et al., *South Africa and the Communist International*, volume 2, pp. 80–2.

52 Davidson et al., *South Africa and the Communist International*, volume 2, pp. 83–4.

53 Davidson et al., *South Africa and the Communist International*, volume 2, pp. 94–9.

54 Davidson et al., *South Africa and the Communist International*, volume 2, pp. 101–12.

55 Draft Statutes of the Communist Party of South Africa (Section of the Communist International), 8 June 1934, Online Comintern Archives, 495/4/442/82-85.

56 'The Party Leadership on the Inner Party Situation', excerpts from report of the Politburo signed by Mofutsanyana, 25 September 1935, Comintern Archives Online, 495/14/347/6.

57 Roux and Roux, *Rebel Pity*, pp. 142–3; Allison Drew, *Discordant Comrades: Identities and Loyalties on the South African Left*, Ashgate, Aldershot, 2000, pp. 170–1.

58 Resolution of the Political Bureau of the CPSA, 27 October 1934, Comintern Archives Online, 495/14/347/28.

59 *Umsebenzi*, 9 February 1935, 16 February 1935. How seriously Marks held such views is doubtful. He maintained his own friendships with ANC leaders and that year visited East London, spending a month staying at Kadalie's house. During his stay he spoke at various meetings of Kadalie's local ICU branch – there was no party organisation in East London at that time, just a few members (JB Marks, interviewed by Sylvia Neame, August 1969, pp. 3–6, Sylvia Neame Papers, Wits Historical Papers).

60 AZ, 'Is There a Class of Native Capitalists', *Umsebenzi*, 13 April 1935.

61 Drew, *Discordant Comrades*, p. 172.

62 *Umsebenzi*, 2 March 1935, 16 March 1935.

63 Henry Dee, 'Clements Kadalie, Trade Unionism, Migration and Race in Southern Africa', PhD dissertation, University of Edinburgh, 2019, pp. 97 and 101.

64 Bill Freund, 'South Africa: The Union Years, 1910–1948', in Robert Ross, Anne Kelk Mager and Bill Nasson (eds), *The Cambridge History of South Africa*, volume 2, Cambridge University Press, New York, pp. 219–23.

65 Baruch Hirson, *Yours for the Union: Class and Community Struggles in South Africa*, Zed Press, London, 1989, p. 38.

66 David Duncan, *The Mills of God: The State and African Labour in South Africa, 1918–1948*, Witwatersrand University Press, Johannesburg, 1995, pp. 194–6.

67 Max Gordon, Report to the Trustees of the Bantu Welfare Trust, 1937, Ambrose Lynn Saffery Papers, Wits Historical Papers, AD 1179, A3.

68 *Umsebenzi*, 20 April 1935.

69 Gilbert Coka, 'The Story of Gilbert Coka', in Margery Perham (ed.), *Ten Africans*, Faber and Faber, London, 1963, p. 314; *Umsebenzi*, 28 September 1935.

70 *Umsebenzi*, 15 July 1935.

71 *Umsebenzi*, 22 June 1935.

72 Davidson et al., *South Africa and the Communist International*, volume 1, p. xix.

73 *Umsebenzi*, 7 September 1935.

74 Roux and Roux, *Rebel Pity*, p. 140.

75 Jonathan Grossman, 'Class Relations and the Communist Party of South Africa, 1921–1950', PhD dissertation, University of Warwick, 1985, p. 195.

76 Andrew Thorpe, 'Comintern "Control" of the Communist Party of Great Britain', *English Historical Review*, 113, 452, 1998, p. 651.

77 RK Naumann, 'The Factional Struggle in the CP South Africa', 1 February 1936, Comintern Archives Online, 495/14/347/36.

78 Information material on South Africa, 2 March 1936, Comintern Archives Online, 495/14/347/76.

79 For texts of the telegrams, see Comintern Archives Online 495/14/347/3-5.

80 *Umsebenzi*, 10 August 1935. The case against Roux was eventually dismissed on appeal in March 1936 (ES Sachs, *The Choice before South Africa*, self-published, London, 1953, p. 79).

81 Davidson et al., *South Africa and the Communist International*, volume 1, p. 18. The speech ended with a reference to the struggle that was 'commencing' to weaken 'the influence of national reformist spreading reformist illusions'. Within the party, its author insisted there persisted 'errors' in the interpretation of an independent Native republic, especially in the denials of 'class opposition and difference of interest' among 'the masses of native people'. South African officials kept a copy of the speech in their files: South African National Archives, ARB 3071, 1103/1.

82 Three months later ex-sailor and French naval Black Sea mutineer André Marty would direct the recruitment of the International Brigade from French party's headquarters in Paris and for the next three years he would be a key figure in the politics of the Spanish Civil War, exercising an 'iron rule'. That he found any time subsequently to pay attention to South African developments, as he did, is remarkable. His treatment of the South Africans was uncharacteristically benign for, as he once boasted, he was responsible for the shooting of 500 of his international brigaders, executed as agents of Fascism-Trotskyism (Anthony Beevor, *The Battle for Spain: The Spanish Civil War, 1936–1939*, Weidenfeld and Nicolson, London, 2006, p. 161; Gabriel Jackson, *The Spanish Republic and the Civil War, 1931–1939*, Princeton University Press, Princeton, 1972, p. 339). Hemingway referred to him as a madman in *For Whom the Bell Tolls*. He was expelled from the French party in 1953, denounced as a 'Titoist agent' (Raymond Carr, *The Spanish Tragedy: The Civil War in Perspective*, Phoenix Press, London, 2000, p. 235).

83 Davidson et al., *South Africa and the Communist International*, volume 2, pp. 173–5.

84 Drew, *Discordant Comrades*, p. 177.

85 'Meeting with Comrade Marty on the South African Question', transcript, 13 November 1935, Online Comintern Archives, 495/14/20/77-78.

86 Davidson et al., *South Africa and the Communist International*, volume 2, p. 189.

87 South African Commission, 1936, transcript, Comintern Archives Online, 495/14/20a/40.

88 Davidson et al., *South Africa and the Communist International*, volume 2, p. 188.

89 South African Commission, 1936, transcript, Comintern Archives Online, 495/14/20a/45-46.

90 Davidson et al., *South Africa and the Communist International*, volume 2, p. 192.

91 South African Commission, 1936, transcript, Comintern Archives Online, 495/14/20a/260.

92 Roth, *The Communist Party of South Africa*, pp. 118–19.

93 Roux and Roux, *Rebel Pity*, p. 98.

94 Davidson et al., *South Africa and the Communist International*, volume 2, p. 195.

95 Davidson et al., *South Africa and the Communist International*, volume 2, p. 182.

96 Davidson et al., *South Africa and the Communist International*, volume 2, p. 183.

97 Davidson et al., *South Africa and the Communist International*, volume 2, p. 184.

98 Davidson et al., *South Africa and the Communist International*, volume 2, p. 195.

99 Davidson et al., *South Africa and the Communist International*, volume 2, pp. 187–200.

100 Davidson et al., *South Africa and the Communist International*, volume 2, pp. 200–10.

101 South African Commission, 1936, transcript, Online Comintern Archives, 495/14/20a/219. The transcript actually reads 'I advise you not ...', but the 'not' is obviously, in the context of the sense of the rest of the paragraph, a mistranscription of 'now'.

102 Drew, *Discordant Comrades*, p. 177.

103 Brian Bunting, *Moses Kotane: South African Revolutionary*, Inkululeko Publications, London, 1975, p. 74.

104 Drew, *Discordant Comrades*, p. 173.

105 Davidson et al., *South Africa and the Communist International*, volume 2, p. 10.

106 In 1937 its members were Harry Pollitt, R Palme Dutt, Ben Bradley and George Hardy (Sheridan Johns, 'Internationalism, Intervention, or Irrelevance? Comintern Emissaries from Moscow to the Communist Party of South Africa, 1929–1937', paper given to the Canadian African Studies Association meeting, Ottawa, 2–5 June 1998, p. 13).

107 Born in Berlin in 1899, Robert Naumann became a toolmaker in 1915. In 1919 he emigrated to the Soviet Union to work at a locomotive works, before attending the German party school in Moscow in 1921. He obtained a post at the new Communist University of the National Minorities of the West (KUNMS) in Moscow, where he taught political economy until 1926, before undertaking advanced studies at the Institute of the Red Professors of the All-Union Communist Party. He began working for Comintern's Anglo-American Secretariat in 1935 while continuing to lecture, helping to train students at the University for the Toilers of the East and at the Lenin School. Naumann was clearly adept at survival within the Comintern's troubled politics during this period, a time when two-thirds of the German communists living in the USSR were executed or imprisoned. He would return to the German Democratic Republic in 1950 to be appointed as a pro-rector at Berlin's Humboldt University, where he led a process of reconstruction of the social sciences in conformity with party doctrine (Peter Erler, 'Robert Naumann', in *Wer war wer in de DDR*, volume 2, Ch. Links Verlag, Berlin, 2010).

108 *South African Worker*, 19 June 1937.

109 The Richter brothers, Maurice and Paul, were originally from Latvia but their family settled in the Orange Free State. The Richters 'were well known in Kroonstad where Paul was known as Pinkie'. Shortly after the Radek–Pyatov trial, the three men were listed by the Communist International Control Commission as 'party wreckers closely associated with the Trotskyist Jacob Berman'. In Comintern's journal Bach was reported 'to have taken part in disruptive factional work in South Africa. The Richters moved in circles hostile both to the party and to the Soviet government and had 'incriminating correspondence' addressed to Berman in their flat. Lazar Bach's family cabled the British Foreign Office to arrange 'representations' to the Soviet government ('Secret OGPU Coup: Eleventh

Hour Bid to Save Three Men from Bullets', *Sunday Express*, Johannesburg, 18 July 1937).

110   Davidson et al., *South Africa and the Communist International*, volume 2, pp. 20 and 252.

111   Andre Marty to Georgi Dimitrov, 21 August 1937, Comintern Archives Online, 495/14/351/9.

112   *South African Worker*, 25 July 1936.

113   George Hardy, *Those Stormy Years*, Lawrence and Wishart, London, 1956, p. 229.

114   Drew, *Discordant Comrades*, p. 179.

115   RK Cope, *Comrade Bill: The Life and Times of WH Andrews, Worker's Leader*, Stewart Printing Company, Cape Town, 1944, p. 330.

116   Diary of a visit to the Soviet Union, entry for 5 August 1937, Notebook, 'Kirby Series Reporter's Book', RK Cope Papers, Wits Historical Papers, A 953.

117   Davidson et al., *South Africa and the Communist International*, volume 2, p. 281.

118   Harry Pollitt to Centre, 20 October 1937, Comintern Archives Online, 495/14/355/123.

119   Hardy, *Those Stormy Years*, p. 236; see also HJ and RE Simons, *Class and Colour in South Africa, 1850–1950*, Penguin, Harmondsworth, 1969, p. 480.

120   Hardy, *Those Stormy Years*, p. 236.

121   Ray Simons, interviewed by Tom Lodge, Cape Town, 1993.

122   Davidson et al., *South Africa and the Communist International*, volume 2, p. 287.

123   Peter Ramutla at a meeting of the Johannesburg District Committee of the CPSA, 9 August 1936, minutes, Comintern Archives Online, 495/14/350/3.

124   Sachs, *The Choice before South Africa*, p. 200.

125   Robert Edgar, *The Making of an African Communist: Edwin Thabo Mofutsanyana and the CPSA, 1927–1939*, University of South Africa Press, Pretoria, 2005, p. 37.

126   Willie Kalk, interview with Luli Callinicos, 19 March 1987, Colin Purkey Papers, A 1984.-

127   Allison Drew, *Between Empire and Revolution: A Life of Sidney Bunting, 1873–1936*, Pickering and Chatto, London, 2007, p. 143.

128   This was at a meeting of Johannesburg's District Committee. On this occasion, Johnny Gomas said he supported Ramutla, for in exchanges with Kalk 'we are considered boys'. Minutes, Johannesburg District Committee, CPSA, 9 August 1936, Comintern Archives Online, 495/14/350/2.

129   Issy Heymann, interviewed by Colin Purkey, 1987, Colin Purkey Papers, A 1984. Willie Kalk was the first South African-born white communist, born in Pretoria in 1900, the son of a German immigrant cabinet maker (Martin Legassick, 'Class and Nationalism in South African Protest: The South African Communist Party and the "Native Republic", 1928–1934', Eastern African Studies Program, Syracuse University, July 1973, p. 3). He started work at the age of 15, first at Bosch Electrical and then in a furniture factory in Johannesburg. By 1924 he was secretary of the furniture union he had helped to organise. He was a foundation member of the ISL, prompted by his opposition to the First World War, and joined the Young Communist League in 1923, becoming friends with Eddie Roux (Roux and Roux, *Rebel Pity*, p. 31). Kalk's brother fought in the Jeppe Commando during the 1922 strike. Between 1927 and 1930 Kalk was in the Soviet Union, learning, he recalled, 'how the party operated in the factory'. He was told he 'was quite good at thinking dialectically', perhaps as a result of his enthusiastic support for Stalin's line during the dispute with Bukharin. He met Zinoviev on one occasion.

130   Simons and Simons, *Class and Colour in South Africa*, p. 479. See also the profile of Wolfson in Bettie du Toit, *Ukubamba Amadolo*, p. 25.

131   Roux and Roux, *Rebel Pity*, p. 98.

132 Roux and Roux, *Rebel Pity*, p. 111.
133 Issy Heymann, interviewed by Colin Purkey, 1983, p. 28, Colin Purkey Papers, A 1984.
134 Wolfson, report to CPGB, 15 March 1937, Comintern Archives Online, 495/14/355/53.
135 Rusty Bernstein, *Memory against Forgetting*, Viking Penguin, London, 1999, p. 24.
136 Basner, *Am I an African?*, p. 54.
137 Allison Drew, *South Africa's Radical Tradition: A Documentary History*, volume 1: *1907–1950*, University of Cape Town Press, Cape Town, 1996, pp. 239–40.
138 The Farmers' and Workers' Party was a breakaway group from the Labour Party formed in 1936. Its programme offered detailed proposals to improve the livelihoods of white tenant farmers. It accepted racial segregation but called for extensions to the African reserves. It failed to win seats in the 1938 election and collapsed shortly thereafter.
139 Davidson et al, *South Africa and the Communist International*, volume 2, p. 231.
140 Davidson et al., *South Africa and the Communist International*, volume 2, p. 214.
141 National Conference of the CPSA, September 1936, resolutions, Comintern Archives Online, 295/14/360.
142 Grossman, 'Class Relations', p. 284.
143 Davidson et al., *South Africa and the Communist International*, volume 2, p. 238.
144 Communist Party of South Africa, *Organise a People's Front in South Africa*, Johannesburg, September 1936.
145 Simons and Simons, *Class and Colour in South Africa*, p. 483.
146 Gana Makabeni at that stage may have been working with Max Gordon (see Peter Abrahams, *Tell Freedom*, Faber and Faber, 1954, pp. 258–9). Baruch Hirson, though, thinks that Makabeni was not working with Gordon (*Yours for the Union*, p. 44). He is unclear whether Makabeni rejoined the party – and Makabeni certainly remained fairly independent, sometimes siding with party critics during the 1940s.
147 *South African Worker*, 10 October 1936.
148 Simons, *All My Life and All My Strength*, p. 93.
149 Davidson et al., *South Africa and the Communist International*, volume 2, p. 230.
150 Davidson et al., *South Africa and the Communist International*, volume 2, p. 246.
151 Davidson et al., *South Africa and the Communist International*, volume 2, p. 272.
152 Draft resolution of British Commission on South Africa, 15 March 1938, Comintern Archives Online, 495/14/355/90-100.
153 Davidson et al., *South Africa and the Communist International*, volume 2, p. 287.
154 Minutes of meeting of the CPSA held in Johannesburg, 31 December 1938 to 1 January 1939, p. 19, Simons Papers, UCT Manuscripts and Archives, BC 1081.
155 Communist Party of South Africa, *Communism and the Native Question*, CPSA Secretariat, Johannesburg District Committee, 1938.
156 Davidson et al., *South Africa and the Communist International*, volume 2, pp. 243–4.
157 Davidson et al., *South Africa and the Communist International*, volume 2, p. 264.
158 Davidson et al., *South Africa and the Communist International*, volume 2, p. 229.
159 Pauline Podbrey, *White Girl in Search of the Party*, Hadeda Books, Pietermaritzburg, 1993, p. 107.
160 For a profile of George Sachs, see Royal College of Surgeons, Plarr's Lives of the Fellows, George Isak Sacks, 1901–1981, 2015, https://livesonline.rcseng.ac.uk/client/en_GB/lives/search/detailnonmodal/ent:$002f$002fSD_ASSET$002f0$002fSD_ASSET:379090/one.
161 George left the party in 1946 but his former comrades kept the newspaper going and Brian Bunting, Sidney's son, succeeded Betty Radford as editor.

162 Hymie Barsel, interviewed by Colin Purkey, transcript, p. 9, Colin Purkey Papers, A 1984.

163 South African Commission, 1936, transcript, Comintern Archives Online, 495/14/20a/48.

164 Draft resolution of the Tasks of the CPSA, 23 February 1936, Comintern Archives Online, 495/20/658/94.

165 Bill Freund makes the point that female GWU members may have been loyal to Sachs as a union leader but when it came to voting, they followed their husbands' lead in supporting Malanite nationalists, as Solly Sachs discovered to his cost when he stood for parliament in 1943 (Freund, 'South Africa: The Union Years', p. 229).

166 Grossman, 'Class Relations', p.230.

167 Grossman, 'Class Relations', p. 247.

168 Grossman, 'Class Relations', p. 296.

169 Hymie Barsel, interviewed by Colin Purkey, transcript, Colin Purkey Papers, A 1984.

170 Ray Alexander, interviewed by Tom Lodge, 1993.

171 Issy Heymann, interviewed by Luli Callinicos, 31 May 1987, Colin Purkey Papers, A 1984.

172 Wolfson to CPGB, report, 19 November 1937, Comintern Archives Online, 495/14/350/122.

173 Hymie Barsel, interviewed by Colin Purkey, p. 15, Colin Purkey Papers, A 1984.

174 Davidson et al., *South Africa and the Communist International*, volume 2, p. 263.

175 Drew, *Discordant Comrades*, p. 181.

176 Sachs v. Moore and 22 others in the Supreme Court of South Africa, judgment, 13 January 1938, Comintern Archives Online, 495/13/357/1-4.

177 Central Committee minutes, 31 December 1937 to 3 January 1938, Comintern Archives Online, 495/14/355/140.

178 Davidson et al., *South Africa and the Communist International*, volume 2, p. 243.

179 Davidson et al., *South Africa and the Communist International*, volume 2, p. 252.

180 Politburo meeting minutes, 16 November 1936, Comintern Archives Online, 495/14/350/19.

181 Communist Party of South Africa, *Vereeniging: Who is to Blame?*, Johannesburg, 1937.

182 Report of the Vereeniging Location Riots Commission, 1937, roneo, p. 29. File: Vereeniging Location Native Riots, South African National Archives, NTS 7671_87. 332.

183 Vereeniging Native Riots Commission, Minutes of Evidence, pp. 378 and 82. File: Vereeniging Location Native Riots, South African National Archives, NTS 7671_ 87. 332.

184 Vereeniging Native Riots Commission, Minutes of Evidence, p. 362. File: Vereeniging Location Native Riots, South African National Archives, NTS 7671_ 87. 332.

185 Sylvia Neame, *The Congress Movement: The Unfolding of the Congress Alliance, 1912–1961*, HSRC Press, Cape Town, 2015, volume 3, p. 140.

186 Bunting, *Moses Kotane*, p. 83.

187 Basner, *Am I an African?*, p. 93.

188 Basner, *Am I an African?*, p. 94.

189 Davidson et al., *South Africa and the Communist International*, volume 2, p. 72.

190 Basner, *Am I an African?*, pp. 82–3.

191 JB Marks, interviewed by Sylvia Neame, August 1969, p. 9, Sylvia Neame Papers.

192 Politburo minutes, 10 February 1937, Comintern Archives Online, 495/14/350/10.

193 JB Marks, interviewed by Sylvia Neame, August 1969, p. 9, Sylvia Neame Papers.

194 Basner, *Am I an African?*, p. 83. He may well have had useful contacts, but for many former ICU followers, Mote would have been regarded as a traitor, as he had appeared as a state witness in the trial of ICU leaders in Bloemfontein in 1922.

195 Basner, *Am I an African?*, p. 87.

196 Robert Naumann to André Marty, 29 August 1937, Comintern Archives Online, 495/14/351/13.

197 CM Tatz, *Shadow and Substance in South Africa*, University of Natal Press, Pietermaritzburg, 1962, pp. 2–93.

198 Basner, *Am I an African?*, p. 89; Roux and Roux, *Rebel Pity*, p. 148.

199 Unsigned letter to CPGB from party headquarters, Johannesburg, 23 April 1937, Comintern Archives Online, 495/14/351/8.

200 'The African National Unity Committee Supports This Candidate', Basner election leaflet, Comintern Archives Online, 495/14/359/182-183.

201 Untitled minutes of CPGB Colonial Committee meeting, 15 October 1937, Comintern Archives Online, 495/14/350/51.

202 *South African Worker*, 27 November 1937.

203 *South African Worker*, 10 July 1937.

204 *South African Worker*, 17 July 1937.

205 *Umsebenzi*, 15 January 1938

206 Bernstein, *Memory against Forgetting*, p. 31.

207 Basner, *Am I an African?*, p. 107.

208 *South African Worker*, 19 June 1937.

209 Philip Bonner and Noor Nieftagodien, *Alexandra: A History*, Witwatersrand University Press, Johannesburg, 2008, p. 54.

210 Davidson et al., *South Africa and the Communist International*, volume 2, p. 241.

211 Politburo minutes, 16 November 1936, Comintern Archives Online, 495/14/350/19.

212 ES Sachs to Harry Pollitt, 6 September 1937, Comintern Archives Online, 495/14/350/49.

213 Successful in the sense that wages afterwards did increase and the strike itself prompted the Amalgamated Engineering Union to support the subsequent organisation of unskilled labour (Wolfson to CPGB, 19 November 1937, Comintern Archives Online, 495/14/350/100).

214 Bill Freund, *Insiders and Outsiders: The Indian Working Class of Durban, 1910–1990*, James Currey, Oxford, 1995, pp. 60–1; Profile of George Ponnen, Naidoo Papers, University of Durban-Westville.

215 Davidson et al., *South Africa and the Communist International*, volume 2, p. 263.

216 Central Committee minutes, 31 December 1937 – 3 January 1938, Comintern Archives Online, 495/14/355/141.

217 Vishnu Padayachee, S Vawda and P Tichman, *Indian Workers and Trade Unions in Durban, 1930–1950*, Report no. 20, ISER, Durban-Westville, 1985, pp. 159–69.

218 Simons, *All My Life and All My Strength*, p. 44.

219 Simons, *All My Life and All My Strength*, p. 91.

220 Simons, *All My Life and All My Strength*, p. 89.

221 Robert H Davies, *Capital, State and White Labour in South Africa, 1900–1960*, Harvester Press, Brighton, 1979, pp. 262–5.

222 Roger Field, Martin Klammer and Blanche La Guma, *In the Dark with My Dress on Fire: My Life in Cape Town, London, Havana and Home Again*, Jacana Media, Johannesburg, 2011, p. 29; Alex La Guma, *Jimmy La Guma: A Biography*, Friends of the South African Library, Cape Town, 1997, p. 69.

223 Drew, *Discordant Comrades*, p. 14.

224 Gavin Lewis, *Between the Wire and the Wall: A History of South African 'Coloured'*

Politics, St. Martin's Press, New York, 1987 pp. 179–80.

225   Lewis, *Between the Wire and the Wall*, pp. 179–80, Abrahams, *Tell Freedom*, p. 275.

226   Doreen Musson, *Johnny Gomas: Voice of the Working Class*, Buchu Books, Cape Town, 1987, p. 85.

227   Lewis, *Between the Wire and the Wall*, p. 184.

228   Crain Soudien, *The Cape Radicals*, Witwatersrand University Press, Johannesburg, 2019, pp. 69–70.

229   Minutes, Central Committee Meeting, 29 December 1938, Simons Papers, BC 1081, 0.12.1, p. 9.

230   Lewis, *Between the Wire and the Wall*, p. 184.

231   Lewis, *Between the Wire and the Wall*, p. 183.

232   Drew, *Discordant Comrades*, p. 216.

233   Baruch Hirson, *The Cape Town Intellectuals: Ruth Schechter and Her Circle, 1907–1934*, Witwatersrand University Press, Johannesburg, 2001, p. 171.

234   Field, Klammer and La Guma, *In the Dark with My Dress on Fire*, p. 29; La Guma, *Jimmy La Guma*, p. 69.

235   Musson, *Johnny Gomas*, p. 88.

236   Abrahams, *Tell Freedom*, p. 275.

237   Davidson et al., *South Africa and the Communist International*, volume 2, p. 299.

238   CPGB, Colonial Committee, London, minutes, 21 February 1939, Comintern Archives Online, 495/14/360a/7.

239   Comintern Archives Online, 495.14.352.6; 495.14.352.101.

240   Davidson et al., *South Africa and the Communist International*, volume 2, pp. 225–6.

241   Roux and Roux, *Rebel Pity*, pp. 204–5.

242   Davidson et al., *South Africa and the Communist International*, volume 2, pp. 259–66.

243   Davidson et al., *South Africa and the Communist International*, volume 2, p. 249.

244   Naumann to Marty, 4 May 1937, Comintern Archives Online, 495/14/351/6.

245   Wolfson to CPGB, report, 19 November 1937, Comintern Archives Online, 495/14/350/112.

246   Roux and Roux, *Rebel Pity*, pp. 131–2.

247   Roth, *The Communist Party of South Africa*, p. 126. Roth cites Comintern archive documentation. Roux was to be given a chance to recant and whether he was actually expelled is uncertain. He and his wife, Win, remained friends with Moses Kotane, sharing an apartment with him in Clifton.

248   Abrahams, *Tell Freedom*, p. 274.

249   Davidson et al., *South Africa and the Communist International*, volume 2, pp. 275–6.

250   Davidson et al., *South Africa and the Communist International*, volume 2, p. 279.

251   Johns, 'Internationalism, Intervention or Irrelevance?', pp. 14–15.

252   'On the Situation of the CPSA', in Davidson et al., *South Africa and the Communist International*, volume 2, p. 288.

253   Carr, *The Spanish Tragedy*, p. 203.

254   Davidson et al., *South Africa and the Communist International*, volume 2, p. 284.

255   Moses Kotane to Brian Bunting, 15 March 1956, SP Bunting Papers, Wits Historical Papers, A 949, 8.1.2.1.

256   Minutes of meeting of the CPSA, 29 December 1938 to 1 January 1939, Johannesburg, Simons Papers, BC 1081, 0.12.1, p. 4.

257   Davidson et al., *South Africa and the Communist International*, volume 2, p. 223.

258   Davidson et al., *South Africa and the Communist International*, volume 2, p. 223.

259   Davidson et al., *South Africa and the Communist International*, volume 2, p. 220.

260   Davidson et al., *South Africa and the Communist International*, volume 2, p. 253.

261   Davidson et al., *South Africa and the Communist International*, volume 2, p. 258.

262   *Umsebenzi*, 26 February 1938.

263 Roth, *The Communist Party in South Africa*, p. 181.

264 Davidson et al., *South Africa and the Communist International*, volume 2, pp. 289–97.

265 To his comrades Basner explained his grounds for resignation in more detail, criticising the 'immorality and opportunism' of the Soviet–German pact. 'Leave me alone and I'll leave you alone' were his parting words when he left the 'aggregate' meeting (Bernstein, *Memory against Forgetting*, p. 32).

266 Davidson et al., *South Africa and the Communist International*, volume 2, pp. 297–300.

267 Bernstein, *Memory against Forgetting*, p. 28.

268 Minutes of meeting of the CPSA, 29 December 1938 to 1 January 1939, Johannesburg, Simons Papers, BC 1081, 0.12.1.

269 David Lovell and Kevin Windle, *Our Unswerving Loyalty: A Documentary Survey of Relations between the Communist Party of Australia and Moscow, 1920–1940*, Australian National University Press, Canberra, 2008, pp. 339–66.

270 Oleka Drachewych, 'The Comintern and the Communist Parties of South Africa, Canada and Australia on the Questions of Imperialism, Nationalism and Race', PhD dissertation, McMasters University, July 2017 (file: /drachewych_oleksa_m_2017september_PhD.pdf), p. 162.

271 Thomas Buchanan, 'The Dark Millions in the Colonies Are Unavenged: Anti-Fascism and Anti-Imperialism in the 1930s', *Contemporary European History*, 25, 4, 2016.

272 James Mah Yi Hong, 'Liminalities of Colonial Understandings towards Malayan Communism, 1919–1941', BA Honours dissertation, Department of History, National University of Singapore, 2018, https://d1wqtxts1xzle7.cloudfront.net/58532478/Liminalities_of_Colonial_Understandings_towards_Malayan_Communism__1919-1941.pdf.

Chapter 5

1 Bill Nasson, *South Africa at War, 1939-1945*, Jacana Media, Johannesburg, 2012, p. 13.

2 Jill Nattrass, *The South African Economy*, Oxford University Press, Cape Town, 1981, p. 165.

3 D Hobart Houghton, *The South African Economy*, Oxford University Press, Cape Town, 1973.

4 Hobart Houghton, *The South African Economy*, p. 122.

5 HJ and RE Simons, *Class and Colour in South Africa, 1850-1950*, Harmondsworth, Penguin, 1969, p. 555. For more data on these developments, see Peter Alexander, 'African Trade Unions and the South African State, 1937–1947: The Recognition Debate Reassessed', African Studies seminar paper no. 320, African Studies Institute, University of the Witwatersrand, 10 August 1992, p. 2.

6 Nicoli Nattrass, 'Economic Growth in the 1940s', in Saul Dubow and Alan Jeeves (eds), *South Africa's 1940s: Worlds of Possibilities*, Double Storey, Cape Town, 2005, pp. 26–7.

7 AW Stadler, 'Birds in the Cornfield: Squatter Movements in Johannesburg, 1944–1947', *Journal of Southern African Studies*, 6, 1, 1979.

8 This first found expression in Proclamation 31 of 1939, which outlined a programme of livestock limitation and land conservation measures.

9 Cherryl Walker, *Women and Resistance in South Africa*, Onyx Press, London, 1982, p. 70.

10 Deborah Posel, 'The Apartheid Project, 1948–1970', in Robert Ross, Anne Kelk Mager and Bill Nasson (eds), *The Cambridge History of South Africa*, volume 2: *1885–1994*, Cambridge University Press, New York, 2011, p. 324.

11 Leonard Thompson and Monica Wilson (eds), *The Oxford History of South Africa*, volume 2, Oxford University Press, Oxford, 1971, p. 199.

12 Nattrass, 'Economic Growth in the 1940s', p. 26.

13 Simons and Simons, *Class and Colour*, p. 556.

14 J Gomas, 'The War and Segregation', *Freedom*, June 1940, reprinted in Brian Bunting (ed.), *South African Communists Speak: Documents from the History of the South African Communist Party, 1915–1980*, Inkululeko Publications, London, 1981, p. 151.

15 Nasson, *South Africa at War*, p. 9.

16 For examples of expressions of pro-Russian sentiment by government spokesmen, see Brian Bunting, *Moses Kotane, South African Revolutionary*, Inkululeko Publications, London, 1975, pp. 113–14.

17 Friends of the Soviet Union, *Soviet Exhibition, Durban, June 30 – July 14, 1945*, leaflet, p. 4.

18 Simons and Simons, *Class and Colour*, p. 540; Stephen Clingman, *Bram Fischer: Afrikaner Revolutionary*, David Philip, Cape Town, 1998, p. 158 and *Inkululeko* (Johannesburg), 3 December 1945.

19 Minutes of the FSU Executive, 7 February 1944, Douglas Thompson Papers, Wits Historical Papers, A 1906, AC3.3.

20 *Freedom*, 2, 8 June 1944.

21 RK Cope, *Comrade Bill: The Life and Times of WH Andrews, Workers' Leader*, Stewart Printing Company, Cape Town, 1944. As well as sponsoring this tribute through a 'WH Andrews Biography Fund', the CPSA also commissioned a bust of their chairman. In addition to his biography to Andrews, Cope also composed a poetic 'ode' to the party's restored hero. Quite apart from electoral considerations there may have been a desire to atone for the expulsion of Andrews in 1931. See Wilfrid Harrison, *Memoirs of a Socialist in South Africa*, Stewart Printing Company, Cape Town, 1947.

22 See profile of Edwin Mofutsanyana, *Inkululeko*, 17 June 1942. For apprehensions about air raids, see Nasson, *South Africa at War*, p. 71.

23 Taffy Adler, 'Lithuania's Diaspora: The Johannesburg Jewish Workers' Club, 1928–1948', *Journal of Southern African Studies*, 6, 1, 1980, p. 77; Cope, *Comrade Bill*, p. 331.

24 Pauline Podbrey belonged to the Durban Liberal Study group before her recruitment into the party in 1940. Among the students she recalls that she joined in selling *Umsebenzi* were Sarah Carneson, David Kitson, Sylvester Stein, Athol Thorne and Pauline Urry (Pauline Podbrey, *White Girl in Search of a Party*, University of KwaZulu-Natal Press, Pietermaritzburg, 1993, pp. 58 and 94).

25 J Morkel, 'The War and South Africa', reprinted in Brian Bunting (ed.), *South African Communists Speak: Documents from the History of the South African Communist Party, 1915–1980*, Inkululeko Publications, London, 1981, pp. 147–50.

26 Bunting, *South African Communists Speak*, p. 136.

27 Communist Party of South Africa, *Must We Fight?*, Stewart Printing Company, Cape Town, 1939, p. 15, Phyllis Naidoo Papers, University of KwaZulu-Natal Documentation Centre, 2277/28. Oswald Pirow, the Minister of Defence, was the Nazi sympathiser the pamphlet was referring to.

28 Editorial, *Inkululeko*, 15 November 1939, p. 1.

29 G Radebe, *Freedom Is Being Murdered!*, Johannesburg District Committee, 1939, in Hyman Papers, Wits Historical Papers, H 3323.

30 Editorial, *Inkululeko*, 6 September 1939, p. 1.

31 For example, the Australian Communist Party initially supported enlistment after the government's declaration of war on Germany, changing course only two weeks later in reaction to the Soviet occupation of eastern Poland (Craig Johnston, 'The "Leading War Party": Communists and World War Two', *Labour History*, 39, 1980, pp. 63–4). For detail on the South African party's initial hesitation on what its

line should be after learning about the German–Soviet Pact, see Rusty Bernstein, *Memory against Forgetting*, Viking Penguin, London, 1999, pp. 35–6. Initially, Johannesburg's communists were almost persuaded by an argument from George Findlay that despite the Pact, the war against Germany was an anti-fascist struggle.

32 Ray Alexander, interviewed by Tom Lodge, Cape Town, 1993.

33 Michael Harmel, 'Vereeniging', *The Rhodian*, XV, 2, Summer 1937, pp. 29–31.

34 Another contributor to *The Rhodian* ('Indifference: An Old Snobbery', XV, Winter 1937) suggests that Harmel was in the party.

35 All the details in this paragraph about Michael Harmel's early life are from Milan Oralek, 'Michael Harmel (1915–1974): A South African Communist and His Discourse', PhD, School of English, Victoria University, Wellington, New Zealand, 2020. A sketch is supplied in Norman Levy, *The Final Prize: My Life in the Anti-Apartheid Struggle*, South African History Online, Cape Town, 2011, p. 68: 'Michael Harmel, a serious man in his early forties, somewhat soulful in expression for the revolutionary he was, was renowned for his political insights, which were often brilliant and sometimes after the event.'

36 'The Communist Party's Policy on the War Now', statement by the Politburo of the Communist Party, 1940 (reprinted in Bunting, *South African Communists Speak*, p. 160).

37 The NEUF was formed in March 1938 at a conference sponsored by the National Liberation League, a mainly coloured organisation founded by James La Guma in Cape Town in 1935. At the inception of the NEUF, both communist and Trotskyist-influenced coloured radicals were elected to the Front's National Council.

38 Bunting, *South African Communists Speak*, pp. 97–8; Alan Brooks, 'From Class Struggle to National Liberation: The Communist Party of South Africa, 1940–1950', MA dissertation, University of Sussex, 1967, pp. 23–5.

39 Basner's decision to resign from the party is explained in a transcript of a tape-recorded biography which is kept in the Institute of Commonwealth Studies, University of London; see Basner Papers, B 28. See also Miriam Basner, *Am I an African? The Political Memoirs of Hyman Basner*, Witwatersrand University Press, Johannesburg, 1993, pp. 97–8.

40 Roger Field, *Alex La Guma: A Literary and Political Biography*, James Currey, Woodbridge, 2010, pp. 40–1. La Guma had allowed his party membership to 'lapse' shortly before, after disagreements over whether whites should help lead the National Liberation League (pragmatically he believed they should withdraw to play a role behind the scenes). La Guma served in Ethiopia and North Africa in the Cape Malay Corps as a company sergeant. Demobilised only in 1947, he rejoined the CPSA on his return to Cape Town (Alex La Guma, *Jimmy La Guma: A Biography*, Friends of the South African Library, Cape Town, 1997, pp. 69–73).

41 According to his first biographer, Bram Fischer was 'deeply worried' by the Pact. The source for this information is not attributed. See Naomi Mitchison, *A Life for Africa: The Story of Bram Fischer*, Merlin Press, London, 1973. Stephen Clingman's biography makes no such suggestion (*Bram Fischer*, p. 154).

42 The Simonses argue that the party needed 'no prompting from outside to define its attitude', but Morkel in his report states that at the time of the German–Soviet Pact the party 'was asked to be cautious in its attitude to the war that was ahead, and not rush in with support'. See Simons and Simons, *Class and Colour*, p. 528 and Bunting, *South African Communists Speak*, p. 149. This is the only evidence of any effort by the Soviet Union to influence the party during the 1940s, Alan Brooks thinks ('From Class Struggle to National Liberation', p. 24). But Rusty Bernstein, when interviewed by Tony Karon in 1986, was certain that by late

1939 there was no direct communication with Comintern, and rather the South Africans were taking their prompts from the British party, with which it was still in frequent contact (Tony Karon, 'The CPSA's Programme in Wartime and After', unpublished paper, Department of Economic History, University of Cape Town, September 1987, p. 4). Any direct contact with the Comintern ended in 1938, well before Comintern's dissolution on 15 May 1943. Comintern's newsletter, *World New and Views*, was still carrying reports about South Africa in December 1939, though (see Bell Keats, 'South Africa: Against Smuts and Herzog–Malan', *World News and Views*, 19, 56, 2 December 1939, p. 1122), written by a member of the CPGB.

43 Gomas, 'The War and Segregation', p. 151.
44 Rusty and Hilda Bernstein, interviewed by Don Pinnock, 1993, transcript, p. 13, Ruth First Papers, Mayibuye Archives.
45 Karon, 'The CPSA's Programme in Wartime and After', p. 6.
46 Charles Dugmore, 'Dadoo Limited versus Krugersdorp Town Council, 1920', Postgraduate Forum Colloquium on Justice, Policy and Change in Southern Africa, 3 October 1998, pp. 11–13. Dadoo's clothing firm was continuing to trade in the 1990s from premises in central Johannesburg.
47 ES Reddy, 'Dadoo, Gandhi and the South African Struggle', *Mainstream*, 16 September 1939, p. 24.
48 Statement by Dr YM Dadoo, 6 September 1940, NEUF, Johannesburg.
49 According to Basner's biographer, Marks was expelled from the party in 1937 or 1938 for neglecting his duties as a party member. Marks had been preoccupied with financial difficulties as well as campaigning on behalf of Basner in the 1939 Native Senator elections. These were years of considerable disaffection with the party's policies among its black members. Marks rejoined the CPSA during the war. See Z Nkosi, 'The Life of a Revolutionary', *Sechaba*, October 1972.
50 *Inkululeko*, 3 March 1941
51 Brooks, 'From Class Struggle to National Liberation', p. 39.
52 See 'The Communist Party's Policy on the War Now', in Bunting, *South African Communists Speak*, p. 154.
53 Editorial, 'People's Programme', *Freedom / Vryheid*, 7, 10 March 1941, pp. 2–4, David Everatt Papers, Wits Historical Papers, A 2521, Ed.
54 Interview with Edwin Mofutsanyana by Bob Edgar, Lesotho, 1982, transcript, p. 38. (Transcript provided to author.)
55 Quoted in Nasson, *South Africa at War*, p. 58.
56 Statement by Dr YM Dadoo, 6 September 1940, NEUF, Johannesburg.
57 *Inkululeko*, 5 May 1941.
58 Transcripts of speeches at party public meetings, Johannesburg, 23 June 1941 and 7 July 1941, Hyman Papers, H 3323, 2.3.
59 'How to Beat Hitler', *Inkululeko*, 7 August 1941.
60 'How to Beat Hitler', *Inkululeko*, 7 August 1941. Dadoo actually quoted Dimitrov in one speech he made on 9 June 1940 at the inaugural meeting of the Transvaal Indian National Youth Organisation (Frene Ginwala Papers, microfilm, DT 764, E3 Gin).
61 Extracts reprinted in Bunting, *South African Communists Speak*, p. 172.
62 Report of the Central Committee to the Communist Party Conference, 14–16 January 1944, reprinted in Bunting, *South African Communists Speak*, p. 184.
63 'The Strike of African Workers and Compulsory Arbitration', statement by the Central Committee of the CPSA, 31 December 1942, reprinted in Bunting, *South African Communists Speak*, p. 117.
64 Bunting, *South African Communists Speak*, p. 113.

65 South Africa did not manufacture newsprint until 1961 and wartime supplies were especially restricted. A 'paper famine' affected even the major commercial newspapers and no fresh periodicals were allowed to begin publication. From the end of 1940 the allocation of newsprint was controlled by a specially appointed official, Colonel JJ Kruger, who worked in conjunction with the Newspaper Press Union to decide who should receive how much. All the party's publications received adequate quotas through the war. After the war the shortages continued and *The Guardian* was denied paper in 1951 (Adrian Hadland, 'The World Paper Famine and the South African Press, 1938–1955', *South African Journal of Economic History*, 20, 1, 2005, pp. 47–63).

66 Brian Bunting, interviewed by Tom Lodge, 27 February 1985.

67 For circulation statistics, see Brooks, 'From Class Struggle to National Liberation', p. 45.

68 The quotation is from an interview with a veteran activist conducted in 1985. Iain Edwards, 'Recollections: The Communist Party and Worker Militancy in Durban, early 1940s', *South African Labour Bulletin*, 11, 4, 1986, p. 68.

69 For descriptions of Trotskyist agitation against the party's new pro-war policy, see A Manson, C Sideris and D Cachalia, *An Oral History of the Life of William Barney Ngakane*, SAIRR, Johannesburg, 1982, pp. 42–5; Bunting, *Moses Kotane*, pp. 119–25.

70 Johannesburg District Committee, *Arm the People*, CPSA, Johannesburg, 1942, reprinted in A Lerumo, *Fifty Fighting Years: The South African Communist Party, 1921–1971*, rev. edn, Inkululeko Publications, London, 1980, pp. 119–25.

71 'Death from the Skies', leaflet issued by the City and Suburban branch of the CPSA, Johannesburg, 1941, Hyman Basner Papers, 2.3.

72 Barry White, 'The Role of the Springbok Legion', *Kleio*, XXV, 1993, p. 99.

73 *Inkululeko*, 20 September 1942.

74 *Inkululeko*, 23 January 1943.

75 Moses Kotane, 'Rigid Discipline and Mass Membership', *Freedom*, 3, 10 December 1944.

76 *Inkululeko*, 23 January 1943 and Simons and Simons, *Class and Colour*, p. 538.

77 AP Mda, 'Report on Communist Activities among the Natives in Johannesburg', *Catholic Times*, July 1942.

78 *The Guardian*, 24 November 1949. The date was mentioned in a death notice of Aaron Molefi, one of its founders.

79 Brooks, 'From Class Struggle to National Liberation', p. 39.

80 Albie Sachs, interviewed by Tom Lodge, 22 November 2018.

81 *The Guardian,* 2 July 1942.

82 George Findlay, Diary, 18 June 1944, Findlay Papers, Wits Historical Papers, A 1002.

83 Ray Alexander, interviewed by Tom Lodge, Cape Town, 1993.

84 Thomas Karis and Gwendoline Carter, *From Protest to Challenge*, volume 2, Hoover Institution, Stanford, 1973, pp. 107 and 408.

85 *Inkululeko*, 8 September 1941.

86 Dominic Fortescue, 'The Communist Party of South Africa and the African Working Class in the 1940s', *International Journal of African Historical Studies*, 24, 3, 1991, p. 490.

87 In 1945, in two of the main district committees elected that year, in Durban of the 11 members, three were white and the rest Indian, and in Cape Town, of 12 members, 10 were white and two African (*Inkululeko*, 34, 14 April 1945). The Johannesburg District Committee elected in mid-1947 was constituted by eight whites, one Indian and four Africans, three of them members since the 1920s (*Inkululeko*, 113, May 1947). By this stage the party in Johannesburg was employing an African full-time organiser, SJ Mogumotsi, a district committee

member; his activities were focused mainly on African branches and African recruitment. The Central Committee elected in January 1947 included two Africans (Kotane and Mofutsanyana) and four Indians and eleven whites (*Inkululeko*, 106, January 1947). The Central Committee elected in 1949 included three Africans, Arthur Damane joining Kotane and Mofutsanyana on the committee (*Inkululeko*, 146, 22 January 1949). The Central Committee for 1950, the CPSA's last elected body, included three Africans, Kotane, JB Marks and Mofutsanyana, ten whites, three Indians and one coloured person, James La Guma, now back in the party fold (*Inkululeko*, 181, 21 January 1949).

88   Moses Kotane, 'Defects in Party Education', *Freedom*, September 1942, reprinted in Bunting, *South African Communists Speak*, p. 73.

89   For precise figures, see Brooks, 'From Class Struggle to National Liberation', pp. 47 and 113–14.

90   Brian Bunting, interviewed by Tom Lodge, 27 February 1985.

91   Bernstein, *Memory against Forgetting*, pp. 66–7.

92   *Freedom*, 11 September 1944.

93   Arnold Selby, interviewed by Sylvia Neame, Berlin, May 1985, Sylvia Neame Papers, Wits Historical Papers, A 2729.

94   Fortescue, 'The Communist Party of South Africa and the African Working Class', p. 491.

95   Fortescue, 'The Communist Party of South Africa and the African Working Class', p. 491.

96   Ray Alexander, 'Building the Party in the Factories', *Freedom*, 11, September 1942, p. 5.

97   Edwards, 'Recollections', p. 71.

98   Vishnu Padayachee, Shahid Vawda and Paul Tichman, 'Trade Unions and the Communist Party in Durban: A Reply to Iain Edwards', *South African Labour Bulletin*, 11, 7, 1986, pp. 52–6.

99   Report by the Investigation Officer of the SAP into the Activities of the SAP (1947), in Union of South Africa, House of Assembly Debates, volume 8, 9 to 25 June 1953, columns 7953–9.

100   Simons and Simons, *Class and Colour*, p. 536.

101   During the 1930s it only attempted to participate in a parliamentary election once, in 1932 in Germiston, when it tried to register JB Marks as a candidate, as a protest against the exclusion of blacks from the franchise.

102   Bunting, *South African Communists Speak*, p. 113.

103   Communist Party of South Africa, *We South Africans*, Cape Town, 1943, p. 34.

104   Communist Party of South Africa, *We South Africans*, p. 37.

105   *The Guardian*, 20 May 1943.

106   Sheridan Johns, 'South African Communists on the Hustings: Why Participate in Elections', paper delivered at the Canadian Research Consortium for Southern Africa (CRCSA), Montreal, Quebec, 22 March 1996, p. 21.

107   Johns, 'South African Communists at the Hustings', p. 22.

108   Albie Sachs, interviewed by Tom Lodge, 18 November 2018.

109   As was reported at the conference that year: 'Our participation in the elections of 1942–1943 is only a beginning of a new period in the history of the South African people. Our experience has shown that our party can gain the goodwill and support of large sections. Our members who have been elected to the City Councils of Cape Town and East London are the first of a future body of Communists on parliamentary and other representative organs' (*Communists in Conference: The 1943–1944 National Conference of the CPSA*, CPSA, Cape Town, 1944, p. 9).

110   *The Guardian*, 29 July 1943.

111   See Leslie Witz, 'A Case of Schizophrenia: The Rise and Fall of the Independent

Labour Party', paper given at the University of the Witwatersrand, History Workshop, 1984, p. 29.

112 Levy, *The Final Prize*, p. 14.

113 Rusty and Hilda Bernstein, interviewed by Don Pinnock, 1993, transcript, p. 18, Ruth First Papers.

114 Hilda and Rusty Bernstein, interviewed by Stephen Clingman, 4 September 1984, African Studies Institute interview transcripts, Oral History Collection, no. 371, Wits Historical Papers.

115 Hilda Watts, *Have You Met Hilda Watts?*, Sholto Douglas Printer, Johannesburg, October 1944.

116 Hilda Watts, *A Straight Talk on Municipal Affairs by Hilda Watts*, October 1944.

117 Hilda Watts, *Rebuild Johannesburg by Councillor Hilda Watts*, Communist Party South Africa, September 1945, p. 3.

118 *Inkululeko*, 29 October 1945.

119 Hilda Watts, *Rebuild Johannesburg*, p. 7. Hilda's husband, Rusty, who both before and after joining up worked as an architect, probably supplied the pictures.

120 Communist Party of South Africa, *Johannesburg Tomorrow*, CPSA Johannesburg District, 1945.

121 B O'Brien, 'Should Communists Contest Municipal Elections', *Freedom*, 5, 1, February 1946.

122 Rusty Bernstein and Hilda Bernstein, interviewed by Maureen Tayal, London, 23 August 1983. See also *The Guardian*, 15 August 1946.

123 Johns, 'South African Communists at the Hustings', p. 25.

124 Jack Simons speaking at the party conference in Cape Town, December 1944, quoted by Bunting, *Moses Kotane*, p. 122.

125 Brooks, 'From Class Struggle to National Liberation', p. 56.

126 Report of the Central Committee to the CPSA Conference, 14–16 January 1944, excerpts in *Freedom*, January 1944.

127 *Inkululeko*, 14 July 1945.

128 CPSA, *Meet the Communists*, Stewart Printing, Cape Town, 1942.

129 JEN Tchamase, *An African Speaks*, CPSA, Cape Town, October 1945, quoted in Bunting, *South African Communists Speak*, p. 126.

130 *The Guardian*, 6 March 1947,

131 Karon, 'The CPSA's Programme in Wartime and After', p. 32, citing *The Guardian* reports.

132 White, 'The Springbok Legion', pp. 98–9.

133 Neil Redfern, 'A British Version of "Browderism": British Communists and the Teheran Conference of 1943', *Science and Society*, 66, 3, 2002, pp. 362–7.

134 HJ Simons, 'Planning and Control under Capitalism', *Freedom*, 2, 7, May 1944; L Bernstein, 'We're Not in a Vacuum: A Reply to George Findlay', *Freedom*, 2, 8, June 1944; RK Cope, 'The Browder Thesis', *Freedom*, 2, 8, June 1944; Archie Levitan, 'Post-war Perspectives: A Reply to RK Cope and Some Others', *Freedom*, 3, 9, September 1944.

135 Rusty Bernstein, *Letter from Italy*, CPSA, Johannesburg, 1945, pp. 7 and 2, Bernstein Papers, Wits Historical Papers, A 3299, A8.1.

136 George Findlay, 'Browderism', Pretoria District Committee, 3 May 1944, copy in Findlay Papers, 5.44.

137 George Findlay, Diary, 18 June 1944, Findlay Papers.

138 George Findlay, Diary, 27 April 1944, 11 July 1944, Findlay Papers.

139 George Findlay Diary, 16 July 1944, 3 August 1944, Findlay Papers.

140 Earl Browder, 'A Great Leader', *The Guardian*, 9 May 1945.

141 *What Next? A Policy for South Africa*, CPSA, 1944, David Everatt Papers, A 2521, Ed.

142   *We South Africans*, CPSA, Cape Town, 1943, p. 34.

143   *Inkululeko*, 12 November 1945,

144   Memo of meeting between representatives of the NEC of the SALP and the CC of the CPSA, Trades Hall, Johannesburg, 1 September 1943, Simons Papers, UCT Manuscripts and Archives, BC 1081, 05.

145   *Inkululeko*, 3 December 1945

146   George Findlay, 'On United Fronts', *Forward*, 4, 6, December 1945, pp. 22–5.

147   Rodney Davenport, *South Africa: A Modern History*, Macmillan, London, 1977, p. 241.

148   It may be possible to see in this phrase an oblique reference to the efforts to establish a Non-European Unity Movement by opponents of the Communist Party and the ANC, some of whom had been previously associated with Dadoo in the NEUF. Baruch Hirson suggests that the anti-pass campaign's timing may have been influenced by a concern to pre-empt the launching of the NEUM. See IB Tabata, *The Awakening of the People*, Spokesmen Books, Nottingham, 1974, pp. 95–103; B Hirson, 'Prices, Homes and Transport', unpublished paper, n. 99.

149   Circular letter from Mofutsanyana and Dadoo, joint convenors, Anti-Pass Committee, 23 November 1943, South African Institute of Race Relations Papers, Wits Historical Papers, AD 843, B51.2.

150   The members of the committee were the following: ET Mofutsanyana, JB Marks, SM Moema, CS Ramohanoe, YM Dadoo, DW Bopape, J Palmer (Mpama), AEP Fish, J Xaba, E Mokoena, O Monongoaha, V Pillay, EP Mafethe, and A Mabuse. At least ten of these people had been, or were at the time, members of the CPSA.

151   Tabata alleges that initially Xuma opposed the campaign, viewing it as an improper attempt to usurp the leadership role of the ANC. Tabata, *Awakening*, p. 96.

152   *Inkululeko*, 10 June 1944.

153   Brooks, 'From Class Struggle to National Liberation', p. 97.

154   *Inkululeko*, 24 June 1944.

155   For a full treatment of the local tensions that led to this incident, see Hilary Sapire, 'The Stay-Away of the Brakpan Location', University of the Witwatersrand, History Workshop paper, 1984.

156   *Inkululeko*, 9 September 1944.

157   *Inkululeko*, 24 February 1945.

158   *Inkululeko*, 10 March 1945 and 24 March 1945.

159   Tabata, *Awakening*, p. 96. Tabata's chronology may be confused. Here it is possible that he may be describing events in a post-war effort to revive the campaign.

160   See Sapire, 'The Stay-Away at Brakpan' and *Inkululeko*, 10 June 1944. In both centres the restriction of lodgers' permits was used by the municipal authorities as a means of controlling the influx of African migrants into the towns.

161   Philip Bonner, 'Eluding Capture: African Grassroots Struggles in 1940s Benoni', in Saul Dubow and Alan Jeeves (eds), *South Africa's 1940s: Worlds of Possibilities*, Double Storey, Cape Town, 2005, pp. 178–83.

162   *Inkululeko*, 26 October 1943.

163   Tabata, *Awakening of the People*, p. 98 and Edward Roux, *Time Longer than Rope*, University of Wisconsin Press, Madison, 1964, p. 322. Both books were first published in 1948.

164   As their name implied, the Boards had no executive powers, and the four elected members were balanced by official nominees. The vote was confined to municipal tenants, and participation in Board elections among eligible voters was very low. Mofutsanyana won his seat in 1942 with 159 votes (*Inkululeko*, 12 January 1942).

165   *South African Worker*, 26 September 1936.

166   As referred to by Roux.

167 The most detailed examination of the role of different political organisations in the Alexandra boycotts is by Baruch Hirson, 'Prices, Homes and Transport'. See also Alfred Stadler, 'A Long Way to Walk', African Studies Institute, University of the Witwatersrand, seminar paper, 1979.

168 Communist Party of South Africa, *They Marched to Victory: The Story of the Alexandra Bus Boycott*, Stewart Printing Company, Cape Town, 1944, pp. 20–1.

169 Edward Roux, 'The Alexandra Bus Boycott', *Trek*, 21 September 1945.

170 *Inkululeko*, 28 July 1945.

171 *Inkululeko*, 93, 11 March 1946.

172 Kevin John French, 'James Mpanza and the Sofasonke Party in the Development of Local Politics in Soweto', MA dissertation, University of the Witwatersrand, 1983.

173 Edwin Mofutsanyana, interviewed by Bob Edgar, Lesotho, 1982, transcript, p. 47.

174 Johannesburg District Committee, *Democracy in Action: Proceedings of the Johannesburg District Annual Conference of the Communist Party, March 17th, 18th and 25th, 1945*, CPSA, Johannesburg, 1945, p. 6.

175 Johannesburg District Committee, *Democracy in Action*, p. 7.

176 Police report cited in 'Report by the Investigation Officer of the SAO into the Activities of the SAP (1947) in the Union of South Africa', House of Assembly Debates, volume 8, 9 to 25 June 1953, column 7953.

177 For a description of the room, see Norman Levy, *The Final Prize*, p. 109.

178 O'Brien, 'Should Communists Contest Municipal Elections', p. 13.

179 Miriam Roth, *The Communist Party in South Africa: Racism, Eurocentrism and Moscow, 1921–1950*, Partridge, Johannesburg, 2016, expresses scepticism about *The Guardian*'s reports of communist victories in Advisory Board elections. The example she focuses on is a report in November 1942 about six communists winning seats in the location in East London, and in doing so defeating Clements Kadalie and R Godlo. She cites no other reports.

180 'Bad Conditions in WNT', CPSA, Johannesburg, n.d. (probably August 1941), Hyman Papers, H 3323, 2.3.

181 In the Transvaal, for instance, groups or branches existed in Central Johannesburg, Sophiatown, Western Native Township, Coronation, Orlando, Pimville, University of the Witwatersrand, Ferreirastown, Bertrams, Yeoville, Alexandra, Payneville (Springs), Kliptown, Germiston, Benoni, Brakpan, Nigel, Lady Selborne, Marabastad, Eersterust, Atteridgeville, Pretoria Central, Krugersdorp and Roodepoort.

182 Fortescue, 'The Communist Party of South Africa and the African Working Class', p. 494.

183 Reports in *Inkululeko*, 1943–1946 and *Communists in Conference: The 1943–1944 National Conference of the CPSA*, p. 5.

184 For elaboration of the argument with reference to Port Elizabeth and the East Rand where a high level of cross-affiliation in the leadership of trade unions, the ANC and the CPSA was achieved, see Tom Lodge, *Black Politics in South Africa since 1945*, Longman, London, 1983, pp. 51 and 131–3.

185 *The Guardian*, 17 January 1946. The *Guardian* report suggests the League was re-established in 1945 but Ahmed Kathrada recalled joining it in 1941 when he was interviewed (AM Kathrada, interviewed by Sylvia Neame, 17 December 1995, Sylvia Neame Papers).

186 Ruth First and Harold Wolpe were to travel to Europe at the end of 1945 as conference delegates, and in their absence there was a proposal by Eric Laufer, a Wits law student, to split the League into racial sections. The suggestion was rejected but Laufer apparently had some support from his fellow students (AH Kathrada, interviewed by Sylvia Neame, Sylvia Neame Papers).

187   Don Pinnock, *Ruth First: Voices of Liberation*, Human Sciences Research Council Press, Cape Town, 2012, pp. 8–9.

188   Maliba and the ZCA were not mentioned at all in the party's own first systematic survey of the party's history, A Lerumo's 'After 40 Years', *African Communist*, 7, September 1961, and only in passing in Lerumo's later book-length history. By the time of the publication of Brian Bunting's *South African Communists Speak*, a revised view of Lerumo's importance seems to have developed, for his 1939 pamphlet, originally published by the Johannesburg District Committee, *The Conditions of the Venda People*, is reprinted in full.

189   Baruch Hirson, 'Rural Revolt in South Africa, 1937–1951', *The Societies of Southern Africa in the Nineteenth and Twentieth Century*, volume 8, Institute of Commonwealth Studies, University of London, 1978, pp. 120–2.

190   Peter Delius, 'Sebatakgomo, Migrant Organization, the ANC and the Sekhukhuneland Revolt', *Journal of Southern African Studies*, 15, 4, 1989, pp. 605–9.

191   *Inkululeko*, 14 March 1942, 18 December 1943, 14 August 1944. The Building Workers' Union organiser Jackson Nemkula belonged both to the party and the ZCA, though later he seems to have been expelled from the party, applying in 1949 for reinstatement (Minutes of the CEC, 5 July 1949, Simons Papers, BC 1081, 07).

192   *Inkululeko*, 11 December 1941.

193   *Inkululeko*, 12 January 1942.

194   *Inkululeko*, 19 August 1942.

195   *Inkululeko*, 4 April 1941 and *Communists in Conference: The 1943–1944 National Conference of the CPSA*, 1944.

196   *Inkululeko*, 25 March 1944, 24 November 1944.

197   *Inkululeko*, 15 April 1944. This was after the annual conference in Johannesburg in 1944 had instructed the Central Committee to 'investigate the possibility of organising farm workers and African peasants in the reserves' (Document 80, Bunting, *South African Communists Speak*, p. 80). This was after reports on peasant unrest from the Northern Transvaal by Lionel Bernstein and Alpheus Maliba as well as comments by a delegate from Bloemfontein, who said the party should send organisers into the countryside, otherwise others would do so and 'will lead the people' (*Communists in Conference: The 1943–44 Conference of the CPSA*, p. 8).

198   Ray Alexander, interviewed by Tom Lodge, Cape Town, 1993.

199   *Inkululeko*, 15 April 1944.

200   'Race Oppression and the Class Struggle', Report of the Central Committee to the National Conference, CPSA, 1948, Simons Papers, BC 1081, 0.12.1.

201   Ray Alexander, interviewed by Tom Lodge, Cape Town, 1993.

202   Diary entry, 26 July 1944, Findlay Papers, quoted in Richard Haines, 'Resistance and Acquiescence in the Zoutpansberg, 1936–1945', University of the Witwatersrand, History Workshop paper, 1981, p. 6.

203   Hyman Basner, interviewed by Brian Willan, 1975, transcript, p. 50, Institute of Commonwealth Studies Library, University of London, GB 101 ICS 88.

204   Jack Cope (*Comrade Bill*, pp. 332–3) views the ascendancy of 'reactionaries' within the Trades and Labour Council as being completed by 1940 with the defeat of an anti-war motion, the introduction of a block vote, and the voting out of Bill Andrews.

205   For surveys of African trade union organisation during the first years of the war, see WH Andrews, *Class Struggles in South Africa*, Stewart Printing Company, Cape Town, 1941, p. 54; Friends of Africa, Annual Report, October 1940 – June 1941, Ambrose Lynn Saffery Papers, Wits Historical Papers, D1.

206   Fortescue, 'The Communist Party of South Africa and the African Working Class in the 1940s', p. 486.

207   The argument in this paragraph is drawn from Peter Alexander, 'African Trade

Unions and the South African State', pp. 10–19.

208 'African Trade Unions and the Institute', *Race Relations*, 8, 2, 1941, Saffery Papers, A10.

209 *Communists in Conference: The 1943–44 Conference of the CPSA*, p. 5.

210 Quoted in full by Brooks, 'From Class Struggle to National Liberation', p. 58.

211 Ray Alexander, interviewed by Tom Lodge, Cape Town, 1993.

212 Ray Alexander, *Trades Unions and You*, Stewart Printing Company, Cape Town, n.d. [probably 1944], pp. 13–17.

213 Levy, *The Final Prize*, p. 63.

214 'African Trade Unions and the Institute', *Race Relations*, 8, 2, 1941.

215 *Inkululeko*, 27 March 1943.

216 *Inkululeko*, 14 August 1944 and Friends of Africa, 'Report for January–June 1943', Saffery Papers, D1. In January 1944 the union was unable to prevent power station employees from striking at the Victoria Falls works. The Simonses' narrative does not mention the union's role in persuading the men to return to work (*Class and Colour*, pp. 570–1), stating simply that the strike was broken by the Native Military Corps.

217 Dunbar Moodie, 'The South African State and Industrial Conflict in the 1940s', *International Journal of African Historical Studies*, 21, 1, 1988, pp. 28–44.

218 *Inkululeko*, 23 September 1944, 10 June 1944, 28 January 1946. See also *Socialist Action: Progressive Trade Union Bulletin*, 1, 1, February 1945; and Labour History Group, *Workers at War: CNETU and the 1946 African Mineworkers Strike*, Salt River, April 1983.

219 *Socialist Action: Progressive Trade Union Bulletin*, 1, 2, 1945, pp. 3–4.

220 *Inkululeko*, 11 April 1944. A similar motion was adopted in 1942 by the Port Elizabeth branch of the Non-European United Front (Bunting, *South African Communists Speak*, p. 108).

221 For CPSA participation during the strike in January 1943 of Durban Indian rubber workers, see *Inkululeko*, 24 January 1943. This was not a wage dispute but rather a protest strike after the company had tried to sponsor its own union and had sacked workers. For sympathetic reportage of a National Union of Distributive Workers' shop assistants' strike, supported by the Trades and Labour Council, in which the reporter joined the picket line, see *Inkululeko*, 20 November 1943. Here again the strike grievance was not wage-related but arose from OK Bazaars claiming the right to dismiss workers without consulting the union.

222 See, for example, the favourable *Inkululeko* report on the strike led by the Sweet Workers' Union, 22 November 1942. Here, though, the editorial may have been influenced by the non-strategic nature of the industry. See also a sympathetic *Guardian* report on a sugar mill workers' strike ('General Strike Threatened in Sugar Industry', 28 August 1941, p. 7). Another *Guardian* report refers to HA Naidoo in his capacity of president of the NEUF making a statement supporting action by the Tea, Coffee and Chicory Workers' Union ('NEUF Support for Striking Workers', *The Guardian*, 16 October 1941). There is a reference to an FCWU-supported strike in Paarl in 'Paarl Food Workers Still Need Help', *The Guardian*, 16 October 1941, p. 4. The strike followed the dismissal of the local FCWU chairman.

223 Albie Sachs, interviewed by Tom Lodge, 18 November 2018.

224 Brooks, 'From Class Struggle to National Liberation', p. 68.

225 For references to the existence of and activities by a party-sponsored 'Native' or African Miners' or Mineworkers' Union, see *Umsebenzi*, 18 May 1935; *Umsebenzi*, 8 June 1935 (report on striking miners in Brakpan joining the union); *Umsebenzi*, 14 December 1935 (for statement by AMU secretary, TW Thibedi); *Umsebenzi*, 4 April 1936 (report on the need for better organisation); *Umsebenzi*, 8 August 1936, (as an affiliate to a Coordinating Committee of 'Native Trade Unions'); *Umsebenzi*,

27 February 1937 (report on 'native miners' strike' at Nourse mine, with no reference to the union).

226 Brooks, 'From Class Struggle to National Liberation', p. 69.

227 Anon., *A Distant Clap of Thunder: Fortieth Anniversary of the 1946 Mine Strike*, South African Communist Party, London, 1986, p. 5.

228 Anon, *A Distant Clap of Thunder*, p. 1.

229 JB Marks's expulsion for 'failure of discipline' was reported in the *South African Worker* (*Umsebenzi*), 3 July 1937.

230 *The Guardian*, 17 August 1944; VL Allen, *The History of Black Mineworkers in South Africa*, volume 1, Moor Press, Keighley, 1992, p. 384; Baruch Hirson, *Yours for the Union: Class and Community Struggle in South Africa, 1930–1947*, Zed Books, London, 1989, p. 177. At the trial in 1947 in which the CPSA leadership was charged with sedition for their supposed role in instigating the 1946 strike, this disclosure that the party advised against the mineworkers striking in mid-1944 was used by the defence.

231 Eli Weinberg, 'The African Miners', *Freedom*, 7, 2, May 1944, pp. 11–12.

232 Moodie, 'The South African State and Industrial Conflict', p. 47.

233 Dunbar Moodie, 'The Moral Economy of the Black Miners' Strike of 1946', *Journal of Southern African Studies*, 13, 1, October 1986.

234 Fortescue, 'The Communist Party of South Africa and the African Working Class in the 1940s', p. 487.

235 *Revolutionary Communist*, August 1945, p. 3.

236 *Socialist Action: Progressive Trade Union Bulletin*, 1, 1, February 1945.

237 *Inkululeko*, 11 August 1945; Roux, *Time Longer than Rope*, p. 334.

238 Editorial, 'The Struggle for a Party', *Revolutionary Communist*, Workers' International League, Johannesburg, August 1945, p. 2.

239 For Naidoo's views on this issue, see HA Naidoo, 'Trade Union Separatism', *Forward*, 4, 6 December 1945. Ray Alexander, interviewed by Tom Lodge, Cape Town, 1993.

240 The unions are listed in Phyllis Naidoo, 'George Ponnen: Working Class Hero', 11 January 1996, Phyllis Naidoo Papers, 2093/2014.

241 Podbrey, *White Girl*, p. 71

242 Pauline Podbrey, interviewed by Maureen Tayal, London, 8 August 1983, African Studies Institute, Oral History Collection, University of the Witwatersrand.

243 Pauline Podbrey, *White Girl*, p. 77.

244 *Inkululeko*, 25, 23 January 1943.

245 Natal Rubber Workers' Union, 'Defend the Rights of Our Workmates up North', Universal Printing Works, Durban, [1943], Phyllis Naidoo Papers, 2277/25. The issues in the Dunlop stoppage were complex: the pamphlet was probably a bid to secure white worker support. Most of the strikers were Indian. Management had in the previous year been replacing Indian workers with lower-paid Africans and at the end of the year 13 prominent trade unionists within the factory were dismissed: this action triggered the strike (Edwards, 'Recollections', pp. 74–5).

246 Padayachee, Vawda and Tichman, 'Trade Unions and the Communist Party in Durban', p. 60.

247 Podbrey, *White Girl*, p. 96.

248 Brooks, 'From Class Struggle to National Liberation', p. 82

249 Rusty and Hilda Bernstein, interviewed by Don Pinnock, 1993, transcript, p. 38, Ruth First Papers.

250 Jack Simons in his evidence noted that party membership at around 1,800 had been fairly stable. Quoted in *The Guardian*, 13 February 1947.

251 Bernstein, *Memory against Forgetting*, p. 92.

252 Baruch Hirson thinks that Louis Joffe's speech 'was in fact calling for a strike' and that it had a wide impact, being partly responsible for the 'precipitate' wildcat strikes that broke out in individual mines in late April (Hirson, *Yours for the Union*, p. 179).

253 William Beinart, 'Worker Consciousness, Ethnic Particularism and Nationalism', in Shula Marks and Stanley Trapido (eds), *The Politics of Race, Class and Nationalism in 20th Century South Africa*, London, Longman, 1987.

254 Bernstein, *Memory against Forgetting*, p. 93.

255 Hyman Basner's evidence in the sedition trial, quoted in *The Guardian*, 20 February 1947.

256 Jack Simons's evidence in the sedition trial quoted in *The Guardian*, 13 February 1947.

257 Harry Snitcher's evidence quoted in *The Guardian*, 13 February 1947.

258 Evidence at sedition trial, *The Guardian*, 27 February 1947. In Johannesburg, Bram Fischer shared this view. In his evidence at the trial he explained that he thought the proposed strike was so unlikely that he took his family away for a holiday they had planned at the Kruger Park, hurrying back home when the strike began.

259 Jack Simons's evidence, *The Guardian*, 27 February 1947.

260 *The Guardian*, 22 August 1946.

261 Jack Simons's evidence in the sedition trial, quoted in *The Guardian*, 13 February 1947.

262 CPSA Conference, Johannesburg, 29 December 1938 – 1 January 1939, verbatim minutes, p. 27, Simons Papers, BC 1081, 0.12.1.

263 Ray Alexander, interviewed by Tom Lodge, Cape Town, 1993.

264 Moodie, 'The South African State and Industrial Conflict in the 1940s', p. 39.

265 Dan O'Meara, 'The 1946 African Miners' Strike and the Political Economy of South Africa', *Journal of Commonwealth and Comparative Politics*, XII, 2, 1975.

266 George Findlay, 'On United Fronts', *Freedom*, 4, 6, December 1945, p. 26.

267 Ray Alexander, interviewed by Tom Lodge, Cape Town, 1993.

268 'Stimulating Conference', *The Guardian*, 10 January 1946.

269 'Report by the Investigation Officer of the SAO into the Activities of the SAP (1947) in the Union of South Africa', House of Assembly Debates, volume 8, 9 to 25 June 1953, column 7951.

270 Central Committee of the Communist Party of South Africa, *Sam Kahn Speaks*, Pioneer Press, Cape Town, 1949, p. 13.

271 'Reply by Writer', *Freedom*, 5, 1, February 1946.

272 K Luckhardt and N Wall, *Organize or Starve: The History of the South African Congress of Trade Unions*, Lawrence and Wishart, London, 1980, p. 82.

273 Minutes of Central Executive Committee, Cape Town, 12 July 1949, Simons Papers, BC 1081, 07.

274 *Inkululeko*, 174, 24 September 1949.

275 On the Alexandra Tenants' Union, see *Inkululeko*, 123, January 1948.

276 *The Guardian*, 11 April 1946, 2 May 1946, 7 February 1947.

277 'Squatters Demand Land', *Inkululeko*, 107, 2nd issue, January 1947.

278 'Women's Raid on Meat Centres', *The Guardian*, 17 January 1946; 'Communists Raid Shops for Food', *Inkululeko*, 1 June 1946.

279 Johannesburg West Branch of the CPSA, *Smash the Black Market*, Johannesburg, June 1946.

280 Letter from Danie du Plessis to Margaret Ballinger, 25 June 1947, Everatt Papers, A 252, Ed.

281 *Inkululeko*, 113, 1st issue, May 1947.

282 *Inkululeko*, 118, 2nd issue, July 1947; *Inkululeko*, 124, February 1948.

283 *Inkululeko*, 106, January 1947.

284 For a report on the deposition of Chief Sibasa and subsequent ZBA mass meeting and court challenge to the decision, see *Inkululeko*, 102, November 1946;

Inkululeko, 111, 1st issue, April 1947; *Inkululeko*, 118, 2nd issue, July 1947.

285   Minutes of meeting of the Central Committee of the CPSA, Cape Town, 19 July 1949, Simons Papers, BC 1081, 08.1.

286   Fortescue, 'The Communist Party of South Africa and the African Working Class in the 1940s', p. 489.

287   Police attending TARC meetings reported modest-sized audiences of between 100 and 200. Organisers told those present that 'volunteers to join the resistance movement will be told in due course what action to take': perhaps the presence of police observers made them wary about spelling out any plans. Union of South Africa, *Suppression of Communism Act Enquiry into Brian Bunting, Member for Cape Western*, Pretoria, SC 10-53, 1953, p. 16.

288   *Inkululeko*, 134, 30 October 1948.

289   *The Guardian*, 19 November 1942, cited by Fortescue, 'The Communist Party and the African Working Class in the 1940s', p. 490.

290   For details on the party's activities in Langa, see Muchaparara Musemwa, 'Aspects of the Social and Political History of Langa Township, Cape Town, 1927–1948', MA dissertation, Department of History, University of Cape Town, 1993, pp. 153–89.

291   Draft Report of the District Committee to the Annual District Conference, 23 April 1950, Simons Papers, BC 1081, 0.12.3.

292   Workforce statistics in Union of South Africa, *Census, 1946*, Pretoria UG 41, 1954; CNETU affiliation total reported in 'Minute of African Trade Unions', Rheinallt Jones Papers, Wits Historical Papers, Ja2.11.

293   See reports in the *Eastern Province Herald*, 24 April 1948 to 4 June 1948.

294   Govan Mbeki, 'Resistance Politics in Port Elizabeth, New Brighton Township, and the Transkei, 1930–1961', unpublished manuscript, Ben Turok Papers, Rivonia Museum, p. 30.

295   Janet Cherry, 'The Myth of Working Class Defeat: Port Elizabeth in the Post-war Years', *Kronos: Journal of Cape History*, 20, 1, 1993, p. 85.

296   For more detail on the party and trade unions, and the overlap between their leadership and the ANC's, as well as subsequent developments in Port Elizabeth during the early 1950s, see Lodge, *Black Politics in South Africa since 1945*; Cherry, 'The Myth of Working Class Defeat', pp. 66–91.

297   Mbeki, 'Resistance Politics in Port Elizabeth's New Brighton Township and the Transkei', p. 30.

298   *Inkululeko*, 14 April 1945.

299   Mxolise C. Dlamuka, 'Connectedness and Disconnectedness in Thembeyakhe Harry Gwala's Biography, 1920–1995: Rethinking Political Militancy, Mass Mobilisation and Grassroots Struggle in South Africa', PhD dissertation, History Department, University of Western Cape, March 2018, p. 45.

300   Hannah Keal, 'A Life's Work: Hannah Bolton and Durban's Trade Unions, 1944–1974', MA dissertation, University of KwaZulu-Natal, Durban, December 2009, p. 49.

301   Dlamuka, 'Connectedness and Disconnectedness in Thembeyakhe Harry Gwala's Biography', p. 62.

302   Baruch Hirson, 'A Trade Union Organiser in Durban: MB Yengwa, 1943–1944', *The Societies of Southern Africa in the 19th and 20th Centuries*, Institute of Commonwealth Studies, volume 16, University of London, 1990, pp. 37–49. CNETU did not count any of the African unions in Durban among its affiliates (Christopher Merrett, 'Masters and Servants: African Trade Unionism in Pietermaritzburg before the Early 1980s', *Natalia*, 48, 2018).

303   Goolam Vahed, 'The Making of "Indianness": Indian Politics in South Africa during the 1930s and 1940s', *Journal of Natal and Zulu History*, 17, 1997, p. 15.

304   Vahed, 'The Making of "Indianness"', p. 20.

305 Iain Edwards and Tim Nuttall, 'Seizing the Moment: The January 1949 Riots, Proletarian Populism, and the Structures of African Urban Life in Durban in the Late 1940s', paper presented at the History Workshop, University of the Witwatersrand, 6–10 February 1990, p. 11.

306 David Hemson, 'Trade Unions, Labour Circulation, and Class Struggle in Durban, 1940–1959', *Journal of Southern African Studies*, 4, 1, 1977, p. 101.

307 Hemson, 'Trade Unions, Labour Circulation, and Class Struggle in Durban', p. 102. For a different view, see Zakhele Zulu, 'Why I Joined the Communist Party: Impact of the Durban Riots', *African Communist*, 42, 1971, pp. 50–4.

308 Edwards, 'Recollections', p. 82.

309 Dlamuka, 'Connectedness and Disconnectedness in Thembeyakhe Harry Gwala's Biography', p. 77.

310 Hemson, 'Trade Unions, Labour Circulation, and Class Struggle in Durban', p. 93.

311 Dlamuka, 'Connectedness and Disconnectedness in Thembeyakhe Harry Gwala's Biography', p. 78.

312 Naboth Mokgatle, *Autobiography of an Unknown South African*, University of California Press, Berkeley, 1971, pp. 174–80.

313 For the membership statistics, see Baruch Hirson, 'The Mines, the State and African Trade Unions', unpublished seminar paper, p. 24. George Findlay reported at the party's 1944 annual conference that African secretaries led 17 'well-run' unions linked to the Council (*Communists in Conference*, CPSA, Cape Town, January 1944, p. 7).

314 Judicial Commission of Enquiry, Pretoria Municipal Riot of 28 December 1942, Report no. 40, SAIRR Papers, AD 843, B95.3, p. 32.

315 Extract from evidence given by Transvaal CNETU to the Industrial Legislation Commission, Rheinallt Jones Papers, Ja2.11. CNETU figures both at their peak and during their decline were probably overestimations. A figure of 17,000 in 1942 would have represented a very high proportion of Africans in wage employment in Pretoria. The 1948 figures attributed 2,500 workers to the Municipal Workers' Union, three times the total given to the judicial commission of inquiry in 1943 when the union was at its prime.

316 Mokgatle, *Autobiography*, pp. 249 and 264.

317 *Inkululeko*, 111, April 1947.

318 *Inkululeko*, 111, April 1947, p. 274.

319 Findlay Papers.

320 Diary, 27 April 1944, Findlay Papers.

321 Diary, 24 July 1944, Findlay Papers.

322 As noted above, Pretoria provided the setting for the first major defections from the South African Trades and Labour Council in 1948. The portents were visible well before then. George Findlay noted on May Day (Diary, 2 May 1944) anti-African speeches at the Trades Hall: 'Our comrades at the meetings were both frightened and silent.' Rutherford proposed that DPC should support a proposal in the Building Workers' Union that Africans should be admitted into skilled work at half-pay (Diary, 2 May 1944). Later the Building Workers expelled communist members despite rank-and-file protests (Diary, 4 July 1944).

323 Diary, 9 September 1944, Findlay Papers.

324 Diary, volume 1, p. 79, Findlay Papers.

325 Diary, volume 1, p. 54, Findlay Papers.

326 Diary, volume 2, entry for 16 February 1945, Findlay Papers.

327 Diary, 17 July 1945, Findlay Papers.

328 Diary, volume 2, entry for 2 March 1945, Findlay Papers.

329   *The Guardian*, 7 February 1946.

330   *The Guardian*, 4 April 1946.

331   *The Guardian*, 23 May 1946, 29 May 1946, 6 June 1946.

332   *The Guardian*, 25 July 1946, 8 August 1946.

333   *The Guardian*, 22 August 1946.

334   *The Guardian*, 27 February 1947.

335   *The Guardian*, 6 March 1947.

336   Mokgatle, *Autobiography*, p. 281.

337   Republic of South Africa, *Government Gazette*, 16 November 1962, List of people associated with the Communist Party of South Africa. This list is not altogether accurate but in the case of the listed Pretoria members, it has proved correct for those entries which it has been possible to check.

338   The remaining districts were Durban with 115 members, the East Rand with 305, Pretoria with 133, East London with 113 and Port Elizabeth with 75. There remained 30 communists in 'outside areas'. Statistics from Report of the Central Committee to National Conference of the CPSA, 8–10 July 1949, Simons Papers, BC 1081, 0.12.1.

339   Moses Kotane, Affidavit in the matter of the petition of Sam Kahn, Supreme Court, Cape Town, 14 September 1950, p. 3 (document included in Moses Kotane's police file, South African National Archives).

340   Report of the Central Committee to National Conference of the CPSA, 5–8 January 1950, Simons Papers, BC 1081, 0.12.1.

341   Bill Andrews to Solly Sachs, 20 March 1947, Garment Workers' Union Papers, Wits Historical Papers, AH 1092, Bcc.2.1.

342   *The Guardian*, 16 January 1947, cited in Fortescue, 'The Communist Party and the African Working Class in the 1940s', p. 501.

343   Johns, 'South African Communists at the Hustings', p. 26.

344   Johns, 'South African Communists at the Hustings', p. 25.

345   Rusty and Hilda Bernstein, interviewed by Maureen Tayal, London, 23 August 1983. But Brooks suggests that whatever the original intentions may have been, the decision to contest the NRC elections effectively brought the CPSA into alliance with the ANC. Michael Harmel was among those who favoured the party maintaining its boycott stance on the NRC (Brooks, 'From Class Struggle to National Liberation', pp. 73–9).

346   Johns, 'South African Communists at the Hustings', pp. 27–9.

347   Central Committee of the Communist Party of South Africa, *Sam Kahn Speaks: The Parliamentary Record of South Africa's First Communist MP*, p. 38.

348   DY Saks, 'Sam Kahn and the Communist Party', unpublished paper. Sam Kahn did not join the clandestine successor to the banned party though he was among a group who visited the Soviet Union in 1954 and co-authored a leaflet afterwards describing his impressions, focusing on what he perceived to be the happy experiences of the Soviet Jewish community. He evaded arrest during the 1960 state of emergency and left South Africa as an exile, settling in London. He died in a car accident in Israel in 1988 at the age of 77.

349   White, 'The Role of the Springbok Legion', pp. 103–4.

350   Minutes of the Central Committee, CPSA, Cape Town, 9–10 July 1949, Simons Papers, BC 1081, 07.

351   Brooks, 'From Class Struggle to National Liberation', p. 64.

352   Evan Smith, 'Policing Communism across the White Man's World: Anti-Communist Cooperation between Australia, South Africa and Britain in the Early Cold War', *Britain and The World*, 10, 2, 2017, p. 176.

353   'Report by the Investigation Officer of the SAP into the Activities of the SAP

(1947) in Union of South Africa', House of Assembly Debates, volume 8, 9 to 25 June 1953, columns 7946–68.

354   Rusty Bernstein felt the slogan was unrealistic, too far in advance of black workers' expectations, 'not correct at this time'. He was overruled by Moses Kotane (Levy, *The Final Prize*, pp. 70–1).

355   Edwin Mofutsanyana, 'Know Your Organisations: African National Congress', *Fighting Talk*, December 1949, p. 12.

356   Communist Party of South Africa, *The Non-European and the Vote*, Stewart Printing Company, Cape Town, [1948/9], cited in Brooks, 'From Class Struggle to National Liberation', p. 61.

357   Brooks, 'From Class Struggle to National Liberation', p. 62.

358   Letter from Jack Simons to the editor, *Cape Times*, 23 July 1993, Simons Papers, BC 1081.

359   David Everatt, 'Alliance Politics of a Special Type: The Roots of the ANC/SACP Alliance, 1950–1954', *Journal of Southern African Studies*, 18, 1, March 1992, p. 32.

360   Brooks, 'From Class Struggle to National Liberation'.

361   For examples of liberal pessimism, see Paul Rich's discussion of Alfred Hoernlé in his *White Power and the Liberal Conscience*, University of Manchester Press, Manchester, 1984, pp. 66–76.

362   For a recent restatement of this view, see Richard Monroe, 'Lessons of the 1950s', *Inqaba ya Basebenzi*, 13, March–May 1984, p. 9.

363   *Socialist Action: Progressive Trade Union Bulletin*, 1, 1, February 1945, p. 4.

364   Moses Kotane, 'Defects in Party Education', *Freedom*, 11, September 1942, p. 9, cited in Fortescue, 'The Communist Party of South Africa and the African Working Class', p. 498.

365   The obituary of Private Mendel Flior in *Inkululeko*, 8 July 1944 is suggestive. Flior was killed in Italy at the age of 23. Born in Dvinsk in Latvia, he joined the Jewish Workers' Club shortly after his arrival in South Africa in the mid-1930s. As a cabinet maker he became an active trade unionist. He joined the CPSA in 1940. An elder brother died in Spain as a member of the International Brigade.

366   Mokgatle, *Autobiography*, p. 234.

367   Hilda Bernstein, *The World That Was Ours*, Heinemann, London, 1967. She was probably being disingenuous, though: before her recruitment to the South African party, she had belonged to the British Communist Party since 1945. Even so, her professed motivations were probably shared by many of the party's white recruits in the 1940s.

Chapter 6

1   A Lerumo, *Fifty Fighting Years: The South African Communist Party, 1921–1971*, Inkululeko Publications, London, 3rd edn, 1987, pp. 82–98.

2   Brian Bunting (ed.), *South African Communists Speak: Documents from the History of the South African Communist Party, 1915–1980*, Inkululeko Publications, London, 1981, p. 217.

3   Peter Hudson, 'The Freedom Charter and Socialist Strategy in South Africa', *Politikon*, 13, 1, 1986, pp. 75–90; Brigid Lambourne, 'Sowing the Seeds of Alliance: The Evolution of Colonialism of Special Type, 1952–954', History Honours dissertation, Rhodes University, 1990; David Everatt, 'From CPSA to SACP via CST: Socialist Responses to African Nationalism, 1952–1954', in David Everatt, 'The Politics of Nonracialism: White Opposition to Apartheid, 1945–1960', DPhil dissertation, Oxford University, 1990.

4   Brian Bunting, *Moses Kotane: South African Revolutionary*, Inkululeko Publications, London, 1975, p. 224.

5   Gerard Ludi and Blaar Grobbelaar, *The Amazing Mr Fischer*, Nasionale Boekhandel, Cape Town, 1966; Bruno Mtolo, *Umkhonto we Sizwe: The Road to the Left*, Drakensberg Press, Durban, 1966.

6   Raymond Suttner, 'The (Re-)Constitution of the SACP as an Underground Organisation', *Journal of Contemporary African Studies*, 22, 1, 2004.

7   Allison Drew, *Discordant Comrades: Identities and Loyalties on the South African Left*, Ashgate, Ashgate, 2000, p. 270.

8   Report of the Central Committee to the National Conference of the CPSA, 8–10 January 1949, Simons Papers, UCT Manuscript and Archives, 0.12.1.

9   Report of the Central Committee to the National Conference of the CPSA, 6–8 January 1950, Simons Papers, 0.12.1.

10 Report of the District Committee to the Annual District Conference of the CPSA, Cape Town, 23 April 1950, Simons Papers, 0.12.3.

11 Thembeka Mufamadi, *Raymond Mhlaba's Personal Memoirs: Reminiscing from Rwanda and Uganda*, Human Sciences Research Council Press, Pretoria, 2001, pp. 35–73. For more detail and corroboration of the way in which the CPSA built its influence within the ANC's following in Port Elizabeth, see Tom Lodge, *Black Politics in South Africa since 1945*, Longman, London, 1983, pp. 51–4.

12 Lionel ('Rusty') Bernstein, quoted in Peter Delius, 'Sebatakgomo and the Zoutpansberg Balemi Association: The ANC, the Communist Party and Rural Organisation', *Journal of African History*, 34, 1993, p. 310.

13 Full text in the Simons Papers, 0.12.1; extract reprinted in Bunting, *South African Communists Speak*, pp. 200–11.

14 Bunting, *Moses Kotane*, p. 165.

15 Michael Harmel, 'Some Notes on the Communist Party in South Africa', Ronnie Kasrils Papers, Wits Historical Papers, A 3345, A6.1.4.2.

16 Hudson, 'The Freedom Charter', p. 78 and Irina Filatova, 'The Lasting Legacy: The Soviet Theory of National Democratic Revolution and South Africa', *South African Historical Journal*, 64, 3, 2012, pp. 512–13.

17 Lionel 'Rusty' Bernstein, interviewed by Stephen Clingman, 4 September 1984, African Studies Institute Oral History Collection, University of the Witwatersrand.

18 For references to fascism and the need for a united front to fight fascism, see Report of the Central Committee to the National Conference of the CPSA, 8–10 January 1949.

19 David Everatt quotes an article in *Viewpoints and Perspectives* by a white former CPSA member in Cape Town in early 1953 which advocated the 'building of cohesive organisation of the industrial working class in alliance with rural workers and peasants' (David Everatt, *The Roots of Non-Racialism: White Opposition to Apartheid in the 1950s*, Wits University Press, Johannesburg, 2009, p. 84). See also Musson's biography of Johnny Gomas for criticisms of united front strategies within the CPSA during the 1940s by an influential coloured trade unionist (Doreen Musson, *Johnny Gomas: Voice of the Working Class*, Buchu Books, Cape Town, 1989, pp. 104–5).

20 Dominic Fortescue, 'The Communist Party of South Africa and the African Working Class in the 1940s', *International Journal of African Historical Studies*, 24, 3, 1991, p. 487.

21 Barry White, 'The Role of the Springbok Legion', *Kleio*, XXV, 1993, p. 100; Joshua Lazerson, *Against the Tide: Whites in the Struggle against Apartheid*, Westview Press, Boulder, 1994, p. 5.

22 Rica Hodgson, *Foot Soldier for Freedom*, Picador Africa, Johannesburg, 2013, p. 62.

23 Harmel. 'Some Notes on the Communist Party'.

24 Bunting, *Moses Kotane*, p. 191

25 Mufamadi, *Raymond Mhlaba's Personal Memoirs*, p. 95

26 Lionel Bernstein, *Memory against Forgetting*, Viking Penguin, London, 1999, p. 125. Slovo himself confirms that it was the Wits group that took the initiative: 'we made it plain to ex-members of the Central Committee that unless something was done by them, we would jump the gun and form our own Party underground' (Joe Slovo, *Slovo: The Unfinished Autobiography*, Ravan Press, Randburg, 1995, p. 83). Slovo's account corroborates Bernstein's memoir (Joe Slovo, interviewed by Sylvia Neame, Berlin, GDR, 7 April 1986, Sylvia Neame Papers, Wits Historical Papers, A 2729).

27 Everatt, *The Roots of Non-Racialism*, p. 80.

28 Ben Turok, *Nothing but the Truth: Behind the ANC's Struggle Politics*, Jonathan Ball, Johannesburg, 2003, p. 30. Brian Bunting recalled that older Cape Town members were meeting independently of the Modern Youth Society group (Brian Bunting, interviewed by Sylvia Neame, 14 May 1986, Sylvia Neame Papers, A 2729, E1).

29 Albie Sachs, interviewed by Tom Lodge, 22 November 2018.

30 Suttner, 'The (Re-)Constitution of the SACP', p. 43.

31 Naboth Mokgatle, *The Autobiography of an Unknown South African*, Ad Donker, Parklands, 1990, pp. 288–9; A Lerumo, 'Review of Mokgatle's Autobiography', *African Communist*, 48, 1972.

32 In 1954 Mokgatle managed to obtain an invitation to a WFTU gathering in Bucharest. In Vienna, just before embarking on the final stage of his journey, he was informed the invitation has been withdrawn at the request of South Africa communists, Harmel suggests (Lerumo, 'Review'). Mokgatle remained in Europe.

33 Bernstein, *Memory against Forgetting*, p. 129.

34 Bernstein, *Memory against Forgetting*. Slovo provides a full description of the procedure in his memoir (Slovo, *An Unfinished Autobiography*, p. 108).

35 Bernstein, *Memory against Forgetting*, p. 130; Harmel, 'Some Notes on the Communist Party'.

36 Bunting, *Moses Kotane*, p. 173. Brian Bunting, interviewed by Sylvia Neame, London, 14 May 1986, Sylvia Neame Papers, A 2729, E1.

37 Brian Bunting, interviewed by Sylvia Neame, 14 May 1986, Sylvia Neame Papers, A 2729, E1.

38 Moses Kotane, 'Notes on Aspects of the Political Situation in the Republic of South Africa', 9 November 1961, Kasrils Papers, 9 November 1961.

39 Bernstein, *Memory against Forgetting*, p. 123.

40 Suttner, 'The (Re-)Constitution of the SACP', p. 50. For another example of the party's early selectiveness in recruitment, see Norma Kitson, *Where Sixpence Lives*, Hogarth Press, London, 1987, p. 91,

41 Ben Turok, interviewed by Tom Lodge, London, 1985.

42 Bunting, *Moses Kotane*, p. 257.

43 According to his biographer, his 'primary loyalty' remained with the ANC (Elinor Sisulu, *Walter and Albertina Sisulu: In Our Lifetime*, David Philip, Cape Town, 2002, p. 123).

44 See John Pule Motshabi's remarks about his own and David Bopape's reactions in 'Minutes of Africa Group Meeting, 13 May 1982', Simons Papers, 08.1.

45 See JJ Jabulani, 'Why I Joined the Communist Party', *African Communist*, 44, 1971, pp. 79–81.

46 Natoo Babenia, *Memoirs of a Saboteur*, Mayibuye Books, Bellville, 1995, p. 62.

47 Arnold Selby, interviewed by Sylvia Neame, Berlin, 31 May 1985, transcript, p. 11, Sylvia Neame Papers, Wits Historical Papers, A 2729,

48 Rowley Arenstein, interviewed by Iain Edwards, Durban, 1986 (transcript provided to the author). Shamin Marie also noted that 'No major effort was made to extend

[SACTU] membership among Indian workers' (Shamin Marie, *Divide and Profit: Indian Workers in Natal*, Department of Industrial Sociology, University of Natal, Durban, 1986, p. 76).

49 Bettie du Toit, interviewed by Tom Lodge, London, 29 January 1978. See also Bettie du Toit, *Ukubamba Amadolo: Workers' Struggles in the South African Textile Industry*, Onyx Press, London, 1978.

50 Pauline Podbrey, interviewed by Maureen Tayal, London, 8 August 1983, African Studies Institute, Oral History Collection, University of the Witwatersrand.

51 Bill Freund discusses the reasons for declining Indian worker militancy during the 1950s in *Insiders and Outsiders: The Indian Working Class in Durban*, James Currey, London, 1995, pp. 57–61.

52 Moses Kotane, *The Great Crisis Ahead: A Call for Unity*, Pioneer Press, Cape Town, 1957, p. 11.

53 Turok, *Nothing but the Truth*, pp. 53–4.

54 Her autobiography makes only occasional references to SACP activity through the 1950s until her departure into exile in 1955 and it is very evident that, despite attending meetings, trade unions remained her chief commitment (see Ray Alexander Simons, *All My Life and All My Strength*, STE Publishers, Johannesburg, 2004, pp. 196–297.

55 Minutes of CPSA conference, 1938, p. 27, Simons Papers, 0.12.1.

56 Eli Weinberg in *Viewpoints and Perspectives*, 1, 3, February 1954, pp. 22–5, Treason Trial Evidence, Wits Historical Papers, AD 1812, EV2.1.

57 See, for example, Bob Hepple, *Young Man with a Red Tie: A Memoir of Mandela and the Failed Revolution*, Jacana Media, Johannesburg, 2013, p. 29.

58 Ben Turok, interviewed by Tom Lodge, 1985.

59 Hodgson, *Foot Soldier for Freedom*, p. 41.

60 Turok, *Nothing but the Truth*, p. 79.

61 Joe Slovo, interviewed by Sylvia Neame, Berlin, GDR, 7 April 1986, Sylvia Neame Papers, A 2729, H6.4.

62 Brian Bunting, interviewed by Tom Lodge, London, 27 February 1985; Lionel Bernstein, *Letter from Italy*, Communist Party of South Africa, Johannesburg, copy filed in Bernstein Papers, Wits Historical Papers, A 3299, A8.1; Gerald Shaw, 'Wolfie Kodesh, Obituary', *The Guardian*, 13 November 2002; Slovo, *The Unfinished Autobiography*, pp. 29–30.

63 Turok, *Nothing but the Truth*, p. 50.

64 Turok, *Nothing but the Truth*, p. 59.

65 For Unity Movement influence on at least one coloured communist, see Musson, *Johnny Gomas*, pp. 105–6.

66 Ben Turok, interviewed by Baruch Hirson, 30 April 1983, Ben Turok Papers, Rivonia Museum, K/1/1.

67 Turok belonged to this group in 1953. For South Africans resident in London who joined the SACP through the London group, see Padraig O'Malley, *Shades of Difference: Mac Maharaj and the Struggle for South Africa*, Viking, New York, 2007, pp. 82–3: they included Kader Asmal and Mac Maharaj. See also Kitson, *Where Sixpence Lives*, p. 15.

68 Mark Israel, *South African Political Exiles in the United Kingdom*, Macmillan, Basingstoke, 1999, pp. 26–7.

69 Ben Turok, interviewed by son, Ben Turok Papers, K/3.

70 Ben Turok, intervjewed by Baruch Hirson, 30 April 1983, Ben Turok Papers, Rivonia Museum, K/1/1.

71 Bunting, *Moses Kotane*, p. 193.

72 Suttner, 'The (Re-)Constitution of the SACP', p. 53.

73 Rowley Arenstein, interviewed by Iain Edwards, Durban, 1986 (transcript provided to the author).

74 Everatt, *The Roots of Non Racialism*, pp. 82–96.

75 Hudson, 'The Freedom Charter', pp. 78–81.

76 Editorial, *Viewpoints and Perspectives*, 1/3, Treason Trial Papers, Wits Historical Papers, AD 1812, EV2.1.

77 'The Symposium on the National Question', May 1954, Treason Trial Papers, AD 1812, EV2.2.

78 This was a very dogmatic view given that the legislation the ANC was challenging, which included the pass laws, the ban on the Communist Party and the Bantu Authorities Act. It was true that the Group Areas Act had especially severe implications for African property owners and traders.

79 Danie du Plessis, 'The Situation in South Africa Today', *Viewpoints and Perspectives*, 1, 3, February 1954, pp. 39–48.

80 Filatova, 'The Lasting Legacy', pp. 516–18.

81 Rowley Arenstein, interviewed by Iain Edwards, Durban, 1986 (transcript provided to the author).

82 And remained so through the decade and beyond. See Stephen R Davis, *The ANC's War against Apartheid*, Indiana University Press, Bloomington, 2018, p. 57, who cites as his source an interview with Sue Rabkin, who joined the party in the 1970s. See also A Kathrada, *No Bread for Mandela: Memoirs of Ahmed Kathrada*, University of Kentucky Press, Lexington, 2010, p. 90.

83 W Storm and B Storm, *We Meet the Czechoslovaks*, Orbis, Prague, June 1948, p. 5.

84 Storm and Storm, *We Meet the Czechoslovaks*, p .8.

85 Stephen Clingman, *Bram Fischer: Afrikaner Revolutionary*, David Philip, Cape Town, 1998, p. 205. She was initially refused a visa by the Soviet authorities, a telling indication of just how disjointed the SACP's international connections were at this stage; she obtained her Chinese visa with the help of Vella Pillay .

86 Paul Joseph, *Slumboy from the Golden City*, Merlin Press, London, 2018, pp. 91–2. He doesn't mention discussing the Slansky trial with Gustava Fučikova. Two years beforehand she had been a prosecution witness against one of the hanged defendants, Bedřich Reicin, accusing him of being a Gestapo agent. The accusation was false though accepted at the time. See Peter Steiner, 'Making a Czech Hero: Julius Fučik through his Writings', Carl Beck Papers in Russian and East European Studies, no. 1501, University of Pittsburgh, Pittsburgh, 2000, pp. 10–11.

87 Henry R Pike, *A History of Communism in South Africa*, Christian Mission International of South Africa, Germiston, 1988, p. 303.

88 Brian Bunting, *Life is More Joyous: Report of a Visit to the Soviet Union*, South African Society for Peace and Friendship with the Soviet Union, Johannesburg, 1954.

89 Ruth First, *South Africans in the Soviet Union*, Pacific Press, Johannesburg, 1956. Other contributors included Paul Joseph, Walter Sisulu and Duma Nokwe.

90 Kotane, 'Notes on Some Aspects of the Political Situation in the Republic of South Africa'.

91 Sadie Forman and André Odendaal, *A Trumpet from the Housetops: The Selected Writings of Lionel Forman*, Zed Press, London, 1992, pp. 154–6.

92 Forman and Odendaal, *A Trumpet from the Housetops*, p. 179.

93 Forman and Odendaal, *A Trumpet from the Housetops*, p. 182. For an extended discussion of Forman's ideas, see Tom Lodge, 'Lionel Forman's Trumpet: National Communism in South Africa, 1953–59', *Africa*, 63, 4, 1993.

94 Jack Simons was heavily critical: Forman borrowed too heavily from Russian and Austro-Hungarian experience, he thought. See Lodge, 'Lionel Forman's Trumpet', pp. 604–5.

95 H McGee, *Radical Anti-Apartheid Internationalism and Exile: The Life of Elizabeth Mafeking*, Routledge, Abingdon, 2019, pp. 43–4.

96 Forman and Odendaal, *A Trumpet from the Housetops*, pp. 167–9.

97 S Forman, *Lionel Forman: A Life Too Short*, University of Fort Hare Press, Alice, 2008.

98 Forman, *Lionel Forman*, p. 199.

99 Jiri Pelikan, *The Czechoslovak Political Trials, 1950–1954: The Suppressed Report of the Dubček Government's Commission of Inquiry*, Macdonald, London, 1971.

100 Progressive Committee for Jewish Affairs, *Is There Anti-Semitism in Eastern Europe?*, Pacific Press, Johannesburg, 1953, p. 5.

101 Forman and Odendaal, *A Trumpet from the Housetops*, pp. 167–9.

102 M Heimann, *Czechoslovakia: The State that Failed*, Yale University Press, New Haven, 2011, p. 204.

103 Forman, *Lionel Forman*, p. 199.

104 Storm and Storm, *We Meet the Czechoslovaks*, p. 39.

105 Forman, *Lionel Forman*, p. 187.

106 Forman, *Lionel Forman*, p. 191.

107 Albie Sachs, interviewed by Milan Oralek, 27 September 2014 (transcript provided to the author).

108 Forman and Odendaal, *A Trumpet from the Housetops*, p. 182.

109 Storm and Storm, *We Meet the Czechoslovaks*, p. 44.

110 GH Skilling, *Czechoslovakia's Interrupted Revolution*, Princeton University Press, Princeton, 1976, pp. 23–5.

111 For the character of the Czechoslovak party's moral authority during the 1950s, see Matěj Spurný, *Making the Most of Tomorrow*, Karolinum Press, Prague, 2019, pp. 76–84.

112 Reprinted in Bunting, *South African Communists Speak*, pp. 231–41.

113 Turok, *Nothing but the Truth*, p. 59.

114 Sisulu joined the SACP in 1955 according to Harmel's 'Notes' and Beyleveld (by his account in trial evidence) in 1965.

115 Bernstein, *Memory against Forgetting*, pp. 149–55. Slovo confirmed Bernstein's authorship of the first draft in an interview with Sylvia Neame in August 1986 (Neame Papers, A 2729, E1), though he also remembered that the draft was subsequently 'worked on' by the committee, which he thought included himself and Sisulu.

116 Joe Slovo, interviewed by Sylvia Neame, Berlin, GDR, 7 April 1986, transcript, p. 16, Sylvia Neame Papers, A 2729.

117 Norman Levy, *The Final Prize: My Life in the Anti-Apartheid Struggle*, South African History Online, Observatory, Cape Town, 2011, p. 179.

118 Harmel, 'Some Notes on the Communist Party'.

119 Kotane, 'Notes on Aspects of the Political Situation in the Republic of South Africa'.

120 Ben Turok, interviewed by Tom Lodge, London, 1985.

121 Turok, *Nothing but the Truth*, p. 59.

122 Police record of the Congress of the People, Kliptown, Johannesburg, 25–26 June 1955, extracts reproduced in Thomas Karis and Gail M Gerhart, *From Protest to Challenge*, volume 3: *Challenge and Violence, 1953–1964*, Hoover Institution Press, Stanford, 1977.

123 Turok, *Nothing but the Truth*, p. 262.

124 Ben Turok, interviewed by Tom Lodge, London, 1985.

125 Nelson Mandela, 'In Our lifetime', *Liberation*, June 1956.

126 Editorial, *African Communist*, October 1959.

127   Bunting, *Moses Kotane*, p. 224.
128   Wilton Mkwayi and Raymond Mhlaba, interviewed by Barbara Harmel and Philip Bonner, 18 and 27 October 1993, transcripts, Wits Historical Papers.
129   Raymond Suttner and Jeremy Cronin, *30 Years of the Freedom Charter*, Ravan Press, Johannesburg, 1986, p. 109.
130   Reggie Vandeyar, Liz Abrahams and Billy Nair, quoted in Suttner and Cronin, *30 Years of the Freedom Charter*, pp. 39–41.
131   Colin Bundy, *Govan Mbeki*, Jacana Media, Johannesburg, 2012, p. 82
132   Bundy, *Govan Mbeki*, , 2012, p. 36
133   Peter Delius, 'Sebatakgomo and the Zoutpansberg Balemi Association: The ANC, the Communist Party and Rural Organization, 1939–1955', *Journal of African History*, 34, 1993, p. 312.
134   Ben Turok, interviewed by Baruch Hirson, 30 April 1983, Ben Turok Papers, K/1/7.
135   It is unclear whether Horvitch joined the SACP, though he was evidently trusted and respected by its members. The son of Lithuanian immigrants, he was born in 1920 and joined the CPSA at school in Cape Town. He qualified as an architect before working full-time for the party through the war. He was among the defendants in the 1956–61 Treason Trial and left South Africa after the Sharpeville Massacre in 1960. With his family he eventually settled in Britain, where he requalified and practised as an architect in Hampstead. He died in 2005.
136   Kotane, 'Notes on Aspects of the Political Situation in the Republic of South Africa'.
137   Though SACOD membership was open and in Johannesburg included a significant group of people, the SACP leaders would have perceived it as Trotskyist. See Baruch Hirson, *Revolutions in My Life*, Witwatersrand University Press, Johannesburg, 1995, pp. 268–86.
138   Identified as party members in Mufamadi, *Raymond Mhlaba's Personal Memoirs*, p. 41.
139   Indictment, volume 42, Treason Trial Records, AD 1812.
140   Dominic Fortescue, 'The Communist Party of South Africa and the African Working Class in the 1940s', *International Journal of African Political Studies*, 24, 3, 1991.
141   Nair quoted in Suttner and Cronin, *30 Years of the Freedom Charter*, p. 146.
142   Babenia, *Memoirs of a Saboteur*, p. 50.
143   Suttner, 'The (Re-)Constitution of the SACP', p. 55.
144   Brian Bunting, interviewed by Sylvia Neame, London, 14 May 1986, Sylvia Neame Papers, A 2729, E1.
145   Slovo, *An Unfinished Autobiography*, p. 107.
146   Bunting, *Moses Kotane*, p. 180.
147   Musson, *Johnny Gomas*, pp. 108–9.
148   Bernstein, *Memory against Forgetting*, p. 190.
149   Turok, *Nothing but the Truth*, pp. 90–1.
150   Bunting, *Moses Kotane*, p. 230.
151   *New Age*, 4 April 1957.
152   Obet T Motshabi, 'Obituary: John Pule Motshabi', *Sechaba*, May 1989.
153   Turok, *Nothing but the Truth*, p. 90.
154   Moses Kotane, *The Great Crisis Ahead: A Call to Unity*, New Age Publication, Pioneer Press, Woodstock, 1957.
155   Socialist League of Africa (Baruch Hirson), 'A Critical Discussion: South Africa: Ten Years of the Stay at Home', *International Socialism* (London), 5, Summer 1961.
156   Bernstein, *Memory against Forgetting*, p. 15.
157   See Billy Nair on holding 'mass meetings directly in the factories' in Suttner and Cronin, *30 Years of the Freedom Charter*, pp. 41–2.
158   Rowley Arenstein, interviewed by Iain Edwards, Durban, 1986 (transcript provided to author).

159 Turok, *Nothing but the Truth*, p. 90.

160 As he told Baruch Hirson in his interview on 30 April 1983 (Ben Turok Papers, K/1/7), on the whole trade union organisers 'were low level cadres, they did the job but they were very union oriented, obsessed with day to day matters like wage agreements and not interested in national or revolutionary politics'.

161 Hirson, *Revolutions in My Life*, p. 283. For Du Toit's argument, see her *Ukubamba Amadolo*, pp. 126–7. After leaving South Africa, she was refused asylum by the Tanzanians after they consulted with local ANC officials, who included Moses Kotane, about her freedom fighter status (Miriam Basner, interviewed by Tom Lodge, Presteigne, 14 September 1984). This was despite party members helping her to leave South Africa and offering her hospitality during her transit through Bechuanaland (Hodgson, *Foot Soldier for Freedom*, p. 131).

162 See Dan Thloome, 'Lessons of the Stay-Away', *Liberation*, 32, August 1958, pp. 10–13.

163 Bunting, *Moses Kotane*, p. 198.

164 Bernstein, *Memory against Forgetting*, p. 131.

165 Turok, *Nothing but the Truth*, p. 48.

166 Joe Slovo, interviewed by Sylvia Neame, Berlin, GDR, 7 April 1986, Sylvia Neame Papers.

167 As Fred Carneson remarked, 'I don't know what the Nats were doing, putting us together on state expenses. An excellent opportunity to plan our next steps' (Lynn Carneson, *Red in the Rainbow: The Life and Times of Fred and Sarah Carneson*, Zebra Press, Cape Town, 2010, p. 142).

168 Joe Slovo, interviewed by Sylvia Neame, Berlin, GDR, 7 April 1986, Sylvia Neame Papers.

169 On 'D-category' members, see Kitson, *Where Sixpence Lives*, p. 131. See also Clingman, *Bram Fischer*, p. 294. Ben Turok (interviewed by Brian Bunting, 9 October 1973, Ben Turok Papers, J/2/19) thought the D members were especially invaluable during the 1960 Emergency.

170 Ruth First's father, Julius, owned a furniture factory outside Johannesburg, the venue for the party's second congress. His share portfolio helped his daughter re-establish her household in London in exile in 1963 (Alan Wieder, *Ruth First and Joe Slovo in the War against Apartheid*, Monthly Review Press, New York, 2013, p. 145). Ben Turok's father also owned a leather works in Cape Town and Pixie Benjamin's father was the founder of a major engineering firm.

171 Vella Pillay and Yusuf Dadoo, 'The Political Situation in the Union of South Africa', Kasrils Papers, A 3345, A6.1.4.2.

172 Parvathi Raman, 'Yusuf Dadoo: A Son of South Africa', in Saul Dubow and Alan Jeeves (eds), *South Africa's 1940s: Worlds of Possibilities*, Double Storey, Cape Town, 2005, p. 237.

173 For a detailed description of political fundraising among Indians and reference to Dadoo's role as a 'referee', see Hodgson, *Foot Soldier for Freedom*, pp. 77–82.

174 Hodgson, *Foot Soldier for Freedom*, pp. 64–5.

175 Brian Bunting, interviewed by Tom Lodge, London, 27 February 1985.

176 Hodgson, *Foot Soldier for Freedom*, p. 68.

177 Harmel, 'Some Notes on the Communist Party in South Africa'.

178 Michael Harmel, 'Collective Leadership in the Soviet Union', *New Age*, 5 April 1956, reprinted in Bunting, *South African Communists Speak*, p. 244.

179 Hilda Bernstein, interviewed by Padraig O'Malley, transcript, Bernstein Papers, B8.1.

180 Turok, *Nothing but the Truth*, p. 50.

181 Pauline Podbrey, interviewed by Maureen Tayal, London, 8 August 1983, African Studies Institute, Oral History Collection, University of the Witwatersrand.

182   Hirson, *Revolutions in My Life*, p. 225; see also Clingman, *Bram Fischer*, p. 213.

183   Hepple, *Young Man with a Red Tie*, pp. 63–4.

184   Turok, *Nothing but the Truth*, p. 50.

185   Hilda and Lionel Bernstein, interviewed by Stephen Clingman, 4 September 1984.

186   AnnMarie Wolpe, *The Long Way Home*, David Philip, Cape Town, 1994, p. 64. On Joe Slovo's and Ruth First's disagreements over Hungary, see Weider, *Ruth First and Joe Slovo*, pp. 86 and 92.

187   Hepple, *Young Man with a Red Tie*, p. 31.

188   Hepple, *Young Man with a Red Tie*, p. 30.

189   Wieder, *Ruth First and Joe Slovo*, p. 110.

190   For detail, see O'Malley, *Shades of Difference*, p. 85.

191   'Minutes of Africa Group Meeting, 13 May 1982', Simons Papers, 08.1.

192   Turok, *Nothing but the Truth*, p. 90.

193   Bernard Magubane et al., 'The Turn to Armed Struggle', in Bernard Magubane (ed.), *The Road to Democracy in South Africa*, volume 1: *1960–1970*, Zebra Press, Cape Town, and the South African Democracy Education Trust, 2004, especially pp. 60–3 and 80–91.

194   Stephen Ellis, *External Mission: The ANC in Exile, 1960–1990*, Hurst and Company, London, 2012, pp. 9–28.

195   Lerumo, *Fifty Fighting Years*, p. 95.

196   Turok, *Nothing but the Truth*, p. 104.

197   Levy, *The Final Prize*, p. 260.

198   Bernstein, *Memory against Forgetting*, p. 196.

199   Hepple, *Young Man with a Red Tie*, p. 99.

200   Bunting, *Moses Kotane*, p. 255.

201   Pillay and Dadoo, The Political Situation in the Union of South Africa'.

202   Pillay and Dadoo, The Political Situation in the Union of South Africa'.

203   Babenia, *Memoirs of a Saboteur*, p. 53

204   Another account by a member of this group confirms that one of its assigned functions was 'to infiltrate and control leftist youth organisations operating on the Reef' (Ludi and Grobbelaar, *The Amazing Mr Fischer*, p. 31).

205   Personal memory and see Ronnie Kasrils, *Armed and Dangerous: From Undercover Struggle to Freedom*, Jonathan Ball, Johannesburg, 1998, p. 5.

206   Ludi had been involved in Congress of Democrats activities for at least two years, joining the Congress after his recruitment into the police's Special Branch in April 1960. In his most recent memoir he claims that he was able to infiltrate a police colleague 'into the movement' who would visit the party's headquarters, supplying the police with the information that led to the arrests at Rivonia in July 1963. (Gerard Ludi, *The Communisation of the ANC*, Galago, Alberton, 2011, pp. 126–7). Joe Slovo maintained that Ludi was not originally an infiltrator but had been blackmailed into playing such a role to avoid a charge under the Immorality Act after being arrested with a black prostitute (Slovo, *Unfinished Autobiography*, p. 157).

207   Ludi, *The Communisation of the ANC*, p. 18.

208   SACP Central Committee, 'The Revolutionary Way Out', February 1962, text in Lerumo, *Fifty Fighting Years*, p. 154.

209   Jean Middleton, *Convictions: A Woman Political Prisoner Remembers*, Ravan, Randburg, 1998.

210   O'Malley, *Shades of Difference*, pp. 87–110.

211   Middleton, *Convictions*, p. 26.

212   Kotane, 'Notes on Aspects of the Political Situation in the Republic of South Africa'.

213   Mufamadi, *Raymond Mhlaba's Personal Memoirs*, p. 111.

214   Govan Mbeki discusses the influence of peasant 'thinking on military lines' upon

the decision to set up Umkhonto in *The Struggle for Liberation in South Africa*, David Philip, Cape Town, 1992, pp. 88–93.

215 Govan Mbeki, 'Resistance Politics in Port Elizabeth, New Brighton Township, and the Transkei, 1930–1961', p. 65, manuscript, Ben Turok Papers, Rivonia Museum. See also Colin Bundy, *Govan Mbeki*, Jacana Media, Johannesburg, 2012, pp. 97–102.

216 Bundy, *Govan Mbeki*, p. 107.

217 Magubane et al., 'The Turn to Armed Struggle', pp. 70–2.

218 Bernstein, *Memory against Forgetting*, p. 217.

219 Essop Pahad, unpublished biography of Yusuf Dadoo, Mayibuye Centre, University of the Western Cape, pp. 167 and 205–6.

220 Magubane et al., 'The Turn to Armed Struggle', p. 81.

221 Vladimir Shubin, *ANC: A View from Moscow*, Mayibuye Books, Cape Town, 1999, p. 203.

222 The Rivonia farm cost R25,000. Julius First helped to finance the purchase from his own savings. For more detail on how the purchase was organised, see Clingman, *Bram Fischer*, pp. 293–4.

223 Hepple, *Young Man with a Red Tie*, p. 104.

224 Norman Levy agrees with this: 'the matter had been raised briefly' at the conference, he wrote in his memoir (*The Final Prize*, p. 205).

225 South African Communist Party, *International Bulletin*, 1, April 1961, pp. 2–5, Sylvia Neame Papers, A 2729, Q5.3.

226 SACP, *International Bulletin*, 1, April 1961, pp. 13–14.

227 SACP, *International Bulletin*, 1, April 1961, pp. 16–17.

228 Bernstein, *Memory against Forgetting*, p. 225

229 *New Age*, 5 February 1959.

230 'Memorandum', Kasrils Papers, A 3345, A6.1.4.1.

231 Bernstein, *Memory against Forgetting*, p. 227.

232 Kotane, 'Notes on Aspects of the Political Situation in the Republic of South Africa'.

233 Hepple, *Young Man with a Red Tie*, p. 106.

234 Turok, *Nothing but the Truth*, pp. 137 and 199; Bunting, *Moses Kotane*, p. 269.

235 Hepple, *Young Man with a Red Tie*, p. 104.

236 Luthuli writing in the *Golden City Post*, 25 March 1962; see Scott Couper, *Albert Luthuli: Bound by Faith*, University of KwaZulu-Natal Press, Durban, 2010, p. 161.

237 Mbeki, 'Resistance Politics in Port Elizabeth's New Brighton Township', p. 84.

238 On this issue he was probably truthful, for other memoirs, Babenia's for example, offers corroboration. See Mtolo, *Umkhonto we Sizwe*, p. 23.

239 Rowley Arenstein, quoted in *The Star*, 6 July 1990.

240 Arenstein, interview.

241 Babenia, *Memoirs of a Saboteur*, p. 63.

242 See Kasrils, *Armed and Dangerous*, pp. 144–5 for his recollection of Rowley Arenstein's views on the sabotage campaign and the Ponnens' response. For an irreverent description of Ronnie Kasrils's first bomb-making lesson, see Harold Strachan, *Make a Skyf, Man!*, Jacana Media, Johannesburg, 2004 p. 72.

243 Wolfie Kodesh, interviewed by John Carlin, 1995, https://www.pbs.org/wgbh/pages/frontline/shows/mandela/interviews/kodesh.html. Govan Mbeki also referred to the party establishing its own units, separate from those constituted by ANC leaders in *The Struggle for Liberation in South Africa*, p. 90.

244 Hepple, *Young Man with a Red Tie*, p. 106.

245 Bob Hepple, 'Was He or Wasn't He?', *London Review of Books*, 30, 2, 23 January 2014, p. 8.

246 Stephanie Kemp, *Through an Unforgettable Storm: The Forging of a Loyal Cadre*, self-published, 2017, Kindle location 2811.

247 Padraig O'Malley obtained confirmation of Mandela's membership from Brian Bunting as well as 'other sources embargoed until 2030'. He also quotes from his interview with Hilda Bernstein, who may have been present at the meeting as a member of the Johannesburg District Committee (O'Malley, *Shades of Difference*, p. 63).

248 John Pule Motshabi, 'On the Party Bulletin for Internal Circulation Only', 31 March 1980, transcript, Simons Papers, BC 1081, 0.81.

249 'Minutes of Africa Group Meeting, 13 May 1982', Simons Papers, BC 1081, 0. 81.

250 Brian Bunting, interviewed by Sylvia Neame, London, 14 May 1986, Sylvia Neame Papers, A 2729, E1.

251 Hilda Bernstein, interviewed by Padraig O'Malley, 25 August 2994, transcript, Bernstein Papers, B8.1.

252 Nelson Mandela to Barbara Lamb, 1 October 1974, Michael Harmel Papers, Wits Historical Papers, A 3300, B4.

253 Nelson Mandela to the Liquidator, Department of Justice, 23 October 1967, Himie Bernadt Collection of the Legal Papers of Nelson Mandela, Nelson Mandela Foundation.

254 'Memorandum', Kasrils Papers, A 3345, A6.1.4.1. The sixth person referred to may have been Joe Modise. The ANC's obituary of Modise released as a press statement (26 November 2001) stated that he had been a member of Umkhonto's High Command 'since its inception', though this is at odds with other equally authoritative sources. In any case, it is most unlikely that an SACP official would have thought that Modise was about to join the party and he never did. Joe Slovo, though, mentions Joe Modise as one of the co-opted High Command members before 1963 (Slovo, *Unfinished Autobiography*, p. 148). Bruno Mtolo also refers to Modise as a High Command member when he visited Natal regional commanders in September 1962, shortly after Mandela's arrest (Mtolo, *Umkhonto we Sizwe*, p. 48).

255 For an elaboration of this argument, see Paul Landau, 'The M-Plan: Mandela's Struggle to Reorient the African National Congress', in Colin Bundy and William Beinart (eds), *Reassessing Mandela*, Jacana Media, Johannesburg, 2020, pp. 152–5.

256 Hepple, 'Was He or Wasn't He?', p. 8.

257 Kasrils, *Armed and Dangerous*, p. 38.

258 Carneson, *Red in the Rainbow*, pp. 169–70.

259 For a thoughtful review of the court evidence and subsequent recollections by participant, see Davis, *The ANC's War against Apartheid*, pp. 26–57.

260 'Memorandum', Kasrils Papers, A 3345, A6.1.4.1.

261 Bob Hepple also suggests that Mandela's decision to call off the strike may have been a consequence of 'his thoughts and actions' being 'all concentrated in preparing for an armed struggle' (*Young Man with a Red Tie*, p. 46).

262 For detail, see Slovo, *Unfinished Autobiography*, p. 153 and, at length, Strachan, *Make a Skyf, Man!* In Cape Town, Denis Goldberg, Umkhonto's technical officer, borrowed equipment from Fred Carneson's son's toy chemistry set (Carneson, *Red in the Rainbow*, p. 173).

263 There are vivid first-hand accounts of both in Kasrils, *Armed and Dangerous*, pp. 39–43.

264 This was in a letter he wrote to Sylvia Neame in 1964 reviewing her manuscript history of the ICU (Sylvia Neame Papers, A 2729, F). See Paul Landau, 'The ANC, MK and 'the Turn to Violence'', *South African Historical Journal*, 64, 3, 2012, p. 561.

265 For evidence that Bram Fischer may have contributed to the drafting, see Clingman, *Bram Fischer*, p. 284. Joe Slovo told Sylvia Neame when she interviewed him in Berlin on 7 April 1986 that Michael Harmel did most of the writing of *The Road*.

266 Eddy Maloka attributes this apparent contradiction to the difficulty of attempting to reconcile Leninist vanguardism with the requirements of alliance with the ANC.

See his *South African Communist Party: Exile and after Apartheid*, Jacana Media, Joahnnesburg, 2014, p. 24.

267   For quotations, see the text published in Bunting, *South African Communists Speak*, pp. 293–4, 307, 314–15 and 317.

268   Lerumo, *Fifty Fighting Years*, p. 96. Hepple confirms that the draft was circulated to base units, as did Slovo in his interview with Sylvia Neame in August 1986 (Neame Papers, A 2729, E1).

269   Filatova, 'The Lasting Legacy', p. 525.

270   Hepple, *Young Man with a Red Tie*, p. 110

271   'Draft of *South African Road to Freedom*', exhibit AF196, State versus Abraham Fischer, case no. 175/64, pp. 27 and 38.

272   Kitson, *Where Sixpence Lives*, p. 215.

273   Hepple, *Young Man with a Red Tie*, p. 102.

274   Kitson, *Where Sixpence Lives*, p. 133.

275   Bundy, *Govan Mbeki*, p. 113.

276   Garth Benneyworth, 'Rolling up Rivonia', *South African Historical Journal*, 69, 3, 2017.

277   Joel Joffe, *The Rivonia Story*, Mayibuye Books, Bellville, 1995, p. 179

278   Quotations from text as reproduced in Thomas Karis and Gail M Gerhart, *From Protest to Challenge*, volume 3.

279   SACP Central Committee, 'The Revolutionary Way Out', February 1963, reproduced in Lerumo, Fifty Fighting Years, pp. 143–155.

280   Govan Mbeki, *South Africa: The Peasants' Revolt*, Penguin African Library, Harmondsworth, 1964.

281   Ludi and Grobbelaar, *The Amazing Mr Fischer*, p. 40.

282   'The New Year: Some Tasks and Perspectives', Simons Papers, BC 1081, 07.1; evidently a Central Committee document, though unsigned and undated.

283   Bernstein, *Memory against Forgetting*, p. 251.

284   Hepple, *Young Man with a Red Tie*, pp. 117–18.

285   Clingman, *Bram Fischer*, p. 313.

286   Joffe, *The Rivonia Story*, pp. 146–8.

287   Turok, *Nothing but the Truth*, p. 169.

288   See Harold Strachan's comments on Joe Slovo's departure in *Make a Skyf, Man!*, p. 75.

289   Mbeki claimed later it had been adopted by the Central Committee; see Govan Mbeki, 'Resistance Politics in Port Elizabeth's New Brighton Township', p. 93.

290   Babenia, *Memoirs of a Saboteur*, p. 86.

291   Hodgson, *Foot Soldier for Freedom*, pp. 124–38.

292   Mtolo, *Umkhonto we Sizwe*, p. 73. Mtolo's account is obviously questionable, though. Through his testimony the state was trying to prove that the Umkhonto leadership had committed itself to Operation Mayibuye.

293   Alan Brooks's testimony in State vs Fred Carneson, 28 February 1966.

294   Turok, *Nothing but the Truth*, p. 190.

295   Middleton, *Convictions*, p. 24.

296   Paul Trewhela, interviewed by Padraigh O'Malley, 13 June 2004, O'Malley Archive, Nelson Mandela Foundation.

297   Ludi and Grobbelaar, *The Amazing Mr Fischer*, p. 33.

298   Hodgson, *Foot Soldier for Freedom*, p. 127.

299   Minute of a meeting of 12 July 1963 between Michael Harmel and Bohuslav Lastovicka, National Archives, Prague.

300   Karel Sieber and Petr Zídek, *Československo a subsaharská Afrika v letech, 1948–1989*, Ústav Mezinárodnich Vztahu, Prague, 2007, p. 101.

301 Sieber and Zidek, *Československo a subsaharská Afrika v letech, 1948–1989*, p. 103.

302 Mufamadi, *Raymond Mhlaba's Personal Memoirs*, p. 18.

303 Bernstein, *Memory against Forgetting*, p. 252.

304 After the Rivonia raid on 11 July 1963, of the Central Committee Walter Sisulu, Lionel Bernstein, Raymond Mhlaba, Govan Mbeki and Bob Hepple were being held by the police, Nelson Mandela and Ben Turok were in prison, and JB Marks, Dan Thloome, Brian Bunting, Ray Alexander, MP Naicker and Joe Matthews had left South Africa.

305 Interview with Piet Beyleveld, April 1986, transcript, David Everatt Papers, Wits Historical Papers, A 2521,

306 Levy, *The Final Prize*, pp. 309–11.

307 Ludi, *The Communisation of the ANC*, p. 137.

308 Bartholomew Hlapane, testimony of Bartholomew Hlapane before the US Senate Sub-Committee on Security and Terrorism, 25 March 1982. Hlapane's testimony was a composite of the various accounts he had given as a state witness at a succession of security trials through the late 1960s and early 1970s. His reliability as a witness was often questioned but many of the details he offered were subsequently corroborated by memoirs. He provided similar details about the money he received and distributed in his evidence at Bran Fischer's trial, though the sums he specified were different.

309 Clingman, *Bram Fischer*, p. 31.

310 O'Malley, *Shades of Difference*, p. 15.

311 Clingman, *Bram Fischer*, p. 312. Fischer's view was decisive.

312 Though Middleton believed that Ludi's access to information was quite restricted (*Convictions*, p. 37). In an earlier book Ludi suggested his recruitment was later, in May 1963.

313 Middleton, *Convictions*, pp. 23 and 70.

314 Beyleveld was persuaded to testify for the state after the police blackmailed him with filmed evidence of his adultery (Hodgson, *Foot Soldier for Freedom*, p. 192).

315 Turok, *Nothing but the Truth*, p. 61.

316 Mtolo, *Umkhonto we Sizwe*, pp. 116–17.

317 Turok, *Nothing but the Truth*, p. 77.

318 Gregory Houston, 'The Post-Rivonia ANC/SACP Underground', in Bernard Magubane (ed.), *The Road to Democracy in South Africa*, volume 1: *1960–1970*, Zebra Press, Cape Town, and the South African Democracy Education Trust, 2004, p. 619.

319 Kitson, *Where Sixpence Lives*, p. 138. For an oblique description of the role this committee played in supporting the flight out of South Africa of Harold Wolpe and Arthur Goldreich after their escape from prison, see Joffe, *The Rivonia Story*, p. 6.

320 Clingman, *Bram Fischer*, p. 294.

321 Slovo, *Unfinished Autobiography*, p. 160.

322 For detail on the extent to which party networks were engaged in evasion and escape, see Hilda Bernstein, *The World That Was Ours*, Heinemann, London, 1967, pp. 84–5, 88–91 and 97, and AnnMarie Wolpe, *Long Way Home*, p. 212 and Kitson, *Where Sixpence Lives*, pp. 138–40.

323 Middleton, *Convictions*, p. 65.

324 For a description of the public telephone surveillance that finally led to the identification of one of Bram Fischer's helpers, Violet Weinberg, and the subsequent assault that led to her disclosure during her interrogation of his address, see Ludi, *Communisation of the ANC*, pp. 144–5.

325 Houston, 'The Post-Rivonia ANC/SACP Underground', p. 603. Houston cites an interview with Gertrude Shope as his source.

326　Hepple, *Young Man with a Red Tie*, p. 112.

327　Thula Simpson, *Umkhonto we Sizwe: The ANC's Armed Struggle*, Penguin, Johannesburg, 2014, p. 99.

328　Lynne Carneson's biography of her parents suggests that for much of the period between February and December Carneson lived in hiding, confined to a flat in Clifton rented with party funds, 'almost completely isolated' except for occasional visits from 'close comrades' (Carneson, *Red in the Rainbow*, pp. 188–9).

329　See Clingman, *Bram Fischer*, pp. 362–99.

330　For the Fischer family's disillusionment with the London comrades, see Clingman, *Bram Fischer*, pp. 381–2.

331　Houston, 'The Post-Rivonia ANC/SACP Underground', p. 631.

332　Clingman, *Bram Fischer*, p. 343. See also Norman Levy on London's 'ambivalent support'. Interest in his project was clearly limited (*The Final Prize*, p. 370).

333　Eddy Maloka, *The South African Communist Party in Exile, 1963–1965*, African Institute, Pretoria, 2002, p. 12. Maloka cites minutes for the meeting in Prague in May 1965 of the Central Committee but does not indicate this document's archival location.

334　Ben Turok, interviewed by Stephen Clingman, p. 18, Ben Turok Papers.

335　Detail in the above two paragraphs unless otherwise noted is from trial evidence cited in Ludi and Grobbelaar, *The Amazing Mr Fischer*.

336　'Draft Discussion Statement', exhibit AF5, State versus Abraham Fischer, case no. 175/64, p. 5.

337　Houston, 'The Post-Rivonia ANC/SACP Underground', pp. 628–9.

338　By 1975 former SACP members who had set up the Sebatakgomo were once again re-establishing networks in Sekhukhuneland after their release from prison (Peter Delius, *A Lion amongst the Cattle*, James Currey, Oxford, 1996, pp. 175–6).

339　Thomas G Karis, 'South African Liberation: The Communist Factor', *Foreign Affairs*, 65, 2, Winter 1986.

340　Thomas Karis and Gail Gerhart, *From Protest to Challenge*, volume 3, p. 680.

341　Tom Lodge, *Black Politics in South Africa*, London, Longman, 1983. See also especially

342　Philip Bonner, 'Black Trade Unions in South Africa since World War II', in Robert M Price and Carl G Rosberg (eds), *The Apartheid Regime: Political Power and Racial Domination*, David Philip, Cape Town, 1980, p. 183.

343　See especially, Ellis, *External Mission*, p. 76.

Chapter 7

1　Eddy Maloka, *The South African Communist Party: Exile and after Apartheid*, Jacana Media, Johannesburg, 2013, p. 18.

2　Ben Turok, quoted in Stephen Ellis, *External Mission: The ANC in Exile, 1960–1990*, Hurst and Company, London 2012, p. 280.

3　Ellis, *External Mission*, p. 82.

4　Joe Slovo, *Slovo: The Unfinished Autobiography*, Ravan Press, Johannesburg, 1995, p. 145.

5　Raymond Suttner, 'The (Re-)Constitution of the South African Communist Party as an Underground Organisation', *Journal of Contemporary African Studies*, 22, 1, 2004, p. 63.

6　Ray Alexander Simons, manuscript memoir, 1996, p. 3, Jack Simons Papers, UCT Manuscript and Archives, BC 1081.

7　Raymond Suttner, 'The African National Congress Centenary: A Long and Difficult Journey', *International Affairs*, 88, 4, 2012, p. 731.

8　Maloka, *The South African Communist Party*, p. 37.

9   Hugh Macmillan, Stephen Ellis, Arianna Lissoni and Mariya Kurbak, 'Debating the ANC's External Links during the Struggle against Apartheid', *Africa*, 85, 1, 2015, p. 155.

10 Barry Feinberg, interviewed by Sylvia Neame, London, 1 October 1987, Sylvia Neame Papers, Wits Historical Papers, A 2729.

11 AnnMarie Wolpe, *The Long Way Home*, David Philip, Cape Town, 1994, pp. 272–4.

12 Rica Hodgson, *Foot Soldier for Freedom: A Life in South Africa's Liberation Movement*, Picador Africa, Johannesburg, 2010, pp. 143–4.

13 Maloka, *The South African Communist Party*, p. 16.

14 Czech National Archives, Prague, Předsednictvo ÚV KSČ 1962–66, sv. 30, aj. 32, b. 12.

15 'Strive for World Communist Unity', *African Communist*, 16, January–March 1964, pp. 27–35.

16 Barry Feinberg, interviewed by Sylvia Neame (London, 1 October 1987, Sylvia Neame Papers), supplied detail on the divisive impact of the Sino-Soviet dispute among the communists who had belonged to the London group through the 1950s.

17 Vladimir Shubin, 'The Production of History in a Changing South Africa', paper presented at a Conference on the Future of the Past, University of the Western Cape, 10–12 July 1996, p. 7.

18 Karel Sieber and Petr Zídek, *Československo a subsaharská Afrika v letech, 1948– 1989*, Ústav Mezinárodnich Vztahu, Prague, 2007, pp. 100–3.

19 For detail, see Amin Cajee, *Fordsburg Fighter: The Journey of an MK Volunteer*, Face2Face Books, Paarl, 2016.

20 About 300 or so Umkhonto men trained near Moscow in 1963. See Irina Filatova and Apollon Davidson, *The Hidden Thread: Russia and South Africa in the Soviet Era*, Jonathan Ball, Johannesburg, 2013, p. 321.

21 Memo from the Czech Embassy in London concerning the ANC's request for scholarships, 6 September 1962, from the Archives of the Ministry of Foreign Affairs, *Twenty-Five Documents from the Czech Archives Published on the 25th Anniversary of the Establishment of Diplomatic Relations between Czechoslovakia and the Republic of South Africa*, Ministry of Foreign Affairs, Prague, 2016, p. 62.

22 Ronnie Kasrils, *Armed and Dangerous: From Undercover Struggle to Freedom*, Jonathan Ball, Johannesburg, 1998, pp. 100–2.

23 Oliver Tambo to Tom Karis, 6 December 1973, Tom Lodge Papers, Wits Historical Papers.

24 Maloka, *The South African Communist Party*, p. 17.

25 Maloka, *The South African Communist Party*, p. 17.

26 Vladimir Shubin, 'Soviet–South African Relations: A Critique of the Critique', paper given at the Conference of the SAAPS, Bloemfontein, 20–22 October 1993, p. 2.

27 Shubin, 'Soviet–South African Relations', p. 4

28 Shubin, 'Soviet–South African Relations', p. 3

29 Filatova and Davidson, *The Hidden Thread*, pp. 341–2.

30 These transfers for the countries concerned were substantial commitments: for example, the Czech share of this fund was $500,000 a year through the 1960s. Even when divided up amongst the beneficiaries, the allocation to the South Africans would have been a helpful sum. I am grateful to Irina Filatova, who obtained this information from documentation in the Russian State Archive of Contemporary History.

31 Maloka, *The South African Communist Party*, p. 20.

32 Maloka, *The South African Communist Party*, p. 21.

33 Maloka, *The South African Communist Party*, p. 39.

34 Maloka, *The South African Communist Party*, pp. 75–7.

35 Maloka, *The South African Communist Party*, pp. 23–4.

36 Selma Botman, *The Rise of Egyptian Communism, 1939–1970*, Syracuse University Press, Syracuse, 1988, pp. 154–6.

37 A. Gresh, 'The Free Officers and the Comrades: The Sudanese Communist Party and Nimeiri Face to Face, 1969–1971', *International Journal of Middle Eastern Studies*, 21, 1989, p. 404.

38 Ruth First was especially knowledgeable about the Sudanese Communist Party; she had met several of its key personalities while researching her *Power in Africa* (Penguin, Harmondsworth, 1970, pp. 272–7).

39 Anon., 'Reply to the Central Committee of the South African Communist Party Statement "The Enemy Hidden under the Same Colour", February 1976', p. 33 (copy in Tom Lodge Papers).

40 Ellis, citing ANC archival sources, in *External Mission*, p. 33.

41 Kotane is supposed to have replied 'You must humble yourself and subordinate yourself to the cause.' This seems most unlikely: out of keeping with Kotane's personality and his normal relationships with white comrades. The anecdote is recorded in a pamphlet attacking the SACP's influence within the ANC and probably misrepresents Kotane's views though he may well have clashed with Harmel all the same. See 'Reply to the Central Committee of the South African Communist Party Statement "The Enemy Hidden under the Same Colour", February 1976', p. 9. In another version of this exchange, Alfred Kgokong reported Moses Kotane to have said that every revolutionary was expected to 'subordinate himself to the will of the African people without demanding membership' (speech by Alfred Kgokong Mqota, *Ikwezi* (London), 1, 1, November 1975, p. 22).

42 Quotations in this paragraph are from Maloka, *The South African Communist Party*, pp. 108–12.

43 Ben Turok, *Nothing but the Truth: Behind the ANC's Struggle Politics*, Jonathan Ball, Johannesburg, 2003, p. 192.

44 Hugh Macmillan, *The Lusaka Years: The ANC in Exile in Zambia, 1963–1993*, Jacana Media, Johannesburg, pp. 25–6.

45 Ellis, *External Mission*, p. 84.

46 Joe Slovo, interviewed by Sylvia Neame, April 1986, transcript, p. 17, Sylvia Neame Papers, A 2729, H64.

47 According to Nimrod Sejake, a former SACTU organiser who left the ANC after being deported from Tanzania in 1979. For his background, see Nimrod Sejake, 'Workers' Power and the Crisis of Leadership', *Inqaba ya Basebenzi*, 12, November 1983, p. 12.

48 Paul Landau, 'Communist Controlled? Reassessing the Years of ANC Exile', *South African Historical Journal*, 67, 2, 2015, p. 232.

49 This was implied in a Central Committee decision in February 1968 attended by Kotane which authorised the establishment of units where party members were located, where possible (Maloka, *The South African Communist Party*, p. 22).

50 Ellis, *External Mission*, p. 45.

51 Ellis, *External Mission*, p. 96.

52 Ellis, *External Mission*, pp. 53 and 95.

53 Janet Smith and Beauregard Tromp, *Hani: A Life Too Short*, Jonathan Ball, Johannesburg, 2009, p. 36.

54 Smith and Tromp, *Hani*, p. 78; Cajee, *Fordsburg Fighter*, pp. 106–9; Luli Callinicos, *Oliver Tambo: Beyond the Engeni Mountains*, David Philip, Cape Town, 2004, p. 321.

55 Kasrils, *Armed and Dangerous*, pp. 92–4.

56 Ellis, *External Mission*, p. 81.

57 Stephen R Davis, *The ANC's War against Apartheid*, Indiana University Press, Bloomington, 2018, p. 61.

58 Kasrils, *Armed and Dangerous*, p. 98.

59 Smith and Tromp, *Hani*, p. 69.

60 Detail in this paragraph is drawn from Thula Simpson, *Umkhonto we Sizwe*, Penguin, Johannesburg, 2014, pp. 126–68.

61 For example, a Central Committee report on organisation, produced in March 1970, claimed that the Central Executive Committee was 'totally unaware of the Zimbabwe events of 1967 until they hit the world's press' (quoted in *Ikwezi* [London], 2, 1, March 1975, p. 34).

62 Ellis, *External Mission*, p. 99.

63 Kasrils, *Armed and Dangerous*, p. 168. Joe Slovo was, Ronnie Kasrils remembers, 'mortified and angry' about the way that 'Kotane in particular ignored consultation with London' (email from Ronnie Kasrils, 1 April 2021).

64 Ken Keable (ed.), *London Recruits: The Secret War against Apartheid*, Merlin Books, London, 2012.

65 Joe Slovo, 'Latin America and the Ideas of Regis Debray', *African Communist*, 33, second quarter 1968.

66 SACP, 'The Developing Armed Liberation Struggle in Southern Africa', *African Communist*, 34, third quarter 1968, p. 9.

67 Filatova and Davidson, *The Hidden Thread*, p. 324.

68 Howard Barrell, *MK: The ANC's Armed Struggle*, Penguin, Johannesburg, 1990, p. 24.

69 Hugh Macmillan, *Chris Hani*, Jacana Media, Johannesburg, 2014, p. 28.

70 Macmillan, *The Lusaka Years*, p. 22.

71 Cajee, *Fordsburg Fighter*, pp. 103–26.

72 Cajee, *Fordsburg Fighter*, p. 131.

73 The Peace Corps, the memo suggested, was a CIA front and Vuyiswa Nokwe worked for Amitra, an Israeli company which may well have had intelligence connections (Hugh Macmillan, 'The "Hani Memorandum": Introduced and Annotated', *Transformation*, 69, 2009, p. 123).

74 Macmillan, *Chris Hani*, p. 94.

75 Macmillan, *Hani*, p. 55.

76 SACHED (South African Council for Higher Education), a NUSAS-sponsored body that supplied fellowships to enable black South Africans to prepare for and undergo higher education outside South Africa.

77 Essop Pahad in Sifiso Ndlovu and Miranda Strydom (eds), *The Thabo Mbeki I Knew*, Picador Africa, Johannesburg, 2016, p. 91. Mbeki described his own upbringing and party recruitment in *African Communist* in 1971 (J Jabulani, 'Why I Joined the Communist Party', *African Communist*, 44, first quarter 1971). When asked to join, 'I felt an honour has been bestowed upon me'. At school he had been impressed by Russia's role in defending Egypt during the Suez crisis, which was when, he claimed, he began asking and learning about Russia.

78 Mark Gevisser, *Thabo Mbeki: The Dream Deferred*, Jonathan Ball, Johannesburg, 2007, p. 148.

79 Gevisser, *Thabo Mbeki*, p. 264.

80 For detail see Macmillan, 'The "Hani Memorandum"', pp. 108–12.

81 Ellis, *External Mission*, p. 76.

82 Callinicos, *Oliver Tambo*, p. 339.

83 Dirk Kotze, 'Morogoro: Out of the Whirlwind', *Politikon*, 16, 1, June 1989, p. 60.

84 Macmillan, *Hani*, p. 62.

85 Ellis in *External Mission* attributes authorship to Joe Slovo with drafting support from Nokwe and Matthews; he cites no sources. A shorter version using identical language appeared under the authorship of Joe Matthews as 'Armed Struggle in South Africa' in *Marxism Today*, September 1969, pp. 270–2. Slovo told Sylvia

Neame he wrote the first draft by himself with Joe Matthews making a few changes after its review by the ANC's national executive (Joe Slovo, interviewed by Sylvia Neame, April 1986, transcript, pp. 18–19, Sylvia Neame Papers, A 2729, H64). Joe Matthews told Hugh Macmillan that his changes reduced the influence in the document of Che Guevara's thinking as well as a suggestion that without white and Indian participation in the struggle, victory would be impossible (Macmillan, *The Lusaka Years*, p. 78). Stephanie Kemp typed the first drafts of *Strategy and Tactics* to Joe Slovo's dictation (Stephanie Kemp, *Through an Unforgettable Storm: The Forging of a Loyal Cadre*, self-published, 2017, Kindle location 2835).

86 Filatova and Davidson, *The Hidden Thread*, p. 308.
87 Gevisser, *Thabo Mbeki*, p. 104; Ellis, *External Mission*, p. 159.
88 Maloka, *The South African Communist Party*, p. 34.
89 Quoted in Anon., 'Reply to the Central Committee of the South African Communist Party Statement "The Enemy Hidden under the Same Colour"', February 1976', p. 3.
90 This was a reference to Regis Debray's 'foco' thesis, itself the subject of a separate extended critical discussion by Joe Slovo, 'Latin America and the Ideas of Regis Debray', pp. 44–54. Slovo was especially critical of Debray's 'denigration' of the proletariat and orthodox communist parties as well as his assignment of a vanguard role to students and revolutionary intellectuals.
91 'Guerrilla Warfare Is People's War', *Inkululeko / Freedom: Organ of the Central Committee of the South African Communist Party*, 16, April 1975, p. 5.
92 Anon., 'An Analysis of the Freedom Charter, Revolutionary Programme of the African National Congress, Adopted at the Morogoro Conference, 1969', in Anon., *Selected Writings on the Freedom Charter, 1955–1985*, African National Congress, 1985, pp. 5–14.
93 RP Ngcobo, 'The Freedom Charter: A Communist Analysis', *African Communist*, 63, fourth quarter 1975, p. 48.
94 SACP, 'Taking Forward the Resolutions of the 11th Congress: Political Report of the First Plenary Session of the Central Committee of the 11th Congress', 2002, p. 3, Vishwas Satgar Papers, Wits Historical Papers, C.2.2.
95 Maloka, *The South African Communist Party*, p. 34.
96 Maloka, *The South African Communist Party*, p. 34. In fact the meeting was not about anything happening inside South Africa. The meeting mainly focused on 'Africanist' reaction to the Morogoro decision to open up ANC membership to whites, coloureds and Indians. Tambo was especially concerned about the activities of Ambrose Makiwane and Alfred Kgokong in encouraging disaffection (Macmillan, *The Lusaka Years*, pp. 88–9).
97 Maloka, *The South African Communist Party*, p. 36.
98 Ellis, *External Mission*, pp. 95–7. Whether Resha belonged to this group remains questionable. Among the London communist exiles he was often considered a personal friend; he helped advise the Hodgsons' son after he had dropped out of school (Hodgson, *Foot Soldier for Freedom*, p. 161). It was true that at the Morogoro conference Resha had opposed the opening up of the ANC's membership to 'non-Africans'. Paul Landau insists that Resha belonged to the party ('Communist Controlled? Reassessing the Years of ANC Exile', p. 240). Luli Callinicos also refers to Robert Resha as a communist (*Oliver Tambo*, p. 349).
99 Callinicos, *Oliver Tambo*, p. 341.
100 Hugh Macmillan cites an unauthorised and anonymous document written by communists in Dar es Salaam in 1972 which attacked Robert Resha, Jonas Matlou, the Makiwanes, Mazisi Kunene and Mzwai Piliso for preferring a united front with the PAC rather than accepting the non-racial Revolutionary Council. The

document also criticised Alfred Nzo for 'softness' in dealing with such disaffection (Macmillan, *The Lusaka Years*, p. 90).

101 Anon., 'Reply to the Central Committee of the South African Communist Party Statement "The Enemy Hidden under the Same Colour", February 1976', p. 2. The full text of Makiwane's speech is in *Ikwezi* (London), 1, 1, November 1975, p. 24.

102 For Nokwe's role in the decision, see Thomas Karis and Gail M Gerhart, *From Protest to Challenge*, volume 5: *Nadir and Resurgence*, Indiana University Press, Bloomington, 1997, p. 42–3.

103 Landau, 'Communist-Controlled?', citing interview with Ben and Mary Turok, Johannesburg, 26 September 1993, Carter and Karis Papers, Wits Historical Papers.

104 Karis and Gerhart, *From Protest to Challenge*, volume 5, p. 43. For a similar view, see Callinicos, *Oliver Tambo*, p. 351.

105 This was in an interview Sonia Bunting conducted in 1974 for her husband's biography of Moses Kotane. Quoted in Suttner, 'The (Re-)Constitution of the South African Communist Party as an Underground Organisation', p. 63.

106 Keable, *London Recruits*, p. 41.

107 With some justification; as one of his colleagues recalls, he was weak and indecisive 'and tended to have urgent business abroad when trouble was brewing in the college (Christopher R Hill, *Looking In: Some Observations*, Short Run Press, Exeter, 2020, p. 117). See also Sue Donnelly, 'Opposing a Director', blogpost on the LSE website, https://blogs.lse.ac.uk/lsehistory/2019/02/18/the-lse-troubles-opposing-a-director.

108 Ron Press, 'To Change the World! Is Reason Enough? Ron Press His Story', unpublished manuscript, April 1997, pp. 119–20, Ron Press Papers, Wits Historical Papers, A 3239.

109 Press, 'To Change the World!', p. 113.

110 Keable, *London Recruits*, p. 43. John Rose's recollections feature the wrong author: It was Lenin's not Stalin's *Collected Works* Ronnie Kasrils kept on his book shelf (email from Ronnie Kasrils, 1 April 2021).

111 For their subsequent careers and achievements, see Christopher T Husbands, *Sound and Fury: Sociology at the London School of Economics and Political Science, 1904–2015*, Palgrave Macmillan, London, 2015, p. 305.

112 Details in this paragraph are drawn from the autobiographies in Keable, *London Recruits*.

113 Hodgson, *Foot Soldier for Freedom*, p. 195.

114 Alexander Sibeko [Ronnie Kasrils], 'The Underground Voice', *African Communist*, 68, 1, 1977, p. 48.

115 Shubin, 'The Production of History', p. 8.

116 Jamie Miller, *The African Volk: The Apartheid Regime and Its Search for Survival*, Oxford University Press, New York, 2016, pp. 69–70.

117 On Oscar Kambona and the Soviet Union, see Natalia Telepneva, 'Mediators of Liberation: Eastern Bloc Officials and Frelimo, 1958–1965', *Journal of Southern African Studies*, 2017. On the ANC's rift with Nyerere, see Reddy Mampane, interviewed by Tor Sellström, Nordic Africa Institute, https://nai.uu.se/library/resources/liberation-africa/interviews/reddy-mampane-aka-reddy-mazimba.html.

118 Callinicos, *Oliver Tambo*, p. 366.

119 Macmillan, *The Lusaka Years*, pp. 86–7.

120 Barbara Carr, *Loginov: Spy in the Sun*, Howard Timmins, Cape Town, 1969, p. 197. See the discussion of the veracity of Loginov's testimony as recounted by Carr and whether or not he really was a KGB agent in Filatova and Davidson, *The Hidden Thread*, pp. 252–8. On balance, their investigation suggests that his story was truthful.

121 Turok, *Nothing but the Truth*, pp. 219–23.

122 Kemp, *Through an Unforgettable Storm*, Kindle location 2540.

123 Kasrils, *Armed and Dangerous*, p. 112.

124 Keable, *London Recruits*, p. 123.

125 'Report on the Cape', document submitted to the Revolutionary Council meeting in Lusaka, July 1971, File: ANC Mission to Zambia, Papers from the President's Office, ANC Papers, University of Fort Hare.

126 Maloka, *The South African Communist Party*, p. 32

127 Maloka, *The South African Communist Party*, p. 33; Ellis, *External Mission*, p. 88.

128 Hodgson, *Foot Soldier for Freedom*, p.162.

129 Anon., *The Red Flag in South Africa: A Popular History of the South African Communist Party, 1921–1990*, n.d., p. 51.

130 Maloka, *The South African Communist Party*, p. 31.

131 Raymond Suttner, *The ANC Underground in South Africa*, Lynne Rienner Publishers, Boulder, 2009, p. 71.

132 Press, 'To Change the World!', p. 124.

133 The party records that Maloka consulted used pseudonyms to identify the 'party operatives' sent back to South African from London; the documentation suggests at least six people were deployed in this way (Maloka, *The South African Communist Party*, pp. 30–1).

134 Gregory Houston and Bernard Magubane, 'The ANC's Political Underground in the 1970s', in Bernard Magubane (ed.), *The Road to Democracy in South Africa*, volume 2: *1970-1980*, University of South Africa Press, Pretoria, 2006, pp. 439–40.

135 Jeremy Cronin, *Inside*, Ravan Press, Johannesburg, 1983, p. 41.

136 Jeremy Cronin, interviewed by Tom Lodge, 1993.

137 Houston and Magubane, 'The ANC Political Underground in the 1970s', p. 440.

138 Houston and Magubane, 'The ANC Political Underground in the 1970s', p. 441. See also Kemp, *Through an Unforgettable Storm*, Kindle location 2494.

139 Reopened inquest into the death of Ahmed Essop Timol, Judgment, High Court of South Africa, Gauteng Division, Pretoria, case number IQ 01/2017. The judgment is available on https//www: sacp.org.za/docs/misc/2017/Timol-Inquest-Judgment.pdf. See also for commentary and detail from the inquest: James Myburgh, 'The Ahmed Timol Case', *PoliticsWeb*, 17 October 2017, https://www.politicsweb.co.za/news-and-analysis/the-ahmed-timol-case-i. Myburgh argues that Timol's death was an 'induced suicide' brought about by sleep deprivation.

140 All quotations in this paragraph are from Raymond Suttner, *Inside Apartheid's Prisons*, Jacana Media, Johannesburg, 2017, pp. 5–28.

141 Houston and Magubane, 'The ANC Political Underground in the 1970s', p. 538.

142 Houston and Magubane, 'The ANC Political Underground in the 1970s', p. 443.

143 Tim Jenkin, *Escape from Pretoria*, Kliptown Books, London, 1987, pp. 6–21 and 165–74.

144 Kasrils, *Armed and Dangerous*, p. 125.

145 Jenkin, *Escape from Pretoria*, p. 21.

146 Julie Frederickse, *The Unbreakable Thread*, Ravan Press, Johannesburg, 1990, p. 128.

147 Joe Slovo, interviewed by Sylvia Neame, April 1986, transcript, p. 17, Sylvia Neame Papers, A 2729, H64.

148 Padraig O'Malley, *Shades of Difference: Mac Maharaj and the Struggle for South Africa*, Viking Penguin, New York, 2007, p. 211.

149 Rory Riordan, 'The Great Black Shark: Interview with Chris Hani', *Monitor: The Journal of the Human Rights Trust*, Port Elizabeth, December 1990, p. 13.

150 Kemp, *Through an Unforgettable Storm*, Kindle location 2470.

151 Riordan, 'The Great Black Shark', p. 13.

152 Smith and Tromp, *Hani*, p. 129. In one account by Hani, provided in a press interview, he crossed the Botswana border by himself; he does not mention Thomas (Riordan, 'The Great Black Shark', p. 12).

153 Ellis, *External Mission*, p. 91.

154 Suttner, 'The (Re-)Constitution of the SACP', p. 61.

155 Hugh Macmillan, *Jack Simons*, Jacana Media, Johannesburg, 2016, p. 107.

156 They were also members of local trade unions. Because the state's charges rested mainly on alleged SACTU activities, they were acquitted after three years of proceedings. The defence team used expert testimony to argue successfully that SACTU was not a proscribed organisation. See *State versus Mabone Duna and Three Others*, Zwelitsha Regional Court, 1982, Tom Lodge Papers, Wits Historical Papers, A 3104, E5.

157 Themba Ngonyama, 'Transkei', *African Communist*, 88, 1, 1982, p. 39.

158 Jabulani Sithole, 'Contestations over Knowledge Production or Ideological Bullying? A Response to Legassick on the Workers' Movement', *Kronos*, 35, 1, 2009, pp. 225–6. Macmillan dates the establishment of a SACTU office in Lusaka from 1969 (Macmillan, *The Lusaka Years*, p. 98).

159 Press, 'To Change the World!', pp. 134–5.

160 According to the former head of Mozambican national security, Jorge da Costa, who defected to South Africa in mid-1962. See Russell Kay, 'The Da Costa File: The ANC Terror Plan to Destroy South Africa', *Scope Magazine*, 18 February 1983, p. 34.

161 Alexander Sibeko, 'Four Who Were Communists', *African Communist*, 87, 1981, p. 45.

162 Martin Legassick, 'Debating the Revival of the Workers' Movement in the 1970s: The South African Democracy Trust and Post-Apartheid Patriotic History', *Kronos*, 34, 1, November 2008, p. 256.

163 Edward Webster, 'Survey of Unregistered Trade Union Members', seminar paper, African Studies Institute, 1978.

164 Jeremy Gordin, *Zuma: A Biography*, Jonathan Ball, Johannesburg, 2008, p. 28.

165 Phyllis Naidoo, letter to the editor, *Natal Mercury*, 3 November 1997, Phyllis Naidoo Papers, University of KwaZulu-Natal Documentation Centre, 2093/226.

166 Gordin, *Zuma*, p. 28.

167 Legassick, 'Debating the Revival of the Workers' Movement in the 1970s', p. 258.

168 Sithole, 'Contestations over Knowledge Production', pp. 225–7.

169 Macmillan, *The Lusaka Years*, p. 111.

170 Beverley Naidoo, *Death of an Idealist: In Search of Neil Aggett*, Jonathan Ball, Johannesburg, 2012, pp. 84–5.

171 Naidoo, *Death of an Idealist*, p. 85.

172 RE Matajo, 'Obstacles on the Road to Trade Union Unity', *African Communist*, 98, third quarter 1984, p. 53.

173 For detail and background, see Dave Hemson, Martin Legassick and Nicole Ulrich, 'White Activists and the Revival of the Workers' Movement', in South African Democratic Education Trust, *The Road to Democracy in South Africa*, volume 2: *1970–1980*, University of South Africa Press, Pretoria, 2006, pp. 289–98. See also Press, 'To Change the World!', pp. 142–3.

174 Turok, *Nothing but the Truth*, pp. 234–40.

175 Maloka, *The South African Communist Party*, p. 40

176 Stephanie Kemp was a member of the Internal Reconstruction Group. Chaired by Yusuf Dadoo, it also included Joe Slovo, Aziz Pahad, Reg September, Ron Press, Jack Hodgson and Ronnie Kasrils (Kemp, *Through an Unforgettable Storm*, Kindle location 2413).

177 Hodgson, *Foot Soldier for Freedom*, p. 159.

178   Paul Joseph, *Slumboy from the Golden City*, Merlin Press, London, 2018, p. 191.

179   Joseph, *Slumboy from the Golden City*, p. 218.

180   *African Communist*, 35, fourth quarter 1968, pp. 94–7.

181   Interestingly, Nokwe's statement was printed in the ANC's internal bulletin, *Mayibuye*, not the more authoritative and more widely circulated *Sechaba*, which published no statement on the invasion until the 1969 Political Report which referred to reactionary 'acts of provocation' that had prompted the Warsaw Pact's intervention (Scott Thomas, 'The Diplomacy of Liberation: The international Relations of the African National Congress of South Africa, 1960–1985', PhD dissertation, Department of International Relations, London School of Economics, October 1989, pp. 366–7).

182   Pallo Jordan (ed.), *Oliver Tambo Remembered*, Macmillan, Johannesburg, 2007, p. 139.

183   'How the SACP Slanders China', *Ikwezi* (London), 3, 2, August 1978, p. 41.

184   *African Communist*, 35, fourth quarter 1968, p. 12.

185   Brian Bunting (ed.), *South African Communists Speak: Documents from the History of the South African Communist Party*, Inkululeko Publications, London, 1981, p. 316.

186   Interview by Taffy Adler with Helen Lewis, 4 October 1975, Michael Harmel Papers, Wits Historical Papers, A 3300.

187   Yusuf Dadoo, 'Tribute to Michael Harmel: Oration at Funeral in Prague, 24 June 1974', https://www.sahistory.org.za/archive/tribute-michael-harmel-oration-funeral-prague-j.

188   Letters to Barbara Harmel, 28 February 1974 and 24 April 1974, Michael Harmel Papers.

189   Lyndall Shope, interviewed by Milan Oralek, Johannesburg, 29 January 2015 (transcript provided to author by Milan Oralek).

190   World Federation of Trade Unions, *South African Workers and the WFTU: Shoulder to Shoulder*, WFTU, Athens, 2012, pp. 90 and 97.

191   Gertrude Shope, interviewed by Milan Oralek, 29 January 2015.

192   V. Devinatz, 'A Cold War Thaw in the International Working-Class Movement? The WFTU and the ICFTU, 1967–1977', *Science and Society*, 77, 3, 2013, p. 362.

193   P. Waterman, 'Hopeful Traveller: The Itinerary of an Internationalist', *History Workshop*, 35, Spring 1993, pp. 180–1.

194   Their friend Barney Simon 'witnessed their bitter arguments over Czechoslovakia and Joe's stubborn defence of the Russian invasion' (Simon in Slovo, *Unfinished Autobiography*, p. 225).

195   Alan Wieder, *Ruth First and Joe Slovo in the War against Apartheid*, Monthly Review Press, New York, 2013, pp. 172–3.

196   For example, see her reservations about the Soviet notion of an African 'non-capitalist road to socialism' in 'Dialogue', *African Communist*, 56, second quarter 1972, pp. 88–98.

197   Norman Levy, *The Final Prize: My Life in the Anti-Apartheid Struggle*, South African History Online, Observatory, 2011, p. 384.

198   Albie Sachs, interviewed by Milan Oralek, 27 September 2014 (transcript provided to author).

199   Kemp, *Through an Unforgettable Storm*, Kindle location 1921.

200   Kasrils, *Armed and Dangerous*, p. 134.

201   Harold Wolpe, 'Capitalism and Cheap Labour Power in South Africa: From Segregation to Apartheid', *Economy and Society*, 1, 4, 1972, pp. 425–56.

202   Harold Wolpe, 'The Theory of Internal Colonialism: The South African case', in I Oxaal, T Barnett and D Booth (eds), *Beyond the Sociology of Development: Economy and Society in Latin America and Africa*, Routledge, London, 1975.

203   Steven Friedman, *Race, Class and Power: Harold Wolpe and the Radical Critique of*

Apartheid, University of KwaZulu-Natal Press, Pietermaritzburg, 2015, pp. 71–2.

204 Joe Slovo, 'South Africa: No Middle Road', in Basil Davidson, Joe Slovo and Anthony Wilkinson, *Southern Africa: The New Politics of Revolution*, Penguin Books, Harmondsworth, 1976, pp. 136–9. See also Slovo's use of Wolpe's arguments about articulated modes of production.

205 Slovo's text may also have been rejected by *African Communist*, though this seems unlikely (see Friedman, *Race, Class and Power*, p. 71). Publication through Penguin enabled its temporary importation into South Africa before its prohibition. On my first visit to South Africa my baggage was searched and a customs officer picked up the book which he found in my suitcase. He glanced at it briefly, checked it against the list of restricted items and returned it to me, saying that it 'looked very interesting'.

206 Friedman, *Race, Class and Power*, p. 57.

207 Friedman, *Race, Class and Power*, pp. 105–7.

208 Friedman, *Race, Class and Power*, p. 59.

209 Argument and quotations in this paragraph are all drawn from Julian Brown, *The Road to Soweto: Resistance and the Uprising of 16 June 1976*, James Currey, Woodbridge, 2016.

210 Slovo, 'No Middle Road', pp. 140–3.

211 Slovo, 'No Middle Road', p. 204.

212 Summary of a report adopted by the plenary session of the Central Committee of the SACP in *Inkululeko*, 18, December 1975, p. 5, cyclostyled edition circulated in South Africa, Tom Lodge Papers.

213 For examples of the texts, see Jenkin, *Escape from Pretoria*, pp. 21–4.

214 'People's Republic of the Congo Welcomes South African Communists!', *Inkululeko / Freedom*, 18, December 1975, p. 1, cyclostyled edition circulated in South Africa.

215 Yusuf Dadoo in London and Moses Kotane in Moscow remained nominally at the helm but both were ill; in Kotane's case, in hospital.

216 William Mervyn Gumede, *Thabo Mbeki and the Battle for the Soul of the ANC*, Zed Books, London, 2007, p. 43.

Chapter 8

1 Ronnie Kasrils, *Armed and Dangerous: From Undercover Struggle to Freedom*, Jeppestown, Jonathan Ball, 1998, p. 81.

2 Joe Slovo, speech on JB Marks' 80th birthday, 21 March 1983, *African Communist*, 95, fourth quarter 1983.

3 Eddy Maloka, *The South African Communist Party: Exile and after Apartheid*, Jacana Media, Johannesburg, 2014, pp. 89–90.

4 Maloka, *The South African Communist Party*, p. 41.

5 Maloka, *The South African Communist Party*, p. 44.

6 Stephen Ellis, *External Mission: The ANC in Exile, 1960–1990*, Hurst and Company, London, 2012, p. 118.

7 Maloka, *The South African Communist Party*.

8 Ellis, *External Mission*, p. 118; On Simons's impact as a teacher, see Percy Ngonyama, '"Comrade Mzala": Memory Construction and Legacy Preservation', *African Historical Review*, 49, 2, 2017, p. 80.

9 'Diary of Jacks Simons at Novo Catengue camp, January–March 1979', in Thomas Karis and Gail M Gerhart, *From Protest to Challenge*, volume 5: *Nadir and Resurgence*, Indiana University Press, Bloomington, 1997, p. 710.

10 His lecture notes have been published in Marion Sparg (ed.), *Comrade Jack: The Political Lectures and Diary of Jack Simons, Novo Catengue*, STE Publishers,

Johannesburg, 2001.

11 Kasrils, *Armed and Dangerous*, p. 156.

12 Kasrils, *Armed and Dangerous*, p. 157.

13 Barry Gilder, *Songs and Secrets: South Africa from Liberation to Governance*, Jacana Media, Johannesburg, 2012, p. 104.

14 Maloka, *The South African Communist Party*, p. 45; Ellis, *External Mission*, p. 215.

15 Kasrils, *Armed and Dangerous*, p. 150; Irina Filatova and Apollon Davidson, *The Hidden Thread: Russia and South Africa in the Soviet Era*, Jonathan Ball, Cape Town, 2013, p. 326.

16 'Diary of Jacks Simons at Novo Catengue camp, January–March 1979', p. 713.

17 Vladimir Shubin, 'Soviet–South African Relations: A Critique of the Critique', paper presented at the Conference of the SAAPS, Bloemfontein, 20–22 October 1993, p. 5.

18 Gilder, *Songs and Secrets*, p. 103.

19 Kasrils, *Armed and Dangerous*, pp. 164–5.

20 Kasrils, *Armed and Dangerous*, p. 170.

21 Ngonyama, '"Comrade Mzala"', p. 81.

22 Ngonyama, '"Comrade Mzala"', p. 81.

23 Eddy Maloka, 'Mzala: A Revolutionary without Kid Gloves', *African Communist*, 136, 1994, p. 63.

24 A detailed profile is by Blade Nzimande, 'A Prophet of True Radical Transformation', *Sunday Times*, Johannesburg, 25 February 2017.

25 Paul Landau, 'Communist Controlled? Reassessing the Years of ANC Exile', *South African Historical Journal*, 67, 2, 2015, pp. 233–4.

26 For its use, see Thenjiwe Mtintso in Joe Slovo, *Slovo: An Unfinished Autobiography*, Ravan, Randburg, 1995, p. 243.

27 Adam Ashworth, *Witchcraft, Violence and Democracy in South Africa*, University of Chicago Press, Chicago, 2005, p. 69.

28 Stephen R Davis, *The ANC's War against Apartheid*, Indiana University Press, Bloomington, 2018, p. 109.

29 Ron Press, 'To Change the World! Is Reason Enough?', Ron Press Papers, Wits Historical Papers, A 3239, pp. 82–6.

30 Quotations from 'The Green Book, Recommendations of the Politico-Military Strategy Commission', typescript, ANC, Lusaka, 1978, Tom Lodge Papers, Wits Historical Papers.

31 Hugh Macmillan, *Oliver Tambo*, Jacana Media, Johannesburg, 2017, p. 104.

32 Mark Gevisser, *Thabo Mbeki: The Dream Deferred*, Jonathan Ball, Johannesburg, 2007, p. 463.

33 Sol Dubala [Joe Slovo], 'The Two Pillars of Struggle', *African Communist*, 87, 4, 1981, p. 40.

34 Douglas Pike, *Viet Cong: The Organization and Techniques of the National Liberation Front of South Vietnam*, Massachusetts Institute of Technology Press, Cambridge, 1966, pp. 167–8.

35 See Lien-Hang Nguyen, *An International History of the War for Peace in Vietnam*, University of North Carolina Press, Chapel Hill, 2012.

36 Tokyo Sexwale's deposition to the South African police after his capture, quoted in Filatova and Davidson, *The Hidden Thread*, p. 324.

37 For a helpful commentary on the this text, see Davis, *The ANC's War against Apartheid*, pp. 146–50.

38 Kader Asmal and Adrian Hadland with Moira Levy, *Politics in My Blood*, Jacana Media, Johannesburg, 2011, pp. 65–6. A useful introduction to the intricacies of the Irish left is John Mulqueen, *'An Alien Ideology': Cold War Perceptions of the Irish*

Left, Liverpool University Press, Liverpool, 2019. In an oblique acknowledgement of his support, Gerry Adams was invited to join the guard of honour at Nelson Mandela's funeral (see letter by Eoin Dillon, *London Review of Books*, 6 February 2014).

39   Press, 'To Change the World!', p. 146.
40   Thula Simpson, *Umkhonto we Sizwe: The ANC's Armed Struggle*, Penguin, Cape Town, 2016, p. 235.
41   Simpson, *Umkhonto we Sizwe*, p. 244.
42   According to the former head of Mozambican national security, Jorge da Costa, who defected to South Africa in mid-1962. See Russell Kay, 'The Da Costa File: The ANC Terror Plan to Destroy South Africa', *Scope Magazine*, 18 February 1983, p. 29.
43   Simpson, *Umkhonto we Sizwe*, pp. 299 and 313.
44   South African Communist Party, *Internal Party Bulletin*, November 1981, p. 4, Sylvia Neame Papers, Wits Historical Papers, A 2729, Q2-2 2/3.
45   Filatova and Davidson, *The Hidden Thread*, p. 329.
46   Hugh Macmillan, *Oliver Tambo*, Jacana Media, Johannesburg, 2017, p. 104.
47   Simpson, *Umkhonto we Sizwe*, p. 313.
48   Simpson, *Umkhonto we Sizwe*, p. 241.
49   Simpson, *Umkhonto we Sizwe*, p. 241.
50   Simpson, *Umkhonto we Sizwe*, p. 351.
51   Conny Braam, *Operation Vula*, Jacana Media, Johannesburg, 2004, p. 198. See also 'Testimony of Ephraim Mfalapitsa to the Subcommittee on Security and Terrorism, United States Senate', 25 March 1982, Tom Lodge Papers.
52   Kasrils, *Armed and Dangerous*, p. 213.
53   Indeed, South African Military Intelligence had a 'high regard' for Joe Modise. In the negotiations between Umkhonto leaders and the South African military, 'MK leaders (if not their followers) could find very little with which to disagree when the opposition talked of the need for a modern defence force' (Philip Frankel, *Soldiers in a Storm: Armed Forces in South Africa's Democratic Transition*, Westview Press, Boulder, 2000, pp. 21–2). During the negotiations each side perceived the other as 'professional soldiers' (Philip Frankel, *Marching to the Millennium*, South African Department of Defence Communication Service, Pretoria, 1998, p. 13). For Joe Modise's comments on the SADF's qualities as a regular force, 'not a ceremonial army', skilled, sophisticated and 'good in the field also', see interview with Joe Modise, Lusaka, January 1987, Byline Africa, Sandton, p. 20, Tom Lodge Papers.
54   Simpson, *Umkhonto we Sizwe*, p. 432.
55   Simpson, *Umkhonto we Sizwe*, p. 351.
56   Cited by Ellis, *External Mission*, p. 225.
57   Kasrils, *Armed and Dangerous*, pp. 263–5.
58   Simpson, *Umkhonto we Sizwe*, p. 454.
59   'Green Book', p. 10.
60   Macmillan, *Oliver Tambo*, p. 104; also Gevisser, *Thabo Mbeki*, p. 463; Luli Callinicos, *Oliver Tambo: Beyond the Engeni Mountains*, David Philip, Cape Town, 2004, p. 524: 'What struck Tambo most was the connection between the spiritual and material influences on the dedication of the young revolutionaries.' He paid particular attention to testimonies from a priest and a nun, keeping a careful record of what they had to tell him in his notebook.
61   Padraig O'Malley, *Shades of Difference: Mac Maharaj and the Struggle for South Africa*, Viking Penguin, New York, 2007, p. 205.
62   Joe Slovo, 'South Africa: No Middle Road', in Basil Davidson, Joe Slovo and Anthony Wilkinson, *Southern Africa: The New Politics of Revolution*, Penguin

Books, Harmondsworth, 1976, p. 204.

63 Alan Wieder, *Ruth First and Joe Slovo in the War against Apartheid*, Monthly Review Press, New York, 2013, p. 218.

64 Central Committee, SACP, 'The Developing Armed Liberation Struggle in Southern Africa', *African Communist*, 34, 1968, p. 10.

65 Khumalo Migwe, 'Further Contribution on the Arming of the Masses', *African Communist*, 89, 1982, p. 79.

66 Mzala, 'Building Peoples' War', *Sechaba*, September 1986, p. 12.

67 Hugh Trevor, 'The Question of an Uprising of the Whole People', *African Communist*, 97, second quarter 1984, p. 70.

68 Mzala, 'MK: Building People's Forces for Combat and Insurrection', *Sechaba*, November 1986, p. 19. Other visions of the prospective insurrection were less militarist, emphasising, for example, the indispensability of 'large-scale strikes ' in the 'build-up to insurrection' (Trevor, 'The Question of an Uprising of the Whole People', p. 68).

69 South African Communist Party, *Path to Power*, n.p., n.d., pp. 55–7.

70 Maloka, *The South African Communist Party*, p. 96.

71 Andreas Hilger, 'Communism, Decolonisation and the Third World', in Norman Naimark, Sylvio Pons and Sophie Quinn-Judge (eds), *The Cambridge History of Communism*, volume 2: *The Socialist Camp and World Power*, Cambridge University Press, Cambridge, 2017, p. 328.

72 For a local derivative of this argument, see Albert Tshume, 'The Non-capitalist Road to Socialism: Africa's Revolutionary Way Forward', *African Communist*, 56, third quarter 1972, pp. 94–110.

73 Quotations in the above section of this paragraph from Vasily Solodovnikov (one-time director of the Africa Institute in Moscow), Anatoly Adamishin (former Deputy Foreign Minister) and Anatoly Dobrynin (ex-ambassador to Washington) in Filatova and Davidson, *The Hidden Thread*, pp. 226–7.

74 Barbara Carr, *Loginov: Spy in the Sun*, Howard Timmins, Cape Town, 1969.

75 Hilger, 'Communism, Decolonisation and the Third World', p. 330.

76 Hilger, 'Communism, Decolonisation and the Third World', p. 337. See also Marilyn Young and Sophie Quinn-Judge, 'The Vietnam War as a World Event', in Juliane Fürst, Sylvio Pons and Mark Selden (eds), *The Cambridge History of Communism*, volume 3: *Endgames: Late Communism in Global Perspective*, Cambridge University Press, Cambridge, 2017, p. 52.

77 Filatova and Davidson, *The Hidden Thread*, pp. 275–6. MPLA and FRELIMO's formal adoption of Marxism Leninism took place in 1977.

78 More than $1 billion worth of Soviet munitions were sold or given to Ethiopia, Angola, Tanzania, Mozambique and Zambia between 1967 and 1980. See Robert D Grey, 'The Soviet Presence in Africa: An Analysis of Goals', *Journal of Modern African Studies*, 22, 3, September 1984, p. 523.

79 Fred Halliday, *The Making of the Third Cold War*, Verso, London, 1983.

80 Filatova and Davidson, *The Hidden Thread*, p. 227.

81 Filatova and Davidson, *The Hidden Thread*, p. 234.

82 Hilger, 'Communism, Decolonisation and the Third World', p. 331.

83 Stephen M Davis, *Apartheid's Rebels: Inside South Africa's Hidden War*, Yale University Press, New Haven, 1987, pp. 70–1.

84 For detail on the content of such programmes, see Filatova and Davidson, *The Hidden Thread*, pp. 335–9.

85 Vladimir Shubin, *ANC: A View from Moscow*, Mayibuye Books, Cape Town, 1999, p. 311.

86 Filatova and Davidson, *The Hidden Thread*, p. 342. For information on Swedish

funding, see Hugh Macmillan, *The Lusaka Years: The ANC in Exile in Zambia, 1963–1993*, Jacana Media, Johannesburg, p. 100; Reddy Mapane interviewed by Tor Sellström, Nordic Institute of African Studies, https://nai.uu.se/library/resources/liberation-africa/interviews/reddy-mampane-aka-reddy-mazimba.html.

87 Russian archival source cited in Filatova and Davidson, *The Hidden Thread*, p. 241.

88 Essop and Meg Pahad, interviewed by Tom Lodge, 22 September 2019.

89 Czech National Archives, Prague, Předsednictvo ÚV KSČ 1976–81, sv. 77, aj. 81, b. 27.

90 The Czechs maintained an extensive network of Státní Bezpečnost personnel across Africa and recruited 'contacts' within certain liberation movements. See N. Telepneva, 'Codename SEKRETÁŘ: Amilcar Cabral, Czechoslovakia and the Role of Human Intelligence during the Cold War', *International Historical Review*, 2019, https://doi.org/10/1080/07075332.2019.1678508

91 Czech National Archives, Prague, Předsednictvo ÚV KSČ 1976–81, sv. 77, aj. 81, b. 27.

92 Karel Sieber and Petr Zídek, *Československo a subsaharská Afrika v letech, 1948–1989*, Ústav Mezinárodnich Vztahu, Prague, 2007, pp. 110–11.

93 Maloka, *The South African Communist Party*, p. 84.

94 Chris Barron, 'Obituary: Arnold Selby', *Sunday Times* (Johannesburg), 15 September 2002.

95 Hans-Georg Schleicher and Ilona Schleicher, 'Nordic and GDR Solidarity with the Liberation Struggle in Southern Africa', *Jahrbuch Asien-Africa-Lateinamerika*, 28, 3, 2000, p. 319.

96 Hans-Georg Schleicher, 'GDR Solidarity: The German Democratic Republic and the South African Liberation Struggle', in Ben Magubane (ed.), *The Road to Liberation in South Africa*, volume 3: *International Solidarity*, Unisa Press, Pretoria, 2008, pp. 1093 and 1125.

97 Gareth Winrow, 'The GDR in Africa: A Gradual Disengagement?', *Africa Spectrum*, 24, 3, 1989, p. 305; for interviews with East German Anti-Apartheid movement members, see Martin Koch, 'Opposing Apartheid from behind the Berlin Wall', *Germany: News and In-depth Reports*, 15 December 2013, https://p.dw.com/p/1AZqR.

98 Schleicher, 'GDR Solidarity', p. 1131; Schleicher and Schleicher, 'Nordic and GDR Soldarity', p. 1.

99 Gilder, *Songs and Silences*, p. 63.

100 Kasrils, *Armed and Dangerous*, pp. 125 and 130.

101 Christopher Coker, 'Pact, Pox or Proxy: Eastern Europe's Security Relationship with Southern Africa', *Soviet Studies*, 40, 4, 1988, p. 578.

102 Cited in Jeremy Seekings, *The UDF: A History of the United Democratic Front in South Africa, 1983–1991*, David Philip, Cape Town, 2000, p. 32.

103 Gordhan told reporters that he had belonged to the party since the early 1970s; he was an 'informal member', he said, because then the party did not issue membership cards. See 'Gordhan No Longer SACP Member', 27 October 2009, https://www.fin24.com/Economy/Gordhan-no-longer-SACP-member-20091027.

104 Macmillan, *The Lusaka Years*, p. 136.

105 O'Malley, *Shades of Difference*, p. 216.

106 O'Malley, *Shades of Difference*, p. 217.

107 Adrian Hadland and Jovial Rantao, *The Life and Times of Thabo Mbeki*, Zebra Press, Cape Town, 1999, p. 39.

108 Cited in Macmillan, *The Lusaka Years*, p. 111.

109 O'Malley, *Shades of Difference*, p. 205.

110 Wieder, *Ruth First and Joe Slovo*, p. 235.

111 Wieder, *Ruth First and Joe Slovo*, p. 209.

112   Slovo, *Unfinished Autobiography*, p. 245.

113   Kasrils, *Armed and Dangerous*, pp. 193–6.

114   Barbara Hogan Trial Papers, Tom Lodge Papers. See also Beverley Naidoo, *Death of an Idealist: In Search of Neil Aggett*, Jonathan Ball, Johannesburg, 2012, pp. 184–6. The list had in fact been asked for by 'Sipho', a double agent working for the security police, who Barbara Hogan thought was a fellow ANC member.

115   O'Malley, *Shades of Difference*, p. 225. The ANC's claim was surely an exaggeration; the figure is cited from an internal report by Macmillan in *The Lusaka Years*, p. 172.

116   O'Malley, *Shades of Difference*, p. 173.

117   Macmillan, *The Lusaka Years*, p. 168.

118   Gilder, *Songs and Secrets*, p. 81.

119   Kasrils, *Armed and Dangerous*, p. 186.

120   Ellis, *External Mission*, p. 211.

121   Ray Alexander to Moses Kotane, 31 August 1980, Simons Papers, UCT Manuscripts and Archives, B 1081, 8.2.

122   Minutes, party meeting, P Region, 14 August 1982, Simons Papers, B 1081, 8.2.

123   Raymond Suttner, 'The (Re-)Constitution of the South African Communist Party as an Underground Organisation', *Journal of Contemporary African Studies*, 22, 1, 2004, p. 60. Its dominant personality, Mike Roussos, may have done so; he belonged to the party after its legalisation in 1990.

124   Subsequently South African newspapers carried stories citing US and British intelligence to suggest that Ruth First had estranged herself both from the party and from her husband by her 'ultra-leftism' and that Joe Slovo had 'engineered' her assassination (Russell Gault, 'Reports Claim Slovo Responsible for Wife's Letter Bomb Death', *The Star*, 14 July 1984). Joe Slovo was apparently a KGB colonel 'who has a dacha on Lake Baikal' ('Colonel Slovo Lies Low in London', *Sunday Times*, 29 May 1983). Slovo sued both *The Star* and the *Sunday Times* successfully in British courts. Twelve years later security policeman Craig Williamson admitted responsibility for the bomb at the Truth and Reconciliation Commission.

125   Rashid, quoted in Wieder, *Ruth First and Joe Slovo*, p. 243.

126   Wieder, *Ruth First and Joe Slovo*, p. 220.

127   Ellis, *External Mission*, p. 160.

128   Ray Alexander, 'On the Question of the Calling of a "Morogoro-Type" Conference', Jack and Ray Simons Papers, BC 1081, 07.2.

129   Notes on a meeting between ANC and South African businessmen, Mfuwe, Zambia, September 1985, Tom Lodge Papers. It was Oliver Tambo who suggested that nationalisation might be on Zambian lines, though this remark is not attributed in the notes (Macmillan, *The Lusaka Years*, p. 202).

130   Gevisser, *Thabo Mbeki*, p. 502.

131   Though the ANC's acceptance of the EPG proposals was a consequence of Zambian pressure, most ANC leaders, not just communists, disliked the idea of a cessation of hostilities as a precondition and were in any case sceptical about their own organisational ability to rein in their supporters inside South Africa (Macmillan, *The Lusaka Years*, p. 208).

132   Richard Rosenthal, *Mission Improbable*, David Philip, Cape Town, 1998, p. 55.

133   Rosenthal, *Mission Improbable*, p. 107.

134   SACP Politburo discussion document, 'The Developing Situation and Some of Our Strategic and Tactical Objectives', May 1986, Simons Papers, BC 1081, 07.1. The same text was given to journalists by the State President's office on 12 June 1986 (Tom Lodge Papers).

135   David Coetzee, 'The Struggle Goes On: An Exclusive Interview with Joe Slovo',

AfricaAsia magazine, 33, September 1986, p. 16.

136 Howard Barrell, 'All for the Front', *Work in Progress*, 38, 1985, p. 11; *The Guardian Weekly*, 11 August 1985.

137 *Inner Party Bulletin*, September 1985, Sylvia Neame Papers, A 2729, Q2.2 2/3.

138 *Inner Party Bulletin*, January 1986, Sylvia Neame Papers, A 2729, Q2.2 2/3.

139 Joe Slovo, *The South African Working Class and the National Democratic Revolution*, Umsebenzi Discussion Pamphlet, n.p., [1988], p. 15, UKZN Documentation Centre, 1957/44.

140 At their drafting stage the Guidelines were reviewed by a subcommittee constituted by Joe Slovo, Pallo Jordan and Simon Makana, which expressed reservations about their framing in terms of a 'conventional bourgeois democracy' (Macmillan, *The Lusaka Years*, p. 216).

141 Kader Asmal, 'Electoral Systems: A Critical Survey', typescript, ANC in-house seminar, Lusaka, 1–4 March 1988, p. 5, Tom Lodge Papers.

142 Thabo Mbeki, 'Broad Perspectives on Future Economy of South Africa', typescript, ANC in-house seminar, Lusaka, 1–4 March 1988, pp. 8–11, Tom Lodge Papers. Gevisser uses a different source, a video of Mbeki's verbal presentation, which included a 'rather heretical' question on 'What to nationalise and how to do it?' Here Mbeki chose to highlight the risks of nationalisation without the involvement of foreign investors (Gevisser, *Thabo Mbeki*, p. 540).

143 Albie Sachs, 'Post-Apartheid South Africa', *World Policy Journal*, 6, 2, Summer 1989, p. 602.

144 Raymond Suttner, *The Freedom Charter: The People's Charter in the Nineteen-Eighties*, TB Davie Memorial Lecture, University of Cape Town, 1984, pp. 13 and 25.

145 Mzala, 'The Freedom Charter and Its Relevance Today', in African National Congress, *Selected Writings on the Freedom Charter*, Sechaba Publications, London, 1985, p. 100.

146 Dale T McKinley, *The ANC and the Liberation Struggle: A Critical Political Biography*, Pluto Press, London, 1997, p. 78.

147 Mark Gevisser. 'Why is Thabo Mbeki a "Nitemare"', in Daryl Glaser (ed.), *Mbeki and After: Reflections on the Legacy of Thabo Mbeki*, Witwatersrand University Press, Johannesburg, 2010, p. 55.

148 On Mbeki as a cricket enthusiast, see Mpho Mgozi in Ndlovu and Strydom, *The Thabo Mbeki I Knew*, pp. 392–3.

149 William Mervyn Gumede, *Thabo Mbeki and the Battle for the Soul of the ANC*, Zed Books, London, 2007, pp. 40–1.

150 Gevisser, *Thabo Mbeki*, p. 221.

151 Hadland and Rantao, *The Life and Times of Thabo Mbeki*, p. 61. See also Gumede, *Thabo Mbeki and the Battle for the Soul of the ANC*, p. 43.

152 Gumede, *Thabo Mbeki and the Battle for the Soul of the ANC*, p. 43.

153 Gilder, *Songs and Secrets*, p. 97.

154 Gevisser, *Thabo Mbeki*, p. 481.

155 Gevisser, *Thabo Mbeki*, p. 470.

156 Stephanie Kemp, *Through an Unforgettable Storm: The Forging of a Loyal Cadre*, self-published, 2017, Kindle location 3517.

157 Heribert Adam and Kogila Moodley, *The Negotiated Revolution*, Jonathan Ball, Johannesburg, 1993, p. 42.

158 Sara Lorenzini, 'The Socialist Camp and the Challenge of Economic Modernization in the Third World', in Naimark, Pons and Quinn-Judge, *The Cambridge History of Communism*, volume 2, p. 361.

159 Winrich Kühne, *Black Politics in South Africa and the Outlook for Meaningful Negotiations*, Stiftung Wissenschaft und Politik, Ebenhausen, 1987, p. 41.

160 Lorenzini, 'The Socialist Camp and the Challenge of Economic Modernization in the Third World', p. 357; Winrich Kühne, *Die Politik der Sowjetunion in Afrika*, Nomos Verlagsgesellschaft, Baden-Baden, 1982, pp. 297–8; Kühne, *Black Politics in South Africa*, p. 41.

161 Schleicher and Schleicher, 'Nordic and GDR Solidarity', pp. 315–16.

162 James Mark and Tobias Rupprecht, 'Europe's "1989" in Global Context', in Fürst, Pons and Selden, *The Cambridge History of Communism*, volume 3, pp. 238–9.

163 Gleb Starushenko, 'Problems of Struggle against Racism, Apartheid and Colonialism in South Africa', Report presented to the Second Soviet African Conference for Peace, Cooperation and Social Progress, Moscow, USSR Academy of Sciences, the Africa Institute, 24–25 June 1986, p. 9.

164 See Slovo, *The South African Working Class and the National Democratic Revolution*, pp. 34–5.

165 Filatova and Davidson, *The Hidden Thread*, p. 384.

166 Interviewed by Howard Barrell in *Work in Progress*, 48, 1987.

167 Slovo, *The South African Working Class and the National Democratic Revolution*.

168 Janos Radveni, *Psychological Operations and Political Warfare in Long Term Strategic Planning*, Praeger, New York, 1990, pp. 43–5. Radveni, mistakenly, refers to Ramelson as a 'hardliner'.

169 'Oliver Tambo's Visit to the Soviet Union', *Soviet Revue*, Institute for Soviet Studies, University of Stellenbosch, 2, 10, November 1986.

170 *Inner Party Bulletin*, June 1988, Sylvia Neame Papers, A 2729, Q2.2 1/3.

171 African National Congress, Documentation of the Second National Consultative Conference, Kabwe, 16–23 June 1985, p. 36, Tom Lodge Papers.

172 African National Congress, National Consultative Conference, June 1985, Commission on Strategy and Tactics, p. 16.

173 African National Congress, National Consultative Conference, June 1985, Commission on Cadre Policy, Political and Ideological Work, p. 12, Tom Lodge Papers

174 How successful the ANC's and SACP's intelligence were in subverting the South African military remains under-explored. Stephanie Kemp suggests that London-based communists had arranged a meeting with a visiting SADF general as early as 1977 (Kemp, *Through an Unforgettable Storm*, Kindle location 3173).

175 African National Congress, Commission on Strategy and Tactics, p. 18.

176 Gevisser, *Thabo Mbeki*, p. 532.

177 Macmillan, *The Lusaka Years*, p. 193.

178 O'Malley, *Shades of Difference*, p. 219.

179 For example, Quibaxe's commander in 1979, Kenneth Mahamba, was suspected of being a police recruit, and was executed in 1982.

180 For detail, see Ellis, *External Mission*, p. 199. Hugh Macmillan's history of the ANC's Zambian exile is also sceptical about NAT's success in identifying real agents (Macmillan, *The Lusaka Years*, pp. 152–3).

181 Ronnie Kasrils remains convinced that Kenneth Mahamba (Timothy Seremane), a commander at Quibaxe and at Pango camps, was an agent (*Armed and Dangerous*, p. 248) though this is disputed by his family and others. The ANC made a similar claim at the Truth and Reconciliation Commission in 1997. However, in 1998 Hermann Stadler, the former head of the security police's intelligence, confirmed that the police had never head of Mahamba/Seremane and had never recruited him ('The Execution of a Camp Commander', *Mail & Guardian*, 30 October 1998, https://mg.co.za/article/1998-10-30-the-execution-of-a-camp-commander/).

182 Kasrils argues that the more assertive operations against UNITA were morale-raising and that frustrations set in only after Umkhonto 'reverted a defensive role' (*Armed and Dangerous*, p. 250).

183 Ellis, *External Mission*, pp. 158–9.
184 Ellis, *External Mission*, p. 185.
185 Macmillan, *The Lusaka Years*, pp. 162–5.
186 Ellis, *External Mission*, p. 214.
187 Andreas Maercker and Susanne Guski-Leinwand, 'Psychologists' Involvement in Repression: "Stasi" Secret Police Activities in the Former East Germany', *International Perspectives in Psychology*, 7, 2, 2018, p. 113; Mary Beth Stein, 'Narratives of Stasi Detention', *Narrative Culture*, 3, 2, 2016, p. 237. For testimony on the Stasi's use of sleep deprivation, see Anna Funder, *Stasiland: Stories from behind the Berlin Wall*, Granta, London, 2004, pp. 24–6.
188 A subsequent ANC inquiry found no evidence of physical torture (Macmillan, *The Lusaka Years*, p. 246).
189 Ellis, *External Mission*, p. 240.
190 Piliso was also identified as a communist by at least one South African right-wing commentor: Michael Morris, *ANC in Exile: 40 Seniors List*, Terrorism Research Institute, Cape Town, 1986. The claim was repeated in the US Senate's Chairman of the Subcommittee on Security and Terrorism's report on *Soviet, East German and Cuban Involvement in Fomenting Terrorism in Southern Africa* (US Government Printing Office, Washington, 1982, p. 23, citing South African intelligence sources). It seems unlikely. Piliso joined the ANC outside South African in 1961 after training as a pharmacist in London. In the late 1960s he was associated for a while with Tennyson Makiwane's Gang of Eight and he was then the target of SACP criticism.
191 Politburo minutes, 11–12 May 1981, quoted in Maloka, *The South African Communist Party*, p. 47.
192 *Inner Party Bulletin*, April 1986, Sylvia Neame Papers, A 2729, Q2-2 2/3.
193 South African Communist Party, *The Path to Power, Programme of the South African Communist Party*, 1989, p. 58.
194 On Mbeki, see Geraldine J Fraser Moleketi in Ndlovu and Strydom, *The Thabo Mbeki I Knew*, p. 159. On Slovo's contribution, see Thenjiwe Mtintso in Slovo, *The Unfinished Autobiography*, p. 246.
195 *The World Greets the South African Communist Party*, Inkululeko Publications, London, July 1989, pp. 3–4.
196 O'Malley, *Shades of Difference*, p. 282.
197 Wieder, *Ruth First and Joe Slovo*, p. 294.
198 Hermann Stadler, *The Other Side of the Story: A True Perspective*, Contact Publishers, Pretoria, 1997, p. 30.
199 Ellis, *External Mission*, p. 283.
200 O'Malley, *Shades of Difference*, p. 252. South African communists quite often suggested that their relationship with the ANC was comparable to the partnership between Castro's movement and the Cuban party: see, for example, Sol Dubala (Joe Slovo), 'The Two Pillars of Struggle', *African Communist*, 87, 1981, p. 34.
201 O'Malley, *Shades of Difference*, p. 255. For technical details, see Press, 'To Change the World!', pp. 164–7.
202 Conny Braam, *Operation Vula*, Jacana Media, Johannesburg, 2004, p. 63.
203 Braam, *Operation Vula*, p. 269.
204 Braam, *Operation Vula*, p. 42.
205 It is unclear from his own account whether Shaik joined the party; he was a 'committed Marxist' at that time (Moe Shaik, *The ANC Spy Bible: Operating across Enemy Lines*, Tafelberg, Cape Town, 2020, p. 41).
206 Before travelling to Berlin, Joe Slovo warned Shaik that the Stasi would try and recruit him; they didn't, though (Shaik, *The Spy Bible*, p. 104).

207 Alan Wieder suggests she was sent to Johannesburg in 1987 by Joe Slovo 'to engineer the communications networks for the forthcoming Operation Vula' (*Ruth First and Joe Slovo*, p. 273).

208 Braam, *Operation Vula*, p. 140.

209 Ronnie Kasrils, interviewed by Howard Barrell, 19 August 1989, transcript, Barrell Papers, Rhodes House, University of Oxford, cited in Landau, 'Communist Controlled?', p. 29.

210 Seekings, *The UDF*, p. 243.

211 Colin Bundy, *Govan Mbeki*, Jacana Media, Johannesburg, 2012, pp. 139–40.

212 Ken Keable (ed.), *London Recruits: The Secret War against Apartheid*, Merlin Books, London, 2012, p. 309.

213 Gevisser, *Thabo Mbeki*, p. 598.

214 Braam, *Operation Vula*, p. 31.

215 Maloka, *The South African Communist Party*, p. 102.

216 Seekings, *The UDF*, p. 207.

217 Seekings, *The UDF*, p. 48.

218 Seekings, *The UDF*, p. 15.

219 Macmillan, *The Lusaka Years*, p. 172.

220 Hadland and Rantao, *The Life and Times of Thabo Mbeki*, p. 49.

221 Seekings, *The UDF*, p. 199.

222 Central Committee report, SACP 9th Congress, 6–8 April 1995, p. 1, Simons Papers, BC 1081, 08.2.

223 Suttner, 'The (Re-)Constitution of the South African Communist Party', p. 61.

224 Maloka, *The South African Communist Party*, pp. 57–8.

225 Seekings, *The UDF*, p. 313. In his autobiography, Nqakula is vague about when he joined the party though it is evident that he was active in circulating party propaganda in the early 1980s and knew other activists as communists. He was in frequent contact with Chris Hani based in Lesotho during this period (Charles Nqakula, *The People's War: Reflections of an ANC Cadre*, Mutloatse Arts Heritage Trust, Johannesburg, 2017).

226 Seekings, *The UDF*, p. 85.

227 Seekings, *The UDF*, p. 38.

228 Sylvia Neame Papers, Q2-2.1 1/3.

229 Shaik, *The Spy Bible*, p. 161.

230 Ineke van Kessel, *'Beyond Our Wildest Dreams': The United Democratic Front and the Transformation of South Africa*, University Press of Virginia, Charlottesville, 2000.

231 Jeremy Cronin, *Inside*, Ravan Press, Johannesburg, 1983, p. 7.

232 Gavin Evans, 'ANC Spy Bible', *The Conversation*, 29 March 2020. See also Gavin Evans, *Dancing Man Is Dead: A Tale of Fighting Men in South Africa*, Doubleday, London, 2020; and Gavin Evans, interviewed by Howard Barrell, Johannesburg, 28 January 1991, O'Malley Archives.

233 *Inner Party Bulletin*, March 1985, p. 6, Sylvia Neame Papers, A 2729, Q2.2 2/3.

234 Naidoo, *Death of an Idealist*, pp. 81 and 175.

235 For picture, see *The Star*, 5 May 1986.

236 Menzi Duka, *Matthew Goniwe on a South African Frontier*, Institute of Social and Economic Research, Rhodes University, Grahamstown, 2018.

237 Van Kessel, *'Beyond Our Wildest Dreams'*, p. 97.

238 Van Kessel, *'Beyond Our Wildest Dreams'*, p. 145.

239 Isak Niehaus's research on the witchcraft campaigns of this era, conducted in the area around Bushbuckridge, suggests that though the youthful comrades usurped elders' authority, their victims were often identified by older adult residents and were

frequently people who had previously been targets of witchcraft accusations. Niehaus suggests that the actions often reflected communal consensus and were one way in which the Congresses built wider support (Isak Niehaus, *Witchcraft and Politics: Exploring the Occult in the South African Lowveld*, Pluto Press, London, p. 149).

240   Witches were killed in other ways or driven out from their homeplaces. See Van Kessel, *'Beyond Our Wildest Dreams'*, p. 127.

241   Anne Heffernan, 'A History of Youth Politics in Limpopo, 1967–1993', DPhil dissertation, History, University of Oxford, June 2014, p. 236.

242   Heffernan, 'A History of Youth Politics in Limpopo', pp. 216–17.

243   Saleem Badat, *Black Student Politics: From SASO to SANSCO, 1968–1990*, Human Sciences Research Council Press, Pretoria, 1999. p. 313

244   RE Matajo [Ray Alexander], *African Communist*, 1984, cited by DA Kotze, 'Trade Unionism, Working Class Politics and the South African Communist Party', *Politeia*, 8, 1, 1989, p. 26.

245   *Special Inner-Party Bulletin*, July 1980, Sylvia Neame Papers, A 2729 Q2-2 2/3.

246   Editorial, *African Communist*, 89, second quarter 1982, p. 7.

247   David Lewis, 'Black Workers and Trade Unions', in Karis and Gerhart, *From Protest to Challenge*, volume 5, pp. 218–19.

248   Naidoo, *Death of an Idealist*, pp. 166–7.

249   *African Communist*, 95, fourth quarter 1983.

250   RS Nyameko [Ray Alexander], 'Workers' Militancy Demands TU United Front', *African Communist*, 95, fourth quarter 1983, p. 29; Central Committee statement, *African Communist*, 96, first quarter 1984.

251   CC meeting statement, 'Forward to People's Power: The Challenge Ahead', *African Communist*, first quarter 1980.

252   Phil Eidelberg, 'The Unions and the African National Congress', *South African Historical Journal*, 28, May 1993, pp. 278.

253   *Inner Party Bulletin*, April 1986, p. 7, Sylvia Neame Papers, A 2729, Q2-2 2/3.

254   Macmillan, *The Lusaka Years*, p. 211.

255   Press, 'To Change the World!', p. 147.

256   Press, 'To Change the World!', p. 157.

257   Press, 'To Change the World!', p. 148.

258   SACTU argued it should be the channel for any British trade union support for South African unions and in 1982 encouraged the Transport and General Workers' Union to reject a SAAWU appeal to send a delegation during the Wilson Rowntree strike. See Paul Storey, 'Build Direct Links with the Workers' Movement in Other Countries', *Inqaba ya Basebenzi*, 6, May 1982, pp. 38–9. For SACTU's position, see '"Direct Links" – Stinks', *Workers' Unity*, 30, April 1982.

259   *Inner Party Bulletin*, June 1987, Sylvia Neame Papers, A 2729, Q2-2 1/3.

260   To judge from the testimony quoted by Maloka (*The South African Communist Party*, p. 62), not just in COSATU affiliates.

261   *Inner Party Bulletin*, April 1986, Sylvia Neame Papers, A 2729, Q2-2 2/3.

262   Kotze, 'Trade Unionism, Working Class Politics and the South African Communist Party', p. 31.

263   Ndlovu and Strydom, *The Thabo Mbeki I Knew*, p. 142.

264   Gumede, *Thabo Mbeki and the Battle for the Soul of the ANC*, p. 50.

265   Ramaphosa's tribute in Slovo, *The Unfinished Autobiography*, p. 222.

266   'Comrade H' at a Central Committee meeting, quoted in *Inner Party Bulletin*, January 1986, Sylvia Neame Papers, A 2729, Q2.2 2/3.

267   Maloka, *The South African Communist Party*, pp. 58–9.

268   For a useful commentary, see Eidelberg, 'The Unions and the African National Congress', pp. 284–5.

269 Slovo, *The South African Working Class and the National Democratic Revolution*. The 'Chinese wall' phraseology was first used by Francis Meli in his discussion of revolutionary stages in 'Nationalism and Internationalism in South African Liberation', *African Communist*, 57, second quarter 1974, p. 53.

270 Nyawuza, 'New "Marxist" Tendencies and the Battle of Ideas in South Africa!', *African Communist*, 103, fourth quarter 1985, p. 58. For a criticism of the same point, see Langa Mzansi, 'The "Two Stage Theory" and the Balance of Forces', *African Communist*, 104, first quarter 1986, pp. 108–9.

271 For discussion and debate, see 'Workers, Organise and Unite – Join SACP, ANC and MK for Freedom and Socialism', *African Communist*, 112, first quarter 1988, pp. 43–5; 'Draft Workers Charter: Preamble', *African Communist*, 119, fourth quarter 1989, pp. 108–13.

272 Gilder, *Songs and Secrets*, p. 118.

273 Simons Papers, BC 1081, 8.1.

274 Press, 'To Change the World!', p. 140.

275 Moloka, *The South African Communist Party*, p. 55.

276 Rica Hodgson, *Foot Soldier for Freedom: A Life in South Africa's Liberation Movement*, Picador Africa, Johannesburg, 2010, pp. 228–9.

277 Discussion document, 'Role of the Party and Its Place in the NLM', 29 April 1980, Sylvia Neame Papers, A 2729, Q2.1 1/2.

278 CC plenary of 1981, 'Party Work in the Fraternal Organisations', document on accountability, Sylvia Neame Papers, A 2729 Q2.1.

279 Maloka, *The South African Communist Party*, p. 46.

280 Ray Simons, quoted by Ellis in *External Mission*, p. 215.

281 *Inner Party Bulletin*, October 1981, Sylvia Neame Papers, A 2729, Q2-2 2/3.

282 'SACP Holds Its 6th Conference', *African Communist*, 101, second quarter 1985, p. 2.

283 Maloka, *The South African Communist Party*, p. 55.

284 *Inner Party Bulletin*, March 1985, Sylvia Neame Papers, A 2729, Q2.2 2/3.

285 Maloka, *The South African Communist Party*, p. 56.

286 *Inner Party Bulletin*, March 1985, Sylvia Neame Papers, A 2729, Q2.2 2/3.

287 Kasrils, *Armed and Dangerous*, p. 274.

288 Ellis, *External Mission*, p. 178.

289 *Inner Party Bulletin*, January 1986, Sylvia Neame Papers, A 2729 Q2.2 2/3.

290 *Inner Party Bulletin*, April 1986, Sylvia Neame Papers, A 2729, Q2-2 2/3.

291 *Inner Party Bulletin*, June 1988, Sylvia Neame Papers, A 2729, Q2.2 1/3.

292 *Inner Party Bulletin*, January 1988, Sylvia Neame Papers, A 2729, Q2-2 1/3.

293 *Inner Party Bulletin*, April 1986, Sylvia Neame Papers, A 2729, Q2-2 2/3.

294 *Inner Party Bulletin*, January 1986, Sylvia Neame Papers, A 2729, Q2.2 2/3.

295 *Inner Party Bulletin*, January 1988, Sylvia Neame Papers, A 2729, Q2-2 1/3.

296 *Inner Party Bulletin*, April 1986, Sylvia Neame Papers, A 2729, Q2-2 2/3.

297 *Conversations with a Communist*, p. 6, File: Organization, 159, Phyllis Naidoo Papers, UKZN Documentation Centre.

298 Jeremy Seekings to Tom Lodge, 1 August 1986.

299 Anthony Sampson, *Black and Gold: Tycoons, Revolutionaries and Apartheid*, Coronet Books, London, 1987, p. 132.

300 South African Communist Party, *An Alliance Forged in Struggle: Speeches*, Inkululeko Publications, London, 1986; 'Communist Blueprint for South Africa', *The Guardian*, 7 August 1986.

Chapter 9

1 See Anna Grzymala-Busse, 'The Programmatic Turnaround of Communist Successor Parties in East Central Europe', *Communist and Post-Communist Studies*,

35, 2002, pp. 51–66; Sheri Berman and Maria Snegovaya, 'Populism and the Decline of Social Democracy', *Journal of Democracy*, 30, 3, 1999, pp. 5–19.

2   Lukáš Linek, 'Political Regimes and Generational Effect on the Support for the Czech Communist Party', paper presented at the Workshop on the Legacy of Authoritarian Regimes, University of Nottingham, 25 April 2017.

3   Gianfranco Pasquino and Marco Valbruzzi, 'The Italian Democratic Party, Its Nature and Its Secretary', *Revista Española de Ciencia Politica*, 44, July 2017; David Bell, 'The French Communist Party from Revolution to Reform', in Jocelyn Evans (ed.), *The French Party System*, Manchester University Press, Manchester, 2018.

4   Christopher Lingle, 'Apartheid as Racial Socialism', *Kyklos*, 43, 2, 1989, pp. 229–47.

5   Pierre du Toit and Hennie Kotze, *Liberal Democracy and Peace in South Africa: The Pursuit of Freedom and Dignity*, Palgrave Macmillan, Basingstoke, 2011.

6   SACP, Document from an Extended Politburo Meeting, March 1986, Tom Lodge Papers, Wits Historical Papers.

7   Sylvia Neame, *The Congress Movement: The Unfolding of the Congress Alliance*, volume 1: *1917–April 1926*, HSRC Press, Cape Town, 2015, p. xli.

8   These were authorised by Mandela on 13 April 1990 but only after determined argument from Joe Slovo, Chris Hani and Ronnie Kasrils. Mandela's preferred option was joint policing. See 'Inside the ANC', *Foreign Report*, 18 April 1991.

9   Mark Stansfield and Terry van der Walt, 'The Vula Dossier', *Sunday Times* (Johannesburg), 4 November 1990, p. 16.

10 Joe Slovo, quoted in *Business Day*, 26 June 1990.

11 Simon Adams, 'The Party That Time Forgot: The Construction of a Mass Communist Party in South Africa, 1990–1991', paper presented at the annual conference of the African Studies Association of Australasia and the Pacific, Adelaide, 22–29 September 1996, p. 8.

12 *Umsebenzi*, 6, 4, 1990, p. 4.

13 *City Press*, 5 December 1991.

14 Adams, 'The Party That Time Forgot', p. 9.

15 Adams, 'The Party That Time Forgot', p. 10.

16 Charles Nqakula, *The People's War: Reflections of an ANC Cadre*, Mutloatse Arts Heritage Trust, Johannesburg, 2017, p. 315.

17 Jeremy Cronin, 'Building the Legal Mass Party', *South African Labour Bulletin*, 15, 3, September 1990, p. 7.

18 Joe Slovo, interview, *South African Labour Bulletin*, 14, 8, 1990, p. 36.

19 Frank Wilderson, *Incognegro: A Memoir of Exile and Apartheid*, South End Press, Boston, 2008.

20 *African Communist*, 119, 1989, p. 111.

21 Joe Slovo, Interview, *Learn and Teach*, 4, 1990, p. 9.

22 See Jeremy Cronin's interview with Helena Sheehan on 24 January 2002 for his explanation of what communists called 'The Leipzig Way', http://www.comms.dcu.ie/sheehanh/za/cronin02.ht, p. 5.

23 SAPA, 'SACP Reveals Secret Meeting Minutes', *The Star*, 31 July 1990.

24 Simon Adams, 'Between the Negotiated and Unnegotiated Revolution: The "Bop" Uprising and the South African Communist Party', Socialist History Working Papers 2, London Socialist Historians Group, Institute of Historical Research, University of London, 1996.

25 Joe Slovo, *Has Socialism Failed?*, Umsebenzi Discussion Paper, Inkululeko Publications, London, 1990.

26 Slovo, *Has Socialism Failed?*, p. 24.

27 Stephanie Kemp, *Through an Unforgettable Storm: The Forging of a Loyal Cadre*, self-published, 2017, Kindle location: 3818

28   Slovo, *Has Socialism Failed?*, p. 23.

29   Thomas Stanley Kolasa, *The South African Communist Party: Adapting to a Post-Communist Age*, McFarland and Co., Jefferson, NC, 2016, pp. 33 and 151.

30   SACP, 'Building Workers' Power for Democratic Change: Draft Manifesto of the SACP', 1991, unpublished document circulated to members before the eighth congress), Tom Lodge Papers.

31   Jeremy Cronin, interviewed by Tom Lodge, 1993.

32   Joe Slovo, 'What Room for Compromise?', *African Communist*, 130, third quarter 1992.

33   Jeremy Cronin, interviewed by Helena Sheehan, 24 January 2002, transcript, p. 6, http://www.comms.dcu.ie/sheehan/za/cronin02.htm.

34   Colin Bundy, 'Theory of a Special Type', *Work in Progress*, 89, June 1993, p. 17.

35   His daughter Lindiwe has written a poignant memoir about their new life in Dawn Park. Hani was a strict but loving father and her account suggests that the family was made to feel welcome in the neighbourhood. In researching her book, she visited Waluś in prison as well as the sponsor of her father's killing, Clive Derby-Lewis. See Lindiwe Hani and Melinda Ferguson, *Being Chris Hani's Daughter*, MF Books, Johannesburg, 2017.

36   Z. Pallo Jordan, Chris Hani Memorial Lecture, 15 April 2003, p. 1.

37   Dirk Kotze, 'Why Communism Appears to Be Gaining Favour in South Africa', *The Conversation*, 4 August 2015, theconversation.com/why-communism-appears-to-be-gaining-favour-in-south-africa, accessed August 29, 2017; SACP, Organisational Report, 2017, http://www.sacp.org.za/docs /conf/2017/organisational-report.pdf.

38   Editorial, 'Sixty Years On: New Challenges for the African Communist', *African Communist*, 201, December 2019, p. 8; Alex Mashilo, 'Forward to the SNC', *Umsebenzi*, December 2019, p. 4.

39   SACP, Proposed workplan for SACP recruitment, September 2005, Vishwas Satgar Papers, Wits Historical Papers, A 332, 7.2.

40   SACP, 11th Plenary Session of the 11th Congress Central Committee, 18-20 February 2005, volume 1, p. 53, Vishwas Satgar Papers, A 332, C.2.13.

41   SACP, Political Report of the 13th Plenary Session of the 11th Congress Central Committee, 2005, p. 28, Vishwas Satgar Papers, A 3332, C2.4.

42   'Rebuild Our Movement: Political Report to the SNC', *African Communist*, 202, 2020, p. 51.

43   Anon., 'Special National Congress: Massive Increase in SACP Membership', *Umsebenzi*, July 2015, pp. 4–5.

44   Young Communist League, Organisational Report, Third Congress, 2010, SACP website, p. 16.

45   Young Communist League, Organisational Report of the National Committee, Second National Congress, 13–17 December 2006, SACP website, p. 11.

46   Kemp, *Through an Unforgettable Storm*, Kindle location: 4443.

47   Kotze, 'Why Communism Appears to Be Gaining Favour in South Africa'.

48   SACP, Gauteng Province, Secretary's Report to the Seventh Provincial Congress, 5 August 2001, Vishwas Satgar Papers, A 332, B5.5.

49   SACP, Gauteng Province, Secretary's Report to the Seventh Provincial Congress, 5 August 2001, Vishwas Satgar Papers, A 332, B5.5.

50   SACP, Gauteng Province, Organising Report, 1999, Vishwas Satgar Papers, A 332, B.3.

51   Govan Whittles, 'Stalini Faction Caused ANC to Lose Metro – Report', *Mail & Guardian*, 13 January 2017.

52   SACP, Gauteng Province, An Assessment of the Implementation of the SACP Programme and the State of the SACP in the Gauteng Province, 6 July 2001,

Vishwas Satgar Papers, A 332, B5.2.

53 SACP, Gauteng Province, An Assessment of the Implementation of the SACP Programme and the State of the SACP in the Gauteng Province, 6 July 2001, Vishwas Satgar Papers, A 332, B5.2.

54 SACP, Gauteng Province, Organisational Report, 1998, Vishwas Satgar Papers, A 3332, B2.5.

55 Alex Mashilo, 'We Have Not Been Funded by These NUMSA Leaders – SACP', 22 December 2013, www.politicsweb.co.za/archive/we-have-not-been-funded-by-these-numsa-lead.

56 Frans Baleni and Blade Nzimande, quoted in Alexander Beresford, *South Africa's Political Crisis: Unfinished Liberation and Fractured Class Struggles*, Palgrave Macmillan, Basingstoke, 2016, p. 37.

57 Patrick Bond and Shauna Mottiar, 'Movements, Protests and a Massacre in South Africa', *Journal of Contemporary African Studies*, 31, 2, 2013, p. 299.

58 Michelle Williams, 'Energy, Labour and Democracy in South Africa', in Vishwas Satgar (ed.), *The Climate Crisis: South African and Global Democratic Eco-Socialist Alternatives*, Wits University Press, Johannesburg, 2018, p. 242.

59 Raphaël Botiveau, *Organize or Die? Democracy and Leadership in South Africa's National Union of Mineworkers*, Wits University Press, Johannesburg, 2017.

60 Botiveau, *Organize or Die?*, pp. 55–6.

61 Sakhela Buhlungu, *A Paradox of Victory: COSATU and the Democratic Transformation of South Africa*, University of KwaZulu-Natal Press, Scottsville, 2010, pp. 121–9.

62 Trevor Manuel, 'Twenty Years of Economic Policy Making: Putting People First', in Haroon Bhorat, Alan Hirsch, Ravi Kanbur and Mthuli Ncube (eds), *The Oxford Companion to the Economics of South Africa*, Oxford University Press, Oxford, 2014, p. 31.

63 Lawrence Edwards, 'Trade Policy Reform in South Africa', in Haroon Bhorat, Alan Hirsch, Ravi Kanbur and Mthuli Ncube (eds), *The Oxford Companion to the Economics of South Africa*, Oxford University Press, Oxford, 2014, p. 88

64 Bill Freund, *Twentieth Century South Africa: A Developmental History*, Cambridge University Press, Cambridge, p. 195.

65 Anthony Black, 'The Evolution and Impact of Foreign Direct Investment in South Africa since 1994', in Haroon Bhorat, Alan Hirsch, Ravi Kanbur and Mthuli Ncube (eds), *The Oxford Companion to the Economics of South Africa*, Oxford University Press, Oxford, 2014, pp. 96–7.

66 Marion Eeckhout and Nel de Vink, 'Composition of Financial Flows to SSA Countries', African Studies Centre, Leiden, 2014.

67 Jeremy Seekings and Nicoli Nattrass, *Poverty, Politics and Policy in South Africa: Why Has Poverty Persisted after Apartheid?*, Jacana Media, Johannesburg, 2015, pp. 103–6.

68 Edwards, 'Trade Policy Reform in South Africa', p. 90.

69 For a balanced treatment of the government's record on housing delivery, see Ian Palmer, Nishendra Moodley and Susan Parnell, *Building a Capable State: Service Delivery in Post-Apartheid South Africa*, Zed Press, London, 2017, pp. 230–50. The statistics cited in this paragraph are from this text.

70 For press reportage on the quadrupling of commercial maize farming in the Eastern Cape between 2013 and 2017 by 'emergent black farmers', see Wandile Sihlolo, 'Black Farmers of Eastern Cape Reap Harvest of Success', *Business Report* (supplement to *The Star*), 8 July 2018.

71 Data in this paragraph is drawn from Ben Cousins, 'Land and Land Reform in South Africa', in Haroon Bhorat, Alan Hirsch, Ravi Kanbur and Mthuli Ncube

(eds), *The Oxford Companion to the Economics of South Africa*, Oxford University Press, Oxford, 2014, pp. 377–82.

72 Central Committee, 'Key Strategic Tasks for the SACP', *African Communist*, 197, April 2018, p. 21.

73 'Land, Core of Class Struggle', *Umsebenzi*, December 2019, p. 7.

74 Roger Southall, 'Black Empowerment and Present Limits to Democratic Capitalism in South Africa', in Sakhela Buhlungu, John Daniel, Roger Southall and Jessica Lutchman (eds), *South Africa: State of the Nation, 2005–2006*, HSRC Press, Cape Town, 2006, p. 197.

75 Kate Wilkinson, 'Black Ownership of the Johannesburg Stock Exchange', *Africa Check*, 29 August 2017, https://africacheck.org/factsheets/guide-much-sas-stock-exchange-black-owned-know/.

76 Seekings and Nattrass, *Poverty, Politics and Policy in South Africa*, p. 229.

77 See, for example, comments in the SACP's Fourteenth Congress Political Report in 2017.

78 Andrew Whiteford, Dori Posel and Teresa Kelatwang, *A Profile of Poverty, Inequality and Human Development in South Africa*, Human Sciences Research Council, Pretoria, 1995, pp. 19–21.

79 Statistics South Africa, Inequality Trends Report, November 2019, cited in Dennis Webster, 'SA's Income Inequality Is Growing', *Mail & Guardian*, 22 November 2019, p. 15.

80 Statistics South Africa data, cited in Felix Nkunjana, 'Look to China for Economic Solutions in SA', *The Star*, 27 November 2019.

81 Ruchir Sharma, 'The Liberation Dividend', in Haroon Bhorat, Alan Hirsch, Ravi Kanbur and Mthuli Ncube (eds), *The Oxford Companion to the Economics of South Africa*, Oxford University Press, Oxford, 2014, p. 61.

82 Tom Lodge, 'The South African General Election, April 1994: Results, Analysis and Implications', *African Affairs*, 94, October 1995, p. 479.

83 Seekings and Nattrass, *Poverty, Politics and Policy in South Africa*, p. 267.

84 For a favourable assessment of the quality of care available at primary health care clinics, see Shauna Mottiar and Tom Lodge, 'The Role of Community Health Workers in Supporting South Africa's HIV/AIDS Treatment Programme', *African Journal of AIDS Research*, 17, 1, 2018, pp. 54–61.

85 Murray Leibbrandt, Arden Finn and Vimal Ranchhod, 'Post-Apartheid Poverty and Inequality Trends', in Haroon Bhorat, Alan Hirsch, Ravi Kanbur and Mthuli Ncube (eds), *The Oxford Companion to the Economics of South Africa*, Oxford University Press, Oxford, 2014, p. 293–294.

86 Servaas van der Berg, 'Current Poverty and Income Distribution in the Context of South African History,' *Economic History of Developing Regions*, 26, 1, 2011, pp. 120–40.

87 David P Thomas, 'Post-Apartheid Conundrums: Contemporary Debates and Divisions within the South African Communist Party', *Journal of Contemporary African Studies*, 25, 2, 2007, p. 257.

88 Jeremy Cronin, quoted by Thomas in 'Post-Apartheid Conundrums', p. 258.

89 Blade Nzimande, quoted by Thomas in 'Post-Apartheid Conundrums', p. 260.

90 Jeremy Cronin, interviewed by Helena Sheehan, 24 January 2004, transcript, p. 13.

91 SACP, Political Report of the SACP's 11th Congress Central Committee, as Tabled before the 12th Congress, www.org.za/main.php?ID=2754.

92 William Mervin Gumede, 'Mandela Sees Red at Communist Criticism', *Sunday Independent*, 15 June 1997.

93 Kolasa, *The South African Communist Party*, p. 185.

94 Nathi Theledi, 'Testing Our Programme against Slovo's Vision of the NDR', *African Communist*, 202, 2020, p. 97.

95   Quoted in Patrick Bond, 'Gearing Up or Down?', *South African Labour Bulletin*, 20 April 1996.

96   ANC Discussion Document, 'The State and Social Transformation', November 1996, p. 22; Jeremy Cronin and Blade Nzimande 'We Need Transformation, Not a Balancing Act', press release, 2 April 1997.

97   Quoted in 'The Shikota Splitters', *Bua Komanisi: Information Bulletin of the South African Communist Party*, 7, 2, November 2008, p. 7.

98   Kemp, *Through an Unforgettable Storm*, Kindle location: 4419.

99   Vicky Robinson and Rapule Tabane, 'SACP Divided over Zuma', *Mail & Guardian*, 21 April 2006.

100   Sipho Hlongwane, 'SACP: Where to from Here?', *Daily Maverick*, 16 July 2012, www.daily maverick.co.za/article/2012-07-16-analysis-scap-where-to-from-here/.

101   Matuma Letsoalo, 'SACP's "Comrade Crackdown" Takes Control', *Mail & Guardian*, 27 July 2012.

102   SACP, *The South African Road to Socialism: SACP's Five Year Plan. 13th Congress Political Programme of the SACP, 2012*, available as a PDF file on the SACP website.

103   SACP, 'Let's Not Monumentalise the National Development Plan', May 2013, discussion document, www.sacp.org.za/main.php?ID=3972.

104   Central Committee, 'Advancing, Deepening and Defending the National Democratic Revolution', *African Communist*, 195, June 2017, p. 24.

105   SACP, 'Going to the Root: A Radical Second Phase of the National Democratic Revolution', *Bua Komanisi*, 8, 2, October 2014.

106   SACP, Gauteng Province, Provincial Working Committee Minutes, 14 September 2001, Vishwas Satgar Papers, A 332, B5.2.

107   SACP, Gauteng Province, Secretary's Report to the Seventh Provincial Congress, 5 August 2001, Vishwas Satgar Papers, A 332, B5.5.

108   Blade Nzimande, 'Roll Back the Corrupting Intersection between Private Accumulation and Public Service', *Umsebenzi*, October 2009, pp. 3–4.

109   Alex Mashilo, 'Nzimande Was in the Struggle', *Sunday Independent*, 3 August 2015.

110   SNC, 'The Challenges Facing the Trade Union Movement', *African Communist*, 189, 2015, p. 122.

111   Jeremy Cronin, 'Liberals: Are They Really Defending Our Constitution', *Umsebenzi*, November 2020, p. 13.

112   Andrew Chirwa, 'SACP Is Leading Nkandla Cover-Up', *Mail & Guardian*, 12 September 2014.

113   Tom Wilson, 'Graft under Jacob Zuma Cost South Africa $34 Billion, Says Cyril Ramaphosa', *Financial Times*, 14 October 2019, https://www.ft.com/content/e0991464-ee79-11e9-bfa4-b25f11f42901.

114   Kevin Davie, 'Gordhan Starves the Eskom Piranhas', *Mail & Guardian*, 22 November 2019, p. 26.

115   JD Gloeck and H de Jager, 'Fraud Profiles of Public Sector Institutions in South Africa', *South African Journal of Accountability and Auditing Research*, 6, 2005, p. 50.

116   Central Committee, 'After the Election', *African Communist*, 200, August 2019, p. 19.

117   Susan Booysen, *Precarious Power: Compliance and Discontent within Ramaphosa's ANC*, Witwatersrand University Press, Johannesburg, 2001, p. 31; Matuma Letsoalo, 'Our Zuma Mistake', *Mail & Guardian*, 26 June 2015.

118   'Serve the People as a Whole, Build a People's Economy', *Bua Kmanisi*, 12, 2, September 19, pp. 13 and 23.

119   'The South African Road to Socialism', *Bua Komanisi*, 6, 2, June 2007.

120   SACP, Fourteenth Congress Political Report, July 2012, p. 30.

121   Kolasa, *The South African Communist Party*, p. 203.

122   SACP, Report of the Work of the SACP Central Committee Commission on the Party

and State Power, November 2012, www.sacp.org.za.docs/docs/2016/report.html.

123 Thomas, 'Post-Apartheid Conundrums', p. 254.

124 *Bua Komanisi*, 8, 2, October 2014.

125 SACP, 'Going to the Root'.

126 William Mervin Gumede, 'Could the Communist Party Be the Next Opposition?', *Sunday Independent*, 23 June 1996.

127 Rapule Tabane, 'SACP Regions Want to Go It Alone', *Mail & Guardian*, 31 February 2004.

128 Thomas, 'Post-Apartheid Conundrums', p. 262.

129 Thomas, 'Post-Apartheid Conundrums', p. 264.

130 S'thembiso Msomi, 'SACP Refuse to Fight Elections against ANC', *The Star*, 13 March 2005.

131 SACP, Report of the Work of the SACP Central Committee Commission on the Party and State Power, November 2012.

132 Anon., 'Provincial SACP Calls for CC to Act Ahead of Local Elections', *Umsebenzi*, March 2016, pp. 13–14; Hlengiwe Nkonyane, 'SACP must contest elections', *Umsebenzi*, October 2016.

133 SACP, Declaration and Resolutions, 2017, http://www.sacp.org.za/docs/conf/2017/declaration-and-resolutions.pdf.

134 SACP, 'Towards a Reconfigured Alliance', December 2019, p. 15.

135 Matuma Letsoalo, 'Senior Alliance Leaders Discuss Zuma's Removal from Office', *Mail & Guardian*, 4 March 2016.

136 SACP, Augmented Central Committee Report on the Party and State Power, November 2012. http://www.sacp.org.za/main.php?ID=5168.

137 Marianne Merten, 'Cabinet Reshuffle Analysis: Jacob Zuma the Disrupter', *Daily Maverick*, 18 October 2017, http://www.dailymaverick.co.za/article/2017-10-18-cabinet-reshuffle-analysis-jacob-zuma-the-disrupter.

138 KZN PEC Report, 'The Vanguard Role of the SACP', *African Communist*, 202, 2020, pp. 92–3.

139 SACP, Gauteng Province, Seventh Congress Declaration and Resolutions, 4–5 August 2001, Vishwas Satgar Papers, A 3332, B5.5.

140 SACP, Gauteng Province, email from Mazibuko Jara to Trevor Fowler, 24 February 2000, Vishwas Satgar Papers, A 3332, B4.2.

141 SACP, 'Going to the Root'.

142 David Thomas, 'Multiple Layers of Hegemony: Post-Apartheid South Africa and the South African Communist Party', *Canadian Journal of African Studies*, 46, 1, 2012, p. 122.

143 Sheila Barsel, 'Towards Organisational Review and Renewal', *Umsebenzi*, July 2015, pp. 6–7.

144 SACP, 'Strengthen the Vanguard Character of the SACP', *Bua Komanisi*, 9, 3, June 2015.

145 Young Communist League, National Relaunching Congress, National Steering Committee Report, December 2003, p. 9, Vishwas Satgar Papers, A 3332, F7.2.

146 Leslie Holmes, *Post-Communism: An Introduction*, Polity Press, Oxford, 1997, p. 21.

147 I am grateful to Colin Bundy for drawing my attention to this interview.

148 Naboth Mokgatle, *The Autobiography of an Unknown South African*, Ad Donker, Parklands, 1990, pp. 229–32.

149 Gill Hart, *Disabling Globalization: Places of Power in Post-Apartheid South Africa*, University of California Press, Berkeley, 2002.

150 For a view that the NDR continues to shape policy, see Irina Filatova, 'South Africa's Soviet Theoretical Legacy', *Twentieth Century Communism*, 15, Autumn 2018.

Sources and Bibliography

Archives

African National Congress Mission to Zambia, Papers from the President's Office, ANC Papers, University of Fort Hare (when consulted, these were at Wits Historical Papers)

WH Andrews Papers, Mayibuye Archives. University of the Western Cape, MCH06

Lazar Bach Papers, Wits Historical Papers, A 3381

Ballinger Papers, Wits Historical Papers, AD 1178

Himie Bernadt Collection of the Legal Papers of Nelson Mandela, Nelson Mandela Foundation

Bernstein Papers, Wits Historical Papers, A 3299

Brian Bunting Papers, Mayibuye Centre, University of the Western Cape.

SP Bunting Papers, Wits Historical Papers, A 949

Comintern Archives Online (http://sovdoc.rusarchives.ru/#main)

Jack Cope Papers, Wits Historical Papers, A 953

Czech National Archives, Prague, Předsednictvo ÚV KSČ 1962–66

David Everatt Papers, Wits Historical Papers, A 2521

George Findlay Papers, Wits Historical Papers, A 1002

Lionel Forman Papers, UCT Manuscripts and Archives, BC 581

Garment Workers' Union, Wits Historical Papers AH 1092

Frene Ginwala Papers, Wits Historical Papers, Microfilm, DT 764

Michael Harmel Papers, Wits Historical Papers, A 3300

Bartholomew Hlapane, Testimony of Bartholomew Hlapane before the US Senate Subcommittee on Security and Terrorism, 25 March 1982

Hyman Papers, Wits Historical Papers, H 3323

Industrial and Commercial Union Records, 1925–47, Wits Historical Papers, A 924

Ronnie Kasrils Papers, Wits Historical Papers, A 3345

Naidoo Papers, University of KwaZulu-Natal Documentation Centre, Westville

Sylvia Neame Papers, Wits Historical Papers, A 2729

Ron Press Papers, Wits Historical Papers, A 3239

Rheinallt Jones Papers, Wits Historical Papers, A 394

Edward R Roux Papers, Wits Historical Papers, A 2667
Saffery Papers, Wits Historical Papers, AD 1178
Vishwas Satgar Papers, Wits Historical Papers, A 3332
Jack Simons Papers, UCT Manuscripts and Archives, BC 1081
South African Institute of Race Relations Papers, Wits Historical Papers, AD 843
South African National Archives
State v Fred Carneson, 28 February 1966, transcript
State v Abraham Fischer, Case no. 175/64, exhibits
Douglas Thompson Papers, Wits Historical Papers, A 1906
Treason Trial Records, Wits Historical Papers, AD 1812
Ben Turok Papers, Rivonia Museum

Interviews
Ray Adler, interviewed by C Purkey and L Witz, 8–10 May 1990, Johannesburg, Colin Purkey Papers, Wits Historical Papers, A 1984
Dora Alexander, 12 April 1989, interviewed by Colin Purkey and Les Witz, Colin Purkey Papers, Wits Historical Papers, A 1984
Rowley Arenstein, interviewed by Iain Edwards, Durban, 1986, transcript provided to author
Hymie Barsel, interviewed by Colin Purkey, Colin Purkey Papers, Wits Historical Papers, A 1984
Hyman Basner, interviewed by Brian Willan, 1975, Institute of Commonwealth Studies Library, University of London, GB 101 ICS 88
Miriam Basner interviewed by Tom Lodge, Presteigne, 14 September 1984
Hilda Bernstein, interviewed by Padraig O'Malley, 25 August 1994, transcript in Bernstein Papers, A 3299
Lionel Bernstein and Hilda Bernstein, interviewed by Maureen Tayal, London, 23 August 1983, African Studies Institute Oral History Collection, University of the Witwatersrand
Hilda and Lionel Bernstein, interviewed by Stephen Clingman, 4 September 1984, African Studies Institute Oral History Collection, University of the Witwatersrand
Lionel and Hilda Bernstein, interviewed by Don Pinnock, 1993, Ruth First Papers, Mayibuye Archives
Piet Beyleveld, interview, April 1986, David Everatt Papers, Wits Historical Papers, A 2521
Brian Bunting, interviewed by Tom Lodge, London, 27 February 1985
Brian Bunting, interviewed by Sylvia Neame, London, 14 May 1986, Sylvia Neame Papers, Wits Historical Papers, A 2729
Rebecca Bunting, interviewed by Sylvia Neame, 1964, Sylvia Neame Papers, Wits Historical Papers, A 2729
Jeremy Cronin, interviewed by Tom Lodge, 1993
Jeremy Cronin, interviewed by Helena Sheehan, 24 January 2002, http://www.comms.dcu.ie/sheehanh/za/cronin02.ht
Bettie du Toit, interviewed by Tom Lodge, London, 29 January 1978
Gavin Evans, interviewed by Howard Barrell, Johannesburg, 28 January 1991, file:///C:/Users/Tom%20Lodge/Documents/Evans,%20Gavin%20-%20The%20O'Malley%20Archives.html
Barry Feinberg, interviewed by Sylvia Neame, London, 1 October 1987, Sylvia Neame Papers, Wits Historical Papers, A 2729
Johnny Gomas, interviewed by Sylvia Neame, 1962, Sylvia Neame Papers, Wits Historical Papers, A 2729
Issy Heymann, interviewed by Colin Purkey, 1983, Colin Purkey Papers, Wits Historical

Papers, A 1984

Issy Heymann, interviewed by Luli Callinicos, 31 May 1987, Colin Purkey Papers, Wits Historical Papers, A 1984

Willie Kalk, interviewed by Luli Callinicos, 19 March 1987, Colin Purkey Papers, Wits Historical Papers, A 1984

Willie Kalk, interviewed by David Everatt, Orange Grove, 19 March 1987, David Everatt Papers, Wits Historical Papers, A 2521

AM Kathrada, interviewed by Sylvia Neame, 17 December 1995, African Studies Institute Oral History Collection, University of the Witwatersrand

Wolfie Kodesh, interviewed by John Carlin, 1995, https://www.pbs.org/wgbh/pages/frontline/shows/mandela/interviews/kodesh.html

Sam Malkinson, interviewed by Sylvia Neame, 1964, Sylvia Neame Papers, Wits Historical Papers, A 2729

Reddy Mampane interviewed by Tor Sellström, Nordic Africa Institute, https://nai.uu.se/library/resources/liberation-africa/interviews/reddy-mampane-aka-reddy-mazimba.html

JB Marks, interviewed by Sylvia Neame, August 1969, Sylvia Neame Papers, Wits Historical Papers, A 2729

Raymond Mhlaba, interviewed by Barbara Harmel and Philip Bonner, 18 and 27 October 1993, transcripts, Wits Historical Papers, A 3301

Wilton Mkwayi, interviewed by Barbara Harmel and Philip Bonner, 18 and 27 October 1993, transcripts, Wits Historical Papers, A 3301

Edwin Mofutsanyana, interviewed by Bob Edgar, Lesotho, 1982, transcript provided to author

Matya Ozinsky, interviewed by C Purkey, L Witz and S Ozinsky, 21 February 1988, Johannesburg, Colin Purkey Papers, Wits Historical Papers, A 1984

Essop and Meg Pahad, interviewed by Tom Lodge, September 2019

Pauline Podbrey, interviewed by Maureen Tayal, London, 8 August 1983, African Studies Institute Oral History Collection, University of the Witwatersrand.

Albie Sachs, interviewed by Tom Lodge, 22 November 2018

Albie Sachs, interviewed by Milan Oralek, 27 September 2014, transcript provided to author

Bernard Sachs, interviewed by Tom Lodge, London, 1984

Arnold Selby, interviewed by Sylvia Neame, Berlin, 31 May 1985, Sylvia Neame Papers, Wits Historical Papers, A 2729

Lyndall Shope, interviewed by Milan Oralek, 29 January 2015, transcript provided to author

Ray Alexander Simons, interviewed by Tom Lodge, Cape Town, 1993

Joe Slovo, interviewed by Sylvia Neame, Berlin, GDR, 7 April 1986, Sylvia Neame Papers, Wits Historical Papers, A 2729

Paul Trewhela, interviewed by O'Malley, 13 June 2004, https://omalley.nelsonmandela.org/omalley/index.php/site/q/03lv00017/04lv00344/05lv01461/06lv01472.htm

Ben Turok, interviewed by Baruch Hirson, 30 April 1983, Ben Turok Papers, Rivonia Museum

Ben Turok, interviewed by son, Ben Turok Papers, Rivonia Museum

Ben Turok, interviewed by Tom Lodge, London, 1985

Bennie Weinbren, interviewed by Sylvia Neame, 1962, Sylvia Neame Papers, Wits Historical Papers, A 2729

Douglas Wolton, interviewed by Sylvia Neame, 13 May 1960, Sylvia Neame Papers, Wits Historical Papers, A 2729

Douglas Wolton, interviewed by Tom Lodge, 12 September 1984

Official reports and other government publications
Union of South Africa, *Report of the Martial Law Inquiry Judicial Commission*, Pretoria, 1922
Report by the Investigation Officer of the SAP into the Activities of the SAP (1947), in Union of South Africa, *House of Assembly Debates*, volume 8, 9 to 25 June 1953, columns 7946–68
Union of South Africa, *Suppression of Communism Act Enquiry into Brian Bunting, Member for Cape Western*, Pretoria, SC10 1953
Union of South Africa, *Census, 1946*, Pretoria UG41 1954
Republic of South Africa, *Government Gazette*, 16 November 1962, List of people associated with the Communist Party of South Africa
Archives of the Ministry of Foreign Affairs, *Twenty-Five Documents from the Czech Archives Published on the 25th Anniversary of the Establishment of Diplomatic Relations between Czechoslovakia and the Republic of South Africa*, Ministry of Foreign Affairs, Prague, 2016
Reopened inquest into the death of Ahmed Essop Timol, Judgment, High Court of South Africa, Gauteng Division, Pretoria, Case no. IQ 01/2017 (the judgment is available on https//www: sacp.org.za/docs/misc/2017/Timol-Inquest-Judgment.pdf)

Communist Party newspapers and journals
African Communist, 1960–2021
Fighting Talk, 1950–1960
Guardian, The, 1938–1950 (subsequently until 1960, *Advance, Clarion* and *New Age*)
Inkululeko, 1939–1949
International, The, 1915–1921
Liberation, 1950–1960
South African Worker / Umsebenzi, 1921–1938
Umsebenzi, 1980–2020

Books, pamphlets, articles, conference papers, dissertations
Abrahams, Peter, *Tell Freedom*, Faber, London, 1954
Adam, Heribert and Kogila Moodley, *The Negotiated Revolution*, Jonathan Ball, Johannesburg, 1993
Adams, Simon, 'Between the Negotiated and Unnegotiated Revolution: The "Bop" Uprising and the South African Communist Party', Socialist History Working Papers 2, London Socialist Historians Group, Institute of Historical Research, University of London, London, 1996
Adams, Simon, 'The Party That Time Forgot: The Construction of a Mass Communist Party in South Africa, 1990–1991', Annual Conference of the African Studies Association of Australia and the Pacific, Adelaide, 27–29 September 1996
Adams, Simon, 'What's Left? The South African Communist Party after Apartheid', *Review of African Political Economy*, 24, 72, 1997
Adler, Taffy, 'Lithuania's Diaspora: The Johannesburg Jewish Workers' Club, 1928–1948', *Journal of Southern African Studies*, 6, 1, 1980
Adler, Taffy, 'The History of the Jewish Workers' Club', paper presented at the African Studies Institute, Wits University, 1977
Alexander, Peter, 'African Trade Unions and the South African State, 1937–1947: The Recognition Debate Reassessed', African Studies Seminar Paper no. 320, African Studies Institute, University of the Witwatersrand, 10 August 1992
Alexander, Ray, *Trades Unions and You*, Stewart Printing Company, Cape Town, [1994]
Allen, VL, *The History of Black Mineworkers in South Africa*, volume 1, Moor Press, Keighley, Yorkshire, 1992

Andrews, WH, *Class Struggles in South Africa*, Stewart Printing Company, Cape Town, 1941

Anon., 'An Analysis of the Freedom Charter, Revolutionary Programme of the African National Congress, Adopted at the Morogoro Conference, 1969', in *Selected Writings on the Freedom Charter, 1955–1985*, African National Congress, 1985

Anon., 'Inside the ANC', *Foreign Report*, 18 April 1991

Anon., 'Provincial SACP Calls for CC to Act ahead of Local Elections', *Umsebenzi*, March 2016

Anon., 'Reply to the Central Committee of the South African Communist Party Statement Entitled "The Enemy Hidden under the Same Colour"', London, February 1976

Anon., 'Special National Congress: Massive Increase in SACP Membership', *Umsebenzi*, 405, July 2015

Anthony, David, 'Max Yergan in South Africa', *African Studies Review*, 34, 2, 1991

Arad, Yitzhak, *The Holocaust in the Soviet Union*, University of Nebraska Press, Lincoln, 2009

Ashworth, Adam, *Witchcraft, Violence and Democracy in South Africa*, University of Chicago Press, Chicago, 2005

Asmal, Kader and Adrian Hadland with Moira Levy, *Politics in my Blood*, Jacana Media, Johannesburg, 2011

Babenia, Natoo, *Memoirs of a Saboteur*, Mayibuye Books, Bellville, 1995

Badat, Saleem, *Black Student Politics: From SASO to SANSCO, 1968–1990*, Human Sciences Research Council, Pretoria, 1999

Barrell, Howard, 'All for the Front', *Work in Progress*, 38, 1985

Barrell, Howard, *MK: The ANC's Armed Struggle*, Penguin, Johannesburg, 1990

Barron, Chris, 'Obituary: Arnold Selby', *Sunday Times* (Johannesburg), 15 September 2002

Barsel, Sheila, 'Towards Organisational Review and Renewal', *Umsebenzi*, July 2015

Basner, Miriam, *Am I an African? The Political Memoirs of Hyman Basner*, Witwatersrand University Press, Johannesburg, 1993

Beevor, Anthony, *The Battle for Spain: The Spanish Civil War, 1936–1939*, Weidenfeld and Nicolson, London, 2006

Beinart, William, 'Worker Consciousness, Ethnic Particularism and Nationalism', in Shula Marks and Stanley Trapido (eds), *Politics of Race, Class and Nationalism in Twentieth Century South Africa*, Longman, London, 1987

Beliard, Yann, 'A "Labour War" in South Africa: The 1922 Rand Revolution in Sylvia Pankhurst's Workers' Dreadnought', *Labor History*, 57, 1, 2016

Bell, David, 'The French Communist Party from Revolution to Reform', in Jocelyn Evans (ed.), *The French Party System*, Manchester University Press, Manchester, 2018

Bellling, Victoria, 'The Making of a South African Jewish Activist: The Yiddish Diary of Ray Alexander Simons, Latvia, 1927', *Jewish Culture and History*, 15, 1-2, 2014

Benneyworth, Garth, 'Rolling up Rivonia', *South African Historical Journal*, 69, 3, 2017

Beresford, Alexander, *South Africa's Political Crisis: Unfinished Liberation and Fractured Class Struggles*, Palgrave Macmillan, Basingstoke, 2016

Berger, Iris, 'Solidarity Fragmented: Garment Workers of the Transvaal', in Shula Marks and Stanley Trapido (eds), *Class, Race and Nationalism in Twentieth Century South Africa*, Longman, London, 1987

Berland, Oscar, 'The Emergence of a Communist Perspective on the "Negro Question" in America, 1919–1931, Part One', *Science and Society*, 63-4, 1999

Berman, Sheri and Maria Snegovaya, 'Populism and the Decline of Social Democracy', *Journal of Democracy*, 30, 3, 1999

Bernstein, Hilda, *The World That Was Ours*, Heinemann, London, 1967

Bernstein, Lionel, *Letter from Italy*, Communist Party of South Africa, Johannesburg, 1945

Bernstein, Rusty, *Memory against Forgetting*, Viking Penguin, Sandton, 1999

Betts, Paul, James Marks, Idesbald Goddeeris and Kim Christiaens, 'Race, Socialism and Solidarity: Anti-Apartheid in Eastern Europe', in Anna Konieczna and Rob Skinner (eds), *A Global History of Anti-Apartheid*, Palgrave Macmilllan, London, 2019

Black, Anthony, 'The Evolution and Impact of Foreign Direct Investment in South Africa since 1994', in Haroon Bhorat, Alan Hirsch, Ravi Kanbur and Mthuli Ncube (eds), *The Oxford Companion to the Economics of South Africa*, Oxford University Press, Oxford, 2014

Botiveau, Raphaël, *Organize or Die? Democracy and Leadership in South Africa's National Union of Mineworkers*, Wits University Press, Johannesburg, 2017

Bond, Patrick, 'Gearing Up or Down?', *South African Labour Bulletin*, 20 April 1996

Bond, Patrick and Shauna Mottiar, 'Movements, Protests and a Massacre in South Africa', *Journal of Contemporary African Studies*, 31, 2, 2013

Bonner, Philip, 'Black Trade Unions in South Africa since World War II', in Robert M Price and Carl G Rosberg (eds), *The Apartheid Regime: Political Power and Racial Domination*, David Philip, Cape Town, 1980

Bonner, Philip, 'Eluding Capture: African Grassroots Struggles in 1940s Benoni', in Saul Dubow and Alan Jeeves (eds), *South Africa's 1940s: Worlds of Possibilities*, Double Storey, Cape Town, 2005

Bonner, Philip, 'South African Society and Culture, 1910–1948', in Robert Ross, Anne Kelk Mager and Bill Nasson (eds), *The Cambridge History of South Africa*, volume 2: *1885-1994*, Cambridge University Press, New York, 2011

Bonner, Philip, 'The African Mineworkers' Strike', in Belinda Bozzoli (ed.), *Labour, Townships and Protest*, Ravan Press, Johannesburg, 1979

Bonner, Philip, 'The Transvaal Native Congress, 1917–1920: The Radicalisation of the Black Petty Bourgeoisie on the Rand', African Studies Seminar Paper no. 089, African Studies Institute, University of the Witwatersrand, March 1980

Bonner, Philip and Noor Nieftagodien, *Alexandra: A History*, Witwatersrand University Press, Johannesburg, 2008

Booysen, Susan, *Precarious Power: Compliance and Discontent within Ramaphosa's ANC*, Wits University Press, Johannesburg, 2021

Botman, Selma, *The Rise of Egyptian Communism, 1939–1970*, Syracuse University Press, Syracuse, 1988

Bradford, Helen, *A Taste of Freedom The ICU in Rural South Africa, 1924–1930*, Yale University Press, New Haven, 1987

Breckenridge, Keith, 'Fighting for White South Africa: White Working Class Racism and the 1922 Rand Revolt', *South African Historical Journal*, 57, 2007

Brenner, Sydney, 'Where Did the Insult Peruvian Jew Come from', https://www.youtube.com/watch?v=IU9jKTplxZw

Brooks, Alan, 'From Class Struggle to National Liberation: The Communist Party of South Africa, 1940–1950', MA dissertation, University of Sussex, 1967

Brown, Julian, *The Road to Soweto: Resistance and the Uprising of 16 June 1976*, James Currey, Woodbridge, 2016

Buchan, John, *Greenmantle*, Penguin, Harmondsworth, 1956

Buchanan, Thomas, 'The Dark Millions in the Colonies Are Unavenged: Anti-Fascism and Anti-Imperialism in the 1930s', *Contemporary European History*, 25, 4, 2016

Buhle, Paul, 'Daniel DeLeon', in Mari Jo Buhle, Paul Buhle and Dan Georgakas (eds), *The Encyclopedia of the American Left*, Garland Publishing, New York, 1990

Buhlungu, Sakhela, *A Paradox of Victory: COSATU and the Democratic Transformation of*

South Africa, University of KwaZulu-Natal Press, Scottsville, 2010

Bundy, Colin, *Govan Mbeki*, Jacana Media, Johannesburg, 2012

Bundy, Colin, 'Land and Liberation: Popular Protest and the National Liberation Movements in South Africa, 1920–1960', in Shula Marks and Stanley Trapido (eds), *Class, Race and Nationalism in Twentieth Century South Africa*, Longman, London, 1987

Bundy, Colin, *Nelson Mandela*, Jacana Media, Johannesburg, 2014

Bundy, Colin, 'Theory of a Special Type', *Work in Progress*, 89, June 1993

Bunting, Brian (ed.), *Letters to Rebecca: South African Communist Leader SP Bunting to His Wife, 1917–1934*, Mayibuye Books, Bellville, 1996

Bunting, Brian, *Life Is More Joyous: Report of a Visit to the Soviet Union*, South African Society for Peace and Friendship with the Soviet Union, Johannesburg, 1954

Bunting, Brian, *Moses Kotane: South African Revolutionary*, Inkululeko Publications, London, 1975

Bunting, Brian (ed.), *South African Communists Speak: Documents from the History of the South African Communist Party, 1915–1980*, Inkululeko Publications, London, 1981

Cajee, Amin, *Fordsburg Fighter: The Journey of an MK Volunteer*, Face2Face Books, Paarl, 2016

Callinicos, Luli, *Oliver Tambo: Beyond the Engeni Mountains*, David Philip, Cape Town, 2004

Campbell, JT, 'Romantic Revolutionaries: David Ivon Jones, SP Bunting and the Origins of Non-racial Politics in South Africa', *Journal of African History*, 39, 2, 1998

Carneson, Lynn, *Red in the Rainbow: The Life and Times of Fred and Sarah Carneson*, Zebra Press, Cape Town, 2010

Carr, Barbara, *Loginov: Spy in the Sun*, Howard Timmins, Cape Town, 1969

Carr, Raymond, *The Spanish Tragedy: The Civil War in Perspective*, Phoenix Press, London, 2000

Cherry, Janet, 'The Myth of Working Class Defeat: Port Elizabeth in the Post-war Years', *Kronos: Journal of Cape History*, 20, 1, 1993

Chirwa, Andrew, 'SACP Is Leading Nkandla Cover-up', *Mail & Guardian*, 12 September 2014

Clingman, Stephen, *Bram Fischer: Afrikaner Revolutionary*, David Philip, Cape Town, 1998

Cohen, Robin, 'Introduction', in AT Nzula, II Potekhin and AZ Zusmanovich, *Forced Labour in Colonial Africa*, reprint, Zed Press, London, 1979

Cohen, Stephen F, *Bukharin and the Bolshevik Revolution: A Political Biography, 1888–1938*, Oxford University Press, Oxford, 1980

Coka, Gilbert, 'The Story of Gilbert Coka', in Margery Perham (ed.), *Ten Africans*, Faber and Faber, London, 1963

Coker, Christopher, 'Pact, Pox or Proxy: Eastern Europe's Security Relationship with Southern Africa', *Soviet Studies*, 40, 4, 1988

CPSA, *Communism and the Native Question*, CPSA Secretariat, Johannesburg District Committee, 1938

CPSA, *Communists in Conference: The 1943–1944 National Conference of the CPSA*, CPSA, Cape Town, 1944

CPSA, *Election Manifesto*, 1938

CPSA, *Johannesburg Tomorrow*, CPSA Johannesburg District, 1945

CPSA, *Meet the Communists*, Stewart Printing Company, Cape Town, 1942

CPSA, *Must We Fight?*, Stewart Printing Company, Cape Town, 1939

CPSA, *Organise a People's Front in South Africa*, CPSA, Johannesburg, September 1936

CPSA, *The Transvaal Communist, Organ of the Johannesburg District Communist Party*, mimeo, 1939

CPSA, *They Marched to Victory: The Story of the Alexandra Bus Boycott*, Stewart Printing Company, Cape Town, 1944

CPSA, *We South Africans*, CPSA, Cape Town, 1943

CPSA, *What Next? A Policy for South Africa*, CPSA, 1944

CPSA, Central Committee, *Sam Kahn Speaks: The Parliamentary Record of South Africa's First Communist MP*, Pioneer Press, Cape Town, 1949

CPSA, Johannesburg District Committee, *Democracy in Action: Proceedings of the Johannesburg District Annual Conference of the Communist Party, March 17th, 18th and 25th, 1945*, CPSA, Johannesburg, 1945

CPSA, Johannesburg West Branch of the CPSA, *Smash the Black Market*, Johannesburg, June 1946

Cope, RK, *Comrade Bill: The Life and Times of WH Andrews, Workers' Leader*, Stewart Printing Company, Cape Town, 1944

Couper, Scott, *Albert Luthuli: Bound by Faith*, University of KwaZulu-Natal Press, Durban, 2010

Cousins, Ben, 'Land and Land Reform in South Africa', in Haroon Bhorat, Alan Hirsch, Ravi Kanbur and Mthuli Ncube (eds), *The Oxford Companion to the Economics of South Africa*, Oxford University Press, Oxford, 2014

Cronin, Jeremy, 'Building the Legal Mass Party', *South African Labour Bulletin*, 15, 3, 1990

Cronin, Jeremy, *Inside*, Ravan Press, Johannesburg, 1983

Davenport, Rodney, *South Africa: A Modern History*, Macmillan, London, 1977

Davidson, Apollon, 'Komintern i rozhdenie pervoi kompartii v Afrika', in LP Deliusin, MA Persits, AB Reznikov and RA Ul'ianovskii (eds), *Komintern i Vostok*, Nauka, Moscow, 1969

Davidson, Apollo, 'Lenin on South Africa', *African Communist*, 91, 1982

Davidson, Apollon, Irina Filatova, Valentin Gorodnov and Sheridan Johns, *South Africa and the Communist International: A Documentary History*, volume 1: *Socialist Pilgrims to Bolshevik Footsoldiers, 1919–1930;* volume 2: *Bolshevik Footsoldiers to Victims of Bolshevisation, 1931–1939*, Frank Cass, London, 2003

Davidson, Basil, *Report on South Africa*, Jonathan Cape, London, 1952

Davie, Kevin, 'Gordhan Starves the Eskom Piranhas', *Mail & Guardian*, 22 November 2019

Davies, Robert H, *Capital, State and White Labour in South Africa, 1900–1960*, Harvester Press, Brighton, 1979

Davis, Stephen M, *Apartheid's Rebels: Inside South Africa's Hidden War*, Yale University Press, New Haven, 1987

Davis, Stephen R, *The ANC's War against Apartheid*, Indiana University Press, Bloomington, 2018

Dee, Henry, 'Clements Kadalie, Trade Unionism, Migration and Race in Southern Africa', PhD dissertation, University of Edinburgh, 2019

Delius, Peter, *A Lion amongst the Cattle*, James Currey, Oxford, 1996

Delius, Peter, 'Sebatakgomo, Migrant Organisation, the ANC and the Sekhukhuneland Revolt', *Journal of Southern African Studies*, 15, 4, 1989

Devinatz, V, 'A Cold War Thaw in the International Working-Class Movement? The WFTU and the ICFTU, 1967–1977', *Science and Society*, 77, 3, 2013

Dlamuka, Mxolise C, 'Connectedness and Disconnectedness in Thembeyakhe Harry Gwala's Biography, 1920–1995: Rethinking Political Militancy, Mass Mobilisation and Grassroots Struggle in South Africa', PhD dissertation, History, University of Western Cape, March 2018

Drachewych, Oleka, 'The Comintern and the Communist Parties of South Africa, Canada and Australia on the Questions of Imperialism, Nationalism and Race',

PhD Dissertation, McMasters University, July 2017 (file: /drachewych_oleksa_m_2017september_PhD.pdf)

Drew, Allison, *Between Empire and Revolution: A Life of Sidney Bunting, 1873–1936*, Pickering and Chatto, London, 2007

Drew, Allison, *Discordant Comrades: Identities and Loyalties on the South African Left*, Ashgate, Aldershot, 2000

Drew, Allison, *South Africa's Radical Tradition: A Documentary History*, volume 1: *1907–1950*, University of Cape Town Press, Cape Town, 1996

Drew, Allison, 'The New Line in South Africa: Ideology and Perception in a Very Small Communist Party', in Matthew Worley (ed.), *In Search of Revolution: International Communist Parties in the Third Period*, IB Tauris, London, 2004

Drew, Allison, 'Urban Activists and Rural Movements: Communists in South Africa and Algeria', *African Studies*, 66, 2–3, 2007

Dugmore, Charles, 'Dadoo Limited versus Krugersdorp Town Council, 1920', Postgraduate Forum Colloquium on Justice, Policy and Change in Southern Africa, 3 October 1998

Duka, Menzi, *Matthew Goniwe on a South African Frontier*, Institute of Social and Economic Research, Rhodes University, Grahamstown, 2018

Duncan, David, *The Mills of God: The State and African Labour in South Africa, 1918–1948*, Witwatersrand University Press, Johannesburg, 1995

Du Toit, Bettie, *Ukubamba Amadolo: Workers' Struggles in the South African Textile Industry*, Onyx Press, London, 1978

Du Toit, Pierre and Hennie Kotze, *Liberal Democracy and Peace in South Africa: The Pursuit of Freedom and Dignity*, Palgrave Macmillan, Basingstoke, 2011

Edgar, Robert, *Edwin Thabo Mofutsanyana and the CPSA, 1927–1939*, University of South Africa, Pretoria, 2005

Edgar, Robert, 'Notes on the Life and Death of Albert Nzula', *International Journal of African Historical Studies*, 16, 4, 1983

Edwards, Iain, 'Recollections: The Communist Party and Worker Militancy in Durban in the Early 1940s', *South African Labour Bulletin*, 11, 4, 1985

Edwards, Iain and Tim Nuttall, 'Seizing the Moment: The January 1949 Riots, Proletarian Populism, and the Structures of African Urban Life in Durban in the Late 1940s', paper presented at the History Workshop, University of the Witwatersrand, 6–10 February 1990

Edwards, Lawrence, 'Trade Policy Reform in South Africa', in Haroon Bhorat, Alan Hirsch, Ravi Kanbur and Mthuli Ncube (eds), *The Oxford Companion to the Economics of South Africa*, Oxford University Press, Oxford, 2014

Eeckhout, Marion and Nel de Vink, 'Composition of Financial Flows to SSA Countries', African Studies Centre, Leiden, 2014

Eidelberg, Phil, 'The Unions and the African National Congress', *South African Historical Journal*, 28, May 1993

Ellis, Stephen, *External Mission: The ANC in Exile, 1960–1990*, Hurst and Company, London, 2012

Englert, Sai, 'The Rise and the Fall of the Jewish Labour Bund', *International Socialism*, 135, 2012

Erler, Peter, 'Robert Naumann' in *Wer war wer in de DDR*, volume 2, Ch. Links Verlag, Berlin, 2010

Evans, Gavin, 'ANC Spy Bible', *The Conversation*, 29 March 2020

Evans, Gavin, *Dancing Man Is Dead: A Tale of Fighting Men in South Africa*, Doubleday, London, 2020

Everatt, David, 'Alliance Politics of a Special Type: The Roots of the ANC–SACP Alliance, 1950–1954', *Journal of Southern African Studies*, 18, 1, March 1992

Everatt, David, 'The Politics of Nonracialism: White Opposition to Apartheid, 1945–1960', DPhil dissertation, History, Oxford University, 1990

Everatt, David, *The Roots of Non-racialism: White Opposition to Apartheid in the 1950s*, Wits University Press, Johannesburg, 2009

Feldman, Leibl, *The Jews of Johannesburg*, Isaac and Jessie Kaplan Centre, University of Cape Town, Cape Town, 2007

Field, Roger, *Alex La Guma: A Literary and Political Biography*, James Currey, Woodbridge, 2010

Field, Roger, Martin Klammer and Blanche La Guma, *In the Dark with My Dress on Fire: My Life in Cape Town, London, Havana and Home Again*, Jacana Media, Johannesburg, 2011

Filatova, Irina, 'South Africa's Soviet Theoretical Legacy', *Twentieth Century Communism*, 15, Autumn 2018

Filatova, Irina, 'The Lasting Legacy: The Soviet Theory of National Democratic Revolution and South Africa', *South African Historical Journal*, 64, 3, 2012

Filatova, Irina and Apollon Davidson, *The Hidden Thread: Russia and South Africa in the Soviet Era*, Jonathan Ball, Cape Town, 2013

Filatova, Irina and Apollon Davidson, '"We, the South African Bolsheviks": The Russian Revolution and South Africa', *Journal of Contemporary History*, 52, 4, 2017

First, Ruth, *Power in Africa*, Penguin, Harmondsworth, 1970

First, Ruth, *South Africans in the Soviet Union*, Pacific Press, Johannesburg, 1956

First, Ruth and Ann Scott, *Olive Schreiner*, André Deutsch, London, 1980

Flynn, Elizabeth Gurley, 'The Life of Eugene Dennis', *Political Affairs*, 11, 3, 1961

Forman, Sadie, *Lionel Forman: A Life Too Short*, University of Fort Hare Press, Alice, 2008

Forman, Sadie and André Odendaal, *A Trumpet from the Housetops: The Selected Writings of Lionel Forman*, Zed Press, London, 1992

Fortescue, Dominic, 'The Communist Party of South Africa and the African Working Class in the 1940s', *International Journal of African Historical Studies*, 24, 3, 1991

Frankel, Philip, *Marching to the Millennium*, South African Department of Defence Communication Service, Pretoria, 1998

Frankel, Philip, *Soldiers in a Storm: Armed Forces in South Africa's Democratic Transition*, Westview Press, Boulder, 2000

Frederickse, Julie, *The Unbreakable Thread*, Ravan Press, Johannesburg, 1990

French, Kevin John, 'James Mpanza and the Sofasonke Party in the Development of Local Politics in Soweto', MA dissertation, University of the Witwatersrand, 1983

Freund, Bill, *Insiders and Outsiders: The Indian Working Class of Durban, 1910–1990*, James Currey, Oxford, 1995

Freund, Bill, 'Labour Studies and Labour History in South Africa: Perspectives from the Apartheid Era and After', *International Review of Social History*, 58, 2013

Freund, Bill, 'South Africa: The Union Years, 1910–1948', in Robert Ross, Anne Kelk Mager and Bill Nasson (eds), *The Cambridge History of South Africa*, volume 2, Cambridge University Press, New York, 2011

Freund, Bill, *Twentieth Century South Africa: A Developmental History*, Cambridge University Press, Cambridge, 2018

Friedman, Steven, *Race, Class and Power: Harold Wolpe and the Radical Critique of Apartheid*, University of KwaZulu-Natal Press, Pietermaritzburg, 2015

Friends of the Soviet Union, *Soviet Exhibition*, Durban, 30 June–14 July 1945, leaflet

Funder, Anna, *Stasiland: Stories from behind the Berlin Wall*, Granta, London, 2004

Gevisser, Mark, *Thabo Mbeki: The Dream Deferred*, Jonathan Ball, Johannesburg, 2007.

Gevisser, Mark, 'Why Is Thabo Mbeki a "Nitemare"', in Daryl Glaser (ed.), *Mbeki and After: Reflections on the Legacy of Thabo Mbeki*, Witwatersrand University Press,

Johannesburg, 2010

Gilder, Barry, *Songs and Secrets: South African from Liberation to Governance*, Hurst and Company, London, 2012

Gitlin, Marcia, *The Vision Amazing: The Story of South African Zionism*, Menorah Book Club, Johannesburg, 1950

Gleason, David, 'No Land Is Safe from Expropriation', *Business Day*, 18 July 2013

Gloeck JD and H de Jager, 'Fraud Profiles of Public Sector Institutions in South Africa', *South African Journal of Accountability and Auditing Research*, 6, 2005

Gordin, Jeremy, *Zuma: A Biography*, Jonathan Ball, Cape Town, 2008

Gorham, CM, 'Keeping the Red Flag Flying: The International Socialist League of South Africa and the "Bolshevik Pamphlet" Case', BA Honours dissertation, History Department, Rhodes University, October 1990

Gresh, Alain, 'The Free Officers and the Comrades: The Sudanese Communist Party and Nimeiri Face to Face, 1969–1971', *International Journal of Middle East Studies*, 21, 1989

Grey, Robert D, 'The Soviet Presence in Africa: An Analysis of Goals', *Journal of Modern African Studies*, 22, 3, September 1984

Grossman, Jonathan, 'Class Relations and the Communist Party of South Africa, 1921–1950', PhD dissertation, Department of Sociology, University of Warwick, November 1985

Grzymala-Busse, Anna, 'The Programmatic Turnaround of Communist Successor Parties in East Central Europe', *Communist and Post-Communist Studies*, 35, 2002

Gumede, William Mervin, 'Could the Communist Party Be the Next Opposition?', *Sunday Independent*, 23 June 1996

Gumede, William Mervin, 'Mandela Sees Red at Communist Criticism', *Sunday Independent*, 15 June 1997

Gumede, William Mervyn, *Thabo Mbeki and the Battle for the Soul of the ANC*, Zed Books, London, 2007

Hadland, Adrian, 'The World Paper Famine and the South African Press, 1938–1955', *South African Journal of Economic History*, 20, 1, 2005

Hadland, Adrian and Jovial Rantao, *The Life and Times of Thabo Mbeki*, Zebra Press, Cape Town, 2001

Haines, Richard, 'Resistance and Acquiescence in the Zoutpansberg, 1936–1945', University of the Witwatersrand History Workshop paper, 1981

Haliburton, GM, 'Walter Matitta and Josiel Lefela: A Prophet and a Politician in Lesotho', *Journal of Religion in Africa*, 7, 2, 1975

Halliday, Fred, *The Making of the Second Cold War*, Verso, London, 1983

Hani, Lindiwe and Melinda Ferguson, *Being Chris Hani's Daughter*, MF Books, Johannesburg, 2017

Hardy, George, *Those Stormy Years*, Lawrence and Wishart, London, 1956

Harmel, Michael, *Olive Schreiner, 1855–1955*, Real Printing and Publishing, Cape Town, 1955

Harmel, Michael, 'Vereeniging', *The Rhodian*, XV, 2, Summer 1937

Harrison, Wilfrid, *Memoirs of a Socialist in South Africa, 1905–1947*, Stewart Printing Company, Cape Town, 1948

Hart, Gill, *Disabling Globalization: Places of Power in Post-Apartheid South Africa*, University of California Press, Berkeley, 2002

Haywood, Harry, *Black Bolshevik: The Autobiography of an African American Communist*, Liberation Press, Chicago, 1978

Heffernan, Anne, 'A History of Youth Politics in Limpopo, 1967–1993', DPhil dissertation, History, University of Oxford, June 2014

Heimann, M, *Czechoslovakia: The State That Failed*, Yale University Press, New Haven,

2011

Hemson, David, 'Trade Unions, Labour Circulation, and Class Struggle in Durban, 1940–1959', *Journal of Southern African Studies*, 4, 1, 1977

Hemson, David, Martin Legassick and Nicole Ulrich, 'White Activists and the Revival of the Workers' Movement', in South African Democratic Education Trust, *The Road to Democracy in South Africa*, volume 2: *1970-1980*, University of South Africa Press, Pretoria, 2006

Hepple, Bob, *Young Man with a Red Tie: A Memoir of Mandela and the Failed Revolution*, Jacana Media, Johannesburg, 2013

Herd, Norman, *1922: The Revolt on the Rand*, Blue Crane Books, Johannesburg, 1966

Higginson, John, *Collective Violence and the Agrarian Origins of South African Apartheid*, Cambridge University Press, New York, 2015

Hilger, Andreas, 'Communism, Decolonisation and the Third World', in Norman Naimark, Sylvio Pons and Sophie Quinn-Judge (eds), *The Cambridge History of Communism*, volume 2, Cambridge University Press, Cambridge, 2017

Hill, Christopher R, *Looking In: Some Observations*, Short Run Press, Exeter, 2020

Hirson, Baruch, 'A Trade Union Organiser in Durban: MB Yengwa, 1943–1944', *The Societies of South Africa in the 19th and 20th Centuries, Institute of Commonwealth Studies*, volume 16, University of London, 1990

Hirson, Baruch, 'Death of a Revolutionary: Frank Glass, 1901–1988', *Searchlight South Africa*, 1, September 1989

Hirson, Baruch, 'Lies in the Life of Comrade Bill', *Revolutionary History*, 2, 4, 1990

Hirson, Baruch, 'Prices, Homes and Transport', unpublished paper, n.d.

Hirson, Baruch, *Revolutions in My Life*, Witwatersrand University Press, Johannesburg, 1995

Hirson, Baruch, 'Rural Revolt in South Africa, 1937–1951', *Societies of Southern Africa in the Nineteenth and Twentieth Century*, volume 8, Institute of Commonwealth Studies, University of London, 1978

Hirson, Baruch, 'Syndicalists in South Africa', Seminar in Comparative Labour and Working Class History, Institute of Historical Research, University of London, 12 November 1993

Hirson, Baruch, 'The Black Republic Slogan, Part II', *Searchlight South Africa*, 4, February 1990

Hirson, Baruch, *The Cape Town Intellectuals: Ruth Schechter and her Circle, 1907–1934*, Merlin Press, London, 2001

Hirson, Baruch, 'The Mines, the State and African Trade Unions', unpublished seminar paper, n.d.

Hirson, Baruch, *Yours for the Union: Class and Community Struggles in South Africa*, Zed Press, London, 1989

Hirson, Baruch and Gwyn A Williams, *The Delegate for Africa: David Ivon Jones, 1883–1924*, Core Publications, London, 1995

Historicus, 'Albert Nzula: Our First African General Secretary', *African Communist*, 65, 1976

Hlongwane, Sipho, 'SACP: Where to from Here?', *Daily Maverick*, 16 July 2012, www.daily maverick.co.za/article/2012-07-16-analysis-scap-where-to-from-here/

Hobart Houghton, D, *The South African Economy*, Oxford University Press, Cape Town, 1973

Hodgson, Rica, *Foot Soldier for Freedom: A Life in South Africa's Liberation Movement*, Picador Africa, Johannesburg, 2010

Hofmeyr, Willie, 'Rural Popular Organisation and Its Problems: Struggles in the Western Cape, 1929–1930', *Africa Perspective*, 22, 1983

Holmes, Leslie, *Post-Communism: An Introduction*, Polity Press, Oxford, 1997

Houston, Gregory, 'The Post-Rivonia ANC–SACP Underground', in South African Democracy Education Trust, *The Road to Democracy in South Africa*, volume 1: *1960–1970*, Zebra Press, Cape Town, 2004

Houston, Greg and Bernard Magubane, 'The ANC's Political Underground in the 1970s', in Bernard Magubane (ed.), *The Road to Democracy in South Africa*, volume 2: *1970–1980*, University of South Africa Press, Pretoria, 2006

Hudson, Peter, 'The Freedom Charter and Socialist Strategy in South Africa', Politikon, 13, 1, 1986

Husbands, Christopher T, *Sound and Fury: Sociology at the London School of Economics and Political Science, 1904–2015*, Palgrave Macmillan, London, 2015

Hyslop, Jonathan, 'The Imperial Working Class Makes Itself "White": White Labourism in Britain, Australia and South Africa before the First World War', *Journal of Historical Sociology*, 12, 4, 1999

Hyslop, Jonathan, *The Notorious Syndicalist: JT Bain – A Scottish Rebel in Colonial South Africa*, Jacana Media, Johannesburg, 2004

Hyslop, Jonathan, 'The War on War League: A South African Pacifist Movement', *Scientia Militaria*, 44, 1, 2016

Israel, Mark, *South African Political Exiles in the United Kingdom*, Macmillan, Basingstoke, 1999

Israel, Mark and Simon Adams, '"That Spells Trouble": Jews and the Communist Party of South Africa', *Journal of Southern African Studies*, 26, 1, 2000

Jabulani, JJ, 'Why I Joined the Communist Party', *African Communist*, 44, 1971

Jackson, Gabriel, *The Spanish Republic and the Civil War, 1931–1939*, Princeton University Press, Princeton, 1972

Jenkin, Tim, *Escape from Pretoria*, Kliptown Books, London, 1987

Joffe, Joel, *The Rivonia Story*, Mayibuye Books, Bellville, 1995

Johanningsmeier, Edward, 'Communists and Black Freedom Movements in South Africa and the United States, 1919–1950', *Journal of Southern African Studies*, 30, 1, 2004

Johns, Sheridan, 'Imperial Preferences: The Case of the Comintern and South Africa', Western Australian African Studies Seminar, Perth, 7 August 1993

Johns, Sheridan, 'Internationalism, Intervention, or Irrelevance? Comintern Emissaries from Moscow to the Communist Party of South Africa, 1929–1937', Canadian African Studies Association, Ottawa, 2–5 June 1998

Johns, Sheridan, 'Marxism-Leninism in a Multi-racial Environment: The Origins and Early History of the Communist Party of South Africa, 1914–1932', PhD dissertation, Department of Government, Harvard University, 1965

Johns, Sheridan, 'South African Communists on the Hustings: Why Participate in Elections', paper delivered at the Canadian Research Consortium for Southern Africa (CRCSA), Montreal, Quebec, 22 March 1996

Johns, Sheridan, 'The Birth of the Communist Party of South Africa', *International Journal of African Historical Studies*, 9, 3, 1976

Johnston, Craig, 'The "Leading War Party": Communists and World War Two', *Labour History*, 39, 1980

Johnston, FA, 'The IWA on the Rand', in Belinda Bozzoli (ed.), *Labour, Townships and Protest*, Ravan, Johannesburg, 1979

Jones, D Ivon, 'Lenin's First Book', *The Communist Review*, 4, 11, 1924, https://www.marxists.org/archive/jones/1924/03/x01.htm

Jordan, Pallo (ed.), *Oliver Tambo Remembered*, Macmillan, Johannesburg, 2007

Joseph, Paul, *Slumboy from the Golden City*, Merlin Press, London, 2018

Kadalie, Clements, *My Life and the ICU: The Autobiography of a Black Trade Unionist in South Africa*, Frank Cass, London, 1970

Karon, Tony, 'The CPSA's Programme in Wartime and After', unpublished paper,

Department of Economic History, University of Cape Town, September 1987

Karis, Thomas, 'South African Liberation: The Communist Factor', *Foreign Affairs*, 65, 2, Winter 1986

Karis, Thomas and Gwendoline Carter, *From Protest to Challenge*, volume 2, Hoover Institution, Stanford, 1973

Karis, Thomas and Gail M Gerhart, *From Protest to Challenge*, volume 3: *Challenge and Violence, 1953–1964*, Hoover Institution Press, Stanford, 1977

Karis, Thomas and Gail M Gerhart, *From Protest to Challenge*, volume 5: *Nadir and Resurgence*, Indiana University Press, Bloomington, 1997

Kasrils, Ronnie, *Armed and Dangerous: From Undercover Struggle to Freedom*, Jonathan Ball, Johannesburg, 1998

Kathrada, Ahmed, *No Bread for Mandela: Memoirs of Ahmed Kathrada*, University of Kentucky Press, Lexington, 2010

Katz, Elaine N, *A Trade Union Aristocracy: A History of White Workers in the Transvaal and the General Strike of 1913*, African Studies Institute, University of the Witwatersrand, Johannesburg, 1976

Kay, Russell, 'The Da Costa File: The ANC Terror Plan to Destroy South Africa', *Scope Magazine*, 18 February 1983

Keable, Ken (ed.), *London Recruits: The Secret War against Apartheid*, Merlin Books, London, 2012

Keal, Hannah, '"A Life's Work": Hannah Bolton and Durban's Trade Unions, 1944–1974', MA dissertation, University of KwaZulu-Natal, Durban, December 2009

Keats, Bell, 'South Africa: Against Smuts and Herzog–Malan', *World News and Views*, 19, 56, 2 December 1939

Kelley, Robin D, 'The Religious Odyssey of Black Communists in South Africa and the US South: Observations from the 1920s and 1930s', ASA annual meeting, Atlanta, 2–5 November 1989

Kemp, Stephanie, *Through an Unforgettable Storm: The Forging of a Loyal Cadre*, Kindle self-publication, 2017

Kitson, Norma, *Where Sixpence Lives*, Hogarth Press, London, 1987

Kjerland, Kirsten Alsaker and Bjørn Enge Bertelsen, *Navigating Colonial Orders: Norwegian Entrepreneurship in Africa and Oceania*, Berghahn Books, Oxford and New York, 2015

Koch, Martin, 'Opposing Apartheid from behind the Berlin Wall', *Germany: News and In Depth Reports*, 15 December 2013, https://p.dw.com/p/1AZqR

Kolasa, Thomas Stanley, *The South African Communist Party: Adapting to a Post-Communist Age*, McFarland and Co., Jefferson NC, 2016

Kotane, Moses, *The Great Crisis Ahead: A Call to Unity*, A New Age Publication, Pioneer Press, Cape Town, 1957

Kotze, Dirk, 'Morogoro: Out of the Whirlwind', *Politikon*, 16, 1, June 1989

Kotze, Dirk, 'Trade Unionism, Working Class Politics and the South African Communist Party', *Politeia*, 8, 1, 1989

Kotze, Dirk, 'Why Communism Appears to Be Gaining Favour in South Africa', *The Conversation*, 4 August 2015, theconversation.com/why-communism-appears-to-be-gaining-favour-in-south-africa

Krikler, Jeremy, 'Lost Causes of the Rand Revolt', *South African Historical Journal*, 63, 2, 2011

Krikler, Jeremy, *White Rising: The 1922 Insurrection and Racial Killing in South Africa*, Manchester University Press, Manchester, 2005

Kühne, Winrich, *Black Politics in South Africa and the Outlook for Negotiations*, Stiftung Wissenschaft und Politik, Ebenhausen, 1987

Kühne, Winrich, *Die Politik der Sowjetunion in Afrika*, Nomos Verlagsgesellschaft, Baden

Baden, 1982

Kuzio, Taras, 'Transition in Post-Communist States: Triple or Quadruple?', *Politics*, 21, 3, 2001

Labour History Group, *Workers at War: CNETU and the 1946 African Mineworkers Strike*, Salt River, April 1983

La Guma, Alex, *Jimmy La Guma: A Biography*, Friends of the South African Library, Cape Town, 1997

La Hausse, Paul, 'The Dispersal of the Regiments: African Popular Protest in Durban, 1930', *Journal of Natal and Zulu History*, 10, 1987

Lambourne, Brigid, 'Sowing the Seeds of Alliance: The Evolution of Colonialism of Special Type, 1952–1954', History Honours dissertation, Rhodes University, 1990

Landau, Paul, 'Communist Controlled? Reassessing the Years of ANC Exile', *South African Historical Journal*, 67, 2, 2015

Landau, Paul, 'The ANC, MK and "the Turn to Violence"', *South African Historical Journal*, 64, 3, 2012

Landau, Paul, 'The M-Plan: Mandela's Struggle to Re-orient the African National Congress', in Colin Bundy and William Beinart (eds), *Reassessing Mandela*, Jacana Media, Johannesburg, 2020

Lazerson, Joshua, *Against the Tide: Whites in the Struggle against Apartheid*, Westview Press, Boulder CO, 1994

Legassick, Martin, 'Class and Nationalism in South African Protest: The South African Communist Party and the "Native Republic", 1928–1934', Eastern African Studies Program, Syracuse University, July 1973

Legassick, Martin, 'Debating the Revival of the Workers Movement in the 1970s: The South African Democracy Trust and Post-Apartheid Patriotic History', *Kronos*, 34, 1, November 2008

Leibbrandt, Murray, Arden Finn and Vimal Ranchhod, 'Post-Apartheid Poverty and Inequality Trends', in Haroon Bhorat, Alan Hirsch, Ravi Kanbur and Mthuli Ncube (eds), *The Oxford Companion to the Economics of South Africa*, Oxford University Press, Oxford, 2014

Lenin, VI, *Collected Works*, volume 32, Progress Publishers, Moscow, 1977

Lerumo, AB, 'A Century of Oppression: Review of Class and Colour in South Africa', *African Communist*, 40, 1970

Lerumo, AB, *Fifty Fighting Years: The South African Communist Party, 1921–1971*, 3rd edn, Inkululeko Publications, London, 1987

Lerumo, AB, Review of Mokgatle's Autobiography, *African Communist*, 48, 1972

Letsoalo, Matuma, 'Our Zuma Mistake', *Mail & Guardian*, 26 June 2015

Letsoalo, Matuma, 'SACP's "Comrade Crackdown" Takes Control', *Mail & Guardian*, 27 July 2012

Letsoalo, Matuma, 'Senior Alliance Leaders Discuss Zuma's Removal from Office', *Mail & Guardian*, 4 March 2016

Levy, Norman, *The Final Prize: My Life in the Anti-Apartheid Struggle*, South African History Online, Observatory, Cape Town, 2011

Lewis, Gavin, *Between the Wire and the Wall: A History of South African 'Coloured' Politics*, St Martin's Press, New York, 1987

Lewis, Jon, *Industrialisation and Trade Union Organisation in South Africa, 1924–55*, Cambridge University Press, Cambridge, 1984

Lewis, Jon, 'The Germiston By-election of 1932', in P Bonner (ed.), *Working Papers in Southern African Studies*, Ravan Press, Johannesburg, 1981

Lih, Lars T, 'Lenin and Bolshevism', in Stephen A Smith (ed.), *The Oxford Handbook of the History of Communism*, Oxford University Press, Oxford, 2017

Linek, Lukáš, 'Political Regimes and Generational Effect on the Support for the Czech

Communist Party', paper presented at the Workshop on the Legacy of Authoritarian Regimes, University of Nottingham, 25 April 2017

Lingle, Christopher, 'Apartheid as Racial Socialism', *Kyklos*, 43, 2, 1989

Lodge, Tom, *Black Politics in South Africa since 1945*, Longman, London, 1983

Lodge, Tom, 'Lionel Forman's Trumpet: National Communism in South Africa, 1953–59', *Africa*, 63, 4, 1993

Lodge, Tom, 'Political Organizations in Pretoria's African Townships', in Belinda Bozzoli (ed.), *Class, Community and Conflict*, Ravan, Johannesburg, 1987

Lodge, Tom, 'Secret Party: South African Communists between 1950 and 1960', *South African Historical Journal*, 67, 4, 2015

Lodge, Tom, 'The South African General Election, April 1994: Results, Analysis and Implications', *African Affairs*, 94, October 1995

Lorenzini, Sara, 'The Socialist Camp and the Challenge of Economic Modernisation in the Third World', in Norman Naimark, Sylvio Pons and Sophie Quinn-Judge (eds), *The Cambridge History of Communism*, volume 2, Cambridge University Press, Cambridge, 2017

Lovell, David and Kevin Windle, *Our Unswerving Loyalty: A Documentary Survey of Relations between the Communist Party of Australia and Moscow, 1920–1940*, Australian National University, Canberra, 2008

Luckhardt, K and N Wall, *Organize or Starve: The History of the South African Congress of Trade Unions*, Lawrence and Wishart, London, 1980

Ludi, Gerard, *The Communisation of the ANC*, Galago, Alberton, 2011

Ludi, Gerard and Blaar Grobbelaar, *The Amazing Mr Fischer*, Nasionale Boekhandel, Cape Town, 1966

Macmillan, Hugh, *Chris Hani*, Jacana Media, Johannesburg, 2014

Macmillan, Hugh, *Jack Simons*, Jacana Media, Johannesburg, 2016

Macmillan, Hugh, *Oliver Tambo*, Jacana Media, Johannesburg, 2017

Macmillan, Hugh, 'The "Hani Memorandum": Introduced and Annotated', *Transformation*, 69, 2009

Macmillan, Hugh, *The Lusaka Years: The ANC in Exile in Zambia, 1963–1993*, Jacana Media, Johannesburg, 2017

Macmillan, Hugh, Stephen Ellis, Arianna Lissoni and Mariya Kurbak, 'Debating the ANC's External Links during the Struggle against Apartheid', *Africa*, 85, 1, 2015

Maercker, Andreas and Susanne Guski-Leinwand, 'Psychologists' Involvement in Repression: "Stasi" Secret Police Activities in the Former East Germany', *International Perspectives in Psychology*, 7, 2, 2018

Magubane, Bernard, Philip Bonner, Jabulani Sithole, Peter Delius, Janet Cherry, Pat Gibbs and Thozama April, 'The Turn to Armed Struggle', in South African Democratic Education Trust, *The Road to Democracy in South Africa*, volume 1: *1960–1970*, Zebra Press, Cape Town, 2004

Mah Yi Hong, James, 'Liminalities of Colonial Understandings towards Malayan Communism, 1919–1941', BA Honours dissertation, Department of History, National University of Singapore, 2018, https://d1wqtxts1xzle7.cloudfront. net/58532478/Liminalities_of_Colonial_Understandings_towards_Malayan_ Communism__1919-1941.pdf

Maliba, Alpheus, *The Conditions of the Venda People*, Johannesburg District Committee, Communist Party of South Africa, Johannesburg, 1939

Maloka, Eddy, 'Mzala: A Revolutionary without Kid Gloves', *African Communist*, 136, 1994

Maloka, Eddy, *The South African Communist Party: Exile and after Apartheid*, Jacana Media, Johannesburg, 2014

Maloka, Eddy, *The South African Communist Party in Exile, 1963–1965*, Africa Institute,

Pretoria, 2002

Mandela, Nelson, 'In Our Lifetime', *Liberation*, June 1956

Mann, Tom, *Tom Mann's Memoirs*, Spokesman, Nottingham, 2008

Manson, A, C Sidiris and D Cachalia, *An Oral History of the Life of William Barney Ngakane*, SAIRR, Johannesburg, 1982

Mantzaris, EA, 'Radical Community: The Yiddish-Speaking Branch of the International Socialist League, 1918–1920', in Belinda Bozzoli (ed.), *Class, Community and Conflict: South African Perspectives*, Ravan Press, Johannesburg, 1987

Manuel, Trevor, 'Twenty Years of Economic Policy Making: Putting People First', in Haroon Bhorat, Alan Hirsch, Ravi Kanbur and Mthuli Ncube (eds), *The Oxford Companion to the Economics of South Africa*, Oxford University Press, Oxford, 2014

Marie, Shamin, *Divide and Profit: Indian Workers in Natal*, Department of Industrial Sociology, University of Natal, Durban, 1986

Mark, James and Tobias Rupprecht, 'Europe's "1989" in Global Context', in Juliane Fürst, Sylvio Pons and Mark Selden (eds), *The Cambridge History of Communism*, volume 3: *Endgames: Late Communism in Global Perspective*, Cambridge University Press, Cambridge, 2017

Marks, Shula, 'War and Union, 1899–1910', in Robert Ross, Anne Kelk Mager and Bill Nasson (eds), *The Cambridge History of South Africa*, volume 2: *1885–1994*, Cambridge University Press, New York, 2011

Mashilo, Alex, 'Nzimande Was in the Struggle', *Sunday Independent*, 3 August 2015

Mashilo, Alex, 'We Have Not Been Funded by These NUMSA Leaders – SACP', 22 December, 2013, www.politicsdweb.co.za/archive/we-have-not-been-funded-by-these-numsa-lead

Mason, David J, 'Race, Class and National Liberation: Some Implications of the Policy Dilemmas of the International Socialist League and the Communist Party of South Africa', MSc dissertation, Social Sciences, University of Bristol, 1971

Matthews, Joe, 'Armed Struggle in South Africa', *Marxism Today*, September 1969

Mbeki, Govan, *The Struggle for Liberation in South Africa*, David Philip, Cape Town, 1992

McGee, H, *Radical Anti-Apartheid Internationalism and Exile: The Life of Elizabeth Mafeking*, Routledge, Abingdon, 2019

McKinley, Dale, *The ANC and the Liberation Struggle: A Critical Political Biography*, Pluto Press, London, 1997

Mda, AP, 'Report on Communist Activities among the Natives in Johannesburg', *Catholic Times*, July 1942

Mendelsohn, Ezra, 'The Jewish Socialist Movement and the Second International, 1869–1914', Jewish *Social Studies*, 26, 3, July 1964

Merrett, Christopher, 'Masters and Servants: African Trade Unionism in Pietermaritzburg before the Early 1980s', *Natalia*, 48, 2018

Merten, Marianne, 'Cabinet Reshuffle Analysis: Jacob Zuma the Disrupter', *Daily Maverick*, 18 October 2017, http://www.dailymaverick.co.za/article/2017-10-18-cabinet-reshuffle-analysis-jacob-zuma-the-disrupter

Middleton, Jean, *Convictions: A Woman Political Prisoner Remembers*, Ravan, Randburg, 1998

Mildernerová, Kateřina, '"I Feel like Two in One": Complex Belongings among Namibian Czechs', *Modern Africa: Politics, History and Society* (University of Hradec Králové), 6, 2, 2018

Miller, Jamie, *The African Volk: The Apartheid Regime and Its Search for Survival*, Oxford University Press, New York, 2016

Mitchison, Naomi, *A Life for Africa: The Story of Bram Fischer*, Merlin Press, London, 1973

Mokgatle, Naboth, *The Autobiography of an Unknown South African*, University of California Press, Berkeley, 1971

Monroe, Richard, 'Lessons of the 1950s', *Inqaba ya Basebenzi*, 13, March–May 1984

Moodie, Dunbar, 'The Moral Economy of the Black Miners' Strike of 1946', *Journal of Southern African Studies*, 13, 1, October 1986

Moodie, Dunbar, 'The South African State and Industrial Conflict in the 1940s', *International Journal of African Historical Studies*, 21, 1, 1988

Morris, Michael, *ANC in Exile: 40 Seniors List*, Terrorism Research Institute, Cape Town, 1986

Motshabi, Obet T, 'Obituary: John Pule Motshabi', *Sechaba*, May 1989

Mottiar, Shauna and Tom Lodge, 'The Role of Community Health Workers in Supporting South Africa's HIV/AIDS Treatment Programme', *African Journal of AIDS Research*, 17, 1, 2018

Mouton, FA, 'Van matroos tot senator: Die kleuryke en stormagtige politieke loopbaan van SM Pettersen', *Kleio*, 19,1, 1987

Msomi, S'thembiso, 'SACP Refuse to Fight Elections against ANC', *The Star*, 13 March 2005

Mtolo, Bruno, *Umkhonto we Sizwe: The Road to the Left*, Drakensberg Press, Durban, 1966

Muehlenbeck, Philip, *Czechoslovakia in Africa, 1945–1968*, Palgrave Macmillan, Basingstoke, 2016

Mufamadi, Thembeka, *Raymond Mhlaba's Personal Memoirs: Reminiscing from Rwanda and Uganda*, Human Sciences Research Council, Pretoria, 2001

Mulqueen, John, *'An Alien Ideology': Cold War Perceptions of the Irish Left*, Liverpool University Press, Liverpool, 2019

Musemwa, Muchaparara, 'Aspects of the Social and Political History of Langa Township, Cape Town, 1927–1948', MA dissertation, Department of History, University of Cape Town, 1993

Musson, Doreen, *Johnny Gomas: Voice of the Working Class – A Political Biography*, Buchu Books, Cape Town, 1989

Myburgh, James, 'The Ahmed Timol Case', *Politicsweb*, 17 October 2017, https://www. politicsweb.co.za/news-and-analysis/the-ahmed-timol-case-i

Mzala, 'The Freedom Charter and Its Relevance Today', in African National Congress, *Selected Writings on the Freedom Charter*, Sechaba Publications, London, 1985

Naidoo, Beverley, *Death of an Idealist: In Search of Neil Aggett*, Jonathan Ball, Johannesburg, 2012

Nasson, Bill, *South Africa at War, 1939–1945*, Jacana Media, Johannesburg, 2012,

Nattrass, Jill, *The South African Economy*, Oxford University Press, Cape Town, 1981

Nattrass, Nicoli, 'Economic Growth in the 1940s', in Saul Dubow and Alan Jeeves (eds), *South Africa's 1940s: Worlds of Possibilities*, Double Storey, Cape Town, 2005

Ndlovu, Sifiso, 'Johannes Nkosi and the Communist Party of South Africa: Images of Blood River and King Dingaan, 1920s–1930', *History and Theory*, 39, 4, 2000

Ndlovu, Sifiso and Miranda Strydom (eds), *The Thabo Mbeki I Knew*, Picador Africa, Johannesburg, 2016

Neame, Sylvia, *The Congress Movement, The Unfolding of the Congress Alliance, 1912–1961*, volume 1, Human Sciences Research Council Press, Cape Town, 2015

Neame, Sylvia, *The Congress Movement: The Unfolding of the Congress Alliance, 1912–1961*, volume 2, HSRC Press, Cape Town, 2015

Neame, Sylvia, *The Congress Movement, The Unfolding of the Congress Alliance, 1912–1961*, volume 3, HSRC Press, Pretoria, 2016

Ngonyama, Percy, 'Reconstruction and Legacy Preservation', *African Historical Review*, 2017

Nicol, Martin, 'The Transvaal GWU's Assault on Low Wages in Cape Town', in Belinda Bozzoli (ed.), *Class, Community and Conflict*, Ravan Press, Johannesburg, 1987

Niehaus, Isak, *Witchcraft and Politics: Exploring the Occult in the South African Lowveld*, Pluto Press, London, 2001

Nkonyane, Hlengiwe, 'SACP Must Contest Elections', *Umsebenzi*, October 2016

Nkosi, Z, 'The Life of a Revolutionary', *Sechaba*, October 1972

Nkunjana, Felix, 'Look to China for Economic Solutions in SA', *The Star*, 27 November 2019

Nqakula, Charles, *The People's War: Reflections of an ANC Cadre*, Mutloatse Arts Heritage Trust, Johannesburg, 2017

Nuttall, Tim, 'Class, Race and Nation: African Politics in Durban, 1929–1949', PhD dissertation, University of Oxford, 1991

Nzimande, Blade, 'A Prophet of True Radical Transformation', *Sunday Times*, Johannesburg, 25 February 2017

Nzimande, Blade, 'Roll Back the Corrupting Intersection between Private Accumulation and Public Service', *Umsebenzi*, October 2009

Nzula, Albert T, II Potekhin and AZ Zusmanovich, *Forced Labour in Colonial Africa*, Zed Press, London, 1979 [1933]

O'Connor Lysaght, DR, *The Story of the Limerick Soviet: The 1919 General Strike against British Militarism*, The Limerick Soviet Commemoration Committee, Limerick, 2009

O'Malley, Padraig, *Shades of Difference: Mac Maharaj and the Struggle for South Africa*, Viking, New York, 2007

O'Meara, Dan, 'The 1946 African Miners' Strike and the Political Economy of South Africa', *Journal of Commonwealth and Comparative Politics*, XII, 2, 1975

Oralek, Milan, 'Michael Harmel (1915–1974): A South African Communist and His Discourse', PhD dissertation, School of English, Victoria University, Wellington, New Zealand, 2020

Ozinsky, Max, 'For Land and Freedom: The CPSA and the Strategy of United Fronts in the 1930s', paper, Department of Economic History, UCT, 1983

Padayachee, Vishnu, S Vawda and P Tichman, *Indian Workers and Trade Unions in Durban, 1930–1950*, Report no. 20, ISER, Durban-Westville, 1985

Padayachee, Vishnu, Shahid Vawda and Paul Tichman, 'Trade Unions and the Communist Party in Durban in the 1940s: A Reply to Iain Edwards', *South African Labour Bulletin*, 11, 7, 1985

Pahad, Essop, Unpublished manuscript of a biography of Yusuf Dadoo, Mayibuye Centre, University of the Western Cape, n.d.

Palmer, Bryan D, 'Rethinking the Historiography of United States Communism', *American Communist History*, 2, 2, 2003

Palmer, Ian, Nishendra Moodley and Susan Parnell, *Building a Capable State: Service Delivery in Post-Apartheid South Africa*, Zed Press, London, 2017

Pasquino, Gianfranco and Marco Valbruzzi, 'The Italian Democratic Party, Its Nature and Its Secretary', *Revista Española de Ciencia Política*, 44, July 2017

Pelikan, Jiri, *The Czechoslovak Political Trials, 1950–1954: The Suppressed Report of the Dubček Government's Commission of Inquiry*, Macdonald, London, 1971

Pelling, Henry, *A Short History of the Labour Party*, Macmillan, London, 1961

Phillips, Ray E, *The Bantu are Coming: Phases of South Africa's Race Problem*, Student Christian Movement Press, London, 1930

Pike, Douglas, *Viet Cong: The Organization and Techniques of the National Liberation Front of South Vietnam*, Massachusetts Institute of Technology Press, Cambridge MA, 1966

Pike, Henry R, *A History of Communism in South Africa*, Christian Mission International of South Africa, Germiston, 1988

Pinnock, Don, *Ruth First: Voices of Liberation*, Human Sciences Research Council, Cape Town, 2012

Podbrey, Pauline, *White Girl in Search of a Party*, University of KwaZulu-Natal Press, Pietermaritzburg, 1993

Pollitt, Harry, 'The Work of the Communists of South Africa in the Trade Unions', *Communist Review*, December 1932

Posel, Deborah, 'The Apartheid Project, 1948–1970', in Robert Ross, Anne Kelk Mager and Bill Nasson (eds), *The Cambridge History of South Africa*, volume 2: *1885–1994*, Cambridge University Press, New York, 2011

Press, Ron, 'To Change the World! Is Reason Enough?', unpublished autobiography in Ron Press Papers, Wits Historical Papers, A 3239

Pretorius, Fransjohan, 'Life on Commando', in Peter Warwick (ed.), *The South African War: The Anglo-Boer War of 1899–1902*, Longman, London, 1980

Progressive Committee for Jewish Affairs, *Is There Anti-Semitism in Eastern Europe?*, Pacific Press, Johannesburg, 1953

Radveni, Janos, *Psychological Operations and Political Warfare in Long Term Strategic Planning*, Praeger, New York, 1990

Raman, Parvathi, 'Yusuf Dadoo: A Son of South Africa,' in Saul Dubow and Alan Jeeves (eds), *South Africa's 1940s: Worlds of Possibilities*, Double Storey, Cape Town, 2005

Record, Wilson, *The Negro and the Communist Party*, University of North Carolina Press, Chapel Hill, 1951

Reddy, ES, 'Dadoo, Gandhi and the South African Struggle', *Mainstream*, 16 September 1939

Redfern, Neil, 'A British Version of "Browderism": British Communists and the Teheran Conference of 1943', *Science and Society*, 66, 3, 2002

Rich, Paul, *White Power and the Liberal Conscience*, University of Manchester Press, Manchester, 1984

Riordan, Rory, 'The Great Black Shark: Interview with Chris Hani', *Monitor: The Journal of the Human Rights Trust*, Port Elizabeth, December 1990

Robinson, Vicky and Rapule Tabane, 'SACP Divided over Zuma', *Mail & Guardian*, 21 April 2006

Rosenthal, Richard, *Mission Improbable*, David Philip, Cape Town, 1998

Roth, Mia, *The Communist Party in South Africa: Racism, Eurocentrism and Moscow, 1921–1950*, Partridge, Johannesburg, 2016

Roux, Edward, *SP Bunting: A Political Biography*, African Bookman, Cape Town, 1944

Roux, Edward, 'The Alexandra Bus Boycott', *Trek*, 21 September 1945

Roux, Edward, *Time Longer than Rope*, Victor Gollancz, London, 1948

Roux, Edward, *Time Longer than Rope*, University of Wisconsin, Madison, 1964

Roux, Eddie and Win Roux, *Rebel Pity*, Rex Collings, London, 1970

Royal College of Surgeons, Plarrs Lives of the Fellows, George Isak Sacks (1901–1981), 2015, https://livesonline.rcseng.ac.uk/client/en_GB/lives/search/detailnonmodal/ent:$002f$002fSD_ASSET$002f0$002fSD_ASSET:379090/one

Sachs, Albie, 'Post-Apartheid South Africa', *World Policy Journal*, 6, 2, Summer 1989

Sachs, Bernard, *Multitude of Dreams*, Kayor Publishing House, Johannesburg, 1949

Sachs, ES, *An Open Letter to Garment Workers*, Pacific Press, Johannesburg, 1948

Sachs, ES, *Rebels' Daughters*, MacGibbon and Kee, London, 1957

Sachs, ES, *The Choice before South Africa*, self-published, London, 1953

Saks, DY, 'Sam Kahn and the Communist Party', unpublished paper

Sampson, Anthony, *Black and Gold: Tycoons, Revolutionaries and Apartheid*, Coronet Books, London, 1987

Sapire, Hilary, 'The Stay-Away of the Brakpan Location', University of the Witwatersrand History Workshop paper, 1984

Schleicher, Hans, 'GDR Solidarity: The German Democratic Republic and the South African Liberation Struggle', in Ben Magubane (ed.), *The Road to Liberation in South*

Africa, volume 3: *International Solidarity*, Unisa Press, Pretoria, 2008

Schleicher, Hans-Georg and Ilona Schleicher, 'Nordic and GDR Solidarity with the Liberation Struggles in Southern Africa: Between Politico-Ideological Competition and Co-operation', *Jahrbuch Asien-Africa-Lateinamerika*, 28, 3, 2000

Seekings, Jeremy, *The UDF: A History of the United Democratic Front in South Africa, 1981–1991*, David Philip, Cape Town, 2000

Seekings, Jeremy and Nicoli Nattrass, *Poverty, Politics and Policy in South Africa: Why Has Poverty Persisted after Apartheid?*, Jacana Media, Johannesburg, 2015

Sejaka, Nimrod, 'Workers' Power and the Crisis of Leadership', *Inqaba ya Basebenzi*, 12, November 1983

Shaik, Moe, *The ANC Spy Bible: Operating across Enemy Lines*, Tafelberg, Cape Town, 2020

Sharma, Ruchir, 'The Liberation Dividend', in Haroon Bhorat, Alan Hirsch, Ravi Kanbur and Mthuli Ncube (eds), *The Oxford Companion to the Economics of South Africa*, Oxford University Press, Oxford, 2014

Shaw, Gerald, 'Wolfie Kodesh, Obituary', *The Guardian*, 13 November 2002

Shubin, Vladimir, *ANC: A View from Moscow*, Mayibuye Books, Cape Town, 1999

Shubin, Vladimir, 'Soviet–South African Relations: A Critique of the Critique', Conference of the SAAPS, Bloemfontein, 20–22 October 1993

Shubin, Vladimir, 'The Production of History in a Changing South Africa', paper presented at a Conference on the Future of the Past, University of the Western Cape, 10–12 July 1996

Sibeko, A, 'The Underground Voice', *African Communist*, 68, 1, 1977

Sieber, Karel and Petr Zídek, *Československo a subsaharská Afrika v letech, 1948–1989*, Ústav Mezinárodnich Vztahu, Prague, 2007

Sihlolo, Wandile, 'Black Farmers of Eastern Cape Reap Harvest of Success', *Business Report* (supplement to *The Star*), 8 July 2018

Simons, HJ and RE Simons, *Class and Colour in South Africa, 1850–1950*, Penguin, Harmondsworth, 1969

Simpson, Thula, *Umkhonto we Sizwe: The ANC's Armed Struggle*, Penguin, Johannesburg, 2014

Sisulu, Elinor, *Walter and Albertina Sisulu: In Our Lifetime*, David Philip, Cape Town, 2002

Sithole, Jabulani, 'Contestations over Knowledge Production or Ideological Bullying? A Response to Legassick on the Workers' Movement', *Kronos*, 35, 1, 2009

Skilling, GH, *Czechoslovakia's Interrupted Revolution*, Princeton University Press, Princeton, 1976

Slovo, Joe, *An Unfinished Autobiography*, Ravan, Randburg, 1995

Slovo, Joe, *Has Socialism Failed?*, Inkululeko Publications, London, 1990

Slovo, Joe, Interview, *Learn and Teach*, 4, 1990

Slovo, Joe, Interview, *South African Labour Bulletin*, 14, 8, 1990

Slovo, Joe, 'Latin America and the Ideas of Regis Debray', *African Communist*, 33, Second quarter 1968

Slovo, Joe, 'South Africa: No Middle Road', in Basil Davidson, Joe Slovo and Anthony Wilkinson, *Southern Africa: The New Politics of Revolution*, Penguin Books, Harmondsworth, 1976

Slovo, Joe, *The South African Working Class and the NDR*, Umsebenzi Discussion Pamphlet, [1988]

Smith, Evan, 'Policing Communism across the White Man's World: Anti-Communist Cooperation between Australia, South Africa and Britain in the Early Cold War', *Britain and the World*, 10, 2, 2017

Smith, Janet and Beauregard Tromp, *Hani: A Life Too Short*, Jonathan Ball,

Johannesburg, 2009

Smith, Stephen A, 'The Comintern', in Stephen A Smith (ed.), *The Oxford Handbook of the History of Communism*, Oxford University Press, Oxford, 2014

Socialist League of Africa [Baruch Hirson], 'A Critical Discussion: South Africa: Ten Years of the Stay at Home', *International Socialism* (London), 5, Summer 1961

Southall, Roger, 'Black Empowerment and Present Limits to Democratic Capitalism in South Africa', in Sakhela Buhlungu, John Daniel, Roger Southall and Jessica Lutchman (eds), *South Africa: State of the Nation, 2005–2006*, HSRC Press, Cape Town, 2006

Sparg, Marion (ed.), *Comrade Jack: The Political Lectures and Diary of Jack Simons, Novo Catengue*, STE Publishers, Johannesburg, 2001

Spurný, Matěj, *Making the Most of Tomorrow*, Karolinum Press, Prague, 2019

Stadler, AW, 'A Long Way to Walk', African Studies Institute, University of the Witwatersrand seminar paper, 1979

Stadler, AW, 'Birds in the Cornfield: Squatter Movements in Johannesburg, 1944–1947', *Journal of Southern African Studies*, 6, 1, 1979

Stadler, Hermann, *The Other Side of the Story: A True Perspective*, Contact Publishers, Pretoria, 1997

Stansfield, Mark and Terry van der Walt, 'The Vula Dossier', *Sunday Times* (Johannesburg), 4 November 1990

Starushenko, Gleb, 'Problems of Struggle against Racism, Apartheid and Colonialism in South Africa', report presented to the Second Soviet African Conference for Peace, Cooperation and Social Progress, Moscow, USSR Academy of Sciences, Africa Institute, 24–25 June 1986

Steiner, Mary Beth, 'Narratives of Stasi Detention', *Narrative Culture*, 3, 2, 2016

Steiner, Peter, '"Making a Czech Hero": Julius Fučik through his Writings', Carl Beck Papers in Russian and East European Studies, no. 1501, University of Pittsburgh, Pittsburgh, 2000

Storey, Paul, 'Build Direct Links with the Workers' Movement in Other Countries', *Inqaba ya Basebenzi*, 6, May 1982

Storm, W and B Storm, *We Meet the Czechoslovaks*, Orbis, Prague, June 1948

Strachan, Harold, *Make a Skyf, Man!*, Jacana Media, Johannesburg, 2004

Suttner, Raymond, *Inside Apartheid's Prisons*, Jacana Media, Johannesburg, 2017

Suttner, Raymond, 'The African National Congress Centenary: A Long and Difficult Journey', *International Affairs*, 88, 4, 2012

Suttner, Raymond, *The ANC Underground in South Africa*, Lynne Rienner Publishers, Boulder CO, 2009

Suttner, Raymond, 'The Challenge to African National Congress Predominance', *Representation*, 45, 2, 2009

Suttner, Raymond, *The Freedom Charter: The People's Charter in the Nineteen-Eighties*, TB Memorial Lecture, University of Cape Town, 1984

Suttner, Raymond, 'The (Re-)Constitution of the South African Communist Party as an Underground Organisation', *Journal of Contemporary African Studies*, 22, 1, 2004

Suttner, Raymond and Jeremy Cronin, *30 Years of the Freedom Charter*, Ravan, Johannesburg, 1986

Tabane, Rapule, 'SACP Regions Want to Go It Alone', *Mail & Guardian*, 31 February 2004

Tabata, IB, *The Awakening of the People*, Spokesmen Books, Nottingham, 1974

Tatz, CM, *Shadow and Substance in South Africa*, University of Natal Press, Pietermaritzburg, 1962

Telepneva, N, 'Codename SEKRETÁŘ: Amilcar Cabral, Czechoslovakia and the Role of Human Intelligence during the Cold War', *International Historical Review*, 2019, https://doi.org/10/1080/07075332.2019.1678508

Telepneva, Natalia, 'Mediators of Liberation: Eastern Bloc Officials and Frelimo, 1958–1965', *Journal of Southern African Studies*, 2017

Theledi, Nathi, 'Testing Our Programme against Slovo's Vision of the NDR', *African Communist*, 202, 2020

Thloome, Dan, 'Lessons of the Stay-Away', *Liberation*, 32, August 1958

Thomas, David P, 'Post-Apartheid Conundrums: Contemporary Debates and Divisions within the South African Communist Party', *Journal of Contemporary African Studies*, 25, 2, 2007

Thomas, David, 2012. 'Multiple Layers of Hegemony: Post-Apartheid South Africa and the South African Communist Party', *Canadian Journal of African Studies*, 46, 1, 2012

Thomas, Scott, 'The Diplomacy of Liberation: The international Relations of the African National Congress of South Africa, 1960–1985', PhD dissertation, Department of International Relations, London School of Economics, October 1989

Thompson, Leonard and Monica Wilson (eds), *The Oxford History of South Africa*, volume 2, Oxford University Press, Oxford, 1971

Thorpe, Andrew, 'Comintern "Control" of the Communist Party of Great Britain', *English Historical Review*, 113, 452, 1998

Tobias, Henry J, 'The Bund and Lenin until 1903', *Russian Review*, 20, 4, October 1961

Tobias, Henry and Charles Woodhouse, 'Revolutionary Optimism and the Practice of Revolution: The Jewish Bund in 1905', *Jewish Social Studies*, 47, 2, 1985

Touyz, BM, 'White Politics and the Garment Workers' Union, 1930–1953', MA dissertation, Comparative African Government and Law, University of Cape Town, 1979

Turok, Ben, *Nothing but the Truth: Behind the ANC's Struggle Politics*, Jonathan Ball, Johannesburg, 2003

Vahed, Goolam, 'The Making of "Indianness": Indian Politics in South Africa during the 1930s and 1940s', *Journal of Natal and Zulu History*, 17, 1997

Van der Berg, Servaas, 'Current Poverty and Income Distribution in the Context of South African History,' *Economic History of Developing Regions*, 26, 1, 2011

Van der Walt, Lucien, 'Anarchism and Syndicalism in South Africa, 1904–1921: Rethinking the History of Labour and the Left', PhD dissertation, Department of Sociology, University of the Witwatersrand, 2007

Van der Walt, Lucien, 'The First Globalisation and Transnational Labour Activism in Southern Africa: White Labour, the IWW and the ICU, 1904–1934', *African Studies*, 66, 2–3, 2007

Van Kessel, Ineke, *Beyond Our Wildest Dreams: The United Democratic Front and the Transformation of South Africa*, University Press of Virginia, Charlottesville, 2000

Vatlin, Alexander and Stephen A Smith, 'The Comintern', in Stephen A Smith (ed.), *The Oxford Handbook of the History of Communism*, Oxford University Press, Oxford, 2014

Visser, Wessel, 'The South African Labour Movement's Response to Declarations of Martial Law, 1913–1922', *Scientia Militaria: South African Journal of Military History*, 2003

Walker, Cherryl, *Women and Resistance in South Africa*, Onyx Press, London, 1982

Waterman, P, 'Hopeful Traveller: The Itinerary of an Internationalist', *History Workshop*, 35, Spring 1993

Watts, Hilda, *A Straight Talk on Municipal Affairs by Hilda Watts*, October 1944

Watts, Hilda, *Have You Met Hilda Watts?*, Sholto Douglas Printer, Johannesburg, October 1944

Watts, Hilda, *Rebuild Johannesburg by Councillor Hilda Watts*, Communist Party, South Africa, September 1945

Webster, Dennis, 'SA's Income Inequality Is Growing', *Mail & Guardian*, 22 November 2019

Weinberg, Eli, 'Why I Am a Member of the Communist Party', *African Communist*, 87, 1981

Weisfelder, Richard, 'Early Voices of Protest in Basutoland', *African Studies Review*, 17, 2, 1974

Wells, Julia, 'The Day the Town Stood Still: Women in Resistance in Potchefstroom, 1912–1930', in Belinda Bozzoli (ed.), *Town and Countryside in the Transvaal*, Ravan Press, Johannesburg, 1983

White, Barry, 'The Role of the Springbok Legion', *Kleio*, XXV, 1993

Whiteford, Andrew, Dori Posel and Teresa Kelatwang, *A Profile of Poverty, Inequality and Human Development in South Africa*, Human Sciences Research Council, Pretoria, 1995

Whittles, Govan, 'Stalini Faction Caused ANC to Lose Metro – Report', *Mail & Guardian*, 13 January 2017

Wickens, Peter, *The Industrial and Commercial Workers' Union of South Africa*, Oxford University Press, Cape Town, 1978

Wiebel, Jacob and Samuel Admasie, 'Rethinking the Ethiopian Red Terror', *Journal of African History*, 60, 3, 2019

Wieder, Alan, *Ruth First and Joe Slovo in the War against Apartheid*, Monthly Review Press, New York, 2013

Wilderson, Frank, *Incognegro: A Memoir of Exile and Apartheid*, South End Press, Boston, 2008

Wilkinson, Kate, 'Black Ownership of the Johannesburg Stock Exchange', *Africa Check*, 29 August 2017, https://africacheck.org/factsheets/guide-much-sas-stock-exchange-black-owned-know/

Williams, Michelle, 'Energy, Labour and Democracy in South Africa', in Vishwas Satgar (ed.), *The Climate Crisis: South African and Global Democratic Eco-Socialist Alternatives*, Wits University Press, Johannesburg, 2018

Wilson, Tom, 'Graft under Jacob Zuma Cost South Africa $34 Billion, Says Cyril Ramaphosa', *Financial Times*, 14 October 2019, https://www.ft.com/content/e0991464-ee79-11e9-bfa4-b25f11f42901

Winrow, Gareth, 'The GDR in Africa: A Gradual Disengagement?', *Africa Spectrum*, 24, 3, 1989

Witz, Leslie, 'A Case of Schizophrenia: The Rise and Fall of the Independent Labour Party', University of the Witwatersrand, History Workshop, 1984

Wolpe, AnneMarie, *The Long Way Home*, David Philip, Cape Town, 1994

Wolpe, Harold, 'Capitalism and Cheap Labour Power in South Africa: From Segregation to Apartheid', *Economy and Society*, 1, 4, 1972

Wolpe, Harold, 'The Theory of Internal Colonialism: The South African case', in I Oxaal, T Barnett and D Booth (eds), *Beyond the Sociology of Development: Economy and Society in Latin America and Africa*, Routledge, London, 1975

Wolton, Douglas, G, *Whither South Africa?*, Lawrence and Wishart, London, 1947

Yap, Melanie and Dianne Leong Man, *Colour, Confusion and Concessions: The History of the Chinese in South Africa*, Hong Kong University Press, Hong Kong, 1996

Young, Marilyn and Sophie Quinn-Judge, 'The Vietnam War as a World Event', in Juliane Fürst, Sylvio Pons and Mark Selden (eds), *The Cambridge History of Communism*, volume 3: *Endgames: Late Communism in Global Perspective*, Cambridge University Press, Cambridge, 2017

Yudelman, David, *The Emergence of Modern South Africa: State, Capital and the Incorporation of Organized Labour on the South African Gold Fields, 1924–1933*, Greenwood Press, Westport, 1983

Zulu, Zakhele, 'Why I Joined the Communist Party: Impact of the Durban Riots', *African Communist*, 42, 1971

Photo Credits

Index